The Future of Post-Human Transportation

A Preface to a New Theory of Networks and Operations

By

Peter Baofu

CAMBRIDGE SCHOLARS PUBLISHING

The Future of Post-Human Transportation:
A Preface to a New Theory of Networks and Operations,
by Peter Baofu

This book first published 2012

Cambridge Scholars Publishing

12 Back Chapman Street, Newcastle upon Tyne, NE6 2XX, UK

British Library Cataloguing in Publication Data
A catalogue record for this book is available from the British Library

ISBN (10): 1-4438-4049-1, ISBN (13): 978-1-4438-4049-1

To Those in the Future World beyond Networks and Operations

.

BOOKS ALSO BY PETER BAOFU

Category I: Social Sciences and Related Fields

- 51. *The Future of Post-Human Migration* (2012)
- 50. *The Future of Post-Human Criminality* (2012)
- 49. *The Future of Post-Human Geography* (2011)
- 48. *The Future of Post-Human Gambling* (2011)
- 47. *The Future of Post-Human Education* (2011)
- 46. *The Future of Post-Human War and Peace* (2010)
- 45. *The Future of Post-Human Law* (2010)
- 44. *The Future of Post-Human Organization* (2009)
- 43. *The Future of Post-Human Mass Media* (2009)
- 42. *The Rise of Authoritarian Liberal Democracy* (2007)
- 41. *Beyond the World of Titans, and the Remaking of World Order* (2007)
- 40. *Beyond Capitalism to Post-Capitalism* (2005)
- 39. Volume 1: *Beyond Democracy to Post-Democracy* (2004)
- 38. Volume 2: *Beyond Democracy to Post-Democracy* (2004)
- 37. *The Future of Capitalism and Democracy* (2002)

Category II: Formal Sciences and Related Fields

- 36. *The Future of Post-Human Semantics* (2012)
- 35. *The Future of Post-Human Data Analysis* (2011)
- 34. *The Future of Post-Human Computing* (2011)
- 33. *The Future of Post-Human Formal Science* (2010)
- 32. *The Future of Post-Human Language* (2009)
- 31. *The Future of Post-Human Geometry* (2009)
- 30. *The Future of Post-Human Mathematical Logic* (2008)
- 29. *The Future of Information Architecture* (2008)

Category III: Natural Sciences and Related Fields

- 28. *The Future of Post-Human Architecture* (2012)
- 27. *The Future of Post-Human Chemistry* (2011)
- 26. *The Future of Post-Human Acoustics* (2011)
- 25. *The Future of Post-Human Geology* (2010)
- 24. *Beyond Cosmology to Post-Cosmology* (2010)
- 23. *The Future of Post-Human Personality* (2010)
- 22. *The Future of Post-Human Sexuality* (2010)
- 21. *The Future of Post-Human Urban Planning* (2009)
- 20. *The Future of Post-Human Engineering* (2009)
- 19. *The Future of Post-Human Unconsciousness* (2008)
- 18. *The Future of Complexity* (2007)
- 17. *Beyond Nature and Nurture* (2006)
- 16. *The Future of Post-Human Space-Time* (2006)
- 15. *The Future of Post-Human Consciousness* (2004)

Category IV: The Humanities and Related Fields

- 14. *The Future of Post-Human History* (2012)
- 13. *The Future of Post-Human Performing Arts* (2012)
- 12. *The Future of Post-Human Literature* (2011)
- 11. *The Future of Post-Human Humor* (2011)
- 10. *Beyond Ethics to Post-Ethics* (2011)
- 9. *The Future of Post-Human Religion* (2010)
- 8. *The Future of Post-Human Chess* (2010)
- 7. *The Future of Post-Human Martial Arts* (2009)
- 6. *The Future of Post-Human Creative Thinking* (2009)
- 5. *The Future of Post-Human Knowledge* (2008)
- 4. *The Future of Aesthetic Experience* (2007)
- 3. *Beyond Civilization to Post-Civilization* (2006)
- 2. Volume 1: *The Future of Human Civilization* (2000)
- 1. Volume 2: *The Future of Human Civilization* (2000)

CONTENTS

Part One: Introduction

Part Two: Networks

Part Three: Operations

Part Four: Conclusion

TABLES

Category III: Visions on the Mind

Category IV: Visions on History

Category VII. Visions on Society (Socio-Political)

Category VIII. Visions on Society (Socio-Economic)

Category IX: Visions on Culture

ACKNOWLEDGMENTS

Like all other previous books of mine, this one is written to challenge conventional ideas or, more precisely, in the current context, the ones on transportation—and to replace them with an original way of thinking about its future fate (in relation to networks and operations).

Therefore, this book receives no external funding nor help from any formal organization or institution, because of its political incorrectness—as this is something that I often stressed (and repeated) in all my previous books.

My only reward is the wonderful feeling to conceive something original in the history of transportation studies.

And as always, I bear the sole responsibility for the ideas presented in this book.

ABBREVIATIONS

ALD = Peter Baofu. 2007. *The Rise of Authoritarian Liberal Democracy: A Preface to a New Theory of Comparative Political Systems*. Cambridge, England: Cambridge Scholars Publishing, Ltd.

BCIV = Peter Baofu. 2006. *Beyond Civilization to Post-Civilization: Conceiving a Better Model of Life Settlement to Supersede Civilization*. NY: Peter Lang Publishing, Inc.

BCPC = Peter Baofu. 2005. *Beyond Capitalism to Post-Capitalism: Conceiving a Better Model of Wealth Acquisition to Supersede Capitalism*. NY: The Edwin Mellen Press.

BCOS = Peter Baofu. 2010. *Beyond Cosmology to Post-Cosmology: A Preface to a New Theory of Different Worlds*. Cambridge, England: Cambridge International Science Publishing, Ltd.

BDPD1 = Peter Baofu. 2004. Volume 1. *Beyond Democracy to Post-Democracy: Conceiving a Better Model of Governance to Supersede Democracy*. NY: The Edwin Mellen Press.

BDPD2 = Peter Baofu. 2004. Volume 2. *Beyond Democracy to Post-Democracy: Conceiving a Better Model of Governance to Supersede Democracy*. NY: The Edwin Mellen Press.

BEPE = Peter Baofu. 2011. *Beyond Ethics to Post-Ethics: A Preface to a New Theory of Morality and Immorality.* Charlotte, NC: Infomration Age Publishing.

BNN = Peter Baofu. 2006. *Beyond Nature and Nurture: Conceivng a Better Way to Understand Genes and Memes.* Cambridge, England: Cambridge Scholars Publishing, Ltd.

BWT = Peter Baofu. 2007. *Beyond the World of Titans, and the Renaking of World Order: A Preface to a New Logic of Empire-Building.* Cambridge, England: Cambridge Scholars Publishing, Ltd.

FAE = Peter Baofu. 2007. *The Future of Aesthetic Experience: Conceiving a Better Way to Understand Beauty, Ugliness and the Rest.* Cambridge, England: Cambridge Scholars Publishing, Ltd.

FC = Peter Baofu. 2007. *The Future of Complexity: Conceiving a Better Way to Understand Order and Chaos.* London, United Kingdom: World Scientific Publishing Co.

FCD = Peter Baofu. 2002. *The Future of Capitalism and Democracy.* MD: The University Press of America.

FHC1 = Peter Baofu. 2000. Volume 1. *The Future of Human Civilization.* NY: The Edwin Mellen Press.

FHC2 = Peter Baofu. 2000. Volume 2. *The Future of Human Civilization.* NY: The Edwin Mellen Press.

FIA = Peter Baofu. 2008. *The Future of Information Architecture: Conceiving a Better Way to Understand Taxonomy, Network, and Intelligence.* Oxford, England: Chandos Publishing (Oxford) Limited.

FPHA = Peter Baofu. 2011. *The Future of Post-Human Acoustics: A Preface to a New Theory of Sound and Silence.* Cambridge, England: Cambridge International Science Publishing, Ltd.

FPHARCH = Peter Baofu. 2012. *The Future of Post-Human Architecture: A Preface to a New Theory of Form and Function.* Cambridge, England: Cambridge International Science Publishing, Ltd.

FPHC = Peter Baofu. 2004. *The Future of Post-Human Consciousness.* NY: The Edwin Mellen Press.

FPHCHEM = Peter Baofu. 2011. *The Future of Post-Human Chemistry: A Preface to a New Theory of Substances and their Changes.* England: Cambridge Scholars Publishing, Ltd.

FPHCHESS = Peter Baofu. 2010. *The Future of Post-Human Chess: A Preface to a New Theory of Tactics and Strategy.* Cambridge, England: Cambridge International Science Publishing, Ltd.

FPHCOM = Peter Baofu. 2011. *The Future of Post-Human Computing: A Preface to a New Theory of Hardware and Software.* Cambridge, England: Cambridge International Science Publishing, Ltd.

FPHCRIM = Peter Baofu. 2012. *The Future of Post-Human Criminality: A Preface to a New Theory of Heroes and Villaines.* Cambridge, England: Cambridge International Science Publishing, Ltd.

FPHCT = Peter Baofu. 2009. *The Future of Post-Human Creative Thinking: A Preface to a New Theory of Invention and Innovation.* Cambridge, England: Cambridge Scholars Publishing, Ltd.

FPHDA = Peter Baofu. 2011. *The Future of Post-Human Data Analysis: A Preface to a New Theory of Quantitative and Qualitative Research.* Cambridge, England: Cambridge International Science Publishing, Ltd.

FPHE = Peter Baofu. 2009. *The Future of Post-Human Engineering: A Preface to a New Theory of Technology.* Cambridge, England: Cambridge Scholars Publishing, Ltd.

FPHEDU = Peter Baofu. 2011. *The Future of Post-Human Education: A Preface to a New Theory of Teaching and Learning.* Cambridge, England: Cambridge International Science Publishing, Ltd.

FPHFS = Peter Baofu. 2010. *The Future of Post-Human Formal Science: A Preface to a New Theory of Abstraction and Application.* Cambridge, England: Cambridge Scholars Publishing, Ltd.

FPHG = Peter Baofu. 2009. *The Future of Post-Human Geometry: A Preface to a New Theory of Infinity, Symmetry, and Dimensionality.* Cambridge, England: Cambridge Scholars Publishing, Ltd.

FPHGAM = Peter Baofu. 2011. *The Future of Post-Human Gambling: A Preface to a New Theory of Risk and Caution.* Cambridge, England: Cambridge International Science Publishing, Ltd.

FPHGEOG = Peter Baofu. 2011. *The Future of Post-Human Geography: A Preface to a New Theory of Environments and their Interactions.* Cambridge, England: Cambridge International Science Publishing, Ltd.

FPHGEOL = Peter Baofu. 2010. *The Future of Post-Human Geology: A Preface to a New Theory of Statics and Dynamics.* Cambridge, England: Cambridge International Science Publishing, Ltd.

FPHH = Peter Baofu. 2011. *The Future of Post-Human Humor: A Preface to a New Theory of Joking and Laughing.* Cambridge, England: Cambridge International Science Publishing, Ltd.

FPHHIST = Peter Baofu. 2012. *The Future of Post-Human History: A Preface to a New Theory of Universality and Relativity.* Cambridge, England: Cambridge Scholars Publishing, Ltd.

FPHK = Peter Baofu. 2008. *The Future of Post-Human Knowledge: A Preface to a New Theory of Methodology and Ontology.* Oxford, England: Chandos Publishing (Oxford) Limited.

FPHL = Peter Baofu. 2009. *The Future of Post-Human Language: A Preface to a New Theory of Structure, Context, and Learning.* Cambridge, England: Cambridge Scholars Publishing, Ltd.

FPHLAW = Peter Baofu. 2010. *The Future of Post-Human Law: A Preface to a New Theory of Necessity, Contingency, and Justice.* Cambridge, England: Cambridge Scholars Publishing, Ltd.

FPHLIT = Peter Baofu. 2011. *The Future of Post-Human Literature: A Preface to a New Theory of Fiction and Non-Fiction.* Cambridge, England: Cambridge International Science Publishing, Ltd.

FPHMA = Peter Baofu. 2009. *The Future of Post-Human Martial Arts: A Preface to a New Theory of the Body and Spirit of Warriors.* Cambridge, England: Cambridge Scholars Publishing, Ltd.

FPHMIG = Peter Baofu. 2012. *The Future of Post-Human Migration: A Preface to a New Theory of Sameness, Otherness, and Identity.* Cambridge, England: Cambridge Scholars Publishing, Ltd.

FPHML = Peter Baofu. 2008. *The Future of Post-Human Mathematical Logic: A Preface to a New Theory of Rationality.* Cambridge, England: Cambridge Scholars Publishing, Ltd.

FPHMM = Peter Baofu. 2009. *The Future of Post-Human Mass Media: A Preface to a New Theory of Technology.* Cambridge, England: Cambridge Scholars Publishing, Ltd.

FPHO = Peter Baofu. 2009. *The Future of Post-Human Organization: A Preface to a New Theory of Communication, Decision-Making, and Leadership.*.Cambridge, England: Cambridge Scholars Publishing, Ltd.

FPHP = Peter Baofu. 2010. *The Future of Post-Human Personality: A Preface to a New Theory of Normality and Abnormality.* Cambridge, England: Cambridge International Science Publishing, Ltd.

FPHPA = Peter Baofu. 2012. *The Future of Post-Human Performing Arts: A Preface to a New Theory of the Body and its Presence.* Cambridge, England: Cambridge Scholars Publishing, Ltd.

FPHR = Peter Baofu. 2010. *The Future of Post-Human Religion: A Preface to a New Theory of Spirituality.* Cambridge, England: Cambridge International Science Publishing, Ltd.

FPHS = Peter Baofu. 2010. *The Future of Post-Human Sexuality: A Preface to a New Theory of the Body and Spirit of Love-Makers.* Cambridge, England: Cambridge Scholars Publishing, Ltd.

FPHSEM = Peter Baofu. 2012. *The Future of Post-Human Semantics: A Preface to a New Theory of Internality and Externality.* Cambridge, England: Cambridge Scholars Publishing, Ltd.

FPHST = Peter Baofu. 2006. *The Future of Post-Human Space-Time: Conceivng a Better Way to Understand Space and Time.* New York: Peter Lang Publishing, Inc.

FPHTRAN = Peter Baofu. 2012. *The Future of Post-Human Transportation: A Preface to a New Theory of Networks and Operations.* Cambridge, England: Cambridge Scholars Publishing, Ltd.

FPHU = Peter Baofu. 2008. *The Future of Post-Human Unconsciousness: A Preface to a New Theory of Anomalous Experience.* Cambridge, England: Cambridge Scholars Publishing, Ltd.

FPHUP = Peter Baofu. 2009. *The Future of Post-Human Urban Planning: A Preface to a New Theory of Density, Void, and Sustainability.* Cambridge, England: Cambridge Scholars Publishing, Ltd.

FPHWP = Peter Baofu. 2010. *The Future of Post-Human War and Peace: A Preface to a New Theory of Aggression and Pacificity.* Cambridge, England: Cambridge Scholars Publishing, Ltd.

• PART ONE •

Introduction

CHAPTER 1
INTRODUCTION—THE CONVENIENCE OF TRANSPORTATION

> The modern consequences of heavy automotive use contribute to the use of non-renewable fuels, a dramatic increase in the rate of accidental death, social isolation, the disconnection of community, the rise in obesity, the generation of air and noise pollution, urban sprawl, and urban decay.
> —Jane Holtz Kay (1998)

A Story of Two Contrastive Expectations

Can transportation really have such a destructive impact on society that, as Jay Holtz Kay (1998) once forcefully wrote, with the automobile industry as an example, that "the modern consequences of heavy automotive use contribute to the use of non-renewable fuels, a dramatic increase in the rate of accidental death, social isolation, the disconnection of community, the rise in obesity, the generation of air and noise pollution, urban sprawl, and urban decay"? (WK 2012)

This negative expectation from transportation, with the automobile industry as an example here, can be contrasted with an opposing (positive) expectation in the old "glory days" when, as Skip McGoun (2012) thus reminded us, "we have sung songs about the glory and wonder that surrounds the very concept of the car. Examples of this range from the 1909 tune, 'In My Merry Oldsmobile,' to what is considered to be the first rock and roll song, 'Rocket 88,' in 1949....Motion pictures have portrayed...expensive sleek sports cars...associated with wealth and success....One commercial described Hell as being a place where a teenager would have to drive a minivan!"

Contrary to these opposing expectations (and other views as will be discussed in the book), transportation (in relation to both networks and operations) is neither possible (or impossible) nor desirable (or undesirable) to the extent that the respective ideologues (on different sides) would like us to believe.

Of course, this challenge to the opposing expectations from transportation does not mean that transportation is useless, or that those interdisciplinary fields (related to transportation studies) like urban planning, environmental sustainability, migration, tourism, transport economics, traffic engineering, transportation technology, energy efficiency, the tragedy of the commons, and so on are unimportant. Needless to say, neither of these extreme views is reasonable.

Rather, this book offers an alternative (better) way to understand the future of transportation, especially in the dialectic context of networks and operations—while learning from different approaches in the literature but without favoring any one of them (nor integrating them, since they are not necessarily compatible with each other).

More specifically, this book offers a new theory (that is, *the panoramic theory of transportation*) to go beyond the existing approaches in a novel way.

If successful, this seminal project is to fundamentally change the way that we think about transportation in relation to networks and operations from the combined perspectives of the mind, nature, society, and culture, with enormous implications for the human future and what I originally called its "post-human" fate.

Definition and History of Transportation

A good starting point for this inquiry is to provide a working definition of the word "transportation" and to give a brief history of transportation as an introduction hereafter.

Definition

The term "transportation" (or "transport" in brief) refers to "the movement of people, animals and goods from one location to another. Modes of transport include air, rail, road, water, cable, pipeline, and space. The field can be divided into infrastructure, vehicles, and operations." (WK 2012a)

History

Historically, "transport is important since it enables trade between peoples, which in turn establishes civilizations." (WK 2012a)

For instance, "humans' first means of transport were walking and swimming. The domestication of animals introduces a new way to lay the burden of transport on more powerful creatures, allowing heavier loads to be hauled, or humans to ride the animals for higher speed and duration. Inventions such as the wheel and sled helped make animal transport more efficient through the introduction of vehicles. Also water transport, including rowed and sailed vessels, dates back to time immemorial, and was the only efficient way to transport large quantities or over large distances prior to the Industrial Revolution." (WK 2012a)

In antiquity, "the first forms of road transport were horses, oxen or even humans carrying goods over dirt tracks that often followed game trails. Paved roads were built by many early civilizations, including Mesopotamia and the Indus Valley Civilization. The Persian and Roman empires built stone-paved roads to allow armies to travel quickly. Deep roadbeds of crushed stone underneath ensured that the roads kept dry. The medieval Caliphate later built tar-paved roads. The first watercraft were canoes cut out from tree trunks. Early water transport was accomplished with ships that were either rowed or used the wind for propulsion, or a combination of the two. The importance of water has led to most cities, that grew up as sites for trading, being located on rivers or at sea, ofter at the intersection of two bodies of water. Until the Industrial Revolution, transport remained slow and costly, and production and consumption were located as close to each other as feasible." (WK 2012a)

In modern times, "the Industrial Revolution in the 19th century saw a number of inventions fundamentally change transport. With telegraphy, communication became instant and independent of transport. The invention of the steam engine, closely followed by its application in rail transport, made land transport independent of human or animal muscles. Both speed and capacity increased rapidly, allowing specialization through manufacturing being located independent of natural resources. The 19th century also saw the development of the steam ship, that sped up global transport." (WK 2012a)

Later, "with the development of the combustion engine and the automobile at the turn into the 20th century, road transport became more viable, allowing the introduction of mechanical private transport. The first highways were constructed during the 19th century with macadam. Later, tarmac and concrete became the dominant paving material. In 1903, the first controllable airplane was invented, and after World War I, it became a fast way to transport people and express goods over long distances." (WK 2012a; E. Bardi 2006)

And in contemporary times, "after World War II, the automobile and airlines took higher shares of transport, reducing rail and water to freight and short-haul passenger. Spaceflight was launched in the 1950s, with rapid growth until the 1970s, when interest dwindled. In the 1950s, the introduction of containerization gave massive efficiency gains in freight transport, permitting globalization. International air travel became much more accessible in the 1960s, with the commercialization of the jet engine. Along with the growth in automobiles and motorways, this introduced a decline for rail and water transport. After the introduction of the Shinkansen in 1964, high-speed rail in Asia and Europe started taking passengers on long-haul routes from airlines." (WK 2012a; C. Cooper 1998; E. Bardi 2006)

Networks and Operations in Transportation

With the definition and history of transportation (as given above) in mind—this book is to redefine the field in terms of *networks* and *operations*, while addressing the three issues of "infrastructure, vehicles, and operations" (in accordance with the above definition), as explained below (and summarized in *Table 1.1*).

Networks

The term "network," in accordance to the Merriam-Webster dictionary, refers to "a system of lines or channels" or "an interconnected or interrelated chain, group, or system." (MWD 2012)

All these different lines, channels, or groups are linked together at different points of intersection known as "nodes." (WK 2012b)

In the context of transportation, "networks" are understood in this book in regard to (a) infrastructure and (b) vehicles, as explained below.

Infrastructure

Networks in transportation can be understood in relation to "infrastructure," which refers to "the fixed installations necessary for transport, and may be roads, railways, airways, waterways, canals and pipelines, and terminals such as airports, railway stations, bus stations, warehouses, trucking terminals, refueling depots (including fueling docks and fuel stations), and seaports. Terminals may be used both for interchange of passengers and cargo and for maintenance." (WK 2012a)

Thus, transportation infrastructure can come in all shapes and sizes, as illustrated below: (WK 2012c)

- "Road and Highway Networks"—are "structures (bridges, tunnels, culverts, retaining walls), signage and markings, electrical systems (street lighting and traffic lights), edge treatments (curbs, sidewalks, landscaping), and specialized facilities such as road maintenance depots and rest areas."
- "Mass Transit Systems"—are "commuter rail systems, subways, tramways, trolleys and bus transportation."
- "Railways"—are "structures, terminal facilities (rail yards, train stations), level crossings, signalling and communications systems."
- "Canals and Navigable Waterways"—are those requiring "continuous maintenance (dredging, etc.)."
- "Airports"—refers to "air navigational systems" and the like.
- "Bicycle Paths and Pedestrian Walkways"—are "pedestrian bridges, pedestrian underpasses and other specialized structures for cyclists and pedestrians."

Of course, there can be other examples too (like "seaports and lighthouses," "ferries," etc.), so the ones above are illustrative, not exhaustive.

Vehicles

Networks in transportation can also be understood in relation to "vehicles," because infrastructure by itself is not enough; after all, vehicles are needed to travel on transportation networks with the installations (as described above).

The term "vehicle" here refers to "a device that is designed or used to transport people or cargo. Most often vehicles are manufactured, such as bicycles, cars, motorcycles, trains, ships, boats, and aircraft." (WK 2012d; W. Halsey 1979)

In general, there are two main classifications of vehicles.

Firstly, some vehicles are to travel on land, and good examples are shown below: (WK 2012d)

- Ex: bicycles
- Ex: cars
- Ex: motorcycles

- Ex: trains
- Ex: trucks

In addition, "land vehicles are classified broadly by what is used to apply steering and drive forces against the ground: wheeled, tracked, railed, or skied." (WK 2012d)

And secondly, "vehicles that do not travel on land often are called craft," and good examples are shown below: (WK 2012d)

- Ex: watercraft
- Ex: sailcraft
- Ex: aircraft
- Ex: hovercraft
- Ex: spacecraft

Issues like this about networks (in relation to both infrastructure and vehicles) will be analyzed (especially) in Chapter Two on networks and their intricacies.

Operations

But "networks" in transportation are not sufficient without "operations." In fact, "networks" and "operations" often interact in a mutually connected way.

In the context of transportation, the term "operation" refers to "the way the vehicles are operated, and the procedures set for this purpose including financing, legalities and policies." (WK 2012a)

Thus, "operations" are understood in this book in regard to different issues, and three good examples are (a) agency, (b) financing, and (c) legality and policy, as explained below.

Agency

A vehicle requires an agent (like a human driver or, conversely, an automated driver) to operate and drive it on a network in accordance to its installations.

The role of a driver is important, because a person who drives "under the influence of alcohol or drugs," for instance, can end up "injuring or killing someone." (WK 2012e)

Financing

In addition, to operate a vehicle on a network in transportation, or to build an installation for a network in transportation, can be costly, so the issue of "financing" is to be considered carefully.

This is true both for an individual who wants to buy a car and for a government which wants to build a highway, for instance.

A notorious example is the highway project in West Baltimore in the 1970s "that caused the demolition of 20 blocks of row-houses and churches on Baltimore's west side. Entire neighborhoods were wiped out and nearly 3,000 people displaced." (F. Shen 2010)

But for what ends? It turned out to be known as the "Highway to Nowhere," as it was "the stub end of a road that was never used." (F. Shen 2010)

Legality and Policy

Then, there is the issue about legality and policy, because operations are subject to different regulations in regard to different issues like driver's license, traffic congestion, noise pollution, air safety, vehicle maintenance, travel visa requirement, public health, global warming, etc.

Problems like this about operations (in relation to agency, financing, legality and policy) will be analyzed (especially) in Chapter Three on operations and their complications.

General Aspects of Transportation

This introduction to "networks" and "operations" in transportation thus reveals the more complicated nature of transportation.

To illustrate this more complicated nature further, consider some general aspects of transportation below (as summarized in *Table 1.1*).

Modes of Transport

The first general aspect of transportation to be illustrated here in regard to its more complicated nature concerns the "modes of transport." (WK 2012a)

By definition, "a mode of transport" refers to "a solution that makes use of a particular type of vehicle, infrastructure and operation. The transport of a person or of cargo may involve one mode or several modes, with the latter case being called intermodal or multimodal transport. Each mode has its advantages and disadvantages, and will be chosen for a trip on the basis of cost, capability, route, and speed." (WK 2012a)

Hereafter are some most common modes of transport.

Human-Powered

"Human-powered transport" is quite "common in developing countries" and refers to "the transport of people and/or goods using human muscle-power, in the form of walking, running and swimming. Modern technology has allowed machines to enhance human-power. Human-powered transport remains popular for reasons of cost-saving, leisure, physical exercise and environmentalism. Human-powered transport is sometimes the only type available, especially in underdeveloped or inaccessible regions. It is considered an ideal form of sustainable transportation." (WK 2012a)

Animal-Powered

"Animal-powered transport" is also "common in developing countries" and refers to "the use of working animals for the movement of people and goods. Humans may ride some of the animals directly, use them as pack animals for carrying goods, or harness them, alone or in teams, to pull sleds or wheeled vehicles. Animals are superior to people in their speed, endurance and carrying capacity; prior to the Industrial Revolution they were used for all land transport impracticable for people, and they remain an important mode of transport in less developed areas of the world." (WK 2012a)

Air

Air transport refers to different types of aviation; for example, "a fixed-wing aircraft, commonly called airplane," is "a heavier-than-air craft where movement of the air in relation to the wings is used to generate lift. The term is used to distinguish from rotary-wing aircraft, where the movement of the lift surfaces relative to the air generates lift. A gyroplane is both fixed-wing and rotary-wing. Fixed-wing aircraft range from small trainers and recreational aircraft to large airliners and military cargo aircraft." (WK 2012a)

In fact, "the aircraft is the second fastest method of transport, after the rocket. Commercial jets can reach up to 955 kilometres per hour (593 mph), single-engine aircraft 555 kilometres per hour (345 mph)," in our time. (WK 2012a)

Rail

Rail transport refers to "a train" which "runs along a set of two parallel steel rails, known as a railway or railroad. The rails are anchored perpendicular to ties (or sleepers) of timber, concrete or steel, to maintain a consistent distance apart, or gauge. The rails and perpendicular beams are placed on a foundation made of concrete, or compressed earth and gravel in a bed of ballast. Alternative methods include monorail and maglev." (WK 2012a; M. Lay 1992)

Road

Road transport refers to "an identifiable route, way or path between two or more places. Roads are typically smoothed, paved, or otherwise prepared to allow easy travel; though they need not be, and historically many roads were simply recognizable routes without any formal construction or maintenance. In urban areas, roads may pass through a city or village and be named as streets, serving a dual function as urban space easement and route." (WK 2012a)

It is important to remember that "the most common road vehicle is the automobile; a wheeled passenger vehicle that carries its own motor. Other users of roads include buses, trucks, motorcycles, bicycles and pedestrians. As of 2002, there were 590 million automobiles worldwide." (WK 2012a)

Ship

Ship transport refers to "the process of transport a watercraft, such as a barge, boat, ship or sailboat, makes over a body of water, such as a sea, ocean, lake, canal or river. The need for buoyancy unites watercraft, and makes the hull a dominant aspect of its construction, maintenance and appearance." (WK 2012a)

In the older days of "the 19th century, the first steam ships were developed, using a steam engine to drive a paddle wheel or propeller to move the ship. The steam was produced in a boiler using wood or coal and fed through a steam external combustion engine. Now most ships have an internal combustion engine using a slightly refined type of petroleum called bunker fuel. Some ships, such as submarines, use nuclear power to produce the steam. Recreational or educational craft still use wind power, while some smaller craft use internal combustion engines to drive one or more propellers, or in the case of jet boats, an inboard water jet. In shallow draft areas, hovercraft are propelled by large pusher-prop fans." (WK 2012a)

Other Modes

There are also other modes of transport, and good examples include the following: (WK 2012a)

- "Pipeline Transport"—"sends goods through a pipe, most commonly liquid and gases are sent, but pneumatic tubes can also send solid capsules using compressed air. For liquids/gases, any chemically stable liquid or gas can be sent through a pipeline. Short-distance systems exist for sewage, slurry, water and beer, while long-distance networks are used for petroleum and natural gas."
- "Cable Transport"—"is a broad mode where vehicles are pulled by cables instead of an internal power source. It is most commonly used at steep gradient. Typical solutions include aerial tramway, elevators, escalator and ski lifts; some of these are also categorized as conveyor transport."
- "Spaceflight"—"is transport out of Earth's atmosphere into outer space by means of a spacecraft. While large amounts of research have gone into technology, it is rarely used except to put satellites into orbit, and conduct scientific experiments. However, man has landed on the moon, and probes have been sent to all the planets of the Solar System."
- "Suborbital Spaceflight"—"is the fastest of the existing and planned transport systems from a place on Earth to a distant other place on Earth. Faster transport could be achieved through part of a Low Earth orbit, or following that trajectory even faster using the propulsion of the rocket to steer it."

Surely, there can be other modes of transport too, so the examples here are illustrative, not exhaustive.

Functions of Transport

The second general aspect of transportation to be illustrated here in regard to its more complicated nature concerns the "functions of transport." (WK 2012a)

There can be different functions of transport; for instance, "relocation of travelers and cargo are the most common uses of transport. However, other uses exist, such as the strategic and tactical relocation of armed forces during warfare, or the civilian mobility construction or emergency equipment." (WK 2012a)

In general, functions of transport are classified in terms of two main ones, as described below.

Passenger

"Passenger transport, or travel" is normally "divided into public and private transport. Public is scheduled services on fixed routes, while private is vehicles that provide ad hoc services at the riders desire. The latter offers better flexibility, but has lower capacity, and a higher environmental impact. Travel may be as part of daily commuting, for business, leisure or migration." (WK 2012a)

Freight

"Freight transport, or shipping" is "a key in the value chain in manufacturing. With increased specialization and globalization, production is being located further away from consumption, rapidly increasing the demand for transport. While all modes of transport are used for cargo transport, there is high differentiation between the nature of the cargo transport, in which mode is chosen. Logistics refers to the entire process of transferring products from producer to consumer, including storage, transport, transshipment, warehousing, material-handling and packaging, with associated exchange of information." (WK 2012a; S. Chopra 2007; E. Bardi 2006)

One important aspect of freight transport has to do with "containerization," which, "with the standardization of ISO containers on all vehicles and at all ports, has revolutionized international and domestic trade, offering huge reduction in transshipment costs. Traditionally, all cargo had to be manually loaded and unloaded into the haul of any ship or car; containerization allows for automated handling and transfer between modes, and the standardized sizes allow for gains in economy of scale in vehicle operation. This has been one of the key driving factors in international trade and globalization since the 1950s." (WK 2012a; E. Bardi 2006)

Impacts of Transport

And the third general aspect of transportation to be illustrated here in regard to its more complicated nature concerns the "impacts of transport." (WK 2012a)

Hereafter are three most vital impacts of transport.

Economy

In regard to the economy, "transport is a key necessity for specialization—allowing production and consumption of products to occur at different locations. Transport has throughout history been a spur to expansion; better transport allows more trade and a greater spread of people. Economic growth has always been dependent on increasing the capacity and rationality of transport. But the infrastructure and operation of transport has a great impact on the land and is the largest drainer of energy, making transport sustainability a major issue." (WK 2012a; M. Stopford 1997)

Also, "modern society dictates a physical distinction between home and work, forcing people to transport themselves to places of work or study, as well as to temporarily relocate for other daily activities. Passenger transport is also the essence of tourism, a major part of recreational transport. Commerce requires the transport of people to conduct business, either to allow face-to-face communication for important decisions or to move specialists from their regular place of work to sites where they are needed." (WK 2012a)

Planning

In regard to planning, "using models of transport forecasting, planners are able to predict future transport patterns. On the operative level, logistics allows owners of cargo to plan transport as part of the supply chain. Transport as a field is studied through transport economics, the backbone for the creation of regulation policy by authorities. Transport engineering, a sub-discipline of civil engineering, and must take into account trip generation, trip distribution, mode choice and route assignment, while the operative level is handled through traffic engineering." (WK 2012a)

In general, "too much infrastructure and too much smoothing for maximum vehicle throughput means that in many cities there is too much traffic and many—if not all—of the negative impacts that come with it. It is only in recent years that traditional practices have started to be questioned in many places, and as a result of new types of analysis which bring in a much broader range of skills than those traditionally relied on—spanning such areas as environmental impact analysis, public health, sociologists as well as economists who increasingly are questioning the viability of the old mobility solutions." (WK 2012a)

Environment

And in regard to the natural environment, "transport is a major use of energy and burns most of the world's petroleum. This creates air pollution, including nitrous oxides and particulates, and is a significant contributor to global warming through emission of carbon dioxide, for which transport is the fastest-growing emission sector. By subsector, road transport is the largest contributor to global warming. Environmental regulations in developed countries have reduced individual vehicles' emissions; however, this has been offset by increases in the numbers of vehicles and in the use of each vehicle. Some pathways to reduce the carbon emissions of road vehicles considerably have been studied. Energy use and emissions vary largely between modes, causing environmentalists to call for a transition from air and road to rail and human-powered transport, as well as increased transport electrification and energy efficiency." (WK 2012a; J. Fuglestvedt 2008; WI 2008)

Other environmental impacts are, for example, "traffic congestion and automobile-oriented urban sprawl, which can consume natural habitat and agricultural lands. By reducing transportation emissions globally, it is predicted that there will be significant positive effects on Earth's air quality, acid rain, smog and climate change." (WK 2012a)

The Theoretical Debate

These more complicated general aspects of transportation, together with the introduction to "networks" and "operations," then lead us to a more fundamental question concerning the theoretical debate on the very nature of transportation. Indeed, this theoretical debate can also say much about the study of transportation as a discipline over time.

Although there can be many different theoretical approaches in the debate—there are five main ones to be summarized hereafter, and they can be called, in the absence of better words, namely, (a) the *mental* argument, (b) the *natural* argument, (c) the *societal* argument, (d) the *cultural* argument, and (e) the *panoramic* argument (which is my original contribution to the debate), to be elabroated hereafter, respectively.

Lest misunderstanding occurs, three clarifications should be made here, as this is something that I regularly emphasize in my previous books, whenever a theoretical debate is summarized for a topic, *almost verbatim*.

Firstly, there can be other arguments besides the first four here, that is, the "mental," the "natural," the "societal," and the "cultural" arguments (as indicated above). The advantage to select these four here has to do with their illustrative representation of the diverse theories in the literature (which are deemed sufficient for the purpose at hand in this book).

Secondly, the examples (theories) given to illustrate each argument are also supposed to be illustrative, not exhaustive. After all, the arguments will be addressed again in the rest of the book, with other examples (theories) to be introduced.

And thirdly, the four arguments are not necessarily mutually exclusive. For instance, those who advocate the "mental" argument can also consider the "cultural" argument, although they do not focus on the latter.

And the reverse is also true, in that those who make the "cultural" argument can also consider the "mental" argument, although they do not focus on the latter.

In other words, their disagreement is often one in degree, not in kind.

The Mental Argument

With these three clarifications in mind—the first major theoretical approach is called, in the absence of better words, the *mental* argument, which focuses, relatively speaking of course, more on the biological and psychological aspects of transportation.

Thus, the word "mental" in the title of the argument is suggestive, because it refers to the focus on the physiological, biological and psychological aspects of transportation so understood.

But the mental argument has different issues of concern, and different defenders of the argument offer their own distinctive stands on the issues, depending on their own interests.

For illustration, consider two major versions of the mental argument, namely, (a) obesity and mechanized transportation, and (b) DUI and injury/death—to be addressed below, in that order.

Obesity and Mechanized Transportation

The first version of the mental argument has to do with "obesity" and "mechanized transportation" in the context of networks in the study of transportation.

The term "obesity" refers to "a medical condition in which excess body fat has accumulated to the extent that it may have an adverse effect on health, leading to reduced life expectancy and/or increased health problems. Body mass index (BMI), a measurement which compares weight and height, defines people as overweight (pre-obese) if their BMI is between 25 and 30 kg/m^2, and obese when it is greater than 30 kg/m^2." (WK 2012f; D. Haslam 2005; WHO 2000)

In the context of transportation, obesity occurs because of "insufficient exercise" resulting from the "increasing use of mechanized transportation and a greater prevalence of labor-saving technology in the home." (WK 2012f; WHO 2012)

The danger of obesity is that it "increases the likelihood of various diseases, particularly heart disease, type 2 diabetes, obstructive sleep apnea, certain types of cancer, and osteoarthritis." (WK 2012f; D. Haslam 2005)

However, for the critics, this study of obesity and mechanized transportation has some major problems. Consider, for illustration, a few examples below.

Firstly, one main criticism of the study of obesity and mechanized transportation is that there are multiple causes of obesity which need to be examined.

For example, for the critics, obesity can be caused by "diet," "genetics," "sendentary lifestyle," "medical and psychiatric illness," "infectious agents," and "social determinants"; therefore, to blame "mechanized transportation" for the rise of obesity is rather simplistic as an explanation. (WK 2012f)

And secondly, another main criticism of the study of obesity and mechanized transportation is that the causal relationship between obesity and negative health has been questioned too.

For instance, for the critics, "the principal goal of the fat acceptance movement is to decrease discrimination against people who are overweight and obese"; "some in the movement are also attempting to challenge the established relationship between obesity and negative health outcomes." (WK 2012f; NAAFA 2009; A. Pulver 2007)

DUI and Injury/Death

The second version of the mental argument has to do with "DUI" and injury/death in the context of operations in the study of transportation.

The term "driving under the influence (DUI)" (aka "driving while intoxicated [DWI], drunken driving, drunk driving, operating under the influence, drinking and driving, impaired driving") refers to "the act of driving a motor vehicle with blood levels of alcohol in excess of a legal limit. Similar regulations cover driving or operating certain types of machinery while affected by drinking alcohol or taking other drugs." (WK 2012e)

In the context of transportation, DUI is dangerous, because it can lead to "injuring or killing someone while under the influence of alcohol or drugs"; it is thus no wonder that DUI "is a criminal offense in most countries. Convictions do not necessarily involve actual driving of the vehicle." (WK 2012e)

However, for the critics, this study of DUI and injury/death has some major problems. Consider, for illustration, a few examples below.

Firstly, one main criticism of the study of DUI and injury/death is that the test to measure DUI is not without controversy.

For instance, conventionally, DUI is established by such methods like "observed driving symptoms" (e.g., "weaving") and "field sobriety tests" (e.g., "walking a straight line heel-to-toe or standing on one leg for 30 seconds"), together with "the arresting officer's subjective opinion of impairment." (WK 2012e) But these methods can be subjectively or incorrectly followed.

And secondly, another main criticism of the study of DUI and injury/death is that what counts as "guilt" in DUI cases varies from country to country.

For instance, "the laws relating to drunk driving vary between countries and varying blood alcohol content is allowed before a conviction is made." (WK 2012e)

The Natural Argument

The second theoretical approach is called, in the absence of better words, the *natural* argument, which focuses, relatively speaking of course, more on the natural aspects of transporation, especially in relation to the state of nature.

Therefore, the word "natural" in the title of the argument is suggestive, because it refers to the focus on the natural aspects of transportation so understood.

Like the mental argument—the natural argument has different issues of concern, and different defenders of the argument offer their own distinctive stands on the issues, depending on their own interests.

For illustration, consider two major versions of the natural argument, namely, (a) energy and locomotion and (b) air pollution and regulation—to be summarized below, in that order.

Energy and Locomotion

The first version of the natural argument has to do with energy and locomotion in the context of networks in the study of transportation.

The word "locomotion" refers to the movement "by being towed by another vehicle or animal, or by obtaining, converting and using energy," so "it is essential that a vehicle have a source of energy to drive it. Energy can be extracted from the surrounding environment, as in the case of a sailboat, a solar powered car, or a streetcar. Energy can also be stored, in any form, provided it can be converted on demand and the storing medium's energy density and power density are sufficient to meet the vehicle's needs" (as in the case of "batteries"). (WK 2012d)

In any event, "when needed, the energy is taken from the source and consumed by one or more motors or engines….The mechanical energy that motors and engines produce needs to be converted to work by wheels, propellers, nozzles, or similar means. Aside from converting mechanical energy into motions, wheels allow a vehicle to roll along a surface and, with the exception of railed vehicles, to steer. Wheels are ancient technology, with specimens being discovered from over 5000 years ago. Wheels are used in a plethora of vehicles, including motor vehicles, armoured personnel carriers, amphibious vehicles, airplanes, trains, skateboards, and wheelbarrows." (WK 2012d; K. Nice 2011; A. Gasser 2003)

However, for the critics, this study of locomotion and energy has some major problems. Consider, for illustration, a few examples below.

Firstly, one main criticism of the study of locomotion and energy is that the issue of "friction" has yet to be completely resolved.

For instance, it is known that "all or almost all of the energy added by the engine is usually lost as friction; so minimizing frictional losses are very important in many vehicles." (WK 2012d)

And secondly, another main criticism of the study of locomotion and energy is that the braking mechanism of a vehicle can fail, so that a vehicle may not stop at the right time when needed.

For instance, for the critics, although "with no power, most vehicles will come to a stop due to friction," "in many cases…it may be desirable to stop a vehicle faster than it otherwise would." (WK 2012d) Precisely here, the braking mechaism can fail for various reasons.

Air Pollution, and Regulation

And the second version of the natural argument has to do with air pollution and regulation in the context of operations in the study of transportation.

The term "air pollution" refers to "the introduction of chemicals, particulate matter, or biological materials that cause harm or discomfort to humans or other living organisms, or cause damage to the natural environment or built environment, into the atmosphere. The atmosphere is a complex dynamic natural gaseous system that is essential to support life on planet Earth. Stratospheric ozone depletion due to air pollution has long been recognized as a threat to human health as well as to the Earth's ecosystems." (WK 2012h)

In the curent context of transportation, air pollution has been seriously caused by "mobile sources" which include "motor vehicles, marine vessels, aircraft and the effect of sound etc." (WK 2012h)

For this reason, there are two different "legal regulations" to ensure certain "air quality standards. The first class of standards (such as the U.S. National Ambient Air Quality Standards and E.U. Air Quality Directive) set maximum atmospheric concentrations for specific pollutants. Environmental agencies enact regulations which are intended to result in attainment of these target levels. The second class (such as the North American Air Quality Index) take the form of a scale with various thresholds, which is used to communicate to the public the relative risk of outdoor activity." (WK 2012h)

However, for the critics, this study of air pollution and regulation has some major problems. Consider, for illustration, a few examples below.

Firstly, one main criticism of the study of air pollution and regulation is that "mobile sources" are only ones among different sources of air pollution.

For instance, for the critics, one should not blame mobile sources too much for air pollution, since there are many other sources, and good examples include "sulphur oxides" (by volcanoes), "nitrogen oxides" (by thunderstorms), "particular matter" (by dust storms, forest and grassland fires, etc.), and so on. (WK 2012h)

And secondly, another main criticism of the study of air pollution and regulation is that it does not often work, because of disagreements.

For instance, for the critics, "the Air Quality Health Index or 'AQHI'" in Canada is "a federal program jointly coordinated by Health Canada and Environment Canada. However, the AQHI program would not be possible without the commitment and support of the provinces, municipalities and NGOs," which do not always agree. (WK 2012h)

The Societal Argument

The third theoretical approach is called, in the absence of better words, the *societal* argument, which focuses, relatively speaking of course, more on the societal aspects of transportation (e.g., organizational, institutional, structural, and technological issues).

In this sense, the word "societal" in the title of the argument is suggestive, because it refers to the societal aspects of transportation so understood.

Like the mental and natural arguments—the societal argument has different issues of concern, and different defenders of the argument offer their own distinctive stands on the issues, depending on their own interests.

For illustration, consider two major versions of the societal argument, namely, (a) technology, and car manufacturing, and (b) air safety, and criminal acts—to be summarized in what follows, in that order.

Technology, and Car Manufacturing

The first version of the societal argument has to do with "technology" and "car manufacturing" in the context of networks in the study of transportation.

The term "technology" in the context of car manufacturing refers to the advances in making "varied energy sources and materials, which are being developed in order to make automobiles more energy efficient with reduced regulated emissions. Cars are being developed in many different ways. With rising gas prices, now the future of cars is leaning towards fuel efficiency, energy-savers, hybrid vehicles, battery electric vehicles, and fuel-cell vehicles." (WK 2012i)

However, for the critics, this study of technology and car manufacturing in the context of transportation has some major problems. Consider, for illustration, a few examples below.

Firstly, one main criticism of this study of technology and car manufacturing is that the latter only intensifies the problem of "automobile dependency." (WK 2012j)

For instance, Peter Newman and Jeff Kenworthy argued against "automobile dependency" by pointing out the current "predicament of most cities in the United States, Canada, Australia and New Zealand, and to a lesser extent, large cities in Europe. Automobile dependency implies that cities where automobiles are the predominant transport deny their residents not only freedom of choice about the way they live and move around the city but also that the culture of automobile use has produced a kind of addiction to them." (WK 2012j)

And secondly, another main criticism of this study of technology and car manufacturing is that the automobile industry has contributed to a lot of social ills.

For instance, Jay Holtz Kay (1998) once forcefully argued that "the modern consequences of heavy automotive use contribute to the use of non-renewable fuels, a dramatic increase in the rate of accidental death, social isolation, the disconnection of community, the rise in obesity, the generation of air and noise pollution, urban sprawl, and urban decay." (WK 2012)

Air Safety, and Criminal Acts

And the second version of the societal argument has to do with "air safety" and "criminal acts" in the context of operations in the study of transportation.

The term "air safety" refers to the "investigation and categorization of flight failures, and the prevention of such failures through regulation, education and training. It can also be applied in the context of campaigns that inform the public as to the safety of air travel." (WK 2012k)

In cases involving criminal acts, air safety can become an important issue, when, for example, "since the September 11, 2001 attacks, stricter airport and airline security measures are in place to prevent terrorism"; in other cases, "aircraft, whether passenger planes or military aircraft, are sometimes attacked in both peacetime and war. Examples of this include," say, "the Soviet Air Defence Forces shot down Korean Air Lines Flight 007" in 1983. (WK 2012k)

However, for the critics, this study on air safety and criminal acts has some major problems. Consider, for illustration, a few examples below.

Firstly, one main criticism of the study on air safety and criminal acts is that what counts as "criminal" is in the eyes of the beholder.

For instance, for the critics, when "the Soviet Air Defence Forces shot down Korean Air Lines Flight 007" in 1983, it was portrayed as criminal in the American mainstream media during the Cold War, since, "on 5 September 1983, U.S. President Ronald Reagan condemned the shooting down of the airplane as the 'Korean airline massacre,' a 'crime against humanity [that] must never be forgotten' and an 'act of barbarism ... [and] inhuman brutality.'" (WK 2012l) The Soviet Union, on the other hand, accused the U.S. of recklessly using the civilian aircraft for "a spy mission." (WK 2012l; SPT 1983)

And secondly, another main criticism of the study on air safety and criminal acts is that each opposing side on the fence does what it accuses the other side of doing.

For instance, a few years after "the Soviet Air Defence Forces shot down Korean Air Lines Flight 007" in 1983, "the United States Navy shot down Iran Air Flight 655" in 1988. (WK 2012k)

The Cultural Argument

The fourth theoretical approach is called, in the absence of better words, the *cultural* argument, which focuses, relatively speaking of course, more on the cultural aspects of transportation (e.g., issues in relation to values and beliefs).

Therefore, the word "cultural" in the title of the argument is suggestive, because it refers to the focus on the cultural aspects of transportation so understood.

Like the mental, natural, and societal arguments—the cultural argument has different issues of concern, and different defenders of the argument offer their own distinctive stands on the issues, depending on their own interests.

For illustration, consider two major versions of the cultural argument, namely, (a) car culture, and individualism and (b) New Pedestrianism, and the anti-sedentary lifestyle—to be summarized in what follows, in that order.

Car Culture, and Individualism

The first version of the cultural argument has to do with "car culture" and "individualism" in the context of networks in the study of transportation.

The term "car culture" refers to a culture in which "automobiles were incorporated into artworks including music, books and movies. Between 1905 and 1908, more than 120 songs were written in which the automobile was the subject. Novels celebrating the political effects of motorization included Free Air by Sinclair Lewis. Where earlier mass media had made heroes of Casey Jones, Allan Pinkerton and other dutiful protectors of public transport, new road movies offered heroes who found freedom and equality on the open road." (WK 2012; K. Jackson 1987)

George Monbiot (2005), for instance, argued that "widespread car culture has shifted voter's preference to the right of the political spectrum. He thinks that car culture has contributed to an increase in individualism and fewer social interactions between members of different socioeconomic classes." (WK 20102)

However, for the critics, the study of car culture and individualism has some major problems. Consider, for illustration, a few examples below.

Firstly, one main criticism of the study of car culture and individualism is that the U.S. had long been an individualist culture even before the invention of the automobiles.

For instance, a good example is "the Bill of Rights" which is "the collective name for the first ten amendments to the United States Constitution. These limitations serve to protect the natural rights of liberty and property." (WK 2012m)

And secondly, another main criticism of the study of car culture and individualism is that whether or not individualism is desirable for a culture to have is a relative value judgement.

For instance, what is bad for Monbiot in regard to individualism may well be entirely desirable for those who believe in libertarianism.

New Pedestrianism, and the Anti-Sedentary Lifestyle

And the second version of the cultural argument has to do with "New Pedestrianism" and the anti-sedentary lifestyle in the context of operations in the study of transportation.

The term "New Pedestrianism (NP)" refers to a term used by Michael E. Arth in 1999 to "respect…traditional town design,…[and] seek…to further reduce the negative impact of the automobile, the use of which has increased dramatically since WWII. By eliminating the front street and replacing it with a tree-lined pedestrian lane, emphasis is placed on low-impact alternative travel such as walking and cycling. Pedestrian lanes are usually 12 to 15 feet (5 m) wide, with one smooth side for rolling conveyances such as bicycles, Segways, and skates and the other, narrower, textured side for pedestrians and wheelchairs. Eliminating the automobile street from the front allows for intimate scale plazas, fountains, pocket parks, as well as an unspoiled connection to natural features such as lakes, streams, and forests that may border or be included in a Pedestrian Village." (WK 2012m)

However, for the critics, the study of New Pedestrianism and the anti-sedentary lifestyle has some major problems. Consider, for illustration, a few examples below.

Firstly, one main criticism of the study of New Pedestrianism and the anti-sedentary lifestyle is that its ideology is persuasive, relative to its supporters.

For instance, those who accept New Pedestrianism tends to also support an anti-sedentary lifestyle associated with it for walking and cycling—but NP does not draw a lot of support from those who are still in love with the car culture and all its convenience.

And secondly, another main criticism of the study of New Pedestrianism and the anti-sedentary lifestyle is that it can get too radical at times.

For instance, in 2007, "Arth proposed that a Pedestrian Village be built for the adult homeless in Volusia County, Florida," but "the proposal… garner[ed] derision from some quarters by being called either a 'resort for the homeless' or a 'gulag reservation,'" or even a "leper colony" by Rebbecca Mahoney (2007). (WK 2012n)

The Panoramic Argument

And fifthly, unlike the previous four arguments (viz., the mental, the natural, the societal, and the cultural)—the fifth one to be introduced here can be called, in the absence of better words again, the *panoramic* argument, which learns from all other theoretical approaches (which include the previous four arguments and also other examples as will be introduced in the rest of this book), without, however, favoring any of them, nor trying to integrate them (as they are not necessarily compatible with each other, as the introduction of the theoretical debate in the previous sub-sections has shown).

The Panoramic Theory of Transportation

My *panoramic* argument can be more precisely called *the panoramic theory of transportation*, since it is to propose a new theory of networks and operations in the study of transportation.

My *panoramic theory of transportation* has four major distinct features.

Firstly, my theory makes good use of all theoretical approaches to the study of transportation in relation to networks and operations, be they about the mental argument, the natural argument, the societal argument, or the cultural argument—especially from the most comprehensive combined perspectives of the mind, nature, society, and culture (as will be dealt with in Chapter Two and Chapter Three).

Secondly, just like many other theories of mine in my previous books, my theory here does not heavily favor any specific theory over others in the literature, nor trying to integrate them (as they are not necessarily compatible with each other).

Thirdly, my theory treats the issue of transportation in the distinctive dialectic context of no networks without operations, and vice versa.

And fourthly, it contains twenty-six major theses, namely, (a) the first thesis: the formalness-informalness principle, (b) the second thesis: the absoluteness-relativeness principle, (c) the third thesis: the partiality-totality principle, (d) the fourth thesis: the predictability-unpredictability principle, (e) the fifth thesis: the explicability-inexplicability principle, (f) the sixth thesis: the fiction-reality principle, (g) the seventh thesis: the finiteness-transfiniteness principle, (h) the eighth thesis: the preciseness-vagueness principle, (i) the ninth thesis: the simpleness-complicatedness principle, (j) the tenth thesis: the openness-hiddenness principle, (k) the eleventh thesis: the denseness-emptiness principle, (l) the twelfth thesis: the change-constancy principle, (m) the thirteenth thesis: the order-chaos principle, (n) the fourteenth thesis: the slowness-quickness principle, (o) the fifteenth thesis: the expansion-contraction principle, (p) the sixteenth thesis: the theory-praxis principle, (q) the seventeenth thesis: the convention-novelty principle, (r) the eighteenth thesis: the evolution-transformation principle, (s) the nineteenth thesis: the symmetry-asymmetry principle, (t) the twentieth thesis: the softness-hardness principle, (u) the twenty-first thesis: the seriousness-playfulness principle, (v) the twenty-second thesis: the activeness-inactiveness principle, (w) the twenty-third thesis: the regression-progression principle, (x) the twenty-fourth thesis: the sameness-difference principle, (y) the twenty-fifth thesis: the stability-reaction principle, and (z) the twenty-sixth thesis: the post-human panorama—to be elaborated in the rest of the book, with a summary in the concluding chapter.

Because of the last thesis on "the post-human panorama," the word "panoramic" in the title of my theory are suggestive, because it refers to a comprehensive analysis of transportation, so as to explore multiple views regarding the dialectic interactions between networks and operations in the study of transportation (together with other debates as will be discussed in the rest of the book), and calls for a need to transcend them by future advanced humans and later post-humans in the context of the great transformations of transportation in the future world (as will be discussed in the concluding chapter, Chapter Four).

With this clarification in mind—the seminal project here, if successful, will fundamentally change the way that we think about networks and operations in the study of transportation (together with other debates as will be discussed in the rest of the book), from the combined perspectives of the mind, nature, society, and culture, with enormous implications for the human future and what I originally called its "post-human" fate.

Theory and Meta-Theory

The *panoramic* argument, or *the panoramic theory of transportation*, presupposes some kind of meta-theory, in special relation to methodology and ontology—just as all theories, either explicitly or implicitly, require their own versions of meta-theory.

Meta-Theory

As so often clarified in my previous books—theory and meta-theory, broadly speaking, can be further classified into different categories, as shown below:

- On Theory
  - —Ex: in relation to the mind
  - —Ex: in relation to nature
  - —Ex: in relation to society
  - —Ex: in relation to culture
- On Meta-Theory
  - —Ex: in relation to methodology
  - —Ex: in relation to ontology

Each category, in its turn, can then be further sub-divided into different levels of analysis—which will be elaborated in the next two sections (and summarized in *Table 4.43*).

With this reminder in mind, I already proposed (in my previous books) my distinctive contribution to meta-theory, namely, methodology (like "theory of methodological holism," "complex theory of data analysis," and "critical-dialectic theory of formal science," for instance) and ontology (like "theory of existential dialectics" and "contrastive theory of rationality," for instance).

The next two sections are to introduce my meta-theory—especially, existential dialectics and sophisticated methodological holism, respectively—to be repeated, *often verbatim* (with only a few updated revisions), from my previous works, as this is something that I often do in each new book of mine as an introduction to some background information for the convenience of the readers.

In the process, I shall also introduce my numerous new theories (or to be exact, 59 of them in 51 books so far, as of January 2012) in relation to the four categories of the mind, nature, society, and culture in the context of theory (as also summarized in *Table 4.43*).

A Unified Theory of Everything

In the end, my distinctive contribution to both meta-theory and theory serves as a foundation to unify all domains of knowledge (i.e., the social sciences, the formal sciences, the natural sciences, and the humanities) for an overarching understanding of all forms of reality (by way of some ontological principles at the meta-theoretical level and the comprehensive perspectives of the mind, nature, society, and culture at the theoretical level—as will be explained in the next two sections).

This is so, without commiting the sins of reductionism and reverse-reductionism (as often seen in many holistic approaches, with the fad of systems approach as a most recent notorious example, as already critically explained in *The Future of Post-Human Formal Science*, or *FPHFS*), since my distinctive contribution makes good use of different schools of thought without heavily favoring any of them nor trying to integrate them (as they are not necessarily compatible with each other), so as to include (or adjust for) heterogeneity, conflict, subjectivity, and complexity, for example.

In this sense, the word "unified" does not have to mean an integrative approach, in a narrow sense, nor a systems approach, in a broad one, both of which I have critically rebuked (in my previous books), while learning from them.

This overarching project (consisting of numerous theories of mine, as will be summarized in the next section), thus, constitutes my grand unifed theory of everything in the world and beyond.

The Logic of Existential Dialectics

To start, the ontology of existential dialectics can be summarized in this section—*often verbatim* (with only a few updated revisions), from my previous works, as this is something that I regularly do in each new book of mine as an introduction to some background information for the convenience of the readers.

After all, this book, like all others of mine, is in conversation with all previous ones of mine, for the final aim to converge all of them into a larger grand project on the future of intelligent life, both here on earth and there in deep space unto multiverses.

The summary can be organized in relation to (a) the conception of existential dialectics (or its ontics), (b) the syntax of existential dialectics (or its ontomethodology and ontologic), (c) the semantics of existential dialectics (or its ontosemantics), and (d) the pragmatics of existential dialectics (or its ontopragmatics), respectively hereafter—again *often verbatim*.

This means that, for those readers who had read some of my previous books, the summary below is really not much new (*almost verbatim*, with only some updated revisions).

But for those who have never read my previous books, it is a good review of them.

The Conception of Existential Dialectics (or Its Ontics)

This ontology was originally designated as "existential dialectics" in *Beyond Capitalism to Post-Capitalism* (herein abbreviated as *BCPC*), although it was already analyzed in other books of mine like the 2 volumes of *The Future of Human Civilization* (*FHC*), *The Future of Capitalism and Democracy* (*FCD*), *The Future of Post-Human Consciousness* (*FPHC*), and the 2 volumes of *Beyond Democracy to Post-Democracy* (*BDPD*).

Lest any confusion occurs, it is important to stress at the outset that the word 'existential' in "existential dialectics" has nothing to do with Existentialism, which I rebuked in *FHC*, *FCD*, and also *FPHC*. Instead, the word here merely refers to the existence of intelligent life (both primitive and advanced) in a broad sense.

Some Basic Concepts

The conception of existential dialectics (or its ontics) makes use of different concepts (like "sets," "elements," "relations," "operations," "functions," "truth values," "axioms," "postulates," and "principles"—as shown in *Table 4.3*), which are important for the understanding of any logic of ontology.

That clarified—existential dialectics, as a language of ontology, can be analyzed in different ways that a language, as an analogy, is often analyzed, namely, in relation to phonology ("the study of patterns of a language's sounds"), phonetics ("the study of the physical aspects of sounds of human language"), morphonology ("the study of the internal structure of words"), syntax ("the study of how words combine to form grammatical sentences"), semantics ("the study of the meaning of words [lexical semantics] and fixed word combinations [phraseology]"), and pragmatics ("the study of how utterances are used…literally, figuratively, or otherwise…in communicative acts"). (WK 2007)

But since my theory of existential dialectics makes use of the English language for communication here, it does not propose a new way to make the patterns of a language's sounds (as in phonology), to study the physical aspects of sounds (as in phonetics), or even to strive for a new organization of the internal structure of words for the English language (as in morphonology).

For this reason, the language of existential dialectics to be analyzed hereafter is not concerned with the phonological, phonetic, and morphonological aspects of the English language. Instead, the analysis will explore the syntax, semantics, and pragmatics of existential dialectics as a language of ontology to improve our understanding of reality.

The Ontic Dispute

But first, there is an ontic dispute to be addressed, which is related to what I called "the dilemma of ontology" as introduced earlier in *Sec. 1.4* of *The Future of Post-Human Knowledge* (*FPHK*).

A good point of departure concerns what I want to call *the ontic dispute*, on how to understand the very nature of ontology.

Traditionally, scholars in the field used to study the conception of ontology in terms of its entities (e.g., material objects, abstract numbers), properties (e.g., duration, plurality), and relationships (e.g., causation).

This is a good starting point, but it suffers from different problems. Consider three examples of bias below, which are quite common in the literature, and the recent version (of treating concepts and principles in ontology on the basis of "plurality," "dynamism," "duration," "interaction," "life," "consciousness," and "volition") by Reginald Firehammer (2005) only constitutes a latest addition to this old (impoverishing) tradition.

Firstly, the classification of entities, properties, and relationships is too material-centric, in often focusing more on the existence of material entities than on non-material ones.

Secondly, the classification is too anthropo-centric, in often favoring the factor of human agency in depicting reality.

And lastly, the classification is too confused among the three categories relating to each other, in often lumping them together without adequate consideration of their intricated interrelationships (both in relation to each and in relation to all).

A good alternative is precisely what I want to offer in this debate, that is, a new classification of ontological entities, properties, and their relationships in terms of *method*, *structure*, *process*, *agency*, and *outcome* instead. Let me explicate what these words mean below.

In relation to "method"—it concerns how ontology is to be studied. In this sense, the word 'method' here should not be confused with the different usage of the same term 'method' as a technique of investigation in the context of methodology (as already introduced in *Sec. 1.2* of *FPHK*).

In relation to "structure"—it concerns what the general patterns of entities, properties, and relationships are.

In relation to "process"—it concerns how these general patterns change over time.

In relation to "agency"—it concerns how agency affects any change of these general patterns over time (without putting, however, too much emphasis on the role of human agency).

And in relation to "outcome"—it concerns what the outputs of this change over time are.

The Syntax of Existential Dialectics (or Its Ontomethodology and Ontologic)

The syntax of existential dialectics, analogously speaking, refers here to the structure of an ontology which can be studied by way of combining ideas into complex relationships like ontological principles to depict reality in the world—and can be analyzed in seven sub-sections, namely, (a) the selection criteria, (b) further clarifications on classification, (c) ontomethodology, (d) ontologic, (e) the principles as short cuts, (f) the principles as family resemblances, and (g) the dialectic constraints imposed by the principles, respectively hereafter.

The Selection Criteria

To start, not any pair of relationship can be chosen as an ontological principle in existential dialectics; otherwise, there could be billions of them under the sky.

Six illustrations below suffice to clarify this point.

(a) Firstly, an ontological principle cannot *overlap* with other principles, in that it is too closely related with other ones.

Of course, one cannot totally rule out any relationship between two entities, especially in a complex world of everything being linked to everything else—but the comparison here is relative, not absolute.

In this sense, the flexibility-inflexibility pair cannot be an ontological principle, since it has something closely in common with other ones (like the simpleness-complicatedness principle, for instance).

As an illustration, something which is flexible in interpretation is more likely to allow multiple viewpoints and thus makes the overall picture more complicated than otherwise (simple).

(b) Secondly, an ontological principle cannot be *redundant* in relation to other principles, in that it somehow duplicates other principles.

In this sense, for instance, the directness-indirectness pair cannot be an ontological principle, because it somehow duplicates other ontological principles (like the preciseness-vagueness principle, for instance).

As an illustration, something which is direct means to be right to the point and does not need to go to an unnecessarily long loop—so it is less vague, in being clearer about the thing in question.

(c) Thirdly, an ontological principle cannot be *derived* from other ones—as if it is a child-parent relationship.

In this sense, the convenience-inconvenience pair cannot be an ontological principle, because it can be derived from other ones (like the slowness-quickness principle, for instance).

For instance, something which is convenient already implies that it can be obtained quickly (rather than slowly)—all things considered.

(d) Fourthly, an ontological principle cannot be *trivial* (or *parochial*)—as if it is only one component competing with other ones for inclusion in a set.

In this sense, the consistency-inconsistency pair cannot be an ontological principle, because its validity is limited (or parochial), as it can be easily challenged and replaced by opposing major (not minor) theories (e.g., the correspondence theory of truth, the pragmatic theory of truth, the semantic theory of truth, the disclosedness theory of truth, and whatnot), not just in accordance to the consistency (or coherence) theory of truth (for consistency).

Thus, the consistency argument is only one among different opposing arguments in relation to the logic of what constitutes "truth."

(e) Fifthly, an ontological principle cannot be *one-sided*, that is, part of one side (category) of a dialectic pair.

In this sense, the extroversion-introversion pair cannot be an ontological principle, since it is part of the side (category) of "normality" in the normality-abnormaltiy pair (because both extroversion and introversion are two different "normal" personality traits in psychology).

In addition, the normality-abnormality pair is already related to the symmetry-asymmetry principle, the density-emptiness principle, the convention-novelty principle, and the same-difference principle (as will be explained in the section on "the principles as family resemblances" later).

(f) And sixthly, an ontological principle cannot be *misleading*, in that the two apparent opposites are not really opposites at all, upon closer examination.

In this sense, the east-west pair cannot be an ontological principle, since east and west are not really opposites, as there are also north, south, and center to form a set of five opposing elements.

By the same logic, the left-right pair cannot be an ontological principle, since left and right (width) are not really opposites, as there are also top and bottom (height), back and front (depth), and center to form a set of seven elements in four categories. In the field of visual design, this set of seven elements is known as "form" (as opposed to "function"), as addressed in *FPHARCH*. (WK 2011nn)

Although these six examples (criteria) are not exhaustive, they illustrative the selectiveness of any ontological principle to be existentially dialectic.

Further Clarifications on Classification

Lest any misunderstanding carelessly occurs, some further clarifications on classification should be made here (and summarized in *Table 4.8*).

(a) Firstly, the total number of ontological principles is unknown, to be discovered later, as our knowledge of the world becomes more advanced.

Consequently, the principles as introduced in my books are not exhaustive, with new ones being added, whenever more of them are discovered in later research.

At least, future generations can pick up where I leave off and continue the discovery.

In this sense, my work should be treated as a pioneering effort for the development of a systematic, comprehensive analysis of a new general ontology for the future of knowledge.

(b) Secondly, the principles are not rigidly classified, as they can be reclassified in a different way.

For instance, the preciseness-vagueness principle is classified under the category of "structure" but can be reclassified under the category of "method," although in so doing, it has a different meaning in the context of method.

The same logic applies to the same-difference principle under the category of "outcome," which can be reclassified under the category of "structure," although in so doing, once more, it has a different meaning in the context of structure.

(c) Thirdly, the principles are to be understood together, not that each prinicple is to be treated independently of others. After all, the principles are mutually constraining, in that they work together as a whole.

(d) Fourthly, the principles are relevant to all subject matters, but some principles are, relatively speaking of course, more useful to some subject matters than others under certain conditions—as implied in the symmetry-asymmetry principle.

(e) And fifthly, the principles constitute only two levels of analysis, this time, at the ontological and methodological levels—while other levels of analysis (from the perspectives of the mind, nature, society, and culture) are also needed, in order to understand reality in its totality (as explained in the section on "sophisticated methodological holism," so as to avoid the dual dangers of reductionism and reverse-reductionism).

Ontomethodology

With these selection criteria and clarifications in mind—the syntax of existential dialectics can be divided into two main smaller sections for analysis, since they are related to each other in the context of some fundamental principles, that is, (a) ontomethodology and (b) ontologic, to be addressed hereafter, respectively.

In the context of ontomethodology, some ontological principles are proposed here in relation to the nature of methodology, which however is tied up with the general issue of ontology in the context of knowledge.

In this sense, ontomethodology (in the context of these ontological principles in the category of method) are related with ontologic in general (in the context of ontological principles in general).

Some good instances of ontological principles involving ontomethodology include the formalness-informalness principle, the absoluteness-relativeness principle, the partiality-totality principle, the predictability-unpredictability principle, the explicability-inexplicability principle, and the fiction-reality principle, which will be introduced in conjunction with ontological principles in the ontologic of existential dialectics in general hereafter.

Ontologic

With this clarification of the relationship between ontomethodology and ontologic in mind (which is comparable to the relationship between methodology and ontology as described in *Sec. 1.3* of *FPHK*)—the first three principles in existential dialectics were introduced in *BCPC*. And more principles were later added to the logic in my subsequent books (like *FC*, *FAE*, and others), as explained below.

More specifically, in *BCPC*, I proposed three principles (based on previous works of mine, not just something out of the blue) for the ontological logic, namely, (a) the regression-progression principle on the direction of history, (b) the symmetry-asymmetry principle on the relationships among existents, and (c) the change-constancy principle on the alteration of things—or in a more elegant term, the dynamics of space-time (in *FC*).

In *The Future of Complexity* (*FC*), I added three more principles, on top of the three aforementioned, namely, (d) the partiality-totality principle on the relationships between parts and whole, (e) the order-chaos principle on the pattern of things, and (f) the predictability-unpredictability principle on the occurrence of things—as part of the ontological logic of existential dialectics.

In *The Future of Aesthetic Experience* (or simply *FAE*), another principle is added, namely, (g) the evolution-transformation principle (on the multiple kinds of agency).

Also in *FAE*, I then reclassified the 7 principles into four categories, namely, (i) in relation to method, for the partiality-totality principle and the predictability-unpredictability principle, (ii) in relation to process, for the change-constancy principle and the order-chaos principle, (iii) in relation to agency, for the symmetry-asymmetry principle and the evolution-transformation principle, and (iv) in relation to outcome, for the regression-progression principle.

In *The Rise of Authoritarian Liberal Democracy* (*ALD*), I added two more principles, namely, (h) the softness-hardness principle on the force of agency (which is to be classified under the category about agency) and (i) the same-difference principle on the metamorphosis of change (which is to be classified under the category about outcome).

In *The Future of Information Architecture* (*FIA*), I introduce three additional principles, that is, (j) the simpleness-complicadness principle on the interconnection among things, (k) the preciseness-vagueness principle on the refinement of things, and (l) the slowness-quickness principle on the speed of change—with the first two in relation to structure and the third in relation to process.

In *The Future of Post-Human Unconsciousness* (*FPHU*), I added three more principles, that is, (m) the openness-hidden principle on the detection of things, in relation to structure, (n) the explicability-inexplicability principle on the underlying mechanisms of things, in relation to method, and (o) the expansion-contraction principle on the growth of things, in relation to process.

In *The Future of Post-Human Knowledge* (*FPHK*), I added one more principle, that is, (p) the absoluteness-relativeness principle on the multiplicity of entities, in relation to method.

In *The Future of Post-Human Mathematical Logic* (*FPHML*), I added one more principle, that is, (q) the formalness-informalness principle on the formal requirements of systems, in relation to method.

In *The Future of Post-Human Engineering* (*FPHE*), I added one more principle, that is, (r) the theory-praxis principle on the duality of knowledge, in relation to agency.

In *The Future of Post-Human Creative Thinking* (*FPHCT*), I added one more principle, that is, (s) the convention-novelty principle on the nature of creative thinking, in relation to agency.

In *The Future of Post-Human Geometry* (*FPHG*) here, I added one more principle, that is, (t) the finiteness-transfiniteness principle on the nature of numbers, in relation to structure.

In *The Future of Post-Human Urban Planning* (*FPHUP*), I added one more principle, that is, (u) the denseness-emptiness principle on the distribution of entities in space, in relation to structure.

In *The Future of Post-Human Humor* (*FPHH*), I added one more principle, that is, (v) the seriousness-playfulness principle on the extent of seriousness, in relation to agency.

In *The Future of Post-Human Literature* (*FPHLIT*), I added one more principle, that is, (w) the fiction-reality principle on the different faces of reality, in relation to method.

In *The Future of Post-Human Chemistry* (*FPHCHEM*), I added one more principle, that is, (x) the stability-reaction principle on the feedback mechanism for further changes, in relation to outcome.

And in *The Future of Post-Human Transportation* (*FPHTRAN*), I add one more principle, that is, (x) the activeness-inactiveness principle on the extent of activeness, in relation to agency.

With this update, there are twenty-five principles so far in existential dialectics, that is:

- six principles in the category of "method"—viz., the formalness-informalness principle, the absoluteness-relativeness principle, the partiality-totality principle, the predictability-unpredictability principle, the explicability-inexplicability principle, and the fiction-reality principle
- five principles in the category of "structure"—viz., the finiteness-transfiniteness principle, the simpleness-complicatedness principle, the preciseness-vagueness principle, the openness-hiddenness principle, and the denseness-emptiness principle

- four principles in the category of "process"—viz., the change-constancy principle, the slowness-quickness principle, the order-chaos principle, and the expansion-contraction principle
- seven principles in the category of "agency"—viz., the theory-praxis principle, the convention-novelty principle, the symmetry-asymmetry principle, the evolution-transformation principle, the softness-hardness principle, the seriousness-playfulness principle, and the activeness-inactiveness principle
- three principles in the category of "outcome"—viz., the regression-progression principle, the same-difference principle, and the stability-reaction principle

There can be more than twenty-five principles in existential dialectics, but they are what I have discovered so far (as summarized in *Table 4.4*).

The Principles as Short Cuts

Yet, these principles should be treated with caution, lest misunderstanding occurs, since they do not constitute rigid dualities (or dichotomies).

The reason is that each pair in an ontological principle consists of two opposites, which are, however, merely short cuts both for multiple variations and degrees, as well as for different interactions with multiple other entities unlike them.

In this light, each pair can end up having hundred (or even thousand, if not more) different versions, which interact with hundred (or even thousand, if not more) other entities—as summarized in *Table 4.5*.

There are two clarifications here.

Firstly, this conception of shortcuts is not mutually exclusive nor absolute, in that the opposites can come in all shapes and sizes, with different degrees. For instance, by analogy, just as there are different degrees of the two colors "white" and "black"—there are likewise different degrees of the opposites in each ontological pair, to the extent that there can be multiple entities (not only two) interacting with each other in each pair.

And secondly, this conception of shortcuts do not ignore other possible entities in interacting with the two opposites (with their different versions) in each pair. For instance, by analogy, there are not only the two colors "white" and "black" as opposites, since there are other colors too besides them like "yellow," "green," "purple," or else. The same logic can be applied to each ontological pair, in that they also interact with other entities, not with only two of them (with their different versions).

Therefore, with these two clarifications in mind—each pair in an ontological principle serves only as an abbreviation for something more complicated and, therefore, although it contains two opposites, it should not be confused as a duality (dualism).

Existential dialectics rejects any dualism (or dichotomy) as too rigid and instead allows the multiplicity of entities, to the extent that between the two opposites in each pair exist many other alternatives to choose from. They are named in that short form for aesthetic elegance only, instead of listing all possible entities between the two opposites in the title (which would be too cumbersome and sound extremely awkward).

To be dialectic is to go beyond any rigid dichotomy and transcend into something different altogether in the long haul. One may be tempted to call the dialectic logic here with a different name like existential "multilectics" (instead of "dialectics"), but this naming is incorrect (or even misleading), for the two reasons aforestated.

After all, all the possible entities between any two opposites in an ontological pair are still about the two opposites, although each ontological pair come in all shapes and sizes (with different degrees) and do not exist by themselves but also interact with other entities unlike them. The virtue of revealing an ontological pair is to show how they relate within themselves (in multiple versions) and also interact with others unlike them (also in multiple versions).

This will be clear in a later sub-section titled "the dialectic constraints imposed by the principles."

The Principles as Family Resemblances

In addition, each ontological principle is generic, with some other comparable ontological pairs to be put in the same family (like a *family resemblance*)—as summarized in *Table 4.6*.

Ludwig Wittgenstein (1953) once suggested the idea of "family resemblance" in explaining different games classified under the same family called *games*.

Why should, for instance, playing football and chess as playing "games," when it is well understood that football is not the same as chess? The answer is that, although each game is different and has different rules, many of them (though not all) share, more or less, some commonalites (e.g., scoring as necessary for winning).

And this is so, even though some games share more than some others in any given selection of critieria, and no two games are exactly identical. So, Wittgenstein's point here is that there is no essential core which is common to all games, and the best that one can look for is some characteristics which are common to many (but not all) games. (A. Biletzki 2006)

(a) Appropriate Family Resemblances

In the context of existential dialectics, I want to distinguish two types of family resemblances, and, in the absence of better words, let me call them (a) *appropriate* family resemblances and (b) *inappropriate* family resemblances.

In regard to appropriate family resemblances—good examples include some of the pairs as already explained in an earlier section on selection criteria, like the flexibility-inflexibility pair, which can be put in the family resemblance of the simpleness-complicatedness principle, although the two pairs are not exactly identical. Likewise, the directness-indirectness pair can be put in the family resemblance of the preciseness-vagueness principle, although, again, the two pairs are not exactly identical.

In this sense, which specific pair in a family should be used to designate the name of the family can be at times a bit arbitrary, but with good reason.

For illustration, in the context of method, the partiality-totality principle can take the different form like individualisticness-holisticness, just as the explicability-inexplicability principle can take the different form like underlyingness-regularness—although each two pairs are not exactly identical and have slightly different meanings and usages.

A more comprehensive listing of this family resemblance for all other principles is shown in *Table 4.6* on the syntax of existential dialectics.

In fact, this section on family resemblances overlaps with the semantics of existential dialectics, which will be introduced later in the next section (and summarized in *Table 4.11*).

(b) Inappropriate Family Resemblances

However, there are some family resemblances which are not appropriate, and let me distinugish them by calling them, in the absence of better words, (b1) *inadequate* family resemblances, (b2) *compound* family resemblances, (b3) *one-sided* family resemblances, and (b4) *vague* family resemblances (as summarized in *Table 4.10*).

(b1) In regard to "inadequate" family resemblances—there are some pairs which are not adequate, because they fail the test of selection criteria (as already pointed out in an earlier section), especially in relation to the criterion of not being *trivial* (or *parochial*)—as if it is only one component competing with other ones for inclusion in a set.

For instance, the *consistency-inconsistency* pair is inadequate, because it is only one component competing with other ones for inclusion in the larger set of the formalness-informalenss principle (like the *completeness-incompleteness* pair and the *soundness-unsoundness* pair, as discussed in my book titled *The Future of Post-Human Mathematical Logic*, or *FPHML* in short).

The same is true for the *cognition-noncognition* pair, which is related with both the completeness-incompleteness pair and the soundness-unsoundness pair in the larger set of the formalness-informalenss principle.

(b2) In regard to "compound" (or non-atomic) family resemblances—there are some pairs which are not appropriate for a different reason, because they fail the test of selection criteria (as already pointed out in an earlier section), especially in relation to the criterion of not *overlapping* with other principles, in that it is too closely related with other ones.

For instance, the *normality-abnormality* pair is compound (and thus inappropriate), because it overlaps with several other principles, like the symmetry-asymmetry principle, the density-emptiness principle, the convention-novelty principle, and the same-difference principle, for instance (as already discussed in *FPHP*).

The normality-abnormality pair overlaps with the symmetry-asymmetry principle, because being "abnormal" (say, for those with mental illnesses) is often treated not equally by others who are "normal." So, the relationship reveals the symmetry-asymmetry principle.

The normality-abnormality pair also overlaps with the density-emptiness principle, because being "abnormal" (say, for those with mental illnesses) is often not as dense in the overall (not local) distribution of a population as those who are "normal." So, the relationship reveals the density-emptiness principle.

The normality-abnormality pair also overlaps with the convention-novelty principle, because being "abnormal" (say, for those with mental illnesses) often exhibits non-conventional (non-conformist) ideas and behaviors when contrasted with those who are "normal." So, the relationship reveals the convention-novelty principle.

The normality-abnormality pair also overlaps with the same-difference principle, because being "abnormal" (say, for those with mental illnesses) shares some similarities in outcome when compared with those who are "normal" (in that both contribute to the control and regulation of human thoughts and behaviors in society, albeit in different ways). Yet, being "abnormal" also has something different from being "normal," in that abnormal thoughts and behaviors follow a different pattern when contrasted with those which are normal. So, the relationship reveals the same-difference principle.

(b2.1) There is a special case of compound family resemblances (as summarized in *Table 4.10*), which can be called, in the absence of better words, *one-sided and compound* family resemblances.

For instance, the extroversion-introversion pair is a good example of *one-sided and compound* family resemblances, because, firstly, it is "one-sided," in being part of the side (category) of "normality" in the normality-abnormality pair—and, secondly, the normality-abnormality pair is in turn "compounded," because it is related to the symmetry-asymmetry principle, the density-emptiness principle, the convention-novelty principle, and the same-difference principle, as already explained above.

(b3) In regard to "one-sided" family resemblances—there are some pairs which are not appropriate for another different reason, because they fail the test of selection criteria (as already pointed out in an earlier section), especially in relation to the criterion of not being *one-sided*, that is, part of one side (category) of a dialectic pair.

For instance, the extroversion-introversion pair cannot be an ontological principle, since it is part of the side (category) of "normality" in the normality-abnormaltiy pair (because both extroversion and introversion are two different "normal" personality traits in psychology).

By the same logic, the vision-blindness pair and the sound-silence pair cannot be ontological principles, because the pairs are part of the side (category) of "asymmetry" in the symmetry-asymmetry principle (since being able to see and hear for some individuals and being unable to see or hear for others are two contrastive abilities in the world of animals and humans, for instance).

These illustrations of indequate, compound, and one-sided family resemblances show how difficult it is to come up with an ontological principle in existential dialectics out of the blue, because many of them violate the selection criteria in one way or the other. It is all too easy to join two opposing words and simply make them into a pair, but it is all too difficult to pass the test of the selection criteria to be qualified as an ontological principle in existential dialectics.

(b4) And in regard to "vague" family resemblances—there are some pairs which are not appropriate for still another different reason, because the terms in the pairs are vague in meaning, so that they are inappropriate family resemblances if defined in some particular ways, although they can be appropriate family resemblances if defined in other particular ways.

For instance, such pairs like shortness-longness, narrowness-broadness, smallness-largeness, smallness-greatness, microness-macroness, and littleness-muchness can be understood in at least three different meanings and thus have three different possibilities. The first possibility is that they are one-sided as part of finiteness (in the finiteness-transfiniteness principle), if both opposites are defined on a finite scale. The second possibility is that they are one-sided as part of transfiniteness (in the finiteness-transfiniteness principle) if both opposites are defined on a transfinite scale. And the third possibility is that they are appropriate family resemblances in relation to the finiteness-transfiniteness principle if one opposite is defined on a finite scale and the other opposite is defined on a transfinite scale.

Other examples of inappropriate family resemblances are shown in *Table 4.10* on "The Syntax of Existential Dialectics VII: Types of Inappropriate Family Resemblances."

The Dialectic Constraints Imposed by the Principles

The principles, as they constitute the syntax of existential dialectics, are dialectic in character, such that, when they are applied, they impose dialectic constraints on how reality is to be understood.

Consider, say, the symmetry-asymmetry principle as an illustration here, in order to summarize two main characters of the dialectic constraints in question (as summarized in *Table 4.7*).

Firstly, to be dialectic here is to go beyond the narrow dichotomies (and, for that matter, any rigid multi-dimensional classificatory scheme), be they about "self" vs. "world," "freedom" vs. "unfreedom," "barbarity" vs. "civilization," "individuality" vs. "communality," and so on.

One way to do so (to go beyond) is to consider them all in terms of co-existence (without heavily favoring one over the rest). For instance, my theory of "post-civilization" (to be summarized later in the section on the pragmatics of existential dialectics) is to go beyond barbarity and civilization in terms of understanding barbarity and civilization as being co-existent.

And the same logic can be said in relation to my theories of "post-democracy," "post-capitalsm," and others (also to be introduced later in the section on the pragmatics of existential dialectics), in regard to freedom vs. unfreedom, equality vs. inequality, communality vs. individuality, spirituality vs. materiality, and so on.

But to consider them all (in the dichotomies—and, for that matter, in any rigid multi-dimensional classifactory scheme) as co-existent is not the same as to imply that the opposing categories in any classificatory scheme are all equal, since, in accordance to the symmetry-asymmetry principle (as an illustration here), if they are equal in terms of being considered as co-existent, they are asymmetric in terms of being unequal in dialectic interaction (e.g., X can be more dominant than Y in case A, or Y is more dominant than X in case B), although in some special cases, they can be relatively equal (e.g., X and Y are relatively equal in case C).

For this reason, there are different versions of "post-democracy" and "post-capitalism" in my theories. As an illustration, in version I of the theory of post-democracy, freedom is more dominant than equality, whereas in version II of the theory of post-democracy, equality is more so than freedom.

But this "X more than Y" has to be understood in the context of dialectic logic (not in symbolic logic, as conventionally understood), in that both "X" and "Y" are important in post-democracy (in the context of dialectic logic), but in an asymmetry way.

By contrast, in symbolic logic, it often favors one over the other—be it in regard to privileging freedom over equality (in Fascism), favoring freedom relatively more than equality (in Liberal Democracy), or favoring equality relatively more than freedom (in Socialist Democracy). In regard to the latter two cases (about Liberal Democracy and Socialist Democracy), the difference between dialectic logic and symbolic logic can be one in degree, not in kind—in this sense, albeit not in other senses.

The same reasoning can be said about the relatonships between individuality and communality, between spirituality and materiality, and between formal legalism and informal legalism in the different versions of my theory of "post-capitalism."

Secondly, to be dialectic is to go beyond the narrow dichotomies (and, for that matter, any rigid multi-dimensional classificatory scheme) in another way, this time, in a transcendent way, that is, in exploring other possibilities or even other issues not considered within the narrow confines of narrow dichotomies (and, for that matter, any rigid multi-dimensional classificatory scheme).

As an analogy, in this second meaning, to go beyond the narrow dichotomy of "black" vs. "white" is not just to choose both "black" and "white" (as in the first meaning) but also to explore other options (e.g., "green," "purple," "blue," etc.—and, alternatively, "shade," "line," "curve," etc.).

By the same reasoning, to go beyond "democracy" is to transcend democracy (as in version III of my theory of "post-democracy") and to explore other possibilties of lifeforms (e.g., "floating consciousness," "hyper-spatial consciousness," etc., to live beyond the narrow obsession with freedom and equality).

This dialectic character of the principles in existential dialectics has important implications for the pragmatics of existential dialectics (as will be clear shortly, in the section on the pragmatics of existential dialectics).

The Semantics of Existential Dialectics (or Its Ontosemantics)

The syntax of existential dialectics so understood in terms of ontological principles only gives us the structure of ontology in the world, in an abstract (general) sense. These principles by themselves do not tell us the specific meanings in a given context.

In order to grasp the specific meanings of the principles in a given context, it is necessary to study the semantics of existential dialectics (as summarized in *Table 4.11*).

And the analysis of the ontological principles as family resemblances in the previous section on syntax is only a starting point (and thus overlaps a bit with the semantics of existential dialectics here).

For this reason, I have often gone to great lengths in my previous books on different subjects to explain the specific meanings of the principles when applied in different contexts.

Consider two examples below for illustration, which are not exhaustive.

In *FPHST*, for instance, I used the first three principles (i.e., the change-constancy principle, the regression-progression principle, and the symmetry-asymmetry principle) to propose "the perspectival theory of space-time," for a better way to understand space and time—especially, though not exclusively, in relation to future post-human history (as summarized in *Table 1.3*, *Table 1.4*, *Table 1.5*, and *Table 1.6*).

In so doing, I had to introduce concepts and theories specific to the field of physics and other related fields (e.g., "absolute space" and "absolute time" in "classical mechanics" and "relative space-time" in "the theory of relativity").

And in *BNN*, I also exploited the three principles to propose the "transcendent" approach to the study of genes and memes as a new way to understand the interaction between nature and nurture.

In so doing, I had to explore concepts and theories in the world of evolutionary biology (e.g., "mutation," "variation," "adaptation," "selection," and "inheritance" in classical evolutionary theory) and neural biology (e.g., "chromosome," "gene," "DNA," "RNA," "protein," "neuron," "neural network," and "behavior").

Other examples, besides these two here, are given in other books of mine on different topics.

Therefore, this semantic dimension of existential dialectics is important, since, in each of my books when the ontological principles are used, each principle becomes relevant in a different meaning when contextualized within a given case study in question.

In this book, for instance, the principles are relevant in relation to a different subject matter (as summarized in the concluding chapter), and they can be shown in all shapes and sizes (since they are also to be treated as "short cuts," as indicated before), without, however, being reduced to "specific ontology" (as opposed to "general ontology"), as explained in *Table 4.9*.

In the technical jargons of semantics, these exercises perform two essential functions of translation (or interpretation), namely, (a) "intensive" interpretation (about the properties or relations of the principles in existential dialectics), and (b) "extensive" interpretation (about the classes or cases to which the properties and relations of the principles in existential dialectics are applied). (WK 2011oo)

But there are limits of translation (or interpretation), and an excellent example is that "there is a problem with the 'objectivity' of translation, as it is relative to different cultural (or sub-cultural) contexts. For instance, one of the still unresolved problems in linguistics is: 'Is there an objective gauge for the quality of translation?'" (*FPHCOM* & WK 2011pp) And the problems of "radical translation" by W. V. Quine and "radical interpretation" by Donald Davidson are another well-known examples, as already discussed in *FPHSEM*.

This is one serious problem about the logic of translation and interpretation that I already addressed in *Sec. 2.5.2* of *FPHSEM*, *Sec. 3.5.1* of *FPHCOM* (and also, for that matter, in *FHC*, in the context of hermeneutics).

The Pragmatics of Existential Dialectics (or Its Ontopragmatics)

Even the semantics of existential dialectics is not enough to understand reality, since semantics by itself does not tell us the nature of intentionality and interests in relation to the matrix of power formations and conflicting interests when existential dialectics as an ontology is applied.

Surely, one cannot completely separate the pragmatics of existential dialectics from its semantics (and for that matter, its syntax), but the point here is to give each a more elaborated analysis.

For this reason, the pragmatics of existential dialectics needs to be studied too, in special relation to the inclusion of power formation and conflicting interests in the application of the principles of existential dialectics (as summarized in *Table 4.12*).

It is thus no wonder that all my previous books have shown in different ways how and why these ontological principles and their theoretical applications can reveal the future world to come in a way that humans have never known, in a totally different battleground for competing human (and later post-human) interests by myriad groups fighting for their own versions of hegemony.

Perhaps a summary of my previous works in relation to existential dialectics and their contributions to my new theories as proposed over the years is deemed revealing here, for the further understanding of the pragmatics of existential dialectics (in close relation to the semantics of existential dialectics too).

That stressed—the following summary in four sub-sections is something that I often do in my previous books too, as a way to introduce the intellectual background of my ideas.

So, for those readers who had read my previous works, the following sub-sections serve as a reminder, as they are repeated hereafter *often verbatim* (with only some updated changes, with the rest kept intact).

These sub-sections are, namely, (a) the two-way street connecting theory with meta-theory, (b) the theoretical application of existential dialectics, (c) direct and indirect applications of existential dialectics, and (d) multiple applications of existential dialectics—to be summaried herefafter, respectively.

The Two-Way Street Connecting Theory and Meta-Theory

However, lest any misunderstanding occurs, it is important to remember that the pragmatics of existential dialectics is not a one-way street (that is, using the ontological principles for theoretical insights in praxis) but a two-way one, namely, (a) from meta-theory to theory, and (b) from theory to meta-theory.

(a) On one side of the street, the ontological principles can inspire some theoretical insights in praxis, that is, in relation to some specific fields.

(b) On the other (opposing) side of the street, however, the study of a subject matter in the specific fields in turn reveals some more hitherto unknown ontological principles to be discovered and identified.

For this reason, three new principles were added in *FC*, one in *FAE*, two in *ALD*, and three in *FIA*, on top of the original three in *BCPC*, for example (as there are more)—after some research on the specific subject matters.

Both theory and meta-theory enrich each other in all my works over the years.

The Theoretical Application of Existential Dialectics

This two-way street connecting theory and meta-theory has contributed to my original construction of many theories in numerous books of mine on numerous fields in all domains of knowledge, which can be classified in terms of specific "meta-theories" (about epistemology, methodology, logic, ontology, etc.) and specific "theories" (about the mind, nature, culture, society, and the rest—as will be further explained later in the sub-section on "the holistic organization of an inquiry" in the section about "sophisticated methodological holism").

The final aim of my numerous new specific theories (on both theory and meta-theory) is to converge all of them (as proposed in my numerous books) into a grand project about the future of intelligent life, both here on earth and in deep space.

In this sense, all these theories of mine serve as a foundation to unify all domains of knowledge for an overarching understanding of all forms of reality (by way of some ontological principles and the comprehensive perspectives of the mind, nature, society, and culture), while allowing for heterogeneity, conflict, subjectivity, and complexity, for example.

With this grand project in mind—the summary of my specific theories on meta-theory are given in this section (on "existential dialectics") and the next (on "sophisticated methodological holism"), whereas the specific theories on theory will be summarized in the following categories of (a) society, (b) culture, (c) the mind, (d) nature, and (e) the rest, as shown below, in that order.

(a) Society

The category of "society" here can be divided into four sub-categories, i.e., (a1) social organizations, (a2) social institutions, (a3) social structure, and (a4) social systems (or trends).

(a1) Social Organizations

In relation to social organizations, I proposed a new thesis on the ambivalent nature of virtual organizations in the future, known as "the theory of e-civic alienation" in *FCD* (and summarized in *Table 4.19*).

And in *FPHO*, another theory called "the combinational theory of organization" was worked out, although it was first proposed in Ch.6 of *ALD*.

(a2) Social Institutions

There are different social institutions, be they about (a2.1) politics, (a2.2) economics, (a2.3) military affairs, (a2.4) mass media, (a2.5) law, (a2.6) education, and (a.7) gambling, for instance.

(a2.1) In relation to politics, I offered different visions on (a2.1.1) political theory, (a2.1.2) comparative politics, and (a2.1.3) international relations, to cite three main ones.

(a2.1.1) In the context of political theory, my vision of a path-breaking political system in future times concerns the different forms of "post-democracy" to supersede democracy unto the post-human age.

My vision of post-democracy was called "the theory of post-democracy" (as summarized in *Table 4.22*, *Table 4.23*, and *Table 4.24*), whereas *Table 4.25* explains the distinctions among democracy, non-democracy, and post-democracy.

And *Table 4.26* stresses the multiple causes of the emergence of post-democracy, while *Table 4.27* clarifies some possible misunderstandings in regard to post-capitalism and post-democracy.

(a2.1.2) In the context of comparative politics, I also showed, in *ALD*, how and why authoritarianism can be an advanced form of liberal democracy (just as it has its own counterpart in non-liberal democracy), or what I originally called "authoritarian liberal democracy" (as summarized in *Table 4.21*), before it is to be superceded by "post-democracy."

(a2.1.3) In the context of international relations (both at the institutional and structural levels), I provided, in *BWT*, "the theory of cyclical progression of empire-building," for a better way to understand the logic of empire-building on earth and beyond—with the rise of what I originally envisioned as "hyper-empires" (like "the Chinese Union" and "the Indian Union"), "meso-empires" (like "the European Union" and "the North American Union") and "micro-empires" (like "the Middle Eastern Union" and "the Latin American Union") in the coming "post-post-Cold War era" as a visionary illustration, as summarized in *Table 4.20*.

This is also related to the issues of "social structure" in (a3), "migration" in (a4,6), "identity" in (b11), and "geography" in (d4), for instance.

In addition, in *FPHWP*, I proposed "the multifaceted theory of war and peace" to understand war and peace, in a small sense—or aggression and pacificity, in a broad sense.

(a2.2) In relation to economics, I also offered another vision, this time to understand the future forms of economic systems, that is, the different forms of "post-capitalism" to supersede capitalism unto the post-human age.

My vision of post-capitalism was referred to (in *FCD*, *BDPD* and *BCPC*) as "the theory of post-capitalism" (as summarized in *Table 4.28*, *Table 4.29*, *Table 4.30*, *Table 4.31*, and *Table 4.32*). And *Table 4.33* clarifies the differences among capitalism, non-capitalism, and post-capitalism, whereas *Table 4.34* shows multiple causes of the emergence of post-capitalism.

This vision on "post-capitalism" constitutes the third theoretical application of existential dialectics, this time, in that there is no wealth without poverty (or the wealth/poverty dialectics).

(a2.3) In relation to military affairs, I also proposed "the multifaceted theory of war and peace" (in *FCD*, although it was first so labeled in *FPHK*) for a new way to understand the causes of war—and, for that matter, the rise and fall of different forms of warfare over time.

This theory was further expanded in *FPHWP*, where I suggested a new way to understand war and peace, in a small sense—or aggression and pacificity, in a broad sense.

(a2.4) In relation to mass media, I also proposed "the totalistic theory of communication" in *The Future of Post-Human Mass Media* (or in short, *FPHMM*).

(a2.5) In relation to law, I also proposed "the reconstruction theory of law" in *The Future of Post-Human Law* (or in short, *FPHLAW*). And in relation to criminality, I proposed "the reflective theory of criminality" in *FPHCRIM* for a different way to understand heroes and villains.

(a2.6) In relation to education, I proposed "the heterodox theory of education" in *The Future of Post-Human Education* (or in short, *FPHEDU*).

(a2.7) And in relation to gambling, I proposed "the detached theory of gambling" in *The Future of Post-Human Gambling* (or in short, *FPHGAM*).

(a3) Social Structure

In relation to social structure, I first proposed two additional theories, that is, "the theory of the cyclical progression of hegemony" in *FCD* (and also in *FPHC* and *BDPD*), and "the theory of the cyclical progression of empire-building" (in *BWT*, as already indicated above)—with important implications for the symmetry-asymmetry princple in existential dialectics, just to cite one example.

In addition, this is also related to the issues of "migration" in (a4,6), "identity" in (b11), and "geography" in (d4), for instance.

Then, in *BNN*, I proposed another theory, namely, "the theory of contrastive advantages" to understand the persistence of social structure by gender, race, ethnicity, or any other groupings.

(a4) Social Systems (or Trends)

In relation to social systems, there are several sub-categories for illustration, which can be about (a4.1) urbanization, (a4.2) technology, (a4.3) demography, (a4.4) the environment, (a4.5) social trends as a whole (which also include the current phenomenon of globalization), and (a4.6) migration.

(a4.1) In relation to urbanization, I proposed "the contingent theory of urban planning" in *FPHUP* for a new way to understand density and void—which is also related to the issues of "social trends" (especially in relation to globalization) in (a4.5), "migration" in (a4.6), and "identity" in (b11).

(a4.2) In relation to technology, I worked out "the ambivalent theory of technology" in *FPHE* for a new way to understand the nature of technology.

Some other books (like *FPHMM*, *FAE*, *FCD*, and *FHC*) also deal with technology, and a good example concerns "the synthetic theory of information architecture" in *FIA* on taxonomy, network, and intelligence, in conjunction with the rise of technology.

(a4.3) In relation to demography, I proposed, first in *FHC* (and later in other books like *FCD*, *FPHC*, *FPHU*, etc.), "the theory of post-humanity," in relation to the "post-human" age at some distant point of "after-postmodernity," long after human extinction, to be eventually superseded by "post-humans" of various forms.

Some good candidates of the post-human lifeforms include, for instance, "thinking robots," "thinking machines," "cyborgs," "genetically altered superior beings," "floating consciousness," "hyper-spatial consciousness," "unfolding unconsciousness," "the hyper-sexual body," and "the hyper-martial body." This post-human vision of mine was first originally worked out in *FHC* and further elaborated in both *FCD*, *FPHC*, *FPHU*, *FPHS*, and *FPHMA*, for instance.

Lest any confusion occurs, I need to emphasize two clarifications here about the term "post-human" as a neologism in my works.

Firstly, the word "post-human" here should *not* be confused with another term which looks similar but has a totally different meaning in the literature of postmodernism, namely, "post-humanism"—which constitutes a critique of "humanism" as tradionally understood (especially, though not exclusively, in relation to the idea of progress in science and reason in the Enlightenment project). (WK 2008)

And secondly, the word "post-human" here should also *not* be confused with a similar term which is used to champion the ideology of technology for the future co-existence between humans and cyborgs in "trans-humanism." (WK 2008a)

Instead, my term "post-human" in relation to "posthuman-ism" also rejects "transhumanism" (especially, though not exclusively, in relation to the promises of technology) and refers to something else altogether, that is, the future extinction of humans and its post-human successors in deep space and beyond unto multiverses.

Later, in *BEPE*, I went further and provided a more comprehensive critique of "transhumanism," together with other issues.

With these two clarifications in mind (as summarized in *Table 1.31*)—in the end, a most fundamental question about intelligent life now has an answer, in that, if asked, "What is the future of human civilization?"—my answer in *FCD* (89) is thus: "As addressed in Ch.7 of *FHC*, a later epoch of the age of after-postmodernity (that is, at some point further away from after-postmodernity) will begin, as what I called the 'post-human' history (with the term 'post-human' originally used in my doctoral dissertation at M.I.T., which was finished in November 1995, under the title *After Postmodernity*, still available at M.I.T. library, and was later revised and published as *FHC*). The post-human history will be such that humans are nothing in the end, other than what culture, society, and nature (with some luck) have shaped them into, to be eventually superseded by post-humans (e.g., cyborgs, thinking machines, genetically altered superior beings, and others), if humans are not destroyed long before then."

(a4.4) In relation to the environment, I also addressed the issue of sustainability, especially in *FHC*, *FCD*, and *FPHUP*. For instance, in *FPHUP*, I specifically proposed a new theory, "the contingent theory of urban planning," on the need to go beyond the contemporoary obsession with sustainability, in the context of not only the environment but also other issues.

In addition, I also proposed "the interventive-reshaping theory of geography" in *FPHGEOG*—which is related to the issues of "migration" in (a4.6), "geography" in (d4), and "geology" in (d5).

(a4.5) In relation to social trends as a whole, I proposed in Ch.9 of *FCD* (367-8), that "civilizational history will continue into the following cyclical progression of expansion, before it is to be superseded (solely as a high probability, since humans might be destroyed sooner either by themselves or in a gigantic natural calamity) by posthumans at some distant point in after-postmodernity (which I already discussed in *FHC*)" unto multiverses (different constellations of universes):

Local → Regional → Global →Solar →
Galactic → Clustery…→ Multiversal

The current phenomeon of "globalization" lies in the third category on the line above and was extensively analyzed in *FCD*, in close connection with "globalism" at the cultural level—in the context of "postmodernity" (which will be introduced later in the section on history).

In *BDPD*, this thesis of mine was referred to as "the theory of the cyclical progression of system integration and fragmentation," at the systemic level—in close relation to another thesis analyzed in Ch.9 of *FCD*, which was called, in the absence of better words, "the multifaceted theory of war and peace" in *FPHK* (as already indicated above).

In *FC*, I also proposed "the dialectic theory of complexity" to account for the factor of uncertainty, which can have a major role to play in the world.

All this is also related to the issues of "urbanization" in (a4.1), "the environment" in (a4.4), "migration" in (a4,6), "identity" in (b11), "geography" in (d4), and "geology" in (d5).

(a4.6) And in relation to migration, I proposed "the resettlement theory of geology" in *FPHGEOL* and "the theory of the cyclical progression of migration" in *FPHMIG*—which are also related to the issues of "social structure" in (a3), "urbanization" in (a4.1), "the environment" in (a4.4), "social trends" in (a4.5), "identity" in (b11), "geography" in (d4), and "geology" in (d5).

(b) Culture

The category of "culture" here can also be divided into different sub-categories like (b1) aesthetics, (b2) religion, (b3) popular (mass) culture, (b4) logic, (b5) civilization as a whole, (b6) ethics, (b7) epistemology (methodology), (b8) metaphysics (ontology), (b9) ideology, (b10) language, and (b11) identity.

(b1) Aesthetics

In relation to aesthetics, I proposed "the transformative theory of aesthetic experience" in *FAE* about some great transformations of aesthetic experience in future history.

In *FPHLIT*, I further proposed "the comparative-impartial theory of literature" for a new way to understand fiction and non-fiction.

In *FPHPA*, I further proposed "the transdisciplinary theory of performing arts" for a new way to understand the body and its presence—which is also related to the issues of "popular (mass) culture" in (b3) and of "the human body" in (c1.2).

And the aesthetic issue also overlaps with (d8) on architecture.

(b2) Religion

In relation to religion, I proposed "the comparative theory of religion" in *FHC* (and also in *FCD*, although it was first so labeled in *FPHK*).

And in *FPHR*, I provided a solid foundation of this theory with a better name, that is, "the comparative-substitutive theory of religion" for a new way to understand spirituality.

(b3) Popular (Mass) Culture

In relation to popular (mass) culture, there are some sub-categories for illustration, which can be, for example, (b3.1) mass culture in general and (b3.2) sports (like chess)—both of which are also related to the issues of "aesthetics" in (b1) and of "the human body" in (c1.2).

(b3.1) In relation to mass culture in general, I proposed, in *FHC*, a new way to understand mass culture in terms of some fundamental dilemmas, which is called, in the absence of better words, "the dualistic theory of mass culture" in *FPHO*.

(b3.2) In relation to sports (like chess), I proposed, in *FPHCHESS*, "the mediative-variative theory of chess" for a new way to understand tactics and strategy (in different traditions).

(b4) Logic

In relation to logic, I also worked out, in *FPHML*, "the contrastive theory of rationality" for a new way to understand rationality and knowledge (in the context of mathematical logic).

(b5) Civilization as a Whole

In relation to civilization as a whole, I also argued, in *FHC*, no freedom without unfreedom (as shown in *Table 4.13*) and no equality without inequality (as shown in *Table 4.14*), especially in relation to the seven dimensions of life existence first worked out in *FHC* (i.e., the technological, the everyday, the true, the holy, the sublime/beautiful, the good, and the just).

Even more interestingly, in *BDPD* and later in *BCIV*, I further revealed a theoretical refinement of existential dialectics, this time, in arguing that there is no civilization without barbarity, with human civilization to be eventually superseded by what I originally analyzed as "post-human post-civilization" (which should not be confused with "post-human civilization"), in the context of the freedom/unfreedom and equality/inequality dialectics.

In the final analysis, civilization cannot live without barbarity and has to learn to co-exist with it in ever new ways. Preposteorus as this may seem to many contemporaries—it is no more imperative to preserve civilization than necessary to destroy barbarity, and the ideal of civilization is essentially bankrupt, to be eventually superseded by "post-civilization" (as summarized in *Tables 4.35-4.43*).

This freedom/unfreedom and equality/inequality dialectics holds in pre-moderny, modernity, postmodernity, and what I orignally called "after-postmodernity" in *FHC* and *FCD*—especially, though not exclusively, in the context of the emergence of "post-humans."

There are two specific theories about "after-postmodernity" here. The first theory about "after-postmodernity" is about the trinity of pre-modernity, modernity, postmodernity, and after-postmodernity at the cultural level—and was called, in *BDPD*, "the theory of the trinity of modernity to its after-postmodern counterpart," although it was first analyzed in *FHC* and later in *FCD* and also *BCIV* (as summarized in *Table 1.34*, *Table 1.35*, *Table 1.36*, and *Table 1.37* and will be elaborated further in the later sub-section on "the rest" about future history).

The second theory about "after-postmodernity" is about pre-modernity, modernity, postmodernity, and after-postmodernity at the historical level. For instance, a conclusion in *FHC*, which is shocking indeed for many contemporaries, is none other than that "[t]he post-human history will therefore mark the end of human history as we know it and, for that matter, the end of human dominance and, practically speaking, the end of humans as well. The entire history of human civilization, from its beginning to the end, can be summarized by four words, linked by three arrows (as already discussed in *FHC*)":

Pre-Modernity → Modernity →
Post-Modernity → After-Postmodernity

In *BDPD*, this thesis of mine was specifically called "the theory of the evolution from pre-modernity to after-postmodernity," at the historical level—as shown in *Table 1.34*, *Table 1.35*, *Table 1.36*, and *Table 1.37* (and will be elaborated further in the later sub-section on "the rest" about future history).

Therefore, "[t]he end of humanity in the coming human extinction is the beginning of post-humanity. To say an untimely farewell to humanity is to foretell the future welcome of post-humanity." (P. Baofu 2002: 89) This thesis of mine was known in *BDPD* as "the theory of post-humanity," at the systemic level—as already indicated in (a4.3) above.

(b6) Ethics

In relation to ethics, I proposed, in *BEPE*, "the theory of post-ethics" for a new way to understand morality and immorality.

(b7) Epistemology (Methodology)

In relation to epistemology (methodology), I proposed "the complex theory of data analysis" in *FPHDA* for a different way to understand quantitative and qualitative research.

In addition, I already proposed "the critical-dialectic theory of formal science" in *FPHFS* and "the theory of methodological holism" in several books (like Ch.1 *FCD*, Ch.1of *FPHC*, *Sec.2.1* and *Sec.2.5* of *BCPC*, *FC*, *FPHK*, etc.) for a different way to do methodology.

(b8) Metaphysics (Ontology)

I also proposed "the theory of existential dialectics" in several books (like *FHC*, *FCD*, *FPHC*, *BDPD*, *FC*, *FAE*, *ALD*, *FIA*, *FPHK*, etc,) and "the contrastive theory of rationality" in *FPHML* for a different way to understand ontology.

(b9) Ideology

The issue about ideology was already discussed under the categories of "social institutions" and of "civilization as a whole," especially in relation to my theories of "post-democracy," "post-capitalism," "post-civilization," and so on.

(b10) Language

I already proposed "the multilogical theory of learning" in *FPHL* for a new way to understand the nature of language structure and context .

And I also worked out, in *FPHSEM*, "the interactive theory of semantics" for a new way to understand internality and externality (in the context of semantics).

(b11) Identity

I propose here "the theory of the cyclical progression of migration" in *FPHMIG* for a new way to understand the nature of sameness, otherness, and identity—which is also related to the issues of "social structure" in (a3), "urbanization" in (a4.1), "social trends" (especially in relation to globalization) in (a4.5), "migration" in (a4.6), religion in (b2), and ideology in (b9).

(c) The Mind

The important vision about "post-humans" (as summarized earlier) brings us to the category of "the mind" here, which, as is often understood in everyday's usage, refers to the "brain" and the "body" (together with their interactions) and has different levels of consciousness which can be both "spiritual" and non-spiritual.

Therefore, the "mind" already presupposes the "brain," "body," and "spirit" (or "soul"), so that one does not fall into the intellectual trap of the "mind-body dualism" as debunked in modern (and especially, postmodern) philosophy (which I already went to great lengths to explain in *The Future of Human Civilization*).

That said—the category of "the mind" can be divided into two sub-categories, namely, in relation to (c1) biology and (c2) psychology.

(c1) Biology

In relation to biology, there are two concerns here, namely, (c1.1) genes and intelligence and (c1.2) the human body.

(c1.1) In relation to genes and intelligence, I worked out "the theory of contrastive advantages" (which was originally proposed in *FCD* and further worked out in *BNN*, as summarized in *Table 1.24*), to show the nature-nurture interactions of multiple levels in action (e.g., the biological, the psychological, the structural, the systemic, the cultural, and others) for humans and post-humans on earth and beyond, to the extent that different groups, be they on the basis of race, gender, ethnicity, class, age, or else, are not equal, on average, and have not been, nor will they be, even if there can be exceptions.

(c1.2) In relation to the human body, for instance, in *FPHMA*, I suggested "the expansive-contractive theory of martial arts," in which two great future transformations of the martial body were envisioned, that is, both "with the hyper-martial body" and "without the body" (as summarized in *Table 1.32*)—although this issue can also be classified under the category of "culture."

In *FPHS*, I proposed "the theory of virtual sexuality," in which three great future transformations of the sexual body were envisioned, that is, "virtual pleasure," "the hyper-sexual body," and "the post-sexual floating mind" (as summarized in *Table 1.33*).

And in *FPHPA*, I further proposed "the transdisciplinary theory of performing arts" for a new way to understand the body and its presence, with seven great future transformations of the body in performing arts—which is also related to the issues of "aesthetics" in (b1) and "popular (mass) culture" in (b3).

(c2) Psychology

In relation to psypchology (which also overlaps with biology too, however), I also proposed some greater transformations of the mind to come in the future, especially though not exclusively in the post-human age.

These greater transformations of the mind in psychology can be further sub-divided into different categories, namely, (c2.1) consciousness, (c2.2) unconsciousness (together with subconsciousness), (c2.3) creativity, (c2.4) learning, (c2.5) aggression and pacificity, (c2.6) personality, (c2.7) humor, and (c2.8) artificial intelligence.

(c2.1) In relation to consciousness, I analyzed, in *FPHC*, the nature of consciousness in relation to the conceptual dimensions of consciousness (as shown in *Table 1.12*), the theoretical levels of consciousness (as shown in *Table 1.13*), the thematic issues of consciousness (as shown in *Table*

1.14), and the different dimensions of human existence (viz., having-ness, belonging-ness, and being-ness) in relation to consciousness (as shown in *Table 1.15*, *Table 1.16*, *Table 1.17*, and *Table 1.18*).

In *BCPC*, the nature of consciousness was further explored in relation to cognition, emotion, and behavior, which can be in consciousness and other mental states (e.g., subconsciousness and unconsciousness), in the context of existential dialectics, as shown in *Table 1.19*, *Table 1.20*, *Table 1.21*, *Table 1.22,* and *Table 1.23*.

In fact, in *FCD*, I already proposed three different theories in relation to the limits of cognition, emotion, and behavior, namely, "the theory of cognitive partiality," "the theory of emotional non-neutrality," and "the theory of behavioral alteration."

Then, I argued that the existence of human consciousness will be superseded one day with "floating consciousness" (as first proposed in *FCD*) and "hyper-spatial consciousness" (as first proposed in *FPHC*) as a climax of evolution in consciousness, after the future extinction of human consciousness (as shown below):

Primordial consciousness → Human consciousness →
Post-human consciousness (with floating consciousness and hyper-spatial consciousness as a climax in the evolution of consciousness)

In *BDPD*, these latest theses of mine were called "the theory of floating consciousness" and "the theory of hyper-spatial consciousness," both at the cosmological and psychological levels (as summarized in *Table 1.26* and *Table 1.25*).

(c2.2) In relation to unconsciousness, for instance, in *FPHU*, the unconsious mind will undergo tremendous change, to the rise of what I originally called "unfolding unconsciousess" in relation to anomalous experience, as a climax of evolution in unconsciousness, in conjunction with the conscious mind (both human now and post-human later), especially at the psychological level, as shown below:

Primordial unconsciousness → Human unconsciousness →
Post-human unconsciousness (with unfolding unconsciousness as a climax in the evolution of unconsciousness)

In *FPHU*, this thesis of mine is called "the theory of unfolding unconsciousness" in a small sense, or "the unfolding theory of anomalous experience," in a larger one, as shown in *Table 1.27* and *Table 1.28*.

(c2.3) In relation to creativity, for instance, in *FPHCT*, I also proposed "the comprehensive theory of creative thinking" to explore the role of creative thinking, in relation to technology and other factors, together with my original proposal of important creative techniques and traits (as shown in *Table 1.29*) and its double nature of desirability and undesirability (as shown in *Table 1.30*).

(c2.4) In relation to learning, for instance, in *FPHL*, I worked out "the multilogical theory of learning" for a new way to understand the nature of structure and context in language, in relation to learning and its future development in the context of the mind.

(c2.5) In relation to aggression (and pacificity), I proposed "the multifaceted theory of war and peace" in *FPHWP* (as mentioned above).

(c2.6) In relation to personality, I worked out "the contrarian theory of personality" in *FPHP* for a new way to understand normality and abnormality.

(c2.7) In relation to humor, I worked out "the metamorphic theory of humor" in *FPHH* for a new way to understand joking and laughing.

(c2.8) And in relation to artificial intelligence, I proposed "the supersession theory of computing" in *FPHCOM* for a new way to understand hardware, software, and the mind.

In addition, I also proposed "the complex theory of data analysis" in *FPHDA* for a different way to understand quantitative and qualitative research in the context of the evolution of new minds.

(d) Nature

The category of "nature" here refers to the state of nature, which can be divided into some sub-categories like (d1) physics, (d2) cosmology, (d3) biology, (d4) geography, (d5) geology, (d6) acoustics, (d7) chemistry, (d8) architecture, and (d9) transportation.

But since biology in (d3) overlaps with biology in (c1)—only the rest of the categories are addressed hereafter.

(d1) Physics

In relation to physics, I also proposed "the perspectival theory of space-time" in *FPHST* (based on *FPHC*) for a new way to understand space and time, as shown in *Table 1.3*, *Table 1.4*, *Table 1.5*, and *Table 1.7.*

In *FPHG* (based on *FPHC* and *FPHST*), I proposed "the selective theory of geometry" for a new way to understand geometry, with implications for the understanding of space-time in the context of infinity, symmetry, and dimensionality for future lifeforms that our world has never known (as shown in *Table 1.6*, *Table 1.7*, *Table 1.8; Table 1.9*, *Table 1.10,* and *Table 1.11*).

And in *FC*, I proposed "the dialectic theory of complexity" for a new way to understand order and chaos in the state of nature and beyond.

(d2) Cosmology

In relation to cosmology, my theories on physics (as indicated above) already have important implications for understanding the nature and the future of the universe (which was also addressed in *FHC*, among other works aforcited).

I also proposed "the theory of hyper-spatial consciousness" in *FPHC* (and also in *FPHG*) for a new way to understand the future evolution of the mind to enter into different dimensions of space-time that our current world has never known.

In addition, in *BCOS*, I proposed "the theory of post-cosmology" for a new way to understand the beginnings and ends of the cosmos and beyond.

(d4) Geography

In relation to geography, I proposed "the theory of the geopower of nature" in *ALD* for a different way to understand the relationships between geography and other entities (like the mind, culture, and society).

I further refined this issue of geography by proposing "the interventive-reshaping theory of geography" in *FPHGEOG*—which is related to the issues of "the environment" in (a4.4), "migration" in (a4.6), and "geology" in (d5).

(d5) Geology

In relation to geology, I proposed "the resettlement theory of geology" in *FPHGEOL* for a different way to understand the relationships between statics and dynamics—which is related to the issues of "the environment" in (a4.4), "migration" in (a4.6), and "geography" in (d4).

(d6) Acoustics

In relation to acoustics, I proposed "the multilateral theory of acoustics" in *FPHA* for a different way to understand the relationships between sound and silence.

(d7) Chemistry

In relation to chemistry, I proposed "the creational theory of chemistry" in *FPHCHEM* for a different way to understand substances and their changes.

(d8) Architecture

In relation to architecture, I proposed "the transcendent theory of architecture" in *FPHARCH* for a different way to understand form and function.

(d9) Transportation

And in relation to transportation, I propose "the panoramic theory of transportation" in *FPHTRAN* for a different way to understand networks and operations.

(e) The Rest

The category of "the rest" here refers to what cannot be strictly classified in any of the previous categories (i.e., society, culture, the mind, and nature). A good illustration of "the rest" refers to (e1) history.

(e1) History

The category of history can be divided into some sub-categories like (e1.1) empirical history and (e.1.2) meta-history.

(e1.1) In relation to empirical history, I proposed "the theory of the evolution from pre-modernity to after-postmodernity" (as first worked out in *FHC* and later in *FCD* and *FPHC*), which overlaps—as a reminder from (b5)—with the issue concerning "civilization as a whole" in (b5).

For instance, in both *FCD* and *FPHC*, I worked out the structure of "post-human civilization" in terms of the trinity of after-postmodernity (i.e., "free-spirited after-postmodernity," "post-capitalist after-postmodernity," and "hegemonic after-postmodernity").

Both conceptually and theoretically, the trinity of after-postmodernity is a sequential extension of the trinity of modernity (i.e., "free-spirited modernity," "capitalist modernity,"and "hegemonic modernity") and the trinity of postmodernity (i.e., "free-spirited postmodernity," "capitalist postmodernity," and "hegemonic postmodernity") as first proposed in *FHC*.

And the trinity of pre-modernity (i.e., "pre-free-spirited pre-modernity," "pre-capitalist pre-modernity" and "hegemonic pre-modernity") was later conceived in *BCIV* to complete the historical set from pre-modernity to after-postmodernity.

In *BDPD*, this thesis about the trinity of pre-modernity, modernity, postmodernity, and after-postmodernity was collectively known as "the theory of the trinity of modernity to its after-postmodern counterpart," at the cultural level—as already so mentioned in (b5) earlier, and summarized in *Table 1.34*, *Table 1.35*, *Table 1.36*, and *Table 1.37*.

At the structural level, all these trinities are subject to the existential constraints (e.g., the freedom/unfreedom and equality/inequality dialectics in the context of "the cyclical progression of hegemony"), be the historical epoch in pre-modernity, modernity, postmodernity, or after-postmodernity in future times. Each of the historical epochs has its ever new ways of coming to terms with the ever new (different) mixtures of freedom/unfreedom and equality/inequality.

This is importantly so, not because, as is falsely assumed in conventional wisdom, one certain way is superior (or better) than another in terms of achieving more freedom and less unfreedom, or more equality with less inequality.

On the contrary, indeed, in each of the historical epochs, each increase of unfreedom greets each freedom achieved, just as each increase of inequality welcomes each equality achieved, albeit in ever new (different) ways. In *BDPD*, this thesis of mine was labeled as "the theory of the cyclical progression of hegemony," at the structural level, though it was first analyzed in *FCD*.

In *BDPD*, more theoretical applications of existential dialectics were further examined, in relation to five main features, in the context of the duality of oppression, namely, (a) that each freedom/equality achieved is also each unfreedom/inequality created, (b) that the subsequent oppressiveness is dualistic, both by the Same against the Others and itself and by the Others against the Same and themselves, (c) that both oppression and self-oppression can be achieved by way of downgrading differences (between the Same and the Others) and of accentuating them, (d) that the relationships are relatively asymmetric among them but relatively symmetric within them, even when the Same can be relatively asymmetric towards itself in self-oppression, and the Others can be likewise towards themselves, and (e) that symmetry and asymmetry change over time, with ever new players, new causes, and new forms, be the locality here on Earth or in deep space unto multiverses—as summarized in *Table.4.13*, *Table 4.14*, *Table 4.15*, and *Table 4.16*.

The same logic also holds both in relation to wealth and poverty (as addressed in *BCPC* and summarized in *Table 4.17* on the wealth/poverty dialectics) and in relation to civilization and barbarity (as addressed in *BCIV* and summarized in *Table 4.18* on the civilization/barbarity dialectics).

In *BDPD*, this thesis on existential dialectics was labeled as "the theory of existential dialectics."

(e.1.2) And in relation to meta-history, I proposed "the multifold theory of history" in *FPHHIST* for a different way to understand universality and relativity (together with other debates).

Direct and Indirect Applications of Existential Dialectics

A different way to appreciate the usefulness of existential dialectics is by way of the analysis of its (a) direct and (b) indirect applications.

(a) In direct applications, on the one hand, the logic of existential dialectics can shed some theoretical insights on diverse phenomena in the world, and good instances are the usage of the principles of existential dialectics for the theoretical insights on the freedom/unfreedom dialectics, the equality/inequality dialectics, and the wealth/poverty dialectics—as introduced earlier in (b5) and (e) in the previous sub-section.

For instance, my books like *FPHST*, *BNN*, *FAE*, *FC*, *FIA*, *FPHU*, *FPHK*, *FPHML*, *FPHE*, *FPHMM*, *FPHCT*, *FPHG*, *FPHUP*, *FPHL*, *FPHO*, *FPHMA*, *FPHS*, *FPHLAW*, *FPHFS*, *FPHWP*, *FPHP*, *BEPE*, *BCOS*, *FPHGEOL*, *FPHCHESS*, *FPHR*, *FPHEDU*, *FPHH*, *FPHA*, *FPHGAM*, *FPHCOM*, *FPHLIT*, *FPHCHEM*, *FPHDA*, *FPHGEOG*, *FPHPA*, *FPHSEM*, *FPHARCH*, *FPHCRIM*, *FPHHIST*, *FPHMIG*, and *FPHTRAN* use the principles to reveal some theoretical insights on the perspectives of space and time (as in *FPHST*), of nature and nurture (as in *BNN*), of beauty and ugliness (as in *FAE*), of order and chaos (as in *FC*), of taxonomy and network (as in *FIA*), of the unconscious mind (as in *FPHU*), of the nature of knowledge (as in *FPHK*), of mathematical logic (as in *FPHML*), of engineering (as in *FPHE*), of mass media (as in *FPHMM*), of creative thinking (as in *FPHCT*), of geometry (as in *FPHG*), of urban planning (as in *FPHUP*), of language (as in *FPHL*), of organization (as in *FPHO*), of martial arts (as in *FPHMA*), of sexuality (as in *FPHS*), of law (as in *FPHLAW*), of formal science (as in *FPHFS*), of aggression and pacificity (as in *FPHWP*), of normality and abnormality (as in *FPHP*). of morality and immorality (as in *BEPE*), of the beginnings and ends of the universe (as in *BOCS*), of statics and dynamics (as in *FPHGEOL*), of tactics and strategy (as in *FPHCHESS*), of secularness and sacredness (as in *FPHR*), of teaching and learning (as in *FPHEDU*), of joking and laughing (as in *FPHH*), of sound and silence (as in *FPHA*), of risk and caution (as in *FPHGAM*), of hardware and software (as in *FPHCOM*), of fiction and non-fiction (as in *FPHLIT*), of substances and their changes (as in *FPHCHEM*), of quantitative and qualitative research (as in *FPHDA*), of environments and their interactions (as in *FPHGEOG*), of the body and its presence (as in *FPHPA*), of internality and externality (as in *FPHSEM*). of form and function (as in *FPHARCH*), of heroes and villains (as in *FPHCRIM*), of universality and relativity (as in *FPHHIST*), of Sameness and Otherness (as in *FPHMIG*). and of networks and operations (as in *FPHTRAN*).

(b) In indirect applications, on the other hand, the theoretical insights can further be used to reveal other phenomena directly from them (viz., the theoretical insights) and therefore indirectly from the principles themselves.

A good illustration is of course the use of the theoretical insights on the freedom/unfreedom and equality/inequality dialectics for the understanding of the civilization/barbarity dialectics.

This distinction between direct and indirect applications may sound a bit academic, since even in indirect applications, the phenomena under study can still be directly related back to the principles themselves.

In the previous example, as an illustration, the civilization/barbarity dialectics can be directly related to the principles of existential dialectics without the intermediate role of the freedom/unfreedom and equality/inequality dialectics.

Multiple Levels of Application

There is another issue to be clarified, however. In other words, the theoretical insights can be applied to multiple levels of analysis—even though, in a given example, it may refer to one level or a few only.

For instance, in the example concerning the freedom/unfreedom dialectics, it can be used at the structural level (e.g., in relation to the theory of the cyclical progression of hegemony), but it can also be exploited for other levels (e.g., the theory of post-capitalism at the institutional level).

All these levels of application should not be misleadingly construed, as I stress this before, as a one-way street (that is, to use the ontological principles for theoretical application at multiple levels of specific analysis) but a two-way one, in which theoretical insights in praxis, when studied in more specific contexts, can in turn refine the nature of existential dialectics (for example, with the addition of new principles).

Sophisticated Methodological Holism

The summary of my original meta-theory on methodology is provided below, again, to be repeated *often verbatim* from my previous works—as this is something I regularly do in each new book to introduce my past works, which are in conversation with this current one.

This means that, for those readers who have not read any of my previous books, the summary below is helpful.

That clarified—this original contribution of mine to the study of methodology takes the form of an approach known as "the theory of methodological holism" or "methodological holism" in short, as already worked out in *FPHC* (2004).

I have made good use of this methodological approach of mine for all of my previous works.

The Confusion of Holism with Systems Approach

Yet, it is imperative to stress at the outset, as I often emphasized this in all my previous books, that my approach of "methodological holism" does not oppose or exclude "methodological individualism" (as some readers may be tempted to assume, as is conventionally understood) but actually includes it.

The confusion here has to do with equating holism with systems approach in general (be it about systems theory, chaos theory, complexity theory, or else), which I debunked, while learning something from it, as already elaborated in *The Future of Complexity* (2007)—and *The Future of Post-Human Formal Science* (2010) is another addition to this critique of the intellectual fad of systems approach.

In other words, my meta-theory of holism, or sophisticated methodological holism in short, makes a distinction between doing holistic work and doing systems work, for two reasons.

The first reason is that holism, in my theory, does not imply systems approach, since it rejects systems approach because of the myriad problems that the literature on systems approach has been unable to resolve, while learning something from it.

And the second reason is that my theory is related to the other theory of mine, that is, existential dialectics, which does not exclude methodological individualism (but includes it, because it simply goes beyond both reductionism and reverse-reductionism in a dialectic way).

For these reasons (and others too, as summarized in *Table 4.1*), my version of methodological holism is *sophisticated*—not *vulgar* as sometimes used by inapt scholars employing the same term.

The Ontological Constraints

Sophisticated methodological holism is subject to some ontological constraints, and some good examples include "the formalness-informalness principle," "the absoluteness-relativeness principle," "the partiality-totality principle," "the predictability-unpredictability principle," "the explicability-inexplicability principle," and "the fiction-reallity principle" in existential dialectics.

Of course, there can be more than six ontological principles in relation to method, but the examples here are sufficient to illustrate the point in question.

With this caveat in mind—the first two were already analyzed in previous books of mine like *FC* and *FAE*, whereas the third one was addressed in *FPHU*, the fourth and fifth ones were accounted for in *FPHK* and *FPHML*, respectively, and the last one was addressed in *FPHLIT*.

For now, it suffices to show that sophisticted methodological holism, because of these ontological constraints on methodology, targets two major sins of methodology, namely, what I call, in the absence of better words, (a) *reductionism* and (b) *reverse-reductionism*—both of which come in all shapes and sizes, to be summarized below (and also shown in *Table 4.2*).

Against the Varieties of Reductionism

There are four versions of reductionism to be summarized here, which sophisticated methodological holism rejects, namely, (a1) conceptual, (a2) theoretical, (a3) methodological, and (a4) ontological forms of reductionism.

(a1) In conceptual reductionism, a good case in point concerns myriad dualities like mind vs. body, self vs. world, democracy vs non-democracy, and the like (as already addressed in *FHC*, *FPHC*, and *BDPD*, for instance).

(a2) In theoretical reductionism, an illuminating case study is best exemplified by what I originally called "the foundation fallacy" in *FPHST*, in any attempt to naively understand space-time from the physical perspective as the foundation and, consequently, to dangerously dismiss (or belittle) other perspectives.

In *FAE*, I elaborated further these versions of reductionism in the literature on aesthetics (e.g., form vs. content, representation vs. expression, critics vs. artists, and externalism vs. internalism).

In *FIA*, I revealed other forms of reductionism in the literature on information architecture (e.g., the constructivist argument and the representational argument).

In *FPHU*, I showed the persistent legacy of reductionism, this time, in the literature on anomalous experience (e.g., the obsession with physics, chemistry, and biology for explaining anomalous experience).

In *FPHE*, I examined another case of reductionism in action, in the context of engineering (e.g., technical constraints vs. normative constraints).

In *FPHMM*, I elaborated one more version of reductionism, in relation to the three domains of communication (e.g., the competing views on sending, connecting, and receiving).

In *FPHCT*, I explored another version of reductionism, in relation to invention and innovation (e.g., the bio-psychological argument vs. the socio-cultural arguments).

In *FPHG*, I identified another version of reductionism, in relation to infinity, symmetry, and dimensionality (e.g., the Euclidean argument vs. the non-Euclidean arguments).

In *FPHUP*, I analyzed another version of reductionism, in relation to density and void (e.g., the engineering argument and the ecology argument).

In *PFHL*, I examined another version of reductionism, in relation to structure and context (e.g., the structuralist argument and the contextualist argument).

In *PFHO*, I explored another version of reductionism, in relation to communcation, decision-making, and leadership (e.g., the rational-system argument vs. the natural-system argument vs. the open-system argument).

In *PFHMA*, I revealed another version of reductionism, in relation to the martial body and spirit (e.g., the spiritual argument vs. the materialist argument vs. the defensive argument).

In *PFHS*, I analyzed another version of reductionism, in relation to the sexual body and spirit (e.g., the naturalist argument vs. the constructivist argument).

In *PFHLAW*, I examined another version of reductionism, in relation to law (e.g., the necessity argument vs. the contengency argument).

In *FPHWP*, I show another version of reductionism, in relation to war and peace (e.g., the aggressivist argument vs. the pacifist argument).

In *BEPE*, I analyzed another version of reductionism, in relation to morality and immorality (e.g., the objectivist argument vs. the non-objectivist argument vs. the skeptical argument).

In *BCOS*, I examined another version of reductionism, in relation to the contested beginnings and speculative ends of the universe (e.g., the scientific argument vs. the religious argument vs. the esoteric argument vs. the metaphysical argument).

In *FPHP*, I showed another version of reductionism, in relation to normality and abnormality (e.g., the natural argument vs. the social argument vs. the cultural argument vs. the mental argument).

In *FPHGEOL*, I scrutinized another version of reductionism, in relation to statics and dynamics (e.g., the catastrophe argument vs. the uniformity argument vs. the revision argument).

In *FPHCHESS*, I showed another version of reductionism, in relation to tactics and strategy (e.g., the natural argument vs. the social argument vs. the cultural argument vs. the mental argument).

In *FPHR*, I revealed another version of reductionism, in relation to secularness and sacredness (e.g., the critical argument vs. the skeptical argument vs. the theist argument).

In *FPHEDU*, I examined another version of reductionism, in relation to teaching and learning (e.g., the teacher-centered argument vs. the student-centered argument vs. the balanced argument).

In *FPHH*, I explored another version of reductionism, in relation to joking and laughing (e.g., the natural argument vs. the social argument vs. the cultural argument vs. the mental argument).

In *FPHA*, I revealed another version of reductionism, in relation to sound and silence (e.g., the natural argument vs. the social argument vs. the cultural argument vs. the mental argument).

In *FPHGAM*, I revealed another version of reductionism, in relation to risk and caution (e.g., the natural argument vs. the social argument vs. the cultural argument vs. the mental argument).

In *FPHCOM*, I showed another version of reductionism, in relation to hardware and software (e.g., the natural argument vs. the social argument vs. the cultural argument vs. the mental argument).

In *FPHLIT*, I proposed another version of reductionism, in relation to fiction and non-fiction (e.g., the natural argument vs. the social argument vs. the cultural argument vs. the mental argument).

In *FPHCHEM*, I proposed another version of reductionism, in relation to substances and their changes (e.g., the natural argument vs. the social argument vs. the cultural argument vs. the mental argument).

In *FPHDA*, I proposed another version of reductionism, in relation to quantitative and qualitative research (e.g., the natural argument vs. the social argument vs. the cultural argument vs. the mental argument).

In *FPHGEOG*, I proposed another version of reductionism, in relation to environments and their interactions (e.g., the natural argument vs. the social argument vs. the cultural argument vs. the mental argument).

In *FPHPA*, I proposed another version of reductionism, in relation to the body and its presence (e.g., the natural argument vs. the social argument vs. the cultural argument vs. the mental argument).

In *FPHSEM*, I proposed another version of reductionism, in relation to internality and externality (e.g., the natural argument vs. the social argument vs. the cultural argument vs. the mental argument).

In *FPHARCH*, I proposed another version of reductionism, in relation to form and function (e.g., the natural argument vs. the social argument vs. the cultural argument vs. the mental argument).

In *FPHCRIM*, I proposed another version of reductionism, in relation to heroes and villains (e.g., the natural argument vs. the social argument vs. the cultural argument vs. the mental argument).

In *FPHHIST*, I proposed another version of reductionism, in relation to universality and relativity (e.g., the natural argument vs. the social argument vs. the cultural argument vs. the mental argument).

In *FPHMIG*, I proposed another version of reductionism, in relation to Sameness and Otherness (e.g., the natural argument vs. the social argument vs. the cultural argument vs. the mental argument).

And in *FPHTRAN*, I propose another version of reductionism, in relation to networks and operations (e.g., the natural argument vs. the social argument vs. the cultural argument vs. the mental argument).

(a3) In methodological reductionism, a good illustration can be the debate between different versions of qualitative and quantitative methods (as already analyzed in *FC* and also *FHC*).

In *FPHML*, I examined similar reductionism, this time, in the literature on mathematical logic (e.g., the obsession with consistency, soundness, and completeness).

And in *FPHFS*, I explored the problems of reductionism in the context of formal science (e.g., the analytical argument, as opposed to the synthetic argument).

(a4) In ontological reductionism, an excellent instance involves another debate, this time between emergentism and reductionism in complexity theory (as addressed in *FC*) and also in psychology (as elaborated in *FPHC*, in the context of Being and Belonging).

But to target against the varieties of reductionism constitutes only a side of the same coin, and the other side concerns the varieties of reverse-reductionism.

Against the Varieties of Reverse-Reductionism

The other side of the same coin is the reverse version of reductionism, which is what I want to call, in the absence of better words, *reverse-reductionism*.

My sophisticated version of methodological holism targets against the varieties of reverse-reductionism (just as it also rejects the ones of reductionism).

Perhaps nothing expresses better the popularity of reverse-reductionim than the "anything-goes" mentality in postmodernism of our time, as shown in the following four versions.

(b1) In conceptual reverse-reductionism, any concept of "art" (e.g., fine art, applied art, outsider art, junk art) is welcome in postmodernism (as already analyzed in Ch.4 of *FHC*—and also in *FAE*).

(b2) In theoretical reverse-reductionism, a variety of art and literary theories co-exist. Take the case of literary studies, as there are now Literary Structuralism, Marxist Literary Criticism, New Criticism, Phenomenology, Hermeneutics, Language-Game Literary Criticism, Feminist Literary Criticism, Reception Theory, Reader Response Criticism, Poststructuralism, Semiotics, Pyschoanalytic Literary Criticism, just to cite some well-known ones, with no one being said to be better than any others (as detailedly analyzed in Ch.4 of *FHC*). (S. Raman 1997)

In *BNN*, I even introduced "the compromise fallacy" as another good illustration of theoretical reverse-reductionism, in misleadingly treating both genetic and environmental approaches as equally valid.

(b3) In methodological reverse-reductionism, multiple methodologies are deemed as acceptable in postmodernism (e.g., doing art without praxis, doing art with praxis, and doing art by sublation), as analyzed in Ch.4 of *FHC*.

And in *FPHFS*, I exposed the problems of reverse-reductionism in the context of formal science in relation to systems theory (e.g., the synthetic argument).

(b4) In ontological reverse-reductionism, no privileged ontology is allowed, and the door is open practically for anything in postmodernism (e.g., the equal status of the ontology of Being vs. that of Becoming, as already addressed in Ch.4 of *FHC*—and also in *FPHC*).

In *FAE*, I also introduced another version of reverse-reductionism, that is, "the pluralist fallacy," in the context of understanding aesthetic experience, for instance—although this fallacy has been committed not exclusively in relation to the ontological level (but also at the conceptual, theoretical, and methodological ones).

These dual dangers against reverse-reductionism (in this sub-section) and reductionism (in the previous sub-section) are something that sophisticated methodological holism rejects. And in *FPHFS*, I addressed these two problems further.

This point about the dual dangers is important enough, since many scholars often favor one against the other, but it is vital to target both.

The Holistic Organization of an Inquiry

With these dual dangers against reductionism and reverse-reductionism in mind—sophisticated methodological holism suggests that an inquiry of any given phenomenon is more complete, if treated in the context of a comprehensive analysis at all relevant levels, which challengingly encompass all the fields of human knowledge, ranging from the natural sciences and formal sciences through the social sciences to the humanities.

This section is something that I had already stressed in all my previous books and repeat (*often verbatim*) hereafter. But, for those readers who had read my previous books, this serves as a reminder.

With this reminder in mind—there are multiple ways to engage in a holistic inquiry with all relevent levels of analysis. Over the years, I have proposed different ways to fulfill this holistic methodological requirement, as repeated in my previous books.

Hereafter is a summary of four major ways, namely, (a) by discipline, (b) by domain, (c) by subject, and (d) by meta-analysis—all of which fulfill the holistic requirement of sophisticated methodological holism on a given issue.

(a) In a holistic organization by discipline, a good illustration is the multiple levels of analysis, namely, (a1) the micro-physical, (a2) the chemical, (a3) the biological, (a4) the psychological, (a5) the organizational, (a6) the institutional, (a7) the structural, (a8) the systemic, (a9) the cultural, (a10) the macro-physical (cosmological), and (a11) other relevant levels, which are either a combination of all these levels or the practical applications with a combination of them.

This holistic organization by discipline is used in *FCD* and *BCPC*, for instance.

(b) In a holistic organization by domain, some good candidates include the classification of different perspectives of analysis in relation to (b1) nature, (b2) the mind, (b3) society, and (b4) culture, as already worked out in *BCIV*, *FPHST*, *FC*, *FAE*, *FPHU*, *FPHK*, *FPHE*, and *FPHFS*, just to cite some examples.

Culture in (b4), in this re-classification, is the same as culture in (a9) and can be further divided into different sub-categories, with good examples like (a9i) epistemology (methodology), (a9ii) aesthetics, (a9iii) ethics, (a9iv) metaphysics (ontology), and (a9v) religion. For clarification, epistemology (methodology) in (a9i) and metaphysics (ontology) in (a9iv) overlap with the category of "meta-theory."

Society in (b3) includes the organizational in (a5), the institutional in (a6), the structural in (a7), and the systemic in (a8).

The mind (b2) has more to do with the chemical in (a2), the biological in (a3), and the psychological in (a4), although it can overlap with (a1), (b3) and (b4), for instance.

It should be stressed that the "mind" here also includes the categories like the "brain," "body," and the "spirit" (or the "soul")—whenever needed in a given context, so that one does not fall into the intellectual trap of the "mind-body dualism" in the history of modern (and especially, postmodern) philosophy, which I already went to great lengths to explain in *The Future of Human Civilization*. After all, in everyday's usage, the "mind" already implies the "brain" and the "body" (together with their interactions) and has different levels of consciousness which can be both "spiritual" and non-spiritual.

And nature in (b1) refers to the micro-physical in (a1) and the macro-physical (cosmological) in (a10), although it can also overlap with (a2), (a3) and (a4).

(c) In a holistic organization by subject, some excellent examples concern the analysis of consciousness in *FPHC* (i.e., on Having, Belonging, and Being); of civilization in *FHC* (i.e., the True, the Holy, the Everyday, the Technological, the Beautiful/Sublime, the Good, and the Just); of international politics in *BWT* (i.e., Hyper-Empires, Meso-Empires, and Micro-Empires); of nature and nurture in *BNN* (i.e., genes and memes); of information architecture in *FIA* (i.e., taxonomy and network); of mathematical logic in *FPHML* (i.e., consistency, soundness, and completeness); of communication in *FPHMM* (i.e., sending, connecting, and receiving); of creative thinking in *FPHCT* (i.e., invention and innovation); of geometry in *FPHG* (i.e., infinity, symmetry, and dimensionality); of urban planning in *FPHUP* (i.e., density and void), of language in *FPHL* (i.e., structure and context), of organization in *FPHO* (i.e., communication, decision-making, and leadership), of martial arts in *FPHMA* (i.e., the martial body and the martial spirit), of sexuality in *FPHS* (i.e., the sexual body and the sexual spirit), of law in *FPHLAW* (i.e., necessity and contingency), of war and peace in *FPHWP* (i.e., aggression and pacificity), of personality in *FPHP* (i.e., normality and abnormality), of ethics in *BEPE* (i.e., morality and immorality), of cosmology in *BCOS* (i.e., the beginnings and ends of the universe), of geology in *FPHGEOL* (i.e., statics and dynamics), of chess in *FPHCHESS* (i.e., tactics and strategy), of religion in *FPHR* (i.e., secularness and sacredness), of education in *FPHEDU* (i.e., teaching and learning), of humor in *FPHH* (i.e., laughing and joking), of acoustics in *FPHA* (i.e., sound and silence), of gambling in *FPHGAM* (i.e., risk and caution), of computing in *FPHCOM* (i.e., hardware and software), of literature in *FPHLIT* (i.e., fiction and non-fiction), of chemistry in *FPHCHEM* (i.e., substances and their changes), of data analysis in *FPHDA* (i.e., quantitative and qualitative research), of geography in *FPHGEOG* (i.e., environments and their interactions), of performing arts in *FPHPA* (i.e., the body and its presence), of semantics in *FPHSEM* (i.e., internality and externality), of architecture in *FPHARCH* (i.e., form and function), of criminality in *FPHCRIM* (i.e., heroes and villains), of history in *FPHHIST* (i.e., universality and relativity), of migration in *FPHMIG* (i.e., Sameness and Otherness) and of transportation in *FPHTRAN* (i.e., networks and operations)—by incorporating all the relevent levels of analysis as cited above in each.

(d) And in a holistic organization by meta-analysis, two good cases in point involve the works on post-capitalism in *BCPC* and on authoritarian liberal democracy in *ALD*, with the classification of analysis in theory and meta-theory.

The essential point to remember here, as I thus stress in all my previous books, is that the multiple levels of analysis can be reorganized in many different ways, insofar as none of the levels (if relevant to an inquiry in question) is ignored or dismissed, to avoid the danger of reductionism (and for that matter, the one of reverse-reductionism, in the opposite direction).

Three Clarifications

Three clarifications are needed here, however, to avoid any hasty misunderstanding.

Firstly, the entities in each classification are not mutually exclusive. For instance, in the holisitc organization by domain, nature in (b1) can also be linked to the chemical in (a2), the biological in (a3), and the systemic in (a8). And the mind (b3) can alternatively be related to the micro-physical in (a1) and the chemical in (a2), for example.

Secondly, there is also the important factor of luck (or uncertainty in conventional usage), but it is already implied or allowed in each of the organizations of an inquiry—especially in relation to the predictability-unpredictability principle and the order-chaos principle in existential dialectics. This topic about uncertainty was already addressed in *FHC*—and more extensively, in *FC*, in the context of order and chaos (and later, to an extent, in *FPHK*, *FPHFS*, and *FPHGAM*, for example).

And lastly, the comparison in a classification is not absolute, but relative, as there are often some shades of gray, not exactly black or white (figuratively speaking).

Some further clarifications and qualifications of sophisticated methodological holism are shown in *Table 4.2*.

Some Distinctive Usefulness

In the end, sophisticated methodological holism—when applied, especially though not exclusively, as illustrated in my numerous works—can enrich the understanding of reality in some distinctive ways. Here are four examples (as revealed in each of my books).

Firstly, it provides a comprehensive analysis of a subject matter, from which much can be learned about reality, both in relation to the perspectives of the mind, nature, society, and culture.

Secondly, it offers a new classification of the subject matter.

Thirdly, it suggests some visions of the future in relation to the subject matter in question.

And fourthly, it proposes some insights on meta-theory (e.g., methodology and ontology) in general—with the clear understanding, however, of the dilemma of specific vs. general ontology (as shown in *Table 4.9* on the syntax of existential dialectics in the context of the dilemma of ontology).

For this very reason, all of these ways are important, without reducing one into the analysis of another. (*FPHCT*)

Chapter Outline

With this summary of my two original meta-theories (on methodology and ontology, *almost verbatim* from my previous works) in mind—this book is organized in four main parts, namely, (a) Part I on the introduction to this book, (b) Part II on networks, (c) Part III on operations, and (d) Part IV on the conclusion of the book.

The book is thus organized in four chapters.

The introductory chapter, that is, Chapter One titled "Introduction—The Convenience of Transportation," begins with a story of two contrastive expectations, provides a definition and history of transportation, and then introduces networks and operations in the study of transportation, as well as the general aspects of transportation—together with the theoretical debate on history, my panoramic theory of transportation, the relationship between theory and meta-theory, existential dialectics, sophisticated methodological holism, and some further clarifications.

Chapter Two titled "Networks and their Intricacies" examines the nature of networks in transportation from the four perspectives of the mind, nature, society, and culture, with a deconstructive critique of each.

Chapter Three titled "Operations and their Complications" explores the nature of opreations in transportation from the four perspectives of the mind, nature, society, and culture, with a constructive assessment of each.

The last chapter titled "Conclusion—The Future of Transportation" summarizes the analysis in the book in the dialectic context of networks and operations in transportation with twenty-six major theses, namely, (a) the first thesis: the formalness-informalness principle, (b) the second thesis: the absoluteness-relativeness principle, (c) the third thesis: the partiality-totality principle, (d) the fourth thesis: the predictability-unpredictability principle, (e) the fifth thesis: the explicability-inexplicability principle, (f) the sixth thesis: the fiction-reality principle, (g) the seventh thesis: the finiteness-transfiniteness principle, (h) the eighth thesis: the preciseness-vagueness principle, (i) the ninth thesis: the simpleness-complicatedness principle, (j) the tenth thesis: the openness-hiddenness principle, (k) the eleventh thesis: the denseness-emptiness principle, (l) the twelfth thesis: the change-constancy principle, (m) the thirteenth thesis: the order-chaos principle, (n) the fourteenth thesis: the slowness-quickness principle, (o) the fifteenth thesis: the expansion-contraction principle, (p) the sixteenth thesis: the theory-praxis principle, (q) the seventeenth thesis: the convention-novelty principle, (r) the eighteenth thesis: the evolution-transformation principle, (s) the nineteenth thesis: the symmetry-asymmetry principle, (t) the twentieth thesis: the softness-hardness principle, (u) the twenty-first thesis: the seriousness-playfulness principle, (v) the twenty-second thesis: the activeness-inactiveness principle, (w) the twenty-third thesis: the regression-progression principle, (x) the twenty-fourth thesis: the sameness-difference principle, (y) the twenty-fifth thesis: the stability-reaction principle, and (z) the twenty-sixth thesis: the post-human panorama—to be elaborated in the rest of the book, with a summary in the concluding chapter.

This seminal project here, if successful, will fundamentally change the way that we think about networks and operations in the study of transportation (together with other debates as will be discussed in the rest of the book), from the combined perspectives of the mind, nature, society, and culture, with enormous implications for the human future and what I originally called its "post-human" fate.

Some Clarifications

However, some additional (last) clarifications are needed.

These clarifications, lest any potential misunderstanding by the readers occurs, refer to (a) the conversation with my previous books, (b) the illustrative selection of case studies and examples, (c) detailed analysis versus overall analysis, (d) three distinctive features of using quotations, (e) two difficulties with understanding, (f) repetition, and (g) the use of neologisms.

These clarifications are something that I also regularly repeat in my previous books too, so these points are repeated hereafter, *often verbatim*—albeit in a different context this time.

In Conversation with My Previous Books

Firstly, my *panoramic theory of transportation* is constructed on the theoretical foundation of my previous books (i.e., *FHC*, *FCD*, *FPHC*, *BDPD*, *BCPC*, *BCIV*, *FPHST*, *BNN*, *BWT*, *FC*, *FAE*, *ALD*, *FIA*, *FPHU*, *FPHK*, *FPHML*, *FPHE*, *FPHMM*, *FPHCT*, *FPHG*, *FPHUP*, *FPHL*, *FPHO*, *FPHMA*, *FPHS*, *FPHLAW*, *FPHFS*, *FPHWP*, *FPHP*, *BCOS*, *BEPE*, *FPHGEOL*, *FPHCHESS*, *FPHR*, *FPHEDU*, *FPHH*, *FPHA*, *FPHGAM*, *FPHCOM*, *FPHLIT*, *FPHCHEM*, *FPHDA*, *FPHGEOG*, *FPHPA*, *FPHSEM*, *FPHARCH*, *FPHCRIM*, *FPHHIST*, and *FPHMIG*—as explicated in "The List of Abbreviations").

For this reason, many of my books have some familiar words in their titles like "The Future of Post-Human ____" or "Beyond ____to ____," as well as some tables for background information—as they constitute a series of books with the final aim to converge all of my original theories on numerous fields into a unified theory of everything (as already summarized in the section on theory and meta-theory in Chapter One).

Just consider the following two illustrations, namely, (a) in relation to other related theoretical debates and (b) in relation to different visions as worked out in my previous books.

(a) The first illustration is that the theoretical debate here also involves a few other related theoretical issues.

These other related theoretical issues have to do with some deeply contested theoretical debates, which, however, I had already gone to great lengths to analyze in my numerous (previous) books, as summarized below. It should also be stressed, lest misunderstanding occurs, that each of the theoretical debates (as listed below) does not exhaust the issues covered in the books, as each book covers more issues than what is listed below (for illustration only).

- On Networks
  –Ex: *The Future of Information Architecture*
- On Planning
  –Ex: *The Future of Post-Human Urban Planning*
  –Ex: *The Future of Capitalism and Democracy*
- On Engineering
  –Ex: *The Future of Post-Human Engineering*
- On the Environment
  –Ex: *The Future of Post-Human Geography*
  –Ex: *The Future of Post-Human Geology*
- On Technology
  –Ex: *The Future of Post-Human Engineering*
  –Ex: 2 volumes, *The Future of Human Civilization*
  –Ex: *The Future of Post-Human Computing*
- On Migration
  –Ex: *The Future of Post-Human Migration*
- On Globalization
  –Ex: *The Future of Capitalism and Democracy*
  –Ex: 2 volumes, *The Future of Human Civilization*
- On Urbanization
  –Ex: *The Future of Post-Human Urban Planning*
- On Civilization
  –Ex: *Beyond Civilization to Post-Civilization*
  –Ex: 2 volumes, *The Future of Human Civilization*
- On Economics
  –Ex: *The Future of Capitalism and Democracy*
  –Ex: 2 volumes, *The Future of Human Civilization*
  –Ex: *Beyond Capitalism to Post-Capitalism*
- On War and Peace
  –Ex: *The Future of Post-Human War and Peace*
  –Ex: 2 volumes, *Beyond Democracy to Post-Democracy*
- On Space Colonization
  –Ex: *The Future of Capitalism and Democracy*
  –Ex: 2 volumes, *The Future of Human Civilization*
- On Epistemology and Ontology
  –Ex: *The Future of Post-Human Knowledge*
  –Ex: *The Future of Post-Human Consciousness*
  –Ex: 2 volumes, *The Future of Human Civilization*
- On Rationality
  –Ex: *The Future of Post-Human Mathematical Logic*
  –Ex: *The Future of Post-Human Humor*

- On Freedom
  –Ex: 2 volumes, *The Future of Human Civilization*
  –Ex: *The Future of Capitalism and Democracy*
  –Ex: *Beyond Capitalism to Post-Capitalism*
  –Ex: 2 volumes, *Beyond Democracy to Post-Democracy*
  –Ex: *Beyond Civilization to Post-Civilization*
- On Communication
  –Ex: *The Future of Post-Human Mass Media*
  –Ex: *The Future of Post-Human Organization*
- On Learning
  –Ex: *The Future of Post-Human Language*
  –Ex: *The Future of Post-Human Education*
- On Psychology
  –Ex: *The Future of Post-Human Unconsciousness*
  –Ex: *The Future of Post-Human Consciousness*
  –Ex: *The Future of Capitalism and Democracy*
  –Ex: *The Future of Post-Human Creative Thinking*
  –Ex: *The Future of Post-Human Personality*
- On Cognition
  –Ex: *The Future of Post-Human Unconsciousness*
  –Ex: *The Future of Post-Human Consciousness*
  –Ex: *The Future of Capitalism and Democracy*
  –Ex: *The Future of Post-Human Creative Thinking*
  –Ex: *The Future of Post-Human Personality*
- On Intuition
  –Ex: *The Future of Post-Human Unconsciousness*
  –Ex: *The Future of Post-Human Consciousness*
  –Ex: *Beyond Capitalism to Post-Capitalism*
  –Ex: *The Future of Capitalism and Democracy*
- On Emotion
  –Ex: *The Future of Post-Human Unconsciousness*
  –Ex: *The Future of Post-Human Consciousness*
  –Ex: *The Future of Aesthetic Experience*
  –Ex: *Beyond Capitalism to Post-Capitalism*
  –Ex: *The Future of Capitalism and Democracy*
  –Ex: *The Future of Post-Human Personality*
- On Behavior
  –Ex: *The Future of Post-Human Language*
  –Ex: *The Future of Post-Human Unconsciousness*
  –Ex: *The Future of Post-Human Consciousness*
  –Ex: *Beyond Capitalism to Post-Capitalism*

–Ex: *The Future of Capitalism and Democracy*
–Ex: *The Future of Post-Human Sexuality*
–Ex: *The Future of Post-Human Personality*
–Ex: *The Future of Post-Human Martial Arts*

- On Being and Belonging
  –Ex: *The Future of Post-Human Consciousness*
  –Ex: 2 volumes, *The Future of Human Civilization*
- On Different Dimensions of Human Existence
  –Ex: 2 volumes, *The Future of Human Civilization*
- On Modernity, Post-Modernity, and After-Postmodernity
  –Ex: 2 volumes, *The Future of Human Civilization*
  –Ex: *Beyond Civilization to Post-Civilization*
- On Pre-Modernity
  –Ex: *Beyond Civilization to Post-Civilization*
- On Spirituality
  –Ex: 2 volumes, *The Future of Human Civilization*
  –Ex: *The Future of Capitalism and Democracy*
  –Ex: *The Future of Post-Human Religion*
  –Ex: *Beyond Civilization to Post-Civilization*
  –Ex: *The Future of Post-Human Sexuality*
  –Ex: *The Future of Post-Human Martial Arts*
  –Ex: *The Future of Post-Human Unconsciousness*
  –Ex: *The Future of Post-Human Consciousness*
  –Ex: *Beyond Ethics to Post-Ethics*

Therefore, those who are interested in these other theoretical issues (and debates) which are related to the current context can consult these other books of mine for more details.

(b) And the second illustration is that one of the major theses of this book concerns the future, be it human and later post-human, which is closely linked with the different visions that I had worked out in my previous books, in relation to the mind, nature, society, and culture.

Of course, for the convenience of the readers, a summary of some of these visions will be provided whenever necessary, as shown in the two sections on meta-theory above (*often verbatim*) and in different tables at the end of this chapter and the concluding chapter, for instance.

Yet, I still expect the readers to read my previous books directly for more details—as this book is written in conversation with my previous ones.

Case Studies and Examples

Secondly, the case studies and examples in the chapters are not exhaustive but solely illustrative. Nor are they necessarily mutually exclusive, as they can be reclassified in a different way. And exceptions are allowed.

One is tempted to assume, however, that, since the case studies and their examples are not exhaustive, more case studies and examples are needed. But the problem here is that just adding more of them does not necessarily change the conclusions to be drawn and may even lead to redundancy.

After all, the case studies and examples used in this book are chosen with care and deemed sufficient for the purpose at hand, even though they are solely illustrative.

Detailed Analysis versus Overall Synthesis

Thirdly, there is a distinction between detailed analysis and overall synthesis, in that the former is, especially though not exclusively, more for the specialized viewpoint of a specific discipline, whereas the latter is, especially though not exclusively, more for the broad horizon of an interdisciplinary approach—relatively speaking, of course.

Or, by analogy, there is a distinction between depicting a "tree" (with tiny details) in a "forest" and viewing the entire "forest" itself (with the broader horizon).

This book, like all previous ones of mine, tries to strike a balance between the two forms of understanding, although this does not imply that the two forms should be exactly equally offered, in an exact 50-50 balance.

Instead, the book, more often than not, does not allow the tiny details to obscure the larger picture in a given case study, because the entire book is inter-disciplinary in nature and tries to look at the entire "forest," not being bogged down with the detailed analysis of an individual "tree" in the forest, by analogy.

In this sense, although detailed analysis can be provided whenever needed for a given case study, the important point to remember is the overall horizon with its broadness of scope.

Three Distinctive Features of Using Quotations

Fourthly, the way that quotes are used in this book (and others of mine) has three distinctive features, as explained below.

The first distinctive feature is that, at the end of each quotation, sometimes there are more than one reference—in which case the first reference is for the original citation, and the rest of the references are for the convenience of the reader for more information about the issue(s) under quotation.

The second distinctive feature is that quotations are used as often as possible, so as to let others speak for themselves, without the nuisance of putting my own words into their mouths. Even more importantly, this allows me to use the original text as an evidence for critical analysis at the end of each section.

And the third distinctive feature is that all these quotations are used for my own purposes, in that I often creatively (or originally) re-organize them for a new way of analyzing the issue(s) in question.

Two Difficulties with Understanding

Fifthly, to understand this book (or any other book of mine) is difficult for two main reasons.

In regard to the first difficulty, this book, just like many other books of mine, is in conceptual and theoretical conversation with other books of mine (51 books, as of January, 2012), so this requires a vast background information on numerous subject matters.

And in regard to the second difficulty, this book also analyzes the subject matter in a way very different from the expectation of a conventional specialist reader, since it examines reality outside the specialist's interest (or outside his or her "comfort zone"), from the four broad perspectives of the mind, nature, society, and culture, such that it covers all domains of knowledge (in the social sciences, the natural sciences, the formal sciences, and the humanities). In other words, those who are truly interested in my project for a unified theory of everything would find many books of mine highly stimulating, but those who are specialists in a subject matter (like physics, geography, chess, and so on, in a strictly specialist sense) will not find them suitable to their specialist taste (or expectation).

Not surprisingly, a conventional specialist reader would find these two difficulties (with understanding) almost practically impossible to overcome, as they almost require the mind of a polymath. Even then, the best advice is that one should still try one's best to understand it.

Repetition

Sixthly, many of my books have something in common, and the reason is to show "the unified theory of everything" in all domains of knowledge.

For this reason, there is certain repetition in all books (especially in regard to the background information, together with the tables, in the introductory chapter and the concluding chapter). Therefore, these books are all titled "The Future of Post-Human ____" (or at times "Beyond ____ to ____") and constitute the "post-human" series.

The Use of Neologisms

And finally, I use different neologisms in my books, mostly to introduce my original concepts and theories, and good instances include those here or elsewhere in my previous books (e.g., "the panoramic theory of transportation," "post-democracy," "hyper-spatial consciousness," "post-capitalism," and whatnot). Needless to say, they are used here solely for our current intellectual convenience, as they will be renamed differently in different ways in future history.

As I thus wrote in *FCD* (508-9), "all these terms 'post-capitalism,' 'post-democracy'…and other ones as introduced in…[the] project (e.g.,…'posthuman elitists,' and 'posthuman counter-elitists,' just to cite a few of them) are more for our current intellectual convenience than to the liking of future humans and post-humans, who will surely invent more tasteful neologisms to call their own eras, entities, and everything else, for that matter. But the didactic point here is to use the terms to foretell what the future might be like, not that its eras and entities must be called so exactly and permanently. After all, William Shakespeare (1995: Act II, Scene II, Line 47) well said long ago: 'What is in a name? That which we call a rose by any other name would smell as sweet.'"

As I had also stressed time and again before, each of the neologisms can be re-written as a different "X," only to be re-named differently by the powers that be in different eras of future history.

With these clarifications for thought in mind—I now proceed to Chapter Two on networks and their intricacies.

Table 1.1. General Characteristics of Transportation

- **Networks and Operations**
  - —Networks
    - Ex: infrastructure
    - Ex: vehicles
  - —Operations
    - Ex: agency
    - Ex: financing
    - Ex: legality and policy

- **Modes of Transport**
  - —Ex: human-powered
  - —Ex: animal-powered
  - —Ex: air
  - —Ex: rail
  - —Ex: road
  - —Ex: ship
  - —Ex: others (e.g., spaceflight, cable, pipeline, etc.)

- **Functions of Transport**
  - —Ex: passenger
  - —Ex: freight

- **Impacts of Transport**
  - —Ex: economy
  - —Ex: planning
  - —Ex: environment

Notes: The categories are solely illustrative (not exhaustive), and the comparison is relative (not absolute), nor are they necessarily mutually exclusive. And some can be easily re-classified elsewhere. As generalities, they allow exceptions.
Source: From *Sec. 1.3* & *Sec. 1.4* of *FPHTRAN*. See book for citations.

Table 1.2. Nine Great Future Transformations of Transportation (Part I)

- **In Relation to the Mind**

  —*New Goals*

  - This search search for "new goals" will give future advanced humans and later their successors, namely, the post-humans, different motivations to improve transportation in a way that current humans cannot—in relation to my previous visions on the future "post-human" supersession of the human mind like "the supersession computing," "metamorphic humor," "the contrarian personality," "the hyper-martial body," "the hyper-sexual body," "floating consciousness," "hyper-spatial consciousness," "thinking machines," "unfolding unconsciousness," "thinking robots," "genetically altered superior beings," "cyborgs," etc.

  —*New Means*

  - This quest for "new means" will give future advanced humans and later their successors, namely, the post-humans, the capacity to find novel options to achieve the goals of transportation in a way that current humans cannot.

- **In Relation to Nature**

  —*New Comparisons*

  - This search for "new comparisons" will give future advanced humans and later their successors, namely, the post-humans, the ability to learn from animals, plants, and the universe, through comparison and contrast, about the future of transportation in a way that current humans cannot.

(continued on next page)

Table 1.2. Nine Great Future Transformations of Transportation (Part II)

- **In Relation to Nature (*cont'd*)**
  - —*New Integrations*
    - This search for "new integrations" will give future advanced humans and later their successors, namely, the post-humans, the ability to live and interact with nature for the future of transportation in a way that current humans cannot, especially in different forms of what I orginally propose here as:

      –Solar Transportation
      –Galactic Transportation
      –Clustery Transportation
      –Cosmic Transportation
      –Multiversal Transportation

      These forms are a further extension of the great future transformations of geology (in *FPHGEOL*), of geography (in *FPHGEOG*), and of migration (in *FPHMIG*) to the realm of transportation—in relation to my previous visions on the future "post-human" adventures into different dimensions of space-time unto multiverses like "the alteration of space-time" (*Table 1.3* & *Table 1.4*), "multiverses" (*Table 1.7* & *Table 1.8*), "hyperspace" (*Table 1.9* & *Table 1.25*), "time travel" (*Table 1.10* & *Table 1.11*), and others.

      This extension is consistent with my other theory, namely, "the theory of the cyclical progression of system integration and fragmentation" in *FCD* (2002)—at the social-systemic level (as already clarified in *Sec. 1.8* and shown below):

      Local → Regional → Global →Solar →
      Galactic → Clustery…→ Multiversal

(continued on next page)

Table 1.2. Nine Great Future Transformations of Transportation (Part III)

- **In Relation to Society**
  - —*New Praxes*
    - This search for “new praxes” will give future advanced humans and later their successors, namely, the post-humans, the ability to engage in practice (like activism, politics, personal experience, etc.) for the future of transportation in a way that current humans cannot.
  - —*New Technologies*
    - This search for “new technologies” will give future advanced humans and later their successors, namely, the post-humans, the ability to come up with different techniques, materials, and experiments for the future of transportation in a way that current humans cannot.
  - —*New Stratifications*
    - This emergence of “new stratifications” will lead future advanced humans and later their successors, namely, the post-humans, to face new inequalities in the future of transportation in a way that current humans cannot.

- **In Relation to Culture**
  - —*New Sub-Fields*
    - This search for “new sub-fields” will give future advanced humans and later their successors, namely, the post-humans, the ability to explore new specialties for the future of transportation in a way that current humans cannot.
  - —*New Interpretations*
    - This search for “new interpretations” will give future advanced humans and later their successors, namely, the post-humans, the ability to come up with different evaluations and views about transportation in a way that current humans cannot.

Notes: The categories and examples are solely illustrative (not exhaustive), and the comparison is relative (not absolute), nor are they necessarily mutually exclusive. And some can be easily re-classified elsewhere. As generalities, they allow exceptions.
Source: From *Ch.4* of *FPHTRAN*. See text for citations.

Table 1.3. The Theoretical Debate on Space-Time (Part I)

- **Isaac Newton's Absolutist (Substantivist) Theory of Space-Time**

  —space and time are independent from each other. The structure of space-time is $E3 \times E1$ (with the structure of space, *P*, as the set of spatial locations in a three-dimensional Euclidean space, *E3*, and the structure of time as the set of temporal moments, *T*, in the one-dimensional real time, *E1*).

  —space and time are also independent from the effects of matter and events. The existence of space and time is possible even in a world absent of matter (and, for that matter, even in a world absent of events), as if they were material objects but with their total unchangingness thorough time.

- **Albert Einstein's Relativist Theory of Space-Time**

  —space and time are interchangeable (not absolute), just as matter and energy are equivalent (not independent) with the famous equation, $E = mc^2$ (as in the special theory of relativity in 1905).

  —space-time and matter-energy are also relative in a grand union (as in the general theory of relativity in 1915). Thus, each pair affects the other pair, as "matter 'tells' spacetime how to curve [in a non-Euclidean geometry] and curved spacetime 'tells' matter how to behave….Space contracts near mass and dilates away from it. Time dilates near mass and contracts away from it. Clocks positioned farther away from the mass of the earth run faster than clocks closer to the earth." (L. Shlain 1991: 328-330)

(continued on next page)

Table 1.3. The Theoretical Debate on Space-Time (Part II)

- **Peter Baofu's Perspectival Theory of Space-Time**
  - —space and time can be understood from multiple perspectives, be they in relation to culture, society, nature, and the mind, with each perspective revealing something about the nature of space-time and simultaneously delimiting its view. This is subject to "the regression-progression principle" in existential dialectics.
  - —each perspective of space and time exists in society and culture with good reasons, with some being more successful and hegemonic (dominant) than others. This is subject to "the symmetry-asymmetry principle" in existential dialectics.
  - —space and time will not last, to be eventually superseded (altered) by post-humans in different forms (e.g.,stretching/shrinking space-time, engineering more dimensions of space-time, and manipulating multiverses), be they here in this universe or in multiverses. Thus, even the physical existence of space-time cannot last forever, with ever more transformations in the process. This is subject to "the change-constancy principle" in existential dialectics.
  - —the conventional wisdom (especially by physicists) of treating the physical perspective of space and time as the foundation of all other perspectives (of space and time) and of regarding them as much less important is a form of reductionism,committing what I call *the foundation fallacy*, in misleadingly dismissing the multiple perspectives of space and time in relation to culture, society, nature, and the mind.

Notes: The examples in each category are solely illustrative (not exhaustive), and the comparison is relative (not absolute), nor are they necessarily mutually exclusive. Some can be easily re-classified elsewhere. As generalities, they allow exceptions.
Source: A summary of *Sec.1.1*, *Sec.1.2*, and *Sec.1.3* of *FPHST*—and, for that matter, the rest of *FPHST*

Table 1.4. Main Reasons for Altering Space-Time

- **The Need to Make New Energy-Matter**
  —Ex: manipulating molecular bonds for new materials
  —Ex: creating nanotechnologies on the atomic scale
  —Ex: engineering the atomic nucleus
  —Ex: restructuring most elementary particles
  —Ex: inventing new forms of matter and energy

- **The Need to Create New Space-Time**
  —Ex: creating "warp drive" (as in science fiction) for space travel
  —Ex: creating "pocket universes"

- **The Need to Conquer the Cosmos unto Multiverses**
  —Ex: spreading floating consciousness and hyper-spatial consciousness, besides other forms that humans have never known, in the cosmos and beyond unto multiverses for ultimate conquest

Notes: The examples in each category are solely illustrative (not exhaustive) nor necessarily mutually exclusive, and the comparison is relative (not absolute). As generalities, they allow exceptions. Also, it should be stressed that the three reasons are all related, in that they all contribute to the evolution of intelligent life in the cosmos unto multiverses in the most distant future beyond our current knowledge.
Sources: A summary of *Sec.6.2* of *FPHST*. See also *FHC*, *FCD*, *FPHC*, *FC*, *FPHU*, and *FPHG*, for example.

Table 1.5. The Technological Frontiers of the Micro-World

- **Type I-Minus**
  —Ex: building structures and mining

- **Type II-Minus**
  —Ex: playing with the genetic makeups of living things

- **Type III-Minus**
  —Ex: manipulating molecular bonds for new materials

- **Type IV-Minus**
  —Ex: creating nanotechnologies on the atomic scale

- **Type V-Minus**
  —Ex: engineering the atomic nucleus

- **Type VI-Minus**
  —Ex: restructuring most elementary particles

- **Type Ω-Minus**
  —Ex: altering the structure of space-time

Notes: As already indicated in *Sec.4.4.2.2* of *FPHC*, the problem with this micro-classification (from Barrow's work) is that the civilization types (with the exception of Type Ω-Minus, for example) are not quite distinct, since many of them can be achieved more or less in a civilization, to the extent that Type II-minus and Type III-minus, just to cite two plausible types, can be historically contemporaneous, relatively speaking, unlike the vast historical distance between, say, Type O and Type I (or Type I and Type II) civilizations. In other words, the micro-classification here is not very useful to understand civilization types but is revealing to see the technological frontiers of the micro-world.
Sources: A reconstruction from J.Barrow (1998:133), as originally shown in *Table 4.7* of *FPHC*. See *FPHC* for more info.

Table 1.6. Finity, Transfinity, and Infinity (Part I)

• **Infinity**

—The term "infinity," which is "symbolically represented with ∞," derives from the Latin *infinitas* (or "unboundedness"), to refer to "several distinct concepts—usually linked to the idea of 'without end'—which arise in philosophy, mathematics, and theology." (WK 2008c)

—In the context of mathematics, "infinity" is often "treated as if it were a number (i.e., it counts or measures things: 'an infinite number of terms') but it is a different type of 'number' from the real numbers. Infinity is related to limits,...large cardinals,...projective geometry, extended real numbers and the absolute Infinite," for instance. (WK 2008c)

• **Transfinity**

—To avoid confusion, my usage of the word "transfinite" (as used here in the ontological principle) is not the same as the one which was originally coined by Georg Cantor to refer to "cardinal numbers or ordinal numbers that are larger than all finite numbers, yet not necessarily absolutely infinite" (in the mind of God), as opposed to "relative" infinity (in the mind of Man). (WK 2008d) In other words, for Cantor, there are two kinds of infinity, "absolute" and "relative"—with "relative" infinity or "transfinity" (in the mind of Man) being dependent on "absolute" infinity (in the mind of God) for its existence.

—By contrast, my usage of the word "transfinite" here differs radically from the one used by Cantor (and other mathematicians) and is more limited, in light of the problems confronting any attempt to understand the idea of infinity, be it by intuition, imagination, and conception (as already shown in the prevous three sub-sections).

—With this clarification in mind, I allow numbers which can be many times larger—or smaller, for that matter—than the finite things that we encounter in daily life, but they do not have to be related to the idea of infinity at all (which may not exist).

(continued on next page)

Table 1.6. Finity, Transfinity, and Infinity (Part II)

• **Transfinity** ***(cont'd)***

—Of course, there may be some *borderline* cases, in which it is not clear whether the number in question is transfinite (in my usage) or simply a mathematical convenience. A good example of a borderline case is the Planck unit of length for "the smallest space possibly measured in nature," which is "less than billionths of trillionths of trillionths of an inch" (or something like 1.6×10^{-35} meters). (P. Baofu 2006a; N. McAleer 1987: 219; WKV 2008; D. Corbett 2008)

—The ideas concerning symmetry and dimensions in the examples above were addressed in Chapter Three and Chapter Four of *FPHG*. For now, it suffices to further add that it is mind-boggling to even conceive or imagine extreme numbers like the Planck unit of length (or others). Does it really exist at all? Or is it merely a mathematical convenience to describe a physical situation that the human mind does not understand properly?

—In any event, "transfinity" (in my usage) can be used as a further extension (of number) to the finite numbers in daily life—albeit with some borderline cases in mind.

• **Finity**

—It refers to numbers which are bounded (that is, with an end), especially (though not exclusively) in relation to things in everyday life.

Source: From *Sec. 1.4* and *Sec. 2.2.3* of *FPHG*

Table 1.7. Theoretical Speculations of Multiverses

• **"Baby Universes" (Ex: Andre Linde and others)**
—Ex: In a flat universe theory, "even if our part of it eventually collapses,…some spots in the cosmos would suddenly start inflating on their own, creating brand-new 'baby universes.'" (P. Baofu 2000: 623)

• **"Parallel Universes" (Ex: Stephen Hawking and others)**
—Ex: In quantum cosmology, there allows the existence of infinite numbers of parallel universes, with tunneling among them. (M. Kaku 1994: 256) Hawking later revised his views on this.

• **"Pocket Universes" (Ex: Alan Guth)**
—Ex: "As the pocket universes live out their lives and recollapse or dwindle away, new universes are generated to take their place....While life in our pocket universe will presumably die out, life in the universe as a whole will thrive for eternity." (A. Guth 1997: 248; P. Baofu 2002: 482)

• **"Brane Worlds" (Ex: Warren Siegel, Lisa Randall, and others)**
—Ex: Our universe is stuck on a membrane of space-time embedded in a larger cosmos, with different brane worlds connecting and/or colliding with each other.

Notes: These examples are solely illustrative (not exhaustive), and some of the items can be reclassified somewhere else. Nor are they always mutually exclusive. Since they are generalities, exceptions are expected.
Source: From *Table 4.8* of *FPHC*

Table 1.8. The Confusion between "Many Worlds" and "Multiverse" (Part I)

- **First Problem**

—The first problem in this second confusion concerns a debate between the "many-worlds" interpretation of quantum mechanics by Hugh Everett (1957) and others, and the Copenhagen interpretation by Niels Bohr and Werner Heisenberg on the effects of quantum states after interacting with an external environment (e.g., by a measuring observer).

—On the one hand, the Copenhagen interpretation of quantum mechanics is more indeterministic in its concern with the probabilities of the outcomes of a wave function after interacting with an external environment (e.g., by a measuring observer using light to detect, for example, "an electron in a particular region around the nucleus at a particular time." (WK 2008e) Each wave function for the state of a particle refers to "a mathematical representation used to calculate the probability for it to be found in a location, or state of motion." (WK 2008f) And the "wavefunction collapse" means that "the act of measurement causes the calculated set of probabilities to 'collapse' to the value defined by the measurement." (WK 2008f)

—On the other hand, the Everett's interrpetation is more deterministic, in rejecting "the objective reality of wavefunction collapse" and "instead explaining the subjective appearance of wavefunction collapse with the mechanism of quantum decoherence." (WK 2008g) The words "quantum decoherence" here refers to "the mechanism by which quantum systems interact with their environments to exhibit probabilistically additive behavior," in such a way that "the quantum nature of the system is simply 'leaked' into the environment." (WK 2008g) For example, "[a]s a result of an interaction, the wave functions of the system and the measuring device become entangled with each other. Decoherence happens when different portions of the system's wavefunction become entangled *in different ways* [italic added] with the measuring device...." (WK 2008g) Thus, for Everett, the appearance of "wavefunction collapse" can be explained by "quantum decoherence" for quantum states to branch out in different independent worlds after interacting with an external environment.

(continued on next page)

Table 1.8. The Confusion between "Many Worlds" and "Multiverse" (Part II)

• **First Problem *(cont'd)***
—Yet, a major criticism against Everett's interpretation is that these different independent worlds in Everett's sense "will never be accessible to us," because of the interference by the measuring observer in an external environment. (WK 2008g)
—For illustration, "once a measurement is done, the measured system becomes entangled with both the physicist who measured it and a huge number of other particles, some of which are photons flying away towards the other end of the universe; in order to prove that the wave function did not collapse one would have to bring all these particles back and measure them again, together with the system that was measured originally. This is completely impractical, but even if one can theoretically do this, it would destroy any evidence that the original measurement took place (including the physicist's memory)." (WK 2008g)
—But then, the critics ask, If these independent worlds in Everett's sense are inaccessible to us, how do we know much of anything really about them?

• **Second Problem**
—What is relevant at the quantum mechanical level may not necessarily apply to the world at the physicsl level.
—In fact, the persistent inability among contemporoary physicists to unifiy the theory of relativity for large objects at the physical level and quantum mechanics for tiny objects at the quantum mechanical level should warn us about the danger of reductionism, by reducing the understanding of different universes ("parallel universes") at the physical level from a generalization of "many worlds" at the quantum mechanical level.

• **Third Problem**
—There is no empirical evidence to suggest that there are infinite (or extremely many) possible worlds in the cosmos as the many-worlds model by Everett would have us to believe.

Source: From *Sec.4.4.1* of *FPHG*

Table 1.9. Hyperspace and Its Challenge (Part I)

• **First Problem**

—Hyperspace for intra- and inter-universal travel is assumed to be possible, on the basis of four main assumptions; although there may be others, these are the often cited ones.

—The first assumption concerns the existence of "entry" and "exit" points in hyperspace, which is easier said than done to enter, go through, and then exit hyperspace.

—For instance, using hyperspace "requires complex calculations…of single or multiple hyperspace jumps and the control of the jump….Peturbations such as those experienced by ship in space from the gravitional field around an object such as a planet or even a star are exacerbated in hyperspatial travel, since mass in real space distorts hyperspace in an equal measure. 'Jumping' near to a gravitational mass is likely to make resulting exit from hyperspace to be highly uncertain, with the level of improbability *i* increasing with the square of the distance to the nearest gravitional 'well.'" (WK 2008h)

—Besides, "[o]nly spaceships equipped with a special force field can enter hyperspace, because exposure to hyperspace even for short period of time is hazardous to unprotected humans." (WK 2008h)

• **Second Problem**

—The second assumption concerns the faster-than-light speed. It is well known that Einstein argued for the speed of light as the ultimate limit, but nowadays phyiscists do allow the violation of this limit under certain conditions (like the hypothetical existence of tachyons, as will be explained further in a later sub-section on time travel).

—Even then, there is a challenge to explain in science fiction "why ships can travel faster than light in hyperspace," and two good arguments are that "hyperspace may be smaller than real space and therefore a star ship's propulsion seems to be greatly multiplied, or else the speed of light in hyperspace is not a barrier as it is in real space. Whatever the reasoning, the general effect is that ships traveling in hyperspace seem to have broken the speed of light, appearing at their destinations much more quickly and without the shift in time that the Theory of Relativity would suggest." (WK 2008h)

(continued on next page)

Table 1.9. Hyperspace and Its Challenge (Part II)

- **Third Problem**
  —The third assumption concerns the speed of time (to be measured, say, by a clock), but this is elaborated in a different section on the related issue of "time travel" (as shown in a different table on time travel).

- **Fourth Problem**
  —The fourth assumption concerns spatial shortcut, as it is possible, because of the curvature of space, in that "the manifold of ordinary three-dimensional space is curved in four or more 'higher' spacial dimensions (a 'hyperspace' in the geometric sense…). This curvature causes certain widely separated points in three-dimensional space to nonetheless be 'adjacent' to each other four-dimensionally. Creating an aperture in 4D space (a wormhole) between these locations can allow instantaneous transit between the two locations; a common comparison is that of a folded piece of paper, where a hole punched through two folded sections is more direct than a line drawn between them on the sheet. This idea probably arose out of certain popular descriptions of General Relativity and/or Riemannian manifolds, and may be the original form from which later concepts of hyperspace arose." (WK 2008h)
  —But this does not mean that hyperpsace is always safe. In fact, "in some science fiction, the danger of hyperspace travel is due to the chance that the route through hyperspace may take a ship too close to a celestial body with a large gravitational field, such as a star. In such scenarios, if a starship passes too close to a large gravitational field while in hyperspace, the ship is forcibly pulled out of hyperspace and reverts to normal space. Therefore, certain hyperspace 'routes' may be mapped out that are safe, not passing too close to stars or other dangers." (WJ 2008h)

Source: From *Sec.4.4.1* of *FPHG*

Table 1.10. The Problems of Time Travel into the Future (Part I)

- **First Problem**
  —The first problem concerns "time dilation under the Theory of Special Relativity" (which separates space-time from mass-energy as special cases). Suppose you are on a moving train and an observer outside the train is watching you along the tracks. As your train moves along at the speed of light (or something close to it), "time, as measured by your watch, ticked along at a slower pace than time measured by the observer. Not only that, distance changed, too. For the observer, a one-foot ruler whizzing by on the train would have measured less than a foot." (NO 2000)
  —In fact, you may not even notice that this slower clicking of the clock; in fact, everything looks normal to you inside the train as it was before: "The weird thing is that, for you on the train, time wouldn't seem to be moving slower and your ruler wouldn't be shorter—all would appear normal." (NO 2008) By contrast, you instead think that "time on the rest of the Earth would appear to be ticking along slower and its rulers would be shorter." (NO 2000) So, both of you insist that the other clock (not his) is clicking more slowly—assuming, of course, an inertial frame of reference.
  —Now, change the story a bit, in that, this time, instead of an "inertial reference frame," acceleration is allowed, and you are on your way to board a spaceship. As an illustration, suppose "[y]ou board a spaceship and take off for deep space. The ship approaches the speed of light. Time for you seems to pass as it always has. It takes you about five seconds to tie your shoe. But to an observer on Earth (assuming he or she could watch you), you are moving at a snail's pace. It takes hours to tie your shoe." (NO 2000) In any event, "you continue on your journey. You slow down, stop, and accelerate back to Earth. You arrive home. You have aged two years during your flight. Two hundred years have passed on Earth. You have successfully travelled forward through time." (NO 2000) In this case, both the observer (if he is still alive) and you agree that you have aged less.

(continued on next page)

Table 1.10. The Problems of Time Travel into the Future (Part II)

- **First Problem *(cont'd)***
  —In other words, when you are back to Earth, a lot of things have changed since, and you may find rather strange to be in a new environment which you hardly recognize, when compared with what you used to think as your city, or the Earth (two years ago, well, in accordance to your time of measurement). This means that you are in the future (two hundred years later), even though you are still relatively young (only two years older). But, can you go back? Well, no. The reason is that "[a]ccording to relativity, you can only move through time in one direction." (NO 2000)

- **Second Problem**
  —The second problem concerns "time dilation under the Theory of General Relativity" (which unifies space-time with mass-energy in a general theory), the same result of time dilation occurs.
  —For instance, when "one clock is deeper in a gravity well than the other," a result is that "the clock deeper in the well" will "tick…more slowly; this effect must be taken into account when calibrating the clocks on the satellites of the Global Positioning System, and it could lead to significant differences in rates of aging for observers at different distances from a black hole." (WK 2008i)
  —More precisely, by way of another example, "it has been calculated that, under general relativity, a person could travel forward in time at a rate four times that of distant observers by residing inside a spherical shell with a diameter of 5 meters and the mass of Jupiter. For such a person, every one second of their 'personal' time would correspond to four seconds for distant observers. Of course, squeezing the mass of a large planet into such a structure is not expected to be within our technological capabilities in the near future." (WK 2008i; R. Gott 2002)
  —The point here, however, is that time travel into the future, in this sense, is allowed, theoretically speaking, but in a very limited way, from the theory of relativity. But one can also ask, What if the theory of relativity were wrong? Well, in that case, there would be a need to find a better theory to explain time travel into the future.

Source: From *Sec.4.4.2* of *FPHG*

Table 1.11. The Problems of Time Travel into the Past (Part I)

- **First Problem**

—The first problem concerns the faster-than-light-speed, since, in accordance to the theory of special relativity, when an object goes faster than the speed of light, something weird can happen, in that, instead of having the clock clicking more slowly, it is moving backward, in relation to some inertial frame of reference—which then raisies the issue of whether time travel into the past is possible at all.

—But the problem here is about the violation of the law of casuality. In everyday language, an excellent illustration of causality violation is that, suppose you travel back into the past and then kill your parents, this then means that you could not have been born. But this is not true, since you are alive.

—Yet, "in the case of a hypothetical signal moving faster than light, there would always be some frames in which the signal was received before it was sent, so that the signal could be said to have moved backwards in time." The violation of casuality exists in this case.

—The first part of the problem is that, in accordance to the theory of special relativity, "it would take an infinite amount of energy to accelerate a slower-than-light object to the speed of light"—let alone the energy needed to propel an object to go faster than the speed of light. (WK 2008i) Although some suggest the possibility of "negative energy," it remains to be seen to what extent this is true.

—And the second part of the problem is that, "although relativity does not forbid the theoretical possibility of tachyons which move faster than light at all times, when analyzed using quantum field theory it seems that it would not actually be possible to use them to transmit information faster than light and there is no evidence for their existence." (WK 2008i; S. Chase 1993)

(continued on next page)

Table 1.11. The Problems of Time Travel into the Past (Part II)

- **Second Problem**
  —The second problem concerns cosmic string and black holes, since it is the theory of general relativity which "extends the special theory to cover gravity, illustrating it in terms of curvature in spacetime caused by mass-energy and the flow of momentum." (WK 2008i)
  —On the other hand, "[g]eneral relativity describes the universe under a system of field equations…and there exist solutions to these equations that permit what are called 'closed time-like curves,' and hence time travel into the past….The first of these was proposed by Kurt Gödel, a solution known as the Gödel metric, but his (and many others') example requires the universe to have physical characteristics that it does not appear to have." (WK 2008i; K. Thorne 1994)
  —But then, the problem now becomes: "Whether general relativity forbids closed time-like curves for all realistic conditions is unknown." (WK 2008i)

- **Third Problem**
  —The third problem concerns wormholes and related ones, and "[w]ormholes are a hypothetical warped spacetime which are also permitted by the Einstein field equations of general relativity, although it would be impossible to travel through a wormhole unless it was what is known as a traversable wormhole." (WK 2008i; M. Visser 1995) In other words, "a wormhole is a hypothetical topological feature of spacetime that is fundamentally a 'shortcut' through space and time. Spacetime can be viewed as a 2D surface, and when 'folded' over, a wormhole bridge can be formed. A wormhole has at least two mouths which are connected to a single throat or tube. If the wormhole is traversable, matter can 'travel' from one mouth to the other by passing through the throat." (WK 2008j)
  —But the problem here is three-fold, as shown in what follows.

(continued on next page)

Table 1.11. The Problems of Time Travel into the Past (Part III)

- **Third Problem *(cont'd)***
  —The first part of the problem is that "there is no observational evidence for wormholes." (WK 2008j)
  —The second part of the problem is that it is not clear how exactly wormholes (and black holes, for that matter) could allow time travel into the past at all.
  —And the third part of the problem is that if using wormholes (and black holes, for that matter) to travel into the past requires something to go faster than light too, then this raises another issue concerning the two problems as previously indicated in the sub-section on the faster-than-light-speed.

- **Fourth Problem**
  —The fourth problem is that some physicists have argued that, even should time travel into the past be possible, by way of these three methods, the person still would not return to the same past history that he exactly experienced before, but in a different one. (WK 2008i)
  —In other words, "strictly speaking," time travel into the past is not "really" possible, in light of these criticisms, so there is no need to worry that one could travel into the past and kill one's parent, as a way to violate the law of casuality.

Source: From *Sec.4.4.2* of *FPHG*

Table 1.12. The Conceptual Dimensions of Consciousness (and Other Mental States)

- **On Heredity and Time**
  —Heredity and the Environment
  —The Past and the Present

- **On Layers of Mental States and Abnormality**
  —Consciousness, Unconsciousness, and Preconsciousness
  —Normality and Paranormality

- **On Organicity and Motivation**
  —Mechanicity and Organicity
  —Primary Motivations and Multiple Motivations

- **On Other (Mostly Epistemic) Considerations**
  —Synthesis and Analysis
  —Situation and the Subject
  —Process and Outcome
  —Reasoning and Other Modes of Thinking
  —Meta-Conceptual Nominalism and Realism

Notes:: These examples are solely illustrative (not exhaustive), and some of the items can be reclassified somewhere else. Nor are they always mutually exclusive. Since they are generalities, exceptions are expected.
Sources: From *FPHC*. A re-construction, but with my own contribution, originally from G.Lindzey & C.Hall, *Introduction to Theories of Personality* (NY: John Wiley & Sons, 1985).

Table 1.13. The Theoretical Levels of Consciousness (and Other Mental States) (Part I)

- **At the Micro-Physical Theoretical Level**
  —Quantum-Mechanics
  —Electromagnetism

- **At the Chemical Theoretical Level**
  —Biochemistry

- **At the Biological Theoretical Level**
  —Evolutionary Biology
  —Neuroscience
  —Artificial Intelligence

- **At the Psychological Theoretical Level**
  —Psychodynamic Psychology
    - Psychoanalytical Psychology
    - Analytical Psychology
    - Socially Oriented Psychology

  —Experimental (Behavioral) Psychology
    - Operant Reinforcement Theory
    - Stimulus-Response Theory
    - Social Learning Theory

  —Cognitive (Gestalt) Psychology
    - Humanist Psychology
    - Existential Psychology
    - Field Theory

  —Psychometric Psychology
    - Idiographics
    - Constitutional Psychology

  —Social Psychology
    - Symbolic Interactive Theory
    - Social Exchange Theory

(continued on next page)

Table 1.13. The Theoretical Levels of Consciousness (and Other Mental States) (Part II)

- **At the Organizational Theoretical Level**
  —Managerial-Bureaucratic Theory
  —Oligarchic Theory
  —Network Theory

- **At the Institutional Theoretical Level**
  —Functionalist Theory
  —Anomic Theory

- **At the Structural Theoretical Level**
  —Conflict Theory
    - Marxian Theory
    - Critical Theory
    - Weberian Theory

  —Games Theory (in Formal Theory)
  —Feminist Theory
    - Feminist Concerns
    - Feminist Hopes

- **At the Systemic Theoretical Level**
  —Equilibrium Theory
  —System Theory
  —Chaos Theory

- **At the Cosmological Theoretical Level**
  —Superluminal Model
  —The Theory of Floating Consciousness

(continued on next page)

Table 1.13. The Theoretical Levels of Consciousness (and Other Mental States) (Part III)

- **At the Cultural Theoretical Level**
  - —Substantive Theories
    - Structuralist Theory
    - Post-Structuralist Theory (in Postmodernism)
  - —Meta-Theories
    - Epistemic Objectivism vs. Epistemic Historicism
    - Epistemic Subjectivism vs. Epistemic Non-Subjectivism
      - –Phenomenology
      - –Ethnomethodology
      - –Hermeneutics
    - Epistemic Relativism vs. Epistemic Absolutism
    - Epistemic Reductionism vs. Epistemic Emergencism

- **At Other Levels**
  - —Structuration Theory
  - —Reflexive Socioanalysis

Notes: These examples are solely illustrative (not exhaustive), and some of the items can be reclassified somewhere else. Nor are they always mutually exclusive. Since they are generalities, exceptions are expected.
Source: From many different sources as indicated in *FPHC*

Table 1.14. The Thematic Issues of Consciousness (and Other Mental States)

- **The Factor of History**
  —Pre-Modernity
  —Modernity
  —Postmodernity
  —After-Postmodernity

- **The Importance of Needs**
  —Having (e.g., the everyday, the technological)
  —Belonging (e.g., the just and the good)
  —Being (e.g., the true, the holy, the sublime/beautiful, and the good)

Notes: These examples are solely illustrative (not exhaustive). Nor are they always mutually exclusive. Since they are generalities, exceptions are expected. Also, some categories overlap with others; for instance, the good is also related with being-ness, just as the everyday can be connected with belong-ness.
Sources: From *FPHC*, based on *FHC* and *FCD*

Table 1.15. Having, Belonging, and Being in Consciousness

• **Having (e.g., About the Everyday and Technological)**
—Ex: Physiological needs (e.g., thirst, hunger, sex)
—Ex: Safety (e.g., stability, freedom from fear and anxiety)

• **Belonging (e.g., About the Good and Just)**
—Ex: Social interaction
—Ex: Friendship, acquaintance
—Ex: Love, family
—Ex: Self-respect, respect from others

• **Being (e.g., About the True, Holy, Beautiful/Sublime, and Good)**
—Ex: Understanding of reality about self and world
—Ex: Spiritual quest for holiness, beauty, sublimity, and goodness

Notes: These examples are solely illustrative (not exhaustive), and some of the items can be reclassified somewhere else. Nor are they always mutually exclusive. Since they are generalities, exceptions are expected.
Sources: From *FPHC*, based on *FHC* and *FCD*

Table 1.16. The Having-Ness of Consciousness (and Other Mental States)

- **At the Micro-Physical Level**
  —Ex: The finer physics of nutrition

- **At the Chemical Level**
  —Ex: Food guide pyramid

- **At the Bio-Psychological Level**
  —Ex: The hierarchy of needs

- **At the Institutional Level**
  —Ex: The production of commodity fetishism

- **At the Organizational Level**
  —Ex: Mass standardization (and customization); bureaucratic rationality

- **At the Structural Level**
  —Ex: The divide between the haves and the have-nots

- **At the Cultural Level**
  —Ex: The bondage of greater expectations

- **At the Systemic Level**
  —Ex: The technological transformation of poverty with transvaluations

- **At the Cosmological Level**
  —Ex: Floating consciousness in deep space without the human physiological needs

Notes: These examples are solely illustrative (not exhaustive), and some of the items can be reclassified somewhere else. Nor are they always mutually exclusive. Since they are generalities, exceptions are expected.
Sources: From *FPHC*. See also *FCD* and *FHC*.

Table 1.17. The Belonging-Ness of Consciousness (and Other Mental States)

- **At the Micro-Physical Level**
  —Ex: Statistical physics and social networks

- **At the Chemical Level**
  —Ex: Olfaction and social relations

- **At the Bio-Psychological Level**
  —Ex: Dual human nature on relationships

- **At the Institutional Level**
  —Ex: Private property and social cleavage

- **At the Organizational Level**
  —Ex: Legal formalism and iron cage

- **At the Structural Level**
  —Ex: Class conflicts and social alienation

- **At the Cultural Level**
  —Ex: Ruthless society and the culture of law

- **At the Systemic Level**
  —Ex: Human extinction and post-human relations

- **At the Cosmological Level**
  —Ex: The transcendence of equality in the cosmos and beyond

Notes: These examples are solely illustrative (not exhaustive), and some of the items can be reclassified somewhere else. Nor are they always mutually exclusive. Since they are generalities, exceptions are expected.
Sources: From *FPHC*. See also *FCD* and *FHC*.

Table 1.18. The Being-Ness of Consciousness (and Other Mental States) (Part I)

- **At the Micro-Physical Level**
  —Ex: Space-time and matter-energy in classical mechanics, quantum mechanics, and the theory of relativity

- **At the Chemical Level**
  —Ex: Drugs and well being

- **At the Biological Level**
  —Ex: Neuroscience and mystical experiences

- **At the Psychological Level**
  —Ex: Reductionism and emergencism

- **At the Institutional Level**
  —Ex: The proliferation of cults and sects, and the corporate-art industry

- **At the Organizational Level**
  —Ex: The organization of ideas in the scheme of things

- **At the Structural Level**
  —Ex: Disciplinary power and control in the order of things

- **At the Systemic Level**
  —Ex: Mutualism and ecological psychology

- **At the Cultural Level**
  —Ex: The recurrence of competing spirits, and floating consciousness as a climax of evolution

(continued on next page)

Table 1.18. The Being-Ness of Consciousness (and Other Mental States) (Part II)

- **At the Cosmological Level**
  —Ex: The search for elsewherewhen, and the evolution of other consciousnesses (e.g., the hyper-spatial consciousness)

Notes: These examples are solely illustrative (not exhaustive), and some of the items can be reclassified somewhere else. Nor are they always mutually exclusive. Since they are generalities, exceptions are expected.
Sources: From *FPHC*. See also *FCD* and *FHC*.

Table 1.19. Cognitive Partiality in Different Mental States

- **The Conscious**
  - —*Biased*
    - Ex: Self-overratingness
    - Ex: Self-modesty
    - Ex: Self-fulfilling prophesy
  - —*Shallow*
    - Ex: Attribution error
    - Ex: Heuristics
    - Ex: Illusory thinking
  - —*Short-term*
    - Ex: Deindividuation
  - —*Materialistic*
    - Ex: Hierarchy of needs

- **The Subconscious**
    - Ex: mental reconstruction
    - Ex: stereotyping

- **The Unconscious**
    - Ex: automatic processing
    - Ex: cognitive intuition

Notes: These examples are solely illustrative (not exhaustive), and some of the items can be reclassified somewhere else. Nor are they always mutually exclusive. Since they are generalities, exceptions are expected. And the comparison is relative, not absolute.
Source: From *BCPC*

Table 1.20. Emotional Non-Neutrality and Behavioral Alteration in Different Mental States

- **The Emotional**
  - —*Conscious*
    - Ex: Feelings
  - —*Subconscious*
    - Ex: Moods
  - —*Unconscious*
    - Ex: Empathy
    - Ex: Instincts

- **The Behavioral**
  - —*Conscious*
    - Ex: Foot-in-the-door
    - Ex: Role playing
    - Ex: Saying-is-believing
  - —*Subconscious*
    - Ex: Discrimination
  - —*Unconscious*
    - Ex: Non-Verbal Communication

Notes: These examples are solely illustrative (not exhaustive), and some of the items can be reclassified somewhere else. Nor are they always mutually exclusive. Since they are generalities, exceptions are expected. And the comparison is relative, not absolute.
Source: From *BCPC*

Table 1.21. The Limits of Intuition in Unconsciousness

- **Cognitive Intuition (or Intuitive Thinking)**
  - —*Features*
    - Ex: mental schemas
    - Ex: expertise
    - Ex: blindsight
  - —*Problems*
    - Ex: inaccurate
    - Ex: non-explanatory
- **Emotional Intuition**
  - —*Features*
    - Ex: empathy
    - Ex: instincts
  - —*Problems*
    - Ex: over-generalized
    - Ex: non-explanatory
- **Behavioral Intuition**
  - —*Features*
    - Ex: prosemics
    - Ex: kinesics
  - —*Problems*
    - Ex: unreliable
    - Ex: non-explanatory

Notes: These examples are solely illustrative (not exhaustive), and some of the items can be reclassified somewhere else. Nor are they always mutually exclusive. Since they are generalities, exceptions are expected. And the comparison is relative, not absolute.
Source: From *BCPC*

Table 1.22. The Wealth/Poverty Dialectics in Different Mental States: The Case of Cognition

- **The Conscious**
  - —*Biased*
    - Ex: If richer in self-serving bias, then poorer in understanding others
  - —*Shallow*
    - Ex: If richer in heuristic thinking, then poorer in comprehending reality
  - —*Short-term*
    - Ex: If richer in short-term tendency, then poorer in long-term planning
  - —*Materialistic*
    - Ex: If richer in physiological obsession, then poorer in spiritual enlightenment

- **The Subconscious**
  - Ex: If richer in mental reconstruction, then poorer in accuracy of recall
  - Ex: If richer in stereotyping, then poorer in understanding groups

- **The Unconscious**
  - Ex: If richer in automatic processing, then poorer in depth of analysis
  - Ex: If richer in cognitive intuition, then poorer in reliability of judgments

Notes: These examples are solely illustrative (not exhaustive), and some of the items can be reclassified somewhere else. Nor are they always mutually exclusive. Since they are generalities, exceptions are expected. And the comparison is relative, not absolute.

Source: From *BCPC*

Table 1.23. The Wealth/Poverty Dialectics in Different Mental States: The Case of Emotion and Behavior

- **Emotion**
  - —*Conscious*
    - Ex: If richer in relying on familiarity and similarity for social attraction, then poorer in having diverse social relations
  - —*Subconscious*
    - Ex: If richer in moodiness, then poorer in sober thinking
  - —*Unconscious*
    - Ex: If richer in empathy, then poorer in task-oriented efficiency
    - Ex: If richer in instincts, then poorer in critical thinking

- **Behavior**
  - —*Conscious*
    - Ex: If richer in foot-in-the-door technique, then poorer in instant Gratification
    - Ex: If richer in role playing, then poorer in identity stability
  - —*Subconscious*
    - Ex: If richer in discriminating, then poorer in social harmony
  - —*Unconscious*
    - Ex: If richer in kinesics and proxemics, then poorer in verbal skills, relatively speaking.

Notes: These examples are solely illustrative (not exhaustive), and some of the items can be reclassified somewhere else. Nor are they always mutually exclusive. Since they are generalities, exceptions are expected. And the comparison is relative, not absolute.
Source: From *BCPC*

Table 1.24. The Theoretical Debate on Nature vs. Nurture (Part I)

- **The Environmental Approach**
  —*Thesis*: It focuses, relatively speaking, more on the environment (culture and society) in explaining the achievement gap among individuals and for that matter, countries or regions, when contrasted with the natural factors.
  —*Discourse*: Examples include Jose Ortega y Gasset ("Man has no nature; what he has is history"), Ashley Montagu ("Man is man because he has no instincts, because everything he is and has become he has learned from his culture, from the man-made part of the environment, from other human beings"), Stephen Jay Gould ("[The] brain [is] capable of a full range of behaviors and predisposed to none"), and Jesse Jackson (who blames white racism for the failure of blacks to close the achievement gap between whites and blacks in America). The works on dependency theory in international political economy (with a Marxian influence) and on the Protestant work ethic (by Max Weber) also point to this environmental direction.

- **The Genetic Approach**
  —*Thesis*: It focuses instead, relatively speaking again, on hereditory factors (e.g., genes and evolution) in explaining the achievement gap among individuals and for that matter, countries or regions, when contrasted with the envrionmental factors.
  —*Discourse*: Examples are Hans Eysenck and William Sheldon (in constitutional psychology), Konrad Lorenz (in his work on innate aggressive human nature), Gary Marcus (on the complexities of human thought by a tiny number of genes) and Robert Plomin, together with Michael Owen and Peter McGuffin (on the genetic basis of complex human behaviors).

(continued on next page)

Table 1.24. The Theoretical Debate on Nature vs. Nurture (Part II)

• **The Compromise Approach**

—*Thesis*: It seeks the middle-of-the-road argument in regard to nature and nurture and regards all differences among individuals and groups as the result of the mixture of both nature and nurture, more or less equally.

—*Discourse*: Examples include C. Murray and R. Herrnstein ("It seems highly likely to us that both genes and environment have something to do with this issue") and Dan Dennett ("Surely 'everyone knows' that the nature-nurture debate was resolved long ago, and neither side wins since everything – is – a – mixture – of – both – and - it's – all – very -complicated….")

• **The Transcendent Approach**

—*Thesis*: It goes beyond both nature and nurture (without, however, committing the compromise fallacy) in showing their closely intertwined interactions in producing the behavioral differences as often seen in individual human endeavors on the micro scale, and for that matter, in country (or regional) endeavors on the macro one—in the context of my five theses, namely, (a) the compromise fallacy, (b) no oppression without self-oppression, (c) no success without failure, (d) the factor of randomness, and (e) the post-human vision, to be elaborated in Chapter Six.

—*Discourse*: Peter Baofu proposed this approach on the basis of his "theory of contrastive advantages" (as an original theoretical contribution to the debate, which was first proposed and analyzed in *The Future of Capitalism and Democracy*). In the end, the human genes will not last, to be eventually superseded by post-human life forms, so the debate between genes and memes has obscured something profoundly important about the future that the world has never known. And the debate is also misleading and faulty in its dichotomy.

Source: From *BNN*. See the book for citations and details.

Table 1.25. Physical Challenges to Hyper-Spatial Consciousness

---

• **The Understanding of a Higher-Dimensional World of Space-Time**
—Ex: 4 for traditional aspects of space-time (e.g., length, width, breadth and time) plus 6 more new dimensions in theory of hyper-space, with profound implications for practical applications to new forms of consciousness.

• **The Mastering of Dark Matter and Dark Energy**
—Ex: "ordinary matter" (e.g., atoms, molecules) as a mere 4.4% of the universe, with 23% made of "cold dark matter" and the rest (about 73%) of mysterious "dark energy," with fundamental significance to questions about the limit of the speed of energy (or info), the availability of energy for use, and the nature of space-time, just to cite some examples.

• **The Exploration of Multiverses**
—Ex: theoretical speculation of other universes (e.g., "baby universes," "gateways" in black holes, "wave function of the universe," "many worlds," "brane worlds"), with potentially seminary discoveries of different physical laws in relation to matter-energy and space-time, and vital differences to the future of post-human conquest of other universes (for the emergence of new forms of consciousness).

Notes: These examples are solely illustrative (not exhaustive), and some of the items can be reclassified somewhere else. Nor are they always mutually exclusive. Since they are generalities, exceptions are expected. The point here is to give a rough picture of the evolution of consciousness to the hyper-spatial consciousness and others totally unknown to current earthlings. As a note of clarification, it makes no difference to my argument as to whether or not the hyper-spatial consciousness may emerge before, during, and after floating consciousness.
Source: From *Table 4.5* of *FPHC*

Table 1.26. The Theory of Floating Consciousness (Part I)

- **At the Micro-Physical Level**
  —Ex: intelligent life without the human physical-chemical system

- **At the Chemical Level**
  —Ex: space radiation and toxins

- **At the Bio-Psychological Level**
  —Ex: exo-biological evolution in deep space
  —Ex: genetic engineering of new beings

- **At the Institutional Level**
  —Ex: post-capitalism
  —Ex: post-democracy

- **At the Organizational Level**
  —Ex: less legal-formalistic routines

- **At the Structural Level**
  —Ex: alien forms of violence

- **At the Cultural Level**
  —Ex: transcending freedom
  —Ex: transcending equality

(continued on next page)

Table 1.26. The Theory of Floating Consciousness (Part II)

- **At the Cosmological Level**
  —Ex: parallel universes
  —Ex: pocket universes

- **At the Systemic Level**
  —Ex: space habitats (in zero-gravity)

Notes: Each example draws from the works of different scholars in the field. For instance, at the cosmological level, the idea of parallel universes is from the theoretical speculation in quantum cosmology by Stephen Hawking and others, while the one of pocket universes comes from the theoretical work of Allan Guth at MIT. And at the institutional level, I proposed post-capitalism and post-democracy in *FCD* (and later, from *BDPD* and *BCPC*). In addition, the examples are solely illustrative (not exhaustive), and some of the items can be reclassified somewhere else. Nor are they always mutually exclusive. Since they are generalities, exceptions are expected.
Sources: From *FPHC*—and, originally, from *FCD*

Table 1.27. The Potential of Unfolding Unconsciousness

- **Superior Senses**
  - —*Through space*
    - Ex: clair-sentience (in feeling)
    - Ex: clair-voyance (in seeing)
    - Ex: clair-audience (in hearing)
    - Ex: clair-austance (in tasting)
    - Ex: clair-alience (in smelling)
    - Ex: clair-cognizance (in knowing)
  - —*Through time*
    - Ex: pre-cognition (in knowing), pre-sentiment (in feeling)
    - Ex: retro-cognition (in knowing), retro-sentiment (in feeling)

- **Superior Contacts**
  - —*With living minds*
    - Ex: telepathy
  - —*With the dead*
    - Ex: mediumship
  - —*With other-living entities*
    - Ex: telekinesis

Notes: The categories and examples are solely illustrative (not exhaustive), and the comparison is relative (not absolute), nor are they necessarily mutually exclusive. And some can be easily re-classified elsewhere. As generalities, they allow exceptions.
Source: A summary of Ch.5 of *FPHU*

Table 1.28. The Future Exploration of Unfolding Unconsciousness

- **In the Context of Nature**
  —Ex: the higher-dimensional space-time in hyperspace theory
  —Ex: the particle-wave interactions in quantum mechanics
  —Ex: the study of brain waves in electromagnetic theory

- **In the Context of the Mind**
  —Ex: the unconscious fantasies in psychoanalysis
  —Ex: the mind-altering drugs in biochemistry
  —Ex: the manipulation of neural activity in neurobiology

- **In the Context of Culture**
  —Ex: the correlation between anomalous experience and moral/religious/aesthetic interests in culture studies
  —Ex: the role of myths and language in epistemology

- **In the Context of Society**
  —Ex: different organizational agendas in anomalous research
  —Ex: the scholarly divide on anomalous study
  —Ex: interests and propaganda in institutioanl research
  —Ex: the transformative power of technology in research on social systems
  —Ex: the natural and non-natural selection of other worlds in exo-biology
  —Ex: the role of the post-human conscious mind in qualitative demography

Notes: The examples in each category are solely illustrative (not exhaustive), and the comparison is relative (not absolute), nor are they necessarily mutually exclusive. And some can be easily re-classified elsewhere. As generalities, they allow exceptions.
Source: A summary of Chs.2-5 of *FPHU*, in conjunction with the rest of the book

Table 1.29. Creative Techniques and Traits

- **Creative Techniques**
  - —*Comprehensiveness*
    - Ex: Broadness of Scope
    - Ex: In-Depth Analysis
    - Ex: Multifaceted Taxonomy
    - Ex: Numerous Theories
  - —*Arrangement*
    - Ex: Separation (or Subtraction)
    - Ex: Combination (or Addition)
    - Ex: Replacement
    - Ex: Accommodation
    - Ex: Reversal
    - Ex: Stretching
  - —*Serendipity*
    - Ex: Play
    - Ex: Chance

- **Creative Traits**
  - —*Openness / Risk*
    - Ex: Ability to welcome new ideas or to do new things, with risk
  - —*Discipline*
    - Ex: Ability to sacrifice whatever it takes to succeed
  - —*Resilience / Confidence*
    - Ex: Ability to take failures to mind, not to heart
  - —*Trust*
    - Ex: Ability to cooperate with others for team work, if necessary

Notes: The examples in the categories are solely illustrative (not exhaustive), and the comparison is relative (not absolute), nor are they necessarily mutually exclusive. And some can be easily re-classified elsewhere. As generalities, they allow exceptions.
Source: From *Sec.4.2* of *FPHCT*. For more details, also read the rest of the book.

Table 1.30. The Desirability of Creativity, and Its Dark Sides (Part I)

- **In Relation to Instrumental Rationality**
  - *—Desirability*
    - Ex: For the sake of efficiency and effectiveness in this capitalist era of our time.
  - *—Undesirability*
    - Ex: What Max Weber (1930) called the "iron cage" of capitalism, where live the "sensualists without heart, specialists without spirit"—or something which the Frankfurt School has forcefully asked us to be freed from.

- **In Relation to Substantive Rationality**
  - *—Desirability*
    - Ex: For the sake of God, the King, Motherland, or other comparable ideals.
  - *—Undesirability*
    - Ex: Domination and oppression of various forms—something which the moderns had struggled to free themselves from in the first place, since the dawn of modernity.

- **In Relation to Autonomous Rationality**
  - *—Desirability*
    - Ex: For the sake of itself, the autonomy of creative endeavor.
  - *—Undesirability*
    - Ex: The decadence of its own degeneration (e.g., the donwsides of postmodernism in our postmodern times, or what Nietzsche once called the unbearable "unreality" and "falseness" of the autonomous artist's "innermost existence"—and, in other cases, the painful suffering from different mental illnesses for those highly creative individuals).

(continued on next page)

Table 1.30. The Desirability of Creativity, and Its Dark Sides (Part II)

Notes: The examples in the categories are solely illustrative (not exhaustive), and the comparison is relative (not absolute), nor are they necessarily mutually exclusive. And some can be easily re-classified elsewhere. As generalities, they allow exceptions.
Also, I already went to great lenghts to explain the desirability and its dark sides of all these three rationalities (although there may be others too) in the two volumes of *FHC*—and, for that matter, *FCD*.
Source: From *Sec.4.9* of *FPHCT*. For more details, also read the rest of the book.

Table 1.31. Posthuman-Ism, Post-Humanism, and Trans-Humanism

- **Post-Humanism**
  —The neologism "post-human" used in my books should *not* be confused with another term which looks similar but has a totally different meaning in the literature of postmodernism, namely, "post-humanism"—which constitutes a critique of "humanism" as tradionally understood (especially, though not exclusively, in relation to the idea of progress in science and reason in the Enlightenment project). (WK 2008)
  —My works reject the project of "postmodernism" and propose the future world of what I orignally called "after-postmodernity" in *FHC* and *FCD*, for instance.

- **Trans-Humanism**
  —Also, the neologism "post-human" used in my books should *not* be confused with a similar term which is used to champion the ideology of technology for the fturue co-existence between humans and cyborgs in "trans-humanism." (WK 2008a)
  —Instead, my term "post-human" in relation to "posthuman-ism" also rejects "trans-humanism" (especially, though not exclusively, in relation to the promises of technology) and refers to something else altogether, that is, the future extinction of humans and its post-human successors in deep space and beyond unto multiverses.
  —Chapter Two of my book on ethics (*BEPE*) provides a more comprehensive critique of trans-humanism.

- **Posthuman-Ism**
  —With these two clarifications in mind, the "post-humans" (as envisioned in my books) can take different forms, and I proposed, in my different books, some of them, such as "unfolding unconsciousness," "floating consciousness," "hyper-spatial consciousness," "thinking machines," "thinking robots," "genetically altered superior beings," "cyborgs," and others (as already analyzed in my previous works).
  —They will evolve in conjunction with other visions of mine in relation to nature, society, and culture.

Sources: From *Sec.1.6* of *FPHE* (and also *BEPE*). For more details, also read the rest of the books (and other books of mine).

Table 1.32. Three Great Future Transformations of the Martial Body (Part I)

- **Virtual Battle**
  —Ex: virtual fight
  —Ex: virtual memory

- **The Hyper-Martial Body**
  —*In relation to the physical dimension*
  - Ex: striking (e.g., punching, kicking, trapping, acupressure-striking, and so on in an amazing way)
  - Ex: grapping (e.g., throwing, pinning, joint-locking, and so on in an amazing way)
  - Ex: running and walking (e.g., on different surfaces)
  - Ex: jumping (e.g., through walls, trees, etc.)
  - Ex: flying (e.g., through space)
  - Ex: enduring pain (e.g., absorbing punches, kicks, and so on in an amazing way)
  - Ex: using extremely advanced hi-tech weapons
  - Ex: healing (e.g., with special energy, etc.)
  - Ex: entering (e.g., into different dimensions of space)
  - Ex: sensing (e.g., in extraordinary ways through space and time, etc.)
  - Ex: wearing hi-tech suits for defensive and offensive purposes (e.g., like a hi-tech armor)

  —*In relation to the mental dimension*
  - Ex: the ability to relax the martial body in a way that current humans cannot.
  - Ex: the ability to concentrate the martial mind in a way that current humans are not accustomed to.
  - Ex: the ability to breathe and be timely in preparing the martial body for fighting in a way that current humans are not good at.

- **The Post-Martial Floating Mind**
  —Ex: the mind without the human body
  —Ex: the quest for spirituality beyond martial arts

(continued on next page)

Table 1.32. Three Great Future Transformations of the Martial Body (Part II)

Notes: The examples in the categories are solely illustrative (not exhaustive), and the comparison is relative (not absolute), nor are they necessarily mutually exclusive. And some can be easily re-classified elsewhere. As generalities, they allow exceptions.
Source: From *Sec. 2.5.1* of *FPHMA*. See text for citations.

Table 1.33. Three Great Future Transformations of the Sexual Body

- **Virtual Pleasure**
  —Ex: virtual Sex
  —Ex: virtual Recall

- **The Hyper-Sexual Body**
  —*In relation to the physical dimension*
  - Ex: the ability to perform differenet sexual positions without the various physical limitations that humans currently have.
  - Ex: the ability to produce unusual amount of sexual energy to endure in sexual acts in a way that humans currently cannot.
  - Ex: the ability to engage in multiple sexual experiences comparable to (but different from) non-human sexuality (e.g., hermaphrodite, monoecious, sex-switching, and many other types) that current humans cannot.

  —*In relation to the mental dimension*
  - Ex: the ability to relax the sexual body in a way that current humans are not accustomed to.
  - Ex: the ability to concentrate the sexual mind in a way that current humans are not good at.
  - Ex: the ability to breathe and be patient in preparing the sexual body for sexuality in a way that current humans are not able to.

- **The Post-Sexual Floating Mind**
  —Ex: the mind without the human body
  —Ex: the quest for spirituality beyond sexuality

Notes: The examples in the categories are solely illustrative (not exhaustive), and the comparison is relative (not absolute), nor are they necessarily mutually exclusive. And some can be easily re-classified elsewhere. As generalities, they allow exceptions.
Source: From *Sec. 3.4.2* of *FPHS*. See text for more info.

Table 1.34. The Trinity of Pre-Modernity

- **Pre-Free-Spirited Pre-Modernity (Pre-Modernism) and Its Internal Split**
  —Competing worldviews and values both within and between linear centric (e.g., Islamic, Christian, Judaic, Imperial Roman) and cyclical-centric (e.g., Confucian, Taoist, Hindu, and Buddhist) orientations
  —Compare modernism with pre-modernism here in relation to the seven dimensions of human existence like the true and the holy (e.g., different versions of epistemic dogmas and religious superstitions), the everyday and the technological (e.g.,different versions of non-technophilism and non-consumerism), the beautiful/sublime (e.g., different versions of aesthetic non-autonomy), and the good and the just (e.g., different versions of moral particularism).

- **Pre-Capitalist Pre-Modernity (Pre-Modernization) and Its Own Discontents**
  —Competing versions of societal arrangements (e.g., feudalism, monarchism, and the holy order)

- **Hegemonic Pre-Modernity and Its Countervailing Forces**
  —Different power centers and their enemies (e.g., the Roman Empire and the "barbarian hordes," the "Holy Crusades" and the Muslims, the Middle Kingdom and the invading tribes, different social castes in India, and warring Greek city-states)

Notes: The examples in each category are solely illustrative (not exhaustive) nor necessarily mutually exclusive, and the comparison is relative (not absolute). As generalities, they allow exceptions. Also, it does not matter what the "base" era is in the analysis of any trinity. And in the present context, the "base" era is modernity (for instance, with its "free-spirited modernity" and the other two parts). So, for pre-modernity, the trinity takes the form of, say, "pre-free-spirited pre-modernity," together with the other two parts.
Sources: From Ch.2 of *BCIV* and also the 2 volumes of *FHC*

Table 1.35. The Trinity of Modernity (Part I)

- **Free-Spirited Modernity (Modernism) and Its Internal Split**

—*On the True and the Holy*
  - The freedom from the dogmas of the past to the better understanding of, and union with, the world and self (Ch.3 of *FHC*)
  - Alternative discourses: about the true (e.g., anti-science discourses) and the holy (non-mainstream theologies) (Ch.3 of *FHC*)

—*On the Technological and the Everyday*
  - The freedom from life harshness to the higher technophilic, consumeristic lifeform (Ch.2 of *FHC*)
  - Alternative discourses: about the everyday (e.g., transcendental mindsets) and the technological (e.g., Arcadianism) (Ch.2 of *FHC*)

—*On the Good and the Just*
  - The freedom from the theo-aristocratic tyranny to the moral universality for a just society (Ch.5 of *FHC*)
  - Alternative discourses: about the just (e.g., Communism, Anarchism) and the good (e.g., Nazism/Fascism, and Zarathustrianism) (Chs.5-6 of *FHC*)

—*On the Beautiful and the Sublime*
  - The freedom from the external distortion of aesthetic pleasure to the boundless infinity of totality in artistic autonomy (Ch.4 of *FHC*)
  - Alternative discourses: about the beautiful/sublime (e.g., kitsch and historical avant-gardism) (Ch.4 of *FHC*)

- **Capitalist Modernity (Modernization) and Its Own Discontents**

—*During the Industrial Revolution*
  - Ex: Marx on the institution of inequality (Ch.1 of *FHC*)

—*During the Modern Rational-Instrumental Epoch*
  - Ex: Weber on the politics of soft liberal institutions (Ch.5 of *FHC*)

—*During the Great Depression*
  - Ex: Keynes on the myth of the free market (Chs.1-3 of *FHC*)

—*During the Cold War*
  - Ex: Lasch on the narcissistic culture industry (Chs.2-3 of *FHC*)

(continued on next page)

Table 1.35. The Trinity of Modernity (Part II)

- **Hegemonic Modernity and Its Countervailing Forces**

—*The Legacies of Colonialism and Imperialism*

  - Ex: European colonization of most of the modern world (Ch.1 of *FHC*)

—*The Struggle for Decolonialization*

  - Ex: The countervailing forces of resentment, rechantment, and regionalism (Chs.1 & 6 of *FHC*)

Notes: The examples in each category are solely illustrative (not exhaustive) nor necessarily mutually exclusive, and the comparison is relative (not absolute). As generalities, they allow exceptions.
Sources: From the 2 volumes of *FHC*—and also from *FCD*

Table 1.36. The Trinity of Post-Modernity

- **Free-Spirited Postmodernity (Postmodernism) and Its Internal Split**

  —*On the True and the Holy*
  - Postmodern performative turn for knowing and its enemies (Ch.3 of *FHC*)
  - Postmodern comparative theology and its opponents (Ch.3 of *FHC*)

  —*On the Technological and the Everyday*
  - Postmodern corporate technological mindset and its adversaries (Ch.2 of *FHC*)
  - Postmodern postmaterialism and its critics (Ch.2 of *FHC*)

  —*On the Good and the Just*
  - Postmodern politics of difference and its foes (Ch.5 of *FHC*)

  —*On the Beautiful and the Sublime*
  - Postmodern deconstruction and its dissenters (Ch.4 of *FHC*)

- **Capitalist Postmodernity (Postmodernization) and Its Own Discontents**

  —*During the Post-Cold War and Beyond*
  - Ex: post-Fordism and its shortcomings (Ch.6 of *FHC*; Chs.6-7 of *FCD*)

- **Hegemonic Postmodernity and Its Countervailing Forces**

  —*The Debate on the Global Village*
  - Ex: uni-civilizationalism vs. multi-civilizationalism (Ch.6 of *FHC*)

  —*The Resistance Movement*
  - Ex: rechantment and the politics of civilizational claims (e.g., Islamic, Confucian and other ethos in relation to the Same) (Ch.6 of *FHC*; Ch.10 of *FCD*)
  - Ex: resentment and the politics of resurgence (e.g., the rising Chinese superpower, the growing EU, and other players in relation to the U.S. and her allies) (Ch.6 of *FHC*; Ch.8 of *FCD*)
  - Ex: regionalism and the politics of inequality (e.g., trans- or international blocs, the North-South divide, NGO's) (Ch.6 of *FHC*; Ch.5 of *FCD*)

Notes: The examples in each category are solely illustrative (not exhaustive) nor necessarily mutually exclusive, and the comparison is relative (not absolute). As generalities, they allow exceptions.
Sources: From *FCD* and the 2 volumes of *FHC*

Table 1.37. The Trinity of After-Postmodernity

- **Free-Spirited After-Postmodernity (After-Postmodernism) and Its Internal Split**
  —The discourse of naked contingency (Ch.10 of *FCD*; Ch.4 of *FPHC*)

- **Post-Capitalist After-Postmodernity (After-Postmodernization) and Its Own Discontents**
  —Different versions of post-capitalism and post-democracy, and their enemies (Ch.10 of *FCD*; Chs.3-4 of *FPHC*)

- **Hegemonic After-Postmodernity and Its Countervailing Forces**
  —The Cyclical Progression of Hegemony in Multiverses (Chs.9-10 of *FCD*; Ch.4 of *FPHC*)

Notes: The examples in each category are solely illustrative (not exhaustive) nor necessarily mutually exclusive, and the comparison is relative (not absolute). As generalities, they allow exceptions.
Sources: From *FCD* and also *FHC*

• PART TWO •

Networks

CHAPTER 2
NETWORKS AND THEIR INTRICACIES

> As long as vehicles, roads, parking lots, garages, and automobile-related businesses cover a significant portion of the landscape and determine the design of nearly everything else, most American cities will continue to be dysfunctional and degraded slumscapes, choked with traffic."[3]
> —Michael E. Arth (2012)

The Feasibility of Networks

The study of transportation involves both networks and operations—as already explained in *Sec. 1.3*.

The relationship between networks and operations is not independent, since networks without operations are blind, just as operations without networks are empty.

Yet, a scholarly danger here is to reduce the analysis of one to that of the other, so this book is to devote a whole chapter on each, with the understanding that the two are related.

The issues concerning networks in the study of transportation are to be addressed in this chapter (Chapter Two), whereas the issues concerning operations in the study of transportation will be analyzed in the next chapter (Chapter Three).

With this dialectic treatment in mind—a good way to examine the intricacies of networks in the study of transportation is by way of the evaluation of the extent to which they are in fact both possible (or impossible) and desirable (or undesirable).

This can be done by way of a comprehensive analysis of networks in the context of transportation from the four perspectives of the mind, nature, society, and culture (in accordance to my sophisticated methodological holism, as explained in *Sec. 1.9*).

In other words, this chapter is organized in four main sections, in relation to (2.2) networks and the mind, (2.3) networks and nature, (2.4) networks and society, and (2.5) networks and culture—to be addressed hereafter, in that order (and summarized in *Table 3.1*).

Networks and the Mind

Networks, when examined from the perspective of the mind, can show us their possibility (or impossibility) and desirability (or undesirability), and this can be shown by way of two case studies, namely, (2.2.1) networks, walkability, and health, and (2.2.2) networks, the bicycle, and the feeling of freedom—to be addressed in what follows, respectively.

Networks, Walkability, and Health

An excellent case study here to understand networks from the perspective of the mind has to do with networks, walkability, and health.

It should be clarified, however, that this section on networks overlaps a bit with the issue of operations (as will be addressed in Chapter Three), because the two issues cannot be completely separated, but the focus here is on networks.

With this clarification in mind—the term "walkability" refers to "a measure of how friendly an area is to walking. Walkability has many health, environmental, and economic benefits. Factors influencing walkability include the presence or absence and quality of footpaths, sidewalks or other pedestrian right-of-ways, traffic and road conditions, land use patterns, building accessibility, and safety, among others. Walkability is an important concept in sustainable urban design." (WK 2012o; TDM 2001; S. Grignaffini 2008)

Definitions of Walkability

Another definition of "walkability" refers to "the extent to which the built environment is friendly to the presence of people living, shopping, visiting, enjoying or spending time in an area." (WK 2012o; S. Abley 2005)

There are different factors that can affect walkability, and good examples are "street connectivity; land use mix; residential density (residential units per area of residential use); 'transparency' which includes amount of glass in windows and doors, as well as orientation and proximity of homes and buildings to watch over the street; plenty of places to go to near the majority of homes; placemaking, street designs that work for people, not just cars and retail floor area ratio." (WK 2012o; L. Frank 2006)

In addition, "major infrastructural factors include access to mass transit, presence and quality of footpaths, buffers to moving traffic (planter strips, on-street parking or bike lanes) and pedestrian crossings, aesthetics, nearby local destinations, air quality, shade or sun in appropriate seasons, street furniture, traffic volume and speed, and wind conditions." (WK 2012o; L. Ramirez 2006)

And "one of the best ways to quickly determine the walkability of a block, corridor or neighborhood is to count the number of people walking, lingering and engaging in optional activities within a space. While this process is a vast improvement upon pedestrian level of service (LOS) indicators recommended within the Highway Capacity Manual, it may not translate well to non-Western locations where the idea of 'optional' activities may be different. In any case, the diversity of people, and especially the presence of children, seniors and people with disabilities, denotes the quality, completeness and health of a walkable space." (WK 2012o; J. Gehl 1996; TRB 2000; R. Lo 2009)

Measurements of Walkability

To define something is one thing, but to measure it is another. In the case of walkability, there are several options, as shown below: (WK 2012o; WALK 2011)

- "PERS"—stands "Pedestrian Environment Review System" as "one way of assessing and measuring walkability…which has been used extensively in the UK."
- "Walk Score"—is "an algorithmically derived walkability index based on the distance to the closest amenity in each of several categories, but does not consider factors such as sidewalk availability, safety of the neighborhood, and topography."
- "Walkonomics"—is "a web-app that combines Open Data and Crowdsourcing to rate and review the walkability of each street. So far every street in England (over 600,000 streets) and New York City have been rated."
- "RateMyStreet"—is "a website that uses Crowdsourcing, Google Maps and a five star rating system to empower local communities to rate the walkability of their local streets. Users can rate a street using eight different categories: Crossing the street, Pavement/Sidewalk

> width, Trip hazards, Wayfinding, Safety from crime, Road safety, Clean/attractive and disabled peoples access."

Of course, there can be other examples, so the examples above are illustrative.

Benefits of Walkability

As an alternative form of transportation, "increased walkability has proven to have many other individual and community health benefits, such as opportunities for increased social interaction, an increase in the average number of friends and associates where people live, reduced crime (with more people walking and watching over neighborhoods, open space and main streets), increased sense of pride, and increased volunteerism." (WK 2012o)

In the current context of transportation, "one of most important benefits of walkability is the decrease of the automobile footprint in the community. Carbon emissions can be reduced if more people choose to walk rather than drive. Walkability has also been found to have many economic benefits, including accessibility, cost savings both to individuals and to the public, increased efficiency of land use, increased livability, economic benefits from improved public health, and economic development, among others." (WK 2012o; T. Littman 2003)

In a case study on walkability, obesity, and health, it was found that obesity occurs because of "insufficient exercise" resulting from the "increasing use of mechanized transportation and a greater prevalence of labor-saving technology in the home." (WK 2012f; WHO 2012)

The danger of obesity is that it "increases the likelihood of various diseases, particularly heart disease, type 2 diabetes, obstructive sleep apnea, certain types of cancer, and osteoarthritis." (WK 2012f; D. Haslam 2005)

Evolutionary Basis of Walkability

In fact, there are some studies on evolutionary biology and walkability, which provided "a principal justification for walkability, as a consideration in urban design and planning," on the basis of "evolutionary…grounds, contending that gait has been vital to the cerebral development in humans." (WK 2012o)

In other words, "after millennia of human development firmly based upon gait, twentieth century automotive and automated metropolis has separated between walking and thinking, and in this sense it has become an agent of regression rather than human progress. Walkability, therefore, is offered as a critical component in contemporary urban design considerations, with implications far beyond the scope of current concerns." (WK 2012o; C. Stanford 2003; A. Akkerman 2007)

Community Planning of Walkability

Because of this claim about the link between the evolutionary basis of walkability and health as a critique of the "twentieth century automotive and automated metropolis"—"many communities have embraced pedestrian mobility as an alternative to older building practices that favor automobiles." (WK 2012o)

There are different ways "to make a community more walkable. Sidewalks should be implemented where there are 'sidewalk gaps' with priority to areas where walking should be encouraged, like around schools or transit stations. When implementing new sidewalks, there are several aspects to consider. For example, the width of the sidewalk is important for walkability. The Americans with Disabilities Act (ADA) requires that sidewalks be at least five feet in width. Obstructions like sign posts and utility poles can decrease the walkable width of the sidewalk, so alternative locations for these obstructions, especially sign posts, should be used. Quality maintenance and proper lighting of sidewalks should be sustained to reduce obstructions, improve safety, and overall encourage walking. Another way to make sidewalks safer is to implement buffers, which are areas of grass between the street and the sidewalk. An additional benefit of buffers is that the vegetation absorbs the carbon dioxide from automobile emissions and assists with water drainage." (WK 2012o)

Another key to walkability is "making crosswalks safer….Curb extensions decrease the radii of the corners of the curb at intersections. Curb extensions calm traffic and decrease the distance pedestrians have to cross. On streets with parking, curb extensions allow pedestrians to see oncoming traffic better where they would be forced to walk into the street to see past parked cars otherwise. Striped crosswalks, or zebra crossings, also provide safer crossings because they provide better visibility for both drivers and pedestrians." (WK 2012o)

Problems with the Study on Walkability and Health

However, for the critics, this study on walkability and health has some major problems. Consider, for illustration, a few examples below.

Firstly, one main criticism of the study on walkability and health is that there are multiple causes of obesity which need to be examined.

For example, for the critics, obesity can be caused by "diet," "genetics," "sendentary lifestyle," "medical and psychiatric illness," "infectious agents," and "social determinants"; therefore, to blame "mechanized transportation" for the rise of obesity is rather simplistic as an explanation. (WK 2012f)

Secondly, another main criticism of the study on walkability and health is that the causal relationship between obesity and negative health has been questioned too.

For instance, for the critics, "the principal goal of the fat acceptance movement is to decrease discrimination against people who are overweight and obese"; "some in the movement are also attempting to challenge the established relationship between obesity and negative health outcomes." (WK 2012f; NAAFA 2009; A. Pulver 2007) In fact, in another study, it was found that there were "discrepancies between residents' health in inner city neighborhoods and suburban neighborhoods with similar walkability measures," so "it has been suggested that further research is needed…." (WK 2012o; R. Lopez 2006)

And thirdly, still another main criticism of the study on walkability and health is that the evolutionary argument is problematic.

For instance, as already explained in *FHC* (2000) and *BNN* (2006), humans, unlike animals, are not blindly and helplessly subject to the laws of nature and have been increasingly dominating nature, albeit with both positive and negative consequences. But this is precisely to challenge the "principal justification for walkability, as a consideration in urban design and planning," on the basis of "evolutionary…grounds" alone.

Beyond Walkability

These criticisms of the study on walkability and health should not be misunderstood as a total rejection of its usefulness but serve to show us the two opposing sides of the debate, such that the possibility (or impossibility) and desirability (or undesirability) of networks (from the perspective of the mind with networks, walkability, and health as a case study here) are not to the extent that the respective defenders would like us to believe.

Furthermore, the analysis of networks, walkability, and health can teach us something important about the ontological principles in existential dialectics, and good examples include the formalness-informalness principle, the absoluteness-relativeness principle, the partiality-totality principle, the predictability-unpredictability principle, the explicability-inexplicability principle, the fiction-reality principle, the finiteness-transfiniteness principle, the preciseness-vagueness principle, the simpleness-complicatedness principle, the openness-hiddenness principle, the denseness-emptiness principle, the change-constancy principle, the order-chaos principle, the slowness-quickness principle, the expansion-contraction principle, the theory-praxis principle, the convention-novelty principle, the evolution-transformation principle, the symmetry-asymmetry principle, the softness-hardness principle, the seriousness-playfulness principle, the activeness-inactiveness principle, the regression-progression principle, the same-difference principle, and the stability-reaction principle.

For instance, in relation to the formalness-informalness principle, if there is formalness (e.g., the formal logical requirement of soundness in a system of ideas, as in the study of walkability and health), there is informalness (e.g., the non-formal existence of unsoundness in the study of walkability and health, as shown in the criticisms that the causal relationship between obesity and negative health has been questioned too, that the evolutionary argument can be problematic, etc.). And the reverse direction also holds true.

In relation to the absoluteness-relativeness principle, if there is absoluteness (e.g., the absolute view of the adovates about "the established relationship between obesity and negative health outcomes"), there is relativeness (e.g., what is right for the advocates in regard to "the established relationship between obesity and negative health outcomes" is not necessarily so for the critics like some in the fat acceptance movement who "are also attempting to challenge the established relationship between obesity and negative health outcomes"). And the reverse direction also holds true.

In relation to the partiality-totality principle, if there is partiality (e.g., the partial view of those who advocate "the established relationship between obesity and negative health outcomes"), there is totality (e.g., the more holistic view of the entire picture of health, such that the whole is not the sum of its parts, that is, it cannot be reduced to the sum of opposing views" like blaming "mechanized transportation" for the rise of obesity and its critics, since obesity can be caused by "diet," "genetics," "sendentary lifestyle" and other sources, and there will emerge new views in the future not yet known today). And the reverse direction also holds true.

In relation to the predictability-unpredictability principle, if there is predictability (e.g., the predictable tendency of the benefits of walkability, such as "opportunities for increased social interaction, an increase in the average number of friends and associates where people live, reduced crime," and so on), there is unpredictability (e.g., the more difficult task to predict exactly the extent to which walkability is beneficial to health in a particular future era, since there were "discrepancies between residents' health in inner city neighborhoods and suburban neighborhoods with similar walkability measures," so it has been suggested that further research is needed....")). And the reverse direction also holds true.

In relation to the explicability-inexplicability principle, if there is explicability (e.g., the explanation by those who blame "mechanized transportation" for the rise of obesity"), there is inexplicability (e.g., the lack of sufficient explanation by those who blame "mechanized transportation" for the rise of obesity," since there are other causes of obesity, like "diet," "genetics," "sendentary lifestyle," and the like). And the reverse direction also holds true.

In relation to the fiction-reality principle, if there is fiction (e.g., the fictional aspect of the argument about the benefits of walkability, insofar as there were "discrepancies between residents' health in inner city neighborhoods and suburban neighborhoods with similar walkability measures," so it has been suggested that further research is needed...."), there is reality (e.g., the realistic aspect of the argument about the benefits of walkability, insofar as there are evidences for "opportunities for increased social interaction, an increase in the average number of friends and associates where people live, reduced crime," and so on). And the reverse direction also holds true.

In relation to the finiteness-transfiniteness principle, if there is finiteness (e.g., the finite number of the causes of obesity, like "diet," "genetics," "sendentary lifestyle," "medical and psychiatric illness," "infectious agents," and so on), there is transfiniteness (e.g., the transfinite number of all the individual humans and animals in the history of the earth that have suffered from health problems due to obesity). And the reverse direction also holds true.

In relation to the preciseness-vagueness principle, if there is preciseness (e.g., the precise identification of four major measurements of walkability, like PERS, Walk Score, etc. in the article aforecited), there is vagueness (e.g., the vagueness in the identification of the four major measurements of walkability, like PERS, Walk Score, etc. in the article aforecited, since it is not clear why there must be only four major measurements, not 5, 6, 7, 8, and so on). And the reverse direction also holds true.

In relation to the simpleness-complicatedness principle, if there is simpleness (e.g., the relatively simple analysis of obesity in relation to "mechanized transportation"), there is complicatedness (e.g., the relatively more complicated analysis of obesity, by challenging the claims and assumptions, as shown in the problems pointed out by the critics as cited). And the reverse direction also holds true.

In relation to the openness-hiddenness principle, if there is openness (e.g., the open exploration of the "established relationship between obesity and negative health outcomes" in the article aforecited), there is hiddenness (e.g., the hidden bias in the analysis of the "established relationship between obesity and negative health outcomes" in the article aforecited, since it does not give sufficient attention to the alternative claim by some in the fat acceptance movement who challenge the "established relationship between obesity and negative health outcomes"). And the reverse direction also holds true.

In relation to the denseness-emptiness principle, if there is denseness (e.g., the relatively denser concentration of obese individuals in "twentieth century automotive and automated metropolis"), there is emptiness (e.g., the relatively less dense, or more empty, concentration of obese individuals in ancient times, "after millennia of human development firmly based upon gait"). And the reverse direction also holds true.

In relation to the change-constancy principle, if there is change (e.g., the ever new ways to understand health, as shown in the study of walkability and health), there is constancy (e.g., the ever constant existence of different problems in the ever new ways to understand health, as shown in the problems with the study of walkability and health pointed out by the critics). And the reverse direction also holds true.

In relation to the order-chaos principle, if there is order (e.g., the more or less orderly appearance of reality, if looked from the simple perspective of blaming "mechanized transportation" for the rise of obesity), there is chaos (e.g,. the more or less chaotic appearance of reality, if looked from the complex perspective of numerous sources of obesity, as well as conflicting findings like the criticism that there were "discrepancies between residents' health in inner city neighborhoods and suburban neighborhoods with similar walkability measures," so it has been suggested that further research is needed…."). And the reverse direction also holds true.

In relation to the slowness-quickness principle, if there is slowness (e.g., the relatively slower speed of an individual to become obese if he makes good use of the benefits of walkability), there is quickness (e.g., the relatively quicker speed of an individual to become obese if he depends too much on mechanized transportation). And the reverse direction also holds true.

In relation to the expansion-contraction principle, if there is expansion (e.g., the relative spread of the use of automobiles in "twentieth century…automated metropolis"), there is contraction (e.g., the relative decline of gait in "twentieth century…automated metropolis"). And the reverse direction also holds true.

In relation to the theory-praxis principle, if there is theory (e.g., the theoretical construction of the benefits of "walkability" in the evolutionary study aforecited), there is praxis (e.g., the practical application of the theoretical research on the benefits of walkability in evolutionary study to the field of urban planning, like those for "pedestrian oriented development"). And the reverse direction also holds true.

In relation to the convention-novelty principle, if there is convention (e.g., the conventional wisdom about the benefits of the "twentieth century automotive and automated metropolis" in the older days), there is novelty (e.g., the alternative novel challenge to the conventional wisdom about the benefits of the "twentieth century automotive and automated metropolis" in the older days, by the new idea of "pedestrian oriented development" for more walkability nowadays). And the reverse direction also holds true.

In relation to the evolution-transformation principle, if there is evolution (e.g., the natural evolution of humans to depend on gait in the state of nature), there is transformation (e.g., the technical transformation of human ability to move around by the invention of "mechanized transportation" nowadays). And the reverse direction also holds true.

In relation to the symmetry-asymmetry principle, if there is symmetry (e.g., the existence of different ways to move around, like walking and driving), there is asymmetry (e.g., the dominance of gait in the state of nature—but the dominance of driving in 20th century metropolis). And the reverse direction also holds true.

In relation to the softness-hardness principle, if there is softness (e.g., the appreciation of walkability by the advocates of "pedestrian oriented development"), there is hardness (e.g., the critique of walkability by the supporters of the car culture). And the reverse direction also holds true.

In relation to the seriousness-playfulness principle, if there is seriousness (e.g., the serious business of those who want to understand the relationship between walkability and health), there is playfulness (e.g., the playful part of those who want to understand the relationship between walkability and health, when they play around with different claims, like blaming "mechanized transportation" for the rise of obesity and suggesting the evolutionary origin of walkability). And the reverse direction also holds true.

In relation to the activeness-inactiveness principle, if there is activeness (e.g., the alertness of those who actively try to be in good health by maintaining the lifestyle of walkability), there is inactiveness (e.g., the relative inactiveness of those who are tired, sleepy, sick, old, or drunken, when they cannot engage in walking too much).

In relation to the regression-progression principle, if there is regression (e.g., the regression made by "mechanized transportation," as shown in the problems with obesity and negative health pointed out by the critics), there is progression (e.g., the progress made by"mechanized transportation," as shown in its convenience for contemporary life in "twentieth century…automated metropolis"). And the reverse direction also holds true.

In relation to the same-difference principle, if there is similarity in outcome (e.g., the contribution to the molding and control of beliefs, values, and behaviors, regardless of whether this be done by way of "pedestrian oriented development" or by way of "car culture"), there is difference in outcome (e.g., the contribution to the molding and control of beliefs, values, and behaviors by way of "pedestrian oriented development" for a relatively more physical lifestyle—but the contribution to the molding and control of beliefs, values, and behaviors by way of "car culture" for a relatively more sedentary lifestyle). And the reverse direction also holds true.

And in relation to the stability-reaction principle, if there is stability (e.g., the relatively more stable condition of the sedentary lifestyle in the older days, when the use of automobiles became widespread in "twentieth century…automated metropolis"), there is reaction (e.g., the relatively more stable condition of the sedentary lifestyle in the older days then led to further changes later on, when, nowadays, there is the "pedestrian oriented development" to replace the car culture). And the reverse direction also holds true.

Networks, the Bicycle, and the Feeling of Freedom

Another way to evaluate the possibility (or impossibility) and desirability (or undesirability) of networks from the perspective of the mind is to explore networks, bicycle, and the feeling of freedom.

It should be clarified, however, that this section on networks overlaps a bit with the issue of operations (as will be addressed in Chapter Three), because the two issues cannot be completely separated, but the focus here is on networks.

With this clarification in mind—the term "bicycle" is also known as "a bike, pushbike, pedal bike, pedal cycle, or cycle" and refers to "a human-powered, pedal-driven, single-track vehicle, having two wheels attached to a frame, one behind the other. A person who rides a bicycle is called a cyclist, or bicyclist." (WK 2012p; OED 1982)

History of the Bicycle

The invention of the bicycle is of modern origins. For instance, in the 19th century, "the Draisienne, Laufmaschine, or dandy horse was the first human means of transport to use only two wheels in tandem and was invented by the German Baron Karl von Drais. It is regarded as the forerunner of the modern bicycle and was introduced by Drais to the public in Mannheim in summer 1817 and in Paris in 1818. Its rider sat astride a wooden frame supported by two in-line wheels and pushed the vehicle along with his/her feet while steering the front wheel." (WK 2012p; CSTM 2006)

In 1839, "the first mechanically-propelled 2-wheel vehicle may have been built by Kirkpatrick MacMillan, a Scottish blacksmith…, although the claim is open to dispute. He is also associated with the first recorded instance of a cycling traffic offence, when a Glasgow newspaper reported in 1842 an accident in which an anonymous 'gentleman from Dumfries-shire... bestride a velocipede... of ingenious design' knocked over a little girl in Glasgow and was fined five shillings." (WK 2012p; D. Herlihy 2004)

By the 1860s, "Frenchmen Pierre Michaux and Pierre Lallement took bicycle design in a new direction by adding a mechanical crank drive with pedals on an enlarged front wheel (the velocipede). Another French inventor by the name of Douglas Grasso had a failed prototype of Pierre Lallement's bicycle several years earlier. Several inventions followed using rear wheel drive, the best known being the rod-driven velocipede by Scotsman Thomas McCall in 1869. The French creation, made of iron and wood, developed into the 'penny-farthing' (historically known as an 'ordinary bicycle,' a retronym, since there was then no other kind)." (WK 2012p; G. Norcliffe 2001)

Later, further "innovations increased comfort and ushered in a second bicycle craze, the 1890s' Golden Age of Bicycles. In 1888, Scotsman John Boyd Dunlop introduced the first practical pneumatic tire, which soon became universal. Soon after, the rear freewheel was developed, enabling the rider to coast. This refinement led to the 1890s invention of coaster brakes. Derailleur gears and hand-operated cable-pull brakes were also developed during these years, but were only slowly adopted by casual riders. By the turn of the century, cycling clubs flourished on both sides of the Atlantic, and touring and racing became widely popular." (WK 2012p)

Yet, “the basic shape and configuration of a typical upright bicycle has changed little since the first chain-driven model was developed around 1885.” (WK 2012p; D. Herlihy 2004)

Prior to the invention of the automobile, “bicycles and horse buggies were the two mainstays of private transportation…, and the grading of smooth roads in the late 19th century was stimulated by the widespread advertising, production, and use of these devices.” (WK 2012p; D. Herlihy 2004)

Technical Aspects of the Bicycle

However, “the bicycle has undergone continual adaptation and improvement since its inception. These innovations have continued with the advent of modern materials and computer-aided design, allowing for a proliferation of specialized bicycle types.” (WK 2012p)

Consider, for illustration, three main technical aspects below.

(a) Types

In regard to “types,” bicycles “can be categorized in different ways: e.g. by function, by number of riders, by general construction, by gearing or by means of propulsion. The more common types include utility bicycles, mountain bicycles, racing bicycles, touring bicycles, hybrid bicycles, cruiser bicycles, and BMX Bikes. Less common are tandems, lowriders, tall bikes, fixed gear, folding models, amphibious bicycles and recumbents (one of which was used to set the IHPVA Hour record).” (WK 2012p)

But, strictly speaking, “unicycles, tricycles and quadracycles are not strictly bicycles, as they have respectively one, three and four wheels, but are often referred to informally as 'bikes.'” (WK 2012p)

(b) Dynamics

In regard to “dynamics,” a bicycle “stays upright while moving forward by being steered so as to keep its center of mass over the wheels. This steering is usually provided by the rider, but under certain conditions may be provided by the bicycle itself.” (WK 2012p; J. Meijaard 2007)

The balancing act is achieved, such that “the combined center of mass of a bicycle and its rider must lean into a turn to successfully navigate it. This lean is induced by a method known as countersteering, which can be performed by the rider turning the handlebars directly with the hands or indirectly by leaning the bicycle.” (WK 2012p; D. Wilson 2004; J. Fajans 2000)

In other cases, “short-wheelbase or tall bicycles, when braking, can generate enough stopping force at the front wheel to flip longitudinally.

The act of purposefully using this force to lift the rear wheel and balance on the front without tipping over is a trick known as a stoppie, endo or front wheelie." (WK 2012p; V. Cossalter 2006)

(c) Performance

And in regard to "performance," the bicycle is "extraordinarily efficient in both biological and mechanical terms. The bicycle is the most efficient human-powered means of transportation in terms of energy a person must expend to travel a given distance." (WK 2012p)

In addition, "from a mechanical viewpoint, up to 99% of the energy delivered by the rider into the pedals is transmitted to the wheels, although the use of gearing mechanisms may reduce this by 10–15%. In terms of the ratio of cargo weight a bicycle can carry to total weight, it is also an efficient means of cargo transportation." (WK2012p; S. Wilson 1973; Fr. Whitt 1982)

Also, "the carbon dioxide generated in the production and transportation of the food required by the bicyclist, per mile traveled, is less than 1/10 that generated by energy efficient cars." (WK 2012p; KEN 1999)

Psychological Impacts of the Bicycle

When examined from the perspective of the mind in the context of transportation, the bicycle has some interesting psychological impacts, and an excellent example concerns the "feeling of "freedom."

For instance, it was found that "the safety bicycle gave women unprecedented mobility, contributing to their emancipation in Western nations. As bicycles became safer and cheaper, more women had access to the personal freedom they embodied, and so the bicycle came to symbolize the New Woman of the late 19th century, especially in Britain and the United States." (WK 2012p)

For this reason, "the bicycle was recognized by 19th-century feminists and suffragists as a 'freedom machine' for women. American Susan B. Anthony said in a New York World interview on February 2, 1896: 'Let me tell you what I think of bicycling. I think it has done more to emancipate women than anything else in the world. It gives women a feeling of freedom and self-reliance. I stand and rejoice every time I see a woman ride by on a wheel...the picture of free, untrammeled womanhood.' In 1895 Frances Willard, the tightly laced president of the Women's Christian Temperance Union, wrote a book called *How I Learned to Ride the Bicycle*, in which she praised the bicycle she learned to ride late in life, and which she named 'Gladys,' for its 'gladdening effect' on her health and political optimism. Willard used a cycling metaphor to urge other suffragists to action, proclaiming, 'I would not waste my life in friction when it could be turned into momentum.'" (WK 2012p)

In addition, "the bicycle craze in the 1890s also led to a movement for so-called rational dress, which helped liberate women from corsets and ankle-length skirts and other restrictive garments, substituting the then-shocking bloomers." (WK 2012p)

Problems with the Study on the Bicycle

However, for the critics, this study on the bicycle has some major problems. Consider, for illustration, a few examples below.

Firstly, one main criticism of this study on the bicycle is that the invention of the bicycle has contributed to new accidents which can injure and kill those involved. Thus, freedom has a price to pay, so to speak.

For example, "a study conducted in 2000 by the Institute for Road Safety Research in the Netherlands found that single bicycle accidents accounted for 47% of all bicycle accidents, collisions with obstacles and animals accounted for 12%, and collisions with other road users accounted for 40%, with the remaining 1% having unknown or unclassified cause. Many bicycle crashes are unreported and therefore not included in official statistics. Prospective studies estimate that less than 10% of bicycle accidents are officially reported. In the United Kingdom cyclists have half of the accident rate (killed and serious injury per km) of motorcyclists and eight times the rate for motorists. Even minor bicycle accidents not involving hospitalisation can cause important costs to the cyclist and to society. The Belgian SHAPES project has recently estimated the cost at 12 €-cent per kilometer cycled. A cyclist who is hit by a car is more likely to be killed than one who just falls off." (WK 2012q; G. Vandenbulcke 2011; J. Aertsens 2010; R. Davis 1993)

Secondly, another main criticism of this study on the bicycle is that the discourse of "freedom" or "emancipation" in the feminist movement in regard to the "freedom machine" is ideological.

For instance, for the critics, it is question-begging to assume that freedom is necessarily "good." In fact, I already went to great lengths to argue in Ch.10 of *FCD*, based on *FHC* (and summarized in *Table 4.13* here), that there is no freedom without unfreedom in what I called "the freedom/unfreedom dialectics."

Thirdly, still another main criticism of this study on the bicycle is that not everyone agrees with the different technical aspects of the bicycle.

For instance, for the critics, whether a bicycle should be equipped with "bicycle lighting at night" and "helmets" are "controversial," as some opponents consider them as "optional" for a bicycle to have. (WK 2012q)

Fourthly, an additional main criticism of this study on the bicycle is that the feminists exaggerated the freedom value of the bicycle.

For instance, it is not clear at all to what extent the bicycle has really contributed to human freedom to the extent of being justifiedly called a "freedom machine." Did this instead reveal an euphoria at the time, with the benefit of historical hindsight? This then reminds us of the comparable euphoria in the old "glory days" of the automobile (as already described in *Sec. 1.1*), but the car culture is now under fire, as it is no longer as liberating as it was once innocently believed to be so in those old "glory days."

And fifthly, another additional main criticism of this study on the bicycle is that the feminists may well be inconsistent in stressing the freedom value of the bicycle while neglecting its tradeoff against equality, contrary to their central cherished goal (of equality between the two genders).

For instance, "George Monbiot writes that widespread car culture has shifted voter's preference to the right of the political spectrum. He thinks that car culture has contributed to an increase in individualism and fewer social interactions between members of different socioeconomic classes." (WK 2012; G. Monbiot 2005) One can apply Monbiot's point to the comparable (though different) context of the bicycle, in that its contribution to individualism (like individual freedom) on the right of the political spectrum does not square well with the value of equality (on the left of the political spectrum).

Beyond the Bicycle

However, these criticisms of the study on the bicycle do not mean a total rejection of its usefulness but serve to show us the two opposing sides of the debate, such that the possibility (or impossibility) and desirability (or undesirability) of networks (from the perspective of the mind with networks, the bicycle, and the feeling of freedom as a case study here) are not to the extent that the respective defenders would like us to believe.

Indeed, the analysis of networks, the bicycle, and the feeling of freedom reveals something insightful about the ontological principles in existential dialectics, and good examples include the formalness-informalness principle, the absoluteness-relativeness principle, the partiality-totality principle, the predictability-unpredictability principle, the explicability-inexplicability principle, the fiction-reality principle, the finiteness-transfiniteness principle, the preciseness-vagueness principle, the simpleness-complicatedness principle, the openness-hiddenness principle, the denseness-emptiness principle, the change-constancy principle, the order-chaos principle, the slowness-quickness principle, the expansion-contraction principle, the theory-praxis principle, the convention-novelty principle, the evolution-transformation principle, the symmetry-asymmetry principle, the softness-hardness principle, the seriousness-playfulness principle, the activeness-inactiveness principle, the regression-progression principle, the same-difference principle, and the stability-reaction principle.

For instance, in relation to the formalness-informalness principle, if there is formalness (e.g., the formal logical requirement of soundness in a system of ideas, as in the study on the bicycle), there is informalness (e.g., the non-formal existence of unsoundness in the study on the bicycle, as shown in the criticisms that the invention of the bicycle has contributed to new accidents which can injure and kill those involved, that there is no freedom without unfreedom in the case of the "freedom machine," that not everyone agrees with the different technical aspects of the bicycle, that the feminists exaggerated the freedom value of the bicycle, etc.). And the reverse direction also holds true.

In relation to the absoluteness-relativeness principle, if there is absoluteness (e.g., the absolute view of those who require a bicycle to be equipped with "bicycle lighting at night" and "helmets"), there is relativeness (e.g., what is right for those who require a bicycle to be equipped with "bicycle lighting at night" and "helmets" is not necessarily so for those who consider them as "optional" for a bicycle to have). And the reverse direction also holds true.

In relation to the partiality-totality principle, if there is partiality (e.g., the partial view of those feminists in regard to the bicycle as a "freedom machine"), there is totality (e.g., the more holistic view of the bicycle, such that the whole is not the sum of its parts, that is, it cannot be reduced to the sum of opposing views like the feminists, the critics, etc., since there will emerge new views in the future not yet known today). And the reverse direction also holds true.

In relation to the predictability-unpredictability principle, if there is predictability (e.g., the predictable tendency of those who favor the invention of helmets to claim it as a protective measure to lessen injury or death in accidents), there is unpredictability (e.g., the more difficult task to predict exactly the extent to which the requirement of helmets will be widespread in a particular future era, since there are those who consider them as "optional" for a bicycle to have). And the reverse direction also holds true.

In relation to the explicability-inexplicability principle, if there is explicability (e.g., the explanation by the feminists that the bicycle is desirable because of its being a "freedom machine"), there is inexplicability (e.g., the lack of sufficient explanation by the feminists that the bicycle is necessarily desirable as a "freedom machine," since, for the critics, the bicycle has also contributed to new accidents which can injure and kill those involved, that there is no freedom without unfreedom, etc.). And the reverse direction also holds true.

In relation to the fiction-reality principle, if there is fiction (e.g., the fictional aspect of bicycle safety, insofar as Colin Buchanan in 1963 reported that "the meagre efforts made to separate cyclists from motor traffic have failed,...not...as helpful as it might have been"), there is reality (e.g., the realistic aspect of bicycle safety, insofar as "the use of appropriately designed segregated space on arterial or interurban routes [so as to separate bicycles from vehicles] appears to be associated with reductions in overall risk"). (WK 2012q; CABE 2006; C. Buchanan 1958) And the reverse direction also holds true.

In relation to the finiteness-transfiniteness principle, if there is finiteness (e.g., the finite number of the most common types of bicycles in history like "utility bicycles, mountain bicycles, racing bicycles, touring bicycles, hybrid bicycles, cruiser bicycles, and BMX Bikes"), there is transfiniteness (e.g., the transfinite number of all the individual bicycles which have ever been produced in history). And the reverse direction also holds true.

In relation to the preciseness-vagueness principle, if there is preciseness (e.g., the precise identification of 7 common types of bicycles like "utility bicycles, mountain bicycles, racing bicycles, touring bicycles, hybrid bicycles, cruiser bicycles, and BMX Bikes" in the article aforecited), there is vagueness (e.g., the vagueness in the identification of the 7 common types of bicycles like "utility bicycles, mountain bicycles, racing bicycles, touring bicycles, hybrid bicycles, cruiser bicycles, and BMX Bikes" in the article aforecited, since it is not clear why there must be only 7, not 8, 9, 10, and so on). And the reverse direction also holds true.

In relation to the simpleness-complicatedness principle, if there is simpleness (e.g., the relatively simple analysis of "freedom machine" by its advocates), there is complicatedness (e.g., the relatively more complicated analysis of "freedom machine," by challenging the claims and assumptions, as shown in the problems pointed out by the critics as cited). And the reverse direction also holds true.

In relation to the openness-hiddenness principle, if there is openness (e.g., the open exploration by Herbert Alker Tripp in 1942 that "if we could segregate pedestrians completely from the wheeled traffic, we could of course abolish pedestrian casualties"), there is hiddenness (e.g., the hidden bias in the argument by Tripp, because Colin Buchanan in 1963 rebuked him by arguing that "the meagre efforts made to separate cyclists from motor traffic have failed,...not...as helpful as it might have been"). (WK 2012q; CABE 2006) And the reverse direction also holds true.

In relation to the denseness-emptiness principle, if there is denseness (e.g., the relatively denser concentration of bicycles as one of the "mainstays of private transportation" nowadays), there is emptiness (e.g., the relatively less dense, or more empty, concentration of horses as one of the "mainstays of private transportatioin" nowadays). And the reverse direction also holds true.

In relation to the change-constancy principle, if there is change (e.g., the ever new ways to move around, as shown in the study on the bicycle), there is constancy (e.g., the ever constant existence of different problems in the ever new ways to move around, as shown in the problems with the bicycle pointed out by the critics). And the reverse direction also holds true.

In relation to the order-chaos principle, if there is order (e.g., the more or less orderly appearance of the bicycle, if looked from the perspective of when it works properly as expected), there is chaos (e.g,. the more or less chaotic appearance of the bicycle, if looked from the perspective of when it does not work properly, especially in accidents which injure or kill those involved). And the reverse direction also holds true.

In relation to the slowness-quickness principle, if there is slowness (e.g., the relatively slower speed of the bicycle, when contrasted with that of the automobile), there is quickness (e.g., the relatively quicker speed of the bicycle, when contrasted with that of walking). And the reverse direction also holds true.

In relation to the expansion-contraction principle, if there is expansion (e.g., the relative spread of the presence of the automobile as a form of transportation nowadays), there is contraction (e.g., the relative decline of the presence of horses as a form of transportation nowadays). And the reverse direction also holds true.

In relation to the theory-praxis principle, if there is theory (e.g., the theoretical construction of "head trauma" in psychology and biology), there is praxis (e.g., the practical application of "head trauma" in psychology and biology to the field of transportation, as shown in the call to "wear helmets, as this may protect riders from head trauma"). (WK 2012p) And the reverse direction also holds true.

In relation to the convention-novelty principle, if there is convention (e.g., the conventional wisdom about using horses as a form of transportation in antiquity), there is novelty (e.g., the alternative novel challenge to the conventional wisdom about about using horses as a form of transportation in antiquity, by the new idea of using bicycles since the 19th century). And the reverse direction also holds true.

In relation to the evolution-transformation principle, if there is evolution (e.g., the natural evolution of humans to walk and run in the state of nature), there is transformation (e.g., the technical transformation of human ability to move around by the invention of the bicycle). And the reverse direction also holds true.

In relation to the symmetry-asymmetry principle, if there is symmetry (e.g., the existence of different forms of transportation, like walking, horse-riding, cycling, etc.), there is asymmetry (e.g., the popularity of hourse-riding in antiquity—but the popularity of cycling in the 19th century and beyond). And the reverse direction also holds true.

In relation to the softness-hardness principle, if there is softness (e.g., the appreciation of the bicycle, as shown in the slogan of "freedom machine" by the feminists), there is hardness (e.g., the critique of the bicycle, as shown in the problems pointed out by the critics as cited). And the reverse direction also holds true.

In relation to the seriousness-playfulness principle, if there is seriousness (e.g., the serious business of the feminists to understand the implications of the invention of the bicycle for women), there is playfulness (e.g., the playful part of the feminists, when they play around with such ideological slogans like "freedom machine," etc., without a serious critique of its ideological basis). And the reverse direction also holds true.

In relation to the activeness-inactiveness principle, if there is activeness (e.g., the alertness of those who actively engage in cycling for different purposes like the feeling of freedom, the benefits of good health, etc.), there is inactiveness (e.g., the relative inactiveness of those who are tired, sleepy, sick, old, or drunken, when they cannot engage in cycling too much).

In relation to the regression-progression principle, if there is regression (e.g., the regression made by the invention of the bicycle, as shown in the accidents pointed out by the critics), there is progression (e.g., the progress made by the invention of the bicycle, as shown in its being a form of private transportation aforecited). And the reverse direction also holds true.

In relation to the same-difference principle, if there is similarity in outcome (e.g., the contribution to the molding and control of beliefs, values, and behaviors, regardless of whether this be done by way of cycling, or by way of walking), there is difference in outcome (e.g., the contribution to the molding and control of beliefs, values, and behaviors by way of cycling for a relatively more mechanical lifeworld—but the contribution to the molding and control of beliefs, values, and behaviors by way of walking for a relatively more naturalistic lifeworld). And the reverse direction also holds true.

And in relation to the stability-reaction principle, if there is stability (e.g., the relatively more stable condition of horse-riding in antiquity, when it was commonly used as a form of transportation), there is reaction (e.g., the stable condition of horse-riding in antiquity then led to further changes later on, when the bicycle became more common in the 19th century and beyond). And the reverse direction also holds true.

Networks and Nature

Networks, when examined from the perspective of nature, can show us their possibility (or impossibility) and desirability (or undesirability), and this can be shown by way of two case studies, namely, (2.3.1) networks, locomotion, and energy, and (2.3.2) networks, spacecraft, and outer space—to be addressed in what follows, respectively.

Networks, Locomotion, and Energy

An excellent case study here to understand networks from the perspective of nature has to do with networks, locomotion, and energy.

The term "locomotion" refers to the motion "achieved by being towed by another vehicle or animal, or by obtaining, converting and using energy. Hybrid and tribrid vehicles have more complicated designs that employ several different paths for energy to take before being used." (WK 2012d)

To understand the nature of locomotion then requires an examination of three major issues, namely, (a) energy sources, (b) motors and engines, and (c) the conversion of energy to work, as analyzed below (and summarized in *Table 2.2*), in that order.

Energy Sources

Energy sources are important, because a vehicle neds to have "a source of energy to drive it. Energy can be extracted from the surrounding environment, as in the case of a sailboat, a solar powered car, or a streetcar. Energy can also be stored, in any form, provided it can be converted on demand and the storing medium's energy density and power density are sufficient to meet the vehicle's needs." (WK 2012d)

There are different types of energy to be used, and hereafter are some good examples:

- Electrical Energy—is seen in "electrified rails and overhead cables" for "subways, railways, trams, and trolleybuses." (WK 2012d)
- Nuclear Energy—is "currently reserved for large ships and submarines, mostly military. Nuclear energy can be released by a nuclear reactor, nuclear battery, or by repeatedly detonating nuclear bombs. There have been two experiments with nuclear powered aircraft, the Tupolev Tu-119 and the Convair X-6." (WK 2012d)
- Mechanical Energy—is a form of energy, "where an elastic band or metal spring is deformed and releases energy as it is allowed to return to its ground state. Systems employing elastic materials suffer from hysteresis and metal springs are too dense to be useful is many cases." (WK 2012d)
- Gravitational Energy—is "a form of energy used in gliders, skis, bobsleds and numerous other vehicles that go down hill. Regenerative braking is an example of capturing kinetic energy where the brakes of a vehicle are augmented with a generator or other means of extracting energy." (WK 2012d; HOW 2011b)
- Solar Energy—is "a more modern development, and several solar vehicles have been successfully built and tested, including Helios, a solar powered aircraft." (WK 2012d)
- Wind Energy—is "used is sailboats and land yachts as the primary source of energy. It is very cheap and fairly easy to use, the main issues being dependence on weather and upwind performance. Balloons also rely on the wind to move horizontally. Aircraft flying in the jet stream may get a boost from high altitude winds." (WK 2012d)
- Human Energy—is "a simple source of energy that requires nothing more than humans. Despite the fact that humans cannot exceed 500 W (0.67 hp) for meaningful amounts of time, the land speed record for human powered vehicles (unpaced) is 133 km/h (83 mph), as of 2009." (WK 2011d; MAPA 2011; WHPSC. 2009)

Surely, there are other examples too, so the ones above are illustrative, not exhaustive.

In any event, nowadays, "the most common type of energy source is fuel. External combustion engines can use almost anything that burns as fuel whilst internal combustion engines and rocket engines are tailor built to burn a specific fuel, typically gasoline, diesel, or ethanol." (WK 2012d)

Another common type of energy source is "batteries," which "have the advantage of being responsive, useful in a wide rage of power levels, environmentally friendly, efficient, simple to install, and easy to maintain. Batteries also facilitate the use of electric motors, which have their own advantages." (WK 2012d; BAT 2011)

Motors and Engines

It is one thing to identify energy sources, but it is another to consume them.

For instance, whenever needed, "energy is taken from the source and consumed by one or more motors or engines. Sometimes there is an intermediate medium, such as the batteries of a diesel submarine." (WK 2012d)

Hereafter are some examples of different engines or motors in transportation:

- Aircraft Engines—are "internal combustion engines used…for aircraft" and "have been superseded by continuous internal combustion engines: gas turbines. Turbine engines are light and, particularly when used on aircraft, efficient. On the other hand, they cost more and require careful maintenance. They also get damaged from ingesting foreign objects and produce a hot exhaust….Pulse jet engines are similar in many ways to turbojets, but they have almost no moving parts. For this reason, they were very appealing to vehicle designers in the past, however their noise, heat, and inefficiency has lend their abandonment. A historical example of a pulse jet in use was the V-1 flying bomb. Pulse jets are still occasionally used in amateur experiments. With the advent of modern technology, the pulse detonation engine has become practical, and was successfully tested on a Rutan VariEze. While the pulse detonation engine is much more efficient that the pulse jet and even turbine engines, it still suffers from extreme noise and vibration levels. Ramjets also have few moving parts, but they only work at high speed meaning that their use is restricted to tip jet helicopters and high speed aircraft such as the Lockheed SR-71 Blackbird." (WK 2012d; TIME 1965; AERO 2002)

- Rocket Engines—are "primarily used on rockets, rocket sleds, and experimental aircraft. Rocket engines are extremely powerful. The heaviest vehicle to ever leave the ground, the Saturn V rocket, was powered by five F-1 rocket engines generating a combined 180 million horsepower (134,226 megawatt). Rocket engines also don't need to 'push off' of anything, a fact that the New York Times denied in error. Rocket engines can be particularly simple, sometimes consisting of nothing more than a catalyst, as in the case of a hydrogen peroxide rocket. This makes them an attractive option for vehicles such as jet packs. Despite their simplicity, rocket engines are often dangerous and susceptible to explosions. The fuel they run off may be flammable, poisonous, corrosive, or cryogenic. They also suffer from poor efficiency. For these reasons, rocket engines are only used when absolutely necessary." (WK 2011d; NASA 2011; HOW 2011c)
- Electric Motors— are "used in motor vehicles, electric bicycles, electric scooters, small boats, subways, trains, trolleybuses, trams and experimental aircraft. Electric motors can be very efficient, over 90% efficiency is common. Electric motors can also be built powerful, reliable, low-maintenance and of arbitrary size. Electric motors can deliver a range of speeds and torques without necessarily using a gearbox (although it may be more economic to use one). Electric motors are limited in their use chiefly by the difficulty of supplying electricity." (WK 2012d)
- Compressed Gas Motors—"have been used on some vehicles experimentally. They are simple, efficient, safe, cheap, reliable, and operate in a variety of conditions. One of the difficulties encountered when using gas motors is the cooling effect of expanding gas. These engines are limited by how quickly they absorb heat from their surroundings. The cooling effect can, however, double as air conditioning. Compressed gas motors also loose effectiveness with falling gas pressure." (WK 2012d; QUA 2011)
- Ion Thrusters—"are used on some satellites and spacecraft. They are only effective in a vacuum, which limits their use to spaceborne vehicles. Ion thrusters run primarily off electricity but they also need a propellant such as caesium, or more recently xenon. Ion thrusters can achieve extremely high speeds and use little propellant; however they are power hungry too. Most ion thrusters built today have small thrusts." (WK 2012d; NASA 2011a; Beoing 2011)

Again, there are other examples too, so the ones above are illustrative, not exhaustive.

Conversion of Energy to Work

These motors and engines have then to convert the "energy" (that they produce) "to work by wheels, propellers, nozzles, or similar means." (WK 2012d)

Consider, for illustration, the following ways to convert energy to work (as summarized in *Table 2.2*):

- Wheels—"allow a vehicle to roll along a surface and, with the exception of railed vehicles, to steer. Wheels are ancient technology, with specimens being discovered from over 5000 years ago. Wheels are used in a plethora of vehicles, including motor vehicles, armoured personnel carriers, amphibious vehicles, airplanes, trains, skateboards, and wheelbarrows." (WK 2012d; HOW 2011d; A. Gasser 2003)
- Nozzles—"are used in conjunction with almost all reaction engines. Vehicles using nozzles include jet aircraft, rockets and personal watercraft. While most nozzles take the shape of a cone or bell, some unorthodox designs have been created such as the aerospike. Some nozzles are intangible, such as the electromagnetic field nozzle of a vectored ion thruster." (WK 2012d; NASA 2011b; LTI 2011)
- Tracks—"are sometimes used instead of wheels to power land vehicles. Continuous tracks have the advantage of a larger contact area, easy repairs on small damage, and high maneuverability. Examples of vehicles using continuous tracks include tanks, snowmobiles, and excavators. Two continuous tracks used together allow for steering. The largest vehicle in the world, the Bagger 288 is propelled by continuous tracks." (WK 2012d; MT 2011)
- Propellers—are used (together with "screws, fans, and rotors") "to move through a fluid. Propellers have been used as toys since ancient times, however it was Leonardo da Vinci who devised what was one of the earliest propeller driven vehicles vehicles, the 'aerial-screw.' In 1661, Toogood & Hays adopted the screw for use as a ship propeller. Since then, the propeller has been tested on many terrestrial vehicles, including the Schienenzeppelin train and numerous cars. In modern times, propellers are most prevalent on watercraft and aircraft, as well as some amphibious vehicles such as hovercraft and ground effect vehicles. Intuitively, propellers cannot work in space as there is no working fluid, however some sources have suggested that since space

is never empty, a propeller could be made to work in space." (WK 2012d; USCFC 2011; R. Sampson 2008; J. Walker 2011)

- Wings—are used "for propulsion. Sailboats and sailplanes are propelled by the forward component of lift generated by their sails/wings. Ornithopters also produce thrust aerodynamically. Ornithopters with large rounded leading edges produce lift by leading-edge suction forces." (WK 2012d; HOW 2011e; NASA 2011c)

Of course, there are other examples too, so the ones above are illustrative, not exhaustive.

Problems with the Study on Locomotion and Energy

However, for the critics, this study on locomotion and energy has some major problems. Consider, for illustration, a few examples below (as summarized in *Table 2.2*).

Firstly, one main criticism of this study on locomotion and energy is that energy sources have disadvantages too.

For example, "batteries have low energy densities, short service life, poor performance at extreme temperatures, long charging times, and difficulties with disposal (although they can usually be recycled). Like fuel, batteries store chemical energy and can cause burns and poisoning in event of an accident. Batteries also loose effectiveness with time. The issue of charge time can be resolved by swapping discharged batteries with charged ones, however this incurs additional hardware cost and may be impractical for larger batteries. Moreover, there would have to be standard batteries in order for battery swapping to work at a gas station. Fuel cells are similar to batteries in that they convert from chemical to electrical energy, but have their own set of advantages and disadvantages." (WK 2012d; BAT 2011; ELEC 2011; HOW 2011 & 2011a)

Secondly, another main criticism of this study on locomotion and energy is that energy conversion is not completely efficient.

For instance, for the critics, the case of fiction is a good example, because "all or almost all of the energy added by the engine is usually lost as friction; so minimising frictional losses are very important in many vehicles. The main sources of friction are rolling friction and fluid drag (air drag or water drag)." (WK 2012d)

And thirdly, still another main criticism of this study on locomotion and energy is that there are tradeoffs for each kind of engines or motors.

For instance, "most motor vehicles have internal combustion engines. They are fairly cheap, easy to maintain, reliable, safe, and small. Since IC engines burn fuel, they have long ranges but pollute the environment. A related engine is the external combustion engine. An example of this are steam engines. Aside from fuel, steam engines also need water, making them impractical for some purposes. Steam engines also need time to warm up, whereas IC engines can usually run right after being started, although this is not recommended in cold conditions. Steam engines burning coal release sulfer into the air causing harmful acid rain." (WK 2012d; KCE 2011)

Beyond Locomotion and Energy

However, these criticisms of the study on locomotion and energy do not entail a total rejection of its usefulness but serve to show us the two opposing sides of the debate, such that the possibility (or impossibility) and desirability (or undesirability) of networks (from the perspective of nature with networks, locomotion, and energy as a case study here) are not to the extent that the respective defenders would like us to believe.

In fact, the analysis of networks, locomotion, and energy reveals valuable info about the ontological principles in existential dialectics, and good examples include the formalness-informalness principle, the absoluteness-relativeness principle, the partiality-totality principle, the predictability-unpredictability principle, the explicability-inexplicability principle, the fiction-reality principle, the finiteness-transfiniteness principle, the preciseness-vagueness principle, the simpleness-complicatedness principle, the openness-hiddenness principle, the denseness-emptiness principle, the change-constancy principle, the order-chaos principle, the slowness-quickness principle, the expansion-contraction principle, the theory-praxis principle, the convention-novelty principle, the evolution-transformation principle, the symmetry-asymmetry principle, the softness-hardness principle, the seriousness-playfulness principle, the activeness-inactiveness principle, the regression-progression principle, the same-difference principle, and the stability-reaction principle.

For instance, in relation to the formalness-informalness principle, if there is formalness (e.g., the formal logical requirement of soundness in a system of ideas, as in the study on locomotion and energy), there is informalness (e.g., the non-formal existence of unsoundness in the study on locomotion and energy, as shown in the criticisms that that energy sources have disadvantages too, that energy conversion is not completely efficient, that there are tradeoffs for each kind of engines or motors, etc.). And the reverse direction also holds true.

In relation to the absoluteness-relativeness principle, if there is absoluteness (e.g., the absolute view that "the total kinetic energy of a system of objects [in transportation, for example] cannot be reduced to zero by a suitable choice of the inertial reference frame, unless all the objects have the same velocity"), there is relativeness (e.g., "the speed, and thus the kinetic energy of a single object is frame-dependent [relative]," as in the example that "a bullet [or vehicle] passing an observer has kinetic energy in the reference frame of this observer," but "the same bullet is stationary from the point of view of an observer moving with the same velocity as the bullet, and so has zero kinetic energy"). (WK 2012r; F. Sears 1968) And the reverse direction also holds true.

In relation to the partiality-totality principle, if there is partiality (e.g., the partial view of locomotion and energy if looked from the perspective of a single energy source and engine), there is totality (e.g., the more holistic view of locomotion and energy, such that the whole is not the sum of its parts, that is, it cannot be reduced to the sum of the opposing views in regard to energy sources, engines, and the conversion of energy to work in the article as cited, since there will emerge new views in the future not yet known today). And the reverse direction also holds true.

In relation to the predictability-unpredictability principle, if there is predictability (e.g., the predictable tendency of those in transportation nowadays to make good use of engines and motors like rocket engines, aircraft engines, electric motors, gas motors, and ion thrusters, for example), there is unpredictability (e.g., the more difficult task to predict exactly the extent to which the five types of engines and motors like rocket engines, aircraft engines, electric motors, gas motors, and ion thrusters will remain influential in a future particular era, since there will be ever new types of engines and motors to be invented for new environments later in history). And the reverse direction also holds true.

In relation to the explicability-inexplicability principle, if there is explicability (e.g., the explanation by those in the study of transportation that "all or almost all of the energy added by the engine is usually lost as friction"), there is inexplicability (e.g., the lack of sufficient explanation by those in the study of transportation of why friction is necessarily hard to overcome). And the reverse direction also holds true.

In relation to the fiction-reality principle, if there is fiction (e.g., the fictional aspect of the study of transportation, insofar as the disadvantages of energy sources are not adequately and seriously considered), there is reality (e.g., the realistic aspect of the study of transportation, insofar as there are advantages for each energy source). And the reverse direction also holds true.

In relation to the finiteness-transfiniteness principle, if there is finiteness (e.g., the finite number of ways to convert energy to work, like the use of wheels, tracks, nozzles, propellers, wings, etc.), there is transfiniteness (e.g., the transfinite number of all the units of work ever converted from energy in history). And the reverse direction also holds true.

In relation to the preciseness-vagueness principle, if there is preciseness (e.g., the precise identification of the five ways to convert energy to work, like the use of wheels, tracks, nozzles, propellers, wings, etc. in the article aforecited), there is vagueness (e.g., the vagueness in the identification of the five ways to convert energy to work, like the use of wheels, tracks, nozzles, propellers, wings, etc. in the article aforecited, since it is not clear why there must be only five, not 7, 11, 13, and so on). And the reverse direction also holds true.

In relation to the simpleness-complicatedness principle, if there is simpleness (e.g., the relatively simple analysis of locomtion and energy by the advocates), there is complicatedness (e.g., the relatively more complicated analysis of locomtion and energy, by challenging the claims and assumptions, as shown in the problems pointed out by the critics as cited). And the reverse direction also holds true.

In relation to the openness-hiddenness principle, if there is openness (e.g., the more open view of a car on the street), there is hiddenness (e.g., the more hidden view of a nuclear submarine deep under the sea). And the reverse direction also holds true.

In relation to the denseness-emptiness principle, if there is denseness (e.g., the relatively denser concentration of wheels used for transportation on earth nowadays), there is emptiness (e.g., the relatively less dense, or more empty, concentration of propellers used in space for transportation nowadays). And the reverse direction also holds true.

In relation to the change-constancy principle, if there is change (e.g., the ever new ways to understand transportation, as shown in the study on locomotion and energy), there is constancy (e.g., the ever constant existence of different problems in the ever new ways to understand transportation, as shown in the problems with locomotion and energy pointed out by the critics). And the reverse direction also holds true.

In relation to the order-chaos principle, if there is order (e.g., the more or less orderly view of rocket engines if examined from the observation that "rocket engines can be particularly simple, sometimes consisting of nothing more than a catalyst, as in the case of a hydrogen peroxide rocket"), there is chaos (e.g,. the more or less chaotic view of rocket engines if examined from the observation that they "are often dangerous and susceptible to explosions" and "the fuel they run off may be flammable, poisonous, corrosive, or cryogenic," with all kinds of uncertainty). (WK 2012d; HOW 2011c) And the reverse direction also holds true.

In relation to the slowness-quickness principle, if there is slowness (e.g., the relatively slower speed of a human-powered vehicle), there is quickness (e.g., the relatively quicker speed of a rocket like the Saturn V rocket). And the reverse direction also holds true.

In relation to the expansion-contraction principle, if there is expansion (e.g., the relative spread of the use of electrical energy for transportation nowadays, as seen in "electrified rails and overhead cables" for "subways, railways, trams, and trolleybuses"), there is contraction (e.g., the relative decline of the use of human-powered vehicles for transportation nowadays). And the reverse direction also holds true.

In relation to the theory-praxis principle, if there is theory (e.g., the theoretical construction of "nuclear energy" in physics), there is praxis (e.g., the practical application of "nuclear energy" to the field of transportation like the "experiments with nuclear powered aircraft" such as "the Tupolev Tu-119 and the Convair X-6"). And the reverse direction also holds true.

In relation to the convention-novelty principle, if there is convention (e.g., the conventional wisdom about using wheels for transportation in antiquity), there is novelty (e.g., the alternative novel challenge to the conventional wisdom about using wheels for transportation in antiquity, by the new idea of using nozzles for "jet aircraft," "rockets" and the like nowadays). And the reverse direction also holds true.

In relation to the evolution-transformation principle, if there is evolution (e.g., the natural evolution of humans to walk and run in the state of nature in a primitive way), there is transformation (e.g., the technical transformation of human ability to move around by the invention of a rocket like the Saturn V rocket). And the reverse direction also holds true.

In relation to the symmetry-asymmetry principle, if there is symmetry (e.g., the existence of different vehicles for transportation, like rockets and human-powered vehicles), there is asymmetry (e.g., rockets are more powerful than human-powered vehicles, because "the heaviest vehicle to ever leave the ground, the Saturn V rocket, was powered by five F-1 rocket engines generating a combined 180 million horsepower [134,226 megawatt]"). And the reverse direction also holds true.

In relation to the softness-hardness principle, if there is softness (e.g., the appreciation of rockets, as shown in the observation that "rocket engines are extremely powerful"), there is hardness (e.g., the critique of rockets, as shown in the observation that "rocket engines are often dangerous and susceptible to explosions"). And the reverse direction also holds true.

In relation to the seriousness-playfulness principle, if there is seriousness (e.g., the serious business of those engineers in transportation to explore new ways to convert energy to work), there is playfulness (e.g., the playful part of those engineers in transportation, when they play around with different creative ways to convert energy to work, like the use of "wheels," "tracks," "nozzles," "propellers," "wings, and so on, so as to see and test which ones work under what conditions better). And the reverse direction also holds true.

In relation to the activeness-inactiveness principle, if there is activeness (e.g., the activeness of vehicles which are in motion), there is inactiveness (e.g., the relative inactiveness of vehicles which break down and are at rest).

In relation to the regression-progression principle, if there is regression (e.g., the regression made by ion thrusters, as shown in the problems that "they are only effective in a vacuum, which limits their use to spaceborne vehicles"), there is progression (e.g., the progress made by ion thrusters, as shown in the benefits that "ion thrusters can achieve extremely high speeds and use little propellant"). And the reverse direction also holds true.

In relation to the same-difference principle, if there is similarity in outcome (e.g., the contribution to the molding and control of beliefs, values, and behaviors, regardless of whether this be done by way of using human energy, or by way of using nuclear energy), there is difference in outcome (e.g., the contribution to the molding and control of beliefs, values, and behaviors by way of using human energy for a relatively more naturalistic lifeworld—but the contribution to the molding and control of beliefs, values, and behaviors by way of using nuclear energy for a relatively more technophilic lifeworld). And the reverse direction also holds true.

And in relation to the stability-reaction principle, if there is stability (e.g., the relatively more stable condition of the use of human energy in the older days, when human-powered vehicles were more common in ancient times), there is reaction (e.g., the use of human energy in the older days then led to further changes later on, when nowadays there are the use of nuclear energy, electrical energy, etc.). And the reverse direction also holds true.

Networks, Spacecraft, and Outer Space

Another excellent case study here to understand networks from the perspective of nature has to do with networks, spacecraft, and outer space.

The term "spacecraft" (or "spaceship") refers to "a craft, vehicle, vessel or machine designed for spaceflight. Spacecraft are used for a variety of purposes, including communications, earth observation, meteorology, navigation, planetary exploration and transportation of humans and cargo." (WK 2012s)

Spacecraft is especially useful for spaceflight in "outer space," which is the "void that exists between celestial bodies, including the Earth." (WK 2012t; B. Dainton 2001)

Spaceflight can take different forms, and current technology allows primarily "sub-oribtal" and "orbital" spaceflights not far from the Earth.

For "sub-orbital" spaceflights—"a spacecraft enters space and then returns to the surface, without having gone into an orbit"; and for "orbital" spaceflights, "spacecraft enter closed orbits around the Earth or around other celestial bodies. Spacecraft used for human spaceflight carry people on board as crew or passengers from start or on orbit (space stations) only, while those used for robotic space missions operate either autonomously or telerobotically. Robotic spacecraft used to support scientific research are space probes. Robotic spacecraft that remain in orbit around a planetary body are artificial satellites. Only a handful of interstellar probes, such as Pioneer 10 and 11, Voyager 1 and 2, and New Horizons, are currently on trajectories that leave our Solar System." (WK 2012s)

In our times, "only a few nations have spaceflight technology," and, "as of 2012, only the U.S., Russia, and China have demonstrated human spaceflight capability." (WK 2012s)

History of Spacecraft

The history of spacecraft began with the Russian spacecraft known as "Спутник-1" (or "Satellite-1" in English), which "was the first artificial satellite. It was launched into an elliptical low Earth orbit by the Soviet Union on 4 October 1957. The launch ushered in new…technological, and scientific developments." (WK 2012s; A. Siddiqi.2003)

Even though "the Sputnik launch was a single event, it marked the start of the Space Age. Apart from its value as a technological first, *Sputnik* also helped to identify the upper atmospheric layer's density, through measuring the satellite's orbital changes. It also provided data on radio-signal distribution in the ionosphere. Pressurized nitrogen in the satellite's false body provided the first opportunity for meteoroid detection.

If a meteoroid penetrated the satellite's outer hull, it would be detected by the temperature data sent back to Earth. *Sputnik 1* was launched during the International Geophysical Year from Site No.1/5, at the 5th Tyuratam range, in Kazakh SSR (now at the Baikonur Cosmodrome). The satellite travelled at 29,000 kilometers (18,000 mi) per hour, taking 96.2 minutes to complete an orbit, and emitted radio signals at 20.005 and 40.002 MHz." (WK 2012s; W. McDougall 2010; L. Swenson 1966)

However, "while *Sputnik 1* was the first spacecraft to orbit the Earth, other man-made objects had previously reached an altitude of 100 km, which is the height required by the international organization Fédération Aéronautique Internationale to count as a spaceflight. This altitude is called the Kármán line. In particular, in the 1940s there were several test launches of the V-2 rocket, some of which reached altitudes well over 100 km." (WK 2012s)

Sub-Systems of Spacecraft

With this short introduction to the history of spacecraft in mind—there are several "subsystems" of a spacecraft to be understood, and these "spacecraft subsystems comprise the spacecraft 'bus' and may include: attitude determination and control (variously called ADAC, ADC or ACS), guidance, navigation and control (GNC or GN&C), communications (Comms), command and data handling (CDH or C&DH), power (EPS), thermal control (TCS), propulsion, and structures. Attached to the bus are typically payloads." (WK 2012s)

For illustration, consider the following eleven sub-systems (as summarized in *Table 2.3*): (WK 2012s; ESA 2004)

- "Life Support"—is vital for "spacecraft intended for human spaceflight," because it "must also include a life support system for the crew."
- "Attitude Control"—is important for "a Spacecraft…to be correctly oriented in space and respond[s] to external torques and forces properly. The attitude control subsystem consists of sensors and actuators, together with controlling algorithms. The attitude control subsystem permits proper pointing for the science objective, sun pointing for power to the solar arrays and earth-pointing for communications."
- Guidance, Navigation and Control"—has three terms. "Guidance refers to the calculation of the commands (usually done by the CDH subsystem) needed to steer the spacecraft where it is desired to be. Navigation means determining a spacecraft's orbital elements or

position. Control means adjusting the path of the spacecraft to meet mission requirements. On some missions, GNC and Attitude Control are combined into one subsystem of the spacecraft."

- "Command and Data Handling"—"receives commands from the communications subsystem, performs validation and decoding of the commands, and distributes the commands to the appropriate spacecraft subsystems and components. The CDH also receives housekeeping data and science data from the other spacecraft subsystems and components, and packages the data for storage on a data recorder or transmission to the ground via the communications subsystem. Other functions of the CDH include maintaining the spacecraft clock and state-of-health monitoring."
- "Power"—refers to "an electrical power generation and distribution subsystem for powering the various spacecraft subsystems. For spacecraft near the Sun, solar panels are frequently used to generate electrical power. Spacecraft designed to operate in more distant locations, for example Jupiter, might employ a Radioisotope Thermoelectric Generator (RTG) to generate electrical power. Electrical power is sent through power conditioning equipment before it passes through a power distribution unit over an electrical bus to other spacecraft components. Batteries are typically connected to the bus via a battery charge regulator, and the batteries are used to provide electrical power during periods when primary power is not available, for example when a Low Earth Orbit (LEO) spacecraft is eclipsed by the Earth."
- "Thermal Control"—"must be engineered to withstand transit through the Earth's atmosphere and the space environment. They must operate in a vacuum with temperatures potentially ranging across hundreds of degrees Celsius as well as (if subject to reentry) in the presence of plasmas. Material requirements are such that either high melting temperature, low density materials such as beryllium and reinforced carbon-carbon or (possibly due to the lower thickness requirements despite its high density) tungsten or ablative carbon/carbon composites are used. Depending on mission profile, spacecraft may also need to operate on the surface of another planetary body. The thermal control subsystem can be passive, dependent on the selection of materials with specific radiative properties. Active thermal control makes use of electrical heaters and certain actuators such as louvers to control temperature ranges of equipments within specific ranges."
- "Propulsion"—may be needed, "depending upon whether or not the mission profile calls for propulsion. The Swift spacecraft is an

example of a spacecraft that does not have a propulsion subsystem. Typically though, LEO spacecraft (for example Terra [EOS AM-1]) include a propulsion subsystem for altitude adjustments (called drag make-up maneuvers) and inclination adjustment maneuvers. A propulsion system is also needed for spacecraft that perform momentum management maneuvers. Components of a conventional propulsion subsystem include fuel, tankage, valves, pipes, and thrusters. The TCS interfaces with the propulsion subsystem by monitoring the temperature of those components, and by preheating tanks and thrusters in preparation for a spacecraft maneuver."

- "Structures"—"must be engineered to withstand launch loads imparted by the launch vehicle, and must have a point of attachment for all the other subsystems. Depending upon mission profile, the structural subsystem might need to withstand loads imparted by entry into the atmosphere of another planetary body, and landing on the surface of another planetary body."
- "Payload"—"is dependent upon the mission of the spacecraft, and is typically regarded as the part of the spacecraft 'that pays the bills.' Typical payloads could include scientific instruments (cameras, telescopes, or particle detectors, for example), cargo, or a human crew."
- "Ground Segment"—"is vital to the operation of the spacecraft. Typical components of a ground segment in use during normal operations include a mission operations facility where the flight operations team conducts the operations of the spacecraft, a data processing and storage facility, ground stations to radiate signals to and receive signals from the spacecraft, and a voice and data communications network to connect all mission elements."
- "Launch Vehicle"—"propels the spacecraft from the Earth's surface, through the atmosphere, and into an orbit, the exact orbit being dependent upon mission configuration. The launch vehicle may be expendable or reusable."

Of course, there can be other sub-systems too, so the ones above are illustrative, not exhaustive.

Types of Spacecraft

Spacecrafts, besides its various sub-systems, also have different types. In general, spacecrafts can be classified as either "manned" or "unmanned," as addressed below (and summarized in *Table 2.3*).

(a) Manned Spacecrafts

Currently, as of 2012, "only three nations have flown manned spacecraft: USSR/Russia, USA, and China," although "India, Japan, Europe/ESA, Iran, DPRK, Denmark, and Romania have plans for manned spacecraft (for manned suborbital rockets)." (WK 2012s)

Historically, "the first manned spacecraft was Vostok 1, which carried Soviet cosmonaut Yuri Gagarin into space in 1961, and completed a full Earth orbit. There were five other manned missions which used a Vostok spacecraft. The second manned spacecraft was named Freedom 7, and it performed a sub-orbital spaceflight in 1961 carrying American astronaut Alan Shepard to an altitude of just over 187 kilometres (116 mi). There were five other manned missions using Mercury spacecraft." (WK 2012s; ENA 2012)

Other manned spacecrafts from the Soviet Union include "the Voskhod, Soyuz, unflown as manned Zond/L1, L3, TKS, and the Salyut and Mir manned space stations. Other American manned spacecraft include the Gemini Spacecraft, Apollo Spacecraft, the Skylab space station, and the Space Shuttle with undetached European Spacelab and private US Spacehab space stations-modules. China developed unflown Shuguang and currently using Shenzhou (the first manned mission was in 2003)." (WK 2012s)

A more international spacecraft, known as "the International Space Station, manned since November 2000, is a joint venture between Russia, the United States, Canada and several other countries." (WK 2012s)

In addition, there are "some reusable vehicles" which "have been designed only for manned spaceflight, and these are often called spaceplanes. The first example of such was the North American X-15 spaceplane, which conducted two manned flights which reached a height over 100 km in the 1960s. The first reusable spacecraft, the X-15, was air-launched on a suborbital trajectory on July 19, 1963." (WK 2012s)

The spaceplane like "the first partially reusable orbital spacecraft, winged non-capsule, the Space Shuttle, was launched by the USA on the 20th anniversary of Yuri Gagarin's flight, on April 12, 1981. During the Shuttle era, six orbiters were built, all of which have flown in the atmosphere and five of which have flown in space. The Enterprise was used only for approach and landing tests, launching from the back of a Boeing 747 SCA and gliding to deadstick landings at Edwards AFB, California. The first Space Shuttle to fly into space was the Columbia, followed by the Challenger, Discovery, Atlantis, and Endeavour." (WK 2012s)

Other spaceplanes are automatic, like "the first automatic partially reusable spacecraft" known as "the Buran (Snowstorm), launched by the USSR on November 15, 1988, although it made only one flight. This spaceplane was designed for a crew and strongly resembled the U.S. Space Shuttle, although its drop-off boosters used liquid propellants and its main engines were located at the base of what would be the external tank in the American Shuttle." (WK 2012s)

And "XCOR Aerospace…plans to initiate a suborbital commercial spaceflight service with the Lynx rocketplane in 2012 through a partnership with RocketShip Tours." (WK 2012s)

(b) Unmanned Spacecrafts

On the other hand, the unmanned spacecrafts come in all shapes and sizes too. Consider, for illustration, the following examples: (WK 2012s)

- "Designed as Manned but Flown as Unmanned only Spacecraft"
  - -Ex: "Zond/L1–lunar flyby capsule"
  - -Ex: "L3 –capsule and lunar lander"
  - -Ex: "TKS–capsule"
  - -Ex: "Buran Soviet shuttle"
- "Semi-Manned—Manned as Space Stations or Part of Space Stations"
  - -Ex: "Progress–unmanned USSR/Russia cargo spacecraft"
  - -Ex: "TKS–unmanned USSR/Russia cargo spacecraft"
  - -Ex: "Automated Transfer Vehicle" –"European cargo spacecraft"
- "Earth Orbit satellites"
  - -Ex: "Explorer 1–first US satellite"
  - -Ex: "Project SCORE–first communications satellite"
  - -Ex: "Sputnik 1–world's first artificial satellite"
  - -Ex: "Sputnik 5–first capsule recovered from orbit"
  - -Ex: "Syncom–first geosynchronous communications satellite"
  - -Ex: "Hubble Space Telescope–biggest orbital observatory"
- "Lunar Probes"
  - -Ex: "Luna 1–first lunar flyby"
  - -Ex: "Luna 2–first lunar impact"
  - -Ex: "Luna 3–first images of lunar far side"
  - -Ex: "Luna 9–first soft landing on the Moon"
  - -Ex: "Luna 10–first lunar orbiter"
  - -Ex: "Luna 16–first unmanned lunar sample retrieval"
  - -Ex: "Surveyor–first US soft lander"
- "Planetary Probes"
  - -Ex: "Cassini-Huygens–first Saturn orbiter+Titan lander"
  - -Ex: "Galileo–first Jupiter orbiter+descent probe"

-Ex: "IKAROS JPN–first solar-sail spacecraft"
-Ex: "Mariner 4–first Mars flyby"
-Ex: "Mariner 9–first Mars orbiter"
-Ex: "Mariner 10–first Mercury flyby, first close up images"
-Ex: "Mars Exploration Rover–a Mars rover"
-Ex: "MESSENGER–first Mercury orbiter (arrival 2011)"
-Ex: "New Horizons–first Pluto flyby (arrival 2015)"
-Ex: "Pioneer 10–first Jupiter flyby, first close up images"
-Ex: "Pioneer Venus–first Venus orbiter+landers"
-Ex: "Venera 4–first soft landing on another planet (Venus)"
-Ex: "Viking 1–first soft landing on Mars"
-Ex: "Voyager 2–first flybys/images of Neptune and Uranus"

- "Other–Deep Space"
  -Ex: "Cluster"
  -Ex: "Deep Space 1"
  -Ex: "Deep Impact"
  -Ex: "Genesis"
  -Ex: "Hayabusa"
  -Ex: "Near Earth Asteroid Rendezvous"
  -Ex: "Stardust"
- "Furthest Spacecraft from the Sun"
  -Ex: "Pioneer 10 at 89.7 AU as of 2005, traveling outward at about 2.6 AU/year"
  -Ex: "Voyager 1 at 106.3 AU as of July 2008, traveling outward at about 3.6 AU/year"
  -Ex: "Voyager 2 at 85.49 AU as of July 2008, traveling outward at about 3.3 AU/year"

Needless to say, there can be other examples too, so the ones above are illustrative, not exhaustive.

Problems with the Study on Spacecraft

However, for the critics, this study on spacecraft has some major problems. Consider, for illustration, a few examples below (as summarized in *Table 2.3*).

Firstly, one main criticism of this study on spacecraft is that the history of spacecraft has been driven by ideology and politics too.

For example, the Sputnik launch started the beginning of the space race between the Soviet Union and the U.S. in their competition for global domination during the Cold War.

Secondly, another main criticism of this study on spacecraft is that it is both technologically challenging and financially costly to build spacecrafts.

For instance, currently, only the three most powerful countries on earth, namely, the U.S., Russia, and China, to "have spaceflight technology" and "have demonstrated human spaceflight capability." (WK 2012s) Even for these powers, things did not always go well; for instance, "lack of funding, complicated by the dissolution of the USSR, prevented any further flights of Buran," the Soviet version of the space shuttle—while the American version of the space shuttle "was retired in 2011 due mainly to its old age and high cost of program reaching over a billion dollars per flight." (WK 2012s)

And thirdly, still another main criticism of this study on spacecraft is that spacecrafts, like other transports, are not immune from accidents or disasters.

For instance, the space shuttle "Challenger…was lost in January 1986," and the other one "Columbia broke up during reentry in February 2003." (WK 2012s)

Beyond Spacecraft

However, these criticisms of the study on spacecraft and outer space should not be taken as a total rejection of its usefulness but serve to show us the two opposing sides of the two opposing sides of the debate, such that the possibility (or impossibility) and desirability (or undesirability) of networks (from the perspective of nature with networks, spacecraft, and outer space as a case study here) are not to the extent that the respective defenders would like us to believe.

Furthermore, the analysis of networks, spacecraft, and outer space can cast a bright light on the ontological principles in existential dialectics, and good examples include the formalness-informalness principle, the absoluteness-relativeness principle, the partiality-totality principle, the predictability-unpredictability principle, the explicability-inexplicability principle, the fiction-reality principle, the finiteness-transfiniteness principle, the preciseness-vagueness principle, the simpleness-complicatedness principle, the openness-hiddenness principle, the denseness-emptiness principle, the change-constancy principle, the order-chaos principle, the slowness-quickness principle, the expansion-contraction principle, the theory-praxis principle, the convention-novelty principle, the evolution-transformation principle, the symmetry-asymmetry principle, the softness-hardness principle, the seriousness-playfulness principle, the activeness-inactiveness principle, the regression-

progression principle, the same-difference principle, and the stability-reaction principle.

For instance, in relation to the formalness-informalness principle, if there is formalness (e.g., the formal logical requirement of soundness and completeness in a system of ideas, as in the study on spacecraft), there is informalness (e.g., the non-formal existence of unsoundness and incompleteness in the study on spacecraft, as shown in the criticisms that its history has been driven by ideology and politics too, that it is both technologically challenging and financially costly to build spacecrafts, that spacecrafts, like other transports, are not immune from accidents or disasters, etc.). And the reverse direction also holds true.

In relation to the absoluteness-relativeness principle, if there is absoluteness (e.g., the absolute view of those on each side of the superpower rivalry in the space race during the Cold War), there is relativeness (e.g., what was glorious for the Soviet Union to launch Sputnik in 1957 was not necessarily so for the U.S. who entered the space race to compete with its superpower rival). And the reverse direction also holds true.

In relation to the partiality-totality principle, if there is partiality (e.g., the partial view of a superpower during the Cold War to win the space race), there is totality (e.g., the more holistic view of the future of spaceflight, such that the whole is not the sum of its parts, that is, it cannot be reduced to the sum of opposing views like those held by the Soviet Union and the United States during the Cold War, since there will emerge new views in the future not yet known today, besides the fact that there were already other views like the international space cooperation as shown in the building of "the International Space Station"). And the reverse direction also holds true.

In relation to the predictability-unpredictability principle, if there is predictability (e.g., the predictable tendency of only the major powers like Russia, the U.S., and China to engaged in "human spaceflights" in the foreseeable future), there is unpredictability (e.g., the more difficult task to predict exactly the extent to which each particular space program by each of the space powers will last or remain influential in a particular future era, since no one foresaw that "lack of funding, complicated by the dissolution of the USSR, prevented any further flights of Buran" and "the American version of the space shuttle "was retired in 2011 due mainly to its old age and high cost of program reaching over a billion dollars per flight"). And the reverse direction also holds true.

In relation to the explicability-inexplicability principle, if there is explicability (e.g., the explanation by those on each side of the two superpowers during the Cold War to argue for the space race), there is inexplicability (e.g., the lack of sufficient explanation by those on each side of the two superpowers during the Cold War of why the space race is necessarily desirable, in light of the financial and human costs involved for the glory of the superpowers at the time, with the benefit of historical hindsight, while each side had huge socioeconomic problems at home). And the reverse direction also holds true.

In relation to the fiction-reality principle, if there is fiction (e.g., the fictional aspect of the space race, insofar as it was driven by politics and ideology in the competition for global domination and glory between the two superpowers during the Cold War), there is reality (e.g., the realistic aspect of the space race, insofar as it had contributed to "technological, and scientific developments" of space exploration). And the reverse direction also holds true.

In relation to the finiteness-transfiniteness principle, if there is finiteness (e.g., the finite number of the categories of celestial bodies for spacecrafts to explore, like moons, planets, solar systems, etc.), there is transfiniteness (e.g., the transfinite number of all the possible individual moons, planets, solar systems, etc. in the universe for spacecrafts to explore). And the reverse direction also holds true.

In relation to the preciseness-vagueness principle, if there is preciseness (e.g., the precise identification of 11 sub-systems of a spacecraft systems in the article aforecited, like "life support," "attitude control," "power," etc.), there is vagueness (e.g., the vagueness in the identification of the 11 sub-systems of a spacecraft systems in the article aforecited, like "life support," "attitude control," "power," etc., since it is not clear why there must be only 11, not 13, 15, 16, 20, and so on). And the reverse direction also holds true.

In relation to the simpleness-complicatedness principle, if there is simpleness (e.g., the relatively simple analysis of the history of spacecraft by its advocates), there is complicatedness (e.g., the relatively more complicated analysis of the history of spacecraft, by challenging the claims and assumptions, as shown in the problems pointed out by the critics as cited). And the reverse direction also holds true.

In relation to the openness-hiddenness principle, if there is openness (e.g., the open exploration of the moon, Mars, Jupiter, Saturn, Venus, etc. by different human spacecrafts in the last few decades), there is hiddenness (e.g., the hidden nature of many other moons and planets in the universe not yet explored by human spacecrafts). And the reverse direction also holds true.

In relation to the denseness-emptiness principle, if there is denseness (e.g., the relatively denser concentration of human spacecrafts in earth orbit, since, "as of June 2011, there are more than 2,000 spacecraft in orbit"), there is emptiness (e.g., the relatively less dense, or more empty, concentration of human spacecrafts in the orbit of Neptune, as of June 2011). And the reverse direction also holds true.

In relation to the change-constancy principle, if there is change (e.g., the ever new ways to design transports, as shown in the study on spacecrafts), there is constancy (e.g., the ever constant existence of different problems in the ever new ways to design transports, as shown in the problems with the history of spacecrafts pointed out by the critics aforecited). And the reverse direction also holds true.

In relation to the order-chaos principle, if there is order (e.g., the more or less orderly reality of spacecrafts, if examined from the vantage point of all the successful spaceflights in the last few decades), there is chaos (e.g,. the more or less chaotic reality of spacecrafts, if examined from the vantage point of all the disastrous spaceflights in the last few decades, as shown in the failures when "the space shuttle "Challenger…was lost in January 1986," and the other one "Columbia broke up during reentry in February 2003"). And the reverse direction also holds true.

In relation to the slowness-quickness principle, if there is slowness (e.g., the relatively slower speed of "human powered vehicles" which can travel up to "133 km/h [83 mph], as of 2009"), there is quickness (e.g., the relatively quicker speed of Sputnik which "travelled at 29,000 kilometers [18,000 mi] per hour, taking 96.2 minutes to complete an orbit" in 1957). (WK 2012d & 2012s) And the reverse direction also holds true.

In relation to the expansion-contraction principle, if there is expansion (e.g., the relative spread of the use of spacecrafts in the last few decades), there is contraction (e.g., the relative decline of the use of pulled rickshaws inte last few decades). And the reverse direction also holds true.

In relation to the theory-praxis principle, if there is theory (e.g., the theoretical construction of rockets and aircrafts in rocket science), there is praxis (e.g., the practical application of rockets and aircrafts in rocket science to the field of politics, like the space race between the two superpowers during the Cold War). And the reverse direction also holds true.

In relation to the convention-novelty principle, if there is convention (e.g., the conventional wisdom of using cars for transportation in modern times), there is novelty (e.g., the alternative novel challenge to the conventional wisdom about using cars for transportation in modern times, by the new idea of using spaceplanes nowadays, like the proposal by

"XCOR Aerospace…to initiate a suborbital commercial spaceflight service" in the foreseeable future). And the reverse direction also holds true.

In relation to the evolution-transformation principle, if there is evolution (e.g., the natural evolution of humans to move around on foot in the state of nature in a primitive way), there is transformation (e.g., the technical transformation of human ability to move around by the invention of spacecrafts). And the reverse direction also holds true.

In relation to the symmetry-asymmetry principle, if there is symmetry (e.g., the existence of different ways to fly, like helicopters and spacecrafts), there is asymmetry (e.g., spacecrafts can fly much higher and faster than helicopters). And the reverse direction also holds true.

In relation to the softness-hardness principle, if there is softness (e.g., the appreciation of spacecrafts by the Soviet Union and the U.S. in their space race during the Cold War), there is hardness (e.g., the critique of spacecrafts by the critics, in regard to the vanity and glory behind the space race, while there were so many different socioeconomic problems at home). And the reverse direction also holds true.

In relation to the seriousness-playfulness principle, if there is seriousness (e.g., the serious business of those in designing spacecrafts), there is playfulness (e.g., the playful part of those in designing spacecrafts, when they play around with different designs, like the Soviet "Spiral Shuttle, the Chinese "Shuguang Project 921-3 shuttle," and the American "Lockheed-Martin VentureStar," etc., all of which were later cancelled, for different reasons). (WK 2012s) And the reverse direction also holds true.

In relation to the activeness-inactiveness principle, if there is activeness (e.g., the activeness of spacecrafts which function well in accordance to its planned mission), there is inactiveness (e.g., the relative inactiveness of spacecrafts which are out of order and do not work).

In relation to the regression-progression principle, if there is regression (e.g., the regression made by spacecrafts, as shown in the problems pointed out by the critics aforecited), there is progression (e.g., the progress made by spacecrafts, as shown in the successful spaceflights aforecited). And the reverse direction also holds true.

In relation to the same-difference principle, if there is similarity in outcome (e.g., the contribution to the molding and control of beliefs, values, and behaviors, regardless of whether this be done by way of engaging in the space race by the two superpowers during the Cold War, or by way of participating in the joint venture like "the International Space Station" among Russia, the U.S., and others nowadays), there is difference in outcome (e.g., the contribution to the molding and control of beliefs, values, and behaviors by way of engaging in the space race for a relatively more competitive lifeworld—but the contribution to the molding and control of beliefs, values, and behaviors by way of participating in the joint venture like "the International Space Station" for a relatively more cooperative lifeworld). And the reverse direction also holds true.

And in relation to the stability-reaction principle, if there is stability (e.g., the relatively more stable condition of the old glory days of the automobile, when cars were more and more used in modern times), there is reaction (e.g., the old glory days of the automobile then led to further changes later on, when the space race has opened up new doors to the use of spacecrafts, including those for commercial use). And the reverse direction also holds true.

Networks and Society

Networks, when examined from the perspective of society, can illuminate their possibility (or impossibility) and desirability (or undesirability), and this can be shown by way of two case studies, namely, (2.4.1) networks, vehicles, and the automobile industry, and (2.4.2) networks, future cars, and technology—to be addressed hereafter.

Networks, Vehicles, and the Automobile Industry

A good case study here to understand networks from the perspective of society has to do with networks, vehicles, and the automobile industry.

The term "automotive industry" refers to an industry which "designs, develops, manufactures, markets, and sells motor vehicles, and is one of the world's most important economic sectors by revenue." (WK 2012u)

However, the term "automotive industry" generally "does not include industries dedicated to automobiles after delivery to the customer, such as repair shops and motor fuel filling stations." (WK 2012u)

History of the Automobile Industry

Historically, "the first practical automobile with a petrol engine was built by Karl Benz in 1885 in Mannheim, Germany. Benz was granted a patent for his automobile on 29 January 1886, and began the first production of automobiles in 1888, after Bertha Benz, his wife, had proved with the first long-distance trip in August 1888 (104 km [65 mi] from Mannheim to Pforzheim and back) that the horseless coach was absolutely suitable for daily use. Since 2008 a Bertha Benz Memorial Route commemorates this event." (WK 2012u)

After that, "in 1889, Gottlieb Daimler and Wilhelm Maybach in Stuttgart designed a vehicle from scratch to be an automobile, rather than a horse-drawn carriage fitted with an engine. They also are usually credited as inventors of the first motorcycle, the Daimler Reitwagen, in 1885, but Italy's Enrico Bernardi, of the University of Padua, in 1882, patented a 0.024 horsepower (17.9 W) 122 cc (7.4 cu in) one-cylinder petrol motor, fitting it into his son's tricycle, making it at least a candidate for the first automobile, and first motorcycle. Bernardi enlarged the tricycle in 1892 to carry two adults." (WK 2012u; G. Georgano 1985)

But for much of the 20th century, it was the U.S.A. which, until 2005, "led the world in total automobile production. In 1929 before the Great Depression, the world had 32,028,500 automobiles in use, and the US automobile industry produced over 90% of them. At that time the U.S. had one car per 4.87 persons. In 2006, Japan narrowly passed the U.S. in production and held this rank until 2009, when China took the top spot with 13.8 million units. By producing 18.3 million units in 2010, China produced nearly twice the number of second place Japan (9.6 million units), with the U.S. in third place with 7.8 million units." (WK 2012u; PSM 1929; OICA 2011)

Production of the Automobile Industry

As the figures above show, the automobile industry has spread around the world, and in 2007, "there were about 806 million cars and light trucks on the road…, consuming over 260 billion US gallons (980,000,000 m^3) of gasoline and diesel fuel yearly. The automobile is a primary mode of transportation for many developed economies." (WK 2012u; PR 2008)

By 2014, "the Detroit branch of Boston Consulting Group predicts that…one-third of world demand will be in the four BRIC markets (Brazil, Russia, India and China)." (WK 2012u)

Other potentially big automotive markets include "Iran and Indonesia. Emerging auto markets already buy more cars than established markets. According to a J.D. Power study, emerging markets accounted for 51 percent of the global light-vehicle sales in 2010. The study expects this trend to accelerate." (WK 2012u; P. Eisenstein 2010; B. Schmitt 2011)

Hereafter is a list of the "top 20 motor vehicle producing countries" in 2010: (WK 2012u; OICA 2011)

Country	*Motor Vehicle Production (Units)*
• China	18,264,667

• Japan	9,605,985
• U.S.A.	7,761,443
• Germany	5,905,985
• South Korea	4,271,941
• Brazil	3,648,358
• India	3,536,783
• Spain	2,387,900
• Mexico	2,345,124
• France	2,227,742
• Canada	2,071,026
• Thailand	1,644,513
• Iran	1,599,454
• Russia	1,403,244
• UK	1,393,463
• Turkey	1,097,554
• Czech Rep.	1,076,385
• Poland	869,736
• Italy	857,359

And hereafter is a list of the top 20 "motor vehicle manufacturing companies by volume" in 2010: (WK 2012u; OICA 2011a)

Companies	*Total Motor vehicle production (Units)*
• Toyota	8,557,351
• GM	8,476,192
• Volkswagen	7,341,065
• Hyundai Motor	5,764,918
• Ford	4,988,031
• Nissan	3,982,162
• Honda	3,643,057
• PSA	3,605,524
• Suzuki	2,892,945
• Renault	2,716,286
• Fiat	2,410,021
• Daimler AG	1,940,465
• Chrysler	1,578,488
• BMW	1,481,253
• Mazda	1,307,540
• Mitsubishi	1,174,383
• Chana Automobile	1,102,683
• Tata	1,011,343

- FAW 896,060
- Geely 802,319

Surely, these numbers are only for the year 2010, so the ranking may change in a different year.

Relations in the Automobile Industry

It is also important to note that "automobile manufacturers" often "hold stakes in other automobile manufacturers. These ownerships can be explored under the detail for the individual companies." (WK 2012u)

For illustration, hereafter are some good examples of "current relationships" in the automobile industry so understood: (WK 2012u)

- "Daimler AG"—"holds a 20% stake in Eicher Motors, a 10.0% stake in KAMAZ, a 10% stake in Tesla Motors, a 6.75% stake in Tata Motors and a 3.1% in the Renault-Nissan Motors alliance. They are in the process of selling back their 40% stake (11% remaining) in McLaren Group. This process will be finalized in 2011."
- "Dongfeng Motor Corporation"—"is involved in joint ventures with several companies around the world, including: Honda (Japan), Hyundai (South Korea), Nissan (Japan), Nissan Diesel (Sweden), and PSA Peugeot Citroen (France)."
- "Fiat"—"holds a 90% stake in Ferrari and a 58.5% stake in Chrysler."
- "Ford Motor Company"—"holds a 3% stake in Mazda and an 8.3% share in Aston Martin."
- "Geely Automobile"—"holds a 23% stake in Manganese Bronze Holdings."
- "General Motors and Shanghai Automotive Industry Corporation (SAIC)"—"have two joint ventures in Shanghai General Motors and SAIC-GM-Wuling Automobile."
- "Hyundai Kia Automotive Group"—"holds a 49.20% stake in Kia Motors (July 2011), that up from a previous 38,67%, but down from the 51% that it acquired in 1998."
- "MAN SE"—"holds a 17.01% voting stake in Scania."
- "Porsche Automobil Holding SE"—"has a 50.74% stake in Volkswagen Group. Due to liquidity problems, Volkswagen Group is now in the process of acquiring Porsche."
- "Renault and Nissan Motors"—"have an alliance involving two global companies linked by cross-shareholding, with Renault holding 44.3% of Nissan shares, and Nissan holding 15% of (non-voting) Renault shares. The alliance holds a 3.1% share in Daimler AG."

- "Renault"—"holds a 25% stake in AvtoVAZ and 20.5% of the voting stakes in Volvo Group."
- "Toyota"—"holds a 51% stake in Daihatsu, and 16.5% in Fuji Heavy Industries, parent company of Subaru."
- "Volkswagen Group"—"holds a 37.73% stake in Scania (68.6% voting rights), and a 53.7% stake in MAN SE (55.9% voting rights). Volkswagen is integrating Scania, MAN and its own truck division into one division."
- "Volkswagen Group"—"has a 49.9% stake in Porsche AG. Volkswagen is in the process of acquiring Porsche, which will be completed in late 2011."
- "Volkswagen Group"—"has a 19.9% stake in Suzuki, and Suzuki has a 5% stake in Volkswagen."

Of course, the examples above are illustrative, not exhaustive.

Problems with the Study on the Automobile Industry

However, for the critics, this study on the automobile industry has some major problems. Consider, for illustration, a few examples below.

Firstly, one main criticism of this study on the automobile industry is that the industry has also contributed to considerable economic costs around the world.

For example, "the global economic cost of MVCs [motor vehicle collisions] was estimated at $518 billion per year in 2003 with $100 billion of that occurring in developing countries. The Center for Disease Control and Prevention estimated the U.S. cost in 2000 at $230 billion." (WK 2012v; UN 2003; CDCP 2011)

Secondly, another main criticism of this study on the automobile industry is that the industry has a destructive impact on society too.

For instance, Jay Holtz Kay (1998) forcefully argued that, with the automobile industry as an example, "the modern consequences of heavy automotive use contribute to the use of non-renewable fuels…, social isolation, the disconnection of community, the rise in obesity, the generation of air and noise pollution, urban sprawl, and urban decay." (WK 2012)

Thirdly, still another main criticism of this study on the automobile industry is that the use of the automobile can be so addictive as to become "automobile-dependent."

For instance, Peter Newman and Jeff Kenworthy used the term "automobile dependency" to show that "cities where automobiles are the predominant transport deny their residents not only freedom of choice about the way they live and move around the city, but also that the culture of automobile use has produced a kind of addiction to them. The analogy is made with addictions to harmful substances and activities because of the well-known law of diminishing returns in relation to increasing use or participation: the more that is used, the less of the desired effect is gained until a point is reached where the substance or activity has to be maintained to remain 'normal', a state of dependency." (WK 2012j)

And fourthly, an additional main criticism of this study on the automobile industry is that it also ignores the negative legal consequences for both individuals and society.

For instance, in regard to individuals, "drivers who are involved in a collision frequently receive one or more traffic citations, usually directly addressing any material violations such as speeding, failure to obey a traffic control device, or driving under the influence of drugs or alcohol. In the event of a fatality, a charge of vehicular homicide is occasionally prosecuted, especially in cases involving alcohol." (WK 2012v) And in regard to society, "due to increase in availability of cable news and Internet news, exposure to such legal actions has increased in recent years, specifically with coverage of cases and class action suits concerning SUV rollovers and recent incidents of sudden acceleration crashes highlighted by the 2010 Toyota Recall. Increased exposure has led to larger class action suits," such that society becomes more addicted to lawsuits for dispute resolution. (WK 2012v)

Beyond the Automobile Industry

However, these criticisms of the study on the automobile industry do not mean to imply a total rejection of its usefulness but serve to show us the two opposing sides of the debate, such that the possibility (or impossibility) and desirability (or undesirability) of networks (from the perspective of society with networks, vehicles, and the automobile industry as a case study here) are not to the extent that the respective defenders would like us to believe.

In addition, the analysis of networks, vehicles, and the automobile industry can teach us something valuable about the ontological principles in existential dialectics, and good examples include the formalness-informalness principle, the absoluteness-relativeness principle, the partiality-totality principle, the predictability-unpredictability principle, the explicability-inexplicability principle, the fiction-reality principle, the finiteness-transfiniteness principle, the preciseness-vagueness principle, the simpleness-complicatedness principle, the openness-hiddenness principle, the denseness-emptiness principle, the change-constancy principle, the order-chaos principle, the slowness-quickness principle, the expansion-contraction principle, the theory-praxis principle, the convention-novelty principle, the evolution-transformation principle, the symmetry-asymmetry principle, the softness-hardness principle, the seriousness-playfulness principle, the activeness-inactiveness principle, the regression-progression principle, the same-difference principle, and the stability-reaction principle.

For instance, in relation to the formalness-informalness principle, if there is formalness (e.g., the formal logical requirement of soundness and completeness in a system of ideas, as in the study on the automobile industry), there is informalness (e.g., the non-formal existence of unsoundness and incompleteness in the study on the automobile industry, as shown in the criticisms that the industry has also contributed to considerable economic costs around the world, that the industry has a destructive impact on society too, that the use of the automobile can be so addictive as to become "automobile-dependent," that the study also ignores the negative legal consequences for both individuals and society, etc.). And the reverse direction also holds true.

In relation to the absoluteness-relativeness principle, if there is absoluteness (e.g., the absolute view of those car manufacturers to make more cars for profits), there is relativeness (e.g., what is good for those car manufacturers to make more cars for profits is not necessarily so for the critics like Jay Holtz Kay, who forcefully argued that, with the automobile industry as an example, "the modern consequences of heavy automotive use contribute to the use of non-renewable fuels…, social isolation, the disconnection of community, the rise in obesity, the generation of air and noise pollution, urban sprawl, and urban decay"). And the reverse direction also holds true.

In relation to the partiality-totality principle, if there is partiality (e.g., the partial view of the automobile industry in the old "glory days"), there is totality (e.g., the more holistic view of the automobile industry, such that the whole is not the sum of its parts, that is, it cannot be reduced to the sum of opposing views like its proponents, the critics, etc., since no one exactly foresaw, for instance, "the modern consequences of heavy automotive use" like the massive "use of non-renewable fuels, a dramatic increase in the rate of accidental death, social isolation, the disconnection of community, the rise in obesity, the generation of air and noise pollution, urban sprawl, and urban decay," just as there will emerge new views in the future not yet known today). And the reverse direction also holds true.

In relation to the predictability-unpredictability principle, if there is predictability (e.g., the predictable tendency of the top three motor vehicle producing countries in the next few years to be China, Japan, and the U.S.), there is unpredictability (e.g., the more difficult task to predict exactly the extent to which these three countries will continue to dominate the motor vehicle production in the farther future, just as no one predicted during the Great Degression that the U.S. would one day drop to number three, when at that time "the US automobile industry produced over 90%" of the motor vehicles worldwide). And the reverse direction also holds true.

In relation to the explicability-inexplicability principle, if there is explicability (e.g., the explanation by the proponents of the automobile industry that it is desirable to spread the use of the automobile), there is inexplicability (e.g., the lack of sufficient explanation by the proponents of the automobile industry of why it is necessarily desirable to spread the use of the automobile, since, for the critics like Peter Newman and Jeff Kenworthy, the automobile industry has contributed to "automobile dependency," in that "cities where automobiles are the predominant transport deny their residents not only freedom of choice about the way they live and move around the city, but also that the culture of automobile use has produced a kind of addiction to them"). And the reverse direction also holds true.

In relation to the fiction-reality principle, if there is fiction (e.g., the fictional aspect of the old "glory days" of the automobile, insofar as the negative consequences were ignored, as shown in the criticisms that it has also contributed to considerable economic costs around the world, that it has a destructive impact on society too, that the use of the automobile can be so addictive as to become "automobile-dependent," that it also ignores the negative legal consequences for both individuals and society, etc.), there is reality (e.g., the realistic aspect of the old "glory days" of the automobile, insofar as the automobile has contributed to the convenience of transporation in modern times). And the reverse direction also holds true.

In relation to the finiteness-transfiniteness principle, if there is finiteness (e.g., the finite number of the types of cars produced in the last few decades), there is transfiniteness (e.g., the transfinite number of all the gallons of gasoline consumed by cars produced in the last few decades, since it was estimated that, in 2007 alone, more than "806 million cars and light trucks on the road…consum[ed]…over 260 billion US gallons"). And the reverse direction also holds true.

In relation to the preciseness-vagueness principle, if there is preciseness (e.g., the precise identification of the top 20 "motor vehicle manufacturing companies by volume" in 2010 in the article aforecited), there is vagueness (e.g., the vagueness in the identification of the top 20 "motor vehicle manufacturing companies by volume" in 2010 in the article aforecited, since it is not clear why there must be only 20 on the list, not 21, 24, 25, 30, and so on). And the reverse direction also holds true.

In relation to the simpleness-complicatedness principle, if there is simpleness (e.g., the relatively simple analysis of the automobile industry by its advocates), there is complicatedness (e.g., the relatively more complicated analysis of the automobile industry, by challenging the claims and assumptions, as shown in the problems pointed out by the critics as cited). And the reverse direction also holds true.

In relation to the openness-hiddenness principle, if there is openness (e.g., the open exploration of the relationship between the automobile and its convenience for transportation in modern life), there is hiddenness (e.g., the hidden bias in the view about the relationship between the automobile and its convenience for transportation in modern life, since, for the critics, there are the serious hidden costs, in that it has also contributed to considerable economic costs around the world, that it has a destructive impact on society too, that the use of the automobile can be so addictive as to become "automobile-dependent," that it also ignores the negative legal consequences for both individuals and society, etc.). And the reverse direction also holds true.

In relation to the denseness-emptiness principle, if there is denseness (e.g., the relatively denser concentration of automobiles on the road nowadays), there is emptiness (e.g., the relatively less dense, or more empty, concentration of horses on the road nowadays). And the reverse direction also holds true.

In relation to the change-constancy principle, if there is change (e.g., the ever new ways to build transports, as shown in the study on the automobile industry), there is constancy (e.g., the ever constant existence of different problems in the ever new ways to build transports, as shown in the problems with the study on the automobile industry pointed out by the critics). And the reverse direction also holds true.

In relation to the order-chaos principle, if there is order (e.g., the more or less orderly reality of the automobile industry, insofar as it shows the ranking of the top 20 "motor vehicle manufacturing companies by volume" in 2010), there is chaos (e.g,. the more or less chaotic reality of the automobile industry, insofar as it is embedded within some highly complex relationships among "automobile manufacturers," such that they "hold stakes in other automobile manufacturers" in different ways, as shown in the examples aforecited). And the reverse direction also holds true.

In relation to the slowness-quickness principle, if there is slowness (e.g., the relatively slower speed of the U.S. in the automible industry to lose its #1 ranking, that is, from 1929 to 2005, when it lost the top spot to Japan), there is quickness (e.g., the relatively quicker speed of Japan in the automible industry to lose its #1 ranking, that is, from 2006 to 2009, when it lost the top spot to Chin). And the reverse direction also holds true.

In relation to the expansion-contraction principle, if there is expansion (e.g., the relative rise of China as the top car manufacturer in the world nowadays), there is contraction (e.g., the relative decline of the U.S. as the #3 car manufacturer in the world nowadays). And the reverse direction also holds true.

In relation to the theory-praxis principle, if there is theory (e.g., the theoretical exploration of "gasoline" as "organic compounds obtained by the fractional distillation of petroleum, enhanced with a variety of additives" in the field of chemistry), there is praxis (e.g., the practical application of gasoline in chemistry to the field of transportation, like its use by the automobile industry). And the reverse direction also holds true.

In relation to the convention-novelty principle, if there is convention (e.g., the conventional way of building a practical automobile when Karl Benz in the early 1880s build "a horse-drawn carriage"), there is novelty (e.g., the alternative novel challenge to the conventional way of building a practical automobile like Benz's "horse-drawn carriage," by the new idea of a better automobile when "in 1889, Gottlieb Daimler and Wilhelm Maybach in Stuttgart designed a vehicle from scratch to be an automobile, rather than a horse-drawn carriage fitted with an engine"). And the reverse direction also holds true.

In relation to the evolution-transformation principle, if there is evolution (e.g., the natural evolution of humans to walk and run in the state of nature), there is transformation (e.g., the technical transformation of human ability to move around by the invention of the automobile and the industry to produce it in large numbers). And the reverse direction also holds true.

In relation to the symmetry-asymmetry principle, if there is symmetry (e.g., the existence of different countries like China, France, and others to produce motor vehicles), there is asymmetry (e.g., China was the top motor vehicle producer in 2010, whereas France was #10 on the list instead). And the reverse direction also holds true.

In relation to the softness-hardness principle, if there is softness (e.g., the appreciation of the automobile industry, as shown in the creation of the

Ford Motor Company in the early 20th century by Henry Ford), there is hardness (e.g., the critique of the automobile industry, as shown in the problems pointed out by the critics like Jay Holtz Kay as cited). And the reverse direction also holds true.

In relation to the seriousness-playfulness principle, if there is seriousness (e.g., the serious business of those pioneers to build motor vehicles), there is playfulness (e.g., the playful part of those pioneers to build motor vehicles, when they played around with different imaginative designs like the "horse-drawn carriage" by Karl Benz, the "one-cylinder petrol motor, fitting it into…[a] tricycle" by Enrico Bernardi, etc.). And the reverse direction also holds true.

In relation to the activeness-inactiveness principle, if there is activeness (e.g., the activeness of automobiles which are driven by drivers on the streets), there is inactiveness (e.g., the relative inactiveness of automobiles which are under repair).

In relation to the regression-progression principle, if there is regression (e.g., the regression made by the automobile industry, as shown in the problem with "automobile dependency" pointed out by the critics like Peter Newman and Jeff Kenworthy), there is progression (e.g., the progress made by the automobile industry, as shown in its contribution to the convenience of modern transportation aforediscussed). And the reverse direction also holds true.

In relation to the same-difference principle, if there is similarity in outcome (e.g., the contribution to the molding and control of beliefs, values, and behaviors, regardless of whether this be done by way of the automobile industry, or by way of New Pedestrianism), there is difference in outcome (e.g., the contribution to the molding and control of beliefs, values, and behaviors by way of the automobile industry for a relatively more corporate lifeworld—but the contribution to the molding and control of beliefs, values, and behaviors by way of New Pedestrianism for a relatively more environment-friendly lifeworld). And the reverse direction also holds true.

And in relation to the stability-reaction principle, if there is stability (e.g., the relatively more stable condition of the U.S. as the top car manufacturer in the world, when it dominated from 1929 until 2005), there is reaction (e.g., the dominance of the U.S. in car manufacturing then led to further changes later on, when Japan replaced the U.S. as the top producer in 2006, just as China in 2009 took the top spot from Japan). And the reverse direction also holds true.

Networks, Future Cars, and Technology

Another good case study here to understand networks from the perspective of society has to do with networks, future cars, and technology.

The term "future car" here refers to a car designed for the future with advanced technologies which are for "varied energy sources and materials" and "are being developed in order to make automobiles more energy efficient with reduced regulated emissions. Cars are being developed in many different ways. With rising gas prices, now the future of cars is leaning towards fuel efficiency, energy-savers, hybrid vehicles, battery electric vehicles, and fuel-cell vehicles." (WK 2012i)

Consider, for illustration, four major advances in future cars based on new technologies, as addressed below (and summarized in *Table 2.4*).

Advanced Control

The first direction to improve future cars is by way of "advanced control," which can come in all shapes and sizes. Consider three examples below.

(a) Platoons of Cars

In regard to the "platoons of cars"—the technology here aims to "group…vehicles into platoons" as "a method of increasing the capacity of roads." (WK 2012x)

For instance, "platoons decrease the distances between cars using electronic, and possibly mechanical, coupling. This capability would allow many cars to accelerate or brake simultaneously. Instead of waiting after a traffic light changes to green for drivers ahead to react, a synchronized platoon would move as one, allowing up to a fivefold increase in traffic throughput if spacing is diminished that much. This system also allows for a closer headway between vehicles by eliminating reacting distance needed for human reaction." (WK 2012x)

In fact, "smart cars with artificial intelligence could automatically join and leave platoons. The automated highway system is a proposal for one such system, where cars organise themselves into platoons of eight to twenty-five." (WK 2012x)

(b) Vehicle Infrastructure Integration

In regard to the "vehicle infrastructure integration" (VII)—the technology here is to "link…road vehicles to their physical surroundings in order to improve road safety." (WK 2012y)

For instance, "this technology can reduce rear-end collisions by tracking obstructions in front or behind the vehicle, automatically applying brakes when needed....VII would provide a direct link between a vehicle on the road and all vehicles within a defined vicinity. The vchicles would be able to communicate with each other, exchanging data on speed, orientation, perhaps even on driver awareness and intent. This could increase safety for nearby vehicles, while enhancing the overall sensitivity of the VII system, for example, by performing an automated emergency maneuver (steering, decelerating, braking) more effectively. In addition, the system is designed to communicate with the roadway infrastructure, allowing for complete, real-time traffic information for the entire network, as well as better queue management and feedback to vehicles. It would ultimately close the feedback loops on what is now an open-loop transportation system." (WK 2012y)

(c) Driverless Cars

In regard to the "driverless cars"—the technology here is to build "an autonomous vehicle capable of fulfilling the human transportation capabilities of a traditional car." (WK 2012z)

For instance, "as an autonomous vehicle, it is capable of sensing its environment and navigating on its own. A human may choose a destination, but is not required to perform any mechanical operation of the vehicle." (WK 2012z)

Alternative Energy Sources

The second direction to improve future cars is by way of alternative "energy sources," because "one major problem in developing cleaner, energy efficient automobiles is the source of power to drive the engine. A variety of alternative fuel vehicles have been proposed or sold, including electric cars, hydrogen cars, compressed-air cars and liquid nitrogen cars." (WK 2012i)

For instance, "in one experiment done to improve the future of cars, an old kind of battery was installed which can not be removed, and recharged in two different ways. First, [it can be recharged] by a generator integrated with the IC and second by removing the cassettes so that they can be recharged off-board in the home." (WK 2012i; D. Charters 2008)

More Energy Efficiency

The third direction to improve future cars is by way of more "energy efficiency" ("energy saver"), because "conventional automobiles operate at about 15% efficiency. The rest of the energy is lost to engine and drive-train inefficiencies and idling. Therefore, the potential to improve fuel efficiency with advanced technologies is enormous. Various technologies have been developed and utilized to increase the energy efficiency of conventional cars or supplement them, resulting in energy savings." (WK 2012i)

For illustration, consider the following examples: (WK 2012i; M. Hanlon 2005)

- "Regenerative braking technology saves and stores energy for future use or as back up power. When conventional brakes are used, 100% of the kinetic energy lost is converted to thermal energy, and dissipated in the form of heat. Regenerative braking recovers some of this energy to recharge the batteries in a hybrid vehicle."
- "BMW's Turbosteamer concept uses energy from the exhaust gases of the traditional Internal Combustion Engine (ICE) to power a steam engine which also contributes power to the automobile. This can increase energy efficiency by up to 15%."
- "Compressed Air Hybrid is an engine made by researchers at Brunel University in Britain, which forces highly compressed air into the engine, which they claim reduces fuel consumption by 30%."
- "Utilization of waste heat from D.W. [is]...useful mechanical energy through exhaust powered steam, stirling engines, thermal diodes, etc."
- "Using computational fluid dynamics in the design stage can produce vehicles which take significantly less energy to push through the air, a major consideration at highway speeds. The Volkswagen 1-litre car and Aptera 2 Series are examples of ultra-low-drag vehicles."

Of course, there can be other examples too, so the ones above are illustrative, not exhaustive.

Better Materials

And the fourth direction to improve future cars is by way of better materials, as this technology tries to build new types of materials to make future cars.

Consider, for illustration, the following three examples: (WK 2012i)

- "Duraluminum, fiberglass, carbon fiber, and carbon nanotubes may totally replace all steel in cars (potentially improving lightness and strength). Aluminum, carbon fiber and fiberglass are currently being used more in cars today."

- "Plastic and foam for the car's shell; foam can provide additional safety for pedestrians,…and can also make the car buoyant."
- "Water-repellant glass"

Again, there can be other examples too, so the ones above are illustrative, not exhaustive.

Problems with the Study on Future Car Technologies

However, for the critics, this study on future car technologies has some major problems. Consider, for illustration, a few examples below (as summarized in *Table 2.4*).

Firstly, one main criticism of this study on future car technologies is that the implementation can be costly.

For example, for the critics, "the costs associated with installing the technology in vehicles and providing communications and power at every intersection are significant. Building out the infrastructure along the roadside without the auto manufacturers' cooperation would be disastrous, as would the reverse situation." (WK 2012y)

Secondly, another main criticism of this study on future car technologies is that they are not so simple as they may sound.

For instance, in the case of advanced control, "drivers would feel less in control of their own driving, being at the hands of computer software, or the lead driver." (WK 2012x) And VII is "limited in that it senses only the distance and speed of vehicles within the direct line of sight. It is almost completely ineffective for angled and left-turn collisions. It may even cause a motorist to lose control of the vehicle in the event of an impending head-on collision. The rear-end collisions covered by today's technology are typically less severe than angle, left-turn, or head-on collisions." (WK 2012y)

Thirdly, still another main criticism of this study on future car technologies is that they are not necessarily effective to enhance security.

For instance, "criminals could tamper with VII units, or remove and/or destroy them regardless of whether they are installed inside vehicles or along the roadside….It also raises concerns regarding the honesty of vehicle technicians performing the inspections. The ability of technicians to identify signs of tampering would be dependent on their knowledge of the VII systems themselves. Magnets, electric shocks, and malicious software (viruses, hacking, or jamming) could be used to damage VII systems—regardless of whether units are located inside vehicle or along the roadside." (WK 2012y)

Fourthly, an additional main criticism of this study on future car technologies is that they are also not necessarily safe to use.

For instance, in regard to alternative energy sources, the appeal of "liquid nitrogen" (for "liquid nitrogen cars") shoud be taken with care, because "the liquid to gas expansion ratio of nitrogen is 1:694 at 20 °C (68 °F)," so "a tremendous amount of force can be generated if liquid nitrogen is rapidly vaporized. In an incident in 2006 at Texas A&M University, the pressure-relief devices of a tank of liquid nitrogen were malfunctioning and later sealed. As a result of the subsequent pressure buildup, the tank failed catastrophically and exploded. The force of the explosion was sufficient to propel the tank through the ceiling immediately above it." (WK 2012aa; B. Mattox 2006)

And fifthly, another additional main criticism of this study on future car technologies is that automated driving can become quite boring.

For instance, for the critics, "VII will increase the automation of the vehicle, reducing the driver's enjoyment. Recreational driving concerns are particularly prevalent among owners of sports cars," and this criticism remains, even though these concerns "could be attenuated by compensating for the presence of vehicles without VII or perhaps by maintaining roadways where vehicles without VII are permitted to travel." (WK 2012y)

Beyond Future Car Technologies

However, these criticisms of the study on future car technologies do not entail a total rejection of its usefulness but serve to show us the two opposing sides of the debate, such that the possibility (or impossibility) and desirability (or undesirability) of networks (from the perspective of society with networks, future cars, and technology as a case study here) are not to the extent that the respective defenders would like us to believe.

In addition, the analysis of networks, future cars, and technology illuminates the important relevance of the ontological principles in existential dialectics, and good examples include the formalness-informalness principle, the absoluteness-relativeness principle, the partiality-totality principle, the predictability-unpredictability principle, the explicability-inexplicability principle, the fiction-reality principle, the finiteness-transfiniteness principle, the preciseness-vagueness principle, the simpleness-complicatedness principle, the openness-hiddenness principle, the denseness-emptiness principle, the change-constancy principle, the order-chaos principle, the slowness-quickness principle, the expansion-contraction principle, the theory-praxis principle, the convention-novelty principle, the evolution-transformation principle, the symmetry-asymmetry principle, the softness-hardness principle, the seriousness-playfulness principle, the activeness-inactiveness principle, the regression-progression principle, the same-difference principle, and the stability-reaction principle.

For instance, in relation to the formalness-informalness principle, if there is formalness (e.g., the formal logical requirement of soundness in a system of ideas, as in the study on future car technologies), there is informalness (e.g., the non-formal existence of unsoundness in the study on future car technologies, as shown in the criticisms that they are not so simple as they may sound, that they are not necessarily effective to enhance security, that they are also not necessarily safe to use, etc.). And the reverse direction also holds true.

In relation to the absoluteness-relativeness principle, if there is absoluteness (e.g., the absolute view of those who advocate more safety to endorse VII), there is relativeness (e.g., what is good for those who advocate more safety to endorse VII is not necessarily so for recreational drivers who argue instead that "VII will increase the automation of the vehicle, reducing the driver's enjoyment"). And the reverse direction also holds true.

In relation to the partiality-totality principle, if there is partiality (e.g., the partial view of an advocate for VII in regard to safety), there is totality (e.g., the more holistic view of the entire vehicle infrastructure as a complex system, such that the whole is not the sum of its parts, that is, it cannot be reduced to the sum of opposing views and interests of different parties in question, since "traffic systems are highly dynamic, with new traffic controls implemented every day and roadways constructed or repaired every year" and there can be random events or accidents not entirely controlled, just as there will emerge new views and phenomena in the future not yet known today). And the reverse direction also holds true.

In relation to the predictability-unpredictability principle, if there is predictability (e.g., the predictable tendency of future cars to have advanced control, alternative energy soruces, energy saver, and new materials), there is unpredictability (e.g., the more difficult task to predict exactly the extent to which each of these new car technologies will be widely used in a particular future era, since there are already various criticisms about their effectiveness and desirability, as pointed out by the critics). And the reverse direction also holds true.

In relation to the explicability-inexplicability principle, if there is explicability (e.g., the explanation by those for VII that it is desirable, because it is safer for driving), there is inexplicability (e.g., the lack of sufficient explanation by those for VII of why it is necessarily desirable, since for recreational drivers, VII can make driving boring, not enjoyful). And the reverse direction also holds true.

In relation to the fiction-reality principle, if there is fiction (e.g., the fictional aspect of future car technologies, insofar as some of the claims are questioned, as shown in the criticisms that they are not so simple as they may sound, that they are not necessarily effective to enhance security, that they are also not necessarily safe to use, etc.), there is reality (e.g., the realistic aspect of future car technologies, insofar as they make some contributions to advanced control, alternative energy soruces, energy saver, and new materials). And the reverse direction also holds true.

In relation to the finiteness-transfiniteness principle, if there is finiteness (e.g., the finite number of the types of alternative fuel vehicles that have been proposed or sold, like "electric cars, hydrogen cars, compressed-air cars and liquid nitrogen cars"), there is transfiniteness (e.g., the transfinite amounts of hydrogen, nitrogen, air, etc. on earth and in the rest of the universe that these future cars can use). And the reverse direction also holds true.

In relation to the preciseness-vagueness principle, if there is preciseness (e.g., the precise identification of four ways in which future cars can be made by new technologies, like advanced control, alternative energy soruces, energy saver, and new materials), there is vagueness (e.g., the vagueness in the identification of the four ways in which future cars can be made by new technologies, like advanced control, alternative energy soruces, energy saver, and new materials, since it is not clear why there must be only four ways, not 5, 6, 7, and so on). And the reverse direction also holds true.

In relation to the simpleness-complicatedness principle, if there is simpleness (e.g., the relatively simple analysis of future car technologies by the advocates), there is complicatedness (e.g., the relatively more complicated analysis of future car technologies, by challenging the claims and assumptions, as shown in the problems pointed out by the critics as cited). And the reverse direction also holds true.

In relation to the openness-hiddenness principle, if there is openness (e.g., the open exploration of future car technologies for safety, efficiency, and so on in the article aforecited), there is hiddenness (e.g., the hidden bias in the analysis of future car technologies in the article aforecited, because they are not so effective and desirable as claimed, as pointed out by the critics aforecited). And the reverse direction also holds true.

In relation to the denseness-emptiness principle, if there is denseness (e.g., the relatively denser concentration of cars with "advanced control" in future tansportation systems), there is emptiness (e.g., the relatively less dense, or more empty, concentration of cars with "advanced control" in the early 20th century tansportation system). And the reverse direction also holds true.

In relation to the change-constancy principle, if there is change (e.g., the ever new ways to ensure safety in transportation, as shown in the study on future car technologies), there is constancy (e.g., the ever constant existence of different problems in the ever new ways to ensure safety in transportation, as shown in the problems with future car technologies pointed out by the critics). And the reverse direction also holds true.

In relation to the order-chaos principle, if there is order (e.g., the more or less orderly appearance of traffic, if looked from the perspective of the "platoons of cars" under advanced control), there is chaos (e.g,. the more or less chaotic appearance of traffic, if looked from the perspective of car collisions, espcially in "angled and left-turn collisions" which are more difficult to control). And the reverse direction also holds true.

In relation to the slowness-quickness principle, if there is slowness (e.g., the relatively slower speed of future cars to use energy, as shown by "ultra-low-drag vehicles" which "take significantly less energy to push through the air"), there is quickness (e.g., the relatively quicker speed of conventional cars to use energy, because "conventional automobiles operate at about 15% efficiency" and "the rest of the energy is lost to engine and drive-train inefficiencies and idling"). And the reverse direction also holds true.

In relation to the expansion-contraction principle, if there is expansion (e.g., the relative spread of the use of advanced control and VII in future transportation systems), there is contraction (e.g., the relative decline of the use of conventional car designs in future transportation systems). And the reverse direction also holds true.

In relation to the theory-praxis principle, if there is theory (e.g., the theoretical construction of energy efficiency in physics), there is praxis (e.g., the practical application of energy efficiency in physics to the field of transportation, like "energy saver" in future car technologies). And the reverse direction also holds true.

In relation to the convention-novelty principle, if there is convention (e.g., the conventional wisdom about driving a car by a human driver), there is novelty (e.g., the alternative novel challenge to the conventional wisdom about driving a car by a human driver, by the new idea of "driverless cars," which allows a car to be driven without human intervention). (WK 2012y) And the reverse direction also holds true.

In relation to the evolution-transformation principle, if there is evolution (e.g., the natural evolution of humans to walk, run, or jump in the state of nature in a primitive way), there is transformation (e.g., the technical transformation of human ability to walk, run, and jump by the invention of "driverless cars" and "planes on autopilot"). And the reverse direction also holds true.

In relation to the symmetry-asymmetry principle, if there is symmetry (e.g., the existence of different car technologies), there is asymmetry (e.g., future car technologies for advanced control, alternative energy soruces, energy saver, and new materials are getting more and popular now than conventional car technologies). And the reverse direction also holds true.

In relation to the softness-hardness principle, if there is softness (e.g., the appreciation of future car technologies, as shown in the support by the advocates in the article aforecited), there is hardness (e.g., the critique of future car technologies, as shown in the problems pointed out by the critics as cited). And the reverse direction also holds true.

In relation to the seriousness-playfulness principle, if there is seriousness (e.g., the serious business of those in future car technologies to achieve safety, efficiency, etc.), there is playfulness (e.g., the playful part of those in future car technologies, when they play around with different experimental designs like hydrogen cars, compressed-air cars, liquid nitrogen cars, etc.). And the reverse direction also holds true.

In relation to the activeness-inactiveness principle, if there is activeness (e.g., the alertness of those future cars which actively pay attention "to their physical surroundings in order to improve road safety"), there is inactiveness (e.g., the relative inactiveness of those future cars which collide with others and no longer work)

In relation to the regression-progression principle, if there is regression (e.g., the regression made by future car technologies, as shown in the problems pointed out by the critics aforecited), there is progression (e.g., the progress made by future car technologies, as shown in their contributions to advanced control, alternative energy soruces, energy saver, and new materials aforecited). And the reverse direction also holds true.

In relation to the same-difference principle, if there is similarity in outcome (e.g., the contribution to the molding and control of beliefs, values, and behaviors, regardless of whether this be done by way of human running, or by way of driverless-driving), there is difference in outcome (e.g., the contribution to the molding and control of beliefs, values, and behaviors by way of human running for a relatively more naturalistic lifeworld—but the contribution to the molding and control of beliefs, values, and behaviors by way of driverless-driving for a relatively more automated lifeworld). And the reverse direction also holds true.

And in relation to the stability-reaction principle, if there is stability (e.g., the relatively more stable condition of conventional automobiles, when a driver was needed to drive them), there is reaction (e.g., the older days of conventional automobiles then led to further changes later on, since, nowadays, there are already car technologies for automated-driving, and this will be more so in the future). And the reverse direction also holds true.

Networks and Culture

Networks, when examined from the perspective of culture, can reveal their possibility (or impossibility) and desirability (or undesirability), and this can be shown by way of two case studies, namely, (2.5.1) networks, TOD, and the ideology of Intelligent Urbanism, and (2.5.2) networks, the automobile, and cultural changes—to be addressed hereafter, in that order.

Networks, TOD, and the Ideology of Intelligent Urbanism

An excellent case study here to understand networks from the perspective of culture has to do with networks, TOD, and the ideology of Intelligent Urbanism.

The term "TOD" stands for "transit-oriented development," which refers to a "mixed-use residential or commercial area designed to maximize access to public transport, and often incorporates features to encourage transit ridership. A TOD neighborhood typically has a center with a transit station or stop (train station, metro station, tram stop, or bus stop), surrounded by relatively high-density development with progressively lower-density development spreading outward from the center. TODs generally are located within a radius of one-quarter to one-half mile (400 to 800 m) from a transit stop, as this is considered to be an appropriate scale for pedestrians." (WK 2012bb)

TOD vs. TPD

But one should not confuse "transit-oriented development" (TOD) with "transit-proximate development" (TPD), because TOD "contains specific features that are designed to encourage public transport use and differentiate the development from urban sprawl. Examples of these features include mixed-use development that will use transit at all times of day, excellent pedestrian facilities such as high quality pedestrian crossings, narrow streets, and tapering of buildings as they become more distant from the public transport node. Another key feature of transit-oriented development that differentiates it from 'transit-proximate development' is reduced amounts of parking for personal vehicles." (WK 2012bb)

By contrast, unlike TOD, "transit-proximate development [TPD] can include results where, despite the location of dense development near transit, the development does not take full advantage of—or fully encourage the use of—the public transport node. For example, transit-proximate development could include buildings with extensive parking facilities typical of suburban locations, a lack of 'mixed-use development' (housing, workplaces and shopping in the same place), or a lack of extensive pedestrian facilities that would make it easier for people to reach the public transport node." (WK 2012cc)

TOD and the Ideology of Intellignet Urbanism

With this distinction in mind—TOD is in fact one of the 10 principles of "Intelligent Urbanism," which has become influential as an ideology in urban planning nowadays. (Wk 2012dd)

Intelligent Urbanism is "composed of a set of ten axioms intended to guide the formulation of city plans and urban designs. They are intended to reconcile and integrate diverse urban planning and management concerns. These axioms include environmental sustainability, heritage conservation, appropriate technology, infrastructure efficiency, placemaking, 'Social Access,' transit oriented development [TOD], regional integration, human scale, and institutional integrity. The term was coined by Prof. Christopher Charles Benninger." (WK 2012dd)

These principles "evolved from the city planning guidelines formulated by the International Congress of Modern Architecture (CIAM), the urban design approaches developed at Harvard's pioneering Urban Design Department under the leadership of Josep Lluis Sert, and the concerns enunciated by Team Ten. It is most prominently seen in plans prepared by Christopher Charles Benninger and his numerous colleagues in the Asian context." (WK 2012dd; C. Benninger 2001)

As an ideology, Intelligent Urbanism values "human scale" for a new human condition with the "pedestrian" as the focus, so as to "promote…the scale of the pedestrian moving on the pathway, as opposed to the scale of the automobile on the expressway. Intelligent urbanism promotes the ground plan of imaginable precincts, as opposed to the imagery of façades and the monumentality of the section. It promotes the personal visibility of places moving on foot at eye level." (WK 2012dd)

In this way, Intelligent Urbanism aims to “remov[e]…artificial barrier and promote…face-to-face contact. Proponents argue that the automobile, single use zoning and the construction of public structures in isolated compounds, all deteriorate the human condition and the human scale of the city.” (WK 2012dd)

Thus, for the ideologues of Intellignet Urbanism, “the trend towards urban sprawl can be overcome by developing pedestrian circulation networks along streets and open spaces that link local destinations. Shops, amenities, day care, vegetable markets and basic social services should be clustered around public transport stops, and at a walkable distance from work places, public institutions, high and medium density residential areas. Public spaces should be integrated into residential, work, entertainment and commercial areas. Social activities and public buildings should orient onto public open spaces. These should be the interchange sites for people on the move, where they can also revert into the realm of 'slowness,' of community life and of human interaction.” (WK 2012dd)

The value of “human scale” in the ideology of Intellignet Urbanism can be accomplished “through building masses that 'step down' to human scale open spaces; by using arcades and pavilions as buffers to large masses; by intermixing open spaces and built masses sensitively; by using anthropometric proportions and natural materials. Traditional building precedents often carry within them a human scale language, from which a contemporary fabric of build may evolve.” (WK 2012dd)

In this sense, Intelligent Urbanism endorses “Transit Oriented Development,” even though “the PIU [Principles of Intelligent Urbanism] goal is not merely to replace the automobile, nor to balance it. These are mundane requirements of planning, which the PIU assumes are found in every design and urban configuration. The PIU goal is to enrich the human condition and to enhance the realm of human possibilities.” (WK 2012dd)

In the end, the value of human scale in the ideology of Intelligent Urbanism is to “facilitat[e]…human behavior toward more tolerant, more peaceful, more accommodating and more sensitive modalities of interaction and conflict resolution. Intelligent urbanism recognizes that 'urbanity' emerges where people mix and interact on a face-to-face basis, on the ground, at high densities and amongst diverse social and economic groups. Intelligent Urbanism nurtures 'urbanity' through designs and plans that foster human scale interaction.” (WK 2012dd)

Examples of TOD

There is no lack of good examples of TOD in action around the world, with its more sensitive value of human scale. For illustration, consider four examples around the world below.

(a) Latin America

For instance, in Guatamala, "in an attempt to control rapid growth of Guatemala City, the municipal government (Municipalidad de Guatemala) headed by long time Mayor Álvaro Arzú, has implemented a plan to control its growth based on transects along its important arterial roads and exhibiting Transit-oriented development (TOD) characteristics. This plan denominated POT (Plan de Ordenamiento Territorial) aims to allow taller building structures of mixed uses to be built next to large arterial roads and gradually decline in height and density as you move away from such. This is simultaneously being implemented along with a bus rapid transit {BRT} system called Transmetro." (WK 2012bb)

In Brazil, the city of Curitiba "was organized into transport corridors very early in its history. Over the years, it has integrated its zoning and transportation to place high density development next to high capacity transportation. Since the failure of its first, rather grandiose, city plan due to lack of funding, Curitiba has focused on working with economical forms of infrastructure, so it has arranged unique adaptations, such as bus routes (inexpensive infrastructure) with routing systems, limited access and speeds similar to subway systems. The source of innovation in Curitiba has been a unique form of participatory city planning that emphasizes public education, discussion and agreement." (WK 2012bb)

(b) North America

In the U.S., like San Francisco, California, "local and regional governments encourage transit-oriented development to decrease traffic congestion, protect natural areas, promote public health and increase housing options. The region has designated Priority Development Areas and Priority Conservation Areas. Current population forecasts] for the region predict that it will grow by 2 million people by 2035 due to both the natural birth rate and job creation, and estimate that 50% of this growth can be accommodated in Priority Development Areas through transit-oriented development. Major transit village projects have been developed over the past 20 years at several stations linked to the Bay Area Rapid Transit (BART) system." (WK 2012bb)

In Canada, "Greater Vancouver has had a strong history of creating new development around its SkyTrain lines and also created the concept of regional town centres around the major stations and transit corridors. Of note is the Metrotown area of the suburb of Burnaby, British Columbia near the Metrotown SkyTrain Station. The areas around stations have spurred the development of billions of dollars of high-density real estate, with multiple highrises near the many stations." (WK 2012bb)

(c) Asia and Oceania

In China, Hong Kong is an interesting example, since "in the mid-20th century, no railway was built until an area was well developed. However, in recent decades, Hong Kong has started to have some TODs, where a railway is built simultaneously with residential development above or nearby. Examples include LOHAS Park, Olympian City, and Tung Chung." (WK 2012bb)

In Australia, "Melbourne…is expected to reach a population of 5 million by 2030 with the overwhelming majority of its residents relying on private automobiles. Since the turn of the century, sporadic efforts have been made by various levels of government to implement transit-oriented development principles. However, a lack of commitment to funding public transport infrastructure, resulting to overcrowding and amending zoning laws has dramatically slowed progress toward sustainable development for the city." (WK 2012bb)

(d) Europe

In France, "the city of Paris has a centuries-long history," as "its main frame dates to this XIXth century. The subway network was made to solve both linkage between the five main train stations and local transportation assets for citizens. The whole area of Paris City is closer than 500 meters from the next subway station. Recent bicycle and car rental systems (Velib and Autolib) ease also transportation, in the very same way that TOD emphasizes." (WK 2012bb)

In the Netherlands, "in the Southern part of the Ranstaad will be built a neighbourhood according to the principles of TOD." (WK 2012bb; F. van der Hoeven 2012)

Problems with the Study on TOD

However, for the critics, this study on TOD has some major problems. Consider, for illustration, a few examples below.

Firstly, one main criticism of this study on TOD is that it is driven with the ideology of Intelligent Urbanism.

For example, for the critics, the value of "human scale" for TOD in the ideology of Intelligent Urbanism is biased for those who favor a more sensitive lifestyle which facilitates "human behavior toward more tolerant, more peaceful, more accommodating and more sensitive modalities of interaction and conflict resolution." But for those who do not favor this more sensitive lifestyle and instead choose a more competitive, dominating modalities of interaction and conflict resolution, TOD is not the solution for their lifeworld.

Secondly, another main criticism of this study on TOD is that "it has the potential to spur gentrification in low-income areas." (WK 2012bb)

For instance, for the critics, "TOD can raise the housing costs of formerly affordable neighborhoods, pushing low- and moderate-income residents farther away from jobs and transit. When this happens, TOD projects can disrupt low-income neighborhoods." (WK 2012bb; PL 2008)

Thirdly, still another main criticism of this study on TOD is that there are alternatives to TOD.

For instance, TPD is an alternative to TOD, even though the two have something in common too.

And fourthly, an additional main criticism of this study on TOD that it has an authoritarian tendency.

For instance, "Peter Gordon, a professor of Urban Planning from University of Southern California, spoke out in favor of suburbanization" and criticized such ideologies like Intelligent Urbanism, New Urbanism, etc. "as ignoring consumer preference and the free market, claiming that cities have moved towards car-oriented development because that is what people want." (WK 2012ee; RM 1998) Other critics made the same comparable point, in that an ideology like Intelligent Urbanism is "a form of centrally-planned, large-scale development, 'instead of allowing the initiative for construction to be taken by the final users themselves.' It has been criticized for asserting universal principles of design instead of attending to local conditions." (WK 2012ee; N. Salingaros 2010; J. Grant 2006)

Beyond TOD

However, these criticisms of TOD do not imply a total rejection of its usefulness but serve to show us the two opposing sides of the debate, such that the possibility (or impossibility) and desirability (or undesirability) of networks (from the perspective of culture with networks, TOD, and the ideology of Intelligent Urbanism as a case study here) are not to the extent that the respective defenders would like us to believe.

Furthermore, the analysis of networks, TOD, and the ideology of Intelligent Urbanism can show us something refreshing about the ontological principles in existential dialectics, and good examples include the formalness-informalness principle, the absoluteness-relativeness principle, the partiality-totality principle, the predictability-unpredictability principle, the explicability-inexplicability principle, the fiction-reality principle, the finiteness-transfiniteness principle, the preciseness-vagueness principle, the simpleness-complicatedness principle, the openness-hiddenness principle, the denseness-emptiness principle, the change-constancy principle, the order-chaos principle, the slowness-quickness principle, the expansion-contraction principle, the theory-praxis principle, the convention-novelty principle, the evolution-transformation principle, the symmetry-asymmetry principle, the softness-hardness principle, the seriousness-playfulness principle, the activeness-inactiveness principle, the regression-progression principle, the same-difference principle, and the stability-reaction principle.

For instance, in relation to the formalness-informalness principle, if there is formalness (e.g., the formal logical requirement of soundness and completeness in a system of ideas, as in TOD), there is informalness (e.g., the non-formal existence of unsoundness and incompleteness in TOD, as shown in the criticisms that it is driven with the ideology of Intelligent Urbanism, that it has the potential to spur "gentrification in low-income areas," that it has an authoritarian tendency, etc.). And the reverse direction also holds true.

In relation to the absoluteness-relativeness principle, if there is absoluteness (e.g., the absolute view of the advocates to favor "human scale" in TOD, as part of the ideology of Intelligent Urbanism), there is relativeness (e.g., what is right for the advocates to favor "human scale" in TOD, as part of the ideology of Intelligent Urbanism is not necessarily so for the libertarian critic like Peter Gordon, who "spoke out in favor of suburbanization" and criticized such ideologies like Intelligent Urbanism, New Urbanism, etc. "as ignoring consumer preference and the free market, claiming that cities have moved towards car-oriented development because that is what people want"). And the reverse direction also holds true.

In relation to the partiality-totality principle, if there is partiality (e.g., the partial view of the advocates of TOD), there is totality (e.g., the more holistic view of the development of public transports, such that the whole is not the sum of its parts, that is, it cannot be reduced to the sum of opposing views like TOD, TPD, the libertarian critique, etc., since there will emerge new views in the future not yet known today). And the reverse direction also holds true.

In relation to the predictability-unpredictability principle, if there is predictability (e.g., the predictable tendency of the advocates of TOD "to maximize access to public transport, and often incorporate…features to encourage transit ridership"), there is unpredictability (e.g., the more difficult task to predict exactly the extent to which TOD will remain influential in a particular future era, because of such problems like spurring "gentrification in low-income areas," together with other problems aforediscussed). And the reverse direction also holds true.

In relation to the explicability-inexplicability principle, if there is explicability (e.g., the explanation by the proponents of TOD, as part of Intelligent Urbanism, that it is desirable to plan for "human scale" with the focus on the "pedestrian," because it can "facilitat[e]...human behavior toward more tolerant, more peaceful, more accommodating and more sensitive modalities of interaction and conflict resolution"), there is inexplicability (e.g., the lack of sufficient explanation by the proponents of TOD, as part of Intelligent Urbanism, that it is desirable to plan for "human scale" with the focus on the "pedestrian," since, for the critics, those who do not favor this more sensitive lifestyle can instead choose a more competitive, dominating modalities of interaction and conflict resolution). And the reverse direction also holds true.

In relation to the fiction-reality principle, if there is fiction (e.g., the fictional aspect of TOD, insofar as it does not seriously consider alternative options like TPD, the libertarian argument for the free market, etc.), there is reality (e.g., the realistic aspect of TOD, insofar as it aims "to maximize access to public transport, and often incorporate...features to encourage transit ridership"). And the reverse direction also holds true.

In relation to the finiteness-transfiniteness principle, if there is finiteness (e.g., the finite number of the types of transit stations or stops like "train station," "metro station," "tram stop," "bus stop," etc.), there is transfiniteness (e.g., the transfinite number of all the individuals in history who have ever used any of the transit stops on earth). And the reverse direction also holds true.

In relation to the preciseness-vagueness principle, if there is preciseness (e.g., the precise identification of four regions of the world to be considered for TOD in the article aforecited), there is vagueness (e.g., the vagueness in the identification of the four regions of the world to be considered for TOD in the article aforecited, since it is not clear why there must be only these 4 regions to be classified, not 5, 6, 7, and so on). And the reverse direction also holds true.

In relation to the simpleness-complicatedness principle, if there is simpleness (e.g., the relatively simple analysis of TOD by its advocates), there is complicatedness (e.g., the relatively more complicated analysis of TOD, by challenging the claims and assumptions, as shown in the problems pointed out by the critics as cited). And the reverse direction also holds true.

In relation to the openness-hiddenness principle, if there is openness (e.g., the open exploration of the value of "human scale" in TOD with the focus on the "pedestrian" in the ideology of Intelligent Urbanism), there is hiddenness (e.g., the hidden bias in TOD for the value of "human scale" with the focus on the "pedestrian" as part of the ideology of Intelligent Urbanism, because, for the critic like Gordon, it has an authoritarian tendency in "ignoring consumer preference and the free market"). And the reverse direction also holds true.

In relation to the denseness-emptiness principle, if there is denseness (e.g., the relatively denser concentration of "mixed-use residential or commercial areas" in order to "maximize access to public transport" in TOD), there is emptiness (e.g., the relatively less dense, or more empty, concentration of "mixed-use residential or commercial areas" in the libertarian response to urban planning as proposed by Gordon). And the reverse direction also holds true.

In relation to the change-constancy principle, if there is change (e.g., the ever new ways to analyze public transports, as shown in the study on TOD), there is constancy (e.g., the ever constant existence of different problems in the ever new ways to analyze public transports, as shown in the problems with TOD pointed out by the critics). And the reverse direction also holds true.

In relation to the order-chaos principle, if there is order (e.g., the more or less orderly reality of public transports, if looked from the vantage point of Intelligent Urbanism for TOD in a nicely designed and planned way), there is chaos (e.g,. the more or less chaotic reality of public transports, if looked from the vantage point of libertarianism "for consumer preference and the free market" in any decision on public transports). And the reverse direction also holds true.

In relation to the slowness-quickness principle, if there is slowness (e.g., the relatively slower speed of a pedestrian to get where he wants to go, if transit stops are not readily available as seen in suburbanization), there is quickness (e.g., the relatively quicker speed of a pedestrian to get where he wants to go, if transit stops are readily available as required by TOD). And the reverse direction also holds true.

In relation to the expansion-contraction principle, if there is expansion (e.g., the relative spread of TOD nowadays in North American and European cities, for instance), there is contraction (e.g., the relative decline of old-fashioned suburbanization nowadays in North American and European cities, for instance). And the reverse direction also holds true.

In relation to the theory-praxis principle, if there is theory (e.g., the theoretical construction of Intelligent Urbanism in urban planning), there is praxis (e.g., the practical application of Intelligent Urbanism in urban planning to the field of transportation, as shown in the arrangement of transit stops in accordance to TOD). And the reverse direction also holds true.

In relation to the convention-novelty principle, if there is convention (e.g., the conventional wisdom about suburbanization in the earlier days), there is novelty (e.g., the alternative novel challenge to the conventional wisdom about suburbanization in the earlier days, by the new idea of TOD for "human scale" with the focus on the "pedestrian" nowadays). And the reverse direction also holds true.

In relation to the evolution-transformation principle, if there is evolution (e.g., the natural evolution of humans to live in small groups, as they mix and interact on a face-to-face basis in the state of nature), there is transformation (e.g., the technical transformation of human ability to interact by the invention of suburbanization, where the value of the "pedestrian" is eroded). And the reverse direction also holds true.

In relation to the symmetry-asymmetry principle, if there is symmetry (e.g., the existence of different ways to arrange "access to public transport"), there is asymmetry (e.g., TOD is more influential now as a way to arrange "access to public transport" than its alternative like suburbanization). And the reverse direction also holds true.

In relation to the softness-hardness principle, if there is softness (e.g., the appreciation of TOD, as shown in its implementation in cities around the world in the article aforecited), there is hardness (e.g., the critique of TOD, as shown in the problems pointed out by the critics as cited). And the reverse direction also holds true.

In relation to the seriousness-playfulness principle, if there is seriousness (e.g., the serious business of those in TOD to focus on the "pedestrian"), there is playfulness (e.g., the playful part of those in TOD, when they play around with different designs of public spaces for people to meet freely, like "parks, gardens, glass-covered gallerias, arcades, courtyards, street side cafes, river- and hill-side stroll ways, and a variety of semi-covered spaces," so as to see and test which ones are better under what circumstances). And the reverse direction also holds true.

In relation to the activeness-inactiveness principle, if there is activeness (e.g., the activeness of those transit-oriented areas which are well-planned according to Intelligent Urbanism and function well), there is inactiveness (e.g., the relative inactiveness of those transit-oriented areas which are badly designed and become dysfunctional or out-of-use over time).

In relation to the regression-progression principle, if there is regression (e.g., the regression made by TOD, as shown in the problems pointed out by the critics), there is progression (e.g., the progress made by TOD, as shown in the contributions to the value of "human scale" for the "pedestrian" aforecited). And the reverse direction also holds true.

In relation to the same-difference principle, if there is similarity in outcome (e.g., the contribution to the molding and control of beliefs, values, and behaviors, regardless of whether this be done by way of suburbanization, or by way of TOD), there is difference in outcome (e.g., the contribution to the molding and control of beliefs, values, and behaviors by way of suburbanization for a relatively more impersonal lifeworld—but the contribution to the molding and control of beliefs, values, and behaviors by way of TOD for a relatively more face-to-face lifeworld). And the reverse direction also holds true.

And in relation to the stability-reaction principle, if there is stability (e.g., the relatively more stable condition of suburbanization in the earlier days, when "many residents of metropolitan regions work within the central urban area, choosing instead to live in satellite communities called suburbs and commute to work via automobile or mass transit"), there is reaction (e.g., suburbanization in the earlier days then led to further changes later on, as TOD is more popular instead nowadays). (WK 2012ff) And the reverse direction also holds true.

Networks, the Automobile, and Cultural Changes

Another way to evaluate the possibility (or impossibility) and desirability (or undesirability) of networks from the perspective of culture concerns networks, the automobile, and cultural changes.

In other words, this section is to examine the subsequent cultural changes due to the rise of the automobile in the 20th century.

The Rise of the Automobile

One of the most significant changes in the 20th century in regard to transportation has to do with the invention of "the automobile," which "rapidly developed from an expensive toy for the rich into the de facto standard for passenger transport in most developed countries." (WK 2012: J. Urrey 2004)

Although "in developing countries, the effects of the automobile have lagged," the locals "are emulating the impacts of developed nations. The development of the automobile built upon the transport revolution started by railways, and like the railways, introduced sweeping changes in employment patterns, social interactions, infrastructure and goods distribution." (WK 2012)

The Convenience of the Automobile

The rise of the automobile has much to do with its inherent convenience.

In the older days before "the appearance of the automobile"—"horses, walking and streetcars were the major modes of transportation within cities. Horses require a large amount of care, and were therefore kept in public facilities that were usually far from residences. The wealthy could afford to keep horses for private use, hence the term carriage trade referred to elite patronage. Horse manure left on the streets also created a sanitation problem." (WK 2012; K. Jackson 1987; S. Strasser 1999)

The automobile thus made a big difference, in that it "made regular medium-distance travel more convenient and affordable, especially in areas without railways. Because automobiles did not require rest, and were faster than horse-drawn conveyances, people were routinely able to travel farther than in earlier times. The construction of highways half a century later continued this revolution in mobility. Some experts suggest that many of these changes began during the Golden age of the bicycle, the preceding era from 1880-1915." (WK 2012; R. Smith 1972)

All over the world, "the automobile has allowed easier access to remote places," and, even in underdeveloped countries like Mexico, "paving of Mexican Federal Highway 1 through Baja California, completing the connection of Cabo San Lucas to California, and convenient access to the outside world for villagers along the route…occurred in the 1950s." (WK 2012)

And "the following developments in retail are partially due to automobile use: drive-thru fast food purchasing" and "gasoline station grocery shopping," for instance. (WK 2012)

Cultural Changes

The convenience of the automobile has brought some major cultural changes around the world.

Consider, for illustration, a few noticeable examples below (as summarized in *Table 2.5*).

(a) In Artworks

In artworks, "automobiles were incorporated into…music, books and movies. Between 1905 and 1908, more than 120 songs were written in which the automobile was the subject. Novels celebrating the political effects of motorization included Free Air by Sinclair Lewis. Where earlier mass media had made heroes of Casey Jones, Allan Pinkerton and other dutiful protectors of public transport, new road movies offered heroes who found freedom and equality on the open road." (WK 2012; K. Jackson 1987)

As Skip McGoun (2012) thus reminded us: "We have sung songs about the glory and wonder that surrounds the very concept of the car. Examples of this range from the 1909 tune, 'In My Merry Oldsmobile,' to what is considered to be the first rock and roll song, 'Rocket 88,' in 1949. Indeed, contemporary music has often used the car as a cultural theme."

On television, "currently there are a number of television shows that cater to the automobile enthusiast. In fact, there is a channel called 'Speed' that focuses heavily on automobiles and racing. Others, such as 'Rides' and 'The American Hot Rod,' focus upon the construction of the car." (S. McGoun 2012)

In films, the movie industry has "portrayed hot rods associated with social outcasts. In other films, expensive sleek sports cars have been associated with wealth and success. How have these portrayals of automobiles impacted our impressions of ourselves and others? One commercial described Hell as being a place where a teenager would have to drive a minivan!" (S. McGoun 2012)

(b) In Sports

In sports, "NASCAR, NHRA, NSRA and other formal sports organizations exist to promote motor sports or the consumption of the automobile culture. It has been said that NASCAR is the number one spectator sport in America and is uniquely American." (S. McGoun 2012)

(c) In Political Culture

In political culture, "George Monbiot writes that widespread car culture has shifted voter's preference to the right of the political spectrum. He thinks that car culture has contributed to an increase in individualism and fewer social interactions between members of different socioeconomic classes." (WK 2012; G. Monbiot 2005)

(d) In Economic Culture

In economic culture, "road building was sometimes also influenced by Keynesian-style...ideologies. In Europe, massive freeway building programs were initiated by a number of social democratic governments after World War II, in an attempt to create jobs and make the automobile available to the working classes. From the 1970s, promotion of the automobile increasingly became a trait of some conservatives. Margaret

Thatcher talked of a 'great car economy,' and increased government spending on roads." (WK 2012)

(e) In Social Culture

And in social culture, "the commodification of identity and issues surrounding consumption appear to be intimately connected with the automobile. Status is an essential element that surrounds the ownership of a car and this is a basic element of our cultural experience." (S. McGoun 2012)

Other relevant impacts include "those associated with gender, race, and ethnicity. Are our conceptions of these qualities associated with the automobile? If so, why and to what extent?" (S. McGoun 2012)

Problems with the Automobile and its Cultural Changes

However, for the critics, the phenomenon of the car culture has some major problems. Consider, for illustration, a few examples below (as summarized in *Table 2.5*).

Firstly, one main criticism of the phenomenon of the car culture is that it also has destructive effects.

For example, for the critics, "the effects of the automobile on everyday life have been a subject of controversy. While the introduction of the mass-produced automobile represented a revolution in mobility and convenience, the modern consequences of heavy automotive use contribute to the use of non-renewable fuels..., social isolation, the disconnection of community, the rise in obesity, the generation of air & noise pollution, urban sprawl, and urban decay." (WK 2012; J. Kay 1998)

Secondly, another main criticism of the phenomenon of the car culture is that the convenience of the automobile comes with a price to pay (in regard to time delay).

For instance, for the critics, altough "worldwide the automobile has allowed easier access to remote places..., average journey times to regularly visited places have increased in large cities, especially in Latin America, as a result of widespread automobile adoption. This is due to traffic congestion and the increased distances between home and work brought about by urban sprawl." (WK 2012; A. Gilbert 1996)

Thirdly, still another main criticism of the phenomenon of the car culture is that it can contribute to the spread of diseases.

For instance, "the origin of HIV explosion in the human population has been hypothesized by CDC researchers to derive in part from more intensive social interactions afforded by new road networks in Central Africa allowing more frequent travel from villagers to cities and higher density development of many African cities in the period 1950 to 1980." (WK 2012; J. McCormick 1997)

Fourthly, an additional main criticism of the phenomenon of the car culture is that it has contributed to "a dramatic increase in the rate of accidental death." (WK 2012; J. Kay 1998)

For instance, "motor vehicle accidents are attributed to 37.5% of accidental deaths in the United States, making them the country's leading cause of accidental death." (WK 2012; B. Best 2012)

And fifthly, another additional main criticism of the phenomenon of the car culture is that the requirement of transportation infrastructure is costly.

For instance, governments often have to "support…the automobile through subsidies for infrastructure," which is not cheap at all; in addition, "the cost of highway police enforcement, recovering stolen cars, and many other factors makes public transport a less economically competitive choice for commuters when considering direct out-of-pocket costs. Consumers often make choices based on the direct out-of-pocket costs and underestimate the indirect costs of car ownership, auto insurance and car maintenance." (WK 2012)

Beyond the Car Culture

These criticisms of the car culture, however, do not suggest a total rejection of its usefulness but serve to show us the two opposing sides of the debate, such that the possibility (or impossibility) and desirability (or undesirability) of networks (from the perspective of culture with networks, the automobile, and cultural changes as a case study here) are not to the extent that the respective defenders would like us to believe.

In addition, the analysis of networks, the automobile, and cultural changes casts a bright light on the ontological principles in existential dialectics, and good examples include the formalness-informalness principle, the absoluteness-relativeness principle, the partiality-totality principle, the predictability-unpredictability principle, the explicability-inexplicability principle, the fiction-reality principle, the finiteness-transfiniteness principle, the preciseness-vagueness principle, the simpleness-complicatedness principle, the openness-hiddenness principle, the denseness-emptiness principle, the change-constancy principle, the order-chaos principle, the slowness-quickness principle, the expansion-contraction principle, the theory-praxis principle, the convention-novelty principle, the evolution-transformation principle, the symmetry-asymmetry principle, the softness-hardness principle, the seriousness-playfulness principle, the activeness-inactiveness principle, the regression-

progression principle, the same-difference principle, and the stability-reaction principle.

For instance, in relation to the formalness-informalness principle, if there is formalness (e.g., the formal logical requirement of soundness, completeness, and consistency in a system of ideas, as in the study on the car culture), there is informalness (e.g., the non-formal existence of unsoundness, incompleteness, and inconsistency in the study on the car culture, as shown in the criticisms that it also has destructive effects, that the convenience of the automobile comes with a price to pay in regard to time delay instead, that it can contribute to the spread of diseases, that it has contributed to "a dramatic increase in the rate of accidental death," that the requirement of transportation infrastructure is costly, etc.). And the reverse direction also holds true.

In relation to the absoluteness-relativeness principle, if there is absoluteness (e.g., the absolute view of those in the old "glory days" of the automobile, as pointed out by Skip McGoun), there is relativeness (e.g., what is desirable for those in the old "glory days" of the automobile is not necessarily so for the critics like J. Kay, who pointed out its destructive effects). And the reverse direction also holds true.

In relation to the partiality-totality principle, if there is partiality (e.g., the partial view of those in the old "glory days" of the automobile, or conversely, the critics like J. Kay), there is totality (e.g., the more holistic view of the car culture, such that the whole is not the sum of its parts, that is, it cannot be reduced to the sum of opposing views like those in the old "glory days" of the automobile, the critics like J. Kay, etc., since there will emerge new views in the future not yet known today, just as there were already alternative views about the car culture by CDC researchers recently that, for instance, "the origin of HIV explosion" was unexpectedly due to "more intensive social interactions afforded by new road networks in Central Africa allowing more frequent travel from villagers to cities and higher density development of many African cities in the period 1950 to 1980"). And the reverse direction also holds true.

In relation to the predictability-unpredictability principle, if there is predictability (e.g., the predictable tendency of the automobile to produce convenience for its users), there is unpredictability (e.g., the more difficult task to predict exactly the extent to which the automobile will remain influential in a particular future era, since there are already numerous criticisms about its negative effects on both society and culture aforecited). And the reverse direction also holds true.

In relation to the explicability-inexplicability principle, if there is explicability (e.g., the explanation by the advocates of the automobile that it is desirable because of its convenience), there is inexplicability (e.g., the lack of sufficient explanation by the advocates of the automobile of why it is necessarily desirable, in light of the numerous serious problems as pointed out by the critics aforecited). And the reverse direction also holds true.

In relation to the fiction-reality principle, if there is fiction (e.g., the fictional aspect of the car culture, insofar as it causes time delays, accidents, etc. often downplayed by its advocates), there is reality (e.g., the realistic aspect of the car culture, insofar as it brings convenience too). And the reverse direction also holds true.

In relation to the finiteness-transfiniteness principle, if there is finiteness (e.g., the finite number of the major modes of transportation in history, like automobiles, horses, walking, streetcars, etc.), there is transfiniteness (e.g., the transfinite number of all the individual cars, horses, streetcars, and walkers that have ever existed in history). And the reverse direction also holds true.

In relation to the preciseness-vagueness principle, if there is preciseness (e.g., the precise identification of five different impacts by the automobile on culture in the article aforecited), there is vagueness (e.g., the vagueness in the identification of the five different impacts by the automobile on culture in the article aforecited, since it is not clear why there must be only 5, not 7, 12, 13, 15, 21, and so on). And the reverse direction also holds true.

In relation to the simpleness-complicatedness principle, if there is simpleness (e.g., the relatively simple analysis of the car culture by its advocates), there is complicatedness (e.g., the relatively more complicated analysis of the car culture, by challenging the claims and assumptions, as shown in the problems pointed out by the critics as cited). And the reverse direction also holds true.

In relation to the openness-hiddenness principle, if there is openness (e.g., the open exploration of "direct out-of-pocket costs" by commuters), there is hiddenness (e.g., the hidden bias in the consideration of "direct out-of-pocket costs" by commuters, because they "often make choices based on the direct out-of-pocket costs and underestimate the indirect costs of car ownership, auto insurance and car maintenance"). And the reverse direction also holds true.

In relation to the denseness-emptiness principle, if there is denseness (e.g., the relatively denser concentration of cars in developed countries), there is emptiness (e.g., the relatively less dense, or more empty, concentration of cars in underdeveloped countries like some parts of China, where "there are currently 184 towns and 54,000 villages that have no access to automobile use…or roads at all"). (WK 2012; CHI 2012) And the reverse direction also holds true.

In relation to the change-constancy principle, if there is change (e.g., the ever new ways to build transports for society and culture, as shown in the study on the automobile and its cultural changes), there is constancy (e.g., the ever constant existence of different problems in the ever new ways to build transports for society and culture, as shown in the problems with the study on the automobile and its cultural changes pointed out by the critics). And the reverse direction also holds true.

In relation to the order-chaos principle, if there is order (e.g., the more or less orderly reality of the car culture, insofar as it brings "status" as "an essential element that surrounds the ownership of a car and this is a basic element of our cultural experience"), there is chaos (e.g,. the more or less chaotic reality of the car culture, insofar as it can also spread diseases and contribute to "a dramatic increase in the rate of accidental death" in a random way, etc.). And the reverse direction also holds true.

In relation to the slowness-quickness principle, if there is slowness (e.g., the relatively slower speed of walking or streetcars), there is quickness (e.g., the relatively quicker speed of the automobile). And the reverse direction also holds true.

In relation to the expansion-contraction principle, if there is expansion (e.g., the relative spread of individualism in a car culture), there is contraction (e.g., the relative decline of close social interactions in a car culture). And the reverse direction also holds true.

In relation to the theory-praxis principle, if there is theory (e.g., the theoretical construction of "the commodification of identity" in culture studies), there is praxis (e.g., the practical application of "the commodification of identity" in culture studies to the field of transportation, when the issue of "the commodification of identity" is "to be intimately connected with the automobile"). And the reverse direction also holds true.

In relation to the convention-novelty principle, if there is convention (e.g., the conventional wisdom about the convenience of the automobile in the older "glory days" of car culture), there is novelty (e.g., the alternative novel challenge to the conventional wisdom about the convenience of the automobile in the older "glory days" of car culture, by the new idea of New Pedestrianism to replace the dominant influence of the car culture). And the reverse direction also holds true.

In relation to the evolution-transformation principle, if there is evolution (e.g., the natural evolution of humans to walk in the state of nature), there is transformation (e.g., the technical transformation of human ability to move around by the invention of the automobile, together with the car culture to glorify it). And the reverse direction also holds true.

In relation to the symmetry-asymmetry principle, if there is symmetry (e.g., the existence of different modes of transportation), there is asymmetry (e.g., a car is faster and more powerful in carrying things than a horse over long distance, on average). And the reverse direction also holds true.

In relation to the softness-hardness principle, if there is softness (e.g., the glorfication of the car culture by its advocates), there is hardness (e.g., the critique of the car culture by its critics like J. Kay). And the reverse direction also holds true.

In relation to the seriousness-playfulness principle, if there is seriousness (e.g., the serious business of those who advocate the convenience of the automobile), there is playfulness (e.g., the playful part of those who advocates the convenience of the automobile, when they play around with different slogans to glorify the car culture, like the 1909 tune "In My Merry Oldsmobile," the first rock and roll song "Rocket 88," or the commercial which "described Hell as being a place where a teenager would have to drive a minivan!"). And the reverse direction also holds true.

In relation to the activeness-inactiveness principle, if there is activeness (e.g., the activeness of those in car cultures who are encouraged to drive around to more areas than otherwise possible), there is inactiveness (e.g., the relative inactiveness of those in alternative cultures who cannot go far from their local regions, because of the lack of adequate transportation).

In relation to the regression-progression principle, if there is regression (e.g., the regression made by the car culture, as shown in the problems pointed out by the critics), there is progression (e.g., the progress made by the car culture, as shown in those positive aspects of its cultural changes afordiscussed). And the reverse direction also holds true.

In relation to the same-difference principle, if there is similarity in outcome (e.g., the contribution to the molding and control of beliefs, values, and behaviors, regardless of whether this be done by way of a walk culture or by way of a car culture), there is difference in outcome (e.g., the contribution to the molding and control of beliefs, values, and behaviors by way of a walk culture for a relatively more social identity—but the contribution to the molding and control of beliefs, values, and behaviors by way of a car culture for a relatively more individualist identity). And the reverse direction also holds true.

And in relation to the stability-reaction principle, if there is stability (e.g., the relatively more stable condition of the old "glory days" of car culture, when there were even "songs about the glory and wonder that surrounds the very concept of the car" like "In My Merry Oldsmobile," etc.), there is reaction (e.g., the old "glory days" of the car culture then led to further changes later on, when the critics like J. Kay question its desirability nowadays). And the reverse direction also holds true.

The Infeasibility of Networks

This comprehensive analysis of the possibility (or impossibility) and desirability (or undesirability) of networks in the context of transportation, from the perspectives of the mind, nature, society, and culture, reveals the different ways in which networks are both possible and desirable, but not to the extent that the spokespersons from each side would like us to believe.

Networks thus have their feasibility, just as they have their infeasibility too, as the other side of the same mirror.

But this is only one part of a larger story, since there is the other side of the story, which concerns operations. Since this chapter already deals with networks, the next chapter will therefore address the issue of operations.

As already stressed at the beginning of this chapter, these dual analyses should not be underestimated, because those on the side of networks often downplay operations merely as the other side of transportation without really appreciating it from the vantage point of operations too.

With this in mind, let's now turn to Chapter Three for the study of operations and their complications —for which we now turn to chapter three.

Table 2.1. Networks and their Intricacies

- **Networks and the Mind**
  —Ex: networks, walkability, and health
  —Ex: networks, the bicycle, and the feeling of freedom

- **Networks and Nature**
  —Ex: networks, locomotion, and energy
  —Ex: networks, spacecraft, and outer space

- **Networks and Society**
  —Ex: networks, vehicles, and the automobile industry
  —Ex: networks, future cars, and technology

- **Networks and Culture**
  —Ex: networks, TOD, and the ideology of Intelligent Urbanism
  —Ex: networks, the automobile, and cultural changes

Notes: The examples in the categories are solely illustrative (not exhaustive), and the comparison is relative (not absolute), nor are they necessarily mutually exclusive. And some can be easily re-classified elsewhere. As generalities, they allow exceptions.
Source: A summary of Ch.2 of *FPHTRAN*

Table 2.2. Networks, Locomotion, and Energy

- **Energy Sources**
  —Ex: electrical energy
  —Ex: nuclear energy
  —Ex: mechanical energy
  —Ex: gravitational energy
  —Ex: solar energy
  —Ex: wind energy
  —Ex: human energy

- **Motors and Engines**
  —Ex: aircraft engines
  —Ex: rocket engines
  —Ex: electric motors
  —Ex: compressed gas motors
  —Ex: ion thrusters

- **Conversion of Energy to Work**
  —Ex: wheels
  —Ex: noozles
  —Ex: tracks
  —Ex: propellers
  —Ex: wings

- **Problems with the Study on Locomotion and Energy**
  —Firstly, one main criticism of this study on locomotion and energy is that energy sources have disadvantages too.
  —Secondly, another main criticism of this study on locomotion and energy is that energy conversion is not completely efficient.
  —And thirdly, still another main criticism of this study on locomotion and energy is that there are tradeoffs for each kind of engines or motors.

Notes: The examples in the categories are solely illustrative (not exhaustive), and the comparison is relative (not absolute), nor are they necessarily mutually exclusive. And some can be easily re-classified elsewhere. As generalities, they allow exceptions.
Source: From *Sec. 2.3.1* of *FPHTRAN.* See book for citations.

Table 2.3. Networks, Spacecraft, and Outer Space

- **Sub-Systems of Spacecraft**
  —Ex: life support
  —Ex: attitude control
  —Ex: guidance, navigation, and control
  —Ex: command and data handling
  —Ex: power
  —Ex: thermal control
  —Ex: propulsion
  —Ex: structure
  —Ex: payload
  —Ex: ground segment
  —Ex: launch vehicle

- **Types of Spacecraft**
  —Ex: manned spacecrafts
  —Ex: unmanned spacecrafts

.

- **Problems with the Study on Spacecraft**
  —Firstly, one main criticism of this study on spacecraft is that the history of spacecraft has been driven by ideology and politics too.
  —Secondly, another main criticism of this study on spacecraft is that it is both technologically challenging and financially costly to build spacecrafts.
  —And thirdly, still another main criticism of this study on spacecraft is that spacecrafts, like other transports, are not immune from accidents or disasters.

Notes: The examples in the categories are solely illustrative (not exhaustive), and the comparison is relative (not absolute), nor are they necessarily mutually exclusive. And some can be easily re-classified elsewhere. As generalities, they allow exceptions.
Source: From *Sec. 2.3.2* of *FPHTRAN.* See book for more details and citations.

Table 2.4. Networks, Future Cars, and Technology

- **Advanced Control**
  —Ex: "platoons of cars"
  —Ex: "vehicle infrastructure integration"
  —Ex: "driverless cars"

- **Alternative Energy Sources**
  —Ex: "electric cars"
  —Ex: "hydrogen cars"

- **More Energy Efficiency**
  —Ex: "regenerative braking technology"
  —Ex: "compressed air hybrid"

- **Better Materials**
  —Ex: "duraluminum, fiberglass, carbon fiber, and carbon nanotubes"
  —Ex: "plastic and foam for the car's shell"

- **Problems with the Study on Future Car Technologies**
  —Firstly, one main criticism of this study on future car technologies is that the implementation can be costly.
  —Secondly, another main criticism of this study on future car technologies is that they are not so simple as they may sound.
  —Thirdly, still another main criticism of this study on future car technologies is that they are not necessarily effective to enhance security.
  —Fourthly, an additional main criticism of this study on future car technologies is that they are also not necessarily safe to use.
  —And fifthly, another additional main criticism of this study on future car technologies is that automated driving can become quite boring.

Notes: The examples are solely illustrative (not exhaustive), and the comparison is relative (not absolute), nor are they necessarily mutually exclusive. And some can be easily re-classified elsewhere. As generalities, they allow exceptions.
Source: From *Sec. 2.4.2* of *FPHTRAN.* See book for citations.

Table 2.5. Networks, the Automobile, and Cultural Changes

- **The Automobile, and Cultural Changes**
  —Ex: in artworks
  —Ex: in sports
  —Ex: in political culture
  —Ex: in economic culture
  —Ex: in social culture

- **Problems with the Automobile and its Cultural Changes**
  —Firstly, one main criticism of the phenomenon of the car culture is that it also has destructive effects.
  —Secondly, another main criticism of the phenomenon of the car culture is that the convenience of the automobile comes with a price to pay (in regard to time delay).
  —Thirdly, still another main criticism of the phenomenon of the car culture is that it can contribute to the spread of diseases.
  —Fourthly, an additional main criticism of the phenomenon of the car culture is that it has contributed to "a dramatic increase in the rate of accidental death." (WK 2012; J. Kay 1998)
  —And fifthly, another additional main criticism of the phenomenon of the car culture is that the requirement of transportation infrastructure is costly.

Notes: The examples are solely illustrative (not exhaustive), and the comparison is relative (not absolute), nor are they necessarily mutually exclusive. And some can be easily re-classified elsewhere. As generalities, they allow exceptions.
Source: From *Sec. 2.5.2* of *FPHTRAN.* See book for citations.

• PART THREE •

Operations

CHAPTER 3
OPERATIONS AND THEIR COMPLICATIONS

> In the U.S., the auto industry is a particularly awful candidate for a bailout. For generations it has represented the epitome of arrogance towards customers and inattentiveness to major societal changes….At every adverse turn, U.S. auto chiefs ran to Washington for help…as if they bore no responsibility….
> —Jeffrey E. Garten (2008)

The Functinality of Operations

The study of transportation invovles both networks and operations—as already indicated in *Sec. 1.3.*

The relationship between networks and operations is close enough, since one cannot be completely separated from the other.

Thus, a scholarly danger here is to reduce the analysis of one to that of the other; with this caveat in mind, this book is to devote a whole chapter on each, with the understanding, of course, that the two are related.

The issues concerning operations in the study of transportation are to be addressed in this chapter (Chapter Three), whereas the issues concerning networks were already analyzed in Chapter Two.

With this dialectic treatment in mind—a good way to examine the appeal of operations and their complications is by way of the evaluation of the extent to which they are in fact both possible (or impossible) and desirable (or undesirable).

This can be done by way of a comprehensive analysis of operations in the context of transpotation from the four perspectives of the mind, nature, society, and culture (in accordance to my sophisticated methodological holism, as explained in *Sec. 1.9*).

In other words, this chapter is organized in four main sections, in relation to (3.2) operations and the mind, (3.3) operations and nature, (3.4) operations and society, and (3.5) operations and culture—to be addressed hereafter, in that order (and summarized in *Table 3.1*).

Operations and the Mind

Operations, when examined from the perspective of the mind, can teach us something about their possibility (or impossibility) and desirability (or undesirability), and this can be shown by way of two case studies, namely, (3.2.1) operations, FOD awareness, and training, and (3.2.2) operations, drunkenness, and driving—to be addressed in what follows, respectively.

Operations, FOD Awareness, and Training

An excellent case study here to understand operations from the perspective of the mind has to do with operations, FOD awareness, and traning.

The term "FOD" stands for "foreign object debris" and refers to "a substance, debris or article alien to a vehicle or system which would potentially cause damage." (WK 2012gg)

FOD in Aviation

FOD is most prevalent in aviation, since "typically, FOD is an aviation term used to describe debris on or around an aircraft or damage done to an aircraft. Foreign Object Damage is any damage attributed to a foreign object (i.e. any object that is not part of the vehicle) that can be expressed in physical or economic terms and may or may not degrade the product's required safety or performance characteristics." (WK 2012gg)

There are different types of FOD in aviation, as shown below (and summarized in *Table 3.2*): (WK 2012gg)

- "Internal FOD"—"is used to refer to damage or hazards caused by foreign objects inside the aircraft."
- "Cockpit FOD"—"might be used to describe a situation where an item gets loose in the cockpit and jams or restricts the operation of the controls."
- "Tool FOD"—"is a serious hazard caused by tools left inside the aircraft after manufacturing or servicing. Tools or other items can get

> tangled in control cables, jam moving parts, short out electrical connections, or otherwise interfere with safe flight. Aircraft maintenance teams usually have strict tool control procedures including toolbox inventories to make sure all tools have been removed from an aircraft before it is released for flight. Tools used during manufacturing are tagged with a serial number so if they are found they can be traced."

And the term "damage" in FOD underwent a shift of meaning over time, since it "was prevalent in military circles, but has since been pre-empted by a definition of FOD that looks at the 'debris.' This shift was made 'official' in the latest FAA Advisory Circulars FAA A/C 150/5220-24 'Airport Foreign Object Debris (FOD) Detection Equipment' (2009) and FAA A/C 150/5210-24 'Airport Foreign Object Debris (FOD) Management.' Eurocontrol, ECAC, and the ICAO have all rallied behind this new definition. As Iain McCreary of Insight SRI put it in a presentation to NAPFI (August 2010), 'You can have debris present without damage, but never damage without debris.' Likewise, FOD prevention systems work by sensing and detecting not the damage but the actual debris. Thus FOD is now taken to mean the debris itself, and the resulting damage is referred to as 'FOD damage.'" (WK 2012gg)

Examples of FOD

There are many different examples of FOD. For illustration, consider the following ones (as summarized in *Table 3.2*): (WK 2012gg)

- "Aircraft Parts, Rocks, Broken Pavement, Ramp Equipment, and Vehicle Parts"—can cause damage "when the aircraft is taking off or landing. The intake suction from a jet engine is powerful enough to suck up loose material lying on the runway, and the winds created by a helicopter or prop-driven aircraft's rotors or by a jet blast can send such objects airborne, creating hazards to nearby personnel."
- "Parts from Ground Vehicles"
- "Garbage, Maintenance Tools, etc."—can be "mistakenly or purposely deposited on tarmac and/or runway surfaces"
- "Hail"—"can break windshields and damage or stop engines."
- "Ice on the Wings, Propellers, or Engine Intakes"
- "Dust or Ash"—can clog…the air intakes (as in sandstorms in desert operating conditions or ash clouds in volcanic eruptions). For helicopters, this is also a major problem during a brownout."

- "Tools, Bolts, Metal Shavings, Lockwire, etc."—can be "mistakenly left behind inside aircraft during the manufacturing process or maintenance."

In other cases, however, for example, "bird strikes (when an aeroplane flies into a bird, the impact can cause severe damage from a bird striking the fuselage, engine, etc.) are not considered to be FOD strikes, unless the bird or wildlife was already dead and lying on the operating surface when the strike occurred. Bird strikes are treated separately." (WK 2012gg)

Examples of FOD Damages

These different examples of FOD as indicated above can cause different types of damages. For illustration, consider the following examples (as summarized in *Table 3.2*): (WK 2012gg)

(a) Damages by Runway Debris

In regard to damages by runway debris—"the crash of a Concorde, Air France Flight 4590, at Charles de Gaulle International Airport near Paris on 25 July 2000 was caused by FOD; in this case a piece of titanium debris on the runway which had been part of a thrust reverser which fell off from a Continental Airlines McDonnell Douglas DC-10 that had taken off about four minutes earlier. All 100 passengers and nine crew on board the flight, as well as four people on the ground, were killed." (WK 2012gg)

A few years later, "a Bombardier Learjet 36A was taking off from Newport News/Williamsburg International Airport Va., on March 26, 2007, when the crew heard a loud 'pop.' Aborting the takeoff, the crew tried to control the 'fishtailing' and activate the drag chute. The chute did not work and the Learjet ran off the runway, its tires blown. Airport personnel reported seeing rocks and pieces of metal on the runway, after the accident. The NTSB said that the Learjet accident was caused by Foreign Object Debris (FOD) on the runway. Failure of the drag chute contributed to the accident."

(b) Damages by Volcanic Ash

In regard to damages by volcanic ash—"on 24 June 1982, British Airways Flight 9 on route to Perth, Australia, flew into a volcanic ash cloud over the Indian Ocean. The Boeing 747-200B suffered engine surges in all four engines until they all failed. The passengers and crew could see a phenomenon known as St. Elmo's fire around the plane. Flight 9 dived down until it exited the cloud allowing the airborne ash to clear the engines, which were then restarted. The cockpit windshield was badly pitted by the ash particles but the aircraft landed safely." (WK 2012gg)

(c) Damages by Item Jettisoned from Aircraft

And in regard to damages by item jettisoned from aircraft—"an unusual case of FOD occurred on 28 September 1981 over Chesapeake Bay. During flight testing of an F/A-18 Hornet, the Naval Air Test Center of the United States Navy was using a Douglas TA-4J Skyhawk as a chase plane to film a jettison test of a bomb rack from the Hornet. The bomb rack struck the right wing of the Skyhawk, shearing off almost half the wing. The Skyhawk caught fire within seconds of being struck; the two persons on board ejected." (WK 2012gg)

Measurement of the Seriousness of FOD

These examples of FOD damages show that FOD is a serious problem. In one estimate, "internationally, FOD costs the aviation industry US$13 billion per year in direct plus indirect costs. The indirect costs are as much as ten times the direct cost value, representing delays, aircraft changes, incurred fuel costs, unscheduled maintenance, and the like…and cause…expensive, significant damage to aircraft and parts and death and injury to workers, pilots and passengers." (WK 2012gg; INS 2012)

In another estimate, "FOD costs major airlines in the United States $26 per flight in aircraft repairs, plus $312 in such additional indirect costs as flight delays, plane changes and fuel inefficiencies." (WK 2012gg; INS 2008)

In addition, "there are other costs that are not as easy to calculate but are equally disturbing," as "UK Royal Air Force Wing Commander and FOD researcher Richard Friend" pointed out, since "from accidents such as the Air France Concorde, Flight AF 4590, there is the loss of life, suffering and effect on the families of those who died, the suspicion of malpractice, guilt, and blame that could last for lifetimes. This harrowing torment is incalculable but should not be forgotten, ever." (WK 2012gg)

Awareness and Training

In order to avoid or minimize future FOD damages, there are courses that all pilots are supposed to take, especially in relation to (a) awareness and (b) training, as described below (and summarized in *Table 3.2*).

(a) Awareness

In regard to awareness—there is a manuel known as the FOD "bible" written by Gary Chaplin, Founder and President of The F.O.D. Control Corporation. (WK 2012gg; FOD 2012)

In his handbook *Make It FOD Free: The Ultimate FOD Prevention Program Manual*, Chaplin provided four basic "elements of a comprehensive campaign" to make people aware of FOD damages: (WK 2012gg)

- "FOD-themed posters, signs and large banners and other visual aids displayed in critical work areas and places where employees are likely to gather."
- "Jackets, caps, coffee mugs, water bottles and other usable items with [FOD] logos affixed, which can be given away as 'prizes' for good FOD-prevention performance."
- "FOD Walks, in which personnel walk down a flightline shoulder-to-shoulder, working together to pick up FOD."
- "'FOD Awareness Week,' a week-long schedule of events—such as training sessions and FOD control equipment displays—targeted to get the workforce involved and increase their knowledge of the FOD Program."

Elsewhere, for instance, "the United States Air Force…is always looking for creative ways to encourage FOD awareness. The 407th Air Expeditionary Group at Ali Air Base in Iraq brings the fun of treasure hunting into its FOD Walks, by hiding a prized 'Golden Bolt' somewhere along the flightline. The Aircraft Maintenance Group at Tinker Air Force Base posts signs that say 'get your five today' or 'what were your five,' to encourage personnel to pick up at least five pieces of FOD every day." (WK 2012gg; P. Hanson 2007; D. Miller 2008)

(b) Training

And in regard to training—it is a different form of awareness by practice; in fact, training can be "an opportunity to highlight areas needing improvement, reinforce some of the rules that are not always being adhered to, introduce new initiatives, and applaud accomplishments. For instance, elements of new employee training should include" the followiong: (WK 2012gg)

- "Don't assume everyone knows what Foreign Object Damage is. Show photos of FOD and pass around samples of debris found at your facility."
- "Identify the FOD SOP (Standard Operating Procedure) and provide a copy of the FOD procedure to each new employee."
- "Emphasize the importance of 'Clean-As-You-Go' and define the rules that apply to daily work routines."

- "Review tool and hardware rules, to include tool crib issued items."
- "Review the Missing Item Report, when to use it and how to submit it."
- "Identify FOD control areas. Show examples of typical FOD charts/metrics."
- "If a borescope is available at your site, discuss who may use it, and general safety rules."
- "Identify other specialized tools used to locate or remove foreign objects."
- "Explain the role of the FOD department and how to contact a representative if needed. Put out the Welcome Mat."

In addition, "formal certification in Foreign Object Elimination (FOE)—Elements of Basic Awareness" can be given to those who finish this training program and "is now available from The National Center for Aerospace & Transportation Technologies, NCATT (www.ncatt.org)," which was previously known as "National Center for Aircraft Technician Training" and "is funded by the National Science Foundation. Certification covers knowledge of the following areas": (WK 2012gg)

- "Basic Terms & Definitions"
- "Housekeeping"
- "Tool Accountability"
- "Hardware Accountability"
- "Lost Items"
- "Physical Entry & Personnel Control"
- "Reporting & Investigating"
- "Material Handling"
- "Parts Protections"
- "Hazardous Materials"
- "Wildlife / Environment"
- "FOD Effects"

Of course, these examples are illustrative, not exhaustive.

Problems with the Study on FOD

However, for the critics, this study on FOD has some major problems. Consider, for illustration, a few examples below (as summarized in *Table 3.2*).

Firstly, one main criticism of the study on FOD is that it is hard to avoid FOD, as it is part of life in aviation.

For example, Richard Friend aptly observed that, "in fact, many factors combine to cause a chain of events that can lead to a failure," even though we should also "remain vigilant and…prevent foreign object debris from causing a problem." (WK 2012gg) In another study, "although airport ground crews regularly clean up runways, the crash of Air France Flight 4590 demonstrated that accidents can still occur: in that case, the crash was said to have been caused by debris left by a flight that had departed only four minutes earlier.' (WK 2012gg)

Secondly, another main criticism of the study on FOD is that FOD detection can be costly and its effectiveness may not be as high as its proponents would like us to believe.

For instance, for the critics, "there is some debate regarding FOD detection systems as the costs can be high and the domain of responsibility is not clear." (WK 2012gg)

Thirdly, still another main criticism of the study on FOD is that different data analyses about FOD can be inconsistent with each other and are thus questionable.

For instance, for the critics, "while that 2007 Insight SRI paper remains the best free public source of data, the new analysis (2010) from Insight SRI offers new numbers. The author of the new report (not free) says 'Readers are cautioned not to rely on or in the future refer to numbers from the 2007-08 Insight SRI paper." (WK 2012gg) And in another study, it was found that "when…indirect costs are added, then the cost of FOD increases by a multiple of up to 10x." (WK 2012gg; INS 2008)

And fourthly, an additional main criticism of the study on FOD is that awareness and training are not enough, as technology is also needed.

For instance, for the critics, different technologies need to be used for FOD detection and prevention, and good examples include the use of "radar" (like "QinetiQ and Trex Aviation Systems"), of "Electro-Optical [visible band imagery (standard CCTV) and low light cameras," of "Xsight's Surface Detection Units" (to be "mounted on the runway edge lights" and are combined with "a millimeter-wave radar sensor and an optic sensor with NIR illumination"), of "radio frequency identification (RFID)," and so on. (WK 2012gg; FAA 2009)

Beyond the Study on FOD

However, these criticisms of the study on FOD should not be misconstrued as a total rejection of its usefulness but serve to show us the two opposing sides of the debate, such that the possibility (or impossibility) and desirability (or undesirability) of operations (from the perspective of the mind with operations, FOD awareness, and training as a case study here) are not to the extent that the respective defenders would like us to believe.

Furthermore, the analysis of operations, FOD awareness, and training can enlighten us about the ontological principles in existential dialectics, and good examples include the formalness-informalness principle, the absoluteness-relativeness principle, the partiality-totality principle, the predictability-unpredictability principle, the explicability-inexplicability principle, the fiction-reality principle, the finiteness-transfiniteness principle, the preciseness-vagueness principle, the simpleness-complicatedness principle, the openness-hiddenness principle, the denseness-emptiness principle, the change-constancy principle, the order-chaos principle, the slowness-quickness principle, the expansion-contraction principle, the theory-praxis principle, the convention-novelty principle, the evolution-transformation principle, the symmetry-asymmetry principle, the softness-hardness principle, the seriousness-playfulness principle, the activeness-inactiveness principle, the regression-progression principle, the same-difference principle, and the stability-reaction principle.

For instance, in relation to the formalness-informalness principle, if there is formalness (e.g., the formal logical requirement of soundness, consistency, and completeness in a system of ideas, as in the study on FOD), there is informalness (e.g., the non-formal existence of unsoundness, inconsistency, and incompleteness in the study on FOD, as shown in the criticisms that it is hard to avoid FOD as it is part of life in aviation, that FOD detection can be costly and its effectiveness may not be as high as its proponents would like us to believe, that different data analyses about FOD can be inconsistent with each other and are thus questionable, that awareness and training are not enough as technology is also needed, etc.). And the reverse direction also holds true.

In relation to the absoluteness-relativeness principle, if there is absoluteness (e.g., the absolute view of those like Chaplin when he argued in the FOD "bible" that "a good Promotion and Awareness Program can significantly help reduce FOD by engaging a workforce with information, feedback and involvement"), there is relativeness (e.g., what is true for Chaplin in regard to the effectiveness of the "Promotion and Awareness Program" is not necessarily so for the critics, who instead point out that it is hard to avoid FOD as it is part of life in aviation, that FOD detection can be costly and its effectiveness may not be as high as its proponents would like us to believe, etc.). And the reverse direction also holds true.

In relation to the partiality-totality principle, if there is partiality (e.g., the partial view of those like Chaplin in regard to the "Promotion and Awareness Program"), there is totality (e.g., the more holistic view of FOD prevention, such that the whole is not the sum of its parts, that is, it cannot be reduced to the sum of opposing views like those by Chaplin, his critics, etc., since there will emerge new views in the future not yet known today, just as there are already other alternative views about FOD as part of life in aviation, which can occur unexpectedly). And the reverse direction also holds true.

In relation to the predictability-unpredictability principle, if there is predictability (e.g., the predictable tendency of those like Chaplin to argue that "a good Promotion and Awareness Program can significantly help reduce FOD by engaging a workforce with information, feedback and involvement"), there is unpredictability (e.g., the more difficult task to predict exactly the extent to which FOD can be detected and prevented on a particular future occasion, since there can be so many factors wich "combine to cause a chain of events that can lead to a failure," in an unexpected way). And the reverse direction also holds true.

In relation to the explicability-inexplicability principle, if there is explicability (e.g., the explanation by the advocates like Chaplin that "FOD Program is essentially a public relations campaign"), there is inexplicability (e.g., the lack of sufficient explanation by the advocates like Chaplin of why FOD Program is necessarily "a public relations campaign," since, for the critics, other factors are also needed, like the use of sophisticated technologies, and so on). And the reverse direction also holds true.

In relation to the fiction-reality principle, if there is fiction (e.g., the fictional aspect of the "Promotion and Awareness Program" by Chaplin, insofar as it ignores many other factors, like the use of different technologies to detect and prevent FOD, etc.), there is reality (e.g., the realistic aspect of the "Promotion and Awareness Program" by Chaplin, insofar as it stresses the importance of "public relations campaign" to prevent FOD). And the reverse direction also holds true.

In relation to the finiteness-transfiniteness principle, if there is finiteness (e.g., the finite number of the types of FOD, as shown in the 7 examples aforecited), there is transfiniteness (e.g., the transfinite number of all the individual pieces of foreign object debris in the history of the earth). And the reverse direction also holds true.

In relation to the preciseness-vagueness principle, if there is preciseness (e.g., the precise identification, by Chaplin, of 4 basic "elements of a comprehensive campaign" to make people aware of FOD damages), there is vagueness (e.g., the vagueness in the identification of the 4 basic "elements of a comprehensive campaign" to make people aware of FOD damages, since it is not clear why there must be only these 4 elements, not 5, 6, 7, 8, and so on). And the reverse direction also holds true.

In relation to the simpleness-complicatedness principle, if there is simpleness (e.g., the relatively simple analysis of FOD prevention by its advocates), there is complicatedness (e.g., the relatively more complicated analysis of FOD prevention, by challenging the claims and assumptions, as shown in the problems pointed out by the critics as cited). And the reverse direction also holds true.

In relation to the openness-hiddenness principle, if there is openness (e.g., the open exploration of different possible types of FOD which can cause damages to aircrafts), there is hiddenness (e.g., the hiddenness of the FOD, since some pieces of foreign object debris like tools and bolts can be carelessly or mistakenly put in the wrong places, such that pilots are caught by surprise when these pieces are flying around all of a sudden). And the reverse direction also holds true.

In relation to the denseness-emptiness principle, if there is denseness (e.g., the relatively denser concentration of concerns with "public relations campaign" for FOD prevention by someone like Chaplin), there is emptiness (e.g., the relatively less dense, or more empty, concentration of concerns with "public relations campaign" for FOD prevention by those who prefer to use sophisticated technologies like "radar," "Electro-Optical [visible band imagery [standard CCTV] and low light cameras," and so on). And the reverse direction also holds true.

In relation to the change-constancy principle, if there is change (e.g., the ever new ways to provide air safety, as shown in the study on FOD), there is constancy (e.g., the ever constant existence of different problems in the ever new ways to provide air safety, as shown in the problems with the study on FOD pointed out by the critics). And the reverse direction also holds true.

In relation to the order-chaos principle, if there is order (e.g., the more or less orderly reality of FOD prevention, if everything follows nicely in accordance to the procedures amd elements in the awareness and training programs afore-described), there is chaos (e.g,. the more or less chaotic reality of FOD prevention, if things go unexpectedly, like the accidents by runway debris, volcanic ash, etc. as described earlier). And the reverse direction also holds true.

In relation to the slowness-quickness principle, if there is slowness (e.g., the relatively slower speed of an aircraft to suffer from potential damages, if the pilots are well trained in formal FOD prevention programs, when confronted with these objects), there is quickness (e.g., the relatively quicker speed of an aircraft to suffer from potential damages when unexpectedly surrounded by FOD, if the pilots are not well trained in formal FOD prevention programs). And the reverse direction also holds true.

In relation to the expansion-contraction principle, if there is expansion (e.g., the relative spread, in terms of proportion, of human-made objects like tools, bolts, aircraft parts, vehicle pieces, etc. which can damage aircrafts, in the modern era of aviation), there is contraction (e.g., the relative decline, in terms of proportion, of natural objects like rocks, dust, ash, etc. which can damage aircrafts, in the modern era of aviation) . And the reverse direction also holds true.

In relation to the theory-praxis principle, if there is theory (e.g., the theoretical construction of "public relations campaign" in communication studies), there is praxis (e.g., the practical application of "public relations campaign" in communication studies to the field of transportation, like the "Promotion and Awareness Program" by Chaplin to prevent FOD). And the reverse direction also holds true.

In relation to the convention-novelty principle, if there is convention (e.g., the conventional wisdom about the FOD "bible" written by Gary Chaplin for the "Promotion and Awareness Program"), there is novelty (e.g., the alternative novel challenge to the conventional wisdom about the FOD "bible" written by Gary Chaplin for the "Promotion and Awareness Program, by the new idea of the critics that awareness and training are not enough, as sophisticated technologies are also needed). And the reverse direction also holds true.

In relation to the evolution-transformation principle, if there is evolution (e.g., the natural evolution of humans to be hit by ice, dust, ash, etc. in the state of nature in a primitive way), there is transformation (e.g., the technical transformation of human ability to be hit by the invention of aircrafts, which suffer from potential FOD damages). And the reverse direction also holds true.

In relation to the symmetry-asymmetry principle, if there is symmetry (e.g., the existence of different Insight SRI reports about FOD), there is asymmetry (e.g., the 2010 Insight SRI report about FOD is now more influential than the 2007 Insight SRI report). And the reverse direction also holds true.

In relation to the softness-hardness principle, if there is softness (e.g., the appreciation of the "public relations campaign" for FOD prevention, as shown by the FOD "bible" written by Gary Chaplin for the "Promotion and Awareness Program"), there is hardness (e.g., the critique of the "public relations campaign" for FOD prevention, as shown in the problems pointed out by the critics as cited, like the argument that sophisticated technologies are also needed, as awareness and training are not enough). And the reverse direction also holds true.

In relation to the seriousness-playfulness principle, if there is seriousness (e.g., the serious business of those who study and measure FOD), there is playfulness (e.g., the playful part of those who study and measure FOD, when they play around with different numbers, as shown the criticism that different data analyses about FOD can be inconsistent with each other). And the reverse direction also holds true.

In relation to the activeness-inactiveness principle, if there is activeness (e.g., the activeness of those aircrafts which are not damaged by FOD and function well), there is inactiveness (e.g., the relative inactiveness of those aircrafts which are damaged by FOD and crash later on)

In relation to the regression-progression principle, if there is regression (e.g., the regression made by the study on FOD, as shown in the problems pointed out by the critics aforecited), there is progression (e.g., the progress made by the study on FOD, as shown in the good "Promotion and Awareness Program" aforecited). And the reverse direction also holds true.

In relation to the same-difference principle, if there is similarity in outcome (e.g., the contribution to the molding and control of beliefs, values, and behaviors, regardless of whether this be done by way of the "public relations campaign" for FOD prevention, or by way of sophisticated technologies for FOD prevention), there is difference in outcome (e.g., the contribution to the molding and control of beliefs, values, and behaviors by way of the "public relations campaign" in regard to FOD prevention for a relatively more psychological worldview—but the contribution to the molding and control of beliefs, values, and behaviors by way of sophisticated technologies in regard to FOD prevention for a relatively more technophilic worldview). And the reverse direction also holds true.

And in relation to the stability-reaction principle, if there is stability (e.g., the relatively more stable condition of the "public relations campaign" for FOD prevention, when people generally accepted the FOD "bible" written by Gary Chaplin for the "Promotion and Awareness Program" in the older days), there is reaction (e.g., the popularity of the FOD "bible" in the older days then led to further changes later on, when nowadays there is a call for the use of sophisticated technologies, as awareness and training are no longer deemed as sufficient). And the reverse direction also holds true.

Operations, Drunkenness, and Driving

Another way to evaluate the possibility (or impossibility) and desirability (or undesirability) of operations from the perspective of the mind is to explore operations, drunkenness, and driving.

The term "drunkenness" is also known as "alcohol intoxication" (or "inebriation") and refers to "a physiological state that occurs when a person has a high level of ethanol (alcohol) in his or her blood." (WK 2012hh)

In general, "common symptoms of alcohol intoxication include slurred speech, euphoria, impaired balance, loss of muscle coordination (ataxia), flushed face, vomiting, reddened eyes, reduced inhibition, and erratic behavior. In severe cases, it can cause coma or death." (WK 2012hh)

Drunkenness in Pathophysiology

In pathophysiology (about "the functional changes associated with a disease or syndrome"), drunkenness is understood in contrast to a condition in which "alcohol is metabolized by a normal liver at the rate of about one ounce (one 'highball,' a normal beer, a regular sized glass of wine) every 90 minutes. An 'abnormal' liver with conditions such as hepatitis, cirrhosis, gall bladder disease, and cancer will have a slower rate of metabolism." (WK 2012hh; DIC 201)

In general, "ethanol [alcohol] is metabolised to acetaldehyde by alcohol dehydrogenase (ADH), which is found in many tissues, including the gastric mucosa. Acetaldehyde is metabolised to acetate by acetaldehyde dehydrogenase (ALDH), which is predominantly found in liver mitochondria. Acetate is used by the muscle cells to produce acetyl-CoA using the enzyme acetyl-CoA synthetase, and the acetyl-CoA is then used in the citric acid cycle. It takes roughly 90 minutes for a healthy liver to metabolize a single ounce, approximately one hour per standard unit." (WK 2012hh; C. Smith 2005)

The effects of "ethanol" in alcohol intoxication are "largely due to its nature as a central nervous system depressant, and are dependent on blood alcohol concentrations," as shown below (and summarized in *Table 3.3*): (WK 2012hh)

- "20–99 mg/dL"—"Impaired coordination and euphoria"
- "100–199 mg/dL"—"Ataxia, poor judgement, labile mood"
- "200–299 mg/dL"—"Marked ataxia, slurred speech, poor judgement, labile mood, nausea and vomiting"
- "300–399 mg/dL"—"Stage 1 anaesthesia, memory lapse, labile mood"
- "400+ mg/dL"—"Respiratory failure, coma"

Under normal circumstances, "as drinking increases, people become sleepy, or fall into a stupor. After a very high level of consumption, the respiratory system becomes depressed and the person will stop breathing. The most important thing for friends who witness someone 'passing out' from too much alcohol is to get them emergency medical treatment. Comatose patients may aspirate their vomit (resulting in vomitus in the lungs, which may cause 'drowning' and later pneumonia if survived). CNS depression and impaired motor co-ordination along with poor judgement increases the likelihood of accidental injury occurring. It is estimated that about one third of alcohol-related deaths are due to accidents (32%), and another 14% are from intentional injury." (WK 2012hh; P. McArdle 2004)

In addition to these problems of "respiratory failure and accidents caused by effects on the central nervous system, alcohol causes significant metabolic derangements. Hypoglycaemia occurs due to ethanol's inhibition of gluconeogenesis, especially in children, and may cause lactic acidosis, ketoacidosis and acute renal failure. Metabolic acidosis is compounded by respiratory failure. Patients may also present with hypothermia." (WK 2012hh)

Drunkenness and Driving

In the context of operations in the study of transportation, drunkenness can be associated with driving under the term "driving under the influence" (DUI), which is also known as "driving while intoxicated (DWI), drunken driving, drunk driving, operating under the influence, drinking and driving, impaired driving" and so on. (WK 2012e)

DUI thus refers to "the act of driving a motor vehicle with blood levels of alcohol in excess of a legal limit. Similar regulations cover driving or operating certain types of machinery while affected by drinking alcohol or taking other drugs. This is a criminal offense in most countries. Convictions do not necessarily involve actual driving of the vehicle." (WK 2012e)

Detection of Drunk Driving

Historically, there are different ways to detect if someone drives under the influence or not. Consider, for illustration, two main examples below (as summarized in *Table 3.3*).

(a) Blood Alcohol Level

Blood alcohol content (BAC) is a way to determine "culpability for the offense to strict liability based on driving while having more than a prescribed amount of blood alcohol, although this does not preclude the simultaneous existence of the older subjective tests. BAC is most conveniently measured as a simple percent of alcohol in the blood by weight." (WK 2012e)

In many cases, "a measurement such as a blood alcohol content in excess of a defined level, such as 0.05% or 0.08% defines the offense, with no need to prove impairment or being under the influence of alcohol. In some jurisdictions, there is an aggravated category of the offense at e.g. 0.12%." (WK 2012e)

(b) Field Sobriety Testing

Another way to determine drunken driving is the use of "field sobriety testing," which is to observe common symptoms in tests like "walking a straight line heel-to-toe or standing on one leg for 30 seconds," together with "the arresting officer's subjective opinion of impairment." (WK 2012e)

In the U.S., "the officer must correctly perform the Field Sobriety Tests (FSTs) that are approved by the National Highway Transportation Safety Administration (NHTSA). The US Department of Transportation explains the Field Sobriety Test as, 'a battery of three tests administered and evaluated in a standardized manner to obtain validated indicators of impairment and establish probable cause for arrest.'" (WK 2012e)

Drunk Driving Law

In many countries, "anyone who is convicted of injuring or killing someone while under the influence of alcohol or drugs can be heavily fined, as in France, in addition to being given a lengthy prison sentence." (WK 2012e)

In other countries like the U.S., "many states…have adopted truth in sentencing laws that enforce strict guidelines on sentencing, different from past practice where prison time was reduced or suspended after sentencing had been issued." (WK 2012e)

Many of these laws on drunk driving "apply also to boating, piloting aircraft, or cycling, possibly with different blood alcohol contents than driving. In some jurisdictions there are separate charges depending on the vehicle used, such as BWI (bicycling while intoxicated), which may carry a lighter sentence. In the United States, local law enforcement agencies made 1,467,300 arrests nationwide for driving under the influence of alcohol in 1996, compared to 1.9 million such arrests during the peak year in 1983. In 1997 an estimated 513,200 DWI offenders were in prison or jail, down from 593,000 in 1990 and up from 270,100 in 1986." (WK 2012e; USBJS 1998 & 1999)

Problems with the Study on DUI

However, for the critics, this study on DUI has some major problems. Consider, for illustration, a few examples below (as summarized in *Table 3.3*).

Firstly, one main criticism of the study on DUI is that the test to measure DUI is not without controversy.

For instance, conventionally, DUI is established by such methods like "observed driving symptoms" (e.g., "weaving"), and "field sobriety tests" (e.g., "walking a straight line heel-to-toe or standing on one leg for 30 seconds"), together with "the arresting officer's subjective opinion of impairment." (WK 2012e) But these methods can be subjectively or incorrectly followed—and even "the validity of the testing equipment/methods and mathematical relationships for the measurement of breath and blood alcohol have been criticized." (WK 2012e; NHTSA 2012)

Secondly, another main criticism of the study on DUI is that what counts as "guilt" in DUI cases varies from country to country.

For instance, "the laws relating to drunk driving vary between countries and varying blood alcohol content is allowed before a conviction is made"; for illustration, the blood/alcohol limit in Kyrgyzstan is 0.05% but it is 0.02% in Mongolia. (WK 2012e & 2012ii)

And thirdly, an additional main criticism of the study on DUI is that there can be alternative causes of non-sobriety other than the use of alcohol.

For instance, for some critics, to "determin[e]…whether someone is intoxicated by alcohol by some means other than a blood-alcohol test, it is necessary to rule out other conditions such as hypoglycemia, stroke, usage of other intoxicants, mental health issues, and so on. It is best if their behavior has been observed while the subject is sober to establish a baseline." (WK 2012ehh)

Beyond DUI

However, these criticisms of the study on DUI do not suggest a total rejection of its usefulness but serve to show us the two opposing sides of the debate, such that the possibility (or impossibility) and desirability (or undesirability) of operations (from the perspective of the mind with operations, drunkenness, and driving as a case study here) are not to the extent that the respective defenders would like us to believe.

In addition, the analysis of operations, drunkenness, and driving shows us something important about the ontological principles in existential dialectics, and good examples include the formalness-informalness principle, the absoluteness-relativeness principle, the partiality-totality principle, the predictability-unpredictability principle, the explicability-inexplicability principle, the fiction-reality principle, the finiteness-transfiniteness principle, the preciseness-vagueness principle, the simpleness-complicatedness principle, the openness-hiddenness principle, the denseness-emptiness principle, the change-constancy principle, the order-chaos principle, the slowness-quickness principle, the expansion-contraction principle, the theory-praxis principle, the convention-novelty principle, the evolution-transformation principle, the symmetry-asymmetry principle, the softness-hardness principle, the seriousness-playfulness principle, the activeness-inactiveness principle, the regression-progression principle, the same-difference principle, and the stability-reaction principle.

For instance, in relation to the formalness-informalness principle, if there is formalness (e.g., the formal logical requirement of soundness in a system of ideas, as in the study on DUI), there is informalness (e.g., the non-formal existence of unsoundness in the study on DUI, as shown in the criticisms that the test to measure DUI is not without controversy, that what counts as "guilt" in DUI cases varies from country to country, that there can be alternative causes of non-sobriety other than the use of alcohol, etc.). And the reverse direction also holds true.

In relation to the absoluteness-relativeness principle, if there is absoluteness (e.g., the absolute view of those police officers who depend on field sobriety tests like "walking a straight line heel-to-toe or standing on one leg for 30 seconds"), there is relativeness (e.g., what is right for those police officers who depend on field sobriety tests like "walking a straight line heel-to-toe or standing on one leg for 30 seconds" is not necessarily so for the critics, who argue that these tests are not reliable and controversial, as they are often combined with "the arresting officer's subjective opinion of impairment"). And the reverse direction also holds true.

In relation to the partiality-totality principle, if there is partiality (e.g., the partial view of those police officers who depend on field sobriety tests), there is totality (e.g., the more holistic view of the detection of drunk driving, such that the whole is not the sum of its parts, that is, it cannot be reduced to the sum of opposing views like field sobriety tests, blood alcohol content tests, the claim of unreliability by the critics, etc., since there will emerge new views in the future not yet known today, just as there are already now altnerative views in some countries, where "it is illegal for an open container of an alcoholic beverage to be in the passenger compartment of a motor vehicle or in some specific area of that compartment" and "may be illegal to be asleep in the driver's seat of a vehicle without any intention to drive"). (WK 2012e) And the reverse direction also holds true.

In relation to the predictability-unpredictability principle, if there is predictability (e.g., the predictable tendency of "the laws relating to drunk driving [to] vary between countries"), there is unpredictability (e.g., the more difficult task to predict exactly the extent to which a particular drunk driving law will last in a particular future historical era, since, for instance, in China, a violation of the blood/alcohol limit of 0.02% in the older days would get "1–3 months license suspension," but, "beginning May 1, 2011, Chinese law now mandates a penal detention up to 6 months for any person convicted of drunken driving"). (WK 2012ii) And the reverse direction also holds true.

In relation to the explicability-inexplicability principle, if there is explicability (e.g., the explanation by the law enforcement authority in some countries that it is illegal "to be asleep in the driver's seat of a vehicle without any intention to drive"), there is inexplicability (e.g., the lack of sufficient explanation by the law enforcement authority in some countries of why it is necessarily desirable to make it illegal "to be asleep in the driver's seat of a vehicle without any intention to drive," since, for the driver, it is better to rest and sleep than to drive under the influence). And the reverse direction also holds true.

In relation to the fiction-reality principle, if there is fiction (e.g., the fictional aspect of "field sobriety tests," insofar as these tests are not reliable and controversial, as they are often combined with "the arresting officer's subjective opinion of impairment"), there is reality (e.g., the realistic aspect of "field sobriety tests," insofar as these tests can help to detect blood/alcohol content to some extent). And the reverse direction also holds true.

In relation to the finiteness-transfiniteness principle, if there is finiteness (e.g., the finite number of the categories of "blood alcohol concentrations," such as "20–99 mg/dL," "100–199 mg/dL," etc.), there is transfiniteness (e.g., the transfinite number of all the individuals in history who have ever had any of the categories of "blood alcohol concentrations"). And the reverse direction also holds true.

In relation to the preciseness-vagueness principle, if there is preciseness (e.g., the precise identification of 5 categories of "blood alcohol concentrations," such as "20–99 mg/dL," "100–199 mg/dL," etc.), there is vagueness (e.g., the vagueness in the identification of the 5 categories of "blood alcohol concentrations," such as "20–99 mg/dL," "100–199 mg/dL," etc., since it is not clear why there must be only 5 categories, not 6, 7, 8, and so on). And the reverse direction also holds true.

In relation to the simpleness-complicatedness principle, if there is simpleness (e.g., the relatively simple analysis of field sobriety tests, blood alcohol content tests, etc. by the advocates), there is complicatedness (e.g., the relatively more complicated analysis of field sobriety tests, blood alcohol content tests, etc., by challenging the claims and assumptions, as shown in the problems pointed out by the critics as cited). And the reverse direction also holds true.

In relation to the openness-hiddenness principle, if there is openness (e.g., the open exploration of the correlation between field sobriety tests and driving under influence), there is hiddenness (e.g., the hidden bias in "field sobriety tests," because these tests are not reliable and controversial, as they are often combined with "the arresting officer's subjective opinion of impairment"). And the reverse direction also holds true.

In relation to the denseness-emptiness principle, if there is denseness (e.g., the relatively denser concentration of alcohol in the blood stream, like those cases of 0.40% in "excessive drinking" as in "alcohol poisoning"), there is emptiness (e.g., the relatively less dense, or more empty, concentration of alcohol in the blood stream, like those cases of less than 0.20%). (WK 2012jj & 2012e) And the reverse direction also holds true.

In relation to the change-constancy principle, if there is change (e.g., the ever new ways to detect DUI, as shown in field sobriety tests, blood alcohol content tests, etc.), there is constancy (e.g., the ever constant existence of different problems in the ever new ways to detect DUI, as shown in the problems with field sobriety tests, blood alcohol content tests, etc. pointed out by the critics). And the reverse direction also holds true.

In relation to the order-chaos principle, if there is order (e.g., the more or less orderly reality of drunk driving law, if examined from the viewpoint of a particular country like Mongolia, where the blood/alcohol limit is 0.2%), there is chaos (e.g,. the more or less chaotic reality of drunk driving law, if examined from the viewpoints of all the countries around the world, which vary greatly and are complicated enough). And the reverse direction also holds true.

In relation to the slowness-quickness principle, if there is slowness (e.g., the relatively slower speed of someone to get drunk if he consumes a small amount of alcohol), there is quickness (e.g., the relatively quicker speed of someone to get drunk if he consumes an extreme level of consumption like "alcohol poisoning"). And the reverse direction also holds true.

In relation to the expansion-contraction principle, if there is expansion (e.g., the relative spread of the use of alcohol nowadays, when contrasted with the period during the Prohibition in the United States from 1919 to 1933), there is contraction (e.g., the relative decline of the use of alcohol during the Prohibition in the United States from 1919 to 1933, when contrasted with the use nowadays). And the reverse direction also holds true.

In relation to the theory-praxis principle, if there is theory (e.g., the theoretical construction of the interdisciplinary approach by the Medical Psychological Assessment in Germany to understand "the fitness for drive"), there is praxis (e.g., the practical application of the interdisciplinary approach by the Medical Psychological Assessment in psychology to the field of law enforcement, like the removal of certain drivers "from traffic until their fitness to drive has been established again"). (WK 2012e) And the reverse direction also holds true.

In relation to the convention-novelty principle, if there is convention (e.g., the conventional wisdom about the use of field sobriety tests in the older days), there is novelty (e.g., the alternative novel challenge to the conventional wisdom about the use of field sobriety tests in the older days, by the new idea of blood alcohol content tests, which are regarded as more "scientific" nowadays). And the reverse direction also holds true.

In relation to the evolution-transformation principle, if there is evolution (e.g., the natural evolution of humans to sleep or to be not in an alert state of mind from time to time in the state of nature), there is transformation (e.g., the technical transformation of human ability to be not in an alert state of mind from time to time by the invention of alcoholic intoxication, as shown in drunk driving, which did not exist in the state of nature). And the reverse direction also holds true.

In relation to the symmetry-asymmetry principle, if there is symmetry (e.g., the existence of different agents in society, like drivers, police officers, etc.), there is asymmetry (e.g., police officers have the power to arrest drivers under the influence). And the reverse direction also holds true.

In relation to the softness-hardness principle, if there is softness (e.g., the appreciation of field sobriety tests, as shown in their use by police officers), there is hardness (e.g., the critique of field sobriety tests by the critics as unreliable and controversial). And the reverse direction also holds true.

In relation to the seriousness-playfulness principle, if there is seriousness (e.g., the serious business of drivers to reach their destination by driving), there is playfulness (e.g., the playful part of drivers, when they play around with the consumption of alcohol and drive under the influence). And the reverse direction also holds true.

In relation to the activeness-inactiveness principle, if there is activeness (e.g., the activeness of those who are sober and able to drive to where they want to go), there is inactiveness (e.g., the relative inactiveness of those who are drunken and fall asleep).

In relation to the regression-progression principle, if there is regression (e.g., the regression made by the use of alcohol, as shown in the problems associated with DUI pointed out by the critics), there is progression (e.g., the progress made by the use of alcohol, as shown in its effects to have fun and relax, as "a central nervous system depressant"). And the reverse direction also holds true.

In relation to the same-difference principle, if there is similarity in outcome (e.g., the contribution to the molding and control of beliefs, values, and behaviors, regardless of whether this be done by way of driving under the influence, or by way of driving with asceticism), there is difference in outcome (e.g., the contribution to the molding and control of beliefs, values, and behaviors by way of driving under the influence for a relatively more epicurean lifeworld—but the contribution to the molding and control of beliefs, values, and behaviors by way of driving with asceticism for a relatively more disciplined lifeworld). And the reverse direction also holds true.

And in relation to the stability-reaction principle, if there is stability (e.g., the relatively more stable condition of the use of field sobriety tests in the older day, when police officers often used them, together with "the arresting officer's subjective opinion of impairment"), there is reaction (e.g., the use of field sobriety tests in the older days then led to further changes later on, when blood alcohol content tests are more used nowadays, because they are regarded as more "scientific"). And the reverse direction also holds true.

Operations and Nature

Operations, when examined from the perspective of nature, can show us their possibility (or impossibility) and desirability (or undesirability), and this can be shown by way of two case studies, namely, (3.3.1) operations, air pollution, and regulation, and (3.3.2) operations, horses, and the carriage—to be addressed in what follows, respectively.

Operations, Air Pollution, and Regulation

A good way to evaluate the possibility (or impossibility) and desirability (or undesirability) of operations from the perspective of nature is to explore operations, air pollution, and regulation.

The term "air pollution" refers to "the introduction of chemicals, particulate matter, or biological materials that cause harm or discomfort to humans or other living organisms, or cause damage to the natural environment or built environment, into the atmosphere." (WK 2012h)

In fact, "indoor air pollution and urban air quality are listed as two of the world's worst pollution problems in the 2008 Blacksmith Institute World's Worst Polluted Places report." (WK 2012h; WORS 2010)

Types of Air Pollution

Air pollution introduces chemicals in the air that "can cause harm to humans and the environment," and these chemicals are known as "air pollutants," which "can be in the form of solid particles, liquid droplets, or gases. In addition, they may be natural or man-made." (WK 2012h; EPA 2006)

In general, "pollutants can be classified as primary or secondary," as described below (and summarized in *Table 3.4*):

- "Primary Pollutants"—"are directly emitted from a process, such as ash from a volcanic eruption, the carbon monoxide gas from a motor vehicle exhaust or sulfur dioxide released from factories."
- "Secondary Pollutants"—"are not emitted directly. Rather, they form in the air when primary pollutants react or interact. An important example of a secondary pollutant is ground level ozone—one of the many secondary pollutants that make up photochemical smog."

Of course, there can be other types. For instance, "some pollutants may be both primary and secondary: that is, they are both emitted directly and formed from other primary pollutants." (WK 2012h)

Sources of Air Pollution

Air pollution can also be classified in terms of its "sources," which refer to "the various locations, activities or factors which are responsible for the releasing of pollutants into the atmosphere. These sources can be classified into two major categories" as shown below (and summarized in *Table 3.4*): (WK 2012h; D. Pennise 2012; WHO. 2011; A. Goldstein 2009)

- "Anthropogenic Sources (Human Activity)"—are "mostly related to burning different kinds of fuel."
  - –"Stationary Sources"—"include smoke stacks of power plants, manufacturing facilities (factories) and waste incinerators, as well as furnaces and other types of fuel-burning heating devices. In developing and poor countries, traditional biomass burning is the major source of air pollutants; traditional biomass includes wood, crop waste and dung."
  - –"Mobile Sources"—"include motor vehicles, marine vessels, aircraft and the effect of sound etc."
  - –"Chemicals, Dust and Controlled Burn Practices"—are often seen "in agriculture and forestry management. Controlled or prescribed burning is a technique sometimes used in forest management, farming, prairie restoration or greenhouse gas abatement. Fire is a natural part of both forest and grassland ecology and controlled fire can be a tool for foresters. Controlled burning stimulates the germination of some desirable forest trees, thus renewing the forest."
  - –"Fumes"—occur "from paint, hair spray, varnish, aerosol sprays and other solvents."
  - –"Waste Deposition"—are common "in landfills, which generate methane. Methane is not toxic; however, it is highly flammable and may form explosive mixtures with air. Methane is also an asphyxiant and may displace oxygen in an enclosed space. Asphyxia or suffocation may result if the oxygen concentration is reduced to below 19.5% by displacement."
  - –"Military" Sources—include "nuclear weapons, toxic gases, germ warfare and rocketry."

- "Natural Sources"
  - –"Dust"—covers "usually large areas of land with little or no vegetation."
  - –"Methane"—is "emitted by the digestion of food by animals, for example cattle."
  - –"Radon Gas"—is "from radioactive decay within the Earth's crust. Radon is a colorless, odorless, naturally occurring, radioactive noble gas that is formed from the decay of radium. It is considered to be a health hazard. Radon gas from natural sources can accumulate in buildings, especially in confined areas such as the basement and it is the second most frequent cause of lung cancer, after cigarette smoking."
  - –"Smoke and Carbon Monoxide"—can also occur from wildfires.
  - –"Vegetation"—"in some regions, emits environmentally significant amounts of VOCs on warmer days. These VOCs react with primary anthropogenic pollutants—specifically, NO_x, SO_2, and anthropogenic organic carbon compounds—to produce a seasonal haze of secondary pollutants."
  - –"Volcanic Activity"—"produces sulfur, chlorine, and ash particulates.

Of course, there can be other exapmles, so the ones above are illustrative, not exhaustive.

Carbon Monoxide in Transportation, and Air Pollution

In the current context of transportation, the most relevant sources of air pollution are "mobile sources" (in the anthropogenic category as listed above) which "include motor vehicles, marine vessels, aircraft and the effect of sound etc." (WK 2012h)

These mobile sources of air pollution often release "carbon monoxide (CO)" into the air, which "is a colourless, odorless, non-irritating but very poisonous gas. It is a product by incomplete combustion of fuel such as natural gas, coal or wood. Vehicular exhaust is a major source of carbon monoxide." (WK 2012h)

(a) Molecular Properties

Carbon monoxide has certain molecular properties; for example, it "has a molar mass of 28.0, which makes it slightly lighter than air, whose average molar mass is 28.8. According to the ideal gas law, CO is therefore less dense than air. Neither gas is 'ideal,' however, so the exact densities and other comparative values depend upon temperature and pressure." (WK 2012kk)

In addition, "the bond length between the carbon atom and the oxygen atom is 112.8 pm. This bond length is consistent with a triple bond, as in molecular nitrogen (N_2), which has a similar bond length and nearly the same molecular mass. Carbon-oxygen double bonds are significantly longer, 120.8 pm in formaldehyde, for example. The boiling point (82 K) and melting point (68 K) are very similar to those of N_2 (77 K and 63 K, respectively). The bond dissociation energy of 1072 kJ/mol is stronger than that of N_2 (942 kJ/mol) and represents the strongest chemical bond known." (WK 2012kk; O. Gilliam 1950; W. Haynes 2010)

(b) Toxicity

Carbon monoxide is dangerous, since its "poisoning is the most common type of fatal air poisoning in many countries. Carbon monoxide is colourless, odorless, and tasteless, but highly toxic. It combines with hemoglobin to produce carboxyhemoglobin, which is ineffective for delivering oxygen to bodily tissues. Concentrations as low as 667 ppm may cause up to 50% of the body's hemoglobin to convert to carboxyhemoglobin. A level of 50% carboxyhemoglobin may result in seizure, coma, and fatality. In the United States, the OSHA limits long-term workplace exposure levels above 50 ppm. Within short time scales, carbon monoxide absorption is cumulative, since the half-life is about 5 h in fresh air." (WK 2012kk; S. Omaye 2002; P. Tikuisis 1992; OSHA 2009)

In general, "the most common symptoms of carbon monoxide poisoning may resemble other types of poisonings and infections, including symptoms such as headache, nausea, vomiting, dizziness, fatigue, and a feeling of weakness. Affected families often believe they are victims of food poisoning. Infants may be irritable and feed poorly. Neurological signs include confusion, disorientation, visual disturbance, syncope and seizures." (WK 2012kk; I. Blumenthal 2001)

In addition, "carbon monoxide binds to other molecules such as myoglobin and mitochondrial cytochrome oxidase. Exposures to carbon monoxide may cause significant damage to the heart and central nervous system, especially to the globus pallidus, often with long-term sequelae. Carbon monoxide may have severe adverse effects on the fetus of a pregnant woman." (WK 2012kk; L. Prockop 2007; S. Blackburn 2007)

(c) Urban Pollution

Carbon monoxide often occurs in urban environments, as "a temporary atmospheric pollutant..., chiefly from the exhaust of internal combustion engines (including vehicles, portable and back-up generators, lawn mowers, power washers, etc.), but also from incomplete combustion of various other fuels (including wood, coal, charcoal, oil, paraffin, propane, natural gas, and trash)." (WK 2012kk)

Earlier, for instance, "during World War II, a gas mixture including carbon monoxide was used to keep motor vehicles running in parts of the world where gasoline and diesel fuel were scarce. External (with few exceptions) charcoal or wood gas generators were fitted, and the mixture of atmospheric nitrogen, carbon monoxide, and smaller amounts of other gases produced by gasification was piped to a gas mixer. The gas mixture produced by this process is known as wood gas." (WK 2012kk)

(d) Legal Regulations

Consequently, because of the toxicity of carbon monoxide, there are different legal regulations in regard to the release of carbon monoxide in the air.

For example, in the U.S. and Canada, "there are two types of air quality standards. The first class of standards (such as the U.S. National Ambient Air Quality Standards and E.U. Air Quality Directive) set maximum atmospheric concentrations for specific pollutants. Environmental agencies enact regulations which are intended to result in attainment of these target levels. The second class (such as the North American Air Quality Index) take the form of a scale with various thresholds, which is used to communicate to the public the relative risk of outdoor activity. The scale may or may not distinguish between different pollutants." (WK 2012h)

Problems with the Study on Air Pollution

However, for the critics, this study on air pollution in transportation has some major problems. Consider, for illustration, a few examples below (as summarized in *Table 3.4*).

Firstly, one main criticism of the study on air pollution in transportation is that "mobile sources" are only ones among different sources of air pollution and should not be blamed too much for air pollution.

For instance, for the critics, one should not blame mobile sources too much for air pollution, since there are many other sources, and good examples include "sulphur oxides" (by volcanoes), "nitrogen oxides" (by thunderstorms), "particular matter" (by dust storms, forest and grassland fires, etc.), and so on. (WK 2012h)

Secondly, another main criticism of the study on air pollution in transportation is that regulations do not often work, because of disagreements.

For instance, for the critics, "the Air Quality Health Index or 'AQHI'" in Canada is "a federal program jointly coordinated by Health Canada and Environment Canada. However, the AQHI program would not be possible without the commitment and support of the provinces, municipalities and NGOs," which do not always agree. (WK 2012h)

And thirdly, an additional main criticism of the study on air pollution in transportation is that the use of carbon monoxide has been used for different ulterior purposes.

For instance, "carbon monoxide was also…used on a small scale during the Holocaust at some Nazi extermination camps, the most notable by gas vans in Chelmno, and in the Action T4 'euthanasia' program." (WK 2012kk)

Beyond Air Pollution

However, these criticisms of the study on air pollution in transportation should not be taken as a total rejection of its usefulness but serve to show us the two opposing sides of the debate, such that the possibility (or impossibility) and desirability (or undesirability) of operations (from the perspective of nature with operations, air pollution, and regulation as a case study here) are not to the extent that the respective defenders would like us to believe.

In addition, the analysis of operations, air pollution, and regulation can reveal something relevant about the ontological principles in existential dialectics, and good examples include the formalness-informalness principle, the absoluteness-relativeness principle, the partiality-totality principle, the predictability-unpredictability principle, the explicability-inexplicability principle, the fiction-reality principle, the finiteness-transfiniteness principle, the preciseness-vagueness principle, the simpleness-complicatedness principle, the openness-hiddenness principle, the denseness-emptiness principle, the change-constancy principle, the order-chaos principle, the slowness-quickness principle, the expansion-contraction principle, the theory-praxis principle, the convention-novelty principle, the evolution-transformation principle, the symmetry-asymmetry principle, the softness-hardness principle, the seriousness-playfulness principle, the activeness-inactiveness principle, the regression-progression principle, the same-difference principle, and the stability-reaction principle.

For instance, in relation to the formalness-informalness principle, if there is formalness (e.g., the formal logical requirement of soundness and completeness in a system of ideas, as in the study on air pollution in transportation), there is informalness (e.g., the non-formal existence of unsoundness and incompleteness in the study on air pollution in transportation, as shown in the criticisms that "mobile sources" are only ones among different sources of air pollution and should not be blamed too much for air pollution, that regulations do not often work because of disagreements, that the use of carbon monoxide has been used for different ulterior purposes, etc.). And the reverse direction also holds true.

In relation to the absoluteness-relativeness principle, if there is absoluteness (e.g., the absolute view of the Nazis, who used carbon monoxide "during the Holocaust at some Nazi extermination camps, the most notable by gas vans in Chelmno, and in the Action T4 'euthanasia' program"), there is relativeness (e.g., what is desirable for the Nazis, who used carbon monoxide "during the Holocaust at some Nazi extermination camps, is not necessarily so for the advocates of the U.S. National Ambient Air Quality Standards in regard to regulations of air pollution and the release of carbon monoxide). And the reverse direction also holds true.

In relation to the partiality-totality principle, if there is partiality (e.g., the partial view of the Nazis, who used carbon monoxide "during the Holocaust at some Nazi extermination camps, the most notable by gas vans in Chelmno, and in the Action T4 'euthanasia' program"), there is totality (e.g., the more holistic view of the future of carbon monoxide, such that the whole is not the sum of its parts, that is, it cannot be reduced to the sum of opposing views of the Nazis, those in USNAAQS, etc., since there will emerge new views in the future not yet known today, just as there are already other views which are both critical to the ones of the Nazis, of those in USNAAQS, etc., as shown in the criticisms by the critics aforecited). And the reverse direction also holds true.

In relation to the predictability-unpredictability principle, if there is predictability (e.g., the predictable tendency of carbon monoxide to be dangerous, since its "poisoning is the most common type of fatal air poisoning in many countries"), there is unpredictability (e.g., the more difficult task to predict exactly the extent to which carbon monoxide will be used in a particular future era, since there are already conflicting uses by those in its past history, like the ones by the Nazis, those in USNAAQS, etc.). And the reverse direction also holds true.

In relation to the explicability-inexplicability principle, if there is explicability (e.g., the explanation by those for "the Air Quality Health Index or 'AQHI'" in Canada that certain regulations of air pollution are desirable), there is inexplicability (e.g., the lack of sufficient explanation by those for "the Air Quality Health Index or 'AQHI'" in Canada of why certain regulations of air pollution are necessarily desirable, since "the AQHI program would not be possible without the commitment and support of the provinces, municipalities and NGOs," which do not always agree). And the reverse direction also holds true.

In relation to the fiction-reality principle, if there is fiction (e.g., the fictional aspect of carbon monoxide, insofar as it is uncritically assumed to be regulated so as to not harm people because of its toxcity, but the Nazis, for example, used carbon monoxide "during the Holocaust at some Nazi extermination camps, the most notable by gas vans in Chelmno, and in the Action T4 'euthanasia' program"), there is reality (e.g., the realistic aspect of carbon monoxide, insofar as it is to be regulated so as to not harm people because of its toxcity, as shown in the regulations in accordance to "the Air Quality Health Index or 'AQHI'" in Canada). And the reverse direction also holds true.

In relation to the finiteness-transfiniteness principle, if there is finiteness (e.g., the finite number of the categories of air pollution, like the 3 categories of "chemicals, particulate matter, and biological materials" in the article aforecited), there is transfiniteness (e.g., the transfinite number of all the possible units of "chemicals, particulate matter, and biological materials" that have ever existed in history). And the reverse direction also holds true.

In relation to the preciseness-vagueness principle, if there is preciseness (e.g., the precise identification of 6 anthropogenic sources of air pollution in the article aforecited), there is vagueness (e.g., the vagueness in the identification of the 6 anthropogenic sources of air pollution in the article aforecited, since it is not clear why there must be only 6 sources, not 7, 8, 9, and so on). And the reverse direction also holds true.

In relation to the simpleness-complicatedness principle, if there is simpleness (e.g., the relatively simple analysis of air pollution in transportation by the advocates), there is complicatedness (e.g., the relatively more complicated analysis of air pollution in transportation, by challenging the claims and assumptions, as shown in the problems pointed out by the critics as cited). And the reverse direction also holds true.

In relation to the openness-hiddenness principle, if there is openness (e.g., the open exploration of "air pollutants," which "can be in the form of solid particles, liquid droplets, or gases"), there is hiddenness (e.g., the hidden nature of some of the air pollutants, like carbon monoxide, which "is a colourless, odorless, non-irritating but very poisonous gas"). And the reverse direction also holds true.

In relation to the denseness-emptiness principle, if there is denseness (e.g., the relatively denser concentration of air, "whose average molar mass is 28.8"), there is emptiness (e.g., the relatively less dense, or more empty, concentration of carbon monoxide, which is less dense than air, because it "has a molar mass of 28.0, which makes it slightly lighter than air, whose average molar mass is 28.8"). And the reverse direction also holds true.

In relation to the change-constancy principle, if there is change (e.g., the ever new ways to understand air pollution in transportation, as shown in the study on air pollution and carbon monoxide), there is constancy (e.g., the ever constant existence of different problems in the ever new ways to study air pollution in transportation, as shown in the problems with the study on air pollution and carbon monoxide pointed out by the critics aforecited). And the reverse direction also holds true.

In relation to the order-chaos principle, if there is order (e.g., the more or less orderly reality of the regulations of air pollution, if looked from the vantage point that there are only two types of air quality standards in the U.S. and Canada aforecited), there is chaos (e.g,. the more or less chaotic reality of the regulations of air pollution, if looked from the vantage point that "the AQHI program would not be possible without the commitment and support of the provinces, municipalities and NGOs," which do not always agree). And the reverse direction also holds true.

In relation to the slowness-quickness principle, if there is slowness (e.g., the relatively slower speed of someone to get sick, if he inhales "concentrations" of carbon monoxide much less than 50 ppm), there is quickness (e.g., the relatively quicker speed of someone to get sick, if he inhales "concentrations" of carbon monoxide "as low as 667 ppm" or more). And the reverse direction also holds true.

In relation to the expansion-contraction principle, if there is expansion (e.g., the relative spread of more regulations of the use of carbon monoxide nowadays), there is contraction (e.g., the relative decline of the deliberate use of carbon monoxide to harm people nowadays, as the Nazis did "during the Holocaust at some Nazi extermination camps, the most notable by gas vans in Chelmno, and in the Action T4 'euthanasia' program"). And the reverse direction also holds true.

In relation to the theory-praxis principle, if there is theory (e.g., the theoretical construction of the molecular properties of carbon monoxide in chemistry in order to understand its toxicity), there is praxis (e.g., the practical application of the molecular properties of carbon monoxide in chemistry to the field of transportation so as to deal with its toxicity, as shown in the regulations of air pollution in accordance to the AQHI program). And the reverse direction also holds true.

In relation to the convention-novelty principle, if there is convention (e.g., the conventional wisdom about the regulations of the use of carbon monoxide, because of its toxcity which can harm people), there is novelty (e.g., the alternative novel challenge to the conventional wisdom about the regulations of the use of carbon monoxide, by the new idea of the Nazis, who used carbon monoxide "during the Holocaust at some Nazi extermination camps, the most notable by gas vans in Chelmno, and in the Action T4 'euthanasia' program"). And the reverse direction also holds true.

In relation to the evolution-transformation principle, if there is evolution (e.g., the natural evolution of CO to occur in nature, via "volcanoes, forest fires, and other forms of combustion"), there is transformation (e.g., the technical transformation of human ability to manufacture CO artificially by the invention of "an internal combustion engine in an enclosed space," for instance). (WK 2012kk) And the reverse direction also holds true.

In relation to the symmetry-asymmetry principle, if there is symmetry (e.g., the existence of different views about the use of carbon monoxide), there is asymmetry (e.g., the push for regulations of the use of carbon monoxide nowadays is more influential than its deliterate use to harm people in the older days by the Nazis, for example). And the reverse direction also holds true.

In relation to the softness-hardness principle, if there is softness (e.g., the appreciation of the regulations of air pollution, as shown in the North American Air Quality Index), there is hardness (e.g., the critique of the regulations of air pollution, as shown in the problems pointed out by the critics as cited). And the reverse direction also holds true.

In relation to the seriousness-playfulness principle, if there is seriousness (e.g., the serious business of those who try to live by engaging in different activities which can contribute to pollution), there is playfulness (e.g., the playful part of those who try to live by engaging in different activities which can contribute to pollution, when they play around with different activities in relation to "smoke stacks of power plants," "controlled burn practices in agriculture and forestry management," "fumes from paint," "waste deposition in landfills," etc., so as to test and see which ones work for them under which circumstances, with what consequences). And the reverse direction also holds true.

In relation to the activeness-inactiveness principle, if there is activeness (e.g., the activeness of those who do not suffer from health problems due to air pollution and are ready to do different tasks), there is inactiveness (e.g., the relative inactiveness of those who get sick because of health problems caused by air pollution).

In relation to the regression-progression principle, if there is regression (e.g., the regression made by the regulations of air pollution, as shown in the problems pointed out by the critics aforecited), there is progression (e.g., the progress made by the regulations of air pollution, as shown in their contribution to better air quality aforecited). And the reverse direction also holds true.

In relation to the same-difference principle, if there is similarity in outcome (e.g., the contribution to the molding and control of beliefs, values, and behaviors, regardless of whether this be done by way of regulations of air pollution, or by way of laissez-faire economics), there is difference in outcome (e.g., the contribution to the molding and control of beliefs, values, and behaviors by way of regulations of air pollution for a relatively more government-oriented lifeworld—but the contribution to the molding and control of beliefs, values, and behaviors by way of laissez-faire economics for a relatively more privatized lifeworld). And the reverse direction also holds true.

And in relation to the stability-reaction principle, if there is stability (e.g., the relatively more stable condition of air pollution in the U.S. during the early decades of industrialization, especially with "the development of steam-powered ships, railways, and later in the 19th century with the internal combustion engine," when there was so much more air pollution if measured in terms of emissions per unit of transport then), there is reaction (e.g., air pollution in the U.S. during the early decades of industrialization then led to further changes later on, when nowadays, there are more regulatons of air pollution, like the U.S. National Ambient Air Quality Standards and E.U. Air Quality Directive). (WK 2012ll) And the reverse direction also holds true.

Operations, Horses, and the Carriage

Another good way to evaluate the possibility (or impossibility) and desirability (or undesirability) of operations from the perspective of nature is to explore operations, horses, and the carriage.

The term "carriage" here refers to "a wheeled vehicle for people, usually horse-drawn"—but "litters (palanquins) and sedan chairs are excluded, since they are wheelless vehicles." (WK 2012mm)

The carriage is thus related to such comparable vehicles like "stagecoach, charabanc and omnibus. Working vehicles such as the (four-wheeled) wagon and (two-wheeled) cart share important parts of the history of the carriage, as does the fast (two-wheeled) chariot." (WK 2012mm; L. Tarr 1969; S. Piggott 1992)

In general, "the carriage is especially designed for private passenger use and for comfort or elegance, though some are also used to transport goods. It may be light, smart and fast or heavy, large and comfortable. Carriages normally have suspension using leaf springs, elliptical springs (in the 19th century) or leather strapping." (WK 2012mm)

History of the Horse-Drawn Carriage

The use of horse-drawn carriages has a long history indeed (as summarized in *Table 3.5*).

(a) Prehistory

In prehistory, "some horsecarts found in Celtic graves show hints that their platform was suspended in a frame, elastically. Four wheeled wagons were used in prehistoric Europe, and their form known from excavations suggests that the basic construction techniques of wheel and undercarriage (that survived until the age of the motor car) were established then." (WK 2012mm; S. Piggott 1983)

(b) Chariot

Later, the carriage was used as "the chariot during the 9th century. Used typically for warfare by Egyptians, the near Easterners and Europeans, it was essentially a two-wheeled light basin carrying one or two passengers, drawn by one to two horses. The chariot was revolutionary and effective because it delivered fresh warriors to crucial areas of battle with swiftness." (WK 2012mm)

(c) Wagons

The carriage was also used by the Romans as "wagons for overland journeys. The kingdoms of the Zhou Dynasty and Warring States were also known to have used carriages as transportation. With the decline of these civilizations these techniques almost disappeared. It is likely that Roman carriages employed some form of suspension on chains or leather straps, as indicated by carriage parts found in excavations." (WK 2012mm)

(d) Medieval Carriage

During the Middle Ages in Europe, "the carriage was typically a four-wheeled wagon type, with a rounded top ('tilt') similar in appearance to the

Conestoga Wagon familiar from the USA. Sharing the traditional form of wheels and undercarriage known since the Bronze Age, it very likely also employed the pivoting fore-axle in continuity from the ancient world. Suspension (on chains) is recorded in visual images and written accounts from the 14th century ('chars branlant' or rocking carriages), and was in widespread use by the 15th century." (WK 2012mm)

Not everyone at the time had regular access to the carriage, because "carriages were largely used by royalty, aristocrats (and especially by women), and could be elaborately decorated and gilded. These carriages were on four wheels often and were pulled by two to four horses depending on how they were decorated (elaborate decoration with gold lining made the carriage heavier). Wood and iron were the primary requirements needed to build a carriage and carriages that were used by non-royalty were covered by plain leather. Another form of the carriage was the pageant wagon of the 14th century. Historians debate on the structure and size of pageant wagons; however, they are generally miniature house-like structures that rest on four to six wheels depending on the size of the wagon. The pageant wagon is significant because up until the 14th century most carriages were on two or 3 wheels; the chariot, rocking carriage, and baby carriage are two examples of carriages which pre-date the pageant wagon." (WK 2012mm)

(e) Coach

Another important innovation of the carriage was "the invention of the suspended carriage or the chariot branlant (though whether this was a Roman or medieval innovation remains uncertain). The 'chariot branlant' of medieval illustrations was suspended by chains rather than leather straps as had been believed. Chains provided a smoother ride in the chariot branlant because the compartment no longer rested on the turning axles. In the 15th century, carriages were made lighter and needed only one horse to haul the carriage. This carriage was designed and innovated in Hungary. Both innovations appeared around the same time and historians believe that people began comparing the chariot branlant and the Hungarian light coach. However, the earliest illustrations of the Hungarian 'Kochi-wagon' do not indicate any suspension, and often the use of three horses in harness. Most importantly, the passengers were typically men and not women." (WK 2012mm)

Especially "under King Mathias Corvinus (1458–90), who enjoyed fast travel, the Hungarians developed fast road transport, and the town of Kocs between Budapest and Vienna became an important post-town, and gave its name to the new vehicle type. The Hungarian coach was highly praised because it was capable of holding 8 men, used light wheels, could be towed by only one horse (it may have been suspended by leather straps, but this is a topic of debate). Ultimately it was the Hungarian coach that generated a greater buzz of conversation than the chariot branlant of France because it was a much smoother ride. Henceforth, the Hungarian coach spread across Europe rather quickly, in part due to Ippolito d'Este of Ferrara (1479–1529), nephew of Mathias' queen Beatrix of Aragon, who as a very junior Archbishopric of Esztergom developed a liking of Hungarian riding and took his carriage and driver back to Italy. Around 1550 the 'coach' made its appearance throughout the major cities of Europe, and the new word entered the vocabulary of all their languages." (WK 2012mm)

(f) Later Development of the Coach

But the coach underwent further changes later on. For instance, "the earliest coaches can be seen at Veste Coburg, Lisbon, and the Moscow Kremlin, and they become a commonplace in European art. It was not until the 17th century that further innovations with steel springs and glazing took place, and only in the 18th century, with better road surfaces, was there a major innovation with the introduction of the steel C-spring." (WK 2012mm)

In the 18th century, "steering systems were truly improved. Erasmus Darwin was a young English doctor who was driving a carriage about 10,000 miles a year to visit patients all over England. Darwin found two essential problems or shortcomings of the commonly used light carriage or Hungarian carriage. First, the front wheels were turned by a rotating front axle, which had been used for years, but these wheels were often quite small and hence the rider, carriage and horse felt the brunt of every bump on the road. Secondly, he recognized the danger of overturning." (WK 2012mm)

Then, "a rotating frontal axle changes a carriage's base from a rectangle to a triangle because the wheel on the inside of the turn is able to turn more sharply than the outside front wheel. Darwin proposed to fix these insufficiencies by proposing a principle in which the two front wheels turn about a centre that lies on the extended line of the back axle. This idea was later patented as Ackerman Steering. Darwin argued that carriages would then be easier to pull and prevent carriages from overturning." (WK 2012mm)

The carriage was "more widely used in North America…with the establishment of European settlers. Early colonial horse tracks quickly grew into roads especially as the colonists extended their territories southwest. Colonists began using carts as these roads and trading increased between the north and south. Eventually carriages or coaches were sought to transport goods as well as people. As in Europe, chariots, coaches and/or carriages were a mark of status. The tobacco planters of the South were some of the first Americans to use the carriage as a form of human transportation. As the tobacco farming industry grew in the southern colonies so did the frequency of carriages, coaches and wagons. Upon the turn of the 18th century wheeled vehicle use in the colonies was at an all-time high. Carriages, coaches and wagons were being taxed based on the number of wheels they had. These taxes were implemented in the South primarily as the South had superior numbers of horses and wheeled vehicles when compared to the North. Europe, however, still used carriage transportation far more often and on a much larger scale than anywhere else in the world." (WK 2012mm)

Structure of the Horse-Drawn Carriage

The horse-drawn carriages is generally constructed on the basis of two main parts, namely, (a) body and (b) undergear, as described below (and summarized in *Table 3.5*).

(a) Body

In regard to the body, "the top cover…called the *head* or *hood*, is often flexible and designed to be folded back when desired. Such a folding top is called a *bellows top* or *calash*. A *hoopstick* forms a light framing member for this kind of hood. The top, roof or second-story compartment of a closed carriage, especially a diligence, was called an *imperial*. A closed carriage may have side windows called *quarter lights* (British) as well as windows in the doors, hence a 'glass coach.' On the forepart of an open carriage, a screen of wood or leather called a *dashboard* intercepts water, mud or snow thrown up by the heels of the horses. The dashboard or carriage top sometimes has a projecting sidepiece called a *wing* (British). A *foot iron* or *footplate* may serve as a carriage step." (WK 2012mm)

A driver of the carriage then "sits on a *box* or *perch*, usually elevated and small. When at the front it is known as a *dickey box*, a term also used for a seat at the back for servants. A footman might use a small platform at the rear called a *footboard* or a seat called a *rumble* behind the body. Some carriages have a moveable seat called a *jump seat*. Some seats had an attached backrest called a *lazyback*." (WK 2012mm)

(b) Undergear

Besides the body, there is the "undergear" of the carriage, also known as "undercarriage,…consisting of the running gear and chassis. The wheels and axles, in distinction from the body, are the *running gear*. Most carriages have either one or two pairs of wheels. On a four-wheeled vehicle, the forward part of the running gear, or *forecarriage*, may be arranged so as to permit the two front wheels to turn independently of the rear wheels. The wheels revolve upon bearings or a spindle at the ends of a fixed bar or beam called an *axle* or *axletree*. In some carriages a *crank axle*, bent twice at a right angle near the ends, allows a low body with large wheels. A guard called a *dirtboard* keeps dirt from the axle arm." (WK 2012mm)

In addition, "the fore axletree and the splinter bar above it (supporting the springs) are united by a piece of wood or metal called a *futchel*, which forms a socket for the pole that extends from the front axle. For strength and support, a rod called the *backstay* may extend from either end of the rear axle to the reach, the pole or rod joining the hind axle to the forward bolster above the front axle. A skid called a drag, *dragshoe*, *shoe* or *skidpan* retards the motion of the wheels. A catch or block called a *trigger* may be used to hold a wheel on a declivity." (WK 2012mm)

Also, "a horizontal wheel or segment of a wheel called a *fifth wheel* sometimes forms an extended support to prevent the carriage from tipping; it consists of two parts rotating on each other about the kingbolt above the fore axle and beneath the body. A block of wood called a *headblock* might be placed between the fifth wheel and the forward spring." (WK 2012mm)

Types of the Horse-Drawn Carriage

The horse-drawn carriage can come in all shapes and sizes, in that "an almost bewildering variety of horse-drawn carriages existed. Arthur Ingram's *Horse Drawn Vehicles since 1760 in Colour* lists 325 types with a short description of each. By the early 19th century one's choice of carriage was only in part based on practicality and performance; it was also a status statement and subject to changing fashions." (WK 2012mm)

Some examples of the types of carriage can include the following: (WK 2012mm)

- Ex: "cabriolet"
- Ex: "calash"
- Ex: "curricle"
- Ex: "dogcart"
- Ex: "dos-à-dos"
- Ex: "fiacre"
- Ex: "fly"
- Ex: "gharry"
- Ex: "gig"

- Ex: “hackney”
- Ex: “hansom”
- Ex: “herdic”
- Ex: “jaunting car”
- Ex: “mail coach”
- Ex: “one-horse carriage”
- Ex: “village cart
- Ex: “voiturette”
- Ex: “wagonette”

Surely, there can be other examples, and the ones above are illustrative, not exhaustive.

Operations of the Horse-Drawn Carriage

To operate a horse-drawn carriage correctly requires some skills which can be learned. Consider, for illustration, the following five major steps (as summarized in *Table 3.5*).

(a) 1st Step: Understand Your Horse

The first step to learn how to operate a horse-drawn carriage correctly, for Therea Bettmann (2011), is to “learn everything you can about horses and driving first. Depending upon your horse experience level, you must first learn and understand their behavior and how to care for them. Basic skills like proper feeding, grooming, handling and overall horsemanship are important. Understanding a horse's body language is also vital. You can tell quite a bit about a horse's mood by the way it hold its ears and head. It is not necessary to know how to ride a horse in order to drive one, but it is necessary to understand verbal commands, physical cues like proper reining, and how to correctly use a driving whip. It is critical to know and understand every part of the harness and carriage before ever setting out to drive one. A lack of horse-sense, carelessness or overconfidence can lead to disastrous results.”

(b) 2nd Step: Use a Willing Horse

The second step to learn how to operate a horse-drawn carriage correctly, for Bettmann (2011), is to “use a horse that is willing and well-trained to drive a carriage. Depending upon whether you plan to drive only along the countryside, travel around town in heavy traffic, or take part in equestrian driving events, your horse should be easy to handle. Well-trained horses respond to light, easy movements from the reins and have usually been introduced to a variety of stimuli, making them more confident and less likely to spook. Poorly trained horses require a strong hold on the reins, which actually incorrectly teaches the driver to be hard-handed. Beginning drivers should practice ground-driving the horse before ever attaching it to a carriage. Ground driving is simply a 'dress rehearsal' for the real event. The driver walks behind the fully harnessed horse while practicing the same verbal and physical commands as he or she would on the carriage—commands such as walk, trot or stop."

(c) 3rd Step: Harness the Horse Correctly

The third step to learn how to operate a horse-drawn carriage correctly, for Bettmann (2011), is to "harness and hitch the horse correctly. Drivers should always have another person assist when hitching their horse, especially when they are new to the procedure. However, it is always the driver's responsibility to check the harness and carriage before ever putting a foot on-board. Equipment failure or poor-fitting harnesses and carriages are the main cause of accidents. Always be sure the reins are attached to the bridle, and have the assisting person stand by the horse's head. This helps to prevent a runaway if the horse should spook while being hitched up. Slowly back the horse up to the vehicle and be sure that all lines, tugs and holdbacks are securely fastened to the carriage. The ramifications of a carriage crash are even more deadly than accidents involving horse and rider. Runaway carriages or crashes can injure the occupants, as well as anyone in the path of the carriage."

(d) 4th Step: Take an Experienced Driver with You

The fourth step to learn how to operate a horse-drawn carriage correctly, for Bettmann (2011), is to "take an experienced driver with you. You should not operate a horse drawn carriage alone until you are fully prepared to do so. Experienced drivers are able to assist or take over in the event of problems. When boarding the carriage always have reins in hand, and keep the whip in hand at all times. Begin driving in less populated areas until you feel comfortable. As you become more confident, you can move to higher traffic areas, but be sure to familiarize yourself and your horse with your surroundings. Manhole covers, sirens, umbrellas, and a variety of other situations can spook even well-trained animals. Always be alert, proactive, and attuned to what is happening around you."

(e) 5th Step: Obey Traffic Rules

And the fifth step to learn how to operate a horse-drawn carriage correctly, for Bettmann (2011), is to "obey all traffic laws and signals when driving in towns and cities. The horse and carriage is like any other vehicle on the road and must follow the same procedures. You are considered a slow-moving vehicle and should always stay as far right as possible. Approved slow-moving emblems (which are large orange triangular signs with red borders) should be attached to the rear of the carriage. Always stay at least 10 to 20 yards behind any vehicle, as well as keeping enough distance between cars at your side. Lights, reflectors and reflective tape are all necessary when driving in traffic, especially at night. Use mechanical turn signals when available, otherwise you must use the same hand-signals used by bicyclists. Left arm fully extended signals a left turn, left arm at a 90 degree angle with hand pointing downward signals a stop, and left arm at a 90 degree angle with hand pointing upward signals a right turn."

Problems with the Study on the Horse-Drawn Carriage

However, for the critics, this study on the horse-drawn carriage in transportation has some major problems. Consider, for illustration, a few examples below (as summarized in *Table 3.5*).

Firstly, one main criticism of the study on the horse-drawn carriage in transportation is that its history is not so clear-cut as it may appear.

For instance, for the critics, in regard to the use of the carriage during the Middle Ages, "historians…debate whether or not pageant wagons were built with pivotal axle systems, which allowed the wheels to turn." (WK 2012mm)

Secondly, another main criticism of the study on the horse-drawn carriage in transportation is that the use of horses for the carriage is controversial for animal right activists.

For instance, for the critics, "organized welfare groups, such as the Humane Society of the United States, and animal rights groups such as People for the Ethical Treatment of Animals, have been known to criticise some horse sports with claims of animal cruelty." (WK 2012nn)

Thirdly, an additional main criticism of the study on the horse-drawn carriage in transportation is that operating a horse-drawn carriage is not as simple as the five steps suggested by Bettmann would like us to believe.

For instance, just as there are risky drivers who disobey rules or drive competitively, there are likewise risky operators (of the horse-drawn carriage). In addition, horse-drawn carriages have been used for different purposes in sports, entertainment, warfare, transportation, and the like, so different rules of engagements and training may apply to particular uses in mind. What makes sense for normal driving in transportation may not be so for "competitive driving" in sports, even in the case of the horse-drawn carriage. (WK 2012mm)

And fourthly, another additional main criticism of the study on the horse-drawn carriage in transportation is that its usefulness in history is limited.

For instance, "carriages and coaches began to disappear as use of steam propulsion began to generate more and more interest and research. Steam power quickly won the battle against animal power" by the early 20th century. (WK 2012mm)

Beyond Horse-Drawn Carriage

However, these criticisms of the study on the horse-drawn carriage in transportation are not to mean a total rejection of its usefulness but serve to show us the two opposing sides of the debate, such that the possibility (or impossibility) and desirability (or undesirability) of operations (from the perspective of nature with operations, horses, and the carriage as a case study here) are not to the extent that the respective defenders would like us to believe.

Besides, the analysis of operations, horses, and the carriage has the scholarly virtue to explore the ontological principles in existential dialectics, and good examples include the formalness-informalness principle, the absoluteness-relativeness principle, the partiality-totality principle, the predictability-unpredictability principle, the explicability-inexplicability principle, the fiction-reality principle, the finiteness-transfiniteness principle, the preciseness-vagueness principle, the simpleness-complicatedness principle, the openness-hiddenness principle, the denseness-emptiness principle, the change-constancy principle, the order-chaos principle, the slowness-quickness principle, the expansion-contraction principle, the theory-praxis principle, the convention-novelty principle, the evolution-transformation principle, the symmetry-asymmetry principle, the softness-hardness principle, the seriousness-playfulness principle, the activeness-inactiveness principle, the regression-progression principle, the same-difference principle, and the stability-reaction principle.

For instance, in relation to the formalness-informalness principle, if there is formalness (e.g., the formal logical requirement of soundness and completeness in a system of ideas, as in the study on the horse-drawn carriage), there is informalness (e.g., the non-formal existence of unsoundness and incompleteness in the study on the horse-drawn carriage, as shown in the criticisms that its history is not so clear-cut as it may appear, that the use of horses for the carriage is controversial for animal right activists, that operating a horse-drawn carriage is not as simple as the five steps suggested by Bettmann would like us to believe, that its usefulness in history is limited, etc.). And the reverse direction also holds true.

In relation to the absoluteness-relativeness principle, if there is absoluteness (e.g., the absolute view of Bettmann in regard to the obediance of traffic rules and the attention to careful driving for horse-riding), there is relativeness (e.g., what is right for Bettmann in regard to the obediance of traffic rules for horse-riding is not necessarily so for those who are risk-taking horse-riders, especially in competitive driving). And the reverse direction also holds true.

In relation to the partiality-totality principle, if there is partiality (e.g., the partial view of Bettmann in regard to the obediance of traffic rules and the attention to careful driving for horse-riding), there is totality (e.g., the more holistic view of horse-riding, such that the whole is not the sum of its parts, that is, it cannot be reduced to the sum of opposing views of Bettmann, her critics, etc., since there will emerge new views in the future not yet known today, just as there are already some debates about future car technologies for safety as discussed in *Sec. 2.4.2*). And the reverse direction also holds true.

In relation to the predictability-unpredictability principle, if there is predictability (e.g., the predictable tendency by those in England in the older days, when they argued in "a newspaper article written in England in 1895 entitled 'Horseflesh vs. Steam,'" which "highlights the death of the carriage as the means of transportation"), there is unpredictability (e.g., the more difficult task for those in England in 1895 to predict that, even by 2012, "carriages are still used for day-to-day transport in the United States by some minority groups such as the Amish," and "they are also still used in the tourism as vehicles for sightseeing in cities such as Bruges, Vienna, and New Orleans"). (WK 2012mm) And the reverse direction also holds true.

In relation to the explicability-inexplicability principle, if there is explicability (e.g., the explanation by the advocates that the use of the horse-drawn carriage is desirable for sports), there is inexplicability (e.g., the lack of sufficient explanation by the advocates of why the use of the horse-drawn carriage is necessarily desirable for sports, since "organized welfare groups, such as the Humane Society of the United States, and animal rights groups such as People for the Ethical Treatment of Animals, have been known to criticise some horse sports with claims of animal cruelty"). And the reverse direction also holds true.

In relation to the fiction-reality principle, if there is fiction (e.g., the fictional aspect of the five steps by Bettmann on how to operate a horse-drawn carriage correctly, insofar as they are too conservative and risk-adverse), there is reality (e.g., the realistic aspect of the five steps by Bettmann on how to operate a horse-drawn carriage correctly, insofar as they stress careful driving and the obediance to traffic laws). And the reverse direction also holds true.

In relation to the finiteness-transfiniteness principle, if there is finiteness (e.g., the finite number of the categories of the horse-drawn carriage, like the 325 types as susggested by Arthur Ingram), there is transfiniteness (e.g., the transfinite number of all the individual carriages that have ever been built, either partly or completely, in history, regardless of how many possible types there are). And the reverse direction also holds true.

In relation to the preciseness-vagueness principle, if there is preciseness (e.g., the precise identification of 325 types of the horse-drawn carriage by Arthur Ingram), there is vagueness (e.g., the vagueness in the identification of the 325 types of the horse-drawn carriage by Arthur Ingram, since it is not clear why there must be only 325 types, not 326, 328, 329, 330, and so on). And the reverse direction also holds true.

In relation to the simpleness-complicatedness principle, if there is simpleness (e.g., the relatively simple analysis of the horse-drawn carriage by the advocates), there is complicatedness (e.g., the relatively more complicated analysis of the horse-drawn carriage, by challenging the claims and assumptions, as shown in the problems pointed out by the critics as cited). And the reverse direction also holds true.

In relation to the openness-hiddenness principle, if there is openness (e.g., an "open" carriage, with no top cover), there is hiddenness (e.g., an "closed" carriage). And the reverse direction also holds true.

In relation to the denseness-emptiness principle, if there is denseness (e.g., the relatively denser concentration of wheels in a horse-drawn carriage when it has six wheels), there is emptiness (e.g., the relatively less dense, or more empty, concentration of wheels in a horse-drawn carriage when it has only 2 wheels). And the reverse direction also holds true.

In relation to the change-constancy principle, if there is change (e.g., the ever new ways to invent transports, as shown in the history of the horse-drawn carriage), there is constancy (e.g., the ever constant existence of different problems in the ever new ways to invent transports, as shown in the problems with the horse-drawn carriage pointed out by the critics). And the reverse direction also holds true.

In relation to the order-chaos principle, if there is order (e.g., the more or less orderly reality of horse-riding if the five steps suggested by Bettmann are correctly followed), there is chaos (e.g., the more or less chaotic reality of horse-riding if the five steps suggested by Bettmann are ignored, such that they lead to "disastrous results"). And the reverse direction also holds true.

In relation to the slowness-quickness principle, if there is slowness (e.g., the relatively slower speed of horse-drawn carriages in antiquity, when they were relatively heavy), there is quickness (e.g., the relatively quicker speed of horse-drawn carriages, when "under King Mathias Corvinus [1458–90], who enjoyed fast travel, the Hungarians developed fast road transport," and "carriages were made lighter and needed only one horse to haul the carriage"). And the reverse direction also holds true.

In relation to the expansion-contraction principle, if there is expansion (e.g., the relative spread of the use of rail transports in the 20th century), there is contraction (e.g., the relative decline of the use of horse-drawn carriages in the 20th century). And the reverse direction also holds true.

In relation to the theory-praxis principle, if there is theory (e.g., the theoretical construction of the "body" and the "undergear" in mechanical engineering), there is praxis (e.g., the practical application of the "body" and the "undergear" in mechanical engineering to the fields of sports and entertainment, as shown in the use of the horse-drawn carriage for "competitive driving" nowadays). And the reverse direction also holds true.

In relation to the convention-novelty principle, if there is convention (e.g., the conventional wisdom about constructing carriages with "two or 3 wheels" in ancient times), there is novelty (e.g., the alternative novel challenge to the conventional wisdom about constructing carriages with "two or 3 wheels" in ancient times, by the new idea of constructing "pageant wagons" which have "four to six wheels depending on the size of the wagon" in early modern times). And the reverse direction also holds true.

In relation to the evolution-transformation principle, if there is evolution (e.g., the natural evolution of humans to walk and run in the state of nature in a primitive way), there is transformation (e.g., the technical transformation of human ability to move around by the invention of the horse-drawn carriage). And the reverse direction also holds true.

In relation to the symmetry-asymmetry principle, if there is symmetry (e.g., the existence of different means of transportation, like carriages and rail transports), there is asymmetry (e.g., rail transports are more powerful than horse-drawn carriages, which "began to disappear as use of steam propulsion began to generate more and more interest" in the 19th century and beyond, when "steam power quickly won the battle against animal power"). And the reverse direction also holds true.

In relation to the softness-hardness principle, if there is softness (e.g., the appreciation of the horse-drawn carriage, as shown in its pervasive use in pre-modern times), there is hardness (e.g., the critique of the horse-drawn carriage, as shown in "a newspaper article written in England in 1895 entitled 'Horseflesh vs. Steam,'" which "highlights the death of the carriage as the means of transportation"). And the reverse direction also holds true.

In relation to the seriousness-playfulness principle, if there is seriousness (e.g., the serious business of those who aim to build carriages for better transports), there is playfulness (e.g., the playful part of of those who aim to build carriages, when they play around with different design options over the ages, like carriages with 1 wheel, 2 wheels, 4 wheels, and 6 wheels—or carriages which are made lighter or heavier, etc.). And the reverse direction also holds true.

In relation to the activeness-inactiveness principle, if there is activeness (e.g., the activeness of those horses which are not tired and in good health, so they can drive a carriage well), there is inactiveness (e.g., the relative inactiveness of those horses which are tired or get sick, so they cannot drive a carriage well).

In relation to the regression-progression principle, if there is regression (e.g., the regression made by the horse-drawn carriage, as shown in the problems pointed out by the critics aforecited), there is progression (e.g., the progress made by the horse-drawn carriage, as shown in its uses for transportation, sports, warfare, and the like aforecited). And the reverse direction also holds true.

In relation to the same-difference principle, if there is similarity in outcome (e.g., the contribution to the molding and control of beliefs, values, and behaviors, regardless of whether this be done by way of walking and running in the state of nature, or by way of the Hungarian light horse-drawn carriage in early modern times), there is difference in outcome (e.g., the contribution to the molding and control of beliefs, values, and behaviors by way of walking and running for a relatively more physical lifeworld—but the contribution to the molding and control of beliefs, values, and behaviors by way of the Hungarian light horse-drawn carriage for a relatively more mechanical lifeworld). And the reverse direction also holds true.

And in relation to the stability-reaction principle, if there is stability (e.g., the relatively more stable condition of the horse-drawn carriage in the older days, when it was widely used for transportation, warfare, and sports for centuries), there is reaction (e.g., the pervasive use of the horse-drawn carriage in the older days led to further changes later on, when nowadays other means of transportation like trains, cars, and aircrafts are more widely used instead). And the reverse direction also holds true.

Operations and Society

Operations, when examined from the perspective of society, can reveal to us their possibility (or impossibility) and desirability (or undesirability) in a powerful way, and this can be shown by way of two case studies, namely, (3.4.1) operations, skyjacking, and terrorism, and (3.4.2) operations, traffic congestion, and urban sprawl—to be addressed hereafter.

Operations, Skyjacking, and Terrorism

A good way to evaluate the possibility (or impossibility) and desirability (or undesirability) of operations from the perspective of society is to explore operations, skyjacking, and terrorism.

The term "skyjacking" is also known as "aircraft hijacking" (or "sky controlling") and refers to "the unlawful seizure of an aircraft by an individual or a group. In most cases, the pilot is forced to fly according to the orders of the hijackers. Occasionally, however, the hijackers have flown the aircraft themselves, such as the September 11 attacks of 2001. In at least one case, a plane was hijacked by the official pilot." (WK 2012oo; CNN 1998; B. Ramon 2000)

In general, "unlike the typical hijackings of land vehicles or ships, skyjacking is not usually committed for robbery or theft. Most aircraft hijackers intend to use the passengers as hostages, either for monetary ransom or for some political or administrative concession by authorities. Motives vary from demanding the release of certain inmates (notably IC-814) to highlighting the grievances of a particular community (notably AF 8969). Hijackers also have used aircraft as a weapon to target particular locations (notably during the September 11, 2001 attacks)." (WK 2012oo)

Terroism and the September 11 Attacks

The September 11, 2011 attacks are a good example of terrorism in the context of operating an aircraft.

On the morning of September 11, 2001, "19 hijackers took control of four commercial airliners (two Boeing 757s and two Boeing 767s) en route to San Francisco or Los Angeles after takeoffs from Boston, Massachusetts, Newark, New Jersey, and Washington, D.C. Planes with long flights were intentionally selected for hijacking because they would be heavily fueled." (WK 2012pp; NAAFA 2009)

These four flights were shown below: (WK 2012pp)

- "American Airlines Flight 11: Left Boston's Logan Airport at 7:59 a.m. enroute to Los Angeles with a crew of 11 and 76 passengers, not including five hijackers. The hijackers flew the plane into the North Tower of the World Trade Center at 8:46 a.m."
- "United Airlines Flight 175: Left Logan Airport at 8:14 a.m. enroute to Los Angeles with a crew of nine and 51 passengers, not including five hijackers. The hijackers flew the plane into the South Tower of the World Trade Center at 9:03 a.m."
- "American Airlines Flight 77: Left Washington Dulles International Airport in Northern Virginia at 8:20 a.m. enroute to Los Angeles with a crew of six and 53 passengers, not including five hijackers. The hijackers flew the plane into the Pentagon at 9:37 a.m."
- "United Airlines Flight 93: Left Newark International Airport at 8:42 a.m. enroute to San Francisco, with a crew of seven and 33 passengers, not including four hijackers. After the passengers revolted the hijackers crashed the plane into the ground near Shanksville, Pennsylvania at 10:03 a.m."

It turned out that "the group's leader Osama bin Laden, who had initially denied involvement, claimed responsibility for the attacks….The United States responded to the attacks by launching the War on Terror and invading Afghanistan to depose the Taliban, which had harbored Al-Qaeda. Many countries strengthened their anti-terrorism legislation and expanded law enforcement powers. In May 2011, after years at large, bin Laden was found and killed." (WK 2012pp; CBC 2004)

Major Effects of the September 11 Attacks

The September 11, 2011 attacks have some major effects on transportation and other areas of society and culture. Consider, for illustration, some main examples below.

(a) Government Regulations

One major effect is the creation of "the Aviation and Transportation Security Act," which "made the federal government, rather than airports, responsible for airport security. The law created a federal security force to inspect passengers and luggage, causing long delays and concern over passenger privacy." (WK 2012pp; R. Beck 2004)

In addition, "the Federal Aviation Administration ordered that airplane cockpits be reinforced to prevent terrorists gaining control of planes, and assigned sky marshals to flights." (WK 2012pp)

Other effects in relation to government regulations include the creation of "the Department of Homeland Security…to coordinate domestic anti-terrorism efforts. The USA Patriot Act gave the federal government greater powers, including the authority to detain foreign terror suspects for a week without charge, to monitor telephone communications, e-mail, and Internet use by terror suspects, and to prosecute suspected terrorists without time restrictions." (WK 2012pp)

(b) Economic aftermath

Another major effect is the economic aftermath, since "the attacks had a significant economic impact on United States and world markets. The stock exchanges did not open on September 11 and remained closed until September 17. Reopening, the Dow Jones Industrial Average (DJIA) fell 684 points, or 7.1%, to 8921, a record-setting one-day point decline. By the end of the week, the DJIA had fallen 1,369.7 points (14.3%), at the time its largest one-week point drop in history. In 2001 dollars, U.S. stocks lost $1.4 trillion in valuation for the week." (WK 2012pp; G. Makinen 2002; B. Barnhart 2001; F. Bob 2001)

Especially in New York City, "about 430,000 job-months and $2.8 billion dollars in wages were lost in the three months after the attacks. The economic effects were mainly on the economy's export sectors The city's GDP was estimated to have declined by $27.3 billion for the last three months of 2001 and all of 2002. The U.S. government provided $11.2 billion in immediate assistance to the Government of New York City in September 2001, and $10.5 billion in early 2002 for economic development and infrastructure needs." (WK 2012pp; M. Dolfman 2004; G. Makinen 2002)

In addition, "hurt were small businesses in Lower Manhattan near the World Trade Center, 18,000 of which were destroyed or displaced, resulting in lost jobs and their consequent wages. Assistance was provided by Small Business Administration loans, federal government Community Development Block Grants, and Economic Injury Disaster Loans. Some 31,900,000 square feet (2,960,000 m^2) of Lower Manhattan office space was damaged or destroyed. Many wondered whether these jobs would return, and if the damaged tax base would recover. Studies of the economic effects of 9/11 show the Manhattan office real-estate market and office employment were less affected than first feared, because of the financial services industry's need for face-to-face interaction." (WK 2012pp; G. Makinen 2002; L. Hensell 2001; J. Parrott 2002; F. Fuerst 2005; J. Russell 2004)

Other costs affect the airline industry, because "North American air space was closed for several days after the attacks and air travel decreased upon its reopening, leading to a nearly 20% cutback in air travel capacity, and exacerbating financial problems in the struggling U.S. airline industry. The September 11 attacks also led indirectly to the U.S. wars in Afghanistan and Iraq, as well as additional homeland security spending, totaling at least $5 trillion." (WK 2012pp; D. Bhadra 2004; T. Heath 2011; S. Khimm 2011)

(c) Health effects

The third major effect has to do with health issues, since "the thousands of tons of toxic debris resulting from the collapse of the Twin Towers contained more than 2,500 contaminants, including known carcinogens. Subsequent debilitating illnesses among rescue and recovery workers are said to be linked to exposure to these carcinogens. The Bush administration ordered the Environmental Protection Agency (EPA) to issue reassuring statements regarding air quality in the aftermath of the attacks, citing national security; however, the EPA did not determine that air quality had returned to pre-September 11 levels until June 2002." (WK 2012pp; A. Gates 2006; A. DePalma 2006; J. Heilprin 2003)

Also, "health effects...extended to residents, students, and office workers of Lower Manhattan and nearby Chinatown. Several deaths have been linked to the toxic dust, and the victims' names will be included in the World Trade Center memorial. Approximately 18,000 people have been estimated to have developed illnesses as a result of the toxic dust. There is also scientific speculation that exposure to various toxic products in the air may have negative effects on fetal development. A notable children's environmental health center is currently analyzing the children whose mothers were pregnant during the WTC collapse, and were living or working nearby. A study of rescue workers released in April 2010 found that all those studied had impaired lung functions, and that 30–40% were reporting little or no improvement in persistent symptoms that started within the first year of the attack." (WK 2012pp; S. Smith 2009; D. Shukman 2011; D. Grady 2010)

(d) Hate Crimes

And the fourth major effect concerns hate crimes, since "numerous incidents of harassment and hate crimes against Muslims and South Asians were reported in the days following the 9/11 attacks. Sikhs were also targeted because Sikh males usually wear turbans, which are stereotypically associated with Muslims. There were reports of verbal abuse, attacks on mosques and other religious buildings (including the firebombing of a Hindu temple), and assaults on people, including one murder: Balbir Singh Sodhi, a Sikh mistaken for a Muslim, was fatally shot on September 15, 2001 in Mesa, Arizona." (WK 2012pp; NYC 2011; IND 2011; CNN 2001 & 2001a)

Also, "according to an academic study, people perceived to be Middle Eastern were as likely to be victims of hate crimes as followers of Islam during this time. The study also found a similar increase in hate crimes against people who may have been perceived as Muslims, Arabs and others thought to be of Middle Eastern origin. A report by the South Asian American advocacy group known as South Asian Americans Leading Together, documented media coverage of 645 bias incidents against Americans of South Asian or Middle Eastern descent between September 11 and September 17. Various crimes such as vandalism, arson, assault, shootings, harassment, and threats in numerous places were documented." (WK 2012pp; BSU 2003; SAALT 2003; J. Thayil 2001)

Problems with the Study on Skyjacking and Terrorism

However, for the critics, this study on skyjacking and terrorism has some major problems. Consider, for illustration, a few examples below.

Firstly, one main criticism of the study on skyjacking and terrorism is that some of the solutions suggesed are too tough (or violent).

For instance, for the critics, after the September 11, 2011 attacks, "several states have stated that they would shoot down hijacked commercial aircraft if it can be assumed that the hijackers intend to use the aircraft in a 9/11-style attack, despite killing innocent passengers on board. According to reports, U.S. fighter pilots have been trained to shoot down hijacked commercial airliners should it become necessary. Other countries such as India, Poland, and Russia have enacted laws or decrees that allow the shooting down of hijacked planes"—but the problem here is about the question of constitutionality, because, for example, "Polish Constitutional Court however, in September 2008, decided that the regulations were unconstitutional and dismissed them," because they were simply too violent. (WK 2012oo; BBC 2003 & 2005)

Secondly, another main criticism of the study on skyjacking and terrorism is that some countermeasures are too intrusive.

For instance, for the critics, after the September 11, 2011 attacks, "the Aviation and Transportation Security Act…created a federal security force to inspect passengers and luggage, causing long delays and concern over passenger privacy." (WK 2012pp)

Thirdly, an additional main criticism of the study on skyjacking and terrorism is that it focuses too much on the supply side of individual terrorism, without sufficient attention to the demand side.

For instance, for the critics, "the United States responded to the attacks by launching the War on Terror and invading Afghanistan to depose the Taliban, which had harbored Al-Qaeda," but this does not really address the causes of the attacks, since "Al-Qaeda and bin Laden cited U.S. support of Israel, the presence of U.S. troops in Saudi Arabia, and sanctions against Iraq as motives for the attacks." (WK 2012pp) This then means that, unless the U.S. fundamentally changes its foreign policy in the Middle East, individual terrorism against it will likely continue.

And fourthly, another additional main criticism of the study on skyjacking and terrorism is that what counts as "criminal" or "terrorist" is in the eyes of the beholder.

For instance, for the critics, the U.S. may rightly consider Osama bin Laden as a "terrorist," but bin Laden regards himself as a "freedom fighter." And the reverse is also true, in that bin Laden condemns the U.S. for its "state terrrorism" in the Middle East, whereas the U.S. regards its foreign policy as one for "freedom." So, as the old saying goes, one person's terrorist is another person's freedom fighter.

Beyond Skyjacking and Terrorism

These criticisms of the study on skyjacking and terrorism should not be misconstrued as a total rejection of its usefulness but serve to show us the two opposing sides of the debate, such that the possibility (or impossibility) and desirability (or undesirability) of operations (from the perspective of society with operations, skyjacking, and terrorism as a case study here) are not to the extent that the respective defenders would like us to believe.

Indeed, the analysis of operations, skyjacking, and terrorism can teach us something valuable about the ontological principles in existential dialectics, and good examples include the formalness-informalness principle, the absoluteness-relativeness principle, the partiality-totality principle, the predictability-unpredictability principle, the explicability-inexplicability principle, the fiction-reality principle, the finiteness-transfiniteness principle, the preciseness-vagueness principle, the simpleness-complicatedness principle, the openness-hiddenness principle, the denseness-emptiness principle, the change-constancy principle, the order-chaos principle, the slowness-quickness principle, the expansion-contraction principle, the theory-praxis principle, the convention-novelty principle, the evolution-transformation principle, the symmetry-asymmetry principle, the softness-hardness principle, the seriousness-playfulness principle, the activeness-inactivess principle, the regression-

progression principle, the same-difference principle, and the stability-reaction principle.

For instance, in relation to the formalness-informalness principle, if there is formalness (e.g., the formal logical requirement of soundness and completeness in a system of ideas, as in the study on skyjacking and terrorism), there is informalness (e.g., the non-formal existence of unsoundness and incompleteness in the study on skyjacking and terrorism, as shown in the criticisms that what counts as “criminal” or “terrorist” is in the eyes of the beholder, that some of the solutions suggesed are too violent and too intrusive, etc.). And the reverse direction also holds true.

In relation to the absoluteness-relativeness principle, if there is absoluteness (e.g., the absolute view of those like Osama bin Laden to get involved in the 9/11 attacks), there is relativeness (e.g., what is desirable for those like Osama bin Laden to get involved in the 9/11 attacks is not necessarily so for the U.S., which responded by “launching the War on Terror and invading Afghanistan to depose the Taliban, which had harbored Al-Qaeda”). And the reverse direction also holds true.

In relation to the partiality-totality principle, if there is partiality (e.g., the partial view of those like bin Laden to be concerned with “the U.S. support of Israel, the presence of U.S. troops in Saudi Arabia, and sanctions against Iraq as motives for the attacks”), there is totality (e.g., the more holistic view of the 9/11 attacks, such that the whole is not the sum of its parts, that is, it cannot be reduced to the sum of opposing views like those of bin Laden and George Bush, since there will emerge new views in the future not yet known today, just as there are already alternative views nowadays like the one by William Pfaff [2003], who refused to side with bin Laden or George Bush and instead argued that “what actually has happened...is something Americans have yet to grasp, and that others have yet to say out loud: People outside the United States have stopped believing the American story [viz., as the world's greatest democracy fighting evil in the world]”). And the reverse direction also holds true.

In relation to the predictability-unpredictability principle, if there is predictability (e.g., the prediction by those in August 2001 who wrote “the President's Daily Briefing,” in which they “warned that bin Laden was planning to exploit his operatives' access to the U.S. to mount a terrorist strike”), there is unpredictability (e.g., the more difficult task for those in August 2001 who wrote “the President's Daily Briefing” to predict exactly or to be “specific enough to identify the plan to use planes as missiles” by the terrorists, or precisely on what date this predicted event was to occur).

(WK 2012pp; T. Blanton 2004; CNN 2004) And the reverse direction also holds true.

In relation to the explicability-inexplicability principle, if there is explicability (e.g., the explanation by the U.S. that it launched "the War on Terror" and invaded "Afghanistan to depose the Taliban, which had harbored Al-Qaeda" for the September 11 attacks), there is inexplicability (e.g., the lack of sufficient explanation by the U.S. of why the war on terror is necessarily justifiable, since, for the critics like William Pfaff [2003], "people outside the United States have stopped believing the American story [viz., as the world's greatest democracy fighting evil in the world]"). And the reverse direction also holds true.

In relation to the fiction-reality principle, if there is fiction (e.g., the fictional aspect of the U.S. war on terror, insofar as it wants "people outside the United States" to believe "the American story [viz., as the world's greatest democracy fighting evil in the world]," as pointed out by William Pfaff), there is reality (e.g., the realistic aspect of the U.S. war on terror, insofar as it used the September 11 attacks as an excuse to invade Afghanistan). And the reverse direction also holds true.

In relation to the finiteness-transfiniteness principle, if there is finiteness (e.g., the finite number of the types of "toxic debris resulting from the collapse of the Twin Towers" after the September 11 attacks, like the "2,500 contaminants, including known carcinogens"), there is transfiniteness (e.g., the transfinite number of the possible individual pieces of toxic contaminants to be found in the history of the earth). And the reverse direction also holds true.

In relation to the preciseness-vagueness principle, if there is preciseness (e.g., the precise identification of four major effects of the September 11 attacks in the article aforecited), there is vagueness (e.g., the vagueness in the identification of the four major effects of the September 11 attacks in the article aforecited, since it is not clear why there must be only 4, not 6, 9, 13, 15, and so on). And the reverse direction also holds true.

In relation to the simpleness-complicatedness principle, if there is simpleness (e.g., the relatively simple analysis of the September 11 attacks from the vantage point of the U.S.), there is complicatedness (e.g., the relatively more complicated analysis of the September 11 attacks, by challenging the claims and assumptions, as shown in the problems pointed out by the critics as cited). And the reverse direction also holds true.

In relation to the openness-hiddenness principle, if there is openness (e.g., the open preaching of al-Qaeda for "global jihad" against Western powers like the U.S.), there is hiddenness (e.g., the hidden nature of al-

Qaeda in its secret planning of the September 11 attacks). And the reverse direction also holds true.

In relation to the denseness-emptiness principle, if there is denseness (e.g., the relatively denser concentration of Arab nationals among the hijackers who took part in the September 11 attacks), there is emptiness (e.g., the relatively less dense, or more empty, concentration of Americans among the hijackers who took part in the September 11 attacks). And the reverse direction also holds true.

In relation to the change-constancy principle, if there is change (e.g., the ever new ways to engage in hijacking, as shown in the 9/11 suicide skyjackings), there is constancy (e.g., the ever constant existence of different problems in the ever new ways to engage in hijacking, as shown in the problems facing skyjackers nowadays, since pilots and flight attendants after the September 11, 2001 attacks are now trained to handle suicide hijackings, so that "future hijackers most likely will encounter greater resistance from passengers and flight crews, making a successful hijacking more unlikely"). And the reverse direction also holds true.

In relation to the order-chaos principle, if there is order (e.g., the more or less orderly nature of the September 11 attacks, when the 19 hijackers carefully planned their attacks beforehand), there is chaos (e.g,. the more or less chaotic nature of the September 11 attacks, when, in the final mintuies of Flight 93, crew and passengers fought with hijackers and "attempted to seize control of the plane from the hijackers after learning through phone calls that similarly hijacked planes had been crashed into buildings that morning," before they all died in a crash shortly after). (WK 2012pp; D. Snyder 2002) And the reverse direction also holds true.

In relation to the slowness-quickness principle, if there is slowness (e.g., the relatively slower speed of the North Tower in the World Trade Center Complex to collapse "after burning for 102 minutes"), there is quickness (e.g., the relatively quicker speed of the South Tower in the World Trade Center Complex to collapse "after burning for 56 minutes"). (WK 2012pp; B. Miller 2002) And the reverse direction also holds true.

In relation to the expansion-contraction principle, if there is expansion (e.g., the expansion of the World Trade Center Complex when it was first built from the ground up to more than 100 floors), there is contraction (e.g., the collapse of the World Trade Center Complex after the September 11 attacks). And the reverse direction also holds true.

In relation to the theory-praxis principle, if there is theory (e.g., the theoretical construction of "global jihad" in accordance to the radical interpretation of the Sunni Muslim movement like al-Qaeda), there is praxis (e.g., the practical application of "global jihad" to the field of skyjacking, as shown in the September 11 attacks by the skyjackers linked to al-Qaeda). And the reverse direction also holds true.

In relation to the convention-novelty principle, if there is convention (e.g., the conventional wisdom of skyjacking in the older days, when "most aircraft hijackers intend to use the passengers as hostages, either for monetary ransom or for some political or administrative concession by authorities"), there is novelty (e.g., the alternative novel challenge to the conventional wisdom about skyjacking in the older days, by the new idea of skyjacking by those in the September 11 attacks, when the attackers engaged in "suicide hijacking"). And the reverse direction also holds true.

In relation to the evolution-transformation principle, if there is evolution (e.g., the natural evolution of humans to fight with each other from time to time in the state of nature in a primitive way), there is transformation (e.g., the technical transformation of human ability to fight with each other by the invention of suicide skyjacking). And the reverse direction also holds true.

In relation to the symmetry-asymmetry principle, if there is symmetry (e.g., the existence of different individuals inside a plane, be they crew, flight attendants, passengers, and skyjackers), there is asymmetry (e.g., skyjackers can use force, weapons, and other means to take over a plane and to fly it according to their orders, contrary to the wishes of the pilots, flight attendants, and passengers). And the reverse direction also holds true.

In relation to the softness-hardness principle, if there is softness (e.g., the appreciation of the September 11 attacks by the 19 skyjackers), there is hardness (e.g., the condemnation of the September 11 attacks by the family members of the victims). And the reverse direction also holds true.

In relation to the seriousness-playfulness principle, if there is seriousness (e.g., the serious business of those 19 skyjackers to engage in suicide skyjacking), there is playfulness (e.g., the playful part of those 19 skyjackers when they played around with different weapons during the attacks, like "mace," "tear gas," "pepper spray," "multi-function hand tools," and "assorted knives and blades" to attack and subdue pilots, flight attendants, and other passengers). (WK 2012pp; J. McKinnon 2001; CNN 2001; J. Wilgoren 2001) And the reverse direction also holds true.

In relation to the activeness-inactivess principle, if there is activeness (e.g., the alertness of those pilots and flight attendants after the September 11, 2001 attacks, when they are now trained to handle suicide hijackings, so that "future hijackers most likely will encounter greater resistance from passengers and flight crews, making a successful hijacking more unlikely"), there is inactiveness (e.g., the relative inactiveness of those pilots and flight attendants before the September 11, 2001 attacks, when they were not trained "to handle suicide hijackings, and the hijackers were able to exploit a weakness in the civil aviation security system"). (WK 2012oo) And the reverse direction also holds true.

In relation to the regression-progression principle, if there is regression (e.g., the regression made by the war on terror, as shown in the problems pointed out by the critics aforecited), there is progression (e.g., the progress made by the war on terror, as shown in the killing of bin Laden in May 2011 aforecited). And the reverse direction also holds true.

In relation to the same-difference principle, if there is similarity in outcome (e.g., the contribution to the molding and control of beliefs, values, and behaviors, regardless of whether this be done by way of global jihad by Osama bin Laden, or by way of the war on terror by George Bush), there is difference in outcome (e.g., the contribution to the molding and control of beliefs, values, and behaviors by way of global jihad for a relatively more radical Islamic worldview—but the contribution to the molding and control of beliefs, values, and behaviors by way of the war on terror by George Bush for a relatively more extreme neoconservative worldview). And the reverse direction also holds true.

And in relation to the stability-reaction principle, if there is stability (e.g., the relatively more stable condition of airport security checks in the older days before the September 11 attacks, when passengers were screened and checked less intrusively), there is reaction (e.g., the relatively less intrusive airport security checks in the older days before the September 11 attacks then led to further changes later on, when passengers are now more extensively checked at airports after the September 11 attacks). And the reverse direction also holds true.

Operations, Traffic Congestion, and Urban Sprawl

Another good way to evaluate the possibility (or impossibility) and desirability (or undesirability) of operations from the perspective of society is to explore operations, traffic congestion, and urban sprawl.

The term "traffic congestion" refers to "a condition on road networks that occurs as use increases, and is characterized by slower speeds, longer trip times, and increased vehicular queueing. The most common example is the physical use of roads by vehicles. When traffic demand is great enough that the interaction between vehicles slows the speed of the traffic stream, this results in some congestion. As demand approaches the capacity of a road (or of the intersections along the road), extreme traffic congestion sets in. When vehicles are fully stopped for periods of time, this is colloquially known as a traffic jam or traffic snarl-up." (WK 2012qq)

Traffic Congestion and Urban Sprawl

Traffic congestion can be worsen by the rise of "urban sprawl," which is also known as "suburban sprawl," which is "a multifaceted concept, which includes the spreading outwards of a city and its suburbs to its outskirts to low-density and auto-dependent development on rural land, high segregation of uses (e.g. stores and residential), and various design features that encourage car dependency." (WK 2012rr)

Urban sprawl in its contribution to traffic congestion can be illustrated in different ways.

For example, in the first way, "urban sprawl is associated with a number of negative environmental and public health outcomes, with the primary result being increased dependence on automobiles." (WK 2012rr)

In the second way, "in the years following World War II, when vehicle ownership was becoming widespread, public health officials recommended the health benefits of suburbs due to soot and industrial fumes in the city center. However, air in modern suburbs is not necessarily cleaner than air in urban neighborhoods. In fact, the most polluted air is on crowded highways, where people in suburbs tend to spend more time. On average, suburban residents generate more per capita pollution and carbon emissions than their urban counterparts because of their increased driving." (WK 2012rr; F. Lefebre 2008; R. Fuller 2011)

And in the third way, "a heavy reliance on automobiles increases traffic throughout the city as well as automobile crashes, pedestrian injuries, and air pollution. Motor vehicle crashes are the leading cause of death for Americans between the ages of five and twenty-four and is the leading accident-related cause for all age groups. Residents of more sprawling areas are at greater risk of dying in a car crash." (WK 2012rr)

Causes of Traffic Congestion

In any event, there have been more in-depth studies on the causes of traffic congestion. For illustration, consider two interesting theories below (as summarized in *Table 3.6*).

(a) Mathematical Theories

In mathematical theories, "some traffic engineers have attempted to apply the rules of fluid dynamics to traffic flow, likening it to the flow of a fluid in a pipe. Congestion simulations and real-time observations have shown that in heavy but free flowing traffic, jams can arise spontaneously, triggered by minor events ('butterfly effects' [in chaos theory]), such as an abrupt steering maneuver by a single motorist. Traffic scientists liken such a situation to the sudden freezing of supercooled fluid. However, unlike a fluid, traffic flow is often affected by signals or other events at junctions that periodically affect the smooth flow of traffic. Alternative mathematical theories exist, such as Boris Kerner's three-phase traffic theory." (WK 2012qq)

Yet, this does not prevent traffic engineers from making good use of models for prediction; for example, "a team of MIT mathematicians has developed a model that describes the formation of 'phantom jams,' in which small disturbances (a driver hitting the brake too hard, or getting too close to another car) in heavy traffic can become amplified into a full-blown, self-sustaining traffic jam. Key to the study is the realization that the mathematics of such jams, which the researchers call 'jamitons,' are strikingly similar to the equations that describe detonation waves produced by explosions, says Aslan Kasimov, lecturer in MIT's Department of Mathematics. That discovery enabled the team to solve traffic-jam equations that were first theorized in the 1950s." (WK 2012qq; SCI 2009)

(b) Economic Theories

And in economic theories, "congested roads can be seen as an example of the tragedy of the commons. Because roads in most places are free at the point of usage, there is little financial incentive for drivers not to over-use them, up to the point where traffic collapses into a jam, when demand becomes limited by opportunity cost. Privatization of highways and road pricing have both been proposed as measures that may reduce congestion through economic incentives and disincentives. Congestion can also happen due to non-recurring highway incidents, such as a crash or roadworks, which may reduce the road's capacity below normal levels." (WK 2012qq)

Similarly, but in a different way, Anthony Downs argued that, "in a capitalist economy, goods can be allocated either by pricing (ability to pay) or by queueing (first-come first-serve); congestion is an example of the latter. Instead of the traditional solution of making the 'pipe' large enough to accommodate the total demand for peak-hour vehicle travel (a supply-side solution), either by widening roadways or increasing 'flow pressure' via automated highway systems, Downs advocates greater use of road pricing to reduce congestion (a demand-side solution, effectively rationing demand), in turn plowing the revenues generated therefrom into public transportation projects." (WK 2012qq)

Negative Impacts of Traffic Congestion

Traffic congestion, regardless of its causes, can have negative impacts, as shown below (and summarized in *Table 3.6*): (WK 2012qq)

- "Wasting Time of Motorists and Passengers ('Opportunity Cost')"—"As a non-productive activity for most people, congestion reduces regional economic health."
- "Delays"—"which may result in late arrival for employment, meetings, and education, resulting in lost business, disciplinary action or other personal losses."
- "Inability to Forecast Travel Time Accurately"—"leading to drivers allocating more time to travel 'just in case,' and less time on productive activities."
- "Wasted Fuel"—"increasing air pollution and carbon dioxide emissions owing to increased idling, acceleration and braking."
- "Wear and Tear"—"on vehicles as a result of idling in traffic and frequent acceleration and braking, leading to more frequent repairs and replacements."
- "Stressed and Frustrated Motorists"—"encouraging road rage and reduced health of motorists."
- "Emergencies"—"blocked traffic may interfere with the passage of emergency vehicles traveling to their destinations where they are urgently needed."
- "Spillover Effect"—"from congested main arteries to secondary roads and side streets as alternative routes are attempted ('rat running'), which may affect neighborhood amenity and real estate prices."

Surely, there can be other examples, so the ones above are illustrative, not exhaustive.

Suggested Solutions

As countermeasures to resolve the problem of traffic congestion, there have been some suggested solutions as shown below (and summarized in *Table 3.6*):

- "Parking Restrictions" —"making motor vehicle use less attractive by increasing the monetary and non-monetary costs of parking, introducing greater competition for limited city or road space." (WK 2012qq; H. Knoflacher 2006)

- "Park and Ride Facilities"—"allowing parking at a distance and allowing continuation by public transport or ride sharing. Park-and-ride car parks are commonly found at metro stations, freeway entrances in suburban areas, and at the edge of smaller cities." (WK 2012qq)
- "Road Pricing"—"charging money for access onto a road/specific area at certain times, congestion levels or for certain road users." (WK 2012qq)
- "Cap and Trade"—"in which only licensed cars are allowed on the roads. A limited quota of car licences are issued each year and traded in a free market fashion. This guarantees that the number of cars does not exceed road capacity while avoiding the negative effects of shortages normally associated with quotas." (WK 2012qq; H. Goddard 1997)
- "Congestion Pricing"—"where a certain area, such as the inner part of a congested city, is surrounded with a cordon into which entry with a car requires payment. The cordon may be a physical boundary (i.e., surrounded by toll stations) or it may be virtual, with enforcement being via spot checks or cameras on the entry routes." (WK 2012qq)
- "Road Space Rationing"—"where regulatory restrictions prevent certain types of vehicles from driving under certain circumstances or in certain areas." (WK 2012qq)
- "Number Plate Restrictions"—"based on days of the week, as practiced in several large cities in the world, such as Athens, Mexico City and São Paulo. In effect, such cities are banning a different part of the automobile fleet from roads each day of the week. Mainly introduced to combat smog, these measures also reduce congestion. A weakness of this method is that richer drivers can purchase a second or third car to circumvent the ban." (WK 2012qq; KonSULT 2008)
- "Permits"—"where only certain types of vehicles (such as residents) are permitted to enter a certain area, and other types (such as through-traffic) are banned. For example, Bertrand Delanoë, the mayor of Paris, has proposed to impose a complete ban on motor vehicles in the city's inner districts, with exemptions only for residents, businesses, and the disabled." (WK 2012qq; J. Henley 2005)
- "Cycling Promotion"—"through legislation, cycle facilities, subsidies, and awareness campaigns. The Netherlands has been pursuing cycle friendly policies for decades, and around a quarter of their commuting is done by bicycle." (WK 2012qq; D. Ogilvie 2004; P. Rietveld 2004)
- "Considerate Driving Behaviour Promotion and Enforcement"—"Driving practices such as tailgating and frequent lane changes can

reduce a road's capacity and exacerbate jams. In some countries signs are placed on highways to raise awareness, while others have introduced legislation against inconsiderate driving." (WK 2012qq)

- "Speed Limit Reductions"—"as practiced on the M25 motorway in London. With lower speeds allowing cars to drive closer together, this increases the capacity of a road. Note that this measure is only effective if the interval between cars is reduced, not the distance itself. Low intervals are generally only safe at low speeds." (WK 2012qq)

Again, there can be other examples, so the ones above are illustrative, not exhaustive.

Problems with the Study on Traffic Congestion and Urban Sprawl

However, for the critics, this study on traffic congestion and urban sprawl has some major problems. Consider, for illustration, a few examples below (as summarized in *Table 3.6*).

Firstly, one main criticism of the study on traffic congestion and urban sprawl is that a traffic jam is still not fully predictable.

For instance, for the critics, "traffic research still cannot fully predict under which conditions a 'traffic jam' (as opposed to heavy, but smoothly flowing traffic) may suddenly occur." (WK 2012qq)

Secondly, another main criticism of the study on traffic congestion and urban sprawl is that there are disagreements on traffic classification.

For instance, for the critics, one study used "the qualitative classification of traffic…in the form of a six letter A-F level of service (LOS) scale defined in the Highway Capacity Manual." (WK 2012qq) But another study used a different classification "with some common spatiotemporal features of traffic congestion found in measured traffic data," which are "qualitatively the same for different highways in different countries measured during years of traffic observations. Common features of traffic congestion are independent on weather, road conditions and road infrastructure, vehicular technology, driver characteristics, day time, etc. Examples of common features of traffic congestion are the features [J] and [S] for, respectively, the wide moving jam and synchronized flow traffic phases found in Kerner' three-phase traffic theory. The common features of traffic congestion can be reconstructed in space and time with the use of the ASDA and FOTO models." (WK 2012qq)

Thirdly, an additional main criticism of the study on traffic congestion and urban sprawl is that the debate is definitional in nature.

For instance, "discussions and debates about sprawl are often obfuscated by the ambiguity associated with the phrase. For example, some commentators measure sprawl only with the average number of residential units per acre in a given area. But others associate it with decentralization (spread of population without a well-defined centre), discontinuity (leapfrog development, as defined below), segregation of uses, and so forth." (WK 2012rr)

Fourthly, another additional main criticism of the study on traffic congestion and urban sprawl is that "rush hour traffic congestion is inevitable." (WK 2012qq)

For instance, for the critics, "a 2011 study in the The American Economic Review indicates that there may be a 'fundamental law of road congestion.' The researchers, from the University of Toronto and the London School of Economics, analyzed data from the U.S. Highway Performance and Monitoring System for 1983, 1993 and 2003, as well as information on population, employment, geography, transit, and political factors. They determined that the number of vehicle-kilometers traveled (VKT) increases in direct proportion to the available lane-kilometers of roadways. The implication is that building new roads and widening existing ones only results in additional traffic that continues to rise until peak congestion returns to the previous level." (WK 2012qq; L. Klein 2012; G. Duranton 2011)

And fifthly, still another additional main criticism of the study on traffic congestion and urban sprawl is that the debate has a subjective dimension.

For instance, for the critics, some individuals consider the debate of traffic congestion as one based on "subjective lifestyle choices, differentiating between car-owning and car-free households." (WK 2012qq)

Beyond Traffic Congestion and Urban Sprawl

These criticisms of the study on traffic congestion and urban sprawl do not imply a total rejection of its usefulness but serve to show us the two opposing sides of the debate, such that the possibility (or impossibility) and desirability (or undesirability) of operations (from the perspective of society with operations, traffic congestion, and urban sprawl as a case study here) are not to the extent that the respective defenders would like us to believe.

In fact, the analysis of operations, traffic congestion, and urban sprawl reveals to us refreshing insights about the ontological principles in existential dialectics, and good examples include the formalness-informalness principle, the absoluteness-relativeness principle, the partiality-totality principle, the predictability-unpredictability principle, the explicability-inexplicability principle, the fiction-reality principle, the finiteness-transfiniteness principle, the preciseness-vagueness principle, the simpleness-complicatedness principle, the openness-hiddenness principle, the denseness-emptiness principle, the change-constancy principle, the order-chaos principle, the slowness-quickness principle, the expansion-contraction principle, the theory-praxis principle, the convention-novelty principle, the evolution-transformation principle, the symmetry-asymmetry principle, the softness-hardness principle, the seriousness-playfulness principle, the activeness-inactivess principle, the regression-progression principle, the same-difference principle, and the stability-reaction principle.

For instance, in relation to the formalness-informalness principle, if there is formalness (e.g., the formal logical requirement of soundness, consistency, and completeness in a system of ideas, as in the study on traffic congestion and urban sprawl), there is informalness (e.g., the non-formal existence of unsoundness, inconsistency, and incompleteness in the study on traffic congestion and urban sprawl, as shown in the criticisms that there are disagreements on traffic classification, that the debate is definitional in nature, that the debate has a subjective dimension, etc.). And the reverse direction also holds true.

In relation to the absoluteness-relativeness principle, if there is absoluteness (e.g., the absolute view of those who defend urban sprawl, as "one suburban Detroit politician defends low-density development as the preferred lifestyle choice of his constituents, calling it '...the American Dream unfolding before your eyes'"), there is relativeness (e.g., what is right for the defenders of urban sprawl is not necessarily so for the critics, who reject it on different grounds, like traffic congestion, negative environmental and public health outcomes, etc.). (WK 2012rr; L. Patterson 2012) And the reverse direction also holds true.

In relation to the partiality-totality principle, if there is partiality (e.g., the partial view of "a single motorist" engaging in "an abrupt steering maneuver" in a heavy but free flowing traffic), there is totality (e.g., the more holistic view of traffic congestion, such that the whole is not the sum of its parts, that is, it cannot be reduced to the sum of opposing views or maneuvers of different single motorists, etc., since, "in heavy but free flowing traffic, jams can arise spontaneously, triggered by minor events ['butterfly effects' in chaos theory], such as an abrupt steering maneuver by a single motorist," so that "traffic research still cannot fully predict under which conditions a 'traffic jam'..may suddenly occur"). And the reverse direction also holds true.

In relation to the predictability-unpredictability principle, if there is predictability (e.g., the predictable tendency of traffic jams to occur in highways), there is unpredictability (e.g., the more difficult task to predict exactly "under which conditions a 'traffic jam' [as opposed to a heavy, but smoothly flowing traffic] may suddenly occur" on a particular occasion). And the reverse direction also holds true.

In relation to the explicability-inexplicability principle, if there is explicability (e.g., the explanation by those who defend urban sprawl on the basis of a "preferred lifestyle choice" like "the American Dream unfolding before your eyes"'), there is inexplicability (e.g., the lack of sufficient explanation by those who defend urban sprawl of why it is necesssrily desirable, since, for the critics, there are alternative lifestyles like a "car-free" household). And the reverse direction also holds true.

In relation to the fiction-reality principle, if there is fiction (e.g., the fictional aspect of the argument by those in favor of the resolution of traffic congestion, as the critics pointed out that traffic jam is still not fully predictable, that "rush hour traffic congestion is inevitable," etc.), there is reality (e.g., the realistic aspect of the argument by those in favor of the resolution of traffic congestion, insofar as there are solutions aforecited which could make at least some improvement). And the reverse direction also holds true.

In relation to the finiteness-transfiniteness principle, if there is finiteness (e.g., the finite number of the categories of vehicles in traffic congestion, like cars, trucks, motorcycles, buses, etc.), there is transfiniteness (e.g., the transfinite number of all the individual users who have ever used cars, trucks, motorcyles, buses, etc. in history). And the reverse direction also holds true.

In relation to the preciseness-vagueness principle, if there is preciseness (e.g., the precise identification of two types of theories to understand traffic congestion in the article aforecited), there is vagueness (e.g., the vagueness in the identification of the two types of theories to understand traffic congestion in the article aforecited, since it is not clear why there must be only 2 types, not 3, 5, 6, 8, and so on). And the reverse direction also holds true.

In relation to the simpleness-complicatedness principle, if there is simpleness (e.g., the relatively simple analysis of urban sprawl and traffic congestion by the defenders), there is complicatedness (e.g., the relatively more complicated analysis of urban sprawl and traffic congestion, by challenging the claims and assumptions, as shown in the problems pointed out by the critics as cited). And the reverse direction also holds true.

In relation to the openness-hiddenness principle, if there is openness (e.g., the open exploration of the relationship between heavy traffic and traffic congestion), there is hiddenness (e.g., the hidden nature of traffic jams, because "traffic research still cannot fully predict under which conditions a 'traffic jam' [as opposed to heavy, but smoothly flowing traffic] may suddenly occur"). And the reverse direction also holds true.

In relation to the denseness-emptiness principle, if there is denseness (e.g., the relatively denser concentration of vehicles in a traffic jam), there is emptiness (e.g., the relatively less dense, or more empty, concentration of vehicles in a desert, on average). And the reverse direction also holds true.

In relation to the change-constancy principle, if there is change (e.g., the ever new ways to expand cities outwards, as shown in the rise of urban sprawl), there is constancy (e.g., the ever constant existence of different problems in the ever new ways to expand cities, as shown in the problems with urban sprawl pointed out by the critics). And the reverse direction also holds true.

In relation to the order-chaos principle, if there is order (e.g., the more or less orderly appearance of traffic, when there is no traffic jam), there is chaos (e.g,. the more or less chaotic appearance of traffic, when there is a massive traffic jam). And the reverse direction also holds true.

In relation to the slowness-quickness principle, if there is slowness (e.g., the relatively slower speed of drivers with speed limit reductions to be enforced), there is quickness (e.g., the relatively quicker speed of drivers without any speed limit reductions). And the reverse direction also holds true.

In relation to the expansion-contraction principle, if there is expansion (e.g., the relative spread of cities to the outskirts into "low-density and auto-dependent developments" nowadays), there is contraction (e.g., the relative decline of "bicycling-oriented" and "pedestrian-oriented" areas in modern cities, when contrasted with those in the older days). And the reverse direction also holds true.

In relation to the theory-praxis principle, if there is theory (e.g., the theoretical construction of' "butterfly effects" in chaos theory), there is praxis (e.g., the practical application of "butterfly effects" in chaos theory to the field of transportation to understand traffic congestion). And the reverse direction also holds true.

In relation to the convention-novelty principle, if there is convention (e.g., the conventional wisdom of urban sprawl by its defenders), there is novelty (e.g., the alternative novel challenge to the conventional wisdom about urban sprawl by its defenders, by the new idea of "bicycling-oriented development" and "pedestrian-oriented development" as countermesures to urban sprawl). And the reverse direction also holds true.

In relation to the evolution-transformation principle, if there is evolution (e.g., the natural evolution of humans to walk and run in the state of nature in a primitive way), there is transformation (e.g., the technical transformation of human ability to walk and run by the invention of automobiles, with auto-dependency in urban sprawl). And the reverse direction also holds true.

In relation to the symmetry-asymmetry principle, if there is symmetry (e.g., the existence of different operators of vehicles in traffic), there is asymmetry (e.g., "in heavy but free flowing traffic, jams can arise spontaneously, triggered by minor events ['butterfly effects'], such as an abrupt steering maneuver by a single motorist," so that a normal motorist who follows the traffic rules and does not make any abrupt moves cannot cause, on average, such a traffic jam but another motorist who makes "an abrupt steering maneuver" can). And the reverse direction also holds true.

In relation to the softness-hardness principle, if there is softness (e.g., the appreciation of urban sprawl, as shown by "one suburban Detroit politician" who "defends low-density development as the preferred lifestyle choice of his constituents, calling it '...the American Dream unfolding before your eyes'"), there is hardness (e.g., the critique of urban sprawl, as shown in the problems pointed out by the critics as cited, who reject it on different grounds, like traffic congestion, negative environmental and public health outcomes, etc.). And the reverse direction also holds true.

In relation to the seriousness-playfulness principle, if there is seriousness (e.g., the serious business of those who want to provide countermeasures to traffic congestion), there is playfulness (e.g., the playful part of those who want to provide countermeasures to traffic congestion, when they play around with different options like "parking restrictions," "park and ride facilities," "road pricing," "cap and trade," "congestion pricing," "road space rationing," "number plate restrictions," "permits," "cycling promotion," "speed limit reductions," etc., so as to test and see which ones are more effective). And the reverse direction also holds true.

In relation to the activeness-inactivess principle, if there is activeness (e.g., the alertness of a single motorist who actively tries to make "an abrupt steering maneuver" to get ahead in traffic), there is inactiveness (e.g., the relative inactiveness of another motorist who simply follows the rules unconsciously and does not make "an abrupt steering maneuver" to get ahead in traffic).

In relation to the regression-progression principle, if there is regression (e.g., the regression made by urban sprawl, as shown in its contribution to traffic congestion and other problems pointed out by the critics), there is progression (e.g., the progress made by urban sprawl, as shown in its contribution to "the preferred lifestyle choice" like "the American Dream unfolding before your eyes"). And the reverse direction also holds true.

In relation to the same-difference principle, if there is similarity in outcome (e.g., the contribution to the molding and control of beliefs, values, and behaviors, regardless of whether this be done by way of car-owning lifestyle, or by way of car-free lifestyle), there is difference in outcome (e.g., the contribution to the molding and control of beliefs, values, and behaviors by way of car-owning lifestyle for a relatively more sedentary lifeworld—but the contribution to the molding and control of beliefs, values, and behaviors by way of car-free lifestyle for a relatively more physical lifeworld). And the reverse direction also holds true.

And in relation to the stability-reaction principle, if there is stability (e.g., the relatively more stable condition of cities in the older days, when they evolved out of rural areas), there is reaction (e.g., cities in the older days then led to further changes later on, when cities grew outwards to suburbs and then to the outskirts into what is now known as urban sprawl). And the reverse direction also holds true.

Operations and Culture

Operations, when examined from the perspective of culture, can cast an illuminating light on their possibility (or impossibility) and desirability (or undesirability), and this can be shown by way of two case studies, namely, (3.5.1) operations, rail transport, and popular culture, and (3.5.2) operations, ship transport, and the art of sailing—to be addressed hereafter, in that order.

Operations, Rail Transport, and Popular Culture

An excellent case study here to understand operations from the perspective of culture has to do with operations, rail transport, and popular culture.

The term "rail transport" refers to "a means of conveyance of passengers and goods by way of wheeled vehicles running on rail tracks.

In contrast to road transport, where vehicles merely run on a prepared surface, rail vehicles are also directionally guided by the tracks on which they run. Track usually consists of steel rails installed on sleepers/ties and ballast, on which the rolling stock, usually fitted with metal wheels, moves. However, other variations are also possible, such as slab track where the rails are fastened to a concrete foundation resting on a prepared subsurface." (WK 2012ss)

History of Rail Transport

The history of rail transport has gone through different changes. Consider, for illustration, a few main ones (in its history) below (as summarized in *Table 3.7*).

(a) Pre-Steam Rail Transport

In Europe, "the earliest known record of a railway…is a stained-glass window in the Minster of Freiburg im Breisgau in Germany, dating from around 1350. In 1515, Cardinal Matthäus Lang wrote a description of the Reisszug, a funicular railway at the Hohensalzburg Castle in Austria. The line originally used wooden rails and a hemp haulage rope, and was operated by human or animal power. The line still exists, albeit in updated form, and is one of the oldest railways still to operate." (WK 2012ss; S. Hylton 2007)

Later, "by 1550, narrow gauge railways with wooden rails were common in mines in Europe. By the 17th century, wooden wagonways were common in the United Kingdom for transporting coal from mines to canal wharfs for transshipment to boats. The world's oldest working railway, built in 1758, is the Middleton Railway in Leeds. In 1764, the first gravity railroad in the United States was built in Lewiston, New York. The first permanent tramway was the Leiper Railroad in 1810." (WK 2012ss)

(b) Steam Rail Transport

Rail transport was later transformed by "the development of the steam engine during the Industrial revolution in the United Kingdom," which "spurred ideas for mobile steam locomotives that could haul trains on tracks." (WK 2012ss)

For instance, "James Watt's patented steam engines of 1769 (revised in 1782) were heavy low-pressure engines which were not suitable for use in locomotives. However, in 1804, using high-pressure steam, Richard Trevithick demonstrated the first locomotive-hauled train in Merthyr Tydfil, United Kingdom. Accompanied with Andrew Vivian, it ran with mixed success, breaking some of the brittle cast-iron plates. Two years later, the first passenger horse-drawn railway was opened nearby between Swansea and Mumbles." (WK 2012ss; BBC 2004 & 2007)

By contrast, "railroads (as they were known in the USA) were built on a far larger scale than those in Continental Europe, both in terms of the distances covered and also in the loading gauge adopted which allowed for heavier locomotives and double-deck trains. The Baltimore and Ohio that opened in 1830 was the first to evolve from a single line to a network in the United States. By 1831, a steam railway connected Albany and Schenectady, New York, a distance of 16 miles, which was covered in 40 minutes." (WK 2012ss; J. Dilts 1996)

Especially, "the years between 1850 and 1890 saw phenomenal growth in the US railroad system, which at its peak constituted one third of the world's total mileage. Although the American Civil War placed a temporary halt to major new developments the conflict did demonstrate the enormous strategic importance of railways at times of war. After the war major developments include the first elevated railway built in New York in 1867 and the symbolically important first transcontinental railway was completed in 1869." (WK 2012ss)

(c) Electrical Rail Transport

The third transformation of rail transport is about "electrification," when "experiments with electrical railways were started by Robert Davidson in 1838. He completed a battery-powered carriage capable of 6.4 km/h (4 mph). The Gross-Lichterfelde Tramway was the first to use electricity fed to the trains en-route, when it opened in 1881. Overhead wires were taken into use in the Mödling and Hinterbrühl Tram in Austria in October 1883. At first, this was taken into use on tramways that, until then, had been horse-drawn tramcars." (WK 2012ss)

But "the first conventional completely electrified railway mainline was the 106 km Valtellina line in Italy that was opened on 4 September 1902. During the 1890s, many large cities, such as London, Paris and New York used the new technology to build rapid transit for urban commuting. In smaller cities, tramways became common and were often the only mode of public transport until the introduction of buses in the 1920s. In North America, interurbans became a common mode to reach suburban areas. At first, all electric railways used direct current but, in 1904, the Stubaital Line in Austria opened with alternating current." (WK 2012ss)

(d) Diesel Rail Transport

Then there was the "dieselisation" of rail transport, especially with the use of gasoline.

To start, "steam locomotives require large pools of labour to clean, load, maintain and run. After World War II, dramatically increased labour costs in developed countries made steam an increasingly costly form of motive power. At the same time, the war had forced improvements in internal combustion engine technology that made diesel locomotives cheaper and more powerful. This caused many railway companies to initiate programmes to convert all unelectrified sections from steam to diesel locomotion." (WK 2012ss)

In general, "diesel locomotives use a diesel engine as the prime mover. The energy transmission may be either diesel-electric, diesel-mechanical or diesel-hydraulic but diesel-electric is dominant." (WK 2012ss)

Types of Rail Transport

Rail transport can come in all shapes and sizes, and hereafter are some main examples (as summarized in *Table 3.7*).

(a) Passenger Train

One main type of rail transport is known as "passenger train," which "travels between stations where passengers may embark and disembark. The oversight of the train is the duty of a guard/train manager. Passenger trains are part of public transport and often make up the stem of the service, with buses feeding to stations. Passenger trains can involve a variety of functions including long distance intercity travel, daily commuter trips, or local urban transit services. They even include a diversity of vehicles, operating speeds, right of way requirements, and service frequency." (WK 2012ss)

Conventionally, "passenger trains usually can be divided into two operations: intercity railway and intracity transit. Whereas as intercity railway involve higher speeds, longer routes, and lower frequency (usually scheduled), intracity transit involves lower speeds, shorter routes, and higher frequency (especially during peak hours)." (WK 2012ss)

On the one hand, "intercity trains are long-haul trains that operate with few stops between cities. Trains typically have amenities such as a dining car. Some lines also provide over-night services with sleeping cars. Some long-haul trains been given a specific name. Regional trains are medium distance trains that connect cities with outlying, surrounding areas, or provide a regional service, making more stops and having lower speeds. Commuter trains serve suburbs of urban areas, providing a daily commuting service. Airport rail links provide quick access from city centres to airports. High-speed rail are special inter-city trains that operate at much higher speeds than conventional railways, the limit being regarded at 200 to 320 km/h. High-speed trains are used mostly for long-haul service and most systems are in Western Europe and East Asia. The speed record is 574.8 km/h (357.2 mph), set by a modified French TGV. Magnetic levitation trains such as the Shanghai airport train usc under-riding magnets which attract themselves upward towards the underside of a guideway and this line has achieved somewhat higher peak speeds in day-to-day operation than conventional high-speed railways." (WK 2012ss)

On the other hand, an "intracity train" like a "rapid transit" is "an intracity system built in large cities and has the highest capacity of any passenger transport system. It is grade separated and commonly built underground or elevated. At street level, smaller trams can be used. Light rails are upgraded trams that have step-free access, their own right-of-way and sometimes sections underground. Monorail systems operate as elevated, medium capacity systems. A people mover is a driverless, grade-separated train that serves only a few stations, as a shuttle. Due to the wide variety of rapid transit systems without much uniformity, route alignment vary widely with diverse right-of-ways (private land, side of road, street median) and geometric characteristics (sharp or broad curves, steep or gentle grades). For instance, the Chicago El trains are designed with extremely short cars to negotiate the sharp curves in the Loop. NJ's PATH have similar-sized cars to accommodate curves in the trans-Hudson tunnels. San Francisco's BART operate large cars on its well-engineered routes." (WK 2012ss)

(b) Freight Train

Another main type of rail transport is known as "freight train," which "hauls cargo using freight cars specialized for the type of goods. Freight trains are very efficient, with economy of scale and high energy efficiency….Authorities often encourage the use of cargo rail transport due to its environmental profile." (WK 2012ss)

Nowadays, "container trains have become the dominant type in the US for non-bulk haulage. Containers can easily be transshipped to other modes, such as ships and trucks, using cranes. This has succeeded the boxcar (wagon-load), where the cargo had to be loaded and unloaded into the train manually. The intermodal containerization of cargo has revolutionized the supply chain logistics industry, reducing ship costs significantly. In Europe, the sliding wall wagon has largely superseded the ordinary covered wagons." (WK 2012ss)

Other types of freight rail transport include "refrigerator cars, stock cars for livestock and autoracks for road vehicles. When rail is combined with road transport, a roadrailer will allow trailers to be driven onto the train, allowing for easy transition between road and rail." (WK 2012ss)

Operations of Rail Transport

Rail transport needs to be operated properly, so the issues concerning its operations are important. Consider, for illustration, some main ones below (as summarized in *Table 3.7*).

(a) Ownership

The first issue of operations is about "ownership"; in the U.S., for instance, "traditionally, the infrastructure and rolling stock are owned and operated by the same company. This has often been by a national railway, while other companies have had private railways. Since the 1980s, there has been an increasing tendency to split up railway companies, with separate companies owning the stock from those owning the infrastructure, particularly in Europe, where this is required by the European Union. This has allowed open access by any train operator to any portion of the European railway network." (WK 2012ss)

In the U.S., "virtually all rail networks and infrastructure are privately-owned with passenger lines, primarily Amtrak, operating as tenants on the freight lines. Consequently, operations must be closely synchronized and coordinated between freight and passenger railways for timeliness of their schedules. Due to this shared system, both are regulated by the Federal Railroad Administration (FRA) and follow the AREMA standards for track work and AAR standards for vehicles." (WK 2012ss)

(b) Financing

The second issue of operations is about "financing"; in general, "the main source of income for railway companies is from ticket revenue (for passenger transport) and shipment fees for cargo. Discounts and monthly passes are sometimes available for frequent travellers. Freight revenue may be sold per container slot or for a whole train. Sometimes, the shipper owns the cars and only rents the haulage. For passenger transport, advertisement income can be significant." (WK 2012ss)

In addition, "government may choose to give subsidies to rail operation, since rail transport has fewer externalities than other dominant modes of transport. If the railway company is state-owned, the state may simply provide direct subsidies in exchange for an increased production. If operations have been privatized, several options are available. Some countries have a system where the infrastructure is owned by a government agency or company—with open access to the tracks for any company that meets safety requirements. In such cases, the state may choose to provide the tracks free of charge, or for a fee that does not cover all costs. This is seen as analogous to the government providing free access to roads. For passenger operations, a direct subsidy may be paid to a public-owned operator, or public service obligation tender may be helt, and a time-limited contract awarded to the lowest bidder." (WK 2012ss)

In the U.S., "Amtrak…is a private railroad company chartered by the government. Similarly, Canada's VIA Rail system operates in the same fashion. As private passenger services lost significant ground in competition to the automobile and airplane and was forced out the market, they became stockholders of Amtrak either with a cash entrance fee or relinquishing their locomotives and rolling stock. Government aid supports Amtrak by supplying start-up capital and makes up for loses at end of the fiscal year." (WK 2012ss; K. EuDaly 2009)

(c) Safety

The third issue of operations is about "safety," because "trains can travel at very high speed, but they are heavy, are unable to deviate from the track and require a great distance to stop. Possible accidents include derailment (jumping the track), a collision with another train or collision with an automobile or other vehicle at level crossings. The latter accounts for the majority of rail accidents and casualties. The most important safety measures to prevent accidents are strict operating rules, e.g. railway signalling and gates or grade separation at crossings. Train whistles, bells or horns warn of the presence of a train, while trackside signals maintain the distances between trains." (WK 2012ss)

For this reason, "an important element in the safety of many high-speed inter-city networks such as Japan's Shinkansen is the fact that trains only run on dedicated railway lines, without level crossings. This effectively eliminates the potential for collision with automobiles, other vehicles and pedestrians, vastly reduces the likelihood of collision with other trains and helps ensure services remain timely." (WK 2012ss)

(d) Maintenance

And the fourth issue of operations is about "maintenance," because "railways must keep up with periodic inspection and maintenance in order to minimize effect of infrastructure failures that can disrupt freight revenue operations and passenger services. Because passengers are considered the most crucial cargo and usually operate at higher speeds, steeper grades, and higher capacity/frequency, their lines are especially important. Inspection practices include track geometry cars or walking inspection. Curve maintenance especially for transit services includes gauging, fastener tightening, and rail replacement. Rail corrugation is a common issue with transit systems due to the high number of light-axle, wheel passages which result in grinding of the wheel/rail interface." (WK 2012ss)

More importantly, "unlike highways or road networks where capacity is disaggregated into unlinked trips over individual route segments, railway capacity is fundamentally considered a network system. As a result, many components are causes and effects of system disruptions. Maintenance must acknowledge the vast array of a route's performance (type of train service, origination/destination, seasonal impacts), line's capacity (length, terrain, number of tracks, types of train control), train's throughput (max speeds, acceleration/deceleration rates), and service features with shared passenger-freight tracks (sidings, terminal capacities, switching routes, and design type)." (WK 2012ss)

Rail Transport in Popular Culture

Rail transport has a special place in popular culture. For illustration, consider the following examples (as summarized in *Table 3.7*).

(a) Films

In films, there are countless examples of trains to be part of the stories, as shown below: (WK 2012tt)

- *Back to the Future Part III*—"the improvised method of propelling the time machine to 88 mph in 1885 was by using a steam locomotive, also Emmett Brown refitted a steam locomotive into a hovertrain as the basis of his new time machine."
- *Brief Encounter* (1945)—"romantic meetings in a train station"
- *Boxcar Bertha* (1972)—"starred Barbara Hershey as a orphan who turns to robbing trains for survival. Martin Scorsese's first feature film."
- *The Cassandra Crossing* (1976)—"passengers aboard a transcontinental train face a threat from carrier of plague virus."
- *Closely Watched Trains*—"in which the story takes places at a railway station in World War II in Czechoslovakia under the Nazi occupation. The film is based on Bohumil Hrabal's novel, directed by Jiří Menzel."
- *Death Line* (1972) and *Creep* (2004)—" both deal with killers on the London Underground."
- *The First Great Train Robbery*—"based on the Great Gold Robbery of 1855."

- *From Russia with Love*—"James Bond novel and film, confrontation on board of the Orient Express."
- *Murder, She Said*—"features extensive railway scenes. Based on the novel 4.50 from Paddington by Agatha Christie."
- *North by Northwest* (1959—"Alfred Hitchcock thriller starring Cary Grant, Eva Marie Saint and James Mason"
- *North West Frontier* (1959)—"A British army officer transports a young prince to safety aboard an antiquated locomotive."
- *Strangers on a Train* (1951)—"Alfred Hitchcock classic thriller"
- *Steamboy* (2004)—"featured extensive railway scenes (including a chase scene between a train, a 'steam automotive' and a steam-powered monowheel) around London and Manchester."
- *Unstoppable* (2010)—"tells the story of a runaway freight train and two men who try to stop it. Inspired by the CSX 8888 incident."

Surely, there can be other examples, so the ones above are illustrative, not exhaustive.

(b) Literature

In literature, there are countless examples of trains to be part of the stories, as shown below: (WK 2012tt)

- *The Adventure of the Lost Locomotive*—"a Solar Pons story about a disappearing train on the Great Northern Railway."
- *Anna Karenina* (by Leo Tolstoy)—"train travel is arguably the most prominent motif of the story."
- *The Dark Tower* (book series) by Stephen King—"the main character Roland of Gilead travels through a series of caves which were once part of an underground railroad system. The characters also ride on a monorail with artificial intelligence."
- *Galaxy Express 999*— "from the manga and anime of the same name by Leiji Matsumoto, this train travels the galaxy from planet to planet."
- *Iron Council* (China Mieville) —"a fantasy book about the building of a cross-continental railway line."
- *The Locomotive*—"dynamic poem for children by Julian Tuwim, filmed by Zbigniew Rybczyński"
- *The Lost Special*—"short story by Arthur Conan Doyle, about the investigation of a special train mysteriously disappearing.
- *Murder on the Orient Express* (book, film)—"describes a train journey from Paris to Istanbul aboard the Orient Express during which a

murder takes place. Hercule Poirot, riding on the train solves the mystery and justice is served."

- *The Mystery of the Blue Train* (book, TV adaptation) —"earlier Poirot story in which a murder takes place on a train"
- *Night on the Galactic Railroad* (novel, film) —"two boys travel on a magical train across the night sky…but there is a deeper meaning to the journey."
- *Strangers on a Train* (novel, film)—"tells the story of how two strangers meet on a train and decide to exchange murders so they can't be tied to each other."

Again, there can be other examples, so the ones above are illustrative, not exhaustive.

(c) Television

And on television, there are countless examples of trains to be part of the stories, as shown below: (WK 2012tt)

- *Atomic Train* (1999)—"a runaway train carrying an atomic bomb into a town"
- *Dad's Army*—"several episodes were set at Walmington-on-Sea railway station or on the local railway line."
- *Digimon Frontier*—"features several train like Digimon called Trailmon that run on monorails."
- *Digimon Tamers–The Runaway Digimon Express*—"features a train like Digimon called Locomon that is controlled by another Digimon causing it to run wild on the railways. It later evolves into a meaner looking Digimon called Grandlocomon."
- *The Flockton Flyer*—"about a family who work on a heritage railway."
- *Oh, Doctor Beeching!*—"set on a railway station threatened with closure"
- *Petticoat Junction*—"set on a rural railway line permanently threatened with closure"
- *Quatermass and the Pit*—"building work on the London Underground unearths artefacts from a race of extraterrestrials"
- *Supertrain*—"a television series on a huge luxury double deckered high speed train"
- *Thomas the Tank Engine and Friends*—"TV Series originated from The Railway Series by the Rev.W.Awdry"
- *Kamen Rider Den-O*—"features the DenLiner, the train that ables to travel time."

Once more, there can be other examples, so the ones above are illustrative, not exhaustive.

Problems with the Study on Rail Transport and Popular Culture

However, for the critics, this study on rail transport and popular culture has some major problems. Consider, for illustration, a few examples below (as summarized in *Table 3.7*).

Firstly, one main criticism of the study on rail transport and popular culture is that the history of rail transport has its ups and downs.

For instance, for the critics, "following the large-scale construction of motorways after the war, rail transport became less popular for commuting and air transport started taking large market shares from long-haul passenger trains. Most tramways were either replaced by rapid transits or buses, while high transshipment costs caused short-haul freight trains to become uncompetitive." (WK 2012ss)

Secondly, another main criticism of the study on rail transport and popular culture is that each rail transport has its own advantages and disadvantages.

For instance, for the critics, freight trains are used "due to its environmental profile," but "their use can be reduced by lack of flexibility, if there is need of transshipment at both ends of the trip due to lack of tracks to the points of pick-up and delivery." (WK 2012ss)

And thirdly, an additional main criticism of the study on rail transport and popular culture is that the stories about trains in popular culture are often questionable.

For instance, for the critics, in the film *Mission: Impossible,* one can "see…a helicopter pursuing a TGV train into the Channel Tunnel which runs between Great Britain and France. In reality this type of train does not travel through the Channel Tunnel, and the tunnel shown in the film has double track whereas the real tunnel has two single bores." (WK 2012tt)

Beyond Rail Transport

These criticisms of rail transport and popular culture do not entail a total rejection of its usefulness but serve to show us the two opposing sides of the debate, such that the possibility (or impossibility) and desirability (or undesirability) of operations (from the perspective of culture with operations, rail transport, and popular culture as a case study here) are not to the extent that the respective defenders would like us to believe.

Furthermore, the analysis of operations, rail transport, and popular culture illuminates the working of the ontological principles in existential dialectics, and good examples include the formalness-informalness principle, the absoluteness-relativeness principle, the partiality-totality principle, the predictability-unpredictability principle, the explicability-inexplicability principle, the fiction-reality principle, the finiteness-transfiniteness principle, the preciseness-vagueness principle, the simpleness-complicatedness principle, the openness-hiddenness principle, the denseness-emptiness principle, the change-constancy principle, the order-chaos principle, the slowness-quickness principle, the expansion-contraction principle, the theory-praxis principle, the convention-novelty principle, the evolution-transformation principle, the symmetry-asymmetry principle, the softness-hardness principle, the seriousness-playfulness principle, the activeness-inactivess principle, the regression-progression principle, the same-difference principle, and the stability-reaction principle.

For instance, in relation to the formalness-informalness principle, if there is formalness (e.g., the formal logical requirement of soundness and completeness in a system of ideas, as in the study on rail transport and popular culture), there is informalness (e.g., the non-formal existence of unsoundness and incompleteness in the study on rail transport and popular culture, as shown in the criticisms that the history of rail transport has its ups and downs, that each rail transport has its own advantages and disadvantages, that the stories about trains in popular culture are often questionable, etc.). And the reverse direction also holds true.

In relation to the absoluteness-relativeness principle, if there is absoluteness (e.g., the absolute view about rail transport in the older days before "the large-scale construction of motorways" and "air transport"), there is relativeness (e.g., what is right for the widespread use of rail transport in the older days before "the large-scale construction of motorways" and "air transport" is not necessarily so for later times, when, after the war, "rail transport became less popular for commuting and air transport started taking large market shares from long-haul passenger trains"). And the reverse direction also holds true.

In relation to the partiality-totality principle, if there is partiality (e.g., the partial view about rail transport in the older days, when it was widely used, before "the large-scale construction of motorways" and "air transport"), there is totality (e.g., the more holistic view of rail transport, such that the whole is not the sum of its parts, that is, it cannot be reduced to the sum of opposing views about its rise and fall, since there will emerge new views in the future not yet known today, just as there are already some signs of a small revival of rail transport again nowadays, as shown by some "cities that closed their old tramways" and "have reopened new light railway systems"). (WK 2012ss) And the reverse direction also holds true.

In relation to the predictability-unpredictability principle, if there is predictability (e.g., the predictable tendency of rail transport to have its ups and downs in future history), there is unpredictability (e.g., the more difficult task to predict exactly the extent to which rail transport will be revived in a particular future historical era). And the reverse direction also holds true.

In relation to the explicability-inexplicability principle, if there is explicability (e.g., the explanation by the supporters of freight trains that they are useful because their "environmental profile"), there is inexplicability (e.g., the lack of sufficient explanation by the supporters of freight trains of why they must be necessarily useful, since, for the critics, "their use can be reduced by lack of flexibility, if there is need of transshipment at both ends of the trip due to lack of tracks to the points of pick-up and delivery"). And the reverse direction also holds true.

In relation to the fiction-reality principle, if there is fiction (e.g., the fictional aspect of the film *Mission: Impossible,* when one can "see…a helicopter pursuing a TGV train into the Channel Tunnel which runs between Great Britain and France," but "in reality this type of train does not travel through the Channel Tunnel"), there is reality (e.g., the realistic aspect of the film *Mission: Impossible,* insofar as there are trains which travel through the Channel Tunnel). And the reverse direction also holds true.

In relation to the finiteness-transfiniteness principle, if there is finiteness (e.g., the finite number of the categories of rail transport, like pre-steam, steam, electrical, and diesel rail transports), there is transfiniteness (e.g., the transfinite number of all the individual pieces of rail transport ever produced in history, regardless of how primitive or incomplete they are). And the reverse direction also holds true.

In relation to the preciseness-vagueness principle, if there is preciseness (e.g., the precise identification of three major ways in which rail transport appears in popular culture in the article aforecited, like in films, on TV, and in literature), there is vagueness (e.g., the vagueness in the identification of the three major ways in which rail transport appears in popular culture in the article aforecited, since it is not clear why there must be only 3 ways, not 5, 7, 8, and so on). And the reverse direction also holds true.

In relation to the simpleness-complicatedness principle, if there is simpleness (e.g., the relatively simple analysis of rail transport by its advocates), there is complicatedness (e.g., the relatively more complicated analysis of rail transport, by challenging the claims and assumptions, as shown in the problems pointed out by the critics as cited). And the reverse direction also holds true.

In relation to the openness-hiddenness principle, if there is openness (e.g., the open exploration of the nature of trains and their portrayal in popular culture), there is hiddenness (e.g., the hidden bias in the portrayal of trains in popular culture, as shown in the film *Mission: Impossible,* when one can "see…a helicopter pursuing a TGV train into the Channel Tunnel which runs between Great Britain and France," but "in reality this type of train does not travel through the Channel Tunnel"). And the reverse direction also holds true.

In relation to the denseness-emptiness principle, if there is denseness (e.g., the relatively denser concentration of concerns with train travel in *Anna Karenina* by Leo Tolstoy), there is emptiness (e.g., the relatively less dense, or more empty, concentration of concerns with train travel in the film *Avatar*). And the reverse direction also holds true.

In relation to the change-constancy principle, if there is change (e.g., the ever new ways to build new types of transportation, as shown in the invention of rail transport), there is constancy (e.g., the ever constant existence of different problems in the ever new ways to build new types of transportation, as shown in the problems with rail transport pointed out by the critics). And the reverse direction also holds true.

In relation to the order-chaos principle, if there is order (e.g., the more or less orderly reality of "many high-speed inter-city networks such as Japan's Shinkansen," because they "only run on dedicated railway lines, without level crossings" and "this effectively eliminates the potential for collision with automobiles, other vehicles and pedestrians," so they "vastly reduces the likelihood of collision with other trains and helps ensure services remain timely"), there is chaos (e.g,. the more or less chaotic reality of trains, when they involve in accidents like "derailment," "a collision with another train," or "collision with an automobile or other vehicle at level crossings"). And the reverse direction also holds true.

In relation to the slowness-quickness principle, if there is slowness (e.g., the relatively slower speed of pre-steam rail transport, when "the line originally used wooden rails and a hemp haulage rope, and was operated by human or animal power"), there is quickness (e.g., the relatively quicker speed of a modified French TGV at the speed record of 574.8

km/h, when contrasted with the pre-steam rail transport). And the reverse direction also holds true.

In relation to the expansion-contraction principle, if there is expansion (e.g., the relative spread of the use of "high-speed inter-city networks" nowadays), there is contraction (e.g., the relative decline of the use of pre-steam rail transports nowadays). And the reverse direction also holds true.

In relation to the theory-praxis principle, if there is theory (e.g., the theoretical construction of electromagnetic force in physics), there is praxis (e.g., the practical application of of electromagnetic force in physics to the field of transportation, like the invention of electrical rail transport). And the reverse direction also holds true.

In relation to the convention-novelty principle, if there is convention (e.g., the conventional wisdom about pre-steam rail transport in the older days), there is novelty (e.g., the alternative novel challenge to the conventional wisdom about pre-steam rail transport in the older days, by the new idea of electrical rail transport in modern times). And the reverse direction also holds true.

In relation to the evolution-transformation principle, if there is evolution (e.g., the natural evolution of humans to move around by foot in the state of nature in a primitive way), there is transformation (e.g., the technical transformation of human ability to move around by the invention of rail transport). And the reverse direction also holds true.

In relation to the symmetry-asymmetry principle, if there is symmetry (e.g., the existence of different players in society, like railroad company, government, etc.), there is asymmetry (e.g., government has the power to provide subsidy to railroad company, as shown in the example that the U.S. government aid "supports Amtrak by supplying start-up capital and makes up for loses at end of the fiscal year"). And the reverse direction also holds true.

In relation to the softness-hardness principle, if there is softness (e.g., the appreciation of steam rail transport, as shown by James Watt's patented steam engines of 1769), there is hardness (e.g., the critique of steam rail transport, as shown by the criticism that "steam locomotives require large pools of labour to clean, load, maintain and run" and "after World War II, dramatically increased labour costs in developed countries made steam an increasingly costly form of motive power"). And the reverse direction also holds true.

In relation to the seriousness-playfulness principle, if there is seriousness (e.g., the serious business of those who build rail transports), there is playfulness (e.g., the playful part of those who build rail transports, when they play around with different designs and innovations over time, as shown in the history of pre-steam, steam, electrical, and diesel rail transports). And the reverse direction also holds true.

In relation to the activeness-inactivess principle, if there is activeness (e.g., the alertness of those safe drivers who actively try to avoid collision by operating a train carefully and paying good attention to other vehicles at level crossings), there is inactiveness (e.g., the relative inattentiveness of those careless drivers who collide with other vehicles at level crossings, and so on). And the reverse direction also holds true.

In relation to the regression-progression principle, if there is regression (e.g., the use of freight trains "can be reduced by lack of flexibility, if there is need of transshipment at both ends of the trip due to lack of tracks to the points of pick-up and delivery"), there is progression (e.g., freight trains are used "due to its environmental profile"). And the reverse direction also holds true.

In relation to the same-difference principle, if there is similarity in outcome (e.g., the contribution to the molding and control of beliefs, values, and behaviors, regardless of whether this be done by way of pre-steam human-powered rail transports, or by way of high-speed magnetic levitation trains), there is difference in outcome (e.g., the contribution to the molding and control of beliefs, values, and behaviors by way of pre-steam human-powered rail transports for a relatively more physical lifeworld—but the contribution to the molding and control of beliefs, values, and behaviors by way of high-speed magnetic levitation trains for a relatively more technophilic lifeworld). And the reverse direction also holds true.

And in relation to the stability-reaction principle, if there is stability (e.g., the relatively more stable condition of pre-steam rail transports in the older days, when people used "wooden rails and a hemp haulage rope,… operated by human or animal power"), there is reaction (e.g., the pre-steam rail transports in the older days then led to further changes later on, when nowadays people use high-speed magnetic levitation trains). And the reverse direction also holds true.

Operations, Ship Transport, and the Art of Sailing

Another way to evaluate the possibility (or impossibility) and desirability (or undesirability) of operations from the perspective of culture concerns operations, ship transport, and the art of sailing.

The term "ship transport" refers to "watercraft carrying people (passengers) or goods (cargo). Sea transport has been the largest carrier of freight throughout recorded history….Transport by water is cheaper than transport by air. Ship transport can be over any distance by boat, ship, sailboat or barge, over oceans and lakes, through canals or along rivers. Shipping may be for commerce, recreation or the military. Virtually any material that can be moved, can be moved by water….'General cargo' is goods packaged in boxes, cases, pallets, and barrels. Containerization revolutionized ship transport in the 1960s." (WK 2012uu)

Meanings of Sailing, and Ship Transport

Ship transport needs to be operated, and a person who "navigates water-borne vessels or assists in their operation, maintenance, or service" is known as "a sailor, mariner, or seaman." (WK 2012vv)

However, the term "sailor, mariner, or seaman" can also be used to "apply to professional mariners, military personnel, and recreational sailors as well as a plethora of other uses. Etymologically, the name preserves the memory of the time when ships were commonly powered by sails, but it applies to the personnel of all vessels, whatever their mode of locomotion." (WK 2012vv)

With these multiple meanings in mind, the term "sailor, mariner, or seaman" has come to refer to different things, as shown below (and summarized in *Table 3.8*): (WK 2012vv)

- "A person who goes out sailing, boating or yachting"
- "A person who practices the art of controlling the motion of a sailing ship or sailboat, across a body of water"
- "An enlisted member of a military naval force"
- "Anyone on a boat"
- "Anyone from a recruit to an admiral in a navy or coast guard"
- "Members of the deck department as opposed to members of other departments in the Merchant Navy"

Surely, there can be other uses too, so the examples above are illustrative, not exhautive.

Categories of Sailing, and Ship Transport

Sailing can also be understood in different categories, in relation to "professions and ranks, each of which carries unique responsibilities which are integral to the successful operation of an ocean-going vessel." (WK 2012vv)

For instance, consider the following "four main categories: the deck department, the engineering department, the steward's department, and other," as shown below (and summarized in *Table 3.8*): (WK 2012vv)

(a) Deck Department

The first category of sailing in accordance to profession and rank is related to the "deck department" of a ship.

General speaking, "officer positions in the deck department include but are not limited to: Master and his Chief, Second, and Third officers. The official classifications for unlicensed members of the deck department are Able seaman and Ordinary seaman. With some variation, the Chief Mate is most often charged with the duties of Cargo Mate. Second Mates are charged with being the medical officer, in case of medical emergency. All Three mates each do Four-Hour AM and PM shifts on the bridge, when underway at sea." (WK 2012vv)

A common deck crew for a ship has the following members: (WK 2012vv)

- "(1) Chief Officer/Chief Mate"
- "(1) Second Officer /Second Mate"
- "(1) Third Officer / Third Mate"
- "(1) Cadet/Officer Cadet"
- "(1) Boatswain"
- "(2-8) Able seamen"
- "(0-3) Ordinary seamen"

Of course, the number in relation to the deck crew can vary from case to case.

(b) Engineering Department

The second category of sailing in accordance to profession and rank is related to the "engineering department" of a ship.

In general, "a ship's engineering department consists of the members of a ship's crew that operates and maintains the propulsion and other systems onboard the vessel. Marine engineering staff also deal with the 'hotel' facilities onboard, notably the sewage, lighting, air conditioning and water systems. Engineering staff manage bulk fuel transfers, from a fuel-supply barge in port. When underway at sea, the second and third engineers will often be occupied with oil transfers from storage tanks, to active working tanks; Cleaning of oil purifiers is another regular task. Engineering staff are requireed to have training in firefighting and first aid. Additional duties include maintaining the ship's boats and performing other nautical tasks. Engineers play a key role in cargo loading/discharging gear and safety systems, though the specific cargo discharge function remains the responsibility of deck officers and deck workers." (WK 2012vv)

A common engineering crew for a ship has the following members: (WK 2012vv)

- "(1) Chief Engineer"
- "(1) Second Engineer / First Assistant Engineer"
- "(1) Third Engineer / Second Assistant Engineer"
- "(1-2) Fourth Engineer / Third Assistant Engineer"
- "(0-2) Fifth Engineer / Junior Engineer"
- "(1-3) QMED (unlicensed qualified rating: Qualified member Engine Dept.)"
- "(1-3) Oiler (unlicensed qualified rating)"
- "(0-3) Greaser/s (unlicensed qualified rating)"
- "(1-5) Entry-level rating (such as Wiper [occupation], Utilityman, etc.)"

Again, the number in relation to the engineering crew can vary from case to case.

(c) Steward's Department

The third category of sailing in accordance to profession and rank is related to the "steward's department" of a ship.

In general, "a typical Steward's department for a cargo ship is a Chief Steward, a Chief Cook, and a Steward's Assistant. All three positions are typically filled by unlicensed personnel." (WK 2012vv)

In terms of duties, "the chief steward directs, instructs, and assigns personnel performing such functions as preparing and serving meals; cleaning and maintaining officers' quarters and steward department areas; and receiving, issuing, and inventorying stores. The chief steward also plans menus; compiles supply, overtime, and cost control records. The steward may requisition or purchase stores and equipment. Galley roles may include baking. A chief steward's duties may overlap with those of the Steward's Assistant, the Chief Cook, and other Steward's Department crewmembers." (WK 2012vv)

In addition, "a person has to have a Merchant Mariner's Document issued by the United States Coast Guard in the United States Merchant Marine in order to serve as a chief steward. All chief cooks who sail internationally are similarly documented by their respective countries because of international conventions and agreements." (WK 2012vv)

(d) Other Departments

There are other categories of sailing in accordance to profession and rank, and good examples include "Junior Assistant Purser, Senior Assistant Purser, Purser, Chief Purser, Medical Doctor, Professional Nurse, Marine Physician Assistant, and Hospital Corpsman. These jobs are considered administrative positions and are therefore regulated by Certificates of Registry issued by the United States Coast Guard. Pilots are also merchant marine officers and are licensed by the Coast Guard." (WK 2012vv)

Art of Sailing, and Ship Transport

All these members on a ship help to operate and maintain it at sea, but sailing a ship like this can be understood as an art—also known as "seamanship," which refers to "the art of operating a ship or boat." (WK 2012ww)

The art of sailing (or seamanship) "involves a knowledge of a variety of topics and development of specialised skills including: navigation and international maritime law; weather, meteorology and forecasting; watchstanding; ship-handling and small boat handling; operation of deck equipment, anchors and cables; ropework and line handling; communications;...engines; execution of evolutions such as towing; cargo handling equipment, dangerous cargoes and cargo storage; dealing with emergencies; survival at sea and search and rescue; fire fighting." (WK 2012ww)

Because of these diverse skills and tasks involved in seamanship, "the degree of knowledge needed within these areas is dependent upon the nature of the work and the type of vessel employed by a mariner. However, the practice of good seamanship should be the goal of all. The deep meaning of the word seamanship derives from the word seaman & ship. Thus it is the seaman who makes a good ship through his qualifications. Above all, Seamanship means Safety onboard and this is managed through continuous training and implementation of good working practices." (WK 2012ww)

For illustration, consider two special skills in the art of sailing below (as summarized in *Table 3.8*).

(a) Navigation

The art of sailing requires the skill and knowledge of navigation.

For instance, "more than just finding a vessel's present location, safe navigation includes predicting future location, route planning and collision avoidance. Nautical navigation in western nations, like air navigation, is based on the nautical mile." (WK 2012ww)

(b) Ship-Handling

The art of sailing also requires the skill of ship-handling, which is about "being able to maneuver a vessel with accuracy and precision. Unlike vehicles on land, a ship afloat is subject to the movements of the air around it and the water in which it floats. Another complicating factor is the mass of a ship that has to be accounted for when stopping and starting." (WK 2012ww)

In general, "ship-handling is about arriving and departing a berth or buoy, maneuvering in confined channels and harbours and in proximity to other ships, whilst at all times navigating safely. Two other types of operations, berthing alongside another ship and replenishment at sea, are occasionally included. A key ability for a ship-handler is an innate understanding of how the wind, tide and swell, the passage of other vessels, as well as the shape of the seabed, will affect a vessel's movement, which, together with an understanding of a specific vessels performance, should allow that vessel a safe passage." (WK 2012ww)

What is important "to low speed maneuvering is an understanding of the configuration and handedness of the propeller(s). An effect known as propeller walk will kick the stern of the vessel to port or starboard depending on the configuration and the type of propeller when large variations on propeller rotation speed or changes of propeller rotation direction take place....In single screw vessels where the rotation of the propeller is reversed on an astern bell, a standard was established that the propeller would turn clockwise when viewed from astern. This would mean that the propeller would turn counterclockwise when going astern and the stern would walk to port. This aided in docking operations, where 'port side to' was the preferred situation and the vessel would be brought to the dock with a small bow-in angle and backing would flatten the angle, slow or stop the vessel and walk it alongside….In addition to being fully conversant with the principles of seamanship and ship-handling a good pilot will have developed his or her sense of 'situational awareness' to a point well beyond that of a member of a ships crew, his reactions will appear to be instinctive, positive and at all times safe." (WK 2012ww)

Problems with the Study on Ship Transport and the Art of Sailing

However, for the critics, this study on ship transport and the art of sailing has some major problems. Consider, for illustration, a few examples below (as summarized in *Table 3.8*).

Firstly, one main criticism of the study on ship transport and the art of sailing is that the history of ship transport has its ups and downs.

For instance, for the critics, in our times, "the importance of sea travel for passengers has decreased due to aviation." (WK 2012tt)

Secondly, another main criticism of the study on ship transport and the art of sailing is that ship transport has its advantages and disadvantages.

For instance, for the critics, , ship transport "is effective for short trips and pleasure cruises" and "is cheaper than transport by air"—but the problem here is that "water transport becomes impractical when material delivery is highly time-critical." (WK 2012tt)

Thirdly, an additional main criticism of the study on ship transport and the art of sailing is that the classification of sailing in relation to profession and ranking is not universal.

For instance, for the critics, "American ships also carry a Qualified Member of the Engine Department. Other possible positions include Motorman, Machinist, Electrician, Refrigeration Engineer, and Tankerman," which are not included in the classification aforecited. (WK 2012vv)

Fourthly, another additional main criticism of the study on ship transport and the art of sailing is that the art of sailing is relative.

For instance, for the critics, there is "an exception" to the general rule in the art of sailing that "the propeller would turn counterclockwise when going astern and the stern would walk to port," as shown in the exceptional example about "the U.S. Sealift class tankers which used a controllable pitch propeller, where the pitch and not the direction of rotation was reversed to go astern," so "these propellers rotated counterclockwise at all times and so the 'walk' was 'normal.'" (WK 2012ww)

Fifthly, still another additional main criticism of the study on ship transport and the art of sailing is that the art of sailing is not suitable for anyone to master.

For instance, for the critics, "professional mariners live on the margins of society, with much of their life spent beyond the reach of land. They face cramped, stark, noisy, and dangerous conditions at sea….Whatever the calling, those who live and work at sea invariably confront social isolation. Findings by the Seafarer's International Research Center indicate a leading cause of mariners leaving the industry is 'almost invariably because they want to be with their families.' U.S. merchant ships typically do not allow family members to accompany seafarers on voyages. Industry experts increasingly recognize isolation, stress, and fatigue as occupational hazards." (WK 2012vv)

And sixthly, one more main criticism of the study on ship transport and the art of sailing is that the art of sailing does not guarantee the non-occurrence of ship accidents.

For instance, for the critics, one good example is the sinking of "the RMS *Titanic*," which "was a British passenger liner that sank in the North Atlantic Ocean on 15 April 1912 after colliding with an iceberg during her maiden voyage from Southampton, England to New York City," and "the sinking of *Titanic* caused the deaths of 1,514 people in one of the deadliest peacetime maritime disasters in history." (WK 2012xx)

Beyond Ship Transport and the Art of Sailing

These criticisms of ship transport and the art of sailing do not mean a total rejection of its usefulness but serve to show us the two opposing sides of the debate, such that the possibility (or impossibility) and desirability (or undesirability) of operations (from the perspective of culture with operations, ship transport, and the art of sailing as a case study here) are not to the extent that the respective defenders would like us to believe.

In addition, the analysis of operations, ship transport, and the art of sailing can teach us something valuable about the ontological principles in existential dialectics, and good examples include the formalness-informalness principle, the absoluteness-relativeness principle, the partiality-totality principle, the predictability-unpredictability principle, the explicability-inexplicability principle, the fiction-reality principle, the finiteness-transfiniteness principle, the preciseness-vagueness principle, the simpleness-complicatedness principle, the openness-hiddenness principle, the denseness-emptiness principle, the change-constancy principle, the order-chaos principle, the slowness-quickness principle, the expansion-contraction principle, the theory-praxis principle, the convention-novelty principle, the evolution-transformation principle, the symmetry-asymmetry principle, the softness-hardness principle, the seriousness-playfulness principle, the activeness-inactivess principle, the regression-progression principle, the same-difference principle, and the stability-reaction principle.

For instance, in relation to the formalness-informalness principle, if there is formalness (e.g., the formal logical requirement of soundness, consistency, and completeness in a system of ideas, as in the study on ship transport and the art of sailing), there is informalness (e.g., the non-formal existence of unsoundness, inconsistency, and incompleteness in the study on ship transport and the art of sailing, as shown in the criticisms that the history of ship transport has its ups and downs, that ship transport has its advantages and disadvantages, that the classification of sailing in relation to profession and ranking is not universal, that the art of sailing is relative, that the art of sailing is not suitable for anyone to master, that the art of sailing does not guarantee the non-occurrence of ship accidents, etc.). And the reverse direction also holds true.

In relation to the absoluteness-relativeness principle, if there is absoluteness (e.g., the absolute view of those sailors who prefer life at sea, because of "sea-going adventure and a chance to see the world"), there is relativeness (e.g., what is right for those sailors who prefer life at sea is not necessarily so for others who "leav[e]…the industry" because "they want to be with their families" and cannot bear "isolation, stress, and fatigue as occupational hazards" of seamanship). And the reverse direction also holds true.

In relation to the partiality-totality principle, if there is partiality (e.g., the partial view of the term "sailor" to "preserve…the memory of the time when ships were commonly powered by sails"), there is totality (e.g., the more holistic view of sailing, such that the whole is not the sum of its parts, that is, it cannot be reduced to the sum of opposing views like the older meaning of the term to preserve "the memory of the time when ships were commonly powered by sails" and the newer meaning for "the personnel of all vessels, whatever their mode of locomotion," etc., since there will emerge new views in the future not yet known today, just as there are already multiple meanings of the term nowadays, as described above). And the reverse direction also holds true.

In relation to the predictability-unpredictability principle, if there is predictability (e.g., the predictable tendency in our times that "the importance of sea travel for passengers has decreased due to aviation"), there is unpredictability (e.g., the more difficult task to predict exactly the extent to which ship transport and the art of sailing will remain in decline in a particular future era, in light of the fact that the history of ship transport has its ups and downs, not exactly predictably). And the reverse direction also holds true.

In relation to the explicability-inexplicability principle, if there is explicability (e.g., the explanation by those sailors who prefer life at sea on the basis of "sea-going adventure and a chance to see the world"), there is inexplicability (e.g., the lack of sufficient explanation by those sailors of why life at sea is necessarily desirable, since others leave the industry because "they want to be with their families" and cannot bear "isolation, stress, and fatigue as occupational hazards" of seamanship). And the reverse direction also holds true.

In relation to the fiction-reality principle, if there is fiction (e.g., the fictional aspect of seamanship, insofar as there are exceptions to its general rules of thumb, as shown in the exceptional example about "the U.S. Sealift class tankers which used a controllable pitch propeller, where the pitch and not the direction of rotation was reversed to go astern"), there is reality (e.g., the realistic aspect of seamanship, insofar as there are rules of thumb like the example that "the propeller would turn counterclockwise when going astern and the stern would walk to port"). And the reverse direction also holds true.

In relation to the finiteness-transfiniteness principle, if there is finiteness (e.g., the finite number of the different uses of the term "sailor" in the history of ship transport, as cited in the article), there is transfiniteness (e.g., the transfinite number of all the individual sailors in the history of ship transport who can fit in the different meanings of the term "sailor"). And the reverse direction also holds true.

In relation to the preciseness-vagueness principle, if there is preciseness (e.g., the precise identification of 4 categories of sailing in ship transport in the article aforecited), there is vagueness (e.g., the vagueness in the identification of the 4 categories of sailing in ship transport in the article aforecited, since it is not clear why there must be only 4 categories, not 5, 6, 7, 8, 13, and so on). And the reverse direction also holds true.

In relation to the simpleness-complicatedness principle, if there is simpleness (e.g., the relatively simple analysis of the art of sailing by its advocates), there is complicatedness (e.g., the relatively more complicated analysis of the art of sailing, by challenging the claims and assumptions, as shown in the problems pointed out by the critics as cited). And the reverse direction also holds true.

In relation to the openness-hiddenness principle, if there is openness (e.g., the open exploration of the RMS *Titanic* for "sea-going adventure and a chance to see the world"), there is hiddenness (e.g., the hidden vulnerability of the RMS *Titanic*, when it "sank in the North Atlantic Ocean on 15 April 1912 after colliding with an iceberg not easily noticeable in the darkness of the night). And the reverse direction also holds true.

In relation to the denseness-emptiness principle, if there is denseness (e.g., the relatively denser concentration of passengres aborad the the RMS *Titanic*, carrying 2,224 people), there is emptiness (e.g., the relatively less dense, or more empty, concentration of passengers aboard the commercial oil tanker *AbQaiq*, by contrast with the RMS *Titanic*). (WK 2012xx) And the reverse direction also holds true.

In relation to the change-constancy principle, if there is change (e.g., the ever new ways to build transportation, as shown in the invention of ship transport), there is constancy (e.g., the ever constant existence of different problems in the ever new ways to build transportation, as shown in the problems with ship transport and the art of sailing pointed out by the critics). And the reverse direction also holds true.

In relation to the order-chaos principle, if there is order (e.g., the more or less orderly sailing of the RMS *Titanic* in the first four days of its journey starting on April 10, 1912), there is chaos (e.g,. the more or less chaotic sinking of the RMS *Titanic* on 15 April 1912 after colliding with an iceberg, which caused the deaths of 1,514 people). And the reverse direction also holds true.

In relation to the slowness-quickness principle, if there is slowness (e.g., the relatively slower speed of ships when powered by sails in the wind), there is quickness (e.g., the relatively quicker speed of ships when powered by a modern nuclear reactor). And the reverse direction also holds true.

In relation to the expansion-contraction principle, if there is expansion (e.g., the relative spread of the use of ships powered by mechanical engines like diesel engines, gas turbine engines, nuclear reactors, etc. on hight seas nowadays), there is contraction (e.g., the relative decline of the use of ships powered by old-fashioned sails on high seas nowadays). And the reverse direction also holds true.

In relation to the theory-praxis principle, if there is theory (e.g., the theoretical construction of nuclear force in physics), there is praxis (e.g., the practical application of nuclear force in physics to the field of transportation, like sailing a ship with a nuclear reactor). And the reverse direction also holds true.

In relation to the convention-novelty principle, if there is convention (e.g., the conventional wisdom sailing a ship in the wind in the older days), there is novelty (e.g., the alternative novel challenge to the conventional wisdom about sailing a ship in the wind in the older days, by the new idea of sailing a ship with a nuclear reactor). And the reverse direction also holds true.

In relation to the evolution-transformation principle, if there is evolution (e.g., the natural evolution of humans to move through water by swimming for a brief time in the state of nature, in a primitive way), there is transformation (e.g., the technical transformation of human ability to cross the oceans by the invention of huge ships). And the reverse direction also holds true.

In relation to the symmetry-asymmetry principle, if there is symmetry (e.g., the existence of different members on a ship, like the Pilot, the Master, etc.), there is asymmetry (e.g., "the general Rule of Thumb is that a Pilot assumes command of a vessel and is not classed as 'an advisor' in the Panama Canal, crossing thc sill of a drydock, or in any port in Russia…or, perhaps, all the old Soviet States," so "when a Pilot is in command, the Master can not take any action, but is limited to advising the Pilot on any circumstance that creates what he considers a dangerous situation"). (WK 2012ww) And the reverse direction also holds true.

In relation to the softness-hardness principle, if there is softness (e.g., the appreciation of seamanship, as shown by those sailors who use it to live at sea), there is hardness (e.g., the critique of of seamanship, as shown in the problems pointed out by the critics as cited). And the reverse direction also holds true.

In relation to the seriousness-playfulness principle, if there is seriousness (e.g., the serious business of those who want to master seamanship), there is playfulness (e.g., the playful part of those who want to master seamanship, when they play around with different techniques and skills including navigation, weather forecasting, watchstanding, ship-handling, operation of deck equipment, anchors and cables, ropework and line handling, communications, cargo handling, dealing with emergencies, survival at sea, search and rescue, fire fighting, etc., so as to test and see which ones work under what conditions for safe sailing). And the reverse direction also holds true.

In relation to the activeness-inactivess principle, if there is activeness (e.g., the alertness of those crew members who actively try to operate a ship safely with a good sense of "situational awareness"), there is inactiveness (e.g., the relative inactiveness of those crew members who are tired, sleepy, sick, or drunken, when they do not have a good sense of "situational awareness" to operate a ship safely).

In relation to the regression-progression principle, if there is regression (e.g., the regression made by seamanship, as shown in the problems with "isolation, stress, and fatigue as occupational hazards" of seamanship pointed out by the critics), there is progression (e.g., the progress made by seamanship, as shown in its contribution to the operation and maintenance of ship transports aforecited). And the reverse direction also holds true.

In relation to the same-difference principle, if there is similarity in outcome (e.g., the contribution to the molding and control of beliefs, values, and behaviors, regardless of whether this be done by way of life at sea, or by way of life in a village), there is difference in outcome (e.g., the contribution to the molding and control of beliefs, values, and behaviors by way of life at sea for a relatively more adventurous lifeworld in diferent places and times—but the contribution to the molding and control of beliefs, values, and behaviors by way of life in a village for a relatively more parochial lifeworld). And the reverse direction also holds true.

And in relation to the stability-reaction principle, if there is stability (e.g., the relatively more stable condition of sailing in the older days, when sailors made good use of wind in sailing), there is reaction (e.g., sailing in the older days then led to further changes later on, when nowadays, sailing can depend on mechanical engines like diesel engines, gas turbine engines, etc.). And the reverse direction also holds true.

The Dysfunctionality of Operations

This comprehensive analysis of the possibility (or impossibility) and desirability (or undesirability) of operations in the context of transportation, from the perspectives of the mind, nature, society, and culture, shows us the different ways in which operations are both possible and desirable, but not to the extent that the spokespersons from each side would like us to believe.

Operations thus have their functionality, just as they have their dysfunctionality too, as the other side of the same coin.

As already discussed in the previous chapter (Chapter Two), the other side of the story concerns networks.

These dual analyses of networks and operations should not be underestimated, because those on the side of networks often downgrade operations merely as the other side of transportation without really appreciating them from the vantage point of operations too—and vice versa.

In any event, with the completion of these dual analyses of networks and operations in transportation here, what then can be concluded about the future of transportation? This is the question which we now turn to the next Chapter, Chapter Four, to answer.

Table 3.1. Operations and their Complications

- **Operations and the Mind**
  —Ex: operations, FOD awareness, and training
  —Ex: operations, drunkenness, and driving

- **Operations and Nature**
  —Ex: operations, air pollution, and regulation
  —Ex: operations, horses, and the carriage

- **Operations and Society**
  —Ex: operations, skyjacking, and terrorism
  —Ex: operations, traffic congestion, and urban sprawl

- **Operations and Culture**
  —Ex: operations, rail transport, and popular culture
  —Ex: operations, ship transport, and the art of sailing

Notes: The examples in the categories are solely illustrative (not exhaustive), and the comparison is relative (not absolute), nor are they necessarily mutually exclusive. And some can be easily re-classified elsewhere. As generalities, they allow exceptions.
Source: A summary of Ch.3 of *FPHTRAN*

Table 3.2. Operations, FOD Awareness, and Training

- **FOD in Aviation**
  —Ex: "internal FOD"
  —Ex: "cockpit FOD"
  —Ex: "tool FOD"

- **Examples of FOD**
  —Ex: aircraft parts, rocks, broken pavement, vehicle parts, etc.
  —Ex: garbage, maintenance tools, etc.
  —Ex: ice on the wings, propellers, engine intakes, etc.
  —Ex: dust, ash, etc.

- **Examples of FOD Damages**
  —Ex: "damages by runway debris"
  —Ex: "damages by volcanic ash"
  —Ex: "damages by item jettisoned from aircraft"

- **Awareness and Training**
  —Ex: "FOD-themed posters, signs and large banners," etc.
  —Ex: "FOD Awareness Week"
  —Ex: "formal certification in Foreign Object Elimination (FOE)"

- **Problems with the Study on FOD**
  —Firstly, one main criticism of the study on FOD is that it is hard to avoid FOD, as it is part of life in aviation.
  —Secondly, another main criticism of the study on FOD is that FOD detection can be costly and its effectiveness may not be as high as its proponents would like us to believe.
  —Thirdly, still another main criticism of the study on FOD is that different data analyses about FOD can be inconsistent with each other and are thus questionable.
  —And fourthly, an additional main criticism of the study on FOD is that awareness and training are not enough, as technology is also needed.

Notes: The examples in the categories are solely illustrative (not exhaustive), and the comparison is relative (not absolute), nor are they necessarily mutually exclusive. And some can be easily re-classified elsewhere. As generalities, they allow exceptions.
Source: From *Sec. 3.2.1* of *FPHTRAN*. See book for citations.

Table 3.3. Operations, Drunkenness, and Driving

- **Drunkenness in Pathophysiology**
  —Ex: "20–99 mg/dL"—"Impaired coordination and euphoria"
  —Ex: "100–199 mg/dL"—"Ataxia, poor judgement, labile mood"
  —Ex: "200–299 mg/dL"—"Marked ataxia, slurred speech, nausea"
  —Ex: "300–399 mg/dL"—"Stage 1 anaesthesia, memory lapse"
  —Ex: "400+ mg/dL"—"Respiratory failure, coma"

- **Detection of Drunk Driving**
  —Ex: "blood alcohol content (BAC)"
  —Ex: "field sobriety testing"

- **Problems with the Study on DUI**
  —Firstly, one main criticism of the study on DUI is that the test to measure DUI is not without controversy.
  —Secondly, another main criticism of the study on DUI is that what counts as "guilt" in DUI cases varies from country to country.
  —And thirdly, an additional main criticism of the study on DUI is that there can be alternative causes of non-sobriety other than the use of alcohol.

Notes: The examples in the categories are solely illustrative (not exhaustive), and the comparison is relative (not absolute), nor are they necessarily mutually exclusive. And some can be easily re-classified elsewhere. As generalities, they allow exceptions.
Source: From *Sec. 3.2.2* of *FPHTRAN*. See book for more details and citations.

Table 3.4. Operations, Air Pollution, and Regulation

- **Types of Air Pollution**
  —Ex: primary pollutants
  —Ex: secondary pollutants

- **Sources of Air Pollution**
  —Ex: anthropogenic sources (human activity)
  —Ex: natural sources

- **Carbon Monoxide in Transportation, and Air Pollution**
  —Ex: molecular properties
  —Ex: toxicity
  —Ex: urban pollution
  —Ex: legal regulations

- **Problems with the Study on Air Pollution**
  —Firstly, one main criticism of the study on air pollution in transportation is that "mobile sources" are only ones among different sources of air pollution and should not be blamed too much for air pollution.
  —Secondly, another main criticism of the study on air pollution in transportation is that regulations do not often work, because of disagreements.
  —And thirdly, an additional main criticism of the study on air pollution in transportation is that the use of carbon monoxide has been used for different ulterior purposes.

Notes: The examples are solely illustrative (not exhaustive), and the comparison is relative (not absolute), nor are they necessarily mutually exclusive. And some can be easily re-classified elsewhere. As generalities, they allow exceptions.
Source: From *Sec. 3.3.1* of *FPHTRAN.* See book for citations.

Table 3.5. Operations, Horses, and the Carriage

- **History of the Horse-Drawn Carriage**
  —Ex: prehistory
  —Ex: chariot
  —Ex: wagons
  —Ex: carriage
  —Ex: coach

- **Structure of the Horse-Drawn Carriage**
  —Ex: body
  —Ex: undergear

- **Operations of the Horse-Drawn Carriage**
  —Ex: understand your horse
  —Ex: use a willing horse
  —Ex: harness the horse correctly
  —Ex: take an experienced driver with you
  —Ex: obey traffic rules

- **Problems with the Study on the Horse-Drawn Carriage**
  —Firstly, one main criticism of the study on the horse-drawn carriage in transportation is that its history is not so clear-cut as it may appear.
  —Secondly, another main criticism of the study on the horse-drawn carriage in transportation is that the use of horses for the carriage is controversial for animal right activists.
  —Thirdly, an additional main criticism of the study on the horse-drawn carriage in transportation is that operating a horse-drawn carriage is not as simple as the five steps suggested by Bettmann would like us to believe.
  —And fourthly, another additional main criticism of the study on the horse-drawn carriage in transportation is that its usefulness in history is limited.

Notes: The examples are solely illustrative (not exhaustive), and the comparison is relative (not absolute), nor are they necessarily mutually exclusive. And some can be easily re-classified elsewhere. As generalities, they allow exceptions.
Source: From *Sec. 3.3.2* of *FPHTRAN*. See book for citations.

Table 3.6. Operations, Traffic Congestion, and Urban Sprawl

- **Causes of Traffic Congestion**
  —Ex: mathematical theories
  —Ex: economic theories

- **Negative Impacts of Traffic Congestion**
  —Ex: "wasting time of motorists and passengers"
  —Ex: "delays"
  —Ex: "inability to forecast travel time accurately"
  —Ex: "wasted fuel"
  —Ex: "stressed and frustrated motorists"

- **Suggested Solutions**
  —Ex: "parking restrictions"
  —Ex: "park and ride facilities"
  —Ex: "road pricing"
  —Ex: "cap and trade"
  —Ex: "considerate driving"

- **Problems with the Study on Traffic Congestion and Urban Sprawl**
  —Firstly, one main criticism of the study on traffic congestion and urban sprawl is that a traffic jam is still not fully predictable.
  —Secondly, another main criticism of the study on traffic congestion and urban sprawl is that there are disagreements on traffic classification.
  —Thirdly, an additional main criticism of the study on traffic congestion and urban sprawl is that the debate is definitional in nature.
  —Fourthly, another additional main criticism of the study on traffic congestion and urban sprawl is that "rush hour traffic congestion is inevitable." (WK 2012qq)
  —And fifthly, the last main criticism of the study on traffic congestion and urban sprawl is that the debate has a subjective dimension.

Notes: The examples are solely illustrative (not exhaustive), and the comparison is relative (not absolute), nor are they necessarily mutually exclusive. And some can be easily re-classified elsewhere. As generalities, they allow exceptions.
Source: From *Sec. 3.4.2* of *FPHTRAN*. See book for citations.

Table 3.7. Operations, Rail Transport, and Popular Culture

- **History of Rail Transport**
  —Ex: pre-steam
  —Ex: steam
  —Ex: electrical
  —Ex: diesel

- **Types of Rail Transport**
  —Ex: passenger train
  —Ex: freight train

- **Operations of Rail Transport**
  —Ex: ownership
  —Ex: financing
  —Ex: safety
  —Ex: maintenance

- **Rail Transport in Popular Culture**
  —Ex: films
  —Ex: literature
  —Ex: television

- **Problems with the Study on Rail Transport and Popular Culture**
  —Firstly, one main criticism of the study on rail transport and popular culture is that the history of rail transport has its ups and downs.
  —Secondly, another main criticism of the study on rail transport and popular culture is that each rail transport has its own advantages and disadvantages.
  —And thirdly, an additional main criticism of the study on rail transport and popular culture is that the stories about trains in popular culture are often questionable.

Notes: The examples are solely illustrative (not exhaustive), and the comparison is relative (not absolute), nor are they necessarily mutually exclusive. And some can be easily re-classified elsewhere. As generalities, they allow exceptions.
Source: From *Sec. 3.5.1* of *FPHTRAN*. See book for citations.

Table 3.8. Operations, Ship Transport, and the Art of Sailing

- **Meanings of Sailing, and Ship Transport**
  —Ex: "a person who goes out sailing, boating or yachting"
  —Ex: "an enlisted member of a military naval force"
  —Ex: "anyone from a recruit to an admiral in a navy or coast guard"

- **Categories of Sailing, and Ship Transport**
  —Ex: deck department
  —Ex: engineering department
  —Ex: steward's department
  —Ex: others (e.g., purser, medical doctor, etc.)

- **Art of Sailing, and Ship Transport**
  —Ex: navigation
  —Ex: ship-handling

- **Problems with the Study on Ship Transport and the Art of Sailing**
  —Firstly, one main criticism of the study on ship transport and the art of sailing is that the history of ship transport has its ups and downs.
  —Secondly, another main criticism of the study on ship transport and the art of sailing is that ship transport has its advantages and disadvantages.
  —Thirdly, an additional main criticism of the study on ship transport and the art of sailing is that the classification of sailing in relation to profession and ranking is not universal.
  —Fourthly, another additional main criticism of the study on ship transport and the art of sailing is that the art of sailing is relative.
  —Fifthly, still another additional main criticism of the study on ship transport and the art of sailing is that the art of sailing is not suitable for anyone to master.
  —And sixthly, one more main criticism of the study on ship transport and the art of sailing is that the art of sailing does not guarantee the non-occurrence of ship accidents.

Notes: The examples are solely illustrative (not exhaustive), and the comparison is relative (not absolute), nor are they necessarily mutually exclusive. And some can be easily re-classified elsewhere. As generalities, they allow exceptions.
Source: From *Sec. 3.5.2* of *FPHTRAN.* See book for citations.

• PART FOUR •

Conclusion

CHAPTER 4
CONCLUSION—THE FUTURE OF TRANSPORTATION

> The mastery of the turn is the story of how aviation became practical as a means of transportation. It is the story of how the world became small.
> __William Langewiesche (BQ 2012)

Beyond Networks and Operations

The analyses of networks (in Chapter Two) and operations (in Chapter Three) show us the extent of their possibility (or impossibility) and desirability (or undesirability) in the study of transportation.

These two analyses are important for the evaluation of the opposing expectations about transportation (as already introduced in *Sec. 1.1* and the rest of the book).

Contrary to these opposing expectations (and other views as already discussed in the book), transportation (in relation to both networks and operations) is neither possible (or impossible) nor desirable (or undesirable) to the extent that the respective ideologues (on different sides) would like us to believe.

Of course, this challenge to the opposing expectations from transportation does not mean that transportation is useless, or that those interdisciplinary fields (related to transportation studies) like urban planning, environmental sustainability, migration, tourism, transport economics, traffic engineering, transportation technology, energy efficiency, the tragedy of the commons, and so on are unimportant. Needless to say, neither of these extreme views is reasonable.

Rather, this book offers an alternative (better) way to understand the future of transportation, especially in the dialectic context of networks and operations—while learning from different approaches in the literature but without favoring any one of them (nor integrating them, since they are not necessarily compatible with each other).

More specifically, this book offers a new theory (that is, *the panoramic theory of transportation*) to go beyond the existing approaches in a novel way.

As a recap from Chapter One, my *panoramic theory of transportation* has four major distinct features.

Firstly, my theory makes good use of all theoretical approaches to the study of transportation in relation to networks and operations, be they about the mental argument, the natural argument, the societal argument, or the cultural argument—especially from the most comprehensive combined perspectives of the mind, nature, society, and culture (as will be dealt with in Chapter Two and Chapter Three).

Secondly, just like many other theories of mine in my previous books, my theory here does not heavily favor any specific theory over others in the literature, nor trying to integrate them (as they are not necessarily compatible with each other).

Thirdly, my theory treats the issue of transportation in the distinctive dialectic context of no networks without operations, and vice versa.

And fourthly, it contains twenty-six major theses, namely, (a) the first thesis: the formalness-informalness principle, (b) the second thesis: the absoluteness-relativeness principle, (c) the third thesis: the partiality-totality principle, (d) the fourth thesis: the predictability-unpredictability principle, (e) the fifth thesis: the explicability-inexplicability principle, (f) the sixth thesis: the fiction-reality principle, (g) the seventh thesis: the finiteness-transfiniteness principle, (h) the eighth thesis: the preciseness-vagueness principle, (i) the ninth thesis: the simpleness-complicatedness principle, (j) the tenth thesis: the openness-hiddenness principle, (k) the eleventh thesis: the denseness-emptiness principle, (l) the twelfth thesis: the change-constancy principle, (m) the thirteenth thesis: the order-chaos principle, (n) the fourteenth thesis: the slowness-quickness principle, (o) the fifteenth thesis: the expansion-contraction principle, (p) the sixteenth thesis: the theory-praxis principle, (q) the seventeenth thesis: the convention-novelty principle, (r) the eighteenth thesis: the evolution-transformation principle, (s) the nineteenth thesis: the symmetry-asymmetry principle, (t) the twentieth thesis: the softness-hardness principle, (u) the twenty-first thesis: the seriousness-playfulness principle, (v) the twenty-second thesis: the activeness-inactiveness principle, (w) the twenty-third thesis: the regression-progression principle, (x) the twenty-fourth thesis: the sameness-difference principle, (y) the twenty-fifth thesis: the stability-reaction principle, and (z) the twenty-sixth thesis: the post-human panorama—to be elaborated in the rest of the book, with a summary in the concluding chapter.

Because of the last thesis on "the post-human panorama," the word "panoramic" in the title of my theory are suggestive, because it refers to a comprehensive analysis of transportation, so as to explore multiple views regarding the dialectic interactions between networks and operations in the study of transportation (together with other debates as discussed in the rest of the book), and calls for a need to transcend them by future advanced humans and later post-humans in the context of the great transformations of transportation in the future world (as will be discussed in this concluding chapter).

With this clarification in mind—the seminal project here, if successful, will fundamentally change the way that we think about networks and operations in the study of transportation (together with other debates as discussed in the rest of the book), from the combined perspectives of the mind, nature, society, and culture, with enormous implications for the human future and what I originally called its "post-human" fate.

In Relation to Method

The first six theses are in relation to method in existential dialectics, as shown below.

1st Thesis: The Formalness-Informalness Principle

The first thesis refers to the formalness-informalness principle (on the formal requirements of logical systems) in the category of "method" in existential dialectics, which was first proposed in *FPHML* (and later, *FPHH*, *FPHGAM*, *FPHSEM*, and other books of mine), in that the formal requirements of a logical system (e.g., consistency, soundness, and completeness) have both usefulness and non-usefulness, to the extent that, if there are formal systems requiring them, there are alternative ones which do not.

The formalness-informalness principle reveals something interesting in existential dialectics, in that it goes beyond both classical and non-classical logics (while learning something from both).

Thus, it does *not* exclude classical logics but simply goes beyond both classical and non-classical logics, while learning something from each. There is no formalness without informalness—and vice versa.

For illustration, existential dialectics can make use of both classical logics under certain conditions (e.g., especially, though not exclusively, when they are clear-cut, etc.) and non-classical logics under alternative conditions (especially, though not exclusively, when they are "unknown," "irrelevant," "ambiguous," "possible," with "different degrees of truth," empirically inconsistent in a desirable way, etc.). (WK 2008u)

For instance, on the one hand, there is formalness (e.g., the formal logical requirement of soundness in a system of ideas, as in the study of walkability and health, in *Sec. 2.2.1*; the formal logical requirement of soundness in a system of ideas, as in the study on the bicycle, in *Sec. 2.2.2*; the formal logical requirement of soundness in a system of ideas, as in the study on locomotion and energy, in *Sec. 2.3.1*; the formal logical requirement of soundness and completeness in a system of ideas, as in the study on spacecraft, in *Sec. 2.3.2*; the formal logical requirement of soundness and completeness in a system of ideas, as in the study on the automobile industry, in *Sec. 2.4.1*; the formal logical requirement of soundness in a system of ideas, as in the study on future car technologies, in *Sec. 2.4.2*; the formal logical requirement of soundness and completeness in a system of ideas, as in TOD, in *Sec. 2.5.1*; the formal logical requirement of soundness, completeness, and consistency in a system of ideas, as in the study on the car culture, in *Sec. 2.5.2*; the formal logical requirement of soundness, consistency, and completeness in a system of ideas, as in the study on FOD, in *Sec. 3.2.1*; the formal logical requirement of soundness in a system of ideas, as in the study on DUI, in *Sec. 3.2.2*; the formal logical requirement of soundness and completeness in a system of ideas, as in the study on air pollution in transportation, in *Sec. 3.3.1*; the formal logical requirement of soundness and completeness in a system of ideas, as in the study on the horse-drawn carriage, in *Sec. 3.3.2*; the formal logical requirement of soundness and completeness in a system of ideas, as in the study on skyjacking and terrorism, in *Sec. 3.4.1*; the formal logical requirement of soundness, consistency, and completeness in a system of ideas, as in the study on traffic congestion and urban sprawl, in *Sec. 3.4.2*; the formal logical requirement of soundness and completeness in a system of ideas, as in the study on rail transport and popular culture, in *Sec. 3.5.1*; and the formal logical requirement of soundness, consistency, and completeness in a system of ideas, as in the study on ship transport and the art of sailing, in *Sec. 3.5.2*).

On the other hand, there is also informalness (e.g., the non-formal existence of unsoundness in the study of walkability and health, as shown in the criticisms that the causal relationship between obesity and negative health has been questioned too, that the evolutionary argument can be problematic, etc., in *Sec. 2.2.1*; the non-formal existence of unsoundness in the study on the bicycle, as shown in the criticisms that the invention of the bicycle has contributed to new accidents which can injure and kill those involved, that there is no freedom without unfreedom in the case of the "freedom machine," that not everyone agrees with the different technical aspects of the bicycle, that the feminists exaggerated the freedom value of the bicycle, etc., in *Sec. 2.2.2*; the non-formal existence of unsoundness in the study on locomotion and energy, as shown in the criticisms that that energy sources have disadvantages too, that energy conversion is not completely efficient, that there are tradeoffs for each kind of engines or motors, etc., in *Sec. 2.3.1*; the non-formal existence of unsoundness and incompleteness in the study on spacecraft, as shown in the criticisms that its history has been driven by ideology and politics too, that it is both technologically challenging and financially costly to build spacecrafts, that spacecrafts, like other transports, are not immune from accidents or disasters, etc., in *Sec. 2.3.2*; the non-formal existence of unsoundness and incompleteness in the study on the automobile industry, as shown in the criticisms that the industry has also contributed to considerable economic costs around the world, that the industry has a destructive impact on society too, that the use of the automobile can be so addictive as to become "automobile-dependent," that the study also ignores the negative legal consequences for both individuals and society, etc., in *Sec. 2.4.1*; the non-formal existence of unsoundness in the study on future car technologies, as shown in the criticisms that they are not so simple as they may sound, that they are not necessarily effective to enhance security, that they are also not necessarily safe to use, etc., in *Sec. 2.4.2*; the non-formal existence of unsoundness and incompleteness in TOD, as shown in the criticisms that it is driven with the ideology of Intelligent Urbanism, that it has the potential to spur "gentrification in low-income areas," that it has an authoritarian tendency, etc., in *Sec. 2.5.1*; the non-formal existence of unsoundness, incompleteness, and inconsistency in the study on the car culture, as shown in the criticisms that it also has destructive effects, that the convenience of the automobile comes with a price to pay in regard to time delay instead, that it can contribute to the spread of diseases, that it has contributed to "a dramatic increase in the rate of accidental death," that the requirement of transportation infrastructure is costly, etc., in *Sec. 2.5.2*; the non-formal existence of unsoundness, inconsistency, and incompleteness in the study on FOD, as shown in the criticisms that it is hard to avoid FOD as it is part of life in aviation, that FOD detection can be costly and its effectiveness may not be as high as its proponents would like us to believe, that different data analyses about FOD can be inconsistent with each other and are thus questionable, that awareness and training are not enough as technology is also needed, etc., in *Sec. 3.2.1*; the non-formal existence of unsoundness in the study on DUI, as shown in the criticisms that the test to measure DUI is not without controversy, that what counts as "guilt" in DUI cases varies from country to country, that there can be alternative causes of non-sobriety other than the use of alcohol, etc., in *Sec. 3.2.2*; the non-formal existence of unsoundness and incompleteness in the study on air pollution in transportation, as shown in the criticisms that "mobile sources" are only ones among different sources of air pollution and should not be blamed too much for air pollution, that regulations do not often work because of disagreements, that the use of carbon monoxide has been used for different ulterior purposes, etc., in *Sec. 3.3.1*; the non-formal existence of unsoundness and incompleteness in the study on the horse-drawn carriage, as shown in the criticisms that its history is not so clear-cut as it may appear, that the use of horses for the carriage is controversial for animal right activists, that operating a horse-drawn carriage is not as simple as the five steps suggested by Bettmann would like us to believe, that its usefulness in history is limited, etc., in *Sec. 3.3.2*; the non-formal existence of unsoundness and incompleteness in the study on skyjacking and terrorism, as shown in the criticisms that what counts as "criminal" or "terrorist" is in the eyes of the beholder, that some of the solutions suggesed are too violent and too intrusive, etc., in *Sec. 3.4.1*; the non-formal existence of unsoundness, inconsistency, and incompleteness in the study on traffic congestion and urban sprawl, as shown in the criticisms that there are disagreements on traffic classification, that the debate is definitional in nature, that the debate has a subjective dimension, etc., in *Sec. 3.4.2*; the non-formal existence of unsoundness and incompleteness in the study on rail transport and popular culture, as shown in the criticisms that the history of rail transport has its ups and downs, that each rail transport has its own advantages and disadvantages, that the stories about trains in popular culture are often questionable, etc., in *Sec. 3.5.1*; and the non-formal existence of unsoundness, inconsistency, and incompleteness in the study on ship transport and the art of sailing, as shown in the criticisms that the history of ship transport has its ups and downs, that ship transport has its advantages and disadvantages, that the classification of sailing in relation to profession and ranking is not universal, that the art of sailing is relative, that the art of sailing is not suitable for anyone to master, that the art of sailing does not guarantee the non-occurrence of ship accidents, etc., in *Sec. 3.5.2*).

And the reverse direction also holds true.

However, it should be stressed (as this is something that I regularly did in my previous books, *almost verbatim*) that there are different shades of gray (or different degrees of truth) in the two opposites, and the classification is not necessarily mutually exclusive either. In fact, even when some combinations of the two occur, they only end up sharing the same dialectic relationship, but in a different degree.

Also, there are some other relationships (as a kind of family resemblance) which have something in common with the principle, but they are not exactly the same but only more or less comparable, which varies from case to case.

Good examples of family resemblance in relation to the principle are logicalness-nonlogicalness, rationality-nonrationality, etc.

2nd Thesis: The Absoluteness-Relativeness Principle

The second thesis refers to the absoluteness-relativeness principle (on the multiplicity of things) in the category of "method" in existential dialectics, which was first proposed in *FPHK*, in that there is the multiplicity of things in reality, be they about entities, qualities (or properties), and relationships. If there is something absolute, there is likewise something relative. And there is no absoluteness without relativeness—and vice versa.

Both absoluteness and relativeness here are also relevant to different modalities often cited in the literature on ontology, such as possibility (e.g., something "can" happen) and its opposite (e.g., impossibility), probability (e.g., something "will" happen) and its opposite (e.g., improbability), and necessity (e.g., something "should" happen) and its opposite (e.g., contingency).

For instance, on the one hand, there is absoluteness (e.g., the absolute view of the adovates about "the established relationship between obesity and negative health outcomes," in *Sec. 2.2.1*; the absolute view of those who require a bicycle to be equipped with "bicycle lighting at night" and "helmets," in *Sec. 2.2.2*; the absolute view that "the total kinetic energy of a system of objects [in transportation, for example] cannot be reduced to zero by a suitable choice of the inertial reference frame, unless all the objects have the same velocity," in *Sec. 2.3.1*; the absolute view of those on each side of the superpower rivalry in the space race during the Cold War, in *Sec. 2.3.2*; the absolute view of those car manufacturers to make more cars for profits, in *Sec. 2.4.1*; the absolute view of those who advocate more safety to endorse VII, in *Sec. 2.4.2*; the absolute view of the advocates to favor "human scale" in TOD, as part of the ideology of

Intelligent Urbanism, in *Sec. 2.5.1*; the absolute view of those in the old "glory days" of the automobile, as pointed out by Skip McGoun, in *Sec. 2.5.2*; the absolute view of those like Chaplin when he argued in the FOD "bible" that "a good Promotion and Awareness Program can significantly help reduce FOD by engaging a workforce with information, feedback and involvement," in *Sec. 3.2.1*; the absolute view of those police officers who depend on field sobriety tests like "walking a straight line heel-to-toe or standing on one leg for 30 seconds," in *Sec. 3.2.2*; the absolute view of the Nazis, who used carbon monoxide "during the Holocaust at some Nazi extermination camps, the most notable by gas vans in Chelmno, and in the Action T4 'euthanasia' program," in *Sec. 3.3.1*; the absolute view of Bettmann in regard to the obediance of traffic rules and the attention to careful driving for horse-riding, in *Sec. 3.3.2*; the absolute view of those like Osama bin Laden to get involved in the 9/11 attacks, in *Sec. 3.4.1*; the absolute view of those who defend urban sprawl, as "one suburban Detroit politician defends low-density development as the preferred lifestyle choice of his constituents, calling it '...the American Dream unfolding before your eyes,'" in *Sec. 3.4.2*; the absolute view about rail transport in the older days before "the large-scale construction of motorways" and "air transport," in *Sec. 3.5.1*; and the absolute view of those sailors who prefer life at sea, because of "sea-going adventure and a chance to see the world," in *Sec. 3.5.2*).

On the other hand, there is relativeness (e.g., what is right for the advocates in regard to "the established relationship between obesity and negative health outcomes" is not necessarily so for the critics like some in the fat acceptance movement who "are also attempting to challenge the established relationship between obesity and negative health outcomes," in *Sec. 2.2.1*; what is right for those who require a bicycle to be equipped with "bicycle lighting at night" and "helmets" is not necessarily so for those who consider them as "optional" for a bicycle to have, in *Sec. 2.2.2*; "the speed, and thus the kinetic energy of a single object is frame-dependent [relative]," as in the example that "a bullet [or vehicle] passing an observer has kinetic energy in the reference frame of this observer," but "the same bullet is stationary from the point of view of an observer moving with the same velocity as the bullet, and so has zero kinetic energy," in *Sec. 2.3.1*; what was glorious for the Soviet Union to launch Sputnik in 1957 was not necessarily so for the U.S. who entered the space race to compete with its superpower rival, in *Sec. 2.3.2*; what is good for those car manufacturers to make more cars for profits is not necessarily so for the critics like Jay Holtz Kay, who forcefully argued that, with the automobile industry as an example, "the modern consequences of heavy automotive use contribute to the use of non-renewable fuels..., social isolation, the disconnection of community, the rise in obesity, the generation of air and noise pollution, urban sprawl, and urban decay," in *Sec. 2.4.1*; what is good for those who advocate more safety to endorse VII is not necessarily so for recreational drivers who argue instead that "VII will increase the automation of the vehicle, reducing the driver's enjoyment," in *Sec. 2.4.2*; what is right for the advocates to favor "human scale" in TOD, as part of the ideology of Intelligent Urbanism is not necessarily so for the libertarian critic like Peter Gordon, who "spoke out in favor of suburbanization" and criticized such ideologies like Intelligent Urbanism, New Urbanism, etc. "as ignoring consumer preference and the free market, claiming that cities have moved towards car-oriented development because that is what people want," in *Sec. 2.5.1*; what is desirable for those in the old "glory days" of the automobile is not necessarily so for the critics like J. Kay, who pointed out its destructive effects, in *Sec. 2.5.2*; what is true for Chaplin in regard to the effectiveness of the "Promotion and Awareness Program" is not necessarily so for the critics, who instead point out that it is hard to avoid FOD as it is part of life in aviation, that FOD detection can be costly and its effectiveness may not be as high as its proponents would like us to believe, etc., in *Sec. 3.2.1*; what is right for those police officers who depend on field sobriety tests like "walking a straight line heel-to-toe or standing on one leg for 30 seconds" is not necessarily so for the critics, who argue that these tests are not reliable and controversial, as they are often combined with "the arresting officer's subjective opinion of impairment," in *Sec. 3.2.2*; what is desirable for the Nazis, who used carbon monoxide "during the Holocaust at some Nazi extermination camps, is not necessarily so for the advocates of the U.S. National Ambient Air Quality Standards in regard to regulations of air pollution and the release of carbon monoxide, in *Sec. 3.3.1*; what is right for Bettmann in regard to the obediance of traffic rules for horse-riding is not necessarily so for those who are risk-taking horse-riders, especially in competitive driving, in *Sec. 3.3.2*; what is desirable for those like Osama bin Laden to get involved in the 9/11 attacks is not necessarily so for the U.S., which responded by "launching the War on Terror and invading Afghanistan to depose the Taliban, which had harbored Al-Qaeda," in *Sec. 3.4.1*; what is right for the defenders of urban sprawl is not necessarily so for the critics, who reject it on different grounds, like traffic congestion, negative environmental and public health outcomes, etc., in *Sec. 3.4.2*; what is right for the widespread use of rail transport in the older days before "the large-scale construction of motorways" and "air transport" is not necessarily so for later times, when, after the war, "rail transport became less popular for commuting and air transport started taking large market shares from long-haul passenger trains," in *Sec. 3.5.1*; and what is right for those sailors who prefer life at sea is not necessarily so for others who "leav[e]…the industry" because "they want to be with their families" and cannot bear "isolation, stress, and fatigue as occupational hazards" of seamanship, in *Sec. 3.5.2*).

And the reverse direction also holds true.

However, it should be stressed (as this is something that I regularly did in my previous books, *almost verbatim*) that there are different shades of gray (or different degrees of truth) in the two opposites, and the classification is not necessarily mutually exclusive either. In fact, even when some combinations of the two occur, they only end up sharing the same dialectic relationship, but in a different degree.

Also, there are some other relationships (as a kind of family resemblance) which have something in common with the principle, but they are not exactly the same but only more or less comparable, which varies from case to case.

Good examples of family resemblance in relation to the principle are uniformity-diversity, internalness-externalness, immanence-transcendence, independence-dependence, isolatedness-interconnectiveness, internality-externality, autonomy-interdependency, universalness-relativeness, and so forth.

3rd Thesis: The Partiality-Totality Principle

The third thesis refers to the partiality-totality principle (on the relationships between whole and parts) in the category of "method" in existential dialectics, which was first proposed in *FC* and later *FPHGEOL*, based on earlier works like *FHC* and *FPHC*), in that any analysis of a phenomenon in the world requires both the examination of the individual parts and the whole of them (with the whole as being not the sum of its parts), without privileging the whole as more important than the parts, or vice-versa (that is, the parts as more important than the whole).

In fact, this principle targets two kinds of misleading methodologies as used over the ages, that is, again in the absence of better words, what I called (in *FHC*, *FPHC* and *FC*) "reductionism" and its opposite, "reverse-reductionism," which can take four major forms in relation to concept, theory, methodology, and ontology (as summarized in *Sec. 1.8*).

Thus, reductionism and reverse-reductionism can be (i) conceptual, (ii) theoretical, (iii) methodological, and (iv) ontological. And the whole is not the sum of its parts, and there is no partiality without totality—and vice versa.

Works on emergence (as in *FC*), gestalt psychology (as in *FPHGEOL*), and the hermeneutic circle (as in *FPHDA*), just to name a few of them, have contributed to the understanding of whole and parts.

For instance, on the one hand, there is partiality (e.g., the partial view of those who advocate "the established relationship between obesity and negative health outcomes," in *Sec. 2.2.1*; the partial view of those feminists in regard to the bicycle as a "freedom machine," in *Sec. 2.2.2*; the partial view of locomotion and energy if looked from the perspective of a single energy source and engine, in *Sec. 2.3.1*; the partial view of a superpower during the Cold War to win the space race, in *Sec. 2.3.2*; the partial view of the automobile industry in the old "glory days," in *Sec. 2.4.1*; the partial view of an advocate for VII in regard to safety, in *Sec. 2.4.2*; the partial view of the advocates of TOD, in *Sec. 2.5.1*; the partial view of those in the old "glory days" of the automobile, or conversely, the critics like J. Kay, in *Sec. 2.5.2*; the partial view of those like Chaplin in regard to the "Promotion and Awareness Program," in *Sec. 3.2.1*; the partial view of those police officers who depend on field sobriety tests, in *Sec. 3.2.2*; the partial view of the Nazis, who used carbon monoxide "during the Holocaust at some Nazi extermination camps, the most notable by gas vans in Chelmno, and in the Action T4 'euthanasia' program," in *Sec. 3.3.1*; the partial view of Bettmann in regard to the obediance of traffic rules and the attention to careful driving for horse-riding, in *Sec. 3.3.2*; the partial view of those like bin Laden to be concerned with "the U.S. support of Israel, the presence of U.S. troops in Saudi Arabia, and sanctions against Iraq as motives for the attacks," in *Sec. 3.4.1*; the partial view of "a single motorist" engaging in "an abrupt steering maneuver" in a heavy but free flowing traffic, in *Sec. 3.4.2*; the partial view about rail transport in the older days, when it was widely used, before "the large-scale construction of motorways" and "air transport," in *Sec. 3.5.1*; and the partial view of the term "sailor" to "preserve…the memory of the time when ships were commonly powered by sails," in *Sec. 3.5.2*).

On the other hand, there is also totality (e.g., the more holistic view of the entire picture of health, such that the whole is not the sum of its parts, that is, it cannot be reduced to the sum of opposing views" like blaming "mechanized transportation" for the rise of obesity and its critics, since obesity can be caused by "diet," "genetics," "sendentary lifestyle" and other sources, and there will emerge new views in the future not yet known today, in *Sec. 2.2.1*; the more holistic view of the bicycle, such that the whole is not the sum of its parts, that is, it cannot be reduced to the sum of opposing views like the feminists, the critics, etc., since there will emerge new views in the future not yet known today, in *Sec. 2.2.2*; the more holistic view of locomotion and energy, such that the whole is not the sum of its parts, that is, it cannot be reduced to the sum of the opposing views in regard to energy sources, engines, and the conversion of energy to work in the article as cited, since there will emerge new views in the future not yet known today, in *Sec. 2.3.1*; the more holistic view of the future of spaceflight, such that the whole is not the sum of its parts, that is, it cannot be reduced to the sum of opposing views like those held by the Soviet Union and the United States during the Cold War, since there will emerge new views in the future not yet known today, besides the fact that there were already other views like the international space cooperation as shown in the building of "the International Space Station," in *Sec. 2.3.2*; the more holistic view of the automobile industry, such that the whole is not the sum of its parts, that is, it cannot be reduced to the sum of opposing views like its proponents, the critics, etc., since no one exactly foresaw, for instance, "the modern consequences of heavy automotive use" like the massive "use of non-renewable fuels, a dramatic increase in the rate of accidental death, social isolation, the disconnection of community, the rise in obesity, the generation of air and noise pollution, urban sprawl, and urban decay," just as there will emerge new views in the future not yet known today, in *Sec. 2.4.1*; the more holistic view of the entire vehicle infrastructure as a complex system, such that the whole is not the sum of its parts, that is, it cannot be reduced to the sum of opposing views and interests of different parties in question, since "traffic systems are highly dynamic, with new traffic controls implemented every day and roadways constructed or repaired every year" and there can be random events or accidents not entirely controlled, just as there will emerge new views and phenomena in the future not yet known today, in *Sec. 2.4.2*; the more holistic view of the development of public transports, such that the whole is not the sum of its parts, that is, it cannot be reduced to the sum of opposing views like TOD, TPD, the libertarian critique, etc., since there will emerge new views in the future not yet known today, in *Sec. 2.5.1*; the more holistic view of the car culture, such that the whole is not the sum of its parts, that is, it cannot be reduced to the sum of opposing views like those in the old "glory days" of the automobile, the critics like J. Kay, etc., since there will emerge new views in the future not yet known today, just as there were already alternative views about the car culture by CDC researchers recently that, for instance, "the origin of HIV explosion" was unexpectedly due to "more intensive social interactions afforded by new road networks in Central Africa allowing more frequent travel from villagers to cities and higher density development of many African cities in the period 1950 to 1980," in *Sec. 2.5.2*; the more holistic view of FOD prevention, such that the whole is not the sum of its parts, that is, it cannot be reduced to the sum of opposing views like those by Chaplin, his critics, etc., since there will emerge new views in the future not yet known today, just as there are already other alternative views about FOD as part of life in aviation, which can occur unexpectedly, in *Sec. 3.2.1*; the more holistic view of the detection of drunk driving, such that the whole is not the sum of its parts, that is, it cannot be reduced to the sum of opposing views like field sobriety tests, blood alcohol content tests, the claim of unreliability by the critics, etc., since there will emerge new views in the future not yet known today, just as there are already now altnerative views in some countries, where "it is illegal for an open container of an alcoholic beverage to be in the passenger compartment of a motor vehicle or in some specific area of that compartment" and "may be illegal to be asleep in the driver's seat of a vehicle without any intention to drive," in *Sec. 3.2.2*; the more holistic view of the future of carbon monoxide, such that the whole is not the sum of its parts, that is, it cannot be reduced to the sum of opposing views of the Nazis, those in USNAAQS, etc., since there will emerge new views in the future not yet known today, just as there are already other views which are both critical to the ones of the Nazis, of those in USNAAQS, etc., as shown in the criticisms by the critics aforecited, in *Sec. 3.3.1*; the more holistic view of horse-riding, such that the whole is not the sum of its parts, that is, it cannot be reduced to the sum of opposing views of Bettmann, her critics, etc., since there will emerge new views in the future not yet known today, just as there are already some debates about future car technologies for safety as discussed in *Sec. 2.4.2* of Chapter Two, in *Sec. 3.3.2*; the more holistic view of the 9/11 attacks, such that the whole is not the sum of its parts, that is, it cannot be reduced to the sum of opposing views like those of bin Laden and George Bush, since there will emerge new views in the future not yet known today, just as there are already alternative views nowadays like the one by William Pfaff [2003], who refused to side with bin Laden or George Bush and instead argued that "what actually has happened...is something Americans have yet to grasp, and that others have yet to say out loud: People outside the United States have stopped believing the American story [viz., as the world's greatest democracy fighting evil in the world]," in *Sec. 3.4.1*; the more holistic view of traffic congestion, such that the whole is not the sum of its parts, that is, it cannot be reduced to the sum of opposing views or maneuvers of different single motorists, etc., since, "in heavy but free flowing traffic, jams can arise spontaneously, triggered by minor events ['butterfly effects' in chaos theory], such as an abrupt steering maneuver by a single motorist," so that "traffic research still cannot fully predict under which conditions a 'traffic jam'..may suddenly occur," in *Sec. 3.4.2*; the more holistic view of rail transport, such that the whole is not the sum of its parts, that is, it cannot be reduced to the sum of opposing views about its rise and fall, since there will emerge new views in the future not yet known today, just as there are already some signs of a small revival of rail transport again nowadays, as shown by some "cities that closed their old tramways" and "have reopened new light railway systems," in *Sec. 3.5.1*; and the more holistic view of sailing, such that the whole is not the sum of its parts, that is, it cannot be reduced to the sum of opposing views like the older meaning of the term to preserve "the memory of the time when ships were commonly powered by sails" and the newer meaning for "the personnel of all vessels, whatever their mode of locomotion," etc., since there will emerge new views in the future not yet known today, just as there are already multiple meanings of the term nowadays, as described above, in *Sec. 3.5.2*).

And the reverse direction also holds true.

However, it should be stressed (as this is something that I regularly did in my previous books, *almost verbatim*) that there are different shades of gray (or different degrees of truth) in the two opposites, and the classification is not necessarily mutually exclusive either. In fact, even when some combinations of the two occur, they only end up sharing the same dialectic relationship, but in a different degree.

Also, there are some other relationships (as a kind of family resemblance) which have something in common with the principle, but they are not exactly the same but only more or less comparable, which varies from case to case.

Good examples of family resemblance in relation to the principle are individualisticness-holisticness, partness-wholeness, analysis-synthesis, and the like.

4th Thesis: The Predictability-Unpredictability Principle

The fourth thesis is called the predictability-unpredictability principle (on the occurrence of events) in the category of "method" in existential dialectics (which was first proposed in *FC* and, later, other books of mine), in that both predictability and unpredictability have a major role to play in the occurrence of things, so that neither determinism nor indeterminism wins the centuries-old fight. There is no predictability without unpredictability—and vice versa.

There are events which are predictable, just as there are those which are not. Or what is regarded as unpredictable at one point in time may turn out to be predictable later, and, conversely, what is deemed as predictable may turn out to not be so predictable. Even in predictability, outcomes are subject to uncertainty, the degree of which varies from case to case.

Works on complexity theory (as in *FC*), quantum mechanics (as in *FPHST* and *FPHG*), frequency probability, subjective (or Bayesian) probability, and "special causes" (as in *FPHGAM*), just to name a few of them, have contributed to the understanding of uncertainity.

For instance, on the one hand, there is predictability (e.g., the predictable tendency of the benefits of walkability, such as "opportunities for increased social interaction, an increase in the average number of friends and associates where people live, reduced crime," and so on, in *Sec. 2.2.1*; the predictable tendency of those who favor the invention of helmets to claim it as a protective measure to lessen injury or death in accidents, in *Sec. 2.2.2*; the predictable tendency of those in transportation nowadays to make good use of engines and motors like rocket engines, aircraft engines, electric motors, gas motors, and ion thrusters, for example, in *Sec. 2.3.1*; the predictable tendency of only the major powers like Russia, the U.S., and China to engaged in "human spaceflights" in the foreseeable future, in *Sec. 2.3.2*; the predictable tendency of the top three motor vehicle producing countries in the next few years to be China, Japan, and the U.S., in *Sec. 2.4.1*; the predictable tendency of future cars to have advanced control, alternative energy soruces, energy saver, and new materials, in *Sec. 2.4.2*; the predictable tendency of the advocates of TOD "to maximize access to public transport, and often incorporate…features to encourage transit ridership," in *Sec. 2.5.1*; the predictable tendency of the automobile to produce convenience for its users, in *Sec. 2.5.2*; the predictable tendency of those like Chaplin to argue that "a good Promotion and Awareness Program can significantly help reduce FOD by engaging a workforce with information, feedback and involvement," in *Sec. 3.2.1*; the predictable tendency of "the laws relating to drunk driving [to] vary between countries," in *Sec. 3.2.2*; the predictable tendency of carbon monoxide to be dangerous, since its "poisoning is the most common type of fatal air poisoning in many countries," in *Sec. 3.3.1*; the predictable tendency by those in England in the older days, when they argued in "a newspaper article written in England in 1895 entitled 'Horseflesh vs. Steam,'" which "highlights the death of the carriage as the means of transportation," in *Sec. 3.3.2*; the prediction by those in August 2001 who wrote "the President's Daily Briefing," in which they "warned that bin Laden was planning to exploit his operatives' access to the U.S. to mount a terrorist strike," in *Sec. 3.4.1*; the predictable tendency of traffic jams to occur in highways, in *Sec. 3.4.2*; the predictable tendency of rail transport to have its ups and downs in future history, in *Sec. 3.5.1*; and the predictable tendency in our times that "the importance of sea travel for passengers has decreased due to aviation," in *Sec. 3.5.2*).

On the other hand, there is unpredictability (e.g., the more difficult task to predict exactly the extent to which walkability is beneficial to health in a particular future era, since there were "discrepancies between residents' health in inner city neighborhoods and suburban neighborhoods with similar walkability measures," so it has been suggested that further research is needed…," in *Sec. 2.2.1*; the more difficult task to predict exactly the extent to which the requirement of helmets will be widespread in a particular future era, since there are those who consider them as "optional" for a bicycle to have, in *Sec. 2.2.2*; the more difficult task to predict exactly the extent to which the five types of engines and motors like rocket engines, aircraft engines, electric motors, gas motors, and ion thrusters will remain influential in a future particular era, since there will be ever new types of engines and motors to be invented for new environments later in history, in *Sec. 2.3.1*; the more difficult task to predict exactly the extent to which each particular space program by each of the space powers will last or remain influential in a particular future era, since no one foresaw that "lack of funding, complicated by the dissolution of the USSR, prevented any further flights of Buran" and "the American version of the space shuttle "was retired in 2011 due mainly to its old age and high cost of program reaching over a billion dollars per flight," in *Sec. 2.3.2*; the more difficult task to predict exactly the extent to which these three countries will continue to dominate the motor vehicle production in the farther future, just as no one predicted during the Great Degression that the U.S. would one day drop to number three, when at that time "the US automobile industry produced over 90%" of the motor vehicles worldwide, in *Sec. 2.4.1*; the more difficult task to predict exactly the extent to which each of these new car technologies will be widely used in a particular future era, since there are already various criticisms about their effectiveness and desirability, as pointed out by the critics, in *Sec. 2.4.2*; the more difficult task to predict exactly the extent to which TOD will remain influential in a particular future era, because of such problems like spurring "gentrification in low-income areas," together with other problems aforediscussed, in *Sec. 2.5.1*; the more difficult task to predict exactly the extent to which the automobile will remain influential in a particular future era, since there are already numerous criticisms about its negative effects on both society and culture aforecited, in *Sec. 2.5.2*; the more difficult task to predict exactly the extent to which FOD can be detected and prevented on a particular future occasion, since there can be so many factors wich "combine to cause a chain of events that can lead to a failure," in an unexpected way, in *Sec. 3.2.1*; the more difficult task to predict exactly the extent to which a particular drunk driving law will last in a particular future historical era, since, for instance, in China, a violation of the blood/alcohol limit of 0.02% in the older days would get "1–3 months license suspension," but, "beginning May 1, 2011, Chinese law now mandates a penal detention up to 6 months for any person convicted of drunken driving," in *Sec. 3.2.2*; the more difficult task to predict exactly the extent to which carbon monoxide will be used in a particular future era, since there are already conflicting uses by those in its past history, like the ones by the Nazis, those in USNAAQS, etc., in *Sec. 3.3.1*; the more difficult task for those in England in 1895 to predict that, even by 2012, "carriages are still used for day-to-day transport in the United States by some minority groups such as the Amish," and "they are also still used in the tourism as vehicles for sightseeing in cities such as Bruges, Vienna, and New Orleans," in *Sec. 3.3.2*; the more difficult task for those in August 2001 who wrote "the President's Daily Briefing" to predict exactly or to be "specific enough to identify the plan to use planes as missiles" by the terrorists, or precisely on what date this predicted event was to occur, in *Sec. 3.4.1*; the more difficult task to predict exactly "under which conditions a 'traffic jam' [as opposed to a heavy, but smoothly flowing traffic] may suddenly occur" on a particular occasion, in *Sec. 3.4.2*; the more difficult task to predict exactly the extent to which rail transport will be revived in a particular future historical era, in *Sec. 3.5.1*; and the more difficult task to predict exactly the extent to which ship transport and the art of sailing will remain in decline in a particular future era, in light of the fact that the history of ship transport has its ups and downs, not exactly predictably, in *Sec. 3.5.2*).

And the reverse direction also holds true.

Again, it should be stressed, however, that there are different shades of gray (or different degrees of truth) in the two opposites, and the classification is not necessarily mutually exclusive either. In fact, even when some combinations of the two occur, they only end up sharing the same dialectic relationship, but in a different degree.

Also, there are some other relationships (as a kind of family resemblance) which have something in common with the principle, but they are not exactly the same but only more or less comparable, which varies from case to case.

Good examples of family resemblance in relation to the principle are sureness-arbitrariness, deterministicness-randomness, likeliness-riskiness, sureness-doubtfulness, deterministicness-indeterministicness, certainty-uncertainty, and so forth.

5th Thesis: The Explicability-Inexplicability Principle

The fifth thesis is called the explicability-inexplicability principle (on the underlying mechanisms of things) in the category of "method" in existential dialectics (which was proposed in *FPHU* and other books of mine), in that both explicability and inexplicability are part of the understanding of things. There is no explicability without inexplicability—and vice versa.

This principle tells us the dual nature of the research dilemma, in that, if reality can be explained in some ways, it also has its other ways which are not quite explainable, at a given point in time.

For instance, on the one hand, there is explicability (e.g., the explanation by those who blame "mechanized transportation" for the rise of obesity," in *Sec. 2.2.1*; the explanation by the feminists that the bicycle is desirable because of its being a "freedom machine," in *Sec. 2.2.2*; the explanation by those in the study of transportation that "all or almost all of the energy added by the engine is usually lost as friction," in *Sec. 2.3.1*; the explanation by those on each side of the two superpowers during the Cold War to argue for the space race, in *Sec. 2.3.2*; the explanation by the proponents of the automobile industry that it is desirable to spread the use of the automobile, in *Sec. 2.4.1*; the explanation by those for VII that it is desirable, because it is safer for driving, in *Sec. 2.4.2*; the explanation by the proponents of TOD, as part of Intelligent Urbanism, that it is desirable to plan for "human scale" with the focus on the "pedestrian," because it can "facilitat[e]…human behavior toward more tolerant, more peaceful, more accommodating and more sensitive modalities of interaction and conflict resolution," in *Sec. 2.5.1*; the explanation by the advocates of the automobile that it is desirable because of its convenience, in *Sec. 2.5.2*; the explanation by the advocates like Chaplin that "FOD Program is essentially a public relations campaign, *in Sec. 3.2.1*; the explanation by the law enforcement authority in some countries that it is illegal "to be asleep in the driver's seat of a vehicle without any intention to drive," in *Sec. 3.2.2*; the explanation by those for "the Air Quality Health Index or 'AQHI'" in Canada that certain regulations of air pollution are desirable, in *Sec. 3.3.1*; the explanation by the advocates that the use of the horse-drawn carriage is desirable for sports, in *Sec. 3.3.2*; the explanation by the

U.S. that it launched "the War on Terror" and invaded "Afghanistan to depose the Taliban, which had harbored Al-Qaeda" for the September 11 attacks, in *Sec. 3.4.1*; the explanation by those who defend urban sprawl on the basis of a "preferred lifestyle choice" like "the American Dream unfolding before your eyes,'" in *Sec. 3.4.2*; the explanation by the supporters of freight trains that they are useful because their "environmental profile," in *Sec. 3.5.1*; and the explanation by those sailors who prefer life at sea on the basis of "sea-going adventure and a chance to see the world," in *Sec. 3.5.2*).

On the other hand, there is inexplicability (e.g., the lack of sufficient explanation by those who blame "mechanized transportation" for the rise of obesity," since there are other causes of obesity, like "diet," "genetics," "sendentary lifestyle," and the like, in *Sec. 2.2.1*; the lack of sufficient explanation by the feminists that the bicycle is necessarily desirable as a "freedom machine," since, for the critics, the bicycle has also contributed to new accidents which can injure and kill those involved, that there is no freedom without unfreedom, etc., in *Sec. 2.2.2*; the lack of sufficient explanation by those in the study of transportation of why friction is necessarily hard to overcome, in *Sec. 2.3.1*; the lack of sufficient explanation by those on each side of the two superpowers during the Cold War of why the space race is necessarily desirable, in light of the financial and human costs involved for the glory of the superpowers at the time, with the benefit of historical hindsight, while each side had huge socioeconomic problems at home, in *Sec. 2.3.2*; the lack of sufficient explanation by the proponents of the automobile industry of why it is necessarily desirable to spread the use of the automobile, since, for the critics like Peter Newman and Jeff Kenworthy, the automobile industry has contributed to "automobile dependency," in that "cities where automobiles are the predominant transport deny their residents not only freedom of choice about the way they live and move around the city, but also that the culture of automobile use has produced a kind of addiction to them," in *Sec. 2.4.1*; the lack of sufficient explanation by those for VII of why it is necessarily desirable, since for recreational drivers, VII can make driving boring, not enjoyful, in *Sec. 2.4.2*; the lack of sufficient explanation by the proponents of TOD, as part of Intelligent Urbanism, that it is desirable to plan for "human scale" with the focus on the "pedestrian," since, for the critics, those who do not favor this more sensitive lifestyle can instead choose a more competitive, violent, dominating modalities of interaction and conflict resolution, in *Sec. 2.5.1*; the lack of sufficient explanation by the advocates of the automobile of why it is necessarily desirable, in light of the numerous serious problems as pointed out by the critics aforecited, in *Sec. 2.5.2*; the lack of sufficient explanation by the advocates like Chaplin of why FOD Program is necessarily "a public relations campaign," since, for the critics, other factors are also needed, like the use of sophisticated technologies, and so on, in *Sec. 3.2.1*; the lack of sufficient explanation by the law enforcement authority in some countries of why it is necessarily desirable to make it illegal "to be asleep in the driver's seat of a vehicle without any intention to drive," since, for the driver, it is better to rest and sleep than to drive under the influence, in *Sec. 3.2.2*; the lack of sufficient explanation by those for "the Air Quality Health Index or 'AQHI'" in Canada of why certain regulations of air pollution are necessarily desirable, since "the AQHI program would not be possible without the commitment and support of the provinces, municipalities and NGOs," which do not always agree, in *Sec. 3.3.1*; the lack of sufficient explanation by the advocates of why the use of the horse-drawn carriage is necessarily desirable for sports, since "organized welfare groups, such as the Humane Society of the United States, and animal rights groups such as People for the Ethical Treatment of Animals, have been known to criticise some horse sports with claims of animal cruelty," in *Sec. 3.3.2*; the lack of sufficient explanation by the U.S. of why the war on terror is necessarily justifiable, since, for the critics like William Pfaff [2003], "people outside the United States have stopped believing the American story [viz., as the world's greatest democracy fighting evil in the world]," in *Sec. 3.4.1*; the lack of sufficient explanation by those who defend urban sprawl of why it is necesssrily desirable, since, for the critics, there are alternative lifestyles like a "car-free" household, in *Sec. 3.4.2*; the lack of sufficient explanation by the supporters of freight trains of why they must be necessarily useful, since, for the critics, "their use can be reduced by lack of flexibility, if there is need of transshipment at both ends of the trip due to lack of tracks to the points of pick-up and delivery," in *Sec. 3.5.1*; and the lack of sufficient explanation by those sailors of why life at sea is necessarily desirable, since others leave the industry because "they want to be with their families" and cannot bear "isolation, stress, and fatigue as occupational hazards" of seamanship, in *Sec. 3.5.2*).

And the reverse direction also holds true.

Once more, it should be stressed, however, that there are different shades of gray (or different degrees of truth) in the two opposites, and the classification is not necessarily mutually exclusive either. In fact, even when some combinations of the two occur, they only end up sharing the same dialectic relationship, but in a different degree.

Also, there are some other relationships (as a kind of family resemblance) which have something in common with the principle, but they are not exactly the same but only more or less comparable, which varies from case to case.

Good examples of family resemblance in relation to the principle are underlyingness-regularness, causation-regularity, causation-correlation, explanation-description, explanation-narration, explanation-interpretation, and so forth.

6th Thesis: The Fiction-Reality Principle

The sixth thesis is called the fiction-reality principle (on the different faces of reality) in the category of "method" in existential dialectics (as first proposed in *FPHLIT*), in that both fiction and reality co-exist. There is no reality without fiction—and vice versa.

This principle tells us the different categories of reality, in that, if there is reality, there is also some fiction in it—just as, if there is fiction, there is also some reality in it.

For instance, on the one hand, there is fiction (e.g., the fictional aspect of the argument about the benefits of walkability, insofar as there were "discrepancies between residents' health in inner city neighborhoods and suburban neighborhoods with similar walkability measures," so it has been suggested that further research is needed...," in *Sec. 2.2.1*; the fictional aspect of bicycle safety, insofar as Colin Buchanan in 1963 reported that "the meagre efforts made to separate cyclists from motor traffic have failed,...not...as helpful as it might have been," in *Sec. 2.2.2*; the fictional aspect of the study of transportation, insofar as the disadvantages of energy sources are not adequately and seriously considered, in *Sec. 2.3.1*; the fictional aspect of the space race, insofar as it was driven by politics and ideology in the competition for global domination and glory between the two superpowers during the Cold War, in *Sec. 2.3.2*; the fictional aspect of the old "glory days" of the automobile, insofar as the negative consequences were ignored, as shown in the criticisms that it has also contributed to considerable economic costs around the world, that it has a destructive impact on society too, that the use of the automobile can be so addictive as to become "automobile-dependent," that it also ignores the negative legal consequences for both individuals and society, etc., in *Sec. 2.4.1*; the fictional aspect of future car technologies, insofar as some of the claims are questioned, as shown in the criticisms that they are not so simple as they may sound, that they are not necessarily effective to enhance security, that they are also not necessarily safe to use, etc., in *Sec.*

2.4.2; the fictional aspect of TOD, insofar as it does not seriously consider alternative options like TPD, the libertarian argument for the free market, etc., in *Sec. 2.5.1*; the fictional aspect of the car culture, insofar as it causes time delays, accidents, etc. often downplayed by its advocates, in *Sec. 2.5.2*; the fictional aspect of the "Promotion and Awareness Program" by Chaplin, insofar as it ignores many other factors, like the use of different technologies to detect and prevent FOD, etc., in *Sec. 3.2.1*; the fictional aspect of "field sobriety tests," insofar as these tests are not reliable and controversial, as they are often combined with "the arresting officer's subjective opinion of impairment," in *Sec. 3.2.2*; the fictional aspect of carbon monoxide, insofar as it is uncritically assumed to be regulated so as to not harm people because of its toxcity, but the Nazis, for example, used carbon monoxide "during the Holocaust at some Nazi extermination camps, the most notable by gas vans in Chelmno, and in the Action T4 'euthanasia' program," in *Sec. 3.3.1*; the fictional aspect of the five steps by Bettmann on how to operate a horse-drawn carriage correctly, insofar as they are too conservative and risk-adverse, in *Sec. 3.3.2*; the fictional aspect of the U.S. war on terror, insofar as it wants "people outside the United States" to believe "the American story [viz., as the world's greatest democracy fighting evil in the world]," as pointed out by William Pfaff, in *Sec. 3.4.1*; the fictional aspect of the argument by those in favor of the resolution of traffic congestion, as the critics pointed out that traffic jam is still not fully predictable, that "rush hour traffic congestion is inevitable," etc., in *Sec. 3.4.2*; the fictional aspect of the film *Mission: Impossible,* when one can "see…a helicopter pursuing a TGV train into the Channel Tunnel which runs between Great Britain and France," but "in reality this type of train does not travel through the Channel Tunnel," in *Sec. 3.5.1*; and the fictional aspect of seamanship, insofar as there are exceptions to its general rules of thumb, as shown in the exceptional example about "the U.S. Sealift class tankers which used a controllable pitch propeller, where the pitch and not the direction of rotation was reversed to go astern," in *Sec. 3.5.2*).

On the other hand, there is reality (e.g., the realistic aspect of the argument about the benefits of walkability, insofar as there are evidences for "opportunities for increased social interaction, an increase in the average number of friends and associates where people live, reduced crime," and so on, in *Sec. 2.2.1*; the realistic aspect of bicycle safety, insofar as "the use of appropriately designed segregated space on arterial or interurban routes [so as to separate bicycles from vehicles] appears to be associated with reductions in overall risk," in *Sec. 2.2.2*; the realistic aspect of the study of transportation, insofar as there are advantages for each energy source, in *Sec. 2.3.1*; the realistic aspect of the space race, insofar as it had contributed to "technological, and scientific developments" of space exploration, in *Sec. 2.3.2*; the realistic aspect of the old "glory days" of the automobile, insofar as the automobile has contributed to the convenience of transporation in modern times, in *Sec. 2.4.1*; the realistic aspect of future car technologies, insofar as they make some contributions to advanced control, alternative energy soruces, energy saver, and new materials, in *Sec. 2.4.2*; the realistic aspect of TOD, insofar as it aims "to maximize access to public transport, and often incorporate…features to encourage transit ridership,"in *Sec. 2.5.1*; the realistic aspect of the car culture, insofar as it brings convenience too, in *Sec. 2.5.2*; the realistic aspect of the "Promotion and Awareness Program" by Chaplin, insofar as it stresses the importance of "public relations campaign" to prevent FOD, in *Sec. 3.2.1*; the realistic aspect of "field sobriety tests," insofar as these tests can help to detect blood/alcohol content to some extent, in *Sec. 3.2.2*; the realistic aspect of carbon monoxide, insofar as it is to be regulated so as to not harm people because of its toxcity, as shown in the regulations in accordance to "the Air Quality Health Index or 'AQHI'" in Canada, in *Sec. 3.3.1*; the realistic aspect of the five steps by Bettmann on how to operate a horse-drawn carriage correctly, insofar as they stress careful driving and the obediance to traffic laws, in *Sec. 3.3.2*; the realistic aspect of the U.S. war on terror, insofar as it used the September 11 attacks as an excuse to invade Afghanistan, in *Sec. 3.4.1*; the realistic aspect of the argument by those in favor of the resolution of traffic congestion, insofar as there are solutions aforecited which could make at least some improvement, in *Sec. 3.4.2*; the realistic aspect of the film *Mission: Impossible,* insofar as there are trains which travel through the Channel Tunnel, in *Sec. 3.5.1*; and the realistic aspect of seamanship, insofar as there are rules of thumb like the example that "the propeller would turn counterclockwise when going astern and the stern would walk to port," in *Sec. 3.5.2*).

And the reverse direction also holds true.

Once more, it should be stressed, however, that there are different shades of gray (or different degrees of truth) in the two opposites, and the classification is not necessarily mutually exclusive either. In fact, even when some combinations of the two occur, they only end up sharing the same dialectic relationship, but in a different degree.

Also, there are some other relationships (as a kind of family resemblance) which have something in common with the principle, but they are not exactly the same but only more or less comparable, which varies from case to case.

Good examples of family resemblance in relation to the principle are fiction-nonfiction, fiction-fact, imagination-fact, imagination-nonfiction, subjectivity-objectivity, and so forth.

In Relation to Structure

The next five theses are in relation to structure in existential dialectics, as shown below.

7th Thesis: The Finiteness-Transfiniteness

The seventh thesis is called the finiteness-transfiniteness principle (on the nature of numbers) in the category of "structure" in existential dialectics (as first proposed in *FPHG*), in that, if there are finite things, there are likewise transfinite ones—and vice versa.

To avoid confusion, my usage of the word "transfinite" here differs radically from the one used by Cantor (and other mathematicians) for "relative" infinity—and is more limited, in light of the problems confronting any attempt to understand the idea of infinity, be it by intuition, imagination, and conception (as detailedly analyzed in *Sec. 2.2.3* of *FPHG*).

Instead, by "transfinity," I allow numbers which can be many times larger—or smaller, for that matter—than the finite things that we encounter in daily life, but they do not have to be related to the idea of infinity at all (which may not exist).

Of course, there may be some *borderline* cases, in which it is not clear whether the number in question is transfinite (in my usage) or simply a mathematical convenience. A good example of a borderline case is the Planck unit of length for "the smallest space possibly measured in nature," which is "less than billionths of trillionths of trillionths of an inch" (or something like 1.6×10^{-35} meters). (P. Baofu 2006a; N. McAleer 1987: 219; WKV 2008; D. Corbett 2008a)

That said—my usage of "transfinity" can also resolve (or better, dissolve) an age-old problem in philosophy known as "Zeno's paradoxes" (as already explained in *Sec. 2.2.3* of *FPHG*).

In any event, in relation to the finiteness-transfiniteness principle, on the other hand, there is finiteness (e.g., the finite number of the causes of obesity, like "diet," "genetics," "sendentary lifestyle," "medical and psychiatric illness," "infectious agents," and so on, in *Sec. 2.2.1*; the finite number of the most common types of bicycles in history like "utility bicycles, mountain bicycles, racing bicycles, touring bicycles, hybrid bicycles, cruiser bicycles, and BMX Bikes," in *Sec. 2.2.2*; the finite number of ways to convert energy to work, like the use of wheels, tracks, nozzles, propellers, wings, etc., in *Sec. 2.3.1*; the finite number of the categories of celestial bodies for spacecrafts to explore, like moons, planets, solar systems, etc., in *Sec. 2.3.2*; the finite number of the types of cars produced in the last few decades, in *Sec. 2.4.1*; the finite number of the types of alternative fuel vehicles that have been proposed or sold, like "electric cars, hydrogen cars, compressed-air cars and liquid nitrogen cars," in *Sec. 2.4.2*; the finite number of the types of transit stations or stops like "train station," "metro station," "tram stop," "bus stop," etc., in *Sec. 2.5.1*; the finite number of the major modes of transportation in history, like automobiles, horses, walking, streetcars, etc., in *Sec. 2.5.2*; the finite number of the types of FOD, as shown in the 7 examples aforecited, in *Sec. 3.2.1*; the finite number of the categories of "blood alcohol concentrations," such as "20–99 mg/dL," "100–199 mg/dL," etc., in *Sec. 3.2.2*; the finite number of the categories of air pollution, like the 3 categories of "chemicals, particulate matter, and biological materials" in the article aforecited, in *Sec. 3.3.1*; the finite number of the categories of the horse-drawn carriage, like the 325 types as susggested by Arthur Ingram, in *Sec. 3.3.2*; the finite number of the types of "toxic debris resulting from the collapse of the Twin Towers" after the September 11 attacks, like the "2,500 contaminants, including known carcinogens," in *Sec. 3.4.1*; the finite number of the categories of vehicles in traffic congestion, like cars, trucks, motorcycles, buses, etc., in *Sec. 3.4.2*; the finite number of the categories of rail transport, like pre-steam, steam, electrical, and diesel rail transports, in *Sec. 3.5.1*; and the finite number of the different uses of the term "sailor" in the history of ship transport, as cited in the article, in *Sec. 3.5.2*).

On the other hand, there is transfinitty (e.g., the transfinite number of all the individual humans and animals in the history of the earth that have suffered from health problems due to obesity, in *Sec. 2.2.1*; the transfinite number of all the individual bicycles which have ever been produced in history, in *Sec. 2.2.2*; the transfinite number of all the units of work ever converted from energy in history, in *Sec. 2.3.1*; the transfinite number of all the possible individual moons, planets, solar systems, etc. in the universe for spacecrafts to explore, in *Sec. 2.3.2*; the transfinite number of all the gallons of gasoline consumed by cars produced in the last few decades, since it was estimated that, in 2007 alone, more than "806 million cars and light trucks on the road…consum[ed]…over 260 billion US gallons," in *Sec. 2.4.1*; the transfinite amounts of hydrogen, nitrogen, air, etc. on earth and in the rest of the universe that these future cars can use, in

Sec. 2.4.2; the transfinite number of all the individuals in history who have ever used any of the transit stops on earth, in *Sec. 2.5.1*; the transfinite number of all the individual cars, horses, streetcars, and walkers that have ever existed in history, in *Sec. 2.5.2*; the transfinite number of all the individual pieces of foreign object debris in the history of the earth, in *Sec. 3.2.1*; the transfinite number of all the individuals in history who have ever had any of the categories of "blood alcohol concentrations," in *Sec. 3.2.2*; the transfinite number of all the possible units of "chemicals, particulate matter, and biological materials" that have ever existed in history, in *Sec. 3.3.1*; the transfinite number of all the individual carriages that have ever been built, either partly or completely, in history, regardless of how many possible types there are, in *Sec. 3.3.2*; the transfinite number of the possible individual pieces of toxic contaminants to be found in the history of the earth, in *Sec. 3.4.1*; the transfinite number of all the individual users who have ever used cars, trucks, motorcyles, buses, etc. in history, in *Sec. 3.4.2*; the transfinite number of all the individual pieces of rail transport ever produced in history, regardless of how primitive or incomplete they are, in *Sec. 3.5.1*; and the transfinite number of all the individual sailors in the history of ship transport who can fit in the different meanings of the term "sailor," in *Sec. 3.5.2*).

And the reverse direction also holds true.

Once more, it should be stressed, however, that there are different shades of gray (or different degrees of truth) in the two opposites, and the classification is not necessarily mutually exclusive either. In fact, even when some combinations of the two occur, they only end up sharing the same dialectic relationship, but in a different degree.

Also, there are some other relationships (as a kind of family resemblance) which have something in common with the principle, but they are not exactly the same but only more or less comparable, which varies from case to case.

Good examples of family resemblance in relation to the principle are boundedness-quasiunboundedness, smallness-largeness, boundedness-unboundedness, microness-macroness, and the like.

8th Thesis: The Preciseness-Vagueness Principle

The eighth thesis is called the preciseness-vagueness principle (on the refinement of things) in the category of "structure" in existential dialectics (which was first out worked out in *FIA*), in that both preciseness and vagueness are important, not that one is better than the other, but that both are used, in different degrees of preference, in accordance to the contextual application from the perspectives of nature, the mind, culture, and society. There is no preciseness without vagueness—and vice versa.

For instance, on the one hand, there is preciseness (e.g., the precise identification of four major measurements of walkability, like PERS, Walk Score, etc. in the article aforecited, in *Sec. 2.2.1*; the precise identification of 7 common types of bicycles like "utility bicycles, mountain bicycles, racing bicycles, touring bicycles, hybrid bicycles, cruiser bicycles, and BMX Bikes" in the article aforecited, in *Sec. 2.2.2*; the precise identification of the five ways to convert energy to work, like the use of wheels, tracks, nozzles, propellers, wings, etc. in the article aforecited, in *Sec. 2.3.1*; the precise identification of 11 sub-systems of a spacecraft systems in the article aforecited, like "life support," "attitude control," "power," etc., in *Sec. 2.3.2*; the precise identification of the top 20 "motor vehicle manufacturing companies by volume" in 2010 in the article aforecited, in *Sec. 2.4.1*; the precise identification of four ways in which future cars can be made by new technologies, like advanced control, alternative energy soruces, energy saver, and new materials, in *Sec. 2.4.2*; the precise identification of four regions of the world to be considered for TOD in the article aforecited, in *Sec. 2.5.1*; the precise identification of five different impacts by the automobile on culture in the article aforecited, in *Sec. 2.5.2*; the precise identification, by Chaplin, of 4 basic "elements of a comprehensive campaign" to make people aware of FOD damages, in *Sec. 3.2.1*; the precise identification of 5 categories of "blood alcohol concentrations," such as "20–99 mg/dL," "100–199 mg/dL," etc., in *Sec. 3.2.2*; the precise identification of 6 anthropogenic sources of air pollution in the article aforecited, in *Sec. 3.3.1*; the precise identification of 325 types of the horse-drawn carriage by Arthur Ingram, in *Sec. 3.3.2*; the precise identification of four major effects of the September 11 attacks in the article aforecited, in *Sec. 3.4.1*; the precise identification of two types of theories to understand traffic congestion in the article aforecited, in *Sec. 3.4.2*; the precise identification of three major ways in which rail transport appears in popular culture in the article aforecited, like in films, on TV, and in literature, in *Sec. 3.5.1*; and the precise identification of 4 categories of sailing in ship transport in the article aforecited, in *Sec. 3.5.2*).

On the other hand, there is vagueness (e.g., the vagueness in the identification of the four major measurements of walkability, like PERS, Walk Score, etc. in the article aforecited, since it is not clear why there must be only four major measurements, not 5, 6, 7, 8, and so on, in *Sec. 2.2.1*; the vagueness in the identification of the 7 common types of bicycles like "utility bicycles, mountain bicycles, racing bicycles, touring bicycles, hybrid bicycles, cruiser bicycles, and BMX Bikes" in the article aforecited, since it is not clear why there must be only 7, not 8, 9, 10, and so on, in *Sec. 2.2.2*; the vagueness in the identification of the five ways to convert energy to work, like the use of wheels, tracks, nozzles, propellers, wings, etc. in the article aforecited, since it is not clear why there must be only five, not 7, 11, 13, and so on, in *Sec. 2.3.1*; the vagueness in the identification of the 11 sub-systems of a spacecraft systems in the article aforecited, like "life support," "attitude control," "power," etc., since it is not clear why there must be only 11, not 13, 15, 16, 20, and so on, in *Sec. 2.3.2*; the vagueness in the identification of the top 20 "motor vehicle manufacturing companies by volume" in 2010 in the article aforecited, since it is not clear why there must be only 20 on the list, not 21, 24, 25, 30, and so on, in *Sec. 2.4.1*; the vagueness in the identification of the four ways in which future cars can be made by new technologies, like advanced control, alternative energy soruces, energy saver, and new materials, since it is not clear why there must be only four ways, not 5, 6, 7, and so on, in *Sec. 2.4.2*; the vagueness in the identification of the four regions of the world to be considered for TOD in the article aforecited, since it is not clear why there must be only these 4 regions to be classified, not 5, 6, 7, and so on, in *Sec. 2.5.1*; the vagueness in the identification of the five different impacts by the automobile on culture in the article aforecited, since it is not clear why there must be only 5, not 7, 12, 13, 15, 21, and so on, in *Sec. 2.5.2*; the vagueness in the identification of the 4 basic "elements of a comprehensive campaign" to make people aware of FOD damages, since it is not clear why there must be only these 4 elements, not 5, 6, 7, 8, and so on, in *Sec. 3.2.1*; the vagueness in the identification of the 5 categories of "blood alcohol concentrations," such as "20–99 mg/dL," "100–199 mg/dL," etc., since it is not clear why there must be only 5 categories, not 6, 7, 8, and so on, in *Sec. 3.2.2*; the vagueness in the identification of the 6 anthropogenic sources of air pollution in the article aforecited, since it is not clear why there must be only 6 sources, not 7, 8, 9, and so on, in *Sec. 3.3.1*; the vagueness in the identification of the 325 types of the horse-drawn carriage by Arthur Ingram, since it is not clear why there must be only 325 types, not 326, 328, 329, 330, and so on, in *Sec. 3.3.2*; the vagueness in the identification of the four major effects of the September 11 attacks in the article aforecited, since it is not clear why there must be only 4, not 6, 9, 13, 15, and so on, in *Sec. 3.4.1*; the vagueness in the identification of the two types of theories to understand traffic congestion in the article aforecited, since it is not clear why there must be only 2 types, not 3, 5, 6, 8, and so on, in *Sec. 3.4.2*; the vagueness in the identification of the three major ways in which rail transport appears in popular culture in the article aforecited, since it is not clear why there must be only 3 ways, not 5, 7, 8, and so on, in *Sec. 3.5.1*; and the vagueness in the identification of the 4 categories of sailing in ship transport in the article aforecited, since it is not clear why there must be only 4 categories, not 5, 6, 7, 8, 13, and so on, in *Sec. 3.5.2*).

And the reverse direction also holds true.

Once more, it should be stressed, however, that there are different shades of gray (or different degrees of truth) in the two opposites, and the classification is not necessarily mutually exclusive either. In fact, even when some combinations of the two occur, they only end up sharing the same dialectic relationship, but in a different degree.

Also, there are some other relationships (as a kind of family resemblance) which have something in common with the principle, but they are not exactly the same but only more or less comparable, which varies from case to case.

Good examples of family resemblance in relation to the principle are clarity-ambiguity, directness-indirectness, quantitativeness-qualitativeness, specificity-obscurity, thickness-thinness, describability-nondescribability, concretness-abstractness, translatability-untranslatability, specificity-generality, clearcutness-transitionalness, and the like.

9th Thesis: The Simpleness-Complicatedness Principle

The ninth thesis refers to the simpleness-complicatedness principle (on the interconnection among things) in the category of "structure" in existential dialectics (which was first out worked out in *FIA*), in that both simpleness and complicatedness are vital, without favoring one over the other, and each is utilized, depending on the basis of the perspectives of nature, the mind, culture, and society. There is no simpleness without complicatedness—and vice versa.

For instance, on the one hand, there is simpleness (e.g., the relatively simple analysis of obesity in relation to "mechanized transportation," in *Sec.2.2.1*; the relatively simple analysis of "freedom machine" by its advocates , in *Sec. 2.2.2*; the relatively simple analysis of locomtion and energy by the advocates, in *Sec. 2.3.1*; the relatively simple analysis of the history of spacecraft by its advocates, in *Sec. 2.3.2*; the relatively simple analysis of the automobile industry by its advocates, in *Sec. 2.4.1*; the relatively simple analysis of future car technologies by the advocates, in *Sec. 2.4.2*; the relatively simple analysis of TOD by its advocates, in *Sec. 2.5.1*; the relatively simple analysis of the car culture by its advocates, in *Sec. 2.5.2*; the relatively simple analysis of FOD prevention by its advocates, in *Sec. 3.2.1*; the relatively simple analysis of field sobriety tests, blood alcohol content tests, etc. by the advocates, in *Sec. 3.2.2*; the relatively simple analysis of air pollution in transportation by the advocates, in *Sec. 3.3.1*; the relatively simple analysis of the horse-drawn carriage by the advocates, in *Sec. 3.3.2*; the relatively simple analysis of the September 11 attacks from the vantage point of the U.S., in *Sec. 3.4.1*; the relatively simple analysis of urban sprawl and traffic congestion by the defenders, in *Sec. 3.4.2*; the relatively simple analysis of rail transport by its advocates, in *Sec. 3.5.1*; and the relatively simple analysis of the art of sailing by its advocates, in *Sec. 3.5.2*).

On the other hand, there is complicatedness (e.g., the relatively more complicated analysis of obesity, by challenging the claims and assumptions, as shown in the problems pointed out by the critics as cited, in *Sec. 2.2.1*; the relatively more complicated analysis of "freedom machine," by challenging the claims and assumptions, as shown in the problems pointed out by the critics as cited, in *Sec. 2.2.2*; the relatively more complicated analysis of locomtion and energy, by challenging the claims and assumptions, as shown in the problems pointed out by the critics as cited, in *Sec. 2.3.1*; the relatively more complicated analysis of the history of spacecraft, by challenging the claims and assumptions, as shown in the problems pointed out by the critics as cited, in *Sec. 2.3.2*; the relatively more complicated analysis of the automobile industry, by challenging the claims and assumptions, as shown in the problems pointed out by the critics as cited, in *Sec. 2.4.1*; the relatively more complicated analysis of future car technologies, by challenging the claims and assumptions, as shown in the problems pointed out by the critics as cited, in *Sec. 2.4.2*; the relatively more complicated analysis of TOD, by challenging the claims and assumptions, as shown in the problems pointed out by the critics as cited, in *Sec .2.5.1*; the relatively more complicated analysis of the car culture, by challenging the claims and assumptions, as shown in the problems pointed out by the critics as cited, in *Sec. 2.5.2*; the relatively more complicated analysis of FOD prevention, by challenging the claims and assumptions, as shown in the problems pointed out by the critics as cited, in *Sec. 3.2.1*; the relatively more complicated analysis of field sobriety tests, blood alcohol content tests, etc., by challenging the claims and assumptions, as shown in the problems pointed out by the critics as cited, in *Sec. 3.2.2*; the relatively more complicated analysis of air pollution in transportation, by challenging the claims and assumptions, as shown in the problems pointed out by the critics as cited, in *Sec. 3.3.1*; the relatively more complicated analysis of the horse-drawn carriage, by challenging the claims and assumptions, as shown in the problems pointed out by the critics as cited, in *Sec. 3.3.2*; the relatively more complicated analysis of the September 11 attacks, by challenging the claims and assumptions, as shown in the problems pointed out by the critics as cited, in *Sec. 3.4.1*; the relatively more complicated analysis of urban sprawl and traffic congestion, by challenging the claims and assumptions, as shown in the problems pointed out by the critics as cited, in *Sec. 3.4.2*; the relatively more complicated analysis of rail transport, by challenging the claims and assumptions, as shown in the problems pointed out by the critics as cited, in *Sec. 3.5.1*; and the relatively more complicated analysis of the art of sailing, by challenging the claims and assumptions, as shown in the problems pointed out by the critics as cited, in *Sec. 3.5.2*).

And the reverse direction also holds true.

Again, it should be stressed, however, that there are different shades of gray (or different degrees of truth) in the two opposites, and the classification is not necessarily mutually exclusive either. In fact, even when some combinations of the two occur, they only end up sharing the same dialectic relationship, but in a different degree.

Also, there are some other relationships (as a kind of family resemblance) which have something in common with the principle, but they are not exactly the same but only more or less comparable, which varies from case to case.

Good examples of family resemblance in relation to the principle are inflexibility-flexibility, standardization-specialization, imperfectness-perfectness, superficiality-depth, shallowness-deepness, economicalness-elaboratedness, plainness-circumspection, onesidedness-multisidedness, succinctness-duplicatedness, and the like.

10th Thesis: The Openness-Hiddenness Principle

The tenth thesis refers to the openness-hiddenenss principle (on the detection of things) in the category of "structure" in existential dialectics (which was already worked out in my previous books, especially in *FPHU*), in that reality has its hidden face, just as it is open to outside view in some other ways. There is no openness without hiddenness—and vice versa.

For instance, on the one hand, there is openness (e.g., the open exploration of the "established relationship between obesity and negative health outcomes" in the article aforecited, in *Sec. 2.2.1*; the open exploration by Herbert Alker Tripp in 1942 that "if we could segregate pedestrians completely from the wheeled traffic, we could of course abolish pedestrian casualties," in *Sec. 2.2.2*; the more open view of a car on the street, in *Sec. 2.3.1*; the open exploration of the moon, Mars, Jupiter, Saturn, Venus, etc. by different human spacecrafts in the last few decades, in *Sec. 2.3.2*; the open exploration of the relationship between the automobile and its convenience for transportation in modern life, in *Sec. 2.4.1*; the open exploration of future car technologies for safety, efficiency, and so on in the article aforecited, in *Sec. 2.4.2*; the open exploration of the value of "human scale" in TOD with the focus on the "pedestrian" in the ideology of Intelligent Urbanism, in *Sec. 2.5.1*; the open exploration of "direct out-of-pocket costs" by commuters, in *Sec. 2.5.2*; the open exploration of different possible types of FOD which can cause damages to aircrafts, in *Sec. 3.2.1*; the open exploration of the correlation between field sobriety tests and driving under influence, in *Sec. 3.2.2*; the open exploration of "air pollutants," which "can be in the form of solid particles, liquid droplets, or gases," in *Sec. 3.3.1*; an "open" carriage, with no top cover, in *Sec. 3.3.2*; the open preaching of al-Qaeda for "global jihad" against Western powers like the U.S., in *Sec. 3.4.1*; the open exploration of the relationship between heavy traffic and traffic congestion, in *Sec. 3.4.2*; the open exploration of the nature of trains and their portrayal in popular culture, in *Sec. 3.5.1*; and the open exploration of the RMS *Titanic* for "sea-going adventure and a chance to see the world," in *Sec. 3.5.2*).

On the other hand, there is hiddenness (e.g., the hidden bias in the analysis of the "established relationship between obesity and negative health outcomes" in the article aforecited, since it does not give sufficient attention to the alternative claim by some in the fat acceptance movement who challenge the "established relationship between obesity and negative health outcomes," in *Sec. 2.2.1*; the hidden bias in the argument by Tripp, because Colin Buchanan in 1963 rebuked him by arguing that "the meagre efforts made to separate cyclists from motor traffic have failed,…not…as helpful as it might have been," in *Sec. 2.2.2*; the more hidden view of a nuclear submarine deep under the sea, in *Sec. 2.3.1*; the hidden nature of many other moons and planets in the universe not yet explored by human spacecrafts, in *Sec. 2.3.2*; the hidden bias in the view about the relationship between the automobile and its convenience for transportation in modern life, since, for the critics, there are the serious hidden costs, in that it has also contributed to considerable economic costs around the world, that it has a destructive impact on society too, that the use of the automobile can be so addictive as to become "automobile-dependent," that it also ignores the negative legal consequences for both individuals and society, etc., in *Sec. 2.4.1*; the hidden bias in the analysis of future car technologies in the article aforecited, because they are not so effective and desirable as claimed, as pointed out by the critics aforecited, in *Sec. 2.4.2*; the hidden bias in TOD for the value of "human scale" with the focus on the "pedestrian" as part of the ideology of Intelligent Urbanism, because, for the critic like Gordon, it has an authoritarian tendency in "ignoring consumer preference and the free market," in *Sec. 2.5.1*; the hidden bias in the consideration of "direct out-of-pocket costs" by commuters, because they "often make choices based on the direct out-of-pocket costs and underestimate the indirect costs of car ownership, auto insurance and car maintenance," in *Sec. 2.5.2*; the hiddenness of the FOD, since some pieces of foreign object debris like tools and bolts can be carelessly or mistakenly put in the wrong places, such that pilots are caught by surprise when these pieces are flying around all of a sudden, in *Sec. 3.2.1*; the hidden bias in "field sobriety tests," because these tests are not reliable and controversial, as they are often combined with "the arresting officer's subjective opinion of impairment," in *Sec. 3.2.2*; the hidden nature of some of the air pollutants, like carbon monoxide, which "is a colourless, odorless, non-irritating but very poisonous gas," in *Sec. 3.3.1*; an "closed" carriage, in *Sec. 3.3.2*; the hidden nature of al-Qaeda in its secret planning of the September 11 attacks, in *Sec. 3.4.1*; the hidden nature of traffic jams, because "traffic research still cannot fully predict under which conditions a 'traffic jam' [as opposed to heavy, but smoothly flowing traffic] may suddenly occur," in *Sec. 3.4.2*; the hidden bias in the portrayal of trains in popular culture, as shown in the film *Mission: Impossible,* when one can "see…a helicopter pursuing a TGV train into the Channel Tunnel which runs between Great Britain and France," but "in reality this type of train does not travel through the Channel Tunnel," in *Sec. 3.5.1*; and the hidden vulnerability of the RMS *Titanic*, when it "sank in the North Atlantic Ocean on 15 April 1912 after colliding with an iceberg not easily noticeable in the darkness of the night, in *Sec. 3.5.2*).

And the reverse direction also holds true.

Again, it should be stressed, however, that there are different shades of gray (or different degrees of truth) in the two opposites, and the classification is not necessarily mutually exclusive either. In fact, even when some combinations of the two occur, they only end up sharing the same dialectic relationship, but in a different degree.

Also, there are some other relationships (as a kind of family resemblance) which have something in common with the principle, but they are not exactly the same but only more or less comparable, which varies from case to case.

Good examples of family resemblance in relation to the principle are overtness-covertness, participation-obstruction, publicness-privateness, openness-closedness, surface-depth, transparency-secrecy, openness-biasedness, , exposition-illusion, and so on.

11th Thesis: The Denseness-Emptiness Principle

The eleventh thesis concerns the denseness-emptiness principle (on the distribution of entities in space) in the category of "structure" in existential dialectics, which is first proposed in *FPHUP*, in that both density and void are needed, in relation to the mind, nature, culture, and society, albeit in different ways. There is no denseness without emptiness—and vice versa.

Lest any misunderstanding occurs, the term "void" is used here only as an approximation of emptiness (depending on the degree of the lack of density), since, in physics, it is well known that "empty" space is not really empty all the way, because it can be full of energy (e.g., random quantum fluctuations at the sub-atomic level, and, for that matter, dark energy in the universe) and matter (e.g., different versions of sub-atomic particles, and, for that matter, dark matter in the universe). (F. Wilczek 2008)

For instance, on the one hand, there is denseness (e.g., the relatively denser concentration of obese individuals in "twentieth century automotive and automated metropolis," in *Sec. 2.2.1*; the relatively denser concentration of bicycles as one of the "mainstays of private transportation" nowadays, in *Sec. 2.2.2*; the relatively denser concentration of wheels used for transportation on earth nowadays, in *Sec. 2.3.1*; the relatively denser concentration of human spacecrafts in earth orbit, since, "as of June 2011, there are more than 2,000 spacecraft in orbit," in *Sec. 2.3.2*; the relatively denser concentration of automobiles on the road nowadays, in *Sec. 2.4.1*; the relatively denser concentration of cars with "advanced control" in future tansportation systems, in *Sec. 2.4.2*; the relatively denser concentration of "mixed-use residential or commercial areas" in order to "maximize access to public transport" in TOD, in *Sec. 2.5.1*; the relatively denser concentration of cars in developed countries, in *Sec. 2.5.2*; the relatively denser concentration of concerns with "public relations campaign" for FOD prevention by someone like Chaplin, in *Sec. 3.2.1*; the relatively denser concentration of alcohol in the blood stream, like those cases of 0.40% in "excessive drinking" as in "alcohol poisoning," in *Sec. 3.2.2*; the relatively denser concentration of air, "whose average molar mass is 28.8," in *Sec. 3.3.1*; the relatively denser concentration of wheels in a horse-drawn carriage when it has six wheels, in *Sec. 3.3.2*; the relatively denser concentration of Arab nationals among the hijackers who took part in the September 11 attacks, in *Sec. 3.4.1*; the relatively denser concentration of vehicles in a traffic jam, in *Sec. 3.4.2*; the relatively denser concentration of concerns with train travel in *Anna Karenina* by Leo Tolstoy, in *Sec. 3.5.1*; and the relatively denser concentration of passengres aborad the the RMS *Titanic*, carrying 2,224 people, in *Sec. 3.5.2*).

On the other hand, there is emptiness (e.g., the relatively less dense, or more empty, concentration of obese individuals in ancient times, "after millennia of human development firmly based upon gait," in *Sec. 2.2.1*; the relatively less dense, or more empty, concentration of horses as one of the "mainstays of private transportatioin" nowadays, in *Sec. 2.2.2*; the relatively less dense, or more empty, concentration of propellers used in space for transportation nowadays, in *Sec. 2.3.1*; the relatively less dense, or more empty, concentration of human spacecrafts in the orbit of Neptune, as of June 2011, in *Sec. 2.3.2*; the relatively less dense, or more empty, concentration of horses on the road nowadays, in *Sec. 2.4.1*; the relatively less dense, or more empty, concentration of cars with "advanced control" in the early 20th century tansportation system, in *Sec. 2.4.2*; the relatively less dense, or more empty, concentration of "mixed-use residential or commercial areas" in the libertarian response to urban planning as proposed by Gordon, in *Sec. 2.5.1*; the relatively less dense, or more empty, concentration of cars in underdeveloped countries like some parts of China, where "there are currently 184 towns and 54,000 villages that have no access to automobile use…or roads at all," in *Sec. 2.5.2*; the relatively less dense, or more empty, concentration of concerns with "public relations campaign" for FOD prevention by those who prefer to use sophisticated technologies like "radar," "Electro-Optical [visible band imagery [standard CCTV] and low light cameras," and so on, in *Sec. 3.2.1*; ., the relatively less dense, or more empty, concentration of alcohol in the blood stream, like those cases of less than 0.20%, in *Sec. 3.2.2*; the relatively less dense, or more empty, concentration of carbon monoxide, which is less dense than air, because it "has a molar mass of 28.0, which makes it slightly lighter than air, whose average molar mass is 28.8," in *Sec. 3.3.1*; the relatively less dense, or more empty, concentration of wheels in a horse-drawn carriage when it has only 2 wheels, in *Sec. 3.3.2*; the relatively less dense, or more empty, concentration of Americans among the hijackers who took part in the September 11 attacks, in *Sec. 3.4.1*; the relatively less dense, or more empty, concentration of vehicles in a desert, on average, in *Sec. 3.4.2*; the relatively less dense, or more empty, concentration of concerns with train travel in the film *Avatar*, in *Sec. 3.5.1*; and the relatively less dense, or more empty, concentration of passengers aboard the commercial oil tanker *AbQaiq*, by contrast with the RMS *Titanic*, in *Sec. 3.5.2*).

And the reverse direction also holds true.

Again, it should be stressed, however, that there are different shades of gray (or different degrees of truth) in the two opposites, and the classification is not necessarily mutually exclusive either. In fact, even when some combinations of the two occur, they only end up sharing the same dialectic relationship, but in a different degree.

Also, there are some other relationships (as a kind of family resemblance) which have something in common with the principle, but they are not exactly the same but only more or less comparable, which varies from case to case.

Good examples of family resemblance in relation to the principle are fullness-voidness, nearness-farness, concentration-dispersion, denseness-nothingness, something-nothing, heaviness-lightness, composition-emptiness, solidness-void, presence-absence, focus-unfocus, emphasis-disemphasis, and the like.

In Relation to Process

The next four theses are in relation to process in existential dialectics, as shown below.

12th Thesis: The Change-Constancy Principle

The twelfth thesis concerns the change-constancy principle (on the alteration of things) in the category of "process" in existential dialectics, which is first named in *BCPC* (and were worked out in my books like *FHC*, *FCD*, and *FPHC)*, in that change occurs over time, although constancy is also allowed.

Old players fade away, and new ones emerges, with ever new causes and ever new forms—and asymmetry undergoes changes over time too, so does symmetry. There is no change without constancy—and vice versa.

For instance, on the one hand, there is change (e.g., the ever new ways to understand health, as shown in the study of walkability and health, in *Sec. 2.2.1*; the ever new ways to move around, as shown in the study on the bicycle, in *Sec. 2.2.2*; the ever new ways to understand transportation, as shown in the study on locomotion and energy, in *Sec. 2.3.1*; the ever new ways to design transports, as shown in the study on spacecrafts, in *Sec. 2.3.2*; the ever new ways to build transports, as shown in the study on the automobile industry, in *Sec. 2.4.1*; the ever new ways to ensure safety in transportation, as shown in the study on future car technologies, in *Sec. 2.4.2*; the ever new ways to analyze public transports, as shown in the study on TOD, in *Sec. 2.5.1*; the ever new ways to build transports for society and culture, as shown in the study on the automobile and its cultural changes, in *Sec. 2.5.2*; the ever new ways to provide air safety, as shown in the study on FOD, in *Sec. 3.2.1*; the ever new ways to detect DUI, as shown in field sobriety tests, blood alcohol content tests, etc., in *Sec. 3.2.2*; the ever new ways to understand air pollution in transportation, as shown in the study on air pollution and carbon monoxide, in *Sec. 3.3.1*; the ever new ways to invent transports, as shown in the history of the horse-drawn carriage, in *Sec. 3.3.2*; the ever new ways to engage in hijacking, as shown in the 9/11 suicide skyjackings, in *Sec. 3.4.1*; the ever new ways to expand cities outwards, as shown in the rise of urban sprawl, in *Sec. 3.4.2*; the ever new ways to build new types of transportation, as shown in the invention of rail transport, in *Sec. 3.5.1*; and the ever new ways to build transportation, as shown in the invention of ship transport, in *Sec. 3.5.2*).

On the other hand, there is constancy (e.g., the ever constant existence of different problems in the ever new ways to understand health, as shown in the problems with the study of walkability and health pointed out by the critics, in *Sec. 2.2.1*; the ever constant existence of different problems in the ever new ways to move around, as shown in the problems with the bicycle pointed out by the critics, in *Sec. 2.2.2*; the ever constant existence of different problems in the ever new ways to understand transportation, as shown in the problems with locomotion and energy pointed out by the critics, in *Sec. 2.3.1*; the ever constant existence of different problems in the ever new ways to design transports, as shown in the problems with the history of spacecrafts pointed out by the critics aforecited, in *Sec. 2.3.2*; the ever constant existence of different problems in the ever new ways to build transports, as shown in the problems with the study on the automobile industry pointed out by the critics, in *Sec. 2.4.1*; the ever constant existence of different problems in the ever new ways to ensure safety in transportation, as shown in the problems with future car technologies pointed out by the critics, in *Sec. 2.4.2*; the ever constant existence of different problems in the ever new ways to analyze public transports, as shown in the problems with TOD pointed out by the critics, in *Sec. 2.5.1*; the ever constant existence of different problems in the ever new ways to build transports for society and culture, as shown in the problems with the study on the automobile and its cultural changes pointed out by the critics, in *Sec. 2.5.2*; the ever constant existence of different problems in the ever new ways to provide air safety, as shown in the problems with the study on FOD pointed out by the critics, in *Sec. 3.2.1*; the ever constant existence of different problems in the ever new ways to detect DUI, as shown in the problems with field sobriety tests, blood alcohol content tests, etc. pointed out by the critics, in *Sec. 3.2.2*; the ever constant existence of different problems in the ever new ways to study air pollution in transportation, as shown in the problems with the study on air pollution and carbon monoxide pointed out by the critics aforecited, in *Sec. 3.3.1*; the ever constant existence of different problems in the ever new ways to invent transports, as shown in the problems with the horse-drawn carriage pointed out by the critics, in *Sec. 3.3.2*; the ever constant existence of different problems in the ever new ways to engage in hijacking, as shown in the problems facing skyjackers nowadays, since pilots and flight attendants after the September 11, 2001 attacks are now trained to handle suicide hijackings, so that "future hijackers most likely will encounter greater resistance from passengers and flight crews, making a successful hijacking more unlikely," in *Sec. 3.4.1*; the ever constant existence of different problems in the ever new ways to expand cities, as shown in the problems with urban sprawl pointed out by the critics, in *Sec. 3.4.2*; the ever constant existence of different problems in the ever new ways to build new types of transportation, as shown in the problems with rail transport pointed out by the critics, in *Sec. 3.5.1*; and the ever constant existence of different problems in the ever new ways to build transportation, as shown in the problems with ship transport and the art of sailing pointed out by the critics, in *Sec. 3.5.2*).

And the reverse direction also holds true.

Again, it should be stressed, however, that there are different shades of gray (or different degrees of truth) in the two opposites, and the classification is not necessarily mutually exclusive either. In fact, even when some combinations of the two occur, they only end up sharing the same dialectic relationship, but in a different degree.

Also, there are some other relationships (as a kind of family resemblance) which have something in common with the principle, but they are not exactly the same but only more or less comparable, which varies from case to case.

Good examples of family resemblance in relation to the principle are dynamicness-staticness, instability-stability, and the like.

13th Thesis: The Order-Chaos Principle

The thirteenth thesis is called the the order-chaos principle (on the pattern of things) in the category of "process" in existential dialectics (as first worked out in *FC*), in that both order and chaos are vital in the process of change in the world.

The preference for order is biased, since it does not give sufficient attention to the vital role of chaos in the transformation of the world (without somehow reducing it for the understanding of order). There is no order without chaos—and vice versa.

The scientific search for order in the world is often a hidden bias in its ontological obsession with order, since chaos is often treated as the "bad" guy, with order as the "good" guy (for the end goal of science).

Neither order nor chaos is the final end of the world, and one is not to be treated as the means for the other in the transformation of things. Both are fundamental in their recurrent dialectical interactions with each other over time, without reducing one for the other.

For instance, on the one hand, there is order (e.g., the more or less orderly appearance of reality, if looked from the simple perspective of blaming "mechanized transportation" for the rise of obesity, in *Sec. 2.2.1*; the more or less orderly appearance of the bicycle, if looked from the perspective of when it works properly as expected, in *Sec. 2.2.2*; the more or less orderly view of rocket engines if examined from the observation that "rocket engines can be particularly simple, sometimes consisting of nothing more than a catalyst, as in the case of a hydrogen peroxide rocket," in *Sec. 2.3.1*; the more or less orderly reality of spacecrafts, if examined from the vantage point of all the successful spaceflights in the last few decades, in *Sec. 2.3.2*; the more or less orderly reality of the automobile industry, insofar as it shows the ranking of the top 20 "motor vehicle manufacturing companies by volume" in 2010, in *Sec. 2.4.1*; the more or less orderly appearance of traffic, if looked from the perspective of the "platoons of cars" under advanced control, in *Sec. 2.4.2*; the more or less orderly reality of public transports, if looked from the vantage point of Intelligent Urbanism for TOD in a nicely designed and planned way, in *Sec .2.5.1*; the more or less orderly reality of the car culture, insofar as it brings "status" as "an essential element that surrounds the ownership of a car and this is a basic element of our cultural experience," in *Sec. 2.5.2*; the more or less orderly reality of FOD prevention, if everything follows nicely in accordance to the procedures amd elements in the awareness and training programs afore-described, in *Sec. 3.2.1*; the more or less orderly reality of drunk driving law, if examined from the viewpoint of a particular country like Mongolia, where the blood/alcohol limit is 0.2%, in *Sec. 3.2.2*; the more or less orderly reality of the regulations of air pollution, if looked from the vantage point that there are only two types of air quality standards in the U.S. and Canada aforecited, in *Sec. 3.3.1*; the more or less orderly reality of horse-riding if the five steps suggested by Bettmann are correctly followed, in *Sec. 3.3.2*; the more or less orderly nature of the September 11 attacks, when the 19 hijackers carefully planned their attacks beforehand, in *Sec. 3.4.1*; the more or less orderly appearance of traffic, when there is no traffic jam, in *Sec. 3.4.2*; the more or less orderly reality of "many high-speed inter-city networks such as Japan's Shinkansen," because they "only run on dedicated railway lines, without level crossings" and "this effectively eliminates the potential for collision with automobiles, other vehicles and pedestrians," so they "vastly reduces the likelihood of collision with other trains and helps ensure services remain timely," in *Sec. 3.5.1*; and the more or less orderly sailing of the RMS *Titanic* in the first four days of its journey starting on April 10, 1912, in *Sec. 3.5.2*).

On the other hand, there is chaos (e.g., the more or less chaotic appearance of reality, if looked from the complex perspective of numerous sources of obesity, as well as conflicting findings like the criticism that there were "discrepancies between residents' health in inner city neighborhoods and suburban neighborhoods with similar walkability measures," so it has been suggested that further research is needed...," in *Sec. 2.2.1*; the more or less chaotic appearance of the bicycle, if looked from the perspective of when it does not work properly, especially in accidents which injure or kill those involved, in *Sec. 2.2.2*; the more or less chaotic view of rocket engines if examined from the observation that they "are often dangerous and susceptible to explosions" and "the fuel they run off may be flammable, poisonous, corrosive, or cryogenic," with all kinds of uncertainty, in *Sec. 2.3.1*; the more or less chaotic reality of spacecrafts, if examined from the vantage point of all the disastrous spaceflights in the last few decades, as shown in the failures when "the space shuttle "Challenger...was lost in January 1986," and the other one "Columbia broke up during reentry in February 2003," in *Sec. 2.3.2*; the more or less chaotic reality of the automobile industry, insofar as it is embedded within some highly complex relationships among "automobile manufacturers," such that they "hold stakes in other automobile manufacturers" in different ways, as shown in the examples aforecited, in *Sec. 2.4.1*; the more or less chaotic appearance of traffic, if looked from the perspective of car collisions, espcially in "angled and left-turn collisions" which are more difficult to control, in *Sec. 2.4.2*; the more or less chaotic reality of public transports, if looked from the vantage point of libertarianism "for consumer preference and the free market" in any decision on public transports, in *Sec. 2.5.1*; the more or less chaotic reality of the car culture, insofar as it can also spread diseases and contribute to "a dramatic increase in the rate of accidental death" in a random way, etc., in *Sec. 2.5.2*; the more or less chaotic reality of FOD prevention, if things go unexpectedly, like the accidents by runway debris, volcanic ash, etc. as described earlier, in *Sec. 3.2.1*; the more or less chaotic reality of drunk driving law, if examined from the viewpoints of all the countries around the world, which vary greatly and are complicated enough, in *Sec. 3.2.2*; the more or less chaotic reality of the regulations of air pollution, if looked from the vantage point that "the AQHI program would not be possible without the commitment and support of the provinces, municipalities and NGOs," which do not always agree, in *Sec. 3.3.1*; the more or less chaotic reality of horse-riding if the five steps suggested by Bettmann are ignored, such that they lead to "disastrous results," in *Sec. 3.3.2*; the more or less chaotic nature of the September 11 attacks, when, in the final mintuies of Flight 93, crew and passengers fought with hijackers and "attempted to seize control of the plane from the hijackers after learning through phone calls that similarly hijacked planes had been crashed into buildings that morning," before they all died in a crash shortly after, in *Sec. 3.4.1*; the more or less chaotic appearance of traffic, when there is a massive traffic jam, in *Sec. 3.4.2*; the more or less chaotic reality of trains, when they involve in accidents like "derailment," "a collision with another train," or "collision with an automobile or other vehicle at level crossings," in *Sec. 3.4.2*; and the more or less chaotic sinking of the RMS *Titanic* on 15 April 1912 after colliding with an iceberg, which caused the deaths of 1,514 people, in *Sec. 3.5.2*).

And the reverse direction also holds true.

Once more, it should be stressed, however, that there are different shades of gray (or different degrees of truth) in the two opposites, and the classification is not necessarily mutually exclusive either. In fact, even when some combinations of the two occur, they only end up sharing the same dialectic relationship, but in a different degree.

Also, there are some other relationships (as a kind of family resemblance) which have something in common with the principle, but they are not exactly the same but only more or less comparable, which varies from case to case.

Good examples of family resemblance in relation to the principle are lawfulness-disorder, order-disorder, pattern-chaos, linearity-nonlinearity, unity-disunity, linearity-irreversalness, etc.

14th Thesis: The Slowness-Quickness Principle

The fourteenth thesis concerns the slowness-quickness principle (on the speed of change) in the category of "process" in existential dialectics (which was first worked out in *FIA*), in that both slowness and quickness co-exist, with their own internal tension, to the extent that each fights for its own relevance with the other, in accordance to the perspectives of nature, the mind, culture, and society, without one being the victor and the other being the vanquished in the long haul. There is no slowness without quickness—and vice versa.

For instance, on the one hand, there is slowness (e.g., the relatively slower speed of an individual to become obese if he makes good use of the benefits of walkability, in *Sec. 2.2.1*; the relatively slower speed of the bicycle, when contrasted with that of the automobile, in *Sec. 2.2.2*; the relatively slower speed of a human-powered vehicle, in *Sec. 2.3.1*; the relatively slower speed of "human powered vehicles" which can travel up to "133 km/h [83 mph], as of 2009," in *Sec. 2.3.2*; the relatively slower speed of the U.S. in the automible industry to lose its #1 ranking, that is, from 1929 to 2005, when it lost the top spot to Japan, in *Sec. 2.4.1*; the relatively slower speed of future cars to use energy, as shown by "ultra-low-drag vehicles" which "take significantly less energy to push through the air," in *Sec. 2.4.2*; the relatively slower speed of a pedestrian to get where he wants to go, if transit stops are not readily available as seen in suburbanization, in *Sec. 2.5.1*; the relatively slower speed of walking or streetcars, in *Sec. 2.5.2*; the relatively slower speed of an aircraft to suffer from potential damages, if the pilots are well trained in formal FOD prevention programs, when confronted with these objects, in *Sec. 3.2.1*; the relatively slower speed of someone to get drunk if he consumes a small amount of alcohol, in *Sec. 3.2.2*; the relatively slower speed of someone to get sick, if he inhales "concentrations" of carbon monoxide much less than 50 ppm, in *Sec. 3.3.1*; the relatively slower speed of horse-drawn carriages in antiquity, when they were relatively heavy, in *Sec. 3.3.2*; the relatively slower speed of the North Tower in the World Trade Center Complex to collapse "after burning for 102 minutes," in *Sec. 3.4.1*; the relatively slower speed of drivers with speed limit reductions to be enforced, in *Sec. 3.4.2*; the relatively slower speed of pre-steam rail transport, when "the line originally used wooden rails and a hemp haulage rope, and was operated by human or animal power," in *Sec. 3.5.1*; and the relatively slower speed of ships when powered by sails in the wind, in *Sec. 3.5.2*).

On the other hand, there is quickness (e.g., the relatively quicker speed of an individual to become obese if he depends too much on mechanized transportation, in *Sec. 2.2.1*; the relatively quicker speed of the bicycle, when contrasted with that of walking, in *Sec. 2.2.2*; the relatively quicker speed of a rocket like the Saturn V rocket, in *Sec. 2.3.1*; the relatively quicker speed of Sputnik which "travelled at 29,000 kilometers [18,000 mi] per hour, taking 96.2 minutes to complete an orbit" in 1957, in *Sec. 2.3.2*; the relatively quicker speed of Japan in the automible industry to lose its #1 ranking, that is, from 2006 to 2009, when it lost the top spot to Chin, in *Sec. 2.4.1*; the relatively quicker speed of conventional cars to use energy, because "conventional automobiles operate at about 15% efficiency" and "the rest of the energy is lost to engine and drive-train inefficiencies and idling," in *Sec. 2.4.2*; the relatively quicker speed of a pedestrian to get where he wants to go, if transit stops are readily available as required by TOD, *in Sec. 2.5.1*; the relatively quicker speed of the automobile, in *Sec. 2.5.2*; the relatively quicker speed of an aircraft to suffer from potential damages when unexpectedly surrounded by FOD, if the pilots are not well trained in formal FOD prevention programs, in *Sec. 3.2.1*; the relatively quicker speed of someone to get drunk if he consumes an extreme level of consumption like "alcohol poisoning," in *Sec. 3.2.2*; the relatively quicker speed of someone to get sick, if he inhales "concentrations" of carbon monoxide "as low as 667 ppm" or more, in *Sec. 3.3.1*; the relatively quicker speed of horse-drawn carriages, when "under King Mathias Corvinus [1458–90], who enjoyed fast travel, the Hungarians developed fast road transport," and "carriages were made lighter and needed only one horse to haul the carriage," in *Sec. 3.3.2*; the relatively quicker speed of the South Tower in the World Trade Center Complex to collapse "after burning for 56 minutes," in *Sec. 3.4.1*; the relatively quicker speed of drivers without any speed limit reductions, in *Sec. 3.4.2*; the relatively quicker speed of a modified French TGV at the speed record of 574.8 km/h, when contrasted with the pre-steam rail transport, in *Sec. 3.5.1*; and the relatively quicker speed of ships when powered by a modern nuclear reactor, in *Sec. 3.5.2*).

And the reverse direction also holds true.

Again, it should be stressed, however, that there are different shades of gray (or different degrees of truth) in the two opposites, and the classification is not necessarily mutually exclusive either. In fact, even when some combinations of the two occur, they only end up sharing the same dialectic relationship, but in a different degree.

Also, there are some other relationships (as a kind of family resemblance) which have something in common with the principle, but they are not exactly the same but only more or less comparable, which varies from case to case.

Good examples of family resemblance in relation to the principle are inconvenience-convenience, passiveness-activenessness, gradualness-abruptness, deceleration-acceleration, difficulty-ease, and the like.

15th Thesis: The Expansion-Contraction Principle

The fifteenth thesis is called the expansion-contraction principle in the category of "process" in existential dialectics, in that entities in the world can both expand in some ways and contract in other ones, as part of their nature. There is no expansion without contraction—and vice versa.

This principle, although not so explicitly called, was already used in my previous works on different topics (e.g., the theory of floating consciousness in *FCD* and *FPHC*, the union of the unions in *BWT*, and the cyclical progression of system fragmentation and integration in *FCD*).

For instance, on the one hand, there is expansion (e.g., the relative spread of the use of automobiles in "twentieth century…automated metropolis," in *Sec. 2.2.1*; the relative spread of the presence of the automobile as a form of transportation nowadays, in *Sec. 2.2.2*; the relative spread of the use of electrical energy for transportation nowadays, as seen in "electrified rails and overhead cables" for "subways, railways, trams, and trolleybuses," in *Sec. 2.3.1*; the relative spread of the use of spacecrafts in the last few decades, in *Sec. 2.3.2*; the relative rise of China as the top car manufacturer in the world nowadays, in *Sec. 2.4.1*; the relative spread of the use of advanced control and VII in future transportation systems, in *Sec. 2.4.2*; the relative spread of TOD nowadays in North American and European cities, for instance, in *Sec. 2.5.1*; the relative spread of individualism in a car culture, in *Sec. 2.5.2*; the relative spread, in terms of proportion, of human-made objects like tools, bolts, aircraft parts, vehicle pieces, etc. which can damage aircrafts, in the modern era of aviation, in *Sec. 3.2.1*; the relative spread of the use of alcohol nowadays, when contrasted with the period during the Prohibition in the United States from 1919 to 1933, in *Sec. 3.2.2*; the relative spread of more regulations of the use of carbon monoxide nowadays, in *Sec. 3.3.1*; the relative spread of the use of rail transports in the 20th century, in *Sec. 3.3.2*; the expansion of the World Trade Center Complex when it was first built from the ground up to more than 100 floors, in *Sec. 3.4.1*; the relative spread of cities to the outskirts into "low-density and auto-dependent developments" nowadays, in *Sec. 3.4.2*; the relative spread of the use of "high-speed inter-city networks" nowadays, in *Sec. 3.5.1*; and the relative spread of the use of ships powered by mechanical engines like diesel engines, gas turbine engines, nuclear reactors, etc. on hight seas nowadays, in *Sec. 3.5.2*).

On the other hand, there is contraction (e.g., the relative decline of gait in "twentieth century…automated metropolis," in *Sec. 2.2.1*; the relative decline of the presence of horses as a form of transportation nowadays, in *Sec. 2.2.2*; the relative decline of the use of human-powered vehicles for transportation nowadays, in *Sec. 2.3.1*; the relative decline of the use of pulled rickshaws inte last few decades, in *Sec. 2.3.2*; the relative decline of the U.S. as the #3 car manufacturer in the world nowadays, in *Sec. 2.4.1*; the relative decline of the use of conventional car designs in future transportation systems, in *Sec. 2.4.2*; the relative decline of old-fashioned suburbanization nowadays in North American and European cities, for instance, in *Sec. 2.5.1*; the relative decline of close social interactions in a car culture, in *Sec. 2.5.2*; the relative decline, in terms of proportion, of natural objects like rocks, dust, ash, etc. which can damage aircrafts, in the modern era of aviation, in *Sec. 3.2.1*; the relative decline of the use of alcohol during the Prohibition in the United States from 1919 to 1933, when contrasted with the use nowadays, in *Sec. 3.2.2*; the relative decline of the deliberate use of carbon monoxide to harm people nowadays, as the Nazis did "during the Holocaust at some Nazi extermination camps, the most notable by gas vans in Chelmno, and in the Action T4 'euthanasia' program," in *Sec. 3.3.1*; the relative decline of the use of horse-drawn carriages in the 20th century, in *Sec. 3.3.2*; the collapse of the World Trade Center Complex after the September 11 attacks, in *Sec. 3.4.1*; the relative decline of "bicycling-oriented" and "pedestrian-oriented" areas in modern cities, when contrasted with those in the older days, in *Sec. 3.4.2*; the relative decline of the use of pre-steam rail transports nowadays, in *Sec. 3.5.1*; and the relative decline of the use of ships powered by old-fashioned sails on high seas nowadays, in *Sec. 3.5.2*).

And the reverse direction also holds true.

Again, it should be stressed, however, that there are different shades of gray (or different degrees of truth) in the two opposites, and the classification is not necessarily mutually exclusive either. In fact, even when some combinations of the two occur, they only end up sharing the same dialectic relationship, but in a different degree.

Also, there are some other relationships (as a kind of family resemblance) which have something in common with the principle, but they are not exactly the same but only more or less comparable, which varies from case to case.

Good examples of family resemblance in relation to the principle are conquest-autarky, rise-fall (or up-down), spread-shrink, extendingness-shorteningness, widening-narrowing, and so forth.

In Relation to Agency

The next seven theses are in relation to agency in existential dialectics, as shown below.

16th Thesis: The Theory-Praxis Principle

The sixteenth thesis is the theory-praxis principle (on the duality of knowledge) in the category of "agency" in existential dialectics (which was first worked out in *FPHE*), in that, if there is theoretical construction, there is likewise its practical application, both technical and normative. There is no theory without praxis—and vice versa.

For instance, on the one hand, there is theory (e.g., the theoretical construction of the benefits of "walkability" in the evolutionary study aforecited, in *Sec. 2.2.1*; the theoretical construction of "head trauma" in psychology and biology, in *Sec. 2.2.2*; the theoretical construction of "nuclear energy" in physics, in *Sec. 2.3.1*; the theoretical construction of rockets and aircrafts in rocket science, in *Sec. 2.3.2*; the theoretical exploration of "gasoline" as "organic compounds obtained by the fractional distillation of petroleum, enhanced with a variety of additives" in the field of chemistry, in *Sec. 2.4.1*; the theoretical construction of energy efficiency in physics, in *Sec. 2.4.2*; the theoretical construction of Intelligent Urbanism in urban planning, in *Sec. 2.5.1*; the theoretical construction of "the commodification of identity" in culture studies, in *Sec. 2.5.2*; the theoretical construction of "public relations campaign" in communication studies, in *Sec. 3.2.1*; the theoretical construction of the interdisciplinary approach by the Medical Psychological Assessment in Germany to understand "the fitness for drive," in *Sec. 3.2.2*; the theoretical construction of the molecular properties of carbon monoxide in chemistry in order to understand its toxicity, in *Sec. 3.3.1*; the theoretical construction of the "body" and the "undergear" in mechanical engineering, in *Sec. 3.3.2*; the theoretical construction of "global jihad" in accordance to the radical interpretation of the Sunni Muslim movement like al-Qaeda, in *Sec. 3.4.1*; the theoretical construction of' "butterfly effects" in chaos theory, in *Sec. 3.4.2*; the theoretical construction of electromagnetic force in physics, in *Sec. 3.5.1*; and the theoretical construction of nuclear force in physics, in *Sec. 3.5.2*).

On the other hand, there is praxis (e.g., the practical application of the theoretical research on the benefits of walkability in evolutionary study to the field of urban planning, like those for "pedestrian oriented development," in *Sec. 2.2.1*; the practical application of "head trauma" in psychology and biology to the field of transportation, as shown in the call to "wear helmets, as this may protect riders from head trauma," in *Sec. 2.2.2*; the practical application of "nuclear energy" to the field of transportation like the "experiments with nuclear powered aircraft" such as "the Tupolev Tu-119 and the Convair X-6," in *Sec. 2.3.1*; the practical application of rockets and aircrafts in rocket science to the field of politics, like the space race between the two superpowers during the Cold War, in *Sec. 2.3.2*; the practical application of gasoline in chemistry to the field of transportation, like its use by the automobile industry, in *Sec. 2.4.1*; the practical application of energy efficiency in physics to the field of transportation, like "energy saver" in future car technologies, in *Sec. 2.4.2*; the practical application of Intelligent Urbanism in urban planning to the field of transportation, as shown in the arrangement of transit stops in accordance to TOD, in *Sec. 2.5.1*; the practical application of "the commodification of identity" in culture studies to the field of transportation, when the issue of "the commodification of identity" is "to be intimately connected with the automobile," in *Sec. 2.5.2*; the practical application of "public relations campaign" in communication studies to the field of transportation, like the "Promotion and Awareness Program" by Chaplin to prevent FOD, in *Sec. 3.2.1*; the practical application of the interdisciplinary approach by the Medical Psychological Assessment in psychology to the field of law enforcement, like the removal of certain drivers "from traffic until their fitness to drive has been established again," in *Sec. 3.2.2*; the practical application of the molecular properties of carbon monoxide in chemistry to the field of transportation so as to deal with its toxicity, as shown in the regulations of air pollution in accordance to the AQHI program, in *Sec. 3.3.1*; the practical application of the "body" and the "undergear" in mechanical engineering to the fields of sports and entertainment, as shown in the use of the horse-drawn carriage for "competitive driving" nowadays, in *Sec. 3.3.2*; the practical application of "global jihad" to the field of skyjacking, as shown in the September 11 attacks by the skyjackers linked to al-Qaeda, in *Sec. 3.4.1*; the practical application of "butterfly effects" in chaos theory to the field of transportation to understand traffic congestion, in *Sec. 3.4.2*; the practical application of of electromagnetic force in physics to the field of transportation, like the invention of electrical rail transport, in *Sec. 3.5.1*;

and the practical application of nuclear force in physics to the field of transportation, like sailing a ship with a nuclear reactor, in *Sec. 3.5.2*).

And the reverse direction also holds true.

Again, it should be stressed, however, that there are different shades of gray (or different degrees of truth) in the two opposites, and the classification is not necessarily mutually exclusive either. In fact, even when some combinations of the two occur, they only end up sharing the same dialectic relationship, but in a different degree.

Also, there are some other relationships (as a kind of family resemblance) which have something in common with the principle, but they are not exactly the same but only more or less comparable, which varies from case to case.

Good examples of family resemblance in relation to the principle are discovery-application, knowledge-action, invention-innovation, theory-intentionality, discourse-action, knowledge-interest, knowledge-motivation, universality-particularity, and so forth.

17th Thesis: The Convention-Novelty Principle

The seventeenth thesis is the convention-novelty principle (on the nature of creative thinking) in the category of "agency" in existential dialectics (which was first worked out in *FPHCT*), in that, if there is conventional wisdom, there is likewise novel challenge, to the extent that both convergent and divergent thinking are part of life. There is no convention without novelty—and vice versa.

As srummarized from *FPHCT* (almost verbatim here), there are (a) "creative techniques" and (b) "creative traits," which, when satisfied—in relation to the larger context of the mind, nature, society, and culture—can be used to enhance creative works.

In addition, creative thinking has its own possibilities and limits (in relation to invention), just as it has its own promises and pitfalls (in relation to innovation)— as already analyzed in *FPHCT*).

In the end, creative thinking has its own desirability and dark sides (as also already analyzed in *FPHCT*).

With these clarifications in mind—there are good empirical examples for the convention-novelty princple.

For instance, on the one hand, there is convention (e.g., the conventional wisdom about the benefits of the "twentieth century automotive and automated metropolis" in the older days, in *Sec. 2.2.1*; the conventional wisdom about using horses as a form of transportation in antiquity, in *Sec. 2.2.2*; the conventional wisdom about using wheels for transportation in antiquity, in *Sec. 2.3.1*; the conventional wisdom of using cars for transportation in modern times, in *Sec. 2.3.2*; the conventional way of building a practical automobile when Karl Benz in the early 1880s build "a horse-drawn carriage," in *Sec. 2.4.1*; the conventional wisdom about driving a car by a human driver, in *Sec. 2.4.2*; the conventional wisdom about suburbanization in the earlier days, in *Sec. 2.5.1*; the conventional wisdom about the convenience of the automobile in the older "glory days" of car culture, in *Sec. 2.5.2*; the conventional wisdom about the FOD "bible" written by Gary Chaplin for the "Promotion and Awareness Program," in *Sec. 3.2.1*; the conventional wisdom about the use of field sobriety tests in the older days, in *Sec. 3.2.2*; the conventional wisdom about the regulations of the use of carbon monoxide, because of its toxcity which can harm people, in *Sec. 3.3.1*; the conventional wisdom about constructing carriages with "two or 3 wheels" in ancient times, in *Sec. 3.3.2*; the conventional wisdom of skyjacking in the older days, when "most aircraft hijackers intend to use the passengers as hostages, either for monetary ransom or for some political or administrative concession by authorities," in *Sec. 3.4.1*; the conventional wisdom of urban sprawl by its defenders, in *Sec. 3.4.2*; the conventional wisdom about pre-steam rail transport in the older days, in *Sec. 3.5.1*; and the conventional wisdom sailing a ship in the wind in the older days, in *Sec. 3.5.2*).

On the other hand, there is novelty (e.g., the alternative novel challenge to the conventional wisdom about the benefits of the "twentieth century automotive and automated metropolis" in the older days, by the new idea of "pedestrian oriented development" for more walkability nowadays, in *Sec. 2.2.1*; the alternative novel challenge to the conventional wisdom about about using horses as a form of transportation in antiquity, by the new idea of using bicycles since the 19th century, in *Sec. 2.2.2*; the alternative novel challenge to the conventional wisdom about using wheels for transportation in antiquity, by the new idea of using nozzles for "jet aircraft," "rockets" and the like nowadays, in *Sec. 2.3.1*; the alternative novel challenge to the conventional wisdom about using cars for transportation in modern times, by the new idea of using spaceplanes nowadays, like the proposal by "XCOR Aerospace…to initiate a suborbital commercial spaceflight service" in the foreseeable future, in *Sec. 2.3.2*; the alternative novel challenge to the conventional way of building a practical automobile like Benz's "horse-drawn carriage," by the new idea of a better automobile when "in 1889, Gottlieb Daimler and Wilhelm Maybach in Stuttgart designed a vehicle from scratch to be an automobile, rather than a horse-drawn carriage fitted with an engine," in *Sec. 2.4.1*; the alternative novel challenge to the conventional wisdom about driving a car by a human driver, by the new idea of "driverless cars," which allows a car to be driven without human intervention, in *Sec. 2.4.2*; the alternative novel challenge to the conventional wisdom about suburbanization in the earlier days, by the new idea of TOD for "human scale" with the focus on the "pedestrian" nowadays, in *Sec. 2.5.1*; the alternative novel challenge to the conventional wisdom about the convenience of the automobile in the older "glory days" of car culture, by the new idea of New Pedestrianism to replace the dominant influence of the car culture, in *Sec. 2.5.2*; the alternative novel challenge to the conventional wisdom about the FOD "bible" written by Gary Chaplin for the "Promotion and Awareness Program, by the new idea of the critics that awareness and training are not enough, as sophisticated technologies are also needed, in *Sec. 3.2.1*; the alternative novel challenge to the conventional wisdom about the use of field sobriety tests in the older days, by the new idea of blood alcohol content tests, which are regarded as more "scientific" nowadays, in *Sec. 3.2.2*; the alternative novel challenge to the conventional wisdom about the regulations of the use of carbon monoxide, by the new idea of the Nazis, who used carbon monoxide "during the Holocaust at some Nazi extermination camps, the most notable by gas vans in Chelmno, and in the Action T4 'euthanasia' program," in *Sec. 3.3.1*; the alternative novel challenge to the conventional wisdom about constructing carriages with "two or 3 wheels" in ancient times, by the new idea of constructing "pageant wagons" which have "four to six wheels depending on the size of the wagon" in early modern times, in *Sec. 3.3.2*; the alternative novel challenge to the conventional wisdom about skyjacking in the older days, by the new idea of skyjacking by those in the September 11 attacks, when the attackers engaged in "suicide hijacking," in *Sec. 3.4.1*; the alternative novel challenge to the conventional wisdom about urban sprawl by its defenders, by the new idea of "bicycling-oriented development" and "pedestrian-oriented development" as countermesures to urban sprawl, in *Sec. 3.4.2*; the alternative novel challenge to the conventional wisdom about pre-steam rail transport in the older days, by the new idea of electrical rail transport in modern times, in *Sec. 3.5.1*; and the alternative novel challenge to the conventional wisdom about sailing a ship in the wind in the older days, by the new idea of sailing a ship with a nuclear reactor, in *Sec. 3.5.2*).

And the reverse direction also holds true.

Again, it should be stressed, however, that there are different shades of gray (or different degrees of truth) in the two opposites, and the classification is not necessarily mutually exclusive either. In fact, even when some combinations of the two occur, they only end up sharing the same dialectic relationship, but in a different degree.

Also, there are some other relationships (as a kind of family resemblance) which have something in common with the principle, but they are not exactly the same but only more or less comparable, which varies from case to case.

Good examples of family resemblance in relation to the principle are convergence-divergence (or convergent thinking vs. divergent thinking), normalness-nonnormalness, conformity-nonconformity, and so on.

18th Thesis: The Evolution-Transformation Principle

The eighteenth thesis refers to the evolution-transformation principle (on the multiple kinds of agency). in the category of "agency" in existential dialectics (which was first worked out in *FAE* and then in other books of mine).

This principle—and the symmetry-asymmetry principle, for instance—are both about agency. More precisely, the word "agency," in a formal definition, refers to "a person or thing through which power is exerted or an end is achieved." (MWD 2007) It therefore does not have to necessarily involve an intelligent lifeform.

Because of this dual meaning in agency, the evolution-transformation principle is more concerned with *the kind of agency*, that is, both about the *evolution* in the state of nature (e.g., an object of natural beauty) and the *transformation* in the world of intelligent lifeforms (e.g., a work of art). There is no evolution without transformation—and vice versa.

In classical Darwinian evolutionary theory (as more detailedly analyzed in *BNN*), evolution is "blind." But in the human world, change often takes place because of the conscious intervention of humans in transforming society and culture, just to cite two instances.

And the transformative part of the principle precisely refers to the other dimension in the dual meaning of agency, in giving technology (as invented by intelligent lifeforms like humans and, soon, post-humans) a major role to play in the change of the world, which is something that I extensively analyzed in *FHC* in the context of the technophilic lifeworld, espeically though not exclusively since modern times. The same theme is also elaborated in many other books of mine.

For instance, on the one hand, there is evolution (e.g., the natural evolution of humans to depend on gait in the state of nature, in *Sec. 2.2.1*; the natural evolution of humans to walk and run in the state of nature, in *Sec. 2.2.2*; the natural evolution of humans to walk and run in the state of nature in a primitive way, in *Sec. 2.3.1*; the natural evolution of humans to move around on foot in the state of nature in a primitive way, in *Sec. 2.3.2*; the natural evolution of humans to walk and run in the state of nature, in *Sec. 2.4.1*; the natural evolution of humans to walk, run, or jump in the state of nature in a primitive way, in *Sec. 2.4.2*; the natural evolution of humans to live in small groups, as they mix and interact on a face-to-face basis in the state of nature, in *Sec. 2.5.1*; the natural evolution of humans to walk in the state of nature, in *Sec. 2.5.2*; the natural evolution of humans to be hit by ice, dust, ash, etc. in the state of nature in a primitive way, in *Sec. 3.2.1*; the natural evolution of humans to sleep or to be not in an alert state of mind from time to time in the state of nature, in *Sec. 3.2.2*; the natural evolution of CO to occur in nature, via "volcanoes, forest fires, and other forms of combustion," in *Sec. 3.3.1*; the natural evolution of humans to walk and run in the state of nature in a primitive way, in *Sec. 3.3.2*; the natural evolution of humans to fight with each other from time to time in the state of nature in a primitive way, in *Sec. 3.4.1*; the natural evolution of humans to walk and run in the state of nature in a primitive way, in *Sec. 3.4.2*; the natural evolution of humans to move around by foot in the state of nature in a primitive way, in *Sec. 3.5.1*; and the natural evolution of humans to move through water by swimming for a brief time in the state of nature, in a primitive way, in *Sec. 3.5.2*).

On the other hand, there is transformation (e.g., the technical transformation of human ability to move around by the invention of "mechanized transportation" nowadays, in *Sec. 2.2.1*; the technical transformation of human ability to move around by the invention of the bicycle, in *Sec. 2.2.2*; the technical transformation of human ability to move around by the invention of a rocket like the Saturn V rocket, in *Sec. 2.3.1*; the technical transformation of human ability to move around by the invention of spacecrafts, in *Sec. 2.3.2*; the technical transformation of human ability to move around by the invention of the automobile and the industry to produce it in large numbers, in *Sec. 2.4.1*; the technical transformation of human ability to walk, run, and jump by the invention of "driverless cars" and "planes on autopilot," in *Sec. 2.4.2*; the technical transformation of human ability to interact by the invention of suburbanization, where the value of the "pedestrian" is eroded, in *Sec. 2.5.1*; the technical transformation of human ability to move around by the invention of the automobile, together with the car culture to glorify it, in *Sec. 2.5.2*; the technical transformation of human ability to be hit by the invention of aircrafts, which suffer from potential FOD damages, in *Sec. 3.2.1*; the technical transformation of human ability to be not in an alert state of mind from time to time by the invention of alcoholic intoxication, as shown in drunk driving, which did not exist in the state of nature, in *Sec. 3.2.2*; the technical transformation of human ability to manufacture CO artificially by the invention of "an internal combustion engine in an enclosed space," for instance, in *Sec. 3.3.1*; the technical transformation of human ability to move around by the invention of the horse-drawn carriage, in *Sec. 3.3.2*; the technical transformation of human ability to fight with each other by the invention of suicide skyjacking, in *Sec. 3.4.1*; the technical transformation of human ability to walk and run by the invention of automobiles, with auto-dependency in urban sprawl, in *Sec. 3.4.2*; the technical transformation of human ability to move around by the invention of rail transport, in *Sec. 3.5.1*; and the technical transformation of human ability to cross the oceans by the invention of huge ships, in *Sec. 3.5.2*).

And the reverse direction also holds true.

Again, it should be stressed, however, that there are different shades of gray (or different degrees of truth) in the two opposites, and the classification is not necessarily mutually exclusive either. In fact, even when some combinations of the two occur, they only end up sharing the same dialectic relationship, but in a different degree.

Also, there are some other relationships (as a kind of family resemblance) which have something in common with the principle, but they are not exactly the same but only more or less comparable, which varies from case to case.

Good examples of family resemblance in relation to the principle are inorganicness-volition, naturalness-technologicalness, naturalness-nonnaturalness, nonwillingness-willingness, inorganicness-motivation, evolution-creation, naturalness-artificialness, and so on.

19th Thesis: The Symmetry-Asymmetry Principle

The nineteenth thesis is labeled as the symmetry-asymmetry principle (on the relationships among existents) in the category of "agency" in existential dialectics (which was also already worked out in my previous books), in that there is no asymmetry without symmetry—and vice versa.

For instance, the Same can be symmetric and asymmetric towards the Others. But in case of asymmetry (as analyzed in *BDPD*), oppression and self-oppression can occur. So, when the Same is asymmetric towards the Others, the Same can also be relatively asymmetric towards itself in self-oppression, just as the Others can be likewise towards themselves. The subsequent oppressiveness is dualistic, as much by the Same against the Others and itself, as by the Others against the Same and themselves. Both oppression and self-oppression can be achieved by way of downgrading differences between the Same and the Others and of accentuating them.

This is true, even though not all forms of asymmetry have to be about oppression and self-oppression.

In addition, from Chapter Three of *FPHG*, symmetry is not perfect, to be understood in an approximate sense under many life circumstances. With this clarification in mind, hereafter are some empirical examples.

For instance, on the one hand, there is symmetry (e.g., the existence of different ways to move around, like walking and driving, in *Sec. 2.2.1*; the existence of different forms of transportation, like walking, horse-riding, cycling, etc., in *Sec. 2.2.2*; the existence of different vehicles for transportation, like rockets and human-powered vehicles, in *Sec. 2.3.1*; the existence of different ways to fly, like helicopters and spacecrafts, in *Sec. 2.3.2*; the existence of different countries like China, France, and others to produce motor vehicles, in *Sec. 2.4.1*; the existence of different car technologies, in *Sec. 2.4.2*; the existence of different ways to arrange "access to public transport," in *Sec. 2.5.1*; the existence of different modes of transportation, in *Sec. 2.5.2*; the existence of different Insight SRI reports about FOD, in *Sec. 3.2.1*; the existence of different agents in society, like drivers, police officers, etc., in *Sec. 3.2.2*; the existence of different views about the use of carbon monoxide, in *Sec. 3.3.1*; the existence of different means of transportation, like carriages and rail transports, in *Sec. 3.3.2*; the existence of different individuals inside a plane, be they crew, flight attendants, passengers, and skyjackers, in *Sec. 3.4.1*; the existence of different operators of vehicles in traffic, in *Sec. 3.4.2*; the existence of different players in society, like railroad company, government, etc., in *Sec. 3.5.1*; and the existence of different members on a ship, like the Pilot, the Master, etc., in *Sec. 3.5.2*).

On the other hand, there is asymmetry (e.g., the dominance of gait in the state of nature—but the dominance of driving in 20th century metropolis, in *Sec. 2.2.1*; the popularity of hourse-riding in antiquity—but the popularity of cycling in the 19th century and beyond, in *Sec. 2.2.2*; rockets are more powerful than human-powered vehicles, because "the heaviest vehicle to ever leave the ground, the Saturn V rocket, was powered by five F-1 rocket engines generating a combined 180 million horsepower [134,226 megawatt]," in *Sec. 2.3.1*; spacecrafts can fly much higher and faster than helicopters, in *Sec. 2.3.2*; China was the top motor vehicle producer in 2010, whereas France was #10 on the list instead, in *Sec. 2.4.1*; future car technologies for advanced control, alternative energy soruces, energy saver, and new materials are getting more and popular now than conventional car technologies, in *Sec. 2.4.2*; TOD is more influential now as a way to arrange "access to public transport" than its alternative like suburbanization, in *Sec. 2.5.1*; a car is faster and more powerful in carrying things than a horse over long distance, on average, in *Sec. 2.5.2*; the 2010 Insight SRI report about FOD is now more influential than the 2007 Insight SRI report, in *Sec. 3.2.1*; police officers have the power to arrest drivers under the influence, in *Sec. 3.2.2*; the push for regulations of the use of carbon monoxide nowadays is more influential than its deliterate use to harm people in the older days by the Nazis, for example, in *Sec. 3.3.1*; rail transports are more powerful than horse-drawn carriages, which "began to disappear as use of steam propulsion began to generate more and more interest" in the 19th century and beyond, when "steam power quickly won the battle against animal power," in *Sec. 3.3.2*; skyjackers can use force, weapons, and other means to take over a plane and to fly it according to their orders, contrary to the wishes of the pilots, flight attendants, and passengers, in *Sec. 3.4.1*; "in heavy but free flowing traffic, jams can arise spontaneously, triggered by minor events ['butterfly effects'], such as an abrupt steering maneuver by a single motorist," so that a normal motorist who follows the traffic rules and does not make any abrupt moves cannot cause, on average, such a traffic jam but another motorist who makes "an abrupt steering maneuver" can, in *Sec. 3.4.2*; government has the power to provide subsidy to railroad company, as shown in the example that the U.S. government aid "supports Amtrak by supplying start-up capital and makes up for loses at end of the fiscal year," in *Sec. 3.5.1*; and "the general Rule of Thumb is that a Pilot assumes command of a vessel and is not classed as 'an advisor' in the Panama Canal, crossing the sill of a drydock, or in any port in Russia…or, perhaps, all the old Soviet States," so "when a Pilot is in command, the Master can not take any action, but is limited to advising the Pilot on any circumstance that creates what he considers a dangerous situation," in *Sec. 3.5.2*).

And the reverse direction also holds true.

Again, for the last time, it should be stressed, however, that there are different shades of gray (or different degrees of truth) in the two opposites, and the classification is not necessarily mutually exclusive either. In fact, even when some combinations of the two occur, they only end up sharing the same dialectic relationship, but in a different degree.

Also, there are some other relationships (as a kind of family resemblance) which have something in common with the principle, but they are not exactly the same but only more or less comparable, which varies from case to case.

Good examples of family resemblance in relation to the principle are balance-extremity, reflexiveness-unreflexiveness, equality-inequality, harmoniousness-unharrmoniousness, center-periphery, compatibility-incompatibility, proportion-disproportion, balance-unbalance, and something like that.

20th Thesis: The Softness-Hardness Principle

The twentieth thesis refers to the softness-hardness principle (on the force of change) in the category of "agency" in existential dialectics (which was first worked out in *ALD*), in that any change by an agent, be it organic (like humans) or non-organic (like natural objects), can occur in a forceful (aggressive) or gentle (pacific) way, which can come in all shapes and sizes, of course. There is no softness without hardness—and vice versa.

For instance, on the one hand, there is softness (e.g., the appreciation of walkability by the advocates of "pedestrian oriented development," in *Sec. 2.2.1*; the appreciation of the bicycle, as shown in the slogan of "freedom machine" by the feminists, in *Sec. 2.2.2*; the appreciation of rockets, as shown in the observation that "rocket engines are extremely powerful," in *Sec. 2.3.1*; the appreciation of spacecrafts by the Soviet Union and the U.S. in their space race during the Cold War, in *Sec. 2.3.2*; the appreciation of the automobile industry, as shown in the creation of the Ford Motor Company in the early 20th century by Henry Ford, in *Sec. 2.4.1*; the appreciation of future car technologies, as shown in the support by the advocates in the article aforecited, in *Sec. 2.4.2*; the appreciation of TOD, as shown in its implementation in cities around the world in the article aforecited, in *Sec. 2.5.1*; the glorfication of the car culture by its advocates, in *Sec. 2.5.2*; the appreciation of the "public relations campaign" for FOD prevention, as shown by the FOD "bible" written by Gary Chaplin for the "Promotion and Awareness Program," in *Sec. 3.2.1*; the appreciation of field sobriety tests, as shown in their use by police officers, in *Sec. 3.2.2*; the appreciation of the regulations of air pollution, as shown in the North American Air Quality Index, in *Sec. 3.3.1*; the appreciation of the horse-drawn carriage, as shown in its pervasive use in pre-modern times, in *Sec. 3.3.2*; the appreciation of the September 11 attacks by the 19 skyjackers, in *Sec. 3.4.1*; the appreciation of urban sprawl, as shown by "one suburban Detroit politician" who "defends low-density development as the preferred lifestyle choice of his constituents, calling it '...the American Dream unfolding before your eyes,'" in *Sec. 3.4.2*; the appreciation of steam rail transport, as shown by James Watt's patented steam engines of 1769, in *Sec. 3.5.1*; and the appreciation of seamanship, as shown by those sailors who use it to live at sea, in *Sec. 3.5.2*).

On the other hand, there is hardness (e.g., the critique of walkability by the supporters of the car culture, in *Sec. 2.2.1*; the critique of the bicycle, as shown in the problems pointed out by the critics as cited, in *Sec. 2.2.2*; the critique of rockets, as shown in the observation that "rocket engines are often dangerous and susceptible to explosions," in *Sec. 2.3.1*; the critique of spacecrafts by the critics, in regard to the vanity and glory behind the space race, while there were so many different socioeconomic problems at home, in *Sec. 2.3.2*; the critique of the automobile industry, as shown in the problems pointed out by the critics like Jay Holtz Kay as cited, in *Sec. 2.4.1*; the critique of future car technologies, as shown in the problems pointed out by the critics as cited, in *Sec. 2.4.2*; the critique of TOD, as shown in the problems pointed out by the critics as cited, in *Sec. 2.5.1*; the critique of the car culture by its critics like J. Kay, in *Sec. 2.5.2*; the critique of the "public relations campaign" for FOD prevention, as shown in the problems pointed out by the critics as cited, like the argument that sophisticated technologies are also needed, as awareness and training are not enough, in *Sec. 3.2.1*; the critique of field sobriety tests by the critics as unreliable and controversial, in *Sec. 3.2.2*; the critique of the regulations of air pollution, as shown in the problems pointed out by the critics as cited, in *Sec. 3.3.1*; the critique of the horse-drawn carriage, as shown in "a newspaper article written in England in 1895 entitled 'Horseflesh vs. Steam,'" which "highlights the death of the carriage as the means of transportation," in *Sec. 3.3.2*; the condemnation of the September 11 attacks by the family members of the victims, in *Sec. 3.4.1*; the critique of urban sprawl, as shown in the problems pointed out by the critics as cited, who reject it on different grounds, like traffic congestion, negative environmental and public health outcomes, etc., in *Sec. 3.4.2*; the critique of steam rail transport, as shown by the criticism that "steam locomotives require large pools of labour to clean, load, maintain and run" and "after World War II, dramatically increased labour costs in developed countries made steam an increasingly costly form of motive power," in *Sec. 3.5.1*; and the critique of of seamanship, as shown in the problems pointed out by the critics as cited, in *Sec. 3.5.2*).

And the reverse direction also holds true.

Again, it should be stressed, however, that there are different shades of gray (or different degrees of truth) in the two opposites, and the classification is not necessarily mutually exclusive either. In fact, even when some combinations of the two occur, they only end up sharing the same dialectic relationship, but in a different degree.

Also, there are some other relationships (as a kind of family resemblance) which have something in common with the principle, but they are not exactly the same but only more or less comparable, which varies from case to case.

Good examples of family resemblance in relation to the principle are peacefulness-violence, cooperation-competition, pacificity-aggression, dovishness-hawkishness, reward-punishment, peace-war, friendliness-unfriendliness, kindness-hostility, love-hatred, acceptance-discrimination, admiration-belittlement, inclusion-exclusion, and the like.

21st Thesis: The Seriousness-Playfulness Principle

The twenty-first thesis refers to the seriousness-playfulness principle (on the extent of seriousness) in the category of "agency" in existential dialectics (which is first worked out in *FPHH*), in that, if there is seriousness, there is also playfulness, especially for any agent with some kind of intelligence life, be it about humans, animals, or, later, post-humans. There is no seriousness without playfulness—and vice versa.

Lest any misunderstanding occurs, the word "playfulness" here should not be confused with other terms like "laughter," "smile," "joke," "tickleness," and "laugh-like vocalization" (in some animals), for instance.

Being playful can come in all shapes and sizes and therefore is not necessarily tied up with any of these terms, alhough it can result from any of them, or a combination of them, or something else altogether.

This principle, together with some other principles (especially though not exclusively, like the formalness-informalness principle), have important implications for what constitutes rationality, be it about "rationality of application" at the practical level or "rationality of knowledge" at the meta-theoretical level (as summarized in *Sec. 4.20* of *FPHH*).

For instance, on the one hand, there is seriousness (e.g., the serious business of those who want to understand the relationship between walkability and health, in *Sec. 2.2.1*; the serious business of the feminists to understand the implications of the invention of the bicycle for women, in *Sec. 2.2.2*; the serious business of those engineers in transportation to explore new ways to convert energy to work, in *Sec. 2.3.1*; ., the serious business of those in designing spacecrafts, in *Sec. 2.3.2*; the serious business of those pioneers to build motor vehicles, in *Sec. 2.4.1*; the serious business of those in future car technologies to achieve safety, efficiency, etc., in *Sec. 2.4.2*; the serious business of those in TOD to focus on the "pedestrian," in *Sec. 2.5.1*; the serious business of those who advocate the convenience of the automobile, in *Sec. 2.5.2*; the serious business of those who study and measure FOD, in *Sec. 3.2.1*; the serious business of drivers to reach their destination by driving, in *Sec. 3.2.2*; the serious business of those who try to live by engaging in different activities which can contribute to pollution, in *Sec. 3.3.1*; the serious business of those who aim to build carriages for better transports, in *Sec. 3.3.2*; the serious business of those 19 skyjackers to engage in suicide skyjacking, in *Sec. 3.4.1*; the serious business of those who want to provide countermeasures to traffic congestion, in *Sec. 3.4.2*; the serious business of those who build rail transports, in *Sec. 3.5.1*; and the serious business of those who want to master seamanship, in *Sec. 3.5.2*).

On the other hand, there is playfulness (e.g., the playful part of those who want to understand the relationship between walkability and health, when they play around with different claims, like blaming "mechanized transportation" for the rise of obesity and suggesting the evolutionary origin of walkability, in *Sec. 2.2.1*; the playful part of the feminists, when they play around with such ideological slogans like "freedom machine," etc., without a serious critique of its ideological basis, in *Sec. 2.2.2*; the playful part of those engineers in transportation, when they play around with different creative ways to convert energy to work, like the use of "wheels," "tracks," "nozzles," "propellers," "wings, and so on, so as to see and test which ones work under what conditions better, in *Sec. 2.3.1*; the playful part of those in designing spacecrafts, when they play around with different designs, like the Soviet "Spiral Shuttle, the Chinese "Shuguang Project 921-3 shuttle," and the American "Lockheed-Martin VentureStar," etc., all of which were later cancelled, for different reasons, in *Sec. 2.3.2*; the playful part of those pioneers to build motor vehicles, when they played around with different imaginative designs like the "horse-drawn carriage" by Karl Benz, the "one-cylinder petrol motor, fitting it into…[a] tricycle" by Enrico Bernardi, etc., in *Sec. 2.4.1*; the playful part of those in future car technologies, when they play around with different experimental designs like hydrogen cars, compressed-air cars, liquid nitrogen cars, etc., in *Sec. 2.4.2*; the playful part of those in TOD, when they play around with different designs of public spaces for people to meet freely, like "parks, gardens, glass-covered gallerias, arcades, courtyards, street side cafes, river- and hill-side stroll ways, and a variety of semi-covered spaces," so as to see and test which ones are better under what circumstances, in *Sec. 2.5.1*; the playful part of those who advocates the convenience of the automobile, when they play around with different slogans to glorify the car culture, like the 1909 tune "In My Merry Oldsmobile," the first rock and roll song "Rocket 88," or the commercial which "described Hell as being a place where a teenager would have to drive a minivan!," in *Sec. 2.5.2*; the playful part of those who study and measure FOD, when they play around with different numbers, as shown the criticism that different data analyses about FOD can be inconsistent with each other, in *Sec. 3.2.1*; the playful part of drivers, when they play around with the consumption of alcohol and drive under the influence, in *Sec. 3.2.2*; the playful part of those who try to live by engaging in different activities which can contribute to pollution, when they play around with different activities in relation to "smoke stacks of power plants," "controlled burn practices in agriculture and forestry management," "fumes from paint," "waste deposition in landfills," etc., so as to test and see which ones work for them under which circumstances, with what consequences, in *Sec. 3.3.1*; the playful part of of those who aim to build carriages, when they play around with different design options over the ages, like carriages with 1 wheel, 2 wheels, 4 wheels, and 6 wheels—or carriages which are made lighter or heavier, etc., in *Sec. 3.3.2*; the playful part of those 19 skyjackers when they played around with different weapons during the attacks, like "mace," "tear gas," "pepper spray," "multi-function hand tools," and "assorted knives and blades" to attack and subdue pilots, flight attendants, and other passengers, in *Sec. 3.4.1*; the playful part of those who want to provide countermeasures to traffic congestion, when they play around with different options like "parking restrictions," "park and ride facilities," "road pricing," "cap and trade," "congestion pricing," "road space rationing," "number plate restrictions," "permits," "cycling promotion," "speed limit reductions," etc., so as to test and see which ones are more effective, in *Sec. 3.4.2*; the playful part of those who build rail transports, when they play around with different designs and innovations over time, as shown in the history of pre-steam, steam, electrical, and diesel rail transports, in *Sec. 3.5.1*; and the playful part of those who want to master seamanship, when they play around with different techniques and skills including navigation, weather forecasting, watchstanding, ship-handling, operation of deck equipment, anchors and cables, ropework and line handling, communications, cargo handling, dealing with emergencies, survival at sea, search and rescue, fire fighting, etc., so as to test and see which ones work under what conditions for safe sailing, in *Sec. 3.5.2*).

And the reverse direction also holds true.

Again, it should be stressed, however, that there are different shades of gray (or different degrees of truth) in the two opposites, and the classification is not necessarily mutually exclusive either. In fact, even when some combinations of the two occur, they only end up sharing the same dialectic relationship, but in a different degree.

Also, there are some other relationships (as a kind of family resemblance) which have something in common with the principle, but they are not exactly the same but only more or less comparable, which varies from case to case.

Good examples of family resemblance in relation to the principle are seriousness-jokingness, seriousness-humorousness, seriousness-wittiness, seriousness-nonseriousness, Apollo-Dionysus, seriousness-restingness, seriousness-relaxedness, and so forth.

22nd Thesis: The Activeness-Inactiveness Principle

The twenty-second thesis refers to the activeness-inactiveness principle (on the extent of activeness) in the category of "agency" in existential dialectics (which is first worked out in *FPHTRAN*), in that, if there is activeness, there is also inactiveness, especially (though not exclusively) for any agent with some kind of intelligence life, be it about humans, animals, or, later, post-humans. There is no activeness without inactiveness—and vice versa.

Being active can come in all shapes and sizes, just as a person (or an animal) can be inactive because he (or it) is tired, old, injured, sick, sleepy (or hibernating), uninterested, in a state of passive inertia (or disposition), etc.—and an object can be inactive because it is at rest, out of work (or order), etc.

This principle, together with some other principles (especially though not exclusively, like the formalness-informalness principle and seriousness-playfulness principle), have important implications for what constitutes rationality, be it about "rationality of application" at the practical level or "rationality of knowledge" at the meta-theoretical level (as summarized in *Sec. 4.20* of *FPHH*).

For instance, on the one hand, there is activeness (e.g., the alertness of those who actively try to be in good health by maintaining the lifestyle of walkability, in *Sec. 2.2.1*; the alertness of those who actively engage in cycling for different purposes like the feeling of freedom, the benefits of good health, etc., in *Sec. 2.2.2*; the activeness of vehicles which are in motion, in *Sec. 2.3.1*; the activeness of spacecrafts which function well in accordance to its planned mission, in *Sec. 2.3.2*; the activeness of automobiles which are driven by drivers on the streets, in *Sec. 2.4.1*; the alertness of those future cars which actively pay attention "to their physical surroundings in order to improve road safety," in *Sec. 2.4.2*; the activeness of those transit-oriented areas which are well-planned according to Intelligent Urbanism and function well, in *Sec. 2.5.1*; the activeness of those in car cultures who are encouraged to drive around to more areas than otherwise possible, in *Sec. 2.5.2*; the activeness of those aircrafts which are not damaged by FOD and function well, in *Sec. 3.2.1*; the activeness of those who are sober and able to drive to where they want to go, in *Sec. 3.2.2*; the activeness of those who do not suffer from health problems due to air pollution and are ready to do different tasks, in *Sec. 3.3.1*; the activeness of those horses which are not tired and in good health, so they can drive a carriage well, in *Sec. 3.3.2*; the alertness of those pilots and flight attendants after the September 11, 2001 attacks, when they are now trained to handle suicide hijackings, so that "future hijackers most likely will encounter greater resistance from passengers and flight crews, making a successful hijacking more unlikely," in *Sec. 3.4.1*; the alertness of a single motorist who actively tries to make "an abrupt steering maneuver" to get ahead in traffic, in *Sec. 3.4.2*; the alertness of those safe drivers who actively try to avoid collision by operating a train carefully and paying good attention to other vehicles at level crossings, in *Sec. 3.5.1*; and the alertness of those crew members who actively try to operate a ship safely with a good sense of "situational awareness," in *Sec. 3.5.2*).

On the other hand, there is inactiveness (e.g., the relative inactiveness of those who are tired, sleepy, sick, old, or drunken, when they cannot engage in walking too much, in *Sec. 2.2.1*; the relative inactiveness of those who are tired, sleepy, sick, old, or drunken, when they cannot engage in cycling too much, in *Sec. 2.2.2*; the relative inactiveness of vehicles which break down and are at rest, in *Sec. 2.3.1*; the relative inactiveness of spacecrafts which are out of order and do not work, in *Sec. 2.3.2*; the relative inactiveness of automobiles which are under repair, in *Sec. 2.4.1*; the relative inactiveness of those future cars which collide with others and no longer work, in *Sec. 2.4.2*; the relative inactiveness of those transit-oriented areas which are badly designed and become dysfunctional or out-of-use over time, in *Sec. 2.5.1*; the relative inactiveness of those in alternative cultures who cannot go far from their local regions, because of the lack of adequate transportation, in *Sec. 2.5.2*; the relative inactiveness of those aircrafts which are damaged by FOD and crash later on, in *Sec. 3.2.1*; the relative inactiveness of those who are drunken and fall asleep, in *Sec. 3.2.2*; the relative inactiveness of those who get sick because of health problems caused by air pollution, in *Sec. 3.3.1*; the relative inactiveness of those horses which are tired or get sick, so they cannot drive a carriage well, in *Sec. 3.3.2*; the relative inactiveness of those pilots and flight attendants before the September 11, 2001 attacks, when they were not trained "to handle suicide hijackings, and the hijackers were able to exploit a weakness in the civil aviation security system," in *Sec. 3.4.1*; the relative inactiveness of another motorist who simply follows the rules unconsciously and does not make "an abrupt steering maneuver" to get ahead in traffic, in *Sec. 3.4.2*; the relative inattentiveness of those careless drivers who collide with other vehicles at level crossings, and so on, in *Sec. 3.5.1*; and the relative inactiveness of those crew members who are tired, sleepy, sick, or drunken, when they do not have a good sense of "situational awareness" to operate a ship safely, in *Sec. 3.5.2*).

And the reverse direction also holds true.

Again, it should be stressed, however, that there are different shades of gray (or different degrees of truth) in the two opposites, and the classification is not necessarily mutually exclusive either. In fact, even when some combinations of the two occur, they only end up sharing the same dialectic relationship, but in a different degree.

Also, there are some other relationships (as a kind of family resemblance) which have something in common with the principle, but they are not exactly the same but only more or less comparable, which varies from case to case.

Good examples of family resemblance in relation to the principle are alertness-unalertness, activeness-decrepidness, alertness-sleepiness, activeness-tiredness, alertness-uninterestedness, awakenness-hibernatedness, alertness-unwareness, soberness-unawareness, soberness-inactiveness, alertness-inactiveness, and so on.

In Relation to Outcome

The next three theses are in relation to outcome in existential dialectics, as shown below.

23rd Thesis: The Regression-Progression Principle

The twenty-third thesis is called the regression-progression princple (on the direction of history) in the category of "outcome" in existential dialectics (which was also already worked out in my previous books), in that neither the cyclical nor the linear views are adequate for explaining many phenomena at all levels. There is no regression without progression—and vice versa.

History progresses to more advanced forms, but with a regressive touch. Examples include no freedom without unfreedom, no equality without inequality, and no civilization without barbarity. This is not an inevitable law, but merely a highly likely empirical trend.

For instance, on the one hand, there is regression (e.g., the regression made by "mechanized transportation," as shown in the problems with obesity and negative health pointed out by the critics, in *Sec. 2.2.1*; the regression made by the invention of the bicycle, as shown in the accidents pointed out by the critics, in *Sec. 2.2.2*; the regression made by ion thrusters, as shown in the problems that "they are only effective in a vacuum, which limits their use to spaceborne vehicles," in *Sec. 2.3.1*; the regression made by spacecrafts, as shown in the problems pointed out by the critics aforecited, in *Sec. 2.3.2*; the regression made by the automobile industry, as shown in the problem with "automobile dependency" pointed out by the critics like Peter Newman and Jeff Kenworthy, in *Sec. 2.4.1*; the regression made by future car technologies, as shown in the problems pointed out by the critics aforecited, in *Sec. 2.4.2*; the regression made by TOD, as shown in the problems pointed out by the critics, in *Sec. 2.5.1*; the regression made by the car culture, as shown in the problems pointed out by the critics, in *Sec. 2.5.2*; the regression made by the study on FOD, as shown in the problems pointed out by the critics aforecited, in *Sec. 3.2.1*; the regression made by the use of alcohol, as shown in the problems associated with DUI pointed out by the critics, in *Sec. 3.2.2*; the regression made by the regulations of air pollution, as shown in the problems pointed out by the critics aforecited, in *Sec. 3.3.1*; the regression made by the horse-drawn carriage, as shown in the problems pointed out by the critics aforecited, in *Sec. 3.3.2*; the regression made by the war on terror, as shown in the problems pointed out by the critics aforecited, in *Sec. 3.4.1*; the regression made by urban sprawl, as shown in its contribution to traffic congestion and other problems pointed out by the critics, in *Sec. 3.4.2*; the use of freight trains "can be reduced by lack of flexibility, if there is need of transshipment at both ends of the trip due to lack of tracks to the points of pick-up and delivery," in *Sec. 3.5.1*; and the regression made by seamanship, as shown in the problems with "isolation, stress, and fatigue as occupational hazards" of seamanship pointed out by the critics, in *Sec. 3.5.2*).

On the other hand, there is progress (e.g., the progress made by"mechanized transportation," as shown in its convenience for contemporary life in "twentieth century…automated metropolis," in *Sec. 2.2.1*; the progress made by the invention of the bicycle, as shown in its being a form of private transportation aforecited, in *Sec. 2.2.2*; the progress made by ion thrusters, as shown in the benefits that "ion thrusters can achieve extremely high speeds and use little propellant," in *Sec. 2.3.1*; the progress made by spacecrafts, as shown in the successful spaceflights aforecited, in *Sec. 2.3.2*; the progress made by the automobile industry, as shown in its contribution to the convenience of modern transportation aforediscussed, in *Sec. 2.4.1*; the progress made by future car technologies, as shown in their contributions to advanced control, alternative energy soruces, energy saver, and new materials aforecited, in *Sec. 2.4.2*; the progress made by TOD, as shown in the contributions to the value of "human scale" for the "pedestrian" aforecited, in *Sec. 2.5.1*; the progress made by the car culture, as shown in those positive aspects of its cultural changes afordiscussed, in *Sec. 2.5.2*; the progress made by the study on FOD, as shown in the good "Promotion and Awareness Program" aforecited, in *Sec. 3.2.1*; the progress made by the use of alcohol, as shown in its effects to have fun and relax, as "a central nervous system depressant," in *Sec. 3.2.2*; the progress made by the regulations of air pollution, as shown in their contribution to better air quality aforecited, in *Sec. 3.3.1*; the progress made by the horse-drawn carriage, as shown in its uses for transportation, sports, warfare, and the like aforecited, in *Sec. 3.3.2*; the progress made by the war on terror, as shown in the killing of bin Laden in May 2011 aforecited, in *Sec. 3.4.1*; the progress made by urban sprawl, as shown in its contribution to "the preferred lifestyle choice" like "the American Dream unfolding before your eyes," in *Sec. 3.4.2*; freight trains are used "due to its environmental profile," in *Sec. 3.5.1*; and the progress made by seamanship, as shown in its contribution to the operation and maintenance of ship transports aforecited, in *Sec. 3.5.2*).

And the reverse direction also holds true.

Again, it should be stressed, however, that there are different shades of gray (or different degrees of truth) in the two opposites, and the classification is not necessarily mutually exclusive either. In fact, even when some combinations of the two occur, they only end up sharing the same dialectic relationship, but in a different degree.

Also, there are some other relationships (as a kind of family resemblance) which have something in common with the principle, but they are not exactly the same but only more or less comparable, which varies from case to case.

Good examples of family resemblance in relation to the principle are undesirability-desirability, risk-opportunity, badness-goodness, cost-benefit, and so on.

24th Thesis: The Same-Difference Principle

The twenty-fourth thesis refers to the same-difference principle (on the metamorphosis of change) in the category of "outcome" in existential dialectics (which was worked out in *ALD* and other books of mine), in that an entity, as it evolves over time, can be both different from and similar to its opposing alternatives and does not have to be solely more different from them over time. There is no similarity without difference—and vice versa.

Opposites are not absolute in a black-or-white fashion; so, an entity can become relatively more similar to (or more different from) its opposite over time.

This is further constrained by another principle, that is, the symmetry-asymmetry principle about the relationships among existents under the category about agency in existential dialectics, in that if there is symmetry (equality) between two entities, there is likewise asymmetry (inequality) emerging in a different way.

For instance, on the one hand, there is similarity in outcome (e.g., the contribution to the molding and control of beliefs, values, and behaviors, regardless of whether this be done by way of "pedestrian oriented development" or by way of "car culture," in *Sec. 2.2.1*; the contribution to the molding and control of beliefs, values, and behaviors, regardless of whether this be done by way of cycling, or by way of walking, in *Sec. 2.2.2*; the contribution to the molding and control of beliefs, values, and behaviors, regardless of whether this be done by way of using human energy, or by way of using nuclear energy, in *Sec. 2.3.1*; the contribution to the molding and control of beliefs, values, and behaviors, regardless of whether this be done by way of engaging in the space race by the two superpowers during the Cold War, or by way of participating in the joint venture like "the International Space Station" among Russia, the U.S., and others nowadays, in *Sec. 2.3.2*; the contribution to the molding and control of beliefs, values, and behaviors, regardless of whether this be done by way of the automobile industry, or by way of New Pedestrianism, in *Sec. 2.4.1*; the contribution to the molding and control of beliefs, values, and behaviors, regardless of whether this be done by way of human running, or by way of driverless-driving, in *Sec. 2.4.2*; the contribution to the molding and control of beliefs, values, and behaviors, regardless of whether this be done by way of suburbanization, or by way of TOD, in *Sec. 2.5.1*; the contribution to the molding and control of beliefs, values, and behaviors, regardless of whether this be done by way of a walk culture or by way of a car culture, in *Sec. 2.5.2*; the contribution to the molding and control of beliefs, values, and behaviors, regardless of whether this be done by way of the "public relations campaign" for FOD prevention, or by way of sophisticated technologies for FOD prevention, in *Sec. 3.2.1*; the contribution to the molding and control of beliefs, values, and behaviors, regardless of whether this be done by way of driving under the influence, or by way of driving with asceticism, in *Sec. 3.2.2*; the contribution to the molding and control of beliefs, values, and behaviors, regardless of whether this be done by way of regulations of air pollution, or by way of laissez-faire economics, in *Sec. 3.3.1*; the contribution to the molding and control of beliefs, values, and behaviors, regardless of whether this be done by way of walking and running in the state of nature, or by way of the Hungarian light horse-drawn carriage in early modern times, in *Sec. 3.3.2*; the contribution to the molding and control of beliefs, values, and behaviors, regardless of whether this be done by way of global jihad by Osama bin Laden, or by way of the war on terror by George Bush, in *Sec. 3.4.1*; the contribution to the molding and control of beliefs, values, and behaviors, regardless of whether this be done by way of car-owning lifestyle, or by way of car-free lifestyle, in *Sec. 3.4.2*; the contribution to the molding and control of beliefs, values, and behaviors, regardless of whether this be done by way of pre-steam human-powered rail transports, or by way of high-speed magnetic levitation trains, in *Sec. 3.5.1*; and the contribution to the molding and control of beliefs, values, and behaviors, regardless of whether this be done by way of life at sea, or by way of life in a village, in *Sec. 3.5.2*).

On the other hand, there is difference in outcome (e.g., the contribution to the molding and control of beliefs, values, and behaviors by way of "pedestrian oriented development" for a relatively more physical lifestyle—but the contribution to the molding and control of beliefs, values, and behaviors by way of "car culture" for a relatively more sedentary lifestyle, in *Sec. 2.2.1*; the contribution to the molding and control of beliefs, values, and behaviors by way of cycling for a relatively more mechanical lifeworld—but the contribution to the molding and control of beliefs, values, and behaviors by way of walking for a relatively more naturalistic lifeworld, in *Sec. 2.2.2*; the contribution to the molding and control of beliefs, values, and behaviors by way of using human energy for a relatively more naturalistic lifeworld—but the contribution to the molding and control of beliefs, values, and behaviors by way of using nuclear energy for a relatively more technophilic lifeworld, in *Sec. 2.3.1*; the contribution to the molding and control of beliefs, values, and behaviors by way of engaging in the space race for a relatively more competitive lifeworld—but the contribution to the molding and control of beliefs, values, and behaviors by way of participating in the joint venture like "the International Space Station" for a relatively more cooperative lifeworld, in *Sec. 2.3.2*; the contribution to the molding and control of beliefs, values, and behaviors by way of the automobile industry for a relatively more corporate lifeworld—but the contribution to the molding and control of beliefs, values, and behaviors by way of New Pedestrianism for a relatively more environment-friendly lifeworld, in *Sec. 2.4.1*; the contribution to the molding and control of beliefs, values, and behaviors by way of human running for a relatively more naturalistic lifeworld—but the contribution to the molding and control of beliefs, values, and behaviors by way of driverless-driving for a relatively more automated lifeworld, in *Sec. 2.4.2*; the contribution to the molding and control of beliefs, values, and behaviors by way of suburbanization for a relatively more impersonal lifeworld—but the contribution to the molding and control of beliefs, values, and behaviors by way of TOD for a relatively more face-to-face lifeworld, in *Sec. 2.5.1*; the contribution to the molding and control of beliefs, values, and behaviors by way of a walk culture for a relatively more social identity—but the contribution to the molding and control of beliefs, values, and behaviors by way of a car culture for a relatively more individualist identity, in *Sec. 2.5.2*; ., the contribution to the molding and control of beliefs, values, and behaviors by way of the "public relations campaign" in regard to FOD prevention for a relatively more psychological worldview—but the contribution to the molding and control of beliefs, values, and behaviors by way of sophisticated technologies in regard to FOD prevention for a relatively more technophilic worldview, in *Sec. 3.2.1*; the contribution to the molding and control of beliefs, values, and behaviors by way of driving under the influence for a relatively more epicurean lifeworld—but the contribution to the molding and control of beliefs, values, and behaviors by way of driving with asceticism for a relatively more disciplined lifeworld, in *Sec. 3.2.2*; the contribution to the molding and control of beliefs, values, and behaviors by way of regulations of air pollution for a relatively more government-oriented lifeworld—but the contribution to the molding and control of beliefs, values, and behaviors by way of laissez-faire economics for a relatively more privatized lifeworld, in *Sec. 3.3.1*; the contribution to the molding and control of beliefs, values, and behaviors by way of walking and running for a relatively more physical lifeworld—but the contribution to the molding and control of beliefs, values, and behaviors by way of the Hungarian light horse-drawn carriage for a relatively more mechanical lifeworld, in *Sec. 3.3.2*; the contribution to the molding and control of beliefs, values, and behaviors by way of global jihad for a relatively more radical Islamic worldview—but the contribution to the molding and control of beliefs, values, and behaviors by way of the war on terror by George Bush for a relatively more extreme neoconservative worldview, in *Sec. 3.4.1*; the contribution to the molding and control of beliefs, values, and behaviors by way of car-owning lifestyle for a relatively more sedentary lifeworld—but the contribution to the molding and control of beliefs, values, and behaviors by way of car-free lifestyle for a relatively more physical lifeworld, in *Sec. 3.4.2*; the contribution to the molding and control of beliefs, values, and behaviors by way of pre-steam human-powered rail transports for a relatively more physical lifeworld—but the contribution to the molding and control of beliefs, values, and behaviors by way of high-speed magnetic levitation trains for a relatively more technophilic lifeworld, in *Sec. 3.5.1*; the contribution to the molding and control of beliefs, values, and behaviors by way of life at sea for a relatively more adventurous lifeworld in diferent places and times—but the contribution to the molding and control of beliefs, values, and behaviors by way of life in a village for a relatively more parochial lifeworld, in *Sec. 3.5.2*).

And the reverse direction also holds true.

Again, it should be stressed, however, that there are different shades of gray (or different degrees of truth) in the two opposites, and the classification is not necessarily mutually exclusive either. In fact, even when some combinations of the two occur, they only end up sharing the same dialectic relationship, but in a different degree.

Also, there are some other relationships (as a kind of family resemblance) which have something in common with the principle, but they are not exactly the same but only more or less comparable, which varies from case to case.

Good examples of family resemblance in relation to the principle are homogeneity-heterogeneity, we-they, similarity-contrast, and so forth.

25th Thesis: The Stability-Reaction Principle

The twenty-fifth thesis is called the stability-reaction princple (on the feedback mechanism for further changes) in the category of "outcome" in existential dialectics (which was first worked out in *FPHCHEM*), in that once an outcome becomes stabilized over time (which varies from case to case), it will undergo further changes in its multifaceted interactions with the outside world (e.g., with other entities, energy, space, and so on).

There is no stability without reaction for further changes—and vice versa.

For instance, on the one hand, there is stability in outcome (e.g., the relatively more stable condition of the sedentary lifestyle in the older days, when the use of automobiles became widespread in "twentieth century…automated metropolis," in *Sec. 2.2.1*; the relatively more stable condition of horse-riding in antiquity, when it was commonly used as a form of transportation, in *Sec. 2.2.2*; the relatively more stable condition of the use of human energy in the older days, when human-powered vehicles were more common in ancient times, in *Sec. 2.3.1*; the relatively more stable condition of the old glory days of the automobile, when cars were more and more used in modern times, in *Sec .2.3.2*; the relatively more stable condition of the U.S. as the top car manufacturer in the world, when it dominated from 1929 until 2005, in *Sec. 2.4.1*; the relatively more stable condition of conventional automobiles, when a driver was needed to drive them, in *Sec. 2.4.2*; the relatively more stable condition of suburbanization in the earlier days, when "many residents of metropolitan regions work within the central urban area, choosing instead to live in satellite communities called suburbs and commute to work via automobile or mass transit," in *Sec. 2.5.1*; the relatively more stable condition of the old "glory days" of car culture, when there were even "songs about the glory and wonder that surrounds the very concept of the car" like "In My Merry Oldsmobile," etc., in *Sec. 2.5.2*; the relatively more stable condition of the "public relations campaign" for FOD prevention, when people generally accepted the FOD "bible" written by Gary Chaplin for the "Promotion and Awareness Program" in the older days, in *Sec. 3.2.1*; the relatively more stable condition of the use of field sobriety tests in the older day, when police officers often used them, together with "the arresting officer's subjective opinion of impairment," in *Sec. 3.2.2*; the relatively more stable condition of air pollution in the U.S. during the early decades of industrialization, especially with "the development of steam-powered ships, railways, and later in the 19th century with the internal combustion engine," when there was so much more air pollution if measured in terms of emissions per unit of transport then, in *Sec. 3.3.1*; the relatively more stable condition of the horse-drawn carriage in the older days, when it was widely used for transportation, warfare, and sports for centuries, in *Sec. 3.3.2*; the relatively more stable condition of airport security checks in the older days before the September 11 attacks, when passengers were screened and checked less intrusively, in *Sec. 3.4.1*; the relatively more stable condition of cities in the older days, when they evolved out of rural areas, in *Sec. 3.4.2*; the relatively more stable condition of pre-steam rail transports in the older days, when people used "wooden rails and a hemp haulage rope,…operated by human or animal power," in *Sec. 3.5.1*; and the relatively more stable condition of sailing in the older days, when sailors made good use of wind in sailing, in *Sec. 3.5.2*).

On the other hand, there is reaction in outcome (e.g., the relatively more stable condition of the sedentary lifestyle in the older days then led to further changes later on, when, nowadays, there is the "pedestrian oriented development" to replace the car culture, in *Sec. 2.2.1*; the stable condition of horse-riding in antiquity then led to further changes later on, when the bicycle became more common in the 19th century and beyond, in *Sec. 2.2.2*; the use of human energy in the older days then led to further changes later on, when nowadays there are the use of nuclear energy, electrical energy, etc., in *Sec. 2.3.1*; the old glory days of the automobile then led to further changes later on, when the space race has opened up new doors to the use of spacecrafts, including those for commercial use, in *Sec. 2.3.2*; the dominance of the U.S. in car manufacturing then led to further changes later on, when Japan replaced the U.S. as the top producer in 2006, just as China in 2009 took the top spot from Japan, in *Sec. 2.4.1*; the older days of conventional automobiles then led to further changes later on, since, nowadays, there are already car technologies for automated-driving, and this will be more so in the future, in *Sec. 2.4.2*; suburbanization in the earlier days then led to further changes later on, as TOD is more popular instead nowadays, in *Sec. 2.5.1*; the old "glory days" of the car culture then led to further changes later on, when the critics like J. Kay question its desirability nowadays, in *Sec. 2.5.2*; the popularity of the FOD "bible" in the older days then led to further changes later on, when nowadays there is a call for the use of sophisticated technologies, as awareness and training are no longer deemed as sufficient, in *Sec. 3.2.1*; the use of field sobriety tests in the older days then led to further changes later on, when blood alcohol content tests are more used nowadays, because they are regarded as more "scientific," in *Sec. 3.2.2*; air pollution in the U.S. during the early decades of industrialization then led to further changes later on, when nowadays, there are more regulatons of air pollution, like the U.S. National Ambient Air Quality Standards and E.U. Air Quality Directive, in *Sec. 3.3.1*; the pervasive use of the horse-drawn carriage in the older days led to further changes later on, when nowadays other means of transportation like trains, cars, and aircrafts are more widely used instead, in *Sec. 3.3.2*; the relatively less intrusive airport security checks in the older days before the September 11 attacks then led to further changes later on, when passengers are now more extensively checked at airports after the September 11 attacks, in *Sec. 3.4.1*; cities in the older days then led to further changes later on, when cities grew outwards to suburbs and then to the outskirts into what is now known as urban sprawl, in *Sec. 3.4.2*; the pre-steam rail transports in the older days then led to further changes later on, when nowadays people use high-speed magnetic levitation trains, in *Sec. 3.5.1*; and sailing in the older days then led to further changes later on, when nowadays, sailing can depend on mechanical engines like diesel engines, gas turbine engines, etc., in *Sec. 3.5.2*).

And the reverse direction also holds true.

Again, it should be stressed, however, that there are different shades of gray (or different degrees of truth) in the two opposites, and the classification is not necessarily mutually exclusive either. In fact, even when some combinations of the two occur, they only end up sharing the same dialectic relationship, but in a different degree.

Also, there are some other relationships (as a kind of family resemblance) which have something in common with the principle, but they are not exactly the same but only more or less comparable, which varies from case to case.

Good examples of family resemblance in relation to the principle are stability-forwardness, normalcy-feedback, balance-forwardness, balance-reaction, consolidation-modification, normalcy-feedback, stability-breakup, rest-motion, and the like.

26th Thesis: The Post-Human Panorama

And the twenty-sixth thesis is about the role of "post-humans," which I originally proposed in my previous books, starting with the first book titled *The Future of Human Civilization* in 2000 and all others afterwards.

As already pointed out in *Sec. 1.8*, I need to emphasize, as this is something that I used to repeat (*almost verbatim*) from my previous books, two clarifications here about the term "post-human" as a neologism in my works.

Firstly, the word "post-human" here should *not* be confused with another term which looks similar but has a totally different meaning in the literature of postmodernism, namely, "post-humanism"—which constitutes a critique of "humanism" as tradionally understood (especially, though not exclusively, in relation to the idea of progress in science and reason in the Enlightenment project). (WK 2008)

My works reject the project of "postmodernism" and propose the future world of what I orignally called "after-postmodernity" in *FHC* and *FCD*, for instance.

And secondly, the word "post-human" here should also *not* be confused with a similar term which is used to champion the ideology of technology for the future co-existence between humans and cyborgs in "trans-humanism." (WK 2008a)

Instead, my term "post-human" in relation to "posthuman-ism" also rejects "transhumanism" (especially, though not exclusively, in relation to the promises of technology) and refers to something else altogether, that is, the future extinction of humans and its post-human successors in deep space and beyond unto multiverses.

My critique of "transhumanism" was more extensively elabroated in *Sec. 2.4.1* of *BEPE*—just as my critique of different futuristic scenarios of fictional artificial intelligence in science fiction was given in *Sec. 3.5.2* of *FPHCOM.*

With these two clarifications in mind (as summarized in *Table 1.31*)—the post-human panorama in the study of transportation can be addressed in relation to five main directions, based on my *panoramic theory of transportation*, as analysed in this book (together with my visions as already worked out in my previous books).

Firstly, the post-human panorama in the study of transportation will learn from my panoramic theory of transportation in relation to the dialectic context of no networks without operations (and vice versa), in the context of transportation.

Secondly, the post-human panorama in the study of transportation will learn from my panoramic theory of transportation in relation to the four perspectives of the mind, nature, society, and culture.

Thirdly, the post-human panorama in the study of transportation will learn from my panoramic theory of transportation in relation to the non-privilege of any specific theory over others in the literature and the non-integration of them all (as they are not necessarily compatible with each other).

Fourthly, the post-human panorama in the study of transportation will have to confront the new challenges as posed by the long-term civilizational development of intelligent life in the distant future, both here on this planet Earth and elsewhere in deep space until multiverses.

As this is something that I regularly pointed out in my previous books for background information (and summarize here, *almost verbatim*, with some updates), I already worked out, in my numerous books, what these new challenges will be and provide different original visions to meet them—especially, in regard to the future evolutions of the mind (e.g., "the supersession computing," "metamorphic humor," "the contrarian personality," "the hyper-martial body," "the hyper-sexual body," "floating consciousness," "hyper-spatial consciousness," "thinking machines," "unfolding unconsciousness," "thinking robots," "genetically altered superior beings," "cyborgs," and others), of nature (e.g., "transdisciplinary architecture," "creational chemistry," "multilateral sound," "resettlement geology," "post-cosmology," "the alteration of space-time," "the creation of new matter-energy," "selective geometry," and the like), of society (e.g., "cyclical-progressive migration," "reflective criminology," "interventive-reshaping geography," "detached gambling," "heterodox education," "multifaceted war and peace," "virtual organizations," different versions of "post-capitalism" and "post-democracy," the movement of "cyclical progression" at both structural and systemic levels, "ambivalent technology," and so forth), and of culture (e.g., "interactive semantics," "transdisciplinary performing arts," "comparative-impartial literature," "post-human mind games," "comparative-substitutive religion," "post-ethics," "post-civilization," "transformative aesthetic experience," "contrastive mathematical-logic," and the whatnot) in history (e.g., "multifold history," the age of "after-postmodernity"), in the context of my approaches in relation to methodology (e.g., "sophisticated methodologial holism," "critical-dialectic formal science," "complex data analysis," etc,) and ontology (e.g., "existential dialectics," "contrastive rationality").

Of course, the examples (as listed above) are not exhaustive but illustrative, since my numerous books have worked out many other visions (as already roughly summarized in *Sec.1.8* and *Sec. 1.9*). Many, though not all, of my visions on the mind, nature, society, culture, history, methodology, and ontology (as cited above) are summarized in the tables as shown in Chapter One and Chapter Four (especially in *Table 4.43* about my original theories on numerous topics).

And finally, or fifthly, the post-human panorama in the study of transportation will learn from my panoramic theory of transportation in regard to the need to go beyond networks and operations (as further elaborated in the next section).

Towards the Post-Human Panorama

This "post-human" panorama in the study of transportation to transcend both networks and operations can be understood in terms of nine great future transformations of transportation, in relation to the mind, nature, society, and culture—as explained below (and summarized in *Table 1.2*).

Nine Great Future Transformations of Transportation

The nine great future transformations of transportation (in relation to the mind, nature, society, and culture) can be explained hereafter, with the caveat, however, that the classification in terms of nine is solely aesthetic and utilitarian (illustrative), as there is no objective basis that it must be classified in term of nine (as this is something that I often stressed and repeated in my previous books, albeit in the context of different topics).

The First Great Future Transformation of Transportation

The first great future transformation of transportation in the post-human era concerns what I originally call *new goals,* in relation to the mind.

This search for "new goals" will give future advanced humans and later their successors, namely, the post-humans, the capacity to be motivated to improve transportation in a way that current humans cannot.

There are already some indications that the future of transportation is moving toward this direction.

Consider, for illustration, the different "goals" as already seen in the history of transportation, such as the quest for freedom in cycling (*Sec. 2.2.2*), the race for space domination (*Sec. 2.3.2*), the goals of efficiency and safety in future car technologies (*Sec. 2.4.2*), the value of human scale (*Sec. 2.5.1*), the search for better air quality (*Sec. 3.3.1*), the freedom from suicide skyjacking (*Sec. 3.4.1*), the ideal of car-free households (*Sec. 3.4.2*), and the joy of "sea-going adventure and a chance to see the world" (*Sec. 3.5.2*), for instance.

More importantly, this future quest for new goals should also be understood in relation to my previous works on the future "post-human" supersession of the human mind from the combined perspectives of the mind, nature, society, and culture—with good examples like "the supersession computing," "metamorphic humor," "the contrarian personality," "the hyper-martial body," "the hyper-sexual body," "floating consciousness," "hyper-spatial consciousness," "thinking machines," "unfolding unconsciousness," "thinking robots," "genetically altered superior beings," "cyborgs," and others.

In any event, all these are just some illustrative (relatively primitive) examples in our time, of course, but the important point to remember here is that the search for different new goals will further transform the study of transportation at the more advanced level in the post-human future that the human world has never known.

The Second Great Future Transformation of Transportation

The second great future transformation of transportation in the post-human era concerns what I originally call *new means,* in relation to the mind.

This quest for "new means" will give future advanced humans and later their successors, namely, the post-humans, the capacity to find novel options to achieve the goals of transportation in a way that current humans cannot.

There are already some indications that the future of transportation is moving toward this direction.

Consider, for illustration, the different "means" as already seen in the history of transportation, such as walking for health benefits (*Sec. 2.2.1*), cycling for the feeling of freedom (*Sec. 2.2.2*), motors and engines for transportation (*Sec. 2.3.1*), space race for the Cold War between the two superpowers (*Sec. 2.3.2*), automobile for convenience (*Sec. 2.4.1*), driverless cars for advanced control (*Sec. 2.4.2*), TOD to alleviate urban sprawl (*Sec. 2.5.1*), automobiles for affordable transportation (*Sec. 2.5.2*), FOD awareness to avoid damage (*Sec. 3.2.1*), drunk driving prevention to save lives (*Sec. 3.2.2*), better air quality for good health (*Sec. 3.3.1*), horse-drawn carriages for transport (*Sec. 3.3.2*), skyjacking for terrorism (*Sec. 3.4.1*), considerate driving to reduce traffic congestion (*Sec. 3.4.2*), rail transport to move passengers and goods (*Sec. 3.5.1*), and ship handling for seamanship (*Sec. 3.5.2*), for instance.

All these are just some illustrative (relatively primitive) examples in our time, of course, but the important point to remember here is that the search for different new means will further transform the study of transportation at the more advanced level in the post-human future that the human world has never known.

The Third Great Future Transformation of Transportation

The third great future transformation of transportation in the post-human era concerns what I originally call *new comparisons*, in relation to nature.

This search for "new comparisons" will give future advanced humans and later their successors, namely, the post-humans, the ability to learn from animals, plants, and the universe, through comparison and contrast, about the study of transportation in a way that current humans cannot.

There are already some indications that the future of transportation is moving toward this direction.

Consider, for illustration, the different forms of comparison and contrast as already seen in the history of transportation, such as the imitation of wind energy from nature (*Sec. 2.3.1*), the correct orientation of a spacecraft in space (*Sec. 2.3.2*), the comparison between natural and man-made air pollution (*Sec. 3.3.1*), the running of horses in nature (*Sec. 3.3.2*), the comparison between nature and traffic in chaos theory (*Sec. 3.4.2*), and the learning of weather, meteorology and forecasting for seamanship (*Sec. 3.5.2*), for instance.

All these are just some illustrative (relatively primitive) examples in our time, of course, but the important point to remember here is that the search for different new comparisons will further transform the study of transportation at the more advanced level in the post-human future that the human world has never known.

The Fourth Great Future Transformation of Transportation

The fourth great future transformation of transportation in the post-human era concerns what I originally call *new integrations*, in relation to nature.

This search for "new integrations" will give future advanced humans and later their successors, namely, the post-humans, the ability to live and interact with nature for the study of transportation in a way that current humans cannot.

There are already some indications that the future of transportation is moving toward this direction.

Consider, for illustration, the different integrations for the study of transportation as already seen in the history of transportation, such as walking and human evolution in nature (*Sec. 2.2.1*), locomotion and energy in nature (*Sec. 2.3.1*), the integration of road vehicles with their physical surroundings (*Sec. 2.4.2*), the awareness of volcanic ash in nature (*Sec. 3.2.1*), the coping with air pollution in its natural and man-made forms (*Sec. 3.3.1*), and the adaptation of life at sea (*Sec. 3.5.2*), for instance.

More importantly, this future quest for new integrations should also be understood in relation to my previous works on the future "post-human" adventures into different dimensions of space-time unto multiverses from the combined perspectives of the mind, nature, society, and culture—with good examples like "the alteration of space-time" (*Table 1.3* and *Table 1.4*), "multiverses" (*Table 1.7* and *Table 1.8*), "hyperspace" (*Table 1.9* and *Table 1.25*), "time travel" (*Table 1.10* and *Table 1.11*), and others.

In addition, in my previous book titled *The Future of Post-Human Geology* (2010), I already envisioned the three great future transformations of geology, namely, "solar geology," "galactic geology," and "cosmic geology," in the context of my "resettlement theory of geology," in that humans and later post-humans will explore and migrate to other planets, solar systems, galaxies, and cosmos in the long haul.

Then, in another book of mine titled *The Future of Post-Human Geography* (2011), I linked the two books together, since geography has much to learn from geology (as in "physical geography," which, as already introduced in *Sec. 1.3* of *FPHGEOG*, relies heavily on the earth sciences) and discussed the search for "new explorations" in the context of the three forms of environments outside the planet Earth, namely, what I originally called "solar geography," "galactic geography," and "cosmic geography"—as a further elaboration of the three great future transformations of geology (in *FPHGEOL*).

Later, in still another book of mine titled *The Future of Post-Human Migration* (2012), I envisioned the future integrations in different forms, namely, what I originally called "solar migration," "galactic migration," "clustery migration," "cosmic migration," and "multiversal migration."

With this background of these previous books of mine, the future integrations in the context of transportation will also undergo different forms, namely, in the absence of better words, what I want to call here:

- Solar Transportation
- Galactic Transportation
- Clustery Transportation
- Cosmic Transportation
- Multiversal Transportation

These forms are a further extension of the great future transformations of geology (in *FPHGEOL*), of geography (in *FPHGEOG*), and of migration (in *FPHMIG*) to the realm of transportation.

This extension is consistent with my other theory, namely, "the theory of the cyclical progression of system integration and fragmentation" in *FCD* (2002)—at the social-systemic level (as already clarified in *Sec. 1.8* and shown below):

Local → Regional → Global →Solar →
Galactic → Clustery…→ Multiversal

All these are just some illustrative (relatively primitive) examples in our time, of course, but the important point to remember here is that the search for different new integrations will further transform transportation at the more advanced level in the post-human future that the human world has never known.

The Fifth Great Future Transformation of Transportation

The fifth great future transformation of transportation in the post-human era concerns what I originally call *new praxes*, in relation to society.

This search for "new praxes" will give future advanced humans and later their successors, namely, the post-humans, the ability to engage in practice (like activism, politics, personal experience, etc.) for the study of transportation in a way that current humans cannot.

There are already some indications that the future of transportation is moving toward this direction.

Consider, for illustration, the different praxes as already seen in history of transportation like the application of physics to convert enegy for work (*Sec. 2.3.1*), the application of rocket science to the realm of the Cold War (*Sec. 2.3.2*), the use of gasoline for automobiles (*Sec. 2.4.1*), the application of new materials for car making (*Sec. 2.4.2*), the application of TOD in the rest of the world (*Sec. 2.5.1*), the application of the automobile for cultural changes (*Sec. 2.5.2*), the use of radar for FOD detection (*Sec. 3.2.1*), the domestication of horses for carriages (*Sec. 3.2.2*), the exploitation of skyjacking for terrorism (*Sec. 3.4.1*), the application of chaos theory to understand traffic jams (*Sec. 3.4.2*), the application of of electromagnetic energy for electrical rail transport (*Sec. 3.5.1*), and the application of nuclear force to a ship with a nuclear reactor (*Sec. 3.5.2*), for instance.

All these are just some illustrative (relatively primitive) examples in our time, of course, but the important point to remember here is that the search for different new praxes will further transform the study of transportation at the more advanced level in the post-human future that the human world has never known.

The Sixth Great Future Transformation of Transportation

The sixth great future transformation of transportation in the post-human era concerns what I originally call *new technologies*, in relation to society.

This search for "new technologies" will give future advanced humans and later their successors, namely, the post-humans, the ability to come up with different techniques, materials, and experiments for the study of transportation in a way that current humans cannot.

There are already some indications that the future of transportation is moving toward this direction.

Consider, for illustration, the use of different technologies as already seen in the history of transportation, such as the invention of bicycles (*Sec. 2.2.2*), the invention of motors and engines (*Sec. 2.3.1*), the invention of spacecrafts (*Sec. 2.3.2*), the invention of the automobile (*Sec. 2.4.1* & *Sec. 2.5.2*), future car technologies (*Sec. 2.4.2*), the technique of TOD (*Sec. 2.5.1*), the technology of radio frequency identification for FOD detection (*Sec. 3.2.1*), the technology for BAC testing (*Sec. 3.2.2*), the invention of horse-drawn carriages (*Sec. 3.3.2*), the skills of skyjacking (*Sec. 3.4.1*), the invention of park and ride facilities (*Sec. 3.4.2*), the invention of rail transport (*Sec. 3.5.1*), and the invention of ship transport (*Sec. 3.5.2*), for instance.

All these are just some illustrative (relatively primitive) examples in our time, of course, but the important point to remember here is that the search for new technologies will further transform the study of transportation at the more advanced level in the post-human future that the human world has never known.

The Seventh Great Future Transformation of Transportation

The seventh great future transformation of transportation in the post-human era concerns what I originally call *new stratifications*, in relation to society.

This emergence of "new stratifications" will lead future advanced humans and later their successors, namely, the post-humans, to face new inequalities for the understanding of transportation in a way that current humans cannot.

There are already some indications that the future of tramsportation is moving toward this direction.

Consider, for illustration, the different inequalities as already seen in the history of transportation, such as the tradeoff between freedom and equality in cycling (*Sec. 2.2.2*), the space race between the U.S. and the U.S.S.R. (*Sec. 2.3.2*), the dominance of the auto market by a few countries (*Sec. 2.4.1*), the gentrification in low-income areas (*Sec. 2.5.1*), different laws on drunk driving in different countries (*Sec. 3.2.2*), the privilege of using carriages by royalty and aristocrats (*Sec. 3.3.2*), the war on terror by the U.S. against al-Qaeda (*Sec. 3.4.1*), the lifestyle choice between car-owning and car-free households (*Sec. 3.4.2*), the competition between train and airplane for the market (*Sec. 3.5.1*), and the rivalry between a Pilot and a Master on a ship (*Sec. 3.5.2*), for instance.

All these are just some illustrative (relatively primitive) examples in our time, of course, but the important point to remember here is that the emergence of new stratifications will further transform the study of transportation at the more advanced level in the post-human future that the human world has never known.

The Eighth Great Future Transformation of Transportation

The eighth great future transformation of transportation in the post-human era concerns what I originally call *new sub-fields*, in relation to culture.

This search for "new sub-fields" will give future advanced humans and later their successors, namely, the post-humans, the ability to explore new specialties for the understanding of transportation in a way that current humans cannot.

There are already some indications that the future of transportation is moving toward this direction.

Consider, for illustration, the different sub-fields as already seen in the history of transportation, such as mechanical engineering for bicycles (*Sec. 2.2.2*), aerospace engineering (*Sec. 2.3.2*), electrical/mechanical engineering for automobiles (*Sec. 2.4.1* & *Sec. 2.5.2*), car robotics (*Sec. 2.4.2*), city planning/urban design (*Sec. 2.5.1*), FOD studies (*Sec. 3.2.1*), pathophysiology in driving (*Sec. 3.2.2*), horse-riding studies (*Sec. 3.3.2*), terrorism studies (*Sec. 3.4.1*), urban studies for urban sprawl (*Sec. 3.4.2*), rail transport studies (*Sec. 3.5.1*), and the research on seamanship (*Sec. 3.5.2*), for instance.

All these are just some illustrative (relatively primitive) examples in our time, of course, but the important point to remember here is that the search for new sub-fields will further transform the study of transportation at the more advanced level in the post-human future that the human world has never known.

The Ninth Great Future Transformation of Transportation

And the ninth great future transformation of transportation in the post-human era concerns what I originally call *new interpretations*, in relation to culture.

This search for "new interpretations" will give future advanced humans and later their successors, namely, the post-humans, the ability to come up with different evaluations and views about the study of transportation in a way that current humans cannot.

There are already some indications that the future of transportation is moving toward this direction.

Consider, for illustration, the different interpretations as already seen in the history of transportation, such as the evolutionary argument for walkability (*Sec. 2.2.1*), the argument about cycling for freedom (*Sec. 2.2.2*), the view about the efficiency of energy conversion (*Sec. 2.3.1*), Sputnik and the Soviet propaganda about the Soviet's superiority (*Sec. 2.3.2*), the argument against auto-dependency (*Sec. 2.4.1* & *Sec. 2.5.2*), the ideology of vehicle automotion (*Sec. 2.4.2*), the ideology of intelligent urbanism (*Sec. 2.5.1*), the new argument against carbon monoxide (*Sec. 3.3.1*), the argument for horse domestication (*Sec. 3.3.2*), the justification of the war on terror (*Sec. 3.4.1*), the argument against urban sprawl (*Sec. 3.4.2*), the obession with trains in popular culture (*Sec. 3.5.1*), and the preservation of the memory of ships by sails (*Sec. 3.5.2*), for instance.

All these are just some illustrative (relatively primitive) examples in our time, of course, but the important point to remember here is that the search for new interpretations will further transform the study of transportation at the more advanced level in the post-human future that the human world has never known.

Enormous Implications

These nine great future transformations of the study of transportation have enormous implications for some soul-searching questions which have challenged some of the best minds in the history of transportation.

For illustration, consider the following fundamental questions in the study of transportation:

- Can transportation really have such a destructive impact on society, as Jay Holtz Kay (1998) once forcefully wrote, with the automobile industry as an example?
- Is transportation really so convenient and desirable, as shown in the old "glory days" of the automobile, as Skip McGoun (2012) once reminded us?
- Are future transportation technologies so effective and efficient, as shown in the examples about future cars (in *Sec. 2.4.2*) and future spacecrafts in deep space (in *Sec. 2.3.2*)?

Questions and disagreements like this will receive new answers in the future history of advanced human and later post-human transportation, at least in two fundamental ways.

The first fundamental way is to examine the relationships between networks and operations—such that their possibility (or impossibility) and desirability (or undesirability) are not to the extent that the respective defenders would like us to believe.

The different views about the study of transportation, as already addressed in *Sec. 1.1*, *Sec. 1.5*, and the rest of the book, are just different ways to understand the nature of transportation, with each from its own vantage point.

Each views has its own merits and defects and is preferred over others by different proponents with their own different interests, but none of them is possible (or impossible) and desirable (or undesirable) to the extent that its respective advocates would like us to believe.

And the second fundamental way is to reflect and then transcend, in the long haul, the debate about networks and operations, such that it will be shifted to different directions, as shown in the nine great future transformations that I have envisioned and outlined above. To transcend them all is to move into these different directions, in conjunction with the various visions of my previous books (as already summarized in *Sec. 1.8* and also earlier in this chapter, with the further help of the tables at this end of Chapter One and this chapter).

Lest any misunderstanding occurs, one must remember that these nine great future transformations of the study of transportation will bring neither utopia nor dystopia, regardless of the current fashionable talks about future transportation like "driverless cars," "flying cars," "spaceships in deep space," etc.—as this is something that I have warned time and again in all of my previous books, almost verbatim. (EC 2012)

In any event, as I so often stressed in my previous books, it is not up to us current humans to decide whether or not, or to what extent, the post-human future of transportation will be for better and for worse, because it will be judged by the values and beliefs of future post-humans on earth and in deep space unto multiverses—in a way that the entire history of the human world has never known.

Thus speaks the future of the study of transportation—and its post-human fate.

Table 4.1. Sophisticated Methodological Holism (Part I)

• "My methodological holism implies the partiality-totality principle in the ontology of existential dialectics (see the table on the partiality-totality principle for summary), which is against the varieties of (a) reductionism and (b) reverse-reductionism, in relation to (i) concept, (ii) theory, (iii) methodology, and (iv) ontology." (*FC*)

• "[M]y methodological holism here is not opposed to methodological individualism but includes it (and, for that matter, other methodologies too)…." (*FPHC*) For this reason (and others too, as summarized hereafter), my version of methodological holism is sophisticated—not vulgar as sometimes used by inapt scholars using the same term. (*FC*)

• "[M]y methodological holism does not democratically presume that all levels are equally valid, as all levels are not created equal. In other words, in relation to issue X, level A may be more relevant than level B, but in relation to Y, level B can be more relevant than level A instead." (*FPHC*) One excellent example of this vulgar democratic presumption is what I called in *BNN* "the compromise fallacy." (*FC*)

• My methodological holism does not presume that a lower level of analysis is more important than a higher level, solely because the former serves as the foundation for the latter—and vice versa, for that matter. One excellent example of this reductionistic presumption is what I called in *FPHST* "the foundation fallacy." (*FPHST*, *FC*)

(continued on next page)

Table 4.1. Sophisticated Methodological Holism (Part II)

• "[M]y methodological holism does not make any a-priori postulation that there must be a definite (and, for that matter, indefinite) number of levels" in any analysis. (*FPHC*) Nor does it dogmatically require that there must be a certain combination of levels of analysis in a given inquiry. (*FC*)

• "[M]ethodological holism, in my usage, does not assume that all levels…can necessarily be integrated, since methodological holism is not aimed to search for the holy grail of 'an integral theory…' (as is the case for Wilber). In other words, it allows that sometimes some levels may experience irreducible gaps between them, to be understood, at best, as empirical correlations, not as causal relations…." (*FPHC*)

• "[D]ifferent levels may overlap and even interact with each other in a given context (but sometimes may not), and the fact that I even proposed different ways of re-classifying the levels (whenever needed) in *FDC* reinforces this point….The dual danger here is either forcefully making different levels interact when they are just different (or, metaphorically speaking, apples and oranges) or inappropriately ignoring their interactions when some situations instead require them." (*FPHC*)

• "[T]o understand different levels from their own (unique) perspectives (as required by my methodological holism) is not the same as trying to reduce them to a preferred level in the process of learning from other levels. This second kind of multidisciplinary work is not genuine and does no justice to the unique complexities and merits inherent at each level." (*FPHC*)

(continued on next page)

Table 4.1. Sophisticated Methodological Holism (Part III)

• "[My] methodological holism walks a fine line between the artificial classification (separation) of levels and the simultaneous incorporation of them, if only for the sake of human scholarly endeavor. It should be reminded that nature does not impose upon itself the academic classification of the levels of analysis as humans have. The enterprise of classification is therefore anthropocentric." (*FPHC*)

• "[M]y methodological holism advocates neither epistemic subjectivism nor epistemic non-subjectivism (e.g., realism, idealism, and historicism), neither epistemic relativism (e.g., subjectivism, historicism) nor epistemic absolutism (e.g., realism, positivism), neither epistemic reductionism nor epistemic emergencism, and neither epistemic objectivism (e.g., realism, idealism) nor epistemic historicism....Neither does methodological holism, in my usage, accept the false meta-conceptual dichotomy between nominalism and realism....These false dichotomies...are to be transcended. In other words, methodological holism does not fully accept epistemic realism, positivism (a form of epistemic idealism), historicism, subjectivism, and reductionism in epistemology and philosophy of science but learns from the strengths and weaknesses of all of the opposing approaches without siding with any of them...." (*FPHC*)

• "Sophisticated methodological holism is subject to the constraints as imposed by the syntax of existential dialectics (e.g., the partiality-totality principle and the predictability-unpredictability principle). Even in predictability, outcomes are subject to uncertainty, the degree of which varies from case to case." (*FC*)

(continued on next page)

Table 4.1. Sophisticated Methodological Holism (Part IV)

• "Sophisticated methodological holism—when applied, especially though not exclusively, as illustrated in my numerous works—can enrich the understanding of reality in some distinctive ways. Here are three examples (as revealed in each of my books)." (*FPHCT*; *FPHL*)

—"Firstly, it provides a comprehensive analysis of a subject matter, from which much can be learned about reality," "both in relation to the perspectives of the mind, nature, society, and culture and also in relation to a new classification of the subject matter."

—"Secondly, it suggests some visions of the future in relation to the subject matter in question."

—"And thirdly, it proposes some insights on meta-theory (e.g., methodology and ontology) in general—with the clear understanding, however, of the dilemma of specific vs. general ontology (as shown in the table on the syntax of existential dialectics in the context of the dilemma of ontology). For this very reason, all of these ways are important, without reducing one into the analysis of another."

• "In the end, my meta-theory (both sophisticated methodological holism and existential dialectics) serves as a foundation to unify all domains of knowledge into *an unified theory of everything* (by way of some ontological principles and the comprehensive perspectives of the mind, nature, society, and culture). This is so, without commiting the sins of reductionism and reverse-reductionism (as often seen in many holistic approaches, with the fad of sysems approach—be it about systems theory, chaos theory, complexity theory, or else—as a most recent notorious example, which I debunked in *The Future of Complexity* and also in *The Future of Post-Human Formal Science*). My distinctive approach makes good use of different schools of thought without favoring any of them nor trying to integrate them (as they are not necessarily compatible with each other), so as to adjust for subjectivity, diversity, conflict, and complexity, for example. In this sense, the word "unified" does not have to mean integrative approach, in a narrow sense, nor systems approach, in a broad one, both of which I reject while learning from them." (*FPHFS*; *FPHS*)

Sources: A summary of *Sec.1.2* in *FPHC*—and also from *BNN*, *FPHST*, *ALD*, *FC*, *FPHCT*, and the rest of all other books of mine. See the books for more detail.

Table 4.2. On Reductionism and Reverse-Reductionism (Part I)

- **The Partiality-Totality Principle**
  —The partiality-totality principle in the ontology of existential dialectics targets against the varieties of reductionism and reverse-reductionism (as already worked out in my previous books).

- **Against the Varieties of Reductionism**
  —*Conceptual Reductionism*
  - Some illustrative instances involve myriad dualities like mind vs. body, self vs. world, democracy vs. non-democracy, and the like (as already addressed in *FHC*, *FPHC*, and *BDPD*, for instance).

  —*Theoretical Reductionism*
  - A fascinating case study concerns what I originally called "the foundation fallacy" in *FPHST*, in any attempt to naively understand space-time from the physical perspective as the foundation and, consequently, to dangerously dismiss other perspectives.
  - In *FAE*, I elaborated further these versions of reductionism in the literature on aesthetics (e.g., form vs. content, representation vs. expression, critics vs. artists, and externalism vs. internalism).
  - In *FIA*, I revealed other forms of reductionism in the literature on information architecture (e.g., the constructivist argument).
  - In *FPHU*, I showed the persistent legacy of reductionism, this time, in the literature on anomalous experience (e.g., the obsession with physics, chemistry, and biology for explaining anomalous experience).
  - In *FPHE*, I examined another case of reductionism in action, in the context of engineering (e.g., technical constraints vs. normative constraints).
  - In *FPHMM*, I elaborated one more version of reductionism, in relation to the three domains of communication (e.g., the competing views on sending, connecting, and receiving).
  - In *FPHCT*, I explored another version of reductionism, in relation to invention and innovation (e.g., the bio-psychological argument vs. the socio-cultural arguments).

(continued on next page)

Table 4.2. On Reductionism and Reverse-Reductionism (Part II)

- **Against the Varieties of Reductionism *(cont'd)***
  - *—Theoretical Reductionism (cont'd)*
    - In *FPHG*, I identify another version of reductionism, in relation to infinity, symmetry, and dimensionality (e.g., the Euclidean argument vs. the non-Euclidean arguments).
    - In *FPHUP*, I analyzed another version of reductionism, in relation to density and void (e.g., the engineering argument and the ecology argument).
    - In *FPHL*, I examined another version of reductionism, in relation to structure and context (e.g., the structuralist argument and the contextualist argument).
    - In *PFHO*, I explored another version of reductionism, in relation to communcation, decision-making, and leadership (e.g., the rational-system argument vs. the natural-system argument).
    - In *PFHMA*, I revealed another version of reductionism, in relation to the martial body and spirit (e.g., the spiritual argument vs. the materialist argument vs. the defensive argument).
    - In *PFHS*, I analyzed another version of reductionism, in relation to the sexual body and spirit (e.g., the naturalist argument vs. the constructivist argument).
    - In *PFHLAW*, I examined another version of reductionism, in relation to law (e.g., the necessity argument vs. the contengency argument).
    - In *FPHWP*, I showed another version of reductionism, in relation to war and peace (e.g., the aggressivist argument vs. the pacifist argument).
    - In *BEPE*, I analyzed another version of reductionism, in relation to morality and immorality (e.g., the objectivist argument vs. the non-objectivist argument vs. the skeptical argument).
    - In *BCOS*, I examined another version of reductionism, in relation to the contested beginnings and speculative ends of the universe (e.g., the scientific argument vs. the religious argument vs. the esoteric argument vs. the metaphysical argument).
    - In *FPHP*, I show another version of reductionism, in relation to normality and abnormality (e.g., the natural argument vs. the social argument vs. the cultural argument vs. the mental argument).

(continued on next page)

Table 4.2. On Reductionism and Reverse-Reductionism (Part III)

- **Against the Varieties of Reductionism *(cont'd)***
  —*Theoretical Reductionism (cont'd)*
  - In *FPHGEOL*, I scrutinized another version of reductionism, in relation to statics and dynamics (e.g., the catastrophe argument vs. the uniformity argument vs. the revision argument).
  - In *FPHCHESS*, I showed another version of reductionism, in relation to tactics and strategy (e.g., the natural argument vs. the social argument vs. the cultural argument vs. the mental argument).
  - In *FPHR*, I revealed another version of reductionism, in relation to secularness and sacredness (e.g., the critical argument vs. the skeptical argument vs. the theist argument).
  - In *FPHEDU*, I examined another version of reductionism, in relation to teaching and learning (e.g., the teacher-centered argument vs. the student-centered argument vs. the balanced argument).
  - In *FPHH*, I explored another version of reductionism, in relation to joking and laughing (e.g., the natural argument vs. the social argument vs. the cultural argument vs. the mental argument).
  - In *FPHA*, I proposed another version of reductionism, in relation to sound and silence (e.g., the natural argument vs. the social argument vs. the cultural argument vs. the mental argument).
  - In *FPHGAM*, I proposed another version of reductionism, in relation to risk and caution (e.g., the natural argument vs. the social argument vs. the cultural argument vs. the mental argument).
  - In *FPHCOM*, I worked out another version of reductionism, in relation to hardware and software (e.g., the natural argument vs. the social argument vs. the cultural argument vs. the mental argument).
  - In *FPHLIT*, I proposed another version of reductionism, in relation to fiction and non-fiction (e.g., the natural argument vs. the social argument vs. the cultural argument vs. the mental argument).
  - In *FPHCHEM*, I proposed another version of reductionism, in relation to substances and their changes (e.g., the natural argument vs. the social argument vs. the cultural argument vs. the mental argument).

(continued on next page)

Table 4.2. On Reductionism and Reverse-Reductionism (Part IV)

- **Against the Varieties of Reductionism *(cont'd)***
  —*Theoretical Reductionism (cont'd)*
  - In *FPHDA*, I proposed another version of reductionism, in relation to quantitative and qualitative research (e.g., the natural argument vs. the social argument vs. the cultural argument vs. the mental argument).
  - In *FPHGEOG*, I proposed another version of reductionism, in relation to environments and their interactions (e.g., the natural argument vs. the social argument vs. the cultural argument vs. the mental argument).
  - In *FPHPA*, I proposed another version of reductionism, in relation to the body and its presence (e.g., the natural argument vs. the social argument vs. the cultural argument vs. the mental argument).
  - In *FPHSEM*, I proposed another version of reductionism, in relation to internality and externality (e.g., the natural argument vs. the social argument vs. the cultural argument vs. the mental argument).
  - In *FPHARCH*, I proposed another version of reductionism, in relation to form and function (e.g., the natural argument vs. the social argument vs. the cultural argument vs. the mental argument).
  - In *FPHCRIM*, I proposed another version of reductionism, in relation to heroes and villains (e.g., the natural argument vs. the social argument vs. the cultural argument vs. the mental argument).
  - In *FPHHIST*, I proposed another version of reductionism, in relation to universality and relativity (e.g., the natural argument vs. the social argument vs. the cultural argument vs. the mental argument).
  - In *FPHMIG*, I proposed another version of reductionism, in relation to Sameness, Otherness, and identity (e.g., the natural argument vs. the social argument vs. the cultural argument vs. the mental argument).

(continued on next page)

Table 4.2. On Reductionism and Reverse-Reductionism (Part V)

- **Against the Varieties of Reductionism *(cont'd)***
  —*Theoretical Reductionism (cont'd)*
  - And in *FPHTRAN*, I propose another version of reductionism, in relation to networks and operations (e.g., the natural argument vs. the social argument vs. the cultural argument vs. the mental argument).

  —*Methodological Reductionism*
  - A good instance concerns the debate between different versions of qualitative and quantitative methods (as already analyzed in *FC* and also *FHC*). In *FPHML*, I examined similar reductionism, this time, in the literature on mathematical logic (e.g., the obsession with consistency, soundness, and completeness). And in *FPHFS*, I also explored the problems of reductionism in the context of formal science (e.g., the analytical argument).

  —*Ontological Reductionism*
  - An excellent example is the debate between emergentism and reductionism in complexity theory and also in psychology (as elaborated in *FPHC*, in the context of Being and Becoming).

- **Against the Varieties of Reverse-Reductionism**
  —*Conceptual Reverse-Reductionism*
  - Any concept of "art" (e.g., fine art, cave art, outsider art, junk art) is deemed acceptable in postmodernism (as already addressed in Ch.4 of *FHC*).

(continued on next page)

Table 4.2. On Reductionism and Reverse-Reductionism (Part VI)

- **Against the Varieties of Reverse-Reductionism *(cont'd)***
  —*Theoretical Reverse-Reductionism*
  - There are numerous art and literary theories co-exist. Take the case of literary studies, as there are now Literary Structuralism, Marxist Literary Criticism, New Criticism, Phenomenology, Hermeneutics, Language-Game Literary Criticism, Feminist Literary Criticism, Reception Theory, Reader Response Criticism, Poststructuralism, Semiotics, Pyschoanalytic Literary Criticism, just to cite some well-known ones, with no one being said to be better than any others (as detailedly analyzed in Ch.4 of *FHC*). (S. Raman 1997) In *BNN*, I even introduced "the compromise fallacy" as another good illustration of theoretical reverse-reductionism, in misleadingly treating both genetic and environmental approaches as equally valid.

  —*Methodological Reverse-Reductionism*
  - There is the "anything-goes" mentality in postmodernism (e.g., doing art without praxis, doing art with praxis, and doing art by sublation), as analyzed in Ch.4 of *FHC*. And in *FPHFS*, I also exposed the problems of reverse-reductionism in the context of formal science in relation to systems theory.

  —*Ontological Reverse-Reductionism*
  - There are likewise no privileged ontology, and the door is open for anything in postmodernism (e.g., the equal status of the ontology of Being vs. that of Becoming, as already addressed in Ch.4 of *FHC*—and also in *FPHC)*. In *FAE*, I also introduced another version of reverse-reductionism, that is, "the pluralist fallacy," in the context of understanding aesthetic experience, for instance—although this fallacy has been committed not exclusively in relation to the ontological level (but also at the conceptual, theoretical, and methodological ones).

Sources: From my previous books.

Table 4.3. The Concepton of Existential Dialectics (Part I)

- **Sets and Elements**
  - —Sets
    - Ex: the Same
    - Ex: the Others
  - —Elements
    - Ex: whites in 20th century America (in the set of "the Same")
    - Ex: Iraq during the U.S. invasion in 2003 (in the set of "the Others")

- **Relations, Operations, Functions**
  - —Relations (e.g., "belongs," "equals to," "is greater than")
    - Ex: symmetric interactions within the Same (or the Others)
    - Ex: asymmetric interactions between the Same and the Others
  - —Operations (e.g., "and," "or," "not," "if…then")
    - Ex: if the Same oppresses the Others, it will also oppress itself.
    - Ex: the Same is not the Others.
  - —Functions (e.g., goals)
    - Ex: the Same is hegemonic in relation to the Others.

- **Truth Values**
  - —"1" if True (in Symbolic Logic)
    - Ex: the proposition that imperial Japan was hegemonic to China during WWII
  - —"0" if False (in Symbolic Logic)
    - Ex: the proposition that Grenada invaded France in 2003
  - —"1" & "0" if Both True and False (in Dialectic Logic)
    - Ex: the proposition that the rabbit-duck picture refers to a duck
  - —"~1" & "~0" if Neither True Nor False (or N/A, in Dialectic Logic)
    - Ex: the proposition that God really exists

(continued on next page)

Table 4.3. The Conception of Existential Dialectics (Part II)

- **Axioms and Postulates**
  - —Axioms
    - Ex: the reflexive axiom—"any quantity is equal to itself"
  - —Postulates
    - Ex: the SSS postulate—"if the three sides of a triangle are congruent to their corresponding parts, then the triangles are congruent"

- **Theorems and Principles**
  - —Theorems (and Principles) in Existential Dialectics
    - *In Relation to Method*
      - –#25: The formalness-informalness principle
      - –#24: The absoluteness-relativeness principle
      - –#23: The partiality-totality principle
      - –#22: The predictability-unpredictability principle
      - –#21: The explicability-inexplicability principle
      - –#20: The fiction-reality principle
    - *In Relation to Structure*
      - –#19: The finiteness-transfiniteness principle
      - –#18: The preciseness-vagueness principle
      - –#17: The simpleness-complicatedness principle
      - –#16: The openness-hiddenness principle
      - –#15: The denseness-emptiness principle
    - *In Relation to Process*
      - –#14: The change-constancy principle
      - –#13: The order-chaos principle
      - –#12: The slowness-quickness principle
      - –#11: The expansion-contraction principle

(continued on next page)

Table 4.3. The Conception of Existential Dialectics (Part III)

• **Theorems and Principles (*cont'd*)**
 —Theorems (and Principles) in Existential Dialectics
 • *In Relation to Agency*
 –#10: The theory-praxis principle
 –#9: The convention-novelty principle
 –#8: The evolution-transformation principle
 –#7: The symmetry-asymmetry principle
 –#6: The softness-hardness principle
 –#5: The seriousness-playfulness principle
 –#4: The activeness-inactiveness principle
 • *In Relation to Outcome*
 –#3: The regression-progression principle
 –#2: The same-difference principle
 –#1: The stability-reaction principle

Notes: The categories and examples in each are solely illustrative (not exhaustive). The comparison is also relative (not absolute), nor are they mutually exclusive. As generalities, they allow exceptions.
Sources: Starting from Ch.6 of *BCPC* and also from other books of mine

Table 4.4. The Syntax of Existential Dialectics I:
The Principles
(Part I)

- **In Relation to Method**

  —*The Formalness-Informalness Principle*

  (On the Formal Requirements of Logical Systems)

  - The formal requirements of a logical system (e.g., consistency, soundness, and completeness) have both usefulness and non-usefulness, to the extent that, if there are formal systems requiring them, there are alternative ones which do not. Thus, it does *not* exclude classical logics but simply goes beyond both classical and non-classical logics, while learning something from each. There is no formalness without informalness—and vice versa.
  - For instance, existential dialectics can make use of both classical logics under certain conditions (e.g., especially, though not exclusively, when they are clear-cut, etc.) and non-classical logics under alternative conditions (especially, though not exclusively, when they are "unknown," "irrelevant," "ambiguous," "possible," with "different degrees of truth," empirically inconsistent in a desirable way, etc.). (WK 2008u)
  - Family resemblance: e.g., logicalness-nonlogicalness, rationality-nonrationality, etc.
  - Sources: From *FPHML*, *FPHH*, *FPHGAM*, *FPHSEM*, and my later books.

(continued on next page)

Table 4.4. The Syntax of Existential Dialectics I: The Principles (Part II)

• **In Relation to Method** ***(cont'd)***

—*The Absoluteness-Relativeness Principle*
(On the Multiplicity of Things)

- There is the multiplicity of things in reality, be they about entities, qualities (or properties), and relationships, such that what is acceptable from one standpoint may not be so from another. For instance, if there is something absolute, there is likewise something relative. There is no absoluteness without relativeness—and vice versa.
- Both absoluteness and relativeness here are also relevant to different modalities often cited in the literature on ontology, such as possibility (e.g., something "can" happen) and its opposite (e.g., impossibility), probability (e.g., something "will" happen) and its opposite (e.g., improbability), and necessity (e.g., something "should" happen) and its opposite (e.g., contingency).
- Family resemblance: e.g., uniformity-diversity, internalness-externalness, immanence-transcendence, independence-dependence, isolatedness-interconnectiveness, autonomy-interdependency, universalness-relativeness, etc.
- Sources: From *FPHK*. See also my later books.

(continued on next page)

Table 4.4. The Syntax of Existential Dialectics I: The Principles (Part III)

- **In Relation to Method *(cont'd)***
  - —*The Partiality-Totality Principle*
    (On the Relationships between Whole and Parts)
    - The whole is not the sum of the parts. There is no partiality without totality—and vice versa.
    - Any inquiry about a phenomenon in the work is to guard against the varieties of (a) reductionism and (b) reverse-reductionism.
    - Reductionism and reverse-reductionism can be (i) conceptual, (ii) theoretical, (iii) methodological, and (iv) ontological.
    - Works on emergence (as in *FC*), gestalt psychology (as in *FPHGEOL*), the hermeneutic circle (as in *FPHDA*), and mental language (as in *FPHSEM*), to name just a few of them, have contributed to the understanding of whole and parts.
    - Family resemblance: e.g., individualisticness-holisticness, partness-wholeness, analysis-synthesis, etc.
    - Sources: Especially from *FC & FPHGEOL*. See also my later books.

(continued on next page)

Table 4.4. The Syntax of Existential Dialectics I: The Principles (Part IV)

- **In Relation to Method *(cont'd)***
  —*The Predictability-Unpredictability Principle*
  (On the Occurrence of Events)
  - Both predictability and unpredictability have a major role to play in the occurrence of things, so that neither determinism nor indeterminism wins the centuries-old fight. There is no predictability without unpredictability—and vice versa.
  - There are events which are predictable, just as there are those which are not. Or what is regarded as unpredictable at one point in time may turn out to be predictable later, and, conversely, what is deemed as predictable may turn out to not be so predictable. Even in predictability, outcomes are subject to uncertainty, the degree of which varies from case to case.
  - Works on complexity theory (as in *FC*), quantum mechanics (as in *FPHST* and *FPHG*), frequency probability, subjective (or Bayesian) probability, and "special causes" (as in *FPHGAM*), just to name a few of them, have contributed to the understanding of uncertainity.
  - Family resemblance: e.g., sureness-arbitrariness, certainty-uncertainty, deterministicness-indeterministicness, sureness-doubtfulness, likeliness-riskiness, deterministicness-randomness, etc.
  - Sources: Especially from *FC* & *FPHGAM.* See also my later books.

(continued on next page)

Table 4.4. The Syntax of Existential Dialectics I: The Principles (Part V)

- **In Relation to Method *(cont'd)***

—*The Explicability-Inexplicability Principle*
(On the Underlying Mechanisms of Things)

- Both explicability and inexplicability are part of the understanding of things. There is no explicability without inexplicability—and vice versa.
- This principle tells us the duality of the research dilemma, in that, if reality can be explained in some ways, it also has its other ways which are not quite explainable, at a given point in time.
- Family resemblance: e.g., underlyingness-regularness, causation-regularness, explanation-interpretation, explanation-description, causation-correlation, explanation-narration, etc.
- Sources: Especially from *FPHU*—and also *FPHC*. See also my later books.

—*The Fiction-Reality Principle*
(On the different faces of Reality)

- If there is reality, there is also fiction, especially for any agent with some kind of intelligence life, be it about humans, animals, or, later, post-humans. There is no reality without fiction—and vice versa.
- The distinction between reality and fiction is not absolute, since there can be a mixture of both. Fiction can have non-fictional elements, just as non-fiction can have fictional ones. So, the distinction is in degree, not in kind.
- Family resemblance: e.g., fiction-nonfiction, fiction-fact, imagination-fact, subjectivity-objectivity, imagination-nonfiction, etc.
- Sources: First from *FPHLIT*.

(continued on next page)

Table 4.4. The Syntax of Existential Dialectics I: The Principles (Part VI)

• **In Relation to Structure**

—*The Finiteness-Transfiniteness Principle*

(On the Nature of Numbers)

- If there are finite things, there are likewise transfinite ones. There is no finiteness without transfiniteness—and vice versa.
- To avoid confusion, my usage of the word "transfinite" here differs radically from the one used by Cantor (and other mathematicians) for "relative" infinity—and is more limited, in light of the problems confronting any attempt to understand the idea of infinity, be it by intuition, imagination, and conception (as detailedly analyzed in *Sec. 2.2.3* of *FPHG*).
- Instead, by "transfinity," I allow numbers which can be many times larger—or smaller, for that matter—than the finite things that we encounter in daily life, but they do not have to be related to the idea of infinity at all (which may not exist).
- Of course, there may be some *borderline* cases, in which it is not clear whether the number in question is transfinite (in my usage) or simply a mathematical convenience. A good example of a borderline case is the Planck unit of length for "the smallest space possibly measured in nature," which is "less than billionths of trillionths of trillionths of an inch" (or something like 1.6×10^{-35} meters).
- That said—my usage of "transfinity" can also resolve (or better, dissolve) an age-old problem in philosophy known as "Zeno's paradoxes" (as already explained in *Sec. 2.2.3* of *FPHG*).
- Family resemblance: e.g., boundedness-quasiunboundedness, smallness-largeness, boundedness-unboundedness, etc.
- Source: From *FPHG*. See also my later books.

(continued on next page)

Table 4.4. The Syntax of Existential Dialectics I: The Principles (Part VII)

- **In Relation to Structure** ***(cont'd)***
  —The Preciseness-Vagueness Principle (On the Refinement of Things)
  - Both preciseness and vagueness are important, not that one is better than the other, but that both are used, in different degrees of preference, in accordance to the contextual application from the perspectives of nature, the mind, culture, and society. Even when both are used in a combination, the dilemma is shifted instead to one of combinational concern. There is no preciseness without vagueness—and vice versa.
  - In relation to taxonomy, preciseness has its taxonomic clarity, just as vagueness has its classificatory flexibility, for instance. And in relation to network, vagueness has its explorative liberty, just as preciseness has its conceptual definitiveness, for instance.
  - Family resemblance: e.g., clarity-ambiguity, directness-indirectness, quantitativeness-qualitativeness, describability-nondescribability, specificity-obscurity, specificity-generality, thickness-thinness, translatability-untranslatability, clearcutness-transitionalness, concreteness-abstractness, etc.
  - Sources: Especially from *FIA*. See also my later books.

(continued on next page)

Table 4.4. The Syntax of Existential Dialectics I: The Principles (Part VIII)

- **In Relation to Structure** ***(cont'd)***
  —*The Simpleness-Complicatedness Principle*
  (On the Interconnection among Things)
  - Both simpleness and complicatedness are vital, without favoring one over the other, in that each is utilized, depending on the basis of the perspectives of nature, the mind, culture, and society. And even when a combination of them is preferred, the dilemma is only shifted to a combinational degree of concern. There is no simpleness without complicatedness—and vice versa.
  - In relation to taxonomy, simpleness has its heuristic usefulness, just as complicatedness has its realistic representation, for instance. And in relation to network, simpleness has its economical attractiveness, just as complicatedness has its practical reliability, for instance.
  - Family resemblance: e.g., inflexibility-flexibility, standardization-specialization, imperfectness-perfectness, superficiality-depth, shallowness-deepness, economicalness-elaboratedness, plainness-circumspection, onesidedness-multisidedness, succinctness-duplicatedness, etc.
  - Sources: Especially from *FIA*. See also my later books.

(continued on next page)

Table 4.4. The Syntax of Existential Dialectics I: The Principles (Part IX)

- **In Relation to Structure *(cont'd)***
  —*The Openness-Hiddenness Principle*
  (On the Detection of Things)
  - Reality has its hidden face, just as it is open to outside view in some other ways. There is no openness without hiddenness—and vice versa.
  - For instance, in the context of anomalous experience, certain aspects of reality can be open for examination (e.g., the experiment with SPECT images, the transmission of telepathemic bit, and the use of metonymies and metaphors). Other aspects, however, remain hidden, and examples include the elusive deeper nature of spiritual reality in the intangible realm, the undetectability of different branched universes, the underlying mechanisms of signals traveling between different folds of physical space-time, and the dependence on language and the bias for science and logic).
  - Family resemblance: e.g., overtness-covertness, publicness-privateness, openness-closedness, transparency-secrecy, openness-biasedness, participation-obstruction, exposition-illusion, surface-depth, etc.
  - Sources: Especially from *FPHU*. See also my later books.

(continued on next page)

Table 4.4. The Syntax of Existential Dialectics I: The Principles (Part X)

• **In Relation to Structure** ***(cont'd)***
 —*The Denseness-Emptiness Principle*
 (On the Distribution of Entities in Space)
 • Both density and void are needed, in relation to the mind, nature, culture, and society, albeit in different ways. There is no denseness without emptiness—and vice versa.
 • For clarity, the term "void" is used here only as an approximation of emptiness (depending on the degree of the lack of density), since, in physics, it is well known that "empty" space is not really empty all the way, because it can be full of energy (e.g., random quantum fluctuations at the sub-atomic level, and, for that matter, dark energy in the universe) and matter (e.g., different versions of sub-atomic particles, and, for that matter, dark matter in the universe).
 • Family resemblance: e.g., fullness-voidness, nearness-farness, concentration-dispersion, denseness-nothingness, presence-absence, focus-unfocus, solidness-void, something-nothing, heaviness-lightness, composition-emptiness, emphasis-disemphasis, etc.
 • Sources: First worked out in *FPHUP*. See also my later books.

• **In Relation to Process**
 —*The Change-Constancy Principle*
 (On the Alteration of Things)
 • Change occurs over time, although constancy is also allowed. There is no change without constancy—and vice versa.
 • Asymmetry undergoes changes over time, so does symmetry.
 • Old players fade away, and new ones emerges, with ever new causes and ever new forms.
 • Family resemblance: e.g., dynamicness-staticness, instability-stability, etc.
 • Sources: First named in *BCPC*. Especially from *FHC*, *FCD*, and *FPHC*. See also other books of mine (from that point on).

(continued on next page)

Table 4.4. The Syntax of Existential Dialectics I: The Principles (Part XI)

- **In Relation to Process** ***(cont'd)***
  —*The Order-Chaos Principle*
  (On the Pattern of Things)
  - Both order and chaos are vital in the process of change in the world. The preference for order is biased, since it does not give sufficient attention to the vital role of chaos in the transformation of the world (without somehow reducing it for the understanding of order). There is no order without chaos—and vice versa.
  - The scientific search for order in the world is often a hidden bias in its ontological obsession with order, since chaos is often treated as the "bad" guy, with order as the "good" guy (for the end goal of science).
  - Neither order nor chaos is the final end of the world, and one is not to be treated as the means for the other in the transformation of things. Both are fundamental in their recurrent dialectical interactions with each other over time, without reducing one for the other.
  - Family resemblance: e.g., lawfulness-disorder, order-disorder, linearity-nonlinearity, linearity-irreversalness, pattern-chaos, unity-disunity, etc.
  - Sources: Especially from *FC*. See also my later books.

(continued on next page)

Table 4.4. The Syntax of Existential Dialectics I: The Principles (Part XII)

- **In Relation to Process *(cont'd)***

—*The Slowness-Quickness Principle*
(On the Speed of Change)

- Both slowness and quickness co-exist, with their own internal tension, to the extent that each fights for its own relevance with the other, in accordance to the perspectives of nature, the mind, culture, and society, without one being the victor and the other being the vanquished in the long haul. Even when both are chosen in other cases, this dilemma is only transferred into something else with a combinational character. There is no slowness without quickness—and vice versa.
- In relation to taxonomy, quickness has its efficient usability, just as slowness has its aesthetic appeal, for instance. And in relation to network, quickness has its adventurous readiness, just as slowness has its risk-adverse convenience, for instance.
- Family resemblance: e.g., inconvenience-convenience, passiveness-activenessness, gradualness-abruptness, deceleration-acceleration, difficulty-ease, etc.
- Sources: Especially from *FIA*. See also my later books.

—*The Expansion-Contraction Principle*
(On the Growth of Things)

- Entities in the world can both expand in some ways and contract in other ones, as part of their nature. There is no expansion without contraction—and vice versa.
- For instance, in the context of anomalous experience, one of its most fascinating expressions is none other than the analysis of different causes of the slow but steady expansion (and, furthermore, if put in a different way, unfolding) of unconsciousness.
- Family resemblance: e.g., conquest-autarky, rise-fall (or up-down), spread-shrink, extendingness-shorteningness, widening-narrowing, etc.
- Sources: Especially from *FPHU*. See also my later books.

(continued on next page)

Table 4.4. The Syntax of Existential Dialectics I: The Principles (Part XIII)

- **In Relation to Agency**
  —*The Theory-Praxis Principle*
  (On the Duality of Knowledge))
  - This has to do with the duality of knowledge in existential dialectics, in that, if there is theoretical construction, there is likewise its practical application, both technical and normative. There is no theory without praxis—and vice versa.
  - Family resemblance: e.g., discovery-application, knowledge-action, invention-innovation, knowledge-motivation, theory-intentionality, universality-particularity, discourse-action, knowledge-interest, etc.
  - Source: Especially from *FPHE*. See also my later books.

(continued on next page)

Table 4.4. The Syntax of Existential Dialectics I: The Principles (Part XIV)

- **In Relation to Agency *(cont'd)***
  —*The Convention-Novelty Principle*
  (On the Nature of Creative Thinking)
  - If there is conventional wisdom, there is likewise novel challenge, to the extent that both convergent and divergent thinking are part of life. There is no convention without novelty—and vice versa.
  - In addition, in this context of the convention-novelty principle, there are, in the absence of better words, what I want to call (a) *creative techniques* and (b) *creative traits*, which, when satisfied—in relation to the larger context of the mind, nature, society, and culture—can be used to enhance creative works. The list of creative techniques and traits (as summarized in *Table 4.1* of *FPHCT*) are not exhaustive, of course, but the examples here constitute a great beginning of understanding the structure of creative thinking.
  - Yet, lest the reader gets carried away by the euphoria about creative thinking in our time, it should be reminded that creative thinking has its own possibilities and limits (as shown in *Table 2.1* of *FPHCT* on invention), just as it has its own promises and pitfalls (as shown in *Table 3.1* of *FPHCT* on innovation). In the end, it should also be stressed that creative thinking has its own desirability and dark sides (as shown in *Table 4.2* of *FPHCT*, *BNN*, and *FPHMIG*).
  - This has important daily implications for an average individual, and the word "average" here allows different degrees of variation from one individual to another in a population, at any given point in history.
  - Family resemblance: e.g., normalness-nonnormalness, conformity-nonconformity, convergence-divergence, etc.
  - Sources: First from *FPHCT*. See also my later books.

(*continued on next page*)

Table 4.4. The Syntax of Existential Dialectics I: The Principles (Part XV)

- **In Relation to Agency** ***(cont'd)***

  —*The Evolution-Transformation Principle*
  (On the Multiple Kinds of Agency)

  - This principle (and the symmetry-asymmetry principle) are both about *the agency of change*. The word "agency," in a formal definition, refers to "a person or thing through which power is exerted or an end is achieved." (MWD 2007b) It therefore does not have to necessarily involve an intelligent lifeform.
  - Because of this dual meaning in agency, the evolution-transformation principle is more concerned with *the multiple kinds of agency*, that is, both about the *evolution* in the state of nature (e.g., an object of natural beauty) and the *transformation* in the world of intelligent lifeforms (e.g., a work of art, an air-conditioner, etc.). There is no evolution without transformation—and vice versa.
  - And the transformative part of the principle precisely refers to the other dimension in the dual meaning of agency, in giving technology a major role to play in the change of the world, which is something that I extensively analyzed in *FHC* in the context of the technophilic lifeworld, espeically though not exclusively since modern times. The same theme is also elaborated in other books of mine.
  - Family resemblance: e.g., nonwillingness-willingness, naturalness-technologicalness, evolution-creation, naturalness-nonnaturalness, inorganicness-volition, naturalness-artificialness, inorganicness-motivation, etc.
  - Sources: Especially from *FAE*. See also other books of mine.

(*continued on next page*)

Table 4.4. The Syntax of Existential Dialectics I: The Principles (Part XVI)

- **In Relation to Agency** ***(cont'd)***
  —*The Symmetry-Asymmetry Principle*
  (On the Relationships among Existents)
  - There is no symmetry without asymmetry—and vice versa.
  - For instance, the Same can be symmetric and asymmetric towards the Others. But in case of asymmetry, oppression and self-oppression can occur. So, when the Same is asymmetric towards the Others, the Same can also be relatively asymmetric towards itself in self-oppression, just as the Others can be likewise towards themselves.
  - The subsequent oppressiveness is dualistic, as much by the Same against the Others and itself, as by the Others against the Same and themselves.
  - Both oppression and self-oppression can be achieved by way of downgrading differences between the Same and the Others and of accentuating them.
  - This is true, even though not all forms of asymmetry have to be about oppression and self-oppression.
  - In addition, from Chapter Three of *FPHG*, symmetry is not perfect, to be understood in an approximate sense under many life circumstances.
  - Family resemblance: e.g., balance-extremity, reflexiveness-unreflexiveness, balance-unbalance, equality-inequality, center-periphery, compatibility-incompatibility, proportion-disproportion, harmoniousness-unharrmoniousness, etc.
  - Sources: From all my books, starting with *FHC*. First named in *BCPC*. See, for instance, *FCD* for more details on the Same and the Others.

(*continued on next page*)

Table 4.4. The Syntax of Existential Dialectics I: The Principles (Part XVII)

- **In Relation to Agency *(cont'd)***

  —The Softness-Hardness Principle

  (On the Force of Change)

  - This has to do with *the force of change* under the category about agency in existential dialectics, in that any change by an agent, be it organic (like humans) or non-organic (like natural objects), can occur in a forceful (aggressive) or gentle (pacific) way, which can come in all shapes and sizes, of course. There is no softness without hardness—and vice versa.
  - Family resemblance: e.g., peacefulness-violence, cooperation-competition, acceptance-discrimination, love-hatred, peace-war, pacificity-aggression, dovishness-hawkishness, reward-punishment, kindness-hostility, admiration-belittlement, inclusion-exclusion, friendliness-unfriendliness, etc.
  - Sources: Especially from *ALD*. See also my later books.

(continued on next page)

Table 4.4. The Syntax of Existential Dialectics I: The Principles (Part XVIII)

- **In Relation to Agency** ***(cont'd)***
  —*The Seriousness-Playfulness Principle*
  (On the Extent of Seriousness)
  - If there is seriousness, there is also playfulness, especially for any agent with some kind of intelligence life, be it about humans, animals, or, later, post-humans. There is no seriousness without playfulness—and vice versa.
  - Lest any misunderstanding occurs, the word "playfulness" here should not be confused with other terms like "laughter," "smile," "joke," "tickleness," and "laugh-like vocalization" (in some animals), for instance.
  - Being playful can come in all shapes and sizes and therefore is not necessarily tied up with any of these terms, alhough it can result from any of them, or a combination of them, or something else altogether.
  - This principle, together with some other principles (especially though not exclusively, like the formalness-informalness principle), have important implications for what constitutes rationality, be it about "rationality of application" at the practical level or "rationality of knowledge" at the meta-theoretical level (as summarized in *Sec. 4.20* of *FPHH*).
  - Family resemblance: e.g., seriousness-jokingness, seriousness-humorousness, seriousness-wittiness, seriousness-nonseriousness, seriousness-relaxedness, seriousness-restingness, Apollo-Dionysus, etc.
  - Sources: First from *FPHH* & *FPHGAM* See also my later books.

(*continued on next page*)

Table 4.4. The Syntax of Existential Dialectics I: The Principles (Part XIX)

- **In Relation to Agency** ***(cont'd)***
  —*The Activeness-Inactiveness Principle*
  (On the Extent of Activeness)
  - If there is activeness, there is also inactiveness, especially (though not exclusively) for any agent with some kind of intelligence life, be it about humans, animals, or, later, post-humans. There is no activeness without inactiveness—and vice versa.
  - Being active can come in all shapes and sizes, just as a person (or an animal) can be inactive because he (or it) is tired, old, injured, sick, sleepy (or hibernating), uninterested, in a state of passive inertia (or disposition), etc.—and an object can be inactive because it is at rest, out of work (or order), etc.
  - This principle, together with some other principles (especially though not exclusively, like the formalness-informalness principle and seriousness-playfulness principle), have important implications for what constitutes rationality, be it about "rationality of application" at the practical level or "rationality of knowledge" at the meta-theoretical level (as summarized in *Sec. 4.20* of *FPHH*).
  - Family resemblance: e.g., alertness-unalertness, activeness-decrepidness, alertness-sleepiness, awakenness-hibernatedness, activeness-tiredness, alertness-uninterestedness, alertness-unwareness, soberness-unawareness, soberness-inactiveness, alertness-inactiveness, etc.
  - Sources: First from *FPHTRAN*

(*continued on next page*)

Table 4.4. The Syntax of Existential Dialectics I: The Principles (Part XX)

- **In Relation to Outcome**

—*The Regression-Progression Principle (On the Direction of History)*

- Neither the cyclical nor the linear views are adequate for explaining many phenomena at all levels. There is regression without progression—and vice versa.
- History progresses to more advanced forms, but with a regressive touch. Examples include no freedom without unfreedom, no equality without inequality, and no civilization without barbarity.
- This is not an inevitable law, but merely a highly likely empirical trend.
- Family resemblance: e.g., cost-benefit, undesirability-desirability, badness-goodness, risk-opportunity, etc.
- Sources: From all my books, starting with *FHC*. First named in *BCPC*.

—*The Same-Difference Principle (On the Metamorphosis of Change)*

- An entity, as it evolves over time, can be both different from and similar to its opposing alternatives and does not have to be solely more different from them over time. There is no similarity without difference—and vice versa.
- Opposites are not absolute in a black-or-white fashion; so, an entity can become relatively more similar to (or more different from) its opposite over time.
- Family resemblance: e.g., homogeneity-heterogeneity, we-they, similarity-contrast, etc.
- Sources: Especially from ALD. See also my later books

(*continued on next page*)

Table 4.4. The Syntax of Existential Dialectics I: The Principles (Part XXI)

- **In Relation to Outcome *(cont'd)***
  —The Stability-Reaction Principle
  (On the Feedback Mechanism for Further Changes)
  - Once an outcome becomes stabilized over time (which varies from case to case), it will undergo further changes in its multifaceted interactions with the outside world (e.g., with other entities, energy, space, and so on).
  - There is no stability without reaction for further changes—and vice versa.
  - Family resemblance: e.g., stability-forwardness, balance-reaction, balance-forwardness, rest-motion, normalcy-feedback, stability-breakup, consolidation-modification, etc.
  - Sources: First from *FPHCHEM.*

Notes: The features in each principle are solely illustrative (not exhaustive). The comparison is also relative (not absolute), nor are they mutually exclusive. As generalities, they allow exceptions.

Table 4.5. The Syntax of Existential Dialectics II: The Principles as Short Cuts (Part I)

• The principles should be treated with caution, lest misunderstanding occurs, since they do not constitute rigid dualities (or dichotomies).

• The reason is that each pair in an ontological principle consists of two opposites, which are, however, merely short cuts both for multiple variations and degrees, as well as for different interactions with multiple other entities unlike them. In this light, each pair can end up having hundred (or even thousand, if not more) different versions, which interact with hundred (or even thousand, if not more) other entities. There are two clarifications here.

• Firstly, this conception of shortcuts is not mutually exclusive nor absolute, in that the opposites can come in all shapes and sizes, with different degrees. For instance, by analogy, just as there are different degrees of the two colors "white" and "black"—there are likewise different degrees of the opposites in each ontological pair, to the extent that there can be multiple entities (not only two) interacting with each other in each pair.

• And secondly, this conception of shortcuts do not ignore other possible entities in interacting with the two opposites (with their different versions) in each pair. For instance, by analogy, there are not only the two colors "white" and "black" as opposites, since there are other colors too besides them like "yellow," "green," "purple," or else. The same logic can be applied to each ontological pair, in that they also interact with other entities, not with only two of them (with their different versions).

• Therefore, with these two clarifications in mind—each pair in an ontological principle serves only as an abbreviation for something more complicated and, therefore, although it contains two opposites, it should not be confused as a duality (dualism).

(continued on next page)

Table 4.5. The Syntax of Existential Dialectics II: The Principles as Short Cuts (Part II)

• Existential dialectics rejects any dualism (or dichotomy) as too rigid and instead allows the multiplicity of entities, to the extent that between the two opposites in each pair exist many other alternatives to choose from. They are named in that short form for aesthetic elegance, instead of listing all possible entities between the two opposites in the title.

• To be dialectic is to go beyond any rigid dichotomy and transcend into something different altogether in the long haul. One may be tempted to call the dialectic logic here with a different name like existential "multilectics" (instead of "dialectics"), but this naming is incorrect (or even misleading), for the two reasons aforestated.

• After all, each ontological pair come in all shapes and sizes (with different degrees) and do not exist by themselves but also interact with other entities unlike them. The virtue of revealing an ontological pair is to show how they relate within themselves (in multiple versions) and also interact with others unlike them (also in multiple versions).

• This will be clear in the table on "the dialectic constraints imposed by the principles."

Source: From Ch.1 of *FPHK*

Table 4.6. The Syntax of Existential Dialectics III: The Principles as Family Resemblances

• Each ontological principle is generic, with some other comparable ontological pairs to be put in the same family (like a *family resemblance*). Ludwig Wittgenstein (1953) once suggested the idea of "family resemblance" in explaining different games classified under the same family called *games*.

• Why should, for instance, playing football and chess as playing "games," when it is well understood that football is not the same as chess? The answer is that, although each game is different and has different rules, many of them (though not all) share, more or less, some commonalites (e.g., scoring as necessary for winning).

• And this is so, even though some games share more than some others in any given selection of critieria, and no two games are exactly identical. So, his point here is that there is no essential core which is common to all games, and the best that one can look for is some characteristics which are common to many (but not all) games. (A. Biletzki 2006)

• By the same logic—in the previous section on selection criteria, the flexibility-inflexibility pair can be put in the family resemblance of the simpleness-complicatedness principle, although the two pairs are not exactly identical. Likewise, the directness-indirectness pair can be put in the family resemblance of the preciseness-vagueness principle, although, again, the two pairs are not exactly identical.

• In this sense, which specific pair in a family should be used to designate the name of the family can be at times a bit arbitrary, but with good reason.

• For illustration, in the context of method, the partiality-totality principle can take the different form like individualisticness-holisticness, just as the explicability-inexplicability principle can take the different form like underlyingness-regularness—although each two pairs are not exactly identical and have slightly different meanings and usages. A more comprehensive listing of this family resemblance for all other principles is shown in the table on the syntax of existential dialectics.

Source: From Ch.1 of *FPHK*

Table 4.7. The Syntax of Existential Dialectics IV: The Dialectic Constraints Imposed by the Principles (Part I)

• **Co-Existent and Asymmetric**

—The principles, as they constitute the syntax of existential dialectics, are dialectic in character, such that, when they are applied, they impose dialectic constraints on how reality is to be understood. Consider, say, the symmetry-asymmetry principle as an illustration here, in order to summarize two main characters of the dialectic constraints in question.

—Firstly, to be dialectic here is to go beyond the narrow dichotomies (and, for that matter, any rigid multi-dimensional classificatory scheme), be they about "self" vs. "world," "freedom" vs. "unfreedom," "barbarity" vs. "civilization," "individuality" vs. "communality," and so on.

—One way to do so (to go beyond) is to consider them all in terms of co-existence (without favoring one over the rest). For instance, my theory of "post-civilization" (to be summarized later in the section on the pragmatics of existential dialectics) is to go beyond barbarity and civilization in terms of understanding barbarity and civilization as being co-existent. And the same logic can be said in relation to my theories of "post-democracy," "post-capitalsm," and others (also to be introduced later in the section on the pragmatics of existential dialectics), in regard to freedom vs. unfreedom, equality vs. inequality, communality vs. individuality, spirituality vs. materiality, and so on.

—But to consider them all (in the dichotomies—and, for that matter, in any rigid multi-dimensional classifactory schme) as co-existent is not the same as to imply that the opposites in any classificatory scheme are all equal, since, in accordance to the symmetry-asymmetry principle (as an illustration here), if they are equal in terms of being considered as co-existent, they are asymmetric in terms of being unequal in dialectic interaction (e.g., X can be more dominant than Y in case A, or Y is more dominant than X in case B).

(continued on next page)

Table 4.7. The Syntax of Existential Dialectics IV: The Dialectic Constraints Imposed by the Principles (Part II)

—For this reason, there are different versions of "post-democracy" and "post-capitalism" in my theories. As an illustration, in version I of the theory of post-democracy, freedom is more dominant than equality, whereas in version II of the theory of post-democracy, equality is more so than freedom.
—But this "X more than Y" has to be understood in the context of dialectic logic (not in conventional logic), in that both "X" and "Y" are important in post-democracy (in the context of dialectic logic), but in an asymmetry way. By contrast, in conventional logic, it often favors one over the other—be it in regard to privileging freedom over equality in Fascism, favoring freedom relatively more than equality in Liberal Democracy, or favoring equality relatively more than freedom in Socialist Democracy. In the latter two cases (about Liberal Democracy and Socialist Democracy), the difference between dialectic logic and conventional logic can be one in degree, not in kind—in this sense, albeit not in other senses.
—The same logic can be said about the relatonships between individuality and communality, between spirituality and materiality, and between formal legalism and informal legalism in the different versions of my theory of post-capitalism.

• **Transcendent**
—Secondly, to be dialectic is to go beyond the narrow dichotomies (and, for that matter, any rigid multi-dimensional classificatory scheme) in another way, this time, in a transcendent way, that is, in exploring other possibilities or even other issues not considered within the narrow confines of narrow dichotomies (and, for that matter, any rigid multi-dimensional classificatory scheme).

(continued on next page)

Table 4.7. The Syntax of Existential Dialectics IV: The Dialectic Constraints Imposed by the Principles (Part III)

—As an analogy, to go beyond the narrow color dichotomy of "black" and "white" is not just to choose both "black" and "white" (as in the first meaning) but also to explore other color options (e.g., "green," "purple," "blue," etc.—and, alternatively, "shade," "line," "curve," etc.). By the same logic, to go beyond "democracy" is to transcend democracy (as in version III of the theory of "post-democracy") and to explore other possibilties of lifeforms (e.g., floating consciousness, hyper-spatial consciousness, etc., to live beyond the narrow obsession with freedom and equality).

—This dialectic character of the principles in existential dialectics has important implications for the pragmatics of existential dialectics (as will be clear shortly, in the section on the pragmatics of existential dialectics).

Notes: The examples here are solely illustrative (not exhaustive). The comparison is also relative (not absolute), nor are they mutually exclusive. As generalities, they allow exceptions.
Sources: First explicitly stated in *ALD*. Also from all other books of mine.

Table 4.8. The Syntax of Existential Dialectics V: Further Clarifications (Part I)

• **Pioneering**

—Firstly, the total number of ontological principles is unknown, to be discovered later, as our knowledge of the world becomes more advanced.

—Consequently, the principles as introduced in my books are not exhaustive, with new ones being added, whenever more of them are discovered in later research.

—At least, future generations can pick up where I leave off and continue the discovery.

—In this sense, my work should be treated as a pioneering effort for the development of a systematic, comprehensive analysis of a new general ontology for the future of knowledge.

• **Flexible**

—Secondly, the principles are not rigidly classified, as they can be reclassified in a different way.

—For instance, the preciseness-vagueness principle is classified under the category of "structure" but can be reclassified under the category of "method," although in so doing, it has a different meaning in the context of method.

—The same logic applies to the same-difference principle under the category of "outcome," which can be reclassified under the category of "structure," although in so doing, once more, it has a different meaning in the context of structure.

• **Mutually Constraining**

—Thirdly, the principles are to be understood together, not that each prinicple is to be analyzed independently of others. After all, the principles are mutually constraining, in that they work together as a whole.

(continued on next page)

Table 4.8. The Syntax of Existential Dialectics V: Further Clarifications (Part II)

- **Selectively Useful**
  —Fourthly, the principles are relevant to all subject matters, but some principles are more useful to some subject matters than others—as implied in the symmetry-asymmetry principle. This is true, even if different studies of the same kind can yield different views about the degree of relevance for each ontological principle, depending on the specific nature of a research in question, needless to say.

- **Anti-Reductionistic**
  —And fifthly, the principles constitute only two levels of analysis, this time, at the ontological and methodological levels—while other levels of analysis (from the perspectives of the mind, nature, society, and culture) are also needed, in order to understand reality in its totality (as explained in the section on "sophisticated methodological holism," so as to avoid the dual dangers of reductionism and reverse-reductionism).

Notes: The examples here are solely illustrative (not exhaustive). The comparison is also relative (not absolute), nor are they mutually exclusive. As generalities, they allow exceptions.
Sources: From my previous books like *FHC*, *FCD*, *FPHC*, *BDPD*, *BCPC*, *BNN*, *FC*, *FAE*, and so on.

Table 4.9. The Syntax of Existential Dialectics VI: The Dilemma of Specific vs. General Ontology (Part I)

• Ontology is often more complicated and imposes some seemingly insurmountable difficulties concerning what constitutes a kind of ontology which can be valid enough to be accepted by the wider intellectual community in question. An excellent example concerns what I want to call *the dilemma of ontology* in relation to the relationship between "specific ontology" and "general ontology." (M. Bunge 1999; R. Corazzon 2007)

• On the one hand, "general ontology," as Mario Bunge (1999) put it, "studies all existents." But, on the other hand, "special ontology studies one genus of thing or process—physical, chemical, biological, social, etc." (M. Bunge 1999; R. Corazzon 2007)

• Consequently, the relationship between the former and the latter is that, as an illustration, "whereas general ontology studies the concepts of space, time, and event, the ontology of the social investigates such general sociological concepts as those of social system, social structure, and social change." (M. Bunge 1999; R. Corazzon 2007)

• With this formal definition in mind, the relationship between the two forms of ontology only poses *the dilemma of ontology*, in that general ontology is possible to the extent that its general contructs must be broad enough to serve as the "lowest common denominator" for all disciplines, but this character of the lowest common denominator is not only hard to find but also its usefulness is limited. (WK 2008b)

• But specific ontology fares no better either, in that its specific constructs primarily serve a specific discipline in question, although other disciplines can appropriate them for their own purposes, but in a different context (especially, though not exclusively, when used as a metaphor from one field to another). For instance, the Kantian category of understanding under the heading of "quantity" constitutes a type of specific ontology, which is specific to the discipline of mathematics, although other disciplines can make use of the categories in their own context.

(continued on next page)

Table 4.9. The Syntax of Existential Dialectics VI: The Dilemma of Specific vs. General Ontology (Part II)

• A solution lies in my proposal of "sophisticated methodological holism," which requires all levels of analysis in any subject matter. See the tables on sophisticated methodological holism, and on reductionism and reverse-reductionism, for more details.

Source: From *Sec. 1.4* of *FPHK*

Table 4.10. The Syntax of Existential Dialectics VII: Types of Inappropriate Family Resemblances (Part I)

- **Inadequate Family Resemblances**
  —Ex: consistency-inconsistency: the formalness-informalenss principle
  —Ex: cognition-noncognition: the formalness-informalness principle

- **Compound Family Resemblances**
  —Ex: reality-nonreality: the formalness-informalness principles, the absoluteness-relativeness principle
  —Ex: normality-abnormality: the symmetry-asymmetry principle, the density-emptiness principle, the convention-novelty principle, the same-difference principle
  —Ex: structure-context: the simpleness-complicatedness principle, the theory-praxis principle
  —Ex: freedom-unfreedom: the expansion-contraction principle
  —Ex: morality-immorality: the denseness-emptiness principle, the symmetry-asymmetry, the same-difference principle
  —Ex: particularness-universalness: the preciseness-vagueness principle, the simpleness-complicatedness principle
  —Ex: pureness-mixedness: the absoluteness-relativeness principle, the simpleness-complicatedness principle, the same-difference principle
  —Ex: shortsightedness-foresightedness: the partiality-totality principle, the simpleness-complicatedness principle
  —Ex: shorttermness-longtermness: the partiality-totality principle, the simpleness-complicatedness principle, the slowness-quickness principle

- **One-Sided Family Resemblances**
  —Ex: sound-silence: asymmetry (in the symmetry-asymmetry principle)
  —Ex: vision-blindness: asymmetry (in the symmetry-asymmetry principle)

(continued on next page)

Table 4.10. The Syntax of Existential Dialectics VII: Types of Inappropriate Family Resemblances (Part II)

- **Vague Family Resemblances**
  —Ex: shortness-longness, narrowness-broadness, smallness-largeness, smallness-greatness, microness-macroness, and littleness-muchness: three different possibilities, namely, (a) finiteness (in the finiteness-transfiniteness principle), if both opposites are defined on a finite scale, (b) transfiniteness (in the finiteness-transfiniteness principle) if both opposites are defined on a transfinite scale, and (c) the finiteness-transfiniteness principle if one opposite is defined on a finite scale and the other opposite is defined on a transfinite scale.

- **One-Sided and Compound Family Resemblances**
  —Ex: extroversion-introversion: one-sided, in being part of the side (category) of "normality" in the normality-abnormality pair. And compounded, because the normality-abnormality pair is in turn related to the symmetry-asymmetry principle, the density-emptiness principle, the convention-novelty principle, the same-difference principle
  —Ex: organizedness-spontaneousness: one-sided, in being part of the side (category) of "normality" in the normality-abnormality pair. And compounded, because the normality-abnormality pair is in turn related to the symmetry-asymmetry principle, the density-emptiness principle, the convention-novelty principle, the same-difference principle
  —Ex: risk-caution: one-sided, in being part of the side (category) of "normality" in the normality-abnormality pair. And compounded, because the normality-abnormality pair is in turn related to the symmetry-asymmetry principle, the density-emptiness principle, the convention-novelty principle, the same-difference principle

Notes: The examples here are solely illustrative (not exhaustive). The comparison is also relative (not absolute), nor are they mutually exclusive. As generalities, they allow exceptions.
Source: First summarized in *BEPE* (and updated in later books)

Table 4.11. The Semantics of Existential Dialectics (Part I)

• **Abstract Structure vs. Specific Meanings**

—The syntax of existential dialectics so understood in terms of ontological principles only gives us the structure of ontology in the world, in an abstract (general) sense. These principles by themselves do not tell us the specific meanings in a given context.

—In order to grasp the specific meanings of the principles in a given context, it is necessary to study the semantics of existential dialectics. And the analysis of the ontological principles as family resemblances in the section on syntax is only a starting point (and thus overlaps a bit with the semantics of existential dialectics here).

—With this caveat in mind, the reason that I have often gone in great lengths in my previous books on different subjects is to explain the specific meanings of the principles when applied in different contexts.

• **Specific Meanings in Specific Fields**

—For instance, in *FPHST*, I used the first three principles (i.e., the change-constancy principle, the regression-progression principle, and the symmetry-asymmetry principle) to propose "the perspectival theory of space-time," for a better way to understand space and time—especially, though not exclusively, in relation to future post-human history (as summarized in *Table 3.6*, *Table 3.7*, *Table 3.8*, and *Table 3.9*). In so doing, I had to introduce concepts and theories specific to the field of physics and other related fields (e.g., "absolute space" and "absolute time" in "classical mechanics" and "relative space-time" in "the theory of relativity").

—In *BNN*, I also exploited the three principles to propose the "transcendent" approach to the study of genes and memes as a new way to understand the interaction between nature and nurture. In so doing, I had to explore concepts and theories in the world of evolutionary theory (e.g., "mutation," "variation," "adaptation," "selection," and "inheritance" in Darwinian evolutionary theory) and neural biology (e.g., "chromosome," "gene," "DNA," "RNA," "protein," "neuron," "neural network," and "behavior").

(continued on next page)

Table 4.11. The Semantics of Existential Dialectics (Part II)

- **Two Types of Translation (Interpretation)**
  —In the technical jargons of semantics, these exercises in my books perform two essential functions of translation (or interpretation), namely, (a) "intensive" interpretation (about the properties or relations of the principles in existential dialectics), and (b) "extensive" interpretation (about the classes or cases to which the properties and relations of the principles in existential dialectics are applied). (WK 2011oo)

- **Limits of Translation (Interpretation)**
  —But there are limits of translation (or interpretation), and an excellent example is that "there is a problem with the 'objectivity' of translation, as it is relative to different cultural (or sub-cultural) contexts. For instance, one of the still unresolved problems in linguistics is: 'Is there an objective gauge for the quality of translation?'" (*FPHCOM* & WK 2011pp)
  —This is one serious problem about the logic of translation and interpretation that I already addressed in *Sec. 3.5.1* of *FPHCOM (*and also, for that matter, in *FHC*, in the context of hermeneutics).

Notes: The categories and examples in each are solely illustrative (not exhaustive). The comparison is also relative (not absolute), nor are they mutually exclusive. As generalities, they allow exceptions.
Sources: First explicitly stated in *ALD* (and later revised in *FPHCOM*). Also from all other books of mine.

Table 4.12. The Pragmatics of Existential Dialectics (Part I)

• **The Two-Way Street Connecting Theory and Meta-Theory**

—The pragmatics of existential dialectics is not a one-way street (that is, using the ontological principles for theoretical insights in praxis) but a two-way one, that is, (a) from meta-theory to theory, and (b) from theory to meta-theory.

—(a) On one side of the street, the ontological principles can inspire some theoretical insights in praxis, that is, in relation to some specific fields.

—(b) On the other (opposing) side of the street, however, the study of a subject matter in the specific fields in turn reveals some more hitherto unknown ontological principles to be discovered and identified. For this reason, three new principles were added in *FC*, one in *FAE*, and two in *ALD*, on top of the original three in *BCPC*—after some research on the specific subject matters.

• **Direct and Indirect Applications**

—*Direct*

- The logic of existential dialectics can shed some theoretical insights on diverse phenomena in the world, and good instances are the pertinent use of the principles of existential dialectics for the theoretical insights on the freedom/unfreedom dialectics, the equality/inequality dialectics, and the wealth/poverty dialectics in my previous works.
- My latest books like *FPHST* and *BNN* also use the principles to reveal some theoretical insights on the perspectives of space and time (as in *FPHST*) and of nature and nurture (as in *BNN*).

—*Indirect*

- The theoretical insights can further be used to reveal other phenomena directly from them (viz., the theoretical insights) and therefore indirectly from the principles themselves. A good instance is the use of the theoretical insights on the freedom/unfreedom and equality/inequality dialectics for the understanding of the civilization/barbarity dialectics.

(continued on next page)

Table 4.12. The Pragmatics of Existential Dialectics (Part II)

- **Direct and Indirect Applications (*cont'd*)**
  - Even in indirect applications, however, a phenomenon under study can still be directly related back to the principles themselves. In the example as cited above, the civilization/barbarity dialectics can be directly related to the principles of existential dialectics without the intermediate role of the freedom/unfreedom and equality/inequality dialectics.

- **Multiple Levels of Application**

  —The theoretical insights can be applied to different levels of analysis, even though in a given example, it may refer to one level only. For instance, in the example concerning the freedom/unfreedom dialectics, it can be used at the structural level (e.g., in relation to the theory of cyclical progression of hegemony), but it can be exploited as well for other levels (e.g., the theory of post-capitalism at the institutional level).

Notes: The categories and examples in each are solely illustrative (not exhaustive). The comparison is also relative (not absolute), nor are they mutually exclusive. As generalities, they allow exceptions.
Sources: From Ch.6 of *BCPC*. See also other books of mine.

Table 4.13. The Freedom-Unfreedom Dialectics (Part I)

• **On Having**

—*In Relation to the Technological*

(1) if freer from submission to Nature, then less free from ecological degradation (Deep and Social Ecology), even if in a hi-tech form

(2) if freer from technological inconvenience / backwardness, then less free from technological control and the loss of privacy

(3) if freer from technological (material) backwardness, then less free from the abusive (barbaric) maltreatment of the primitive Others

—*In Relation to the Everyday*

(1) if freer from abject poverty, then less free from artificial needs/discontents (Frankfurt School)

(2) if freer from sensual suppression, then less free from violent sublimation (Freud)

(3) if freer from the snobbishness of high culture, then less free from the shabbiness (leveling-off effect) of mass culture (Tocqueville)

(4) if freer from the inefficiency of traditional "compassionate economy," then less free from the bondage of a "ruthless [competitive] economy" (Keynes)

(5) if freer from anarchy in the state of nature (system fragmentation), then less free from government regulations and controls in system integration

(continued on next page)

Table 4.13. The Freedom-Unfreedom Dialectics (Part II)

- **On Belonging**
  - *—In Relation to the Good and the Just*
    - (1) if freer from disciplinary society, then less free from society of control (Foucault)
    - (2) if freer from the tyranny of one or a few, then less free from the tyranny of the majority (or sometimes, minority veto)
    - (3) if freer from elitist decision making, then less free from political gridlock/cleavage
    - (4) if freer from arbitrary (discretionary) administration, then less free from bureaucratic irrationality (Weber) and legal trickery (loopholes)

- **On Being**
  - *—In Relation to the True*
    - (1) if freer from unscientific dogmas, then less free from instrumental abyss (nihilism). Or conversely, if freer from meaninglessness, then less free from dogmas.
    - (2) if freer from the bondage of partiality/partisanship (e.g., prejudice, discrimination), then less free from the danger of impartiality and neutrality (e.g., opportunism, unrealisticness, lack of compassion, inaction)
    - (3) if freer from making generalizations, then less free from being unable to understand much of anything
  - *—In Relation to the Holy*
    - (1) if freer from collective conscience, then less free from social loneliness
    - (2) if freer from religious absoluteness, then less free from spiritual emptiness
  - *—In Relation to the Beautiful/Sublime*
    - (1) if freer from artistic non-autonomy, then less free from aesthetic disillusion (deconstruction)

(continued on next page)

Table 4.13. The Freedom-Unfreedom Dialectics (Part III)

Notes: The examples in each category are solely illustrative (not exhaustive), and the comparison is relative (not absolute), nor are they necessarily mutually exclusive. And some can be easily re-classified elsewhere. As generalities, they allow exceptions.
Sources: A reconstruction from Ch.10 of *FCD*, based on *FHC*

Table 4.14. The Equality-Inequality Dialectics (Part I)

- **On Having**
  - —*In Relation to the Technological*
    - (1) if more equal in treating Nature with spiritual unity, then less equal in suppressing the dominant drive to transcend it altogether
  - —*In Relation to the Everyday*
    - (1) if more equal in building social plurality, then less equal in leveling-off effects (e.g., the subsequent relative intolerance of high/intellectual ethos in mass culture industry)
    - (2) if more equal in socioeconomic distribution beyond a certain point, then less equal in efficiency (e.g. resentment, the erosion of work ethics)
    - (3) if more equal in urging an affirmative action program, then less equal in creating victim mentality (in oneself), stigma (from others), reverse discrimination (against the once privileged), and mediocracy (against the more able)

- **On Belonging**
  - —*In Relation to the Good and the Just*
    - (1) if more equal in banning monarchic/oligarchic exclusion, then less equal in producing "the tyranny of the majority" or of "minority veto"
    - (2) if more equal in encouraging participatory decision making, then less equal in inducing political divisiveness (gridlock/cleavage in power blocs) and organizational oligarchy
    - (3) if more equal in institutionalizing a decentralized bureaucracy, then less equal in falling into more territorial/turf politics (intrigues)

(continued on next page)

Table 4.14. The Equality-Inequality Dialectics (Part II)

• **On Being**

—In Relation to the Beautiful / Sublime

(1) if more equal in accepting diverse styles ("anything goes" mentality), then less equal in artistic good quality (in leveling-off effects against the best)

—In Relation to the True

(1) if more equal in tolerating multiple viewpoints (no matter how extreme), then less equal in epistemic standards

—In Relation to the Holy

(1) if more equal in celebrating any cults and sects (no matter how questionable), then less equal in spiritual depth and authenticity

Notes: The examples in each category are solely illustrative (not exhaustive), and the comparison is relative (not absolute), nor are they mutually exclusive. And some can be easily reclassified elsewhere. As generalities, they allow exceptions.
Sources: A reconstruction from Ch.10 of *FCD*, based on *FHC*

Table 4.15. The Duality of Oppression in Existential Dialectics: Oppression and Self-Oppression (Part I)

- **From the Same to the Others and Itself**
  - —The Oppression by the Same against the Others
    - *By way of downgrading differences*
      - –Ex: on judiciary caprice for corporate crimes (*Sec.2.2.1.2.1*)
      - –Ex: on the deceptive politics of liberation (*Sec.3.5*)
      - –Ex: on the humanitarian mystique (*Sec.4.4*)
      - –Ex: on the fad of emotional intelligence (*Sec.5.3*)
    - *By way of accentuating differences*
      - –Ex: on the legal sophistry of self-defense (*Sec.2.3*)
      - –Ex: on the legal semantics of proportionality (*Sec.2.4*)
      - –Ex: on the tricky politics of external threat (*Sec.3.4*)
      - –Ex: on the appeal of the Far Right for democracy (*Sec.5.4*)
      - –Ex: on the democratic axis of evil (*Sec.5.5*)
      - –Ex: on the democratic way of brutality and revenge (*Sec.5.6*)
      - –Ex: on democratic autocracy (*Sec.6.4*)
  - —The Oppression by the Same against Itself
    - *By way of downgrading differences*
      - –Ex: on the politics of fear (*Sec.2.2*)
      - –Ex: on the trickery of compassionate conservatism (*Sec.3.2*)
      - –Ex: on the deceptive politics of patriotism (*Sec.3.3*)
    - *By way of accentuating differences*
      - –Ex: on the caprice of due process on domestic suspects (*Sec.2.2*)
      - –Ex: on the false security/freedom dilemma (*Sec.6.5.2*)

(continued on next page)

Table 4.15. The Duality of Oppression in Existential Dialectics: Oppression and Self-Oppression (Part II)

- **From the Others to the Same and Themselves**
  - —The Oppression by the Others against the Same
    - *By way of downgrading differences*
      - –Ex: on judiciary caprice in the reverse direction (*Sec.2.2.1.2.2*)
      - –Ex: on equal pay (*Sec.6.2.1.1*)
      - –Ex: on equal representation (*Sec.6.2.1.2*)
      - –Ex: on affirmative action program (*Sec.6.3.1.1*)
      - –Ex: on same-sex marriage (*Sec.6.3.1.2*)
    - *By way of accentuating differences*
      - –Ex: on sexual harassment (*Sec.6.2.2.1*)
      - –Ex: on physical violence (*Sec.6.2.2.2*)
      - –Ex: on sexual exploitation (*Sec.6.2.2.3*)
  - —The Oppression by the Others against Themselves
    - *By way of downgrading differences*
      - –Ex: on the reverse-class mystique (*Sec.4.2*)
      - –Ex: on the reverse-black mystique (*Sec.4.3*)
      - –Ex: on self-discrimination by downgrading (*Sec.6.3.2.2*)
    - *By way of accentuating differences*
      - –Ex: on self-discrimination by accentuating (*Sec.6.3.2.1*)

Notes: The examples are solely illustrative (not exhaustive), nor are they mutually exclusive. As generalities, they allow exceptions. Also, both forms of oppression co-exist in all of the examples, so the listing of them are only meant in a relative, not absolute, sense.
Source: A summary of the sections (as cited) in Chs.2-6 of *BDPD*. See text for more info and references.

Table 4.16. The Structure of Existential Dialectics I: The Freedom/Unfreedom and Equality/Inequality Dialectics

---

• Each freedom and equality produces its own unfreedom and inequality, regardless of whether the pair occurs in political society (with the nation-state), in civil society (with some autonomy from the state), or elsewhere (e.g., in the private sphere of individual homes)—and regardless of whether freedom and equality are understood as "negative" or "positive."

• Oppression is dualistic, as much by the Same against the Others and itself, as by the Others against the Same and themselves.

• Both forms of oppression and self-oppression can be achieved by way of downgrading differences (between the Same and the Others) and of accentuating them.

• The relationships are relatively asymmetric between the Same and the Others and relatively symmetric within them. This is true, even when the Same can be relatively asymmetric towards itself in self-oppression, just as the Others can be likewise towards themselves.

• Symmetry and asymmetry change over time, with ever new players, new causes, and new forms.

Notes: The examples in each category are solely illustrative (not exhaustive) nor necessarily mutually exclusive, and the comparison is relative (not absolute). As generalities, they allow exceptions. "Negative" freedom is freedom "from" (e.g., freedom from poverty), whereas "positive" freedom is freedom "to" (e.g., freedom to the state of enlightenment). "Negative" equality is "procedural" equality (e.g., equality of opportunity), while "positive" equality is "substantive" equality (e.g., equality of outcome). Existential dialectics impose constraints on freedom and equality in democracy, non-democracy, and post-democracy. There is no utopia, in the end; even should there be one, dystopia would exist within it.

Sources: From *Table 1.5* of *BDPD*—and also from *FHC*, *FCD*, and *FPHC*

Table 4.17. The Structure of Existential Dialectics II: The Wealth/Poverty Dialectics

• There is no wealth without poverty, just as there is no poverty without wealth.

• The wealth/poverty dialectics occurs in the realms of having, belonging, and being, in relation to the material, relational, and spiritual.

• The wealth/poverty dialectics also expresses itself at the multiple levels of analysis in accordance to methodological holism, be they about the micro-physical, the chemical, the biological, the psychological, the organizational, the institutional, the structural, the systemic, the cultural, and the cosmological.

• The wealth/poverty dialectics is a different manifestation of existential dialectics in general, subject to the principles in its logic of ontology—just as the freedom/unfreedom and equality/inequality dialectics are likewise.

• There is no economic utopia, in the end; even should there be one, dystopia would exist within it.

Notes: The main points here are solely illustrative (not exhaustive) nor necessarily mutually exclusive, and the comparison is relative (not absolute). As generalities, they allow exceptions.
Sources: From *BCPC*. See also *FCD* and *FHC*.

Table 4.18. The Structure of Existential Dialectics III: The Civilization/Barbarity Dialectics

• There is no civilization without barbarity.

• The civilization/barbarity dialectics applies in the four civilizing processes (e.g., the rationalizing process, the pacifying process, the stewardizing process, and the subliming process).

• The civilization/barbarity dialectics is another (different) manifestation of existential dialectics in general, subject to the principles in its logic of ontology—just as the freedom/unfreedom and equality/inequality dialectics and the wealth/poverty dialectics are likewise.

• There is no utopia, in the end; even should there be one, dystopia would exist within it.

Notes: The main points here are solely illustrative (not exhaustive) nor necessarily mutually exclusive, and the comparison is relative (not absolute). As generalities, they allow exceptions.
Sources: From *BCIV*. See also *FCD*, *FHC*, and *BDPD*.

Table 4.19. The Double Sides of Virtual Organizations (Part I)

- **Psychological**
  —Ex: virtual psychosis
  —Ex: impersonality and loneliness in quaternary social relations

- **Organizational**
  —Ex: the race for power and interests
  —Ex: the world of unequal successes
  —Ex: the bureaucratic life of its own
  —Ex: lesser accountability and transparency

- **Economic**
  —Ex: the economic divides
  —Ex: the erosive impact of commercialization

- **Political**
  —Ex: the anti-authoritarian myth
  —Ex: different power struggles among groups (e.g., Conservative, Reformist, Radical)

- **Structural**
  —Ex: different localities (e.g., climates, scenery)
  —Ex: divided domains (e.g., core, peripheral, sub-peripheral)
  —Ex: substitution effect of social capital

- **Systemic**
  —Ex: uneven advances in transportation and communications, and geographical migration

- **Cultural**
  —Ex: conflicting civilizational fabrics (e.g., Confucian, Islamic, Western)
  —Ex: the bias of the Liberal Democratic agenda
  —Ex: the addiction to moral fanaticism

(continued on next page)

Table 4.19. The Double Sides of Virtual Organizations (Part II)

Notes: These categories and examples are solely illustrative (not exhaustive), and some of the items can be reclassified somewhere else. Nor are they mutually exclusive. Since they are generalities, exceptions are expected.
Source: From Ch.7 of *FCD*

Table 4.20. Beyond the World of Titans, and the Remaking of the World Order

- **Hyper-Empires**
  - —Ex: The Chinese Union
  - —Ex: The Indian Union

- **Meso-Empires**
  - —Ex: The European Union
  - —Ex: The North American Union

- **Micro-Empires**
  - —Ex: The Latin American Union
  - —Ex: The Middle Eastern Union

- **The Rest of the World**
  - —Odd Powers
    - Ex: Japan
    - Ex: Russia
  - —The Poor Club
    - Ex: The African Union
  - —Ambivalent Regions
    - Ex: Southeast Asia
    - Ex: Oceania
    - Ex: South Asia
    - Ex: Central Asia
    - Ex: Southern/Eastern Europe
    - Ex: North Africa
    - Ex: Central America
    - Ex: Others (e.g., the Korean peninsula)

Source: A summary of Chs.2-5 (of *BWT*)

Table 4.21. The Origins of Authoritarian Liberal Democracy

- **The Geopower of Nature (Ch.4 of *ALD*)**
  —Ex: Power Character and Geographical Strategy
  —Ex: Living Space and Territorial Expansion
  —Ex: Strategic Heartland and Containment

- **The Biopsychology of the Mind (Ch.5 of *ALD*)**
  —Ex: The Bell Curve and Mass Intelligence
  —Ex: Group Analysis and Mass Knowledge
  —Ex: Groupthink and Elite (Mis)calculation

- **The Disciplinary Control of Society (Ch.6 of *ALD*)**
  —Ex: Social Organizations of Ruthlessness
  —Ex: Social Institutions of Greed
  —Ex: Social Structure of Exclusion
  —Ex: Social Systems of Violence

- **The Molding Force of Culture (Ch.7 of *ALD*)**
  —Ex: The Tradition of Conquest
  —Ex: The Rationalization of Unreason

Notes: The examples in each category are solely illustrative (not exhaustive), and they are also relative (not absolute), nor are they mutually exclusive. As generalities, they allow exceptions.
Source: A summary of Chs.4-7 of *ALD*

Table 4.22. The Theory of Post-Democracy I: The Priority of Freedom over Equality (Part I)

- **Differences**
  - —*For the aggressive Lions (the strong Elitists)*
    - •Setting up rank distinctions among unequals (e.g., between inferior humans and superior post-humans, or later among inferior post-humans and superior ones, relatively speaking)
    - •Yearning for being not only distinguished from unequals, but also the first among equals (the best of the very best)
    - •Soul-searching for a high spiritual culture (not the trashy one for the masses). Mass culture is a dirty joke for them.
  - —*For the manipulative Foxes (the weak Counter-Elitists)*
    - •Seeking a gentle hegemony by way of more communitarian concerns (for inferior humans and, later, inferior post-humans)
    - •Being more sympathetic to less formal-legalistic institutions and values

- **Similarities**
  - —*For both Lions and Foxes*
    - •Exploring different spheres of non-human consciousness in the cosmos (something vastly superior than the human one)
    - •Recognizing the democratic illusions (e.g., no freedom without unfreedom, no equality without inequality, or simply no justice without injustice, and vice versa)

(continued on next page)

Table 4.22. The Theory of Post-Democracy I: The Priority of Freedom over Equality (Part II)

Notes: The two callings and examples in each category are solely illustrative (not exhaustive), since there will be many different post-human value ideals in the distant future of post-human civilization. The comparison is also relative (not absolute) towards post-democracy, so this is not just a version of free-market democracy (nor Fascism/Nazism, as shown in the table later on democracy, non-democracy, and post-democracy). Nor are they mutually exclusive. As generalities, they allow exceptions. And the specific forms of post-human post-democratic ideals need to be further developed in future after-postmodern history, as they will be different from the ones we now know. The point here is to solely give an extremely rough picture of a small part of the world to come that we have never known.

Source: From Ch.10 of *FCD*. Refer to text for more info and references.

Table 4.23. The Theory of Post-Democracy II: The Priority of Equality over Freedom

- **Hybrid Versions of**
  —Ex: the Trans-Feminine Calling
  —Ex: the Trans-Sinitic Calling
  —Ex: the Trans-Islamic Calling
  —Ex: the Trans-Outerspace Calling

- **Qualifications**
  —These four versions of post-capitalist value ideals need not automatically be post-democratic, just as capitalism does not necessarily mean democracy. They are two different entities—though closely related.
  —But up to a certain threshold of elevating equality at the farther expense of freedom, the democratic ideals will be overcome and cease to exist.
  —The overcome will not be socialist or communist, but post-democratic with no freedom without unfreedom and no equality without inequality, subject to the constraints of existential dialectics.

Notes: The callings are solely illustrative (not exhaustive), since there will be many different post-human value ideals in the distant future of post-human lifeforms. The comparison is also relative (not absolute), nor are they mutually exclusive. As generalities, they allow exceptions. And the specific forms of post-human post-democratic ideals need to be further developed in future after-postmodern history, as they will be different from the ones we now know. The point here is to solely give an extremely rough picture of a small part of the world to come that we have never known.
Source: From Ch.10 of *FCD*. Refer to text for more info and references.

Table 4.24. The Theory of Post-Democracy III: The Transcendence of Freedom and Equality (Part I)

- **Transcending Freedom in Floating Existence**
  —*Freedom*: seeking an ultimate elimination of the body. Being without the body. The aim is to transcend freedom in the end into a metaphysical state (i.e., beyond the physique).
  —*Unfreedom*: yet facing difficult trade-offs. The sacrifice of bodily existence and its joyfulness. An eternal boredom in floating existence in dark deep space, though with alternative pleasures. There is no free lunch even in the state of transcending freedom.

- **Transcending Equality in the Rivalry of Cosmic Hegemony**
  —*Inequality*: competing to outlast other lifeforms in floating existence, or just marginalizing them for one's hegemonic expansiveness in the rest of the cosmos (and even beyond). Universalism is only for the mediocre.
  —*Equality*: accepting only those of one's rank as equal partners in the vast spacetime for cosmic supremacy. Even here, the aim is to transcend equality into a metaphysical state.

(continued on next page)

k

Table 4.24. The Theory of Post-Democracy III: The Transcendence of Freedom and Equality (Part II)

Notes: Do not confuse this transcendence of freedom and equality (as one version of post-democracy) with the naïve temptation to transcend the freedom/unfreedom and equality/inequality dialectics. Existential dialectics hold true for freedom and equality in all cultures and societies—past, present, or future (i.e., democracy, non-democracy, and post-democracy), regardless of whether freedom and equality are conventionally understood as "negative" or "positive."
Also, the two features and examples in each are solely illustrative (not exhaustive), since there will be many different post-human value ideals in the distant future of post-human lifeforms. The comparison is also relative (not absolute), nor are they mutually exclusive. As generalities, they allow exceptions. And the specific forms of post-human ideals even for these radically alien floating lifeforms (and others unknown to us) need to be further developed in future after-postmodern history, as they will likely be different from the ones herein illustrated. The point here is to solely give a very rough picture of a small part of the extremely alien world to come that we have never known.
Source: From Ch.10 of *FCD*. Refer to text for more info and references.

Table 4.25. Democracy, Non-Democracy, and Post-Democracy (Part I)

- **Democracy**
  - —*Theoretical Constructs*
    - •The pursuit of freedom and equality (in various degrees), regardless of whether freedom and equality can be understood as "negative" or "positive"
      - (1) more equality than freedom: The relative priority of the good over the right
      - (2) more freedom than equality: The relative priority of the right over the good
  - —*Types*
    - •Only (1): Different versions of communitarian moral universalism
    - •Only (2): Different versions of liberal moral universalism
    - •(1) or (2): Different versions of anarchic (non-nation-state) moral universalism
    - •(1) or (2): Different versions of postmodern moral localism

- **Non-Democracy**
  - —*Theoretical Constructs*
    - •The focus on (1') equality or (2') freedom, but not both, regardless of whether freedom and equality can be understood as "negative" or "positive"
  - —*Types*
    - •Only (1'): Different versions on the Far Left (e.g., Stalinism, Robespierrianism)
    - •Only (2'): Different versions on the Far Right (e.g., Nazism, absolute monarchism)

(continued on next page)

Table 4.25. Democracy, Non-Democracy, and Post-Democracy (Part II)

- **Post-Democracy**
  —*Theoretical Constructs*
  - The priority of (1'') equality over freedom, or (2'') freedom over equality, or (3'') the transcendence of freedom and equality, regardless of whether freedom and equality are "negative" or "positive." In degree, (1'') or (2'') is less than (1') or (2') but more than (1) or (2)—respectively.
  - Like democracy and non-democracy, post-democracy is also subject to the freedom/unfreedom and equality/inequality dialectics (or existential dialectics in general). Unlike them, post-democracy acknowledges the constraints of existential dialectics and no longer value freedom and equality as sacred virtues. There is no utopia, in the end; even were there one, dystopia would exist within it.

  —*Types*
  - (1''): Different versions of trans-Sinitic value ideals
  - (1''): Different versions of trans-feminine value ideals
  - (1''): Different versions of trans-Islamic value ideals
  - (1''): Different versions of trans-outerspace value ideals
  - (2''): Different versions of post-human elitist value ideals
  - (3''): Different versions of the value ideals of floating consciousness (etc.)

(continued on next page)

Table 4.25. Democracy, Non-Democracy, and Post-Democracy (Part III)

Notes: The examples are solely illustrative (not exhaustive), nor are they mutually exclusive. As generalities, they allow exceptions. "Negative" freedom is freedom "from" (e.g., freedom from poverty), whereas "positive" freedom is freedom "to" (e.g., freedom to the state of enlightenment). "Negative" equality is "procedural" equality (e.g., equality of opportunity), while "positive" equality is "substantive" equality (e.g., equality of outcome). Existential dialectics impose constraints on freedom and equality in democracy, non-democracy, and post-democracy, regardless of whether freedom and equality can be understood as "negative" or "positive" in conventional discourse. Therefore, do not confuse the transcendence of freedom and equality in (3'') with the naïve temptation to transcend existential dialectics. There is no utopia, in the end; even should there be one, it would not exist without dystopia embedded within it.
Sources: A summary, based on my previous works, especially Ch.5 of *FHC*, Chs.5-10 of *FCD*, Chs.2-4 of *FPHC*, and Chs.1 & 7 of *BDPD*. The reader should consult the books for more analysis, as this is only a summary here.

Table 4.26. Multiple Causes of the Emergence of Post-Democracy (Part I)

- **At the Micro-Physical Level**
  —Ex: intelligent life without the human physical-chemical system
  —Sources: Ch.7 of *FHC*; Chs.9-10 of *FCD*; Ch.1 of *FPHC*

- **At the Chemical Level**
  —Ex: space radiation and toxins
  —Sources: Ch.7 of *FHC*; Chs.9-10 of *FCD*

- **At the Bio-Psychological Level**
  —Ex: exo-biological evolution in deep space
  —Ex: genetic engineering of new beings
  —Ex: limits of cognitive partiality
  —Ex: illusions of emotional neutrality
  —Ex: human biological inequality
  —Ex: the rise of unfolding unconsciousness
  —Sources: Ch.2 & Chs.9-10 of *FCD*; Ch.7 of *FHC*; Ch.4 of *BCPC*; *FPHU*

- **At the Institutional Level**
  —Ex: the flawed logic of equality
  —Ex: the conflicting nature of governance
  —Sources: Ch. 5 of *FHC*; Chs. 6 & 10 of *FCD*; Ch. 3 of *FPHC*; Chs.2-5 of *BDPD*

- **At the Organizational Level**
  —Ex: e-civic alienation
  —Ex: the dark sides of formal-legalistic routines
  —Sources: Ch.3 of *FHC*; Ch.7 of *FCD*; Ch.3 of *FPHC*

- **At the Structural Level**
  —Ex: ever new forms of inequities, at home and abroad
  —Ex: the emergence of China, women, and Islam as major actors
  —Sources: Chs.5-6 of *FHC*; Chs.7, 9 & 10 of *FCD*; Chs.4-5 of *BDPD*

(continued on next page)

Table 4.26. Multiple Causes of the Emergence of Post-Democracy (Part II)

- **At the Cultural Level**
  —Ex: freedom/unfreedom dialectics
  —Ex: equality/inequality dialectics
  —Ex: system fragmentation and integration
  —Sources: Ch.5 of *FHC*; Chs. 3, 9 & 10 of *FCD*; Ch.4 of *FPHC*; Ch.1 of *BDPD*; Ch.4 of *BCPC*

- **At the Systemic Level**
  —Ex: space habitats (in zero-gravity) and colonization
  —Ex: ultra advanced future info systems
  —Ex: qualitative demography
  —Sources: Ch.7 of *FHC*; Chs.9 &10 of *FCD*

- **At the Cosmological Level**
  —Ex: the colonization of multiverses
  —Ex: the alteration of space-time and the creation of new matter-energy
  —Ex: the expansion of floating consciousness
  —Ex: the spread of hyper-spatial consciousness
  —Sources: Ch.7 of *FHC*; Chs.9 &10 of *FCD*; Ch.4 of *FPHC*; *FPHST*

Notes: The examples in each category are solely illustrative (not exhaustive), and some of the items can be reclassified somewhere else. Nor are they always mutually exclusive. Since they are generalities, exceptions are expected.
Sources: Especially from *FHC*, *FCD*, *FPHC*, *BCPC*, *BDPD*, *FPHST*, and *FPHU*. See also other books and my perspectives on civilizational holism.

Table 4.27. Some Clarifications about Post-Capitalism and Post-Democracy (Part I)

• The prefix "trans-" in the first category of post-capitalism (with its four versions) refers to something "going beyond" (not "uniting" or "combining"). Ex: *Sec.10.3.3* of *FCD*; *Sec.2.4* & *Sec.4.4* of *FPHC*; *Sec.7.2* of *BCPC*

• Such terms like "post-democracy," "post-capitalism," "post-human elitist," "trans-feminine calling," and the like as used in my works are more for our current intellectual convenience than to the liking of future humans and post-humans, who will surely invent more tasteful neologisms to call their own eras, entities, and everything else, for that matter. But the didactic point here is to use the terms to foretell what the future might be like, not that its eras and entities must be called so exactly and permanently.
Ex: *Sec.11.1* of *FCD*; *Sec.7.2* of *BCPC*

• The four versions in the first category of post-capitalist value ideals need not automatically be post-democratic, just as capitalism does not necessarily mean democracy. They are two different entities—though closely related. But up to a certain threshold of elevating equality at the farther expense of freedom, the democratic ideals will be overcome and cease to exist. The same is true for the post-human elitist calling in the second category of post-capitalism in relation to post-democracy, depending on the extent to which freedom is elevated at the expense of equality.
Ex: *Sec.10.4.3.3* of *FCD*; *Table 3.9* of *FPHC*; *Table 7.6* of *BDPD*

• The comparison in each of the three realms of existence in all forms of post-capitalism is not absolute, but relative. Examples include "communal" vs. "individualistic," and the like.
Ex: Notes in *Table 10.8*, *Table 10.9*, *Table 10.10*, & *Table 10.11* of *FCD*; Chs.2-4 of *FPHC*; *Sec.7.2* of *BCPC*

(continued on next page)

Table 4.27. Some Clarifications about Post-Capitalism and Post-Democracy (Part II)

• The emergence of post-capitalism (and post-democracy, for that matter) has multiple causes (to not be reduced to one or only a few).
Ex: Ch.10 of *FCD*, Chs.2-4 of *FPHC*; *Sec.1.3* & *Sec.7.2* of *BCPC* (or *Table 1.8* & *Table 7.11*)

• The specific forms of post-capitalism (and post-democracy, for that matter) need to be further developed in future after-postmodern history, as they will be different from the ones we now know. The point here is to solely give an extremely rough sketch of a world to come that we have never known.
Ex: *Sec.10.3.3* & *Sec.10.4.3.3* of *FCD*; *Table 10.14* & *Table 10.15* of *FCD*; *Sec.7.2* of *BCPC*

• All forms of post-capitalism are not part of a "teleological law," but of "historical trends" only. The same is also true for all forms of post-democracy.
Ex: *Sec.7.1* of *FHC*; *Sec.9.5.3.2* & *Sec.10.3.4.2* of *FCD*; *Sec.7.2* of *BCPC*

• Post-capitalism is not better than capitalism in an "absolute" sense but only fits in better, on the basis of the historical contingency of culture, society, nature, and the mind in some future eras. The same is true for post-democracy in relation to democracy. The term "better" is historically relative.
Ex: *Sec.10.3.3* of *FCD*; *Sec.1.7* of *BDPD*; *Sec.1.5* of *BCPC*

(continued on next page)

Table 4.27. Some Clarifications about Post-Capitalism and Post-Democracy (Part III)

• All forms of post-capitalism and post-democracy are subject to the constraints of existential dialectics. In the process, the dialectic direction is to go beyond the conventional "either-or" dichotomies (e.g., freedom vs. unfreedom, equality vs. inequality, freedom vs. equality, individuality vs. communality, spirituality vs. materiality, formal legalism vs. informal legalism, etc.). As is true in post-civilization, to go beyond the dichotomies is to acknowledge the co-existence of both in each dichotomy, although the degree of scaling one over the over varies from case to case (e.g., the theory of post-capitalism I, the theory of post-capitalism II, the theory of post-democracy I, the theory of post-democracy II, etc.)—but is not to be extreme in largely favoring one over the other, *on average* (all things considered). There is no utopia to be had in the end; even should there be one, dystopia would exist within it.
Ex: Ch.5 of *FHC*; *Sec.10.4.4.2* of *FCD*; *Sec.1.5* of *BDPD*; *Sec.1.3* of *BCPC*; *BCIV*

• All forms of post-capitalism, however different from each other though they are, share one common feature, in that they all inspire for a higher spiritual culture. The same is also true for post-democracy.
Ex: *Sec.10.3*, *Sec.10.4* & *Sec.10.5* of *FCD*; *Chs.2-4* of *FPHC*; *Sec.7.2* of *BCPC*

• All forms of post-capitalism try to avoid the excess in capitalist consumerism by favoring more basic than artificial needs in having, but the quality and quantity of these "basic" needs will be measured by future standards, not by our current ones. Standards are historically relative.
Ex: *Sec.10.3*, *Sec.10.4* & *Sec.10.5* of *FCD*; Ch.2 of *FPHC*; *Sec.7.2* of *BCPC*

(continued on next page)

Table 4.27. Some Clarifications about Post-Capitalism and Post-Democracy (Part IV)

• All forms of post-capitalism make use of a different degree of political authority with advanced info systems in future history and strives for higher spiritual cultures (especially in the post-human age), while acknowledging the constraints of existential dialectics and no longer valuing free market (as in capitalism) and economic control (as in non-capitalism) as sacred virtues.
Ex: *Sec.10.3.4.2*, *Sec.10.3*, *Sec.10.4* & *Sec.10.5* of *FCD*; Chs.2-4 of *FPHC*; *Sec.1.5* of *BDPD*; *Sec.7.2* of *BCPC*

Notes:: The main points here are solely illustrative (not exhaustive) nor necessarily mutually exclusive, and the comparison is relative (not absolute). As generalities, they allow exceptions. The sections as cited are only illustrative (not exhaustive).
Sources: From *FHC*, *FCD*, *FPHC*, and *BDPD*

Table 4.28. The Theory of Post-Capitalism I.1: By Group— Ex: Spiritual/Communal in the Trans-Feminine Calling

• **More Communal Than Individual**
—*Sharing*: learning from others, as different ideas mutually enrich
—*Cooperative*: encouraging a sense of shared leadership and teamwork

• **More Informal-Legalistic Than Formal-Legalistic**
—*Specific*: listening more from the heart than from the head, to know a person as a concrete, not as an abstract, unit
—*Affective*: thinking and acting with others on a more affective tone. Business can mix with an emotional touch.
—*Ascriptive*: hiring (or firing) can be done on the basis of merit (or lack of it), but deep solidarity (sisterhood) is important too.
—*Particularistic*: making decisions on the basis of cost-benefit analysis, but a given group relationship is vital

• **More Spiritual Than Secular**
—*Long-Term Looking*: sharing for a long-term relationship (e.g., love, friendship), not just for a short-term gain
—*Loving/Caring*: showing compassion for the sufferings of others, without quickly blaming and pre-judging
—*Respectful*: showing acceptance about others' feelings (and thoughts)

Notes: The categories and examples are solely illustrative, since there can be different versions, and the comparison is relative (not absolute), nor are they mutually exclusive. As generalities, they allow exceptions. The specific forms of the trans-feminine version need to be further developed in future after-postmodern history, as they will be different from the ones we now know, since the prefix "trans-" here means going beyond or deconstructing the feminine values, while using them as the inspirational point at the beginning.
Source: From Ch.10 of *FCD*. Refer to text for more info and references.

Table 4.29. The Theory of Post-Capitalism I.2: By Nation-State— Ex: Spiritual/Communal in the Trans-Sinitic Calling

- **More Communal Than Individualistic**
  —*Centralized*: being more top-down in management
  —*Collective*: encouraging more group cooperation
  —*Social*: investing in trust and connection

- **More Informal-Legalistic Than Formal-Legalistic**
  —*Specific*: knowing more of those related or connected
  —*Affective*: behaving in a paternalistic, hierarchical way
  —*Ascriptive*: favoring family members and those related
  —*Particularistic*: building connection (guanxi) as imperative

- **More Spiritual Than Secular**
  —*Expansionist*: diffusing civilizational values (e.g., the superiority complex of civilizationalism)
  —*Holistic*: synthesizing things into a panoramic horizon
  —*Historical*: learning from the lessons of the ancient past
  —*Respectful*: deferential to elders and superiors

Notes: The categories and examples are solely illustrative, since there can be different versions, and the comparison is relative (not absolute), nor are they mutually exclusive. As generalities, they allow exceptions. The specific forms of the trans-Sinitic version need to be further developed in future after-postmodern history, as they will be different from the ones we now know, since the prefix "trans-" here means going beyond or deconstructing the Sinitic values, while using them as the inspirational point at the beginning.
Source: From Ch.10 of *FCD*. Refer to text for more info and references.

Table 4.30. The Theory of Post-Capitalism I.3: By Region— Ex: Spiritual/Communal in the Trans-Islamic Calling

• **More Communal Than Individualistic**
—*Collective*: building the webs of relationships to bind individuals
—*Sharing*: cultivating the established "wisdom" through common experience
—*Cooperative*: stressing harmony, solidarity, and commonality

• **More Informal-Legalistic Than Formal-Legalistic**
—*Specific*: making efforts to know well the participants (family and larger community) in matters of common concern
—*Affective*: mixing work with language and ritual on explicit religious (Islamic) ideals, texts, stories, and examples
—*Ascriptive*: privileging local history and custom on relationships among kinship groups
—*Particularistic*: preferring an unbiased insider with ongoing connections to all parties

• **More Spiritual Than Secular**
—*Historical*: learning from the lessons of the past as a source of stability and guidance
—*Deferential*: showing respect for age, experience, status, and leadership in communal affairs
—*Honorable*: emphasizing face, dignity, prestige, and fairness
—*Compassionate*: giving mercy and charity ("Zahah") to others

Notes: The categories and examples are solely illustrative (not exhaustive), and the comparison is relative (not absolute), nor are they mutually exclusive. As generalities, they allow exceptions. The specific forms of the trans-Islamic version need to be further developed in future after-postmodern history, as they will be different from the ones we now know, since the prefix "trans-" here means going beyond or deconstructing the Islamic values, while using them as the inspirational point at the beginning.
Sources: From Ch.10 of *FCD*. Refer to text for more info and references, especially from the works by George Irani (2000) and C. Murphy (September 19, 2001).

Table 4.31. The Theory of Post-Capitalism I.4: By Universe— Ex: Spiritual/Communal in the Trans-Outerspace Calling

- **More Communal Than Individual**
  —*Cooperative*: requiring teamwork in small space habitats
  —*Sharing*: learning from, and enjoying being with, each other in a small group in outer space

- **More Informal-Legalistic Than Formal-Legalistic**
  —*Specific*: knowing more about each other to facilitate living and working together in space, both as fellow astronauts and space-mates
  —*Affective*: being friendly and social to each other as vital to working and living in small space quarters
  —*Ascriptive*: nurturing comaraderie among fellow astronauts as if they are family members over time
  —*Particularistic*: building work relationship with enduring memory in a space mission

- **More Spiritual Than Secular**
  —*Long-Term*: looking beyond selfish materialistic concerns in a precarious space environment with potential life or death
  —*Loving/Caring*: cultivating deep bondage for the success of a long term space mission
  —*Transcendent*: searching for life meaning in outer space

Notes: The calling and examples in each category are solely illustrative (not exhaustive), since there will be many different outer-space value ideals in the distant future of space colonization. The comparison is also relative (not absolute), nor are they mutually exclusive. As generalities, they allow exceptions. And the specific forms of trans-outer-space calling need to be further developed in future after-postmodern history, as they will be different from the ones we now know, since the prefix "trans-" here means going beyond or deconstructing the current outer-space values, while using them as the inspirational point at the beginning. The point here is to solely give an extremely rough picture of a small part of the world to come that we still do not know much about.
Source: From Ch.10 of *FCD*. Refer to text for more info and references.

Table 4.32. The Theory of Post-Capitalism II: Spiritual/Individualistic in the Post-Human Elitist Calling (Part I)

- **More Individualistic Than Communal**
  —Setting up rank distinctions among unequals (e.g., between inferior humans and superior post-humans, or later among inferior post-humans and superior ones, relatively speaking)
  —Yearning for being not only distinguished from unequals, but also the first among equals (the best of the very best)
  —Recognizing the constraints of equality/inequality dialectics (or existential dialectics in general)

- **More Spiritual Than Secular**
  —Soul-searching for a high spiritual culture (not the trashy one for the masses). Mass culture is a dirty joke for them.
  —Exploring different spheres of non-human consciousness in the cosmos (something vastly superior than the human one)
  —Recognizing the constraints of freedom/unfreedom dialectics (or existential dialectics in general)

- **Qualifications**
  —Although post-human elitist post-democracy is comparable to post-human elitist post-capitalism in some respects, the former does not necessarily imply the latter (post-human elitist post-capitalism), just as democracy does not have to entail capitalism. They are two different (though related) entities.
  —But up to a certain threshold of incorporating government intervention with advanced info systems in future civilizations for higher spiritual concerns at the expense of the free market and materialist pursuit, the capitalist ideal will be overcome.
  —The overcome will not be Fascist or feudalistic, but post-capitalist, subject to the constraints of existential dialectics.

(continued on next page)

Table 4.32. The Theory of Post-Capitalism II: Spiritual/Individualistic in the Post-Human Elitist Calling (Part II)

Notes: The calling and examples in each category are solely illustrative (not exhaustive). The comparison is also relative (not absolute), nor are they mutually exclusive. As generalities, they allow exceptions. And the specific forms of post-human elitist post-capitalism need to be further developed in future after-postmodern history, as they will be different from the ones we now know, while using them as the inspirational point at the beginning. The point here is to solely give an extremely rough picture of a small part of the world to come that we still do not know much about.
Sources: From Ch.10 of *FCD* (and also *FPHC*, *BDPD*, and *BCPC*). Refer to the text for more info and references.

Table 4.33. Capitalism, Non-Capitalism, and Post-Capitalism (Part I)

• **Capitalism**
—*Theoretical Constructs*
•Allocation of scarce resources among alternative wants largely by free market for competition (whose characteristics in its ideal form include, for instance, no barrier to entry or exit, homogeneity, perfect information, a large number of buyers/sellers, and perfect factor mobility)
•More formal-legalistic than informal-legalistic, more individualistic than communal, and more material (secular) than spiritual
•Either (1) minimal government or (2) relatively active government
—*Types*
•Only (1): Different versions of market capitalism (e.g., the U.S.)
•Only (2): Different versions of welfare capitalism (e.g., Sweden)

• **Non-Capitalism**
—*Theoretical Constructs*
•Allocation of scarce resources among alternative wants mainly by political authority for policies (which can be regulative, redistributive, symbolic, and participatory)
•More informal-legalistic than formal-legalistic
•Either (1') more individualistic (for the elites), often (though not always) for material (secular) concerns, or (2') more communal (for the masses), often (though not always) for spiritual concerns
—*Types*
•Only (1'): Different versions on the Right (e.g., Fascist corporate-state economy for the glory of the new Rome, medieval lord-vassal-serf economy for the power of the feudalistic order)
•Only (2'): Different versions on the Left (e.g., Soviet command economy for the creation of the New Socialist Man)

(continued on next page)

Table 4.33. Capitalism, Non-Capitalism, and Post-Capitalism (Part II)

• **Post-Capitalism**

—*Theoretical Constructs*

- •Allocation of scarce resources among alternative wants largely by political authority with advanced info systems in future civilizations, subject to existential dialectics. In degree of allocating by authority, post-capitalism is more than capitalism but less than non-capitalism.
- •More spiritual than secular (material)
- •Either (1'') more individualistic or (2") more communal
- •Like capitalism and non-capitalism, post-capitalism is also subject to the freedom/unfreedom and equality/inequality dialectics (or existential dialectics in general). There is no utopia, in the end; even were there one, dystopia would exist within it.
- •Unlike capitalism and non-capitalism, post-capitalism makes use of a different degree of political authority with advanced info systems in future civilizations and strives for higher-spiritual cultures (especially in the post-human age), while acknowledging the constraints of existential dialectics and no longer valuing free market (as in capitalism) and economic control (as in non-capitalism) as sacred virtues.

—*Types*

- •Only (1"): Different versions of post-human elitist value ideals
- •Only (2''): Different versions of trans-Sinitic value ideals
- •Only (2''): Different versions of trans-feminine value ideals
- •Only (2''): Different versions of trans-Islamic value ideals
- •Only (2''): Different versions of trans-outerspace value ideals

---

(continued on next page)

Table 4.33. Capitalism, Non-Capitalism, and Post-Capitalism (Part III)

Notes: The calling and examples in each category are solely illustrative (not exhaustive). The comparison is also relative (not absolute), nor are they mutually exclusive. As generalities, they allow exceptions. And the specific forms of each calling need to be further developed in future after-postmodern history, as they will be different from the ones we now know, while using them as the inspirational point at the beginning. The point here is to solely give an extremely rough picture of a small part of the world to come that we still do not know much about.
Source: From Ch.10 of *FCD*. Refer to the text for more info and references.

Table 4.34. Multiple Causes of the Emergence of Post-Capitalism (Part I)

• **At the Micro-Physical Level**
—Ex: intelligent life without the human physical-chemical system
—Ex: mastering of quantum mechanics, electromagnetism, and other fields for the understanding of a broad range of anomalous experiences and the application for artificial intelligence for spiritual quest
—Sources: Ch.7 of *FHC*; Chs.9-10 of *FCD*; Ch.1 of *FPHC*

• **At the Chemical Level**
—Ex: space radiation and toxins
—Sources: Ch.7 of *FHC*; Chs.9-10 of *FCD*

• **At the Bio-Psychological Level**
—Ex: exo-biological evolution in deep space
—Ex: genetic engineering of new beings
—Ex: limits of human cognition
—Ex: the rise of unfolding unconsciousness
—Sources: Ch.2 & Chs.9-10 of *FCD*; Ch.7 of *FHC*; *FPHU*

• **At the Institutional Level**
—Ex: the flawed logic of the free market
—Ex: the need of a post-autistic economics
—Sources: Ch.10 of *FCD*

• **At the Organizational Level**
—Ex: the dark sides of formal-legalistic routines
—Sources: Ch.3 of *FHC*; Ch.7 of *FCD*; Ch.3 of *FPHC*

• **At the Structural Level**
—Ex: ever new forms of inequities, at home and abroad
—Ex: the emergence of China, women, and Islam as major actors
—Sources: Chs.5-6 of *FHC*; Chs.7, 9 & 10 of *FCD*; Chs.4-5 of *BDPD*

(continued on next page)

Table 4.34. Multiple Causes of the Emergence of Post-Capitalism (Part II)

- **At the Cultural Level**
  —Ex: freedom/unfreedom dialectics
  —Ex: equality/inequality dialectics
  —Sources: Ch.5 of *FHC*; Chs.3 & 10 of *FCD*; Ch.4 of *FPHC*; Ch.1 of *BDPD*

- **At the Systemic Level**
  —Ex: space habitats (in zero-gravity) and colonization
  —Ex: ultra advanced future info systems
  —Ex: qualitative demography
  —Sources: Ch.7 of *FHC*; Chs. 9 & 10 of *FCD*

- **At the Cosmological Level**
  —Ex: the colonization of multiverses
  —Ex: the alteration of space-time and the creation of new matter-energy
  —Ex: the expansion of floating consciousness
  —Ex: the spread of hyper-spatial consciousness
  —Sources: Ch.7 of *FHC*; Chs. 9 & 10 of *FCD*; Ch.4 of *FPHC*; *FPHST*

Notes: The examples in each category are solely illustrative (not exhaustive), and some of the items can be reclassified somewhere else. Nor are they always mutually exclusive. Since they are generalities, exceptions are expected.
Sources: Especially from *FHC*, *FCD*, *FPHC*, *BCPC*, *BDPD*, *FPHST*, and *FPHU*. See also other books and my perspectives on civilizational holism.

Table 4.35. The Theoretical Debate on Civilization

- **The Progressive Theory of Civilization**
  —*Thesis*: The "civilizing" process is "good," as opposed to the "barbarizing" process as something "bad," relatively speaking.
  —*Discourse*: Especially, though not exclusively, in the Enlightenment era and a bit before. Example: Thomas Hobbes—in that the tribes in primitive societies were "savages."

- **The Romantic Theory of Barbarity**
  —*Thesis*: The "civilizing" process is "bad," as opposed to the "barbarizing" process as something "good," relatively speaking.
  —*Discourse*: Especially, though not exclusively, in the Counter-Enlightenment circle. Example: Jean-Jacques Rousseau—in that civilization "corrupts" men, and the "savages" are in fact "noble."

- **The Moderate Theory of Civilization**
  —*Thesis*: The "civilizing" process is "good," but there is a price to pay, especially in systematic (compulsive) self-control.
  —*Discourse*: Especially, though not exclusively, in some late modern and postmodern circles. Example: Norbert Elias—in that social manners become more refined in the civilizing process, but self-control also becomes more systematic.

- **The Theory of Post-Civilization**
  —*Thesis*: The civilizing process is as evil and good as barbarity, and each cannot exist without the other, to be eventually superseded by post-civilization unto the post-human age.
  —*Discourse*: Proposed by Peter Baofu. See the rest of *BCIV* for more analysis.

Source: From *BCIV* on the theoretical debate

Table 4.36. No Freedom Without Unfreedom in the Civilizing Processes (Part I)

- **The Rationalizing Process (at the Level of Culture)**
  —if freer from the dominance of unreason (as in barbarism) in the civilizing process, then less free from the rationalizing process (be it in the form of the principle of either transcendence or immanence)
  —if freer from the principle of immanence in the rationalizing process, then less free from the inclination to commit terror in the name of reason and the relative underdevelopment of non-reason (e.g., in relation to yoga and meditation)
  —if freer from the principle of transcendence in the rationalizing process, then less free from the relative underdevelopment of reason (e.g., in relation to systematic methodology) and the occurrence of oppression in the name of non-reason

- **The Pacifying Process (at the Level of Society)**
  —if freer from the dominance of pillage (as in savagery) in the civilizing process, then less free from the pacifying process (be it in the form of external control or self-control)
  —if freer from self-control in the pacifying process, then less free from the temptation of expansionist oppression and rebellious mindset in external control
  —if freer from external control in the pacifying process, then less free from the gruesome psychological self-torture and conformism in self-control

- **The Stewardizing Process (at the Level of Nature)**
  —if freer from the dominance of nature (as in the state of nature) in the civilizing process, then less free from the stewardizing process (be it in the form of the stewardship of creation or the covenant with nature)
  —if freer from the stewardship of creation in the stewardizing process, then less free from material underdevelopment, relatively speaking, and spiritual exclusion in the covenant with nature
  —if freer from the covenant with nature in the stewardizing process, then less free from ecological degradation and spiritual disconnection from nature in the stewardship of creation

(continued on next page)

Table 4.36. No Freedom Without Unfreedom in the Civilizing Processes (Part II)

- **The Subliming Process (at the Level of the Mind)**
  —if freer from the dominance of spontaneity (as in the wild state of the mind) in the civilizing process, then less free from the subliming process, be it in the form of (cyclical-centric) self-refinement or (linear-centric) self-discipline
  —if freer from (cyclical-centric) self-refinement in the subliming process, then less free from the (linear-centric) self-regimen (as a form of neurosis)
  —if freer from (linear-centric) self-discipline in the subliming process, then less free from the (cyclical-centric) self-torture (equally as a form of neurosis)

Notes: The examples in each category are solely illustrative (not exhaustive), and the comparison is relative (not absolute), nor are they necessarily mutually exclusive. And some can be easily re-classified elsewhere. As generalities, they allow exceptions.
Sources: From *BCIV*. See also *FHC*, *FCD*, *FPHC*, *BDPD*, and *BCPC*.

Table 4.37. No Equality Without Inequality in the Civilizing Processes (Part I)

- **The Rationalizing Process (at the Level of Culture)**
  —if more equal for the role of rationalization in the rationalizing process (of civilizational making), then less equal for that of mythicization (as in barbarism)
  —if more equal for the principle of transcendence in (linear-centric) rationalizing process, then less equal for the principle of immanence
  —if more equal for the principle of immanence in (cyclical-centric) rationalizing process, then less equal for the principle of transcendence

- **The Pacifying Process (at the Level of Society)**
  —if more equal for pacification in civilizational making, then less equal for the institution of pillaging and others (as in savagery)
  —if more equal for external control, relatively speaking, in pacifying process, then less equal for self-control
  —if more equal for self-control, relatively speaking, in pacifying process, then less equal for external-control

- **The Stewardizing Process (at the Level of Nature)**
  —if more equal for stewardship in the stewardizing process (of civilizational making), then less equal for reverent (submissive) existence (as in barbarism)
  —if more equal for the stewardship of creation in (linear- centric) stewardizing process, then less equal for the (cyclical-centric) covenant with nature for harmonious co-existence
  —if more equal for the (cyclical-centric) covenant with nature in the stewardizing process, then less equal for the (linear-centric) stewardship of nature for domination

(continued on next page)

Table 4.37. No Equality Without Inequality in the Civilizing Processes (Part II)

- **The Subliming Process (at the Level of the Mind)**
  —if more equal for the role of reason in the subliming process, then less equal for that of unreason (as in the natural state of wildness)
  —if more equal for the primacy of reason in (linear-centric) subliming process, then less equal for other faculties (e.g., intuition, existential feelings, and analogous thinking) in cyclical-centric one
  —if more equal for the exercise of other faculties (e.g., intuition, existential feelings, and analogous thinking) in cyclical-centric subliming process, then less equal for the role of reason in linear-centric counterpart

Notes: The examples in each category are solely illustrative (not exhaustive), and the comparison is relative (not absolute), nor are they mutually exclusive. And some can be easily reclassified else-where. As generalities, they allow exceptions.
Sources: From *BCIV*. See also *FHC*, *FCD*, *FPHC*, *BDPD*, and *BCPC*.

Table 4.38. Five Theses on Post-Civilization

• Post-civilization no longer treats civilization as good and barbarity as evil (relatively speaking), nor does it nostalgically regard barbarity as good and civilization as evil (relatively speaking again). Civilization is as evil and good as barbarity.

• Post-civilization also no longer accepts the dichotomy between civilization and barbarity. Civilization cannot exist without barbarity. It is no longer necessary to preserve civilization, any more than it is imperative to destroy barbarity. To go beyond civilization and barbarity is to acknowledge the co-existence of both, although the degree of scaling one over the over varies from case to case—but is not to be extreme in largely favoring one over the other, *on average* (subject to the constraints of existential dialectics).

• Post-civilization is thus subject to the constraints of existential dialectics. There is no freedom without unfreedom, and no equality without inequality, for instance. There will be no utopia; even should there be one, there would be dystopia embedded within it.

• Post-civilization will eventually replace civilization (as a form of life settlement), to be dominated by post-capitalist and post-democratic lifeforms here on earth and in deep space (besides other alien lifeforms that we have never known), unto the post-human age in multiverses. Those few post-humans who keep civilization will live in a "post-human civilization," while the rest (the majority), who choose post-civilization, will evolve towards the state of "post-human post-civilization." One therefore should not confuse "post-human civilization" with "post-human post-civilization," as the two are not the same.

• Post-civilization will confront psychosis as a primary problem in the culture of virtuality unto the post-human age, just as civilization has neurosis as a primary one of its own (although both neurosis and psychosis are major problems in both).

Notes: The comparison in each category is relative (not absolute), nor are they necessarily mutually exclusive. And some can be easily re-classified elsewhere. As generalities, they allow exceptions.
Sources: From *BCIV*. See also *FHC*, *FCD*, *FPHC*, *BDPD*, and *BCPC*.

Table 4.39. Barbarity, Civilization, and Post-Civilization

- **The Rationalizing Process (at the Level of Culture)**
  —*Barbarity*
    - More mythicizing than rationalizing, relatively speaking
  —*Civilization*
    - More rationalizing than mythicizing, relatively speaking
  —*Post-Civilization*
    - Beyond the dichotomy, subject to existential dialectics

- **The Pacifying Process (at the Level of Society)**
  —*Barbarity*
    - More pillaging than pacifying, relatively speaking
  —*Civilization*
    - More pacifying than pillaging, relatively speaking
  —*Post-Civilization*
    - Beyond the dichotomy, subject to existential dialectics

- **The Stewardizing Process (at the Level of Nature)**
  —*Barbarity*
    - More revering than stewardizing, relatively speaking
  —*Civilization*
    - More stewardizing than revering, relatively speaking
  —*Post-Civilization*
    - Beyond the dichotomy, subject to existential dialectics

- **The Subliming Process (at the Level of the Mind)**
  —*Barbarity*
    - More impulsing than subliming, relatively speaking
  —*Civilization*
    - More subliming than impulsing, relatively speaking
  —*Post-Civilization*
    - Beyond the dichotomy, subject to existential dialectics

Notes: The comparison in each category is relative (not absolute), nor are they necessarily mutually exclusive. And some can be easily re-classified elsewhere. As generalities, they allow exceptions.
Sources: From *BCIV*. See also *FHC*, *FCD*, *FPHC*, *BDPD*, and *BCPC*.

Table 4.40. Types of Super Civilization in the Cosmos (Part I)

- **Type I**
  —a civilization which gains control of and uses the total energy output "falling on its planet from its sun for interstellar communication" (or, in general, space colonization). For N. Kardashev, who proposed the first three types, human civilization is currently Type Zero (Type O), which is below even Type I, since its present energy consumption for all purposes, let alone for interstellar communication, is still 10,000 times less.

- **Type II**
  —a civilization which gains control of and uses directly the total energy output of its sun for interstellar communication (or, in general, space colonization).

- **Type III**
  —a civilization which gains control of and uses the total energy output of its galaxy for interstellar communication (or, in general, space colonization).

- **Type IV**
  —a civilization which gains control of and uses the total energy output of its cluster of galaxies for interstellar communication (or, in general, space colonization).

- **Type V**
  —a civilization which gains control of and uses the total energy output of its supercluster of galaxies for interstellar communica-tion (or, in general, space colonization).

(continued on next page)

Table 4.40. Types of Super Civilization in the Cosmos (Part II)

- **Type…n**
  —So continues the series in what I call the cyclical progression of hegemony in the cosmos and beyond.

Notes: The Russian astrophysicist Nikolai Kardashev proposed the first three types of super civilization in terms of total energy out-put for interstellar communication. (CSM 1979) I extend his argument further to propose Type IV, Type V, Type VI, and Type…n, in the context of my claim about the cyclical progression of he-gemony in the cosmos and beyond.
Sources: From *Table 9.4* of *FCD.* See *FHC*, *FCD*, and *FPHC* for more info.

Table 4.41. The Civilizational Project from Pre-Modernity to After-Postmodernity (Part I)

	Pre-Modern	*Modern*	*Postmodern*	*After-Postmodern*
Main narratives	•Sacralness •Courtliness •Vitalism •Animism	•Freedom •Equality •Fraternity	•Multiplicity •Hybridization	•Naked contingency •Cyclical progres-sion of hegemony
Main institutions	•Monarchy •Aristocracy •Feudalism •Holy order •Primitivism	•Capitalism •Liberalism •Socialism •Nazism •Fascism	•Capitalism •Liberalism •Postmodern politics of difference	•Post-Capitalism •Post-Democracy •Others
Main techno-logical and economic revolutions	•Agricultural	•Service •Industrial	•Informational	•Biological •Material •Energy •Space •Others

(continued on next page)

Table 4.41. The Civilizational Project from Pre-Modernity to After-Postmodernity (Part II)

	Pre-Modern	*Modern*	*Postmodern*	*After-Postmodern*
Main agents	•Males •Upper strata •Mini-states	•Males •Upper strata •Whites •Empires	•Males •Upper strata •Whites •Others •Supra-states •IO's	•Post-humans •Humans •Others
Main impacts	•Local	•Inter-national	•Global	•Outer-space •Multiverse
Main outcomes	•Towards moderntiy •Rise of linear- & cyclical-centric civiliza-tions	•Towards post-modernity •Dominance of linear-centric civilization	•Towards after-post-moderntiy •Linear-centric civiliza-tion in crisis	•Towards human (& maybe post-human) extinction •Rise of post-civiliza-tion, especially in post-human forms of space-time

Notes: The examples in each category are solely illustrative (not exhaustive) nor necessarily mutually exclusive, and the comparison is relative (not absolute). As generalities, they allow exceptions.

Sources: From *Table 10.16* of *FCD*—and also from *BCIV* on post-civilization (and *FPHST*)

Table 4.42. Civilizational Holism (Part I)

- **At the Micro-Physical Theoretical Level**
  —Ex: Mastering of quantum mechanics, electromagnetism, and other fields for the understanding of a broad range of anomalous experiences and theapplication for artificial intelligence (*Sec.1.4.1* of *FPHC*)

- **At the Chemical Theoretical Level**
  —Ex: Unprecedented expansion of (and violence to) the mind through ever new forms of drugs (and virtual technologies, for that matter) (Ch.9 of *FCD*)

- **At the Biological Theoretical Level**
  —Ex: Humans are not biologically equal, on the basis of race, gender, ethnicity, age, and whatnot. (*Sec.2.6* & Ch.10 of *FCD*; *BNN*) And post-humans will experience the same fate, in an even more amazing way.

- **At the Psychological Theoretical Level**
  —Ex: Human cognitive impartiality and emotional neutrality are quite limited. (*Secs.2.4-2.5* of *FCD*)
  —Ex: Rise of Floating Consciousness (Ch.10 of *FCD*; Chs.1 & 4 of *FPHC*) and Unfolding Unconsciousness (*FPHU*)

- **At the Organizational Theoretical Level**
  —Ex: Administrative colonization of deep space, with less legal-formalism in some corners. (Chs.9-10 of *FCD*)

- **At the Institutional Theoretical Level**
  —Ex: Both capitalism and democracy will not last, to be superseded by different versions of post-capitalism and post-democracy in after-postmodernity. (Ch.10 of *FCD*)

(continued on next page)

Table 4.42. Civilizational Holism
(Part II)

- **At the Structural Theoretical Level**
  —Ex: Social stratification reappears in ever new forms, also with new causes and new players in the cyclical progression of hegemony. (Chs.8-10 of *FCD*)
  —Ex: The world of hyper-empires, and the union of the unions (*BWT*)

- **At the Systemic Theoretical Level**
  —Ex: Outerspace expansion: local → regional → global → solar → galactic → clustery → multiversal (Ch.9 of *FCD*)
  —Ex: Demographic transition: human extinction, and the rise of post-humans (e.g., cyborgs, thinking machines, thinking robots, genetically altered superior beings, floating consciousness, hyper-spatial consciousness) (Ch.4 of *FPHC*; Ch.10 of *FCD*; & Ch.7 of *FHC*)
  —Ex: New technological forces in material sciences, electronic and communication sciences, energy sciences, biosciences, manufacturing and engineering sciences, and space sciences (Ch.10 of *FCD* & Ch.7 of *FHC*)
  —Ex: Systematic dominance towards nature for space colonization (Chs.9-10 of *FCD*; Chs.2 & 7 of *FHC*)

- **At the Cultural Theoretical Level**
  —Ex: The post-human transcendence of freedom and equality (Ch.10 of *FCD*)
  —Ex: Methodological Holism (Ch.1 of *FCD*; Ch.1 of *FPHC*; *Sec.2.1* & *Sec.2.5* of *BCPC*)
  —Ex: The Evolution from Barbarity to Post-Civilization (*BCIV*)

- **At the Cosmological Theoretical Level**
  —Ex: Mastering of dark matter and dark energy, and the exploration of multiverses (Ch.4 of *FPHC*; Ch.10 of *FCD*; & Ch.7 of *FHC*)
  —Ex: Alternation of space-time (*FPHST*)
  —Ex: The emergence of hyper-spatial consciousness (*FPHC*)

(continued on next page)

Table 4.42. Civilizational Holism (Part III)

- **At Other Levels**
  —Ex: Historical: pre-modernity → modernity → postmodernity → after-postmodernity (human distinction, and the rise of post-humans, including floating consciousness, hyper-spatial consciousness, and unfolding unconsciousness) (Ch.7 of *FHC*; Ch.10 of *FCD*; *FPHC*; *FPHU*)

Notes: These examples are solely illustrative (not exhaustive), and some of the items can be reclassified somewhere else. Nor are they always mutually exclusive. Since they are generalities, exceptions are expected. And the comparison is relative, not absolute.
Sources: From *Table 5.1* of *FPHC*—with details from *FHC*, *FCD*, and the rest of my books. Not every aspect in each category as discussed in all my books are presented here, since there are too many issues. For more info, also consult the table on theories on civilizational holism and, of course, the books themselves.

Table 4.43. Theories on Civilizational Holism (Part I)

I. Theories in Relation to Nature

—At the Chemical Theoretical Level

• 60. Creational Theory of Chemistry (Peter Baofu) (*FPHCHEM*)

—At the Macro-Physical (Cosmological) Theoretical Level

• 59. Resettlement Theory of Geology (Peter Baofu) (*FPHGEOL*)

• 58. Theory of Post-Cosmology (Peter Baofu) (*BCOS*)

• 57. Theory of Hyper-Spatial Consciousness (Peter Baofu) (Ch.4 of *FPHC*; *FPHG*)

(• 55). Panoramic Theory of Transportation (Peter Baofu) (*FPHTRAN*)

(• 53). Multilateral Theory of Acoustics (Peter Baofu) (*FPHA*)

(• 52). Selective Theory of Geometry (Peter Baofu) (*FPHG*)

(• 51). Perspectival Theory of Space-Time (Peter Baofu) (*FPHST*)

(• 50). Dialectic Theory of Complexity (Peter Baofu) (*FC*)

(• 29). Theory of Floating Consciousness (Peter Baofu) (Ch.10 of *FCD*; Chs.1 & 4 of *FPHC*)

• 56. Theory of the Geopower of Nature (Ch.4 of *ALD*)—refined as the Interventive-Reshaping Theory of Geography (Peter Baofu) (*FPHGEOG*)

(continued on next page)

Table 4.43. Theories on Civilizational Holism (Part II)

I. Theories in Relation to Nature (*cont'd*)

—At the Micro-Physical Theoretical Level

- • 55. Panoramic Theory of Transportation (Peter Baofu) (*FPHTRAN*)
- • 54. Transcendent Theory of Architecture (Peter Baofu) (*FPHARCH*)
- • 53. Multilateral Theory of Acoustics (Peter Baofu) (*FPHA*)
- • 52. Selective Theory of Geometry (Peter Baofu) (*FPHG*)
- • 51. Perspectival Theory of Space-Time (Peter Baofu) (*FPHST*)
- • 50. Dialectic Theory of Complexity (Peter Baofu) (*FC*)

(continued on next page)

Table 4.43. Theories on Civilizational Holism (Part III)

II. Theories in Relation to Culture
—At the Cultural Theoretical Level

- • 49. Interactive Theory of Semantics (Peter Baofu) (*FPHSEM*)
- • 48. Transdicsiplinary Theory of Performing Arts (Peter Baofu) (*FPHPA*)
- • 47. Comparative-Impartial Theory of Literature (Peter Baofu) (*FPHLIT*)
- • 46. Mediative-Variative Theory of Chess (Peter Baofu) (*FPHCHESS*)
- • 45. Theory of Post-Ethics (Peter Baofu) (*BEPE*)
- • 44. Dualistic Theory of Mass Culture (Peter Baofu) (Ch.2 of *FHC*)
- • 43. Comparative Theory of Religion—also known as the Comparative-Substitutive Theory of Religion (Peter Baofu) (Ch.3 of *FHC*; Ch.9 of *FCD*; Ch.1 of *FPHK*; *FPHR*)
- • 42. Theory of Post-Civilization (Peter Baofu) (*BCIV*)
- • 41. Theory of the Trinity of Modernity to Its After-Postmodern Counterpart (Peter Baofu) (*FHC*; Ch.10 of *FCD*)
- • 40. Transformative Theory of Aesthetic Experience (Peter Baofu) (*FAE*)
- (• 19). Theory of Post-Capitalism (Peter Baofu) (Ch.10 of *FCD*; Chs.2 & 4 of *FPHC*; *BCPC*)
- (• 18). Theory of Post-Democracy (Peter Baofu) (Ch.10 of *FCD*; Chs.3 & 4 of *FPHC*; *BDPD*)
- (• 4). Theory of Existential Dialectics, or the Holistic Theory of Knowledge (Peter Baofu) (*FHC*; *FCD*; *FPHC*; *BDPD*; *FC*; *FAE*; *ALD; FIA; FPHK*; etc,)
- (• 3). Contrastive Theory of Rationality (Peter Baofu) (*FPHML*)
- (• 5). Theory of Methodological Holism (Peter Baofu) (Ch.1 of *FCD*; Ch.1of *FPHC*; *Sec.2.1* & *Sec.2.5* of *BCPC*; *FC*; *FPHK*; etc.)

(continued on next page)

Table 4.43. Theories on Civilizational Holism (Part IV)

III. Theories in Relation to the Mind

—*At the Biological Theoretical Level*

- 39. Theory of Contrastive Advantages (Peter Baofu) (*Sec.2.6* & Ch.10 of *FCD; BNN*)
- (• 29). Theory of Floating Consciousness (Peter Baofu) (Ch.10 of *FCD*; Chs.1 & 4 of *FPHC*)

—*At the Psychological Theoretical Level*

- 38. Complex Theory of Data Analysis (Peter Baofu) (*FPHDA*)
- 37. Supersession Theory of Computing (Peter Baofu) (*FPHCOM*)
- 36. Metamorphic Theory of Humor (Peter Baofu) (*FPHH*)
- 35. Contrarian Theory of Personality (Peter Baofu) (*FPHP*)
- 34. Theory of Virtual Sexuality (Peter Baofu) (*FPHS*)
- 33. Expansive-Contractive Theory of Martial Arts (Peter Baofu) (*FPHMA*)
- 32. Multilogical Theory of Learning (Peter Baofu) (*FPHL*)
- 31. Comprehensive Theory of Creative Thinking (Peter Baofu) (*FPHCT*)
- 30. Theory of Unfolding Unconsciousness—also known as the Unfolding Theory of Anomalous Experience (Peter Baofu) (*FPHU*)
- 29. Theory of Floating Consciousness (Peter Baofu) (Ch.10 of *FCD*; Chs.1 & 4 of *FPHC*)
- 28. Theory of Cognitive Partiality (Peter Baofu) (*Sec.2.4* of *FCD*; *Sec.4.5.1.1* of *BCPC*)
- 27. Theory of Emotional Non-Neutrality (Peter Baofu) (*Sec.2.5* of *FCD*; *Sec.4.5.2* of of *BCPC*)
- 26. Theory of Behavioral Alteration (Peter Baofu) (*Sec.4.5.3* of *BCPC*)

(continued on next page)

Table 4.43. Theories on Civilizational Holism (Part V)

IV. Theories in Relation to Society

—At the Organizational Theoretical Level

- 25. Theory of E-Civic Alienation (Peter Baofu) (Ch.7 of *FCD*)
- 24. Combinational Theory of Organization (Peter Baofu) (*FPHO*; Ch.6 of *ALD*)

—At the Institutional Theoretical Level

- 23. Reflective Theory of Criminality (Peter Baofu) (*FPHCRIM*)
- 22. Detached Theory of Gambling (Peter Baofu) (*FPHGAM*)
- 21. Heterodox Theory of Education (Peter Baofu) (*FPHEDU*)
- 20. Reconstruction Theory of Law (Peter Baofu) (*FPHLAW*)
- 19. Theory of Post-Capitalism (Peter Baofu) (Ch.10 of *FCD*; Chs.2 & 4 of *FPHC*; *BCPC*)
- 18. Theory of Post-Democracy (Peter Baofu) (Ch.10 of *FCD*; Chs.3 & 4 of *FPHC*; *BDPD*)
- 17. Dynamic Theory of Comparative Political Systems (Peter Baofu) (*ALD*)
- (• 8.) Theory of the Cyclical Progression of Empire-Building (Peter Baofu) (*BWT*)

—At the Systemic Theoretical Level

- 16. Theory of the Cyclical Progression of Migration (Peter Baofu) (*FPHMIG*)
- (• 58). Resettlement Theory of Geology (Peter Baofu) (*FPHGEOL*)
- 15. Contingent Theory of Urban Planning (Peter Baofu) (*FPHUP*)
- 14. Totalistic Theory of Communication (Peter Baofu) (*FPHMM*; *FCD*; *FHC*)
- 13. Ambivalent Theory of Technology (Peter Baofu) (*FPHE*; *FCD*; *FHC*)

(continued on next page)

Table 4.43. Theories on Civilizational Holism (Part VI)

IV. Theories in Relation to Society (*cont'd*)

—*At the Systemic Theoretical Level* (cont'd)

- 12. Multifaceted Theory of War and Peace (Peter Baofu) (Ch.9 of *FCD*; Ch.1 of *FPHK*)
- 11. Theory of Post-Humanity (Peter Baofu) (Ch.7 of *FHC*; Chs.3, & 10 of *FCD*; Chs.1, 3 & 4 of *FPHC*; and other books of mine)
- 10. Theory of the Cyclical Progression of System Integration and Fragmentation (Peter Baofu) (Chs.9-10 of *FCD*)
- 9. Synthetic Theory of Information Architecture (Peter Baofu) (*FIA*)

—*At the Structural Theoretical Level*

- 8. Theory of the Cyclical Progression of Hegemony (Peter Baofu) (Chs.9-10 of *FCD*; Chs.1, 3 & 4 of *FPHC*; *BDPD*)
- 7. Theory of the Cyclical Progression of Empire-Building (Peter Baofu) (*BWT*)

V. Meta-Theories (in Relation to Theories)

—*At the Methodological Meta-Theoretical Level*

- (• 49).Interactive Theory of Semantics (Peter Baofu) (*FPHSEM*)
- (• 38). Complex Theory of Data Analysis (Peter Baofu) (*FPHDA*)
- 6. Critical-Dialectic Theory of Formal Science (Peter Baofu) (*FPHFS*)
- 5. Theory of Methodological Holism (Peter Baofu) (Ch.1 of *FCD*; Ch.1of *FPHC*; *Sec.2.1* & *Sec.2.5* of *BCPC*; *FC*; *FPHK*; etc.)

(continued on next page)

Table 4.43. Theories on Civilizational Holism (Part VII)

V. Meta-Theories (in Relation to Theories) (*cont'd*)

—*At the Ontological Meta-Theoretical Level*

- 4. Theory of Existential Dialectics, or the Holistic Theory of Knowledge (Peter Baofu) (*FHC*; *FCD*; *FPHC*; *BDPD*; *FC*; *FAE*; *ALD; FIA; FPHK*; etc,)
- 3. Contrastive Theory of Rationality (Peter Baofu) (*FPHML*)

VI. Theories in Relation to the Rest

—*At the Meta-Historical Level*

- 2. Multifold Theory of History (Peter Baofu) (*FPHHIST*)

—*At the Empirical-Historical Level*

- 1. Theory of the Evolution from Pre-Modernity to After-Postmodernity (Peter Baofu) (*FHC*; Ch.9-10 of *FCD*; *FPHC*)

Notes: All these theories are my constructions, as some of the main contributions of my grant project on civilization and its future. These examples are solely illustrative (not exhaustive), and some of the items can be reclassified somewhere else. Nor are they always mutually exclusive. Since they are generalities, exceptions are expected.

Sources: From my previous books.

Table 4.44. Three Great Future Transformations of Mind Games

- **Virtual Games**
  —Ex: online chess
  —Ex: virtual experience

- **Novel Games**
  —Ex: new chess variants
  —Ex: new chess engines

- **Post-Human Mind Games**
  —Ex: the quest for broader/deeper mental benefits of chess playing
  —Ex: games designed for the evolution of the mind into different body-less forms (e.g., "floating consciousness," "hyper-spatial consciousness," "unfolding unconsciousness")

Notes: The examples in the categories are solely illustrative (not exhaustive), and the comparison is relative (not absolute), nor are they necessarily mutually exclusive. And some can be easily re-classified elsewhere. As generalities, they allow exceptions.
Sources: From *Sec. 4.16* of *FPHCHESS*. See text for more info. Also, consult *FCD* for strategy and tactics in warfare and *FPHO* for strategy and tactics in organization.

BIBLIOGRAPHY

Abley, Stephen. 2005. "Walkability Scoping Paper" (March 21). <http://www.levelofservice.com/walkability-research.pdf>.

Aérostories (AERO). 2002. "The Heart of the SR-71 'Blackbird': The Mighty J-58 Engine." <http://aerostories.free.fr/technique/J58/J58_01/page9.html>.

Aertsens, Joris, et al. 2010. "Commuting by Bike in Belgium, the Costs of Minor Accidents." *Accident Analysis & Prevention*, 42 (6): 2149-2157.

Akkerman, Abraham. 2007. "The City as Humanity's Evolutionary Link: Walking and Thinking in Urban Design." *Structurist* 47/48: 28-33.

Arth, Michael E. 2012. "Labor IX: Urbanism: Hercules Seizes the Belt of Hippolyte" (March 05). <http://michaelearth.com/herc_IX.htm>.

Ball State University (BSU). 2003. "Many Minority Groups Were Victims of Hate Crimes after 9-11" (October 9). <http://www.bsu.edu/news/article/0,1370,-1019-12850,00.html>.

Baofu, Peter. 2012. *The Future of Post-Human Migration: A Preface to a New Theory of Sameness, Otherness, and Identity*. Cambridge, England: Cambridge Scholars Publishing.

_____.2012a. *The Future of Post-Human History: A Preface to a New Theory of Universality and Relativity*. Cambridge, England: Cambridge Scholars Publishing.

_____.2012b. *The Future of Post-Human Criminality: A Preface to a New Theory of Heroes and Villains*. Cambridge, England: Cambridge International Science Publishing, Ltd.

_____.2012c. *The Future of Post-Human Architecture: A Preface to a New Theory of Form and Function*. Cambridge, England: Cambridge International Science Publishing, Ltd.

_____.2012d. *The Future of Post-Human Semantics: A Preface to a New Theory of Internality and Externality*. Cambridge, England: Cambridge Scholars Publishing.

_____.2012e. *The Future of Post-Human Performing Arts: A Preface to a New Theory of the Body and its Presence*. Cambridge, England: Cambridge Scholars Publishing.

_____.2011. *The Future of Post-Human Geography: A Preface to a New Theory of*

Environments and their Interactions. Cambridge, England: Cambridge International Science Publishing, Ltd.

_____.2011a. *The Future of Post-Human Data Analysis: A Preface to a New Theory of Quantiative and Qualitative Research*. Cambridge, England: Cambridge International Science Publishing, Ltd.

_____.2011b. *The Future of Post-Human Chemistry: A Preface to a New Theory of Substances and their Changes*. Cambridge, England: Cambridge Scholars Publishing.

_____.2011c. *The Future of Post-Human Literature: A Preface to a New Theory of Fiction and Non-Fiction*. Cambridge, England: Cambridge International Science Publishing, Ltd.

_____.2011d. *The Future of Post-Human Computing: A Preface to a New Theory of Hardware, Software, and the Mind*. Cambridge, England: Cambridge International Science Publishing, Ltd.

_____.2011e. *The Future of Post-Human Gambling: A Preface to a New Theory of Risk and Caution*. Cambridge, England: Cambridge International Science Publishing, Ltd.

_____.2011f. *The Future of Post-Human Acoustics: A Preface to a New Theory of Sound and Silence*. Cambridge, England: Cambridge International Science Publishing, Ltd.

_____.2011g. *The Future of Post-Human Humor: A Preface to a New Theory of Joking and Laughing*. Cambridge, England: Cambridge International Science Publishing, Ltd.

_____.2011h. *Beyond Ethics to Post-Ethics: A Preface to a New Theory of Morality and Immorality*. Charlotte, NC: Information Age Publishing.

_____.2011i. *The Future of Post-Human Education: A Preface to a New Theory of Teaching and Learning*. Cambridge, England: Cambridge International Science Publishing, Ltd.

_____.2010. *The Future of Post-Human Religion: A Preface to a New Theory of Spirituality*. Cambridge, England: Cambridge International Science Publishing, Ltd.

_____.2010a. *The Future of Post-Human Chess: A Preface to a New Theory of Tactics and Strategy*. Cambridge, England: Cambridge International Science Publishing, Ltd.

_____.2010b. *The Future of Post-Human Geology: A Preface to a New Theory of Statics and Dynamics*. Cambridge, England: Cambridge International Science Publishing, Ltd.

_____.2010c. *Beyond Cosmology to Post-Cosmology: A Preface to a New Theory of Different Worlds*. Cambridge, England: Cambridge International Science Publishing, Ltd.

_____.2010d. *The Future of Post-Human Personality: A Preface to a New Theory of Normality and Abnormality*. Cambridge, England: Cambridge International Science Publishing, Ltd.

_____.2010e. *The Future of Post-Human War and Peace: A Preface to a New Theory of Aggression and Pacificity*. Cambridge, England: Cambridge Scholars Publishing.

_____.2010f. *The Future of Post-Human Formal Science: A Preface to a New Theory of Abstraction and Application*. Cambridge, England: Cambridge Scholars Publishing.

_____.2010g. *The Future of Post-Human Law: A Preface to a New Theory of Necessity, Contingency, and Justice*. Cambridge, England: Cambridge Scholars Publishing.

_____.2010h. *The Future of Post-Human Sexuality: A Preface to a New Theory of the Body and Spirit of Love Makers*. Cambridge, England: Cambridge Scholars Publishing.

_____,2009. *The Future of Post-Human Martial Arts: A Preface to a New Theory of the Body and Spirit of Warriors*. Cambridge, England: Cambridge Scholars Publishing.

_____.2009a. *The Future of Post-Human Organization: A Preface to a New Theory of Communication, Decision-Making, and Leadership*. Cambridge, England: Cambridge Scholars Publishing.

_____.2009b. *The Future of Post-Human Language: A Preface to a New Theory of Structure, Context, and Learning*. Cambridge, England: Cambridge Scholars Publishing.

_____.2009c. *The Future of Post-Human Urban Planning: A Preface to a New Theory of Density, Void, and Sustainability*. Cambridge, England: Cambridge Scholars Publishing.

_____.2009d. *The Future of Post-Human Geometry: A Preface to a New Theory of Infinity, Symmetry, and Dimensionality*. Cambridge, England: Cambridge Scholars Publishing.

_____.2009e. *The Future of Post-Human Creative Thinking: A Preface to a New Theory of Invention and Innovation*. Cambridge, England: Cambridge Scholars Publishing.

_____.2009f. *The Future of Post-Human Mass Media: A Preface to a New Theory of Communication*. Cambridge, England: Cambridge Scholars Publishing.

_____.2009g. *The Future of Post-Human Engineering: A Preface to a New Theory of Technology*. Cambridge, England: Cambridge Scholars Publishing.

_____.2008. *The Future of Post-Human Mathematical Logic: A Preface to a New Theory of Rationality*. Cambridge, England: Cambridge Scholars Publishing.

_____.2008a. *The Future of Post-Human Knowledge: A Preface to a New Theory of Methodology and Ontology*. Oxford, United Kingdom: Chandos Publishing (Oxford) Ltd.

_____.2008b. *The Future of Post-Human Unconsciousness: A Preface to a New Theory of Anomalous Experience*. Cambridge, England: Cambridge Scholars Publishing.

_____.2008c. *The Future of Information Architecture: Conceiving a New Way to Understand Taxonomy, Network, and Intelligence*. Oxford, United Kingdom: Chandos Publishing (Oxford) Ltd.

_____.2007. *The Rise of Authoritarian Liberal Democracy: A Preface to a New Theory of Comparative Political Systems*. Cambridge, England: Cambridge Scholars Publishing.

_____.2007a. *The Future of Aesthetic Experience: Conceiving a Better Way to Beauty, Ugliness, and the Rest*. Cambridge, England: Cambridge Scholars Publishing.

_____.2007b. *The Future of Complexity: Conceiving a Better Way to Understand Order and Chaos*. London, United Kingdom: World Scientific Publishing Co.

_____.2007c. *Beyond the World of Titans, and the Remaking of World Order: A Preface to a New Logic of Empire-Building*. Cambridge, England: Cambridge Scholars Publishing.

_____.2006. *Beyond Nature and Nurture: Conceiving a Better Way to Understand Genes and Memes*. Cambridge, England: Cambridge Scholars Publishing.

_____.2006a. *The Future of Post-Human Space-Time: Conceiving a Better Way to Understand Space and Time*. New York: Peter Lang Publishing, Inc.

_____.2006b. *Beyond Civilization to Post-Civilization: Conceiving a Better Model of Life Settlement to Supersede Civilization*. New York: Peter Lang Publishing, Inc.

_____.2005. *Beyond Capitalism to Post-Capitalism: Conceiving a Better Model of Wealth Acquisition to Supersede Capitalism*. New York: The Edwin Mellen Press.

_____.2004. *The Future of Post-Human Consciousness*. New York: The Edwin Mellen Press.

_____.2004a. *Beyond Democracy to Post-Democracy: Conceiving a Better Model of Governance to Supersede Democracy*. Volume 1. New York: The Edwin Mellen Press.

_____.2004b. *Beyond Democracy to Post-Democracy: Conceiving a Better Model of Governance to Supersede Democracy*. Volume 2. New York: The Edwin Mellen Press.

_____.2002. *The Future of Capitalism and Democracy*. Maryland: The University Press of America.

_____.2000. *The Future of Human Civilization*. Volume 1. New York: The Edwin Mellen Press.

_____.2000a. *The Future of Human Civilization*. Volume 2. New York: The Edwin Mellen Press.

Bardi, Edward; John Coyle; & Robert Novack. 2006. *Management of Transportation*. Mason, OH: Thomson South-Western.

Barnhart, Bill. 2001. "Markets Reopen, Plunge" (September 17). *Chicago Tribune*. <http://www.chicagotribune.com/business/chi-010917markets,0,5287650.story>.

Barrow, John D. 1998. *Impossibility: The Limits of Science and the Science of Limits*. Oxford: Oxford University Press.

Battery University (BAT). 2011. "Comparing the Battery with other Power Sources" (July 23). <http://batteryuniversity.com/learn/article/comparing_the_battery_with_other_power_sources>.

BBC. 2007. "Early Days of Mumbles Railway" (February 15). <http://www.bbc.co.uk/wales/southwest/sites/swansea/pages/mumbles_trainanniv.shtml>.

_____.2005. "Poland to Down Hijacked Aircraft" (January 13). <http://news.bbc.co.uk/2/hi/europe/4172487.stm>.

_____.2004. "Steam Train Anniversary Begins" (February 21). <http://news.bbc.co.uk/2/hi/uk_news/wales/3509961.stm>.

_____.2003. "US Pilots Train Shooting Civilian Planes" (October 03). <http://news.bbc.co.uk/2/hi/americas/3161354.stm>.

Beck, Roger. 2004. "20." *Modern World History*. US: Holt McDougal.

Benninger, C. 2001. "Principles of Intelligent Urbanism." *Ekistics,* 69 (412): 39–65.

Best, Ben. 2012. "Causes of Death" (March 12). <http://www.benbest.com/lifeext/causes.html>.

Bettmann, Theresa. 2011. "How to Operate a Horse-Drawn Carriage" (June 11). <http://www.ehow.com/how_8580312_operate-horsedrawn-carriage.html>.

Biletzki, Anat; & Anat Matar. 2006. "Ludwig Wittgenstein" (Nov. 17). *Stanford Encyclopedia of Philosophy*. <http://plato.stanford.edu/entries/wittgenstein/>.

Beoing. 2011. "NASA—Innovative Engines" (July 22). <http://www.boeing.com/defense-space/space/bss/factsheets/xips/xips.html>.

Bhadra, Dipasis; & Pamela Texter. 2004. "Airline Networks: An Econometric Framework to Analyze Domestic U.S. Air Travel." United States Department of Transportation. <http://www.bts.gov/publications/journal_of_transportation_and_statistics/volume_07_number_01/html/paper_06/>.

Blackburn, Susan Tucker. 2007. *Maternal, Fetal, & Neonatal Physiology: A Clinical Perspective*. Netherlands: Elsevier Health Sciences.

Blanton, Thomas S. 2004. "The President's Daily Brief." (April 12). National Security Archive. <http://www.gwu.edu/~nsarchiv/NSAEBB/NSAEBB116/index.htm>.

Blumenthal, Ivan. 2001. "Carbon Monoxide Poisoning" (June 01). *J R Soc Med* (The Royal Society of Medicine), 94 (6): 270–272. <http://www.ncbi.nlm.nih.gov/pmc/articles/PMC1281520/?tool=pmcentrez>.

Bob, Fernandez. 2001. "U.S. Markets Decline Again" (September 22). *KRTBN Knight Ridder Tribune Business News* (The Philadelphia Inquirer).

BrainyQuotes (BQ). 2012. "William Langewiesche" (April 07). <http://www.brainyquote.com/quotes/keywords/transportation_2.html#xPvpGQq8f1ThAfOM.99>.

Buchanan, Colin. 1958. *Mixed Blessing*. England: L Hill.

Bunge, Mario. 1999. *Dictionary of philosophy*. Amherst, MA: Prometheus Books.

CBC News (CBC). 2004. "Bin Laden Claims Responsibility for 9/11" (October 29). <http://www.cbc.ca/news/world/story/2004/10/29/binladen_message041029.html>.

Canada Science and Technology Museum (CSTM). 2006. "Baron von Drais' Bicycle." <http://www.sciencetech.technomuses.ca/english/collection/cycles2.cfm>.

Center for Disease Control and Prevention (CDCP). 2011 "CDC—Motor Vehicle Safety." <http://www.cdc.gov/MotorVehicleSafety/index.html>.

Charters, Derek; Martin Watkinson; Dave Wykes; & Bob Simpkin. 2008. "H4v-Hybrid Four Wheel Drive Vehicle." Hybrid and Eco-Friendly Vehicle Conference. <http://ieeexplore.ieee.org.libdb.njit.edu:8888/stamp/stamp.jsp?tp=&arnumber=4784369&isnumber=4784367>.

Chase, Scott. 1993. "Tachyons" (March). *Physics FAQ*. <http://math.ucr.edu/home/baez/physics/ParticleAndNuclear/tachyons.html>.

China.org.cn (CHI). 2012. "China Through a Lens: Rural Road Construction Speeded Up'" (March 12). <http://www.china.org.cn/english/2003/May/64719.htm>.

Chopra, Sunil; & Peter Meindl. 2007. *Supply Chain Management*. NJ: Pearson.

CNN. 2007. "French Train Breaks Speed Record" (April 04).

_____.2004. "Transcript of Rice's 9/11 Commission Statement" (May 19). <http://articles.cnn.com/2004-04-08/politics/rice.transcript_1_terrorist-threat-freedom-hating-terrorists-response-across-several-administrations/6?_s=PM:ALLPOLITICS>.

_____.2001. "Hate Crime Reports up in Wake of Terrorist Attacks" (September 17). <http://articles.cnn.com/2001-09-16/us/gen.hate.crimes_1_american-sikh-balbir-singh-sodhi-indian-sikh?_s=PM:US>.

_____.2001a. "Relatives Wait for News as Rescuers Dig" (September 13). <http://articles.cnn.com/2001-09-12/us/family.reacts_1_rescue-teams-rescue-

workers-fire-department?_s=PM:US>.

_____.1998. "Air China Pilot Hijacks his Own Jet to Taiwan" (October 28). <http://web.archive.org/web/20080321171516/http://www.cnn.com/WORLD/asiapcf/9810/28/hijack.china.taiwan.02/index.html>.

Commission for Architecture and the Built Environment (CABE). 2006. "The Cost of Bad Design."

Cooper, Chris; John Fletcher; David Gilbert; Stephen Wanhill, & Rebecca Shepherd. 1998. *Tourism Principles and Practice*. Harlow, England: Longman.

Corazzon, Raul. 2007. "Definitions of Ontology: From Nicolai Hartmann to the Present Time." <http://www.formalontology.it/section_4_two.htm>.

Corbett, Dan. 2008. "Introduction to String Theory" (November 23). *ThinkQuest*. <http://library.thinkquest.org/27930/stringtheory1.htm>.

Cossalter, Vittore. 2006. *Motorcycle Dynamics*. Raleigh, N.C.: Lulu.

Dainton, Barry. 2001. "Conceptions of Void." *Time and Space*. Canada: McGill-Queen's Press.

Davis. R. 1993. "Death on the Streets:Cars and the Mythology of Road Safety." *Leading Edge*.

DePalma, Anthony. 2006. "Tracing Lung Ailments That Rose With 9/11 Dust" (May 13). *The New York Times*. <http://www.nytimes.com/2006/05/13/nyregion/13symptoms.html>.

Dictionary.com (DIC). 2012. "Pathophysiology" (March 14). <http://dictionary.reference.com/browse/Pathophysiology?s=t>.

Dilts, James D. 1996. *The Great Road: The Building of the Baltimore and Ohio, the Nation's First Railroad, 1828-1853*. Palo Alto, CA: Stanford University Press.

Dolfman, Michael L.; & Solidelle F. Wasser. 2004. "9/11 and the New York City Economy." *Monthly Labor Review* 127.

Duranton, Gilles; & Matthew A. Turner. 2011. "The Fundamental Law of Road Congestion: Evidence from U.S. Cities" (October). *American Economic Review*, 101 (6): 2616-52.

Economist, the (EC). 2012. "The Flying Car is (Almost) Here" (April 13). <http://www.economist.com/blogs/babbage/2012/04/flying-car-almost-here>.

Eisenstein, Paul A. 2010. "Building BRIC's: 4 Markets Could Soon Dominate the Auto World" (January 21). <http://www.thedetroitbureau.com/2010/01/building-brics-the-four-markets-that-could-soon-dominate-the-automotive-world/>.

Electropaedia (ELEC). 2011. "Battery Safety" (July 23). <http://www.mpoweruk.com/safety.htm>.

Encyclopedia Astronautica (ENA). 2012. "Vostok" (March 08). <http://www.astronautix.com/craft/vostok.htm>.

Epa.gov. (EPA). 2006. "EPA: Air Pollutants" (June 28). <http://www.epa.gov/ebtpages/airairpollutants.html>.

ESA. 2004. "The Rosetta Ground Segment" (February 17).. <http://www.esa.int/SPECIALS/Rosetta/SEMDV71PGQD_0.html>.

EuDaly, K.; M. Schafer; Jim Boyd; S. Jessup; A. McBridge; & S. Glischinksi. 2009. *The Complete Book of North American Railroading*. Stillwater, MN: Voyageur Press.

Everett, Hugh. 1957. "'Relative State' Formulation of Quantum Mechanics" (July). *Reviews of Modern Physics*, vol. 29, no.3. <http://www.univer.omsk.su/omsk/Sci/Everett/paper1957.html>.

Fajans, Joel. 2000. "Steering in Bicycles and Motorcycles" (July). *American Journal of Physics*, 68 (7): 654–659. <http://socrates.berkeley.edu/~fajans/pub/pdffiles/SteerBikeAJP.PDF>.

Federal Aviation Administration (FAA). 2009. "FAA Advisory Circular" (September 21). <http://www.faa.gov/documentLibrary/media/Advisory_Circular/draft_150_5220_xx.pdf>.

Firehammer, Reginald. 2005. "Basic Principles of Ontology" (January 05). <http://usabig.com/autonomist/philosophy/ontology2.html>.

F.O.D. Control Corporation (FOD). 2012. "FOD—FOREIGN OBJECT DAMAGE or FOREIGN OBJECT DEBRIS" (March 12). <http://www.fodcontrol.com/>.

Frank, Lawrence, et al. 2006. "Many Pathways from Land Use to Health." *Journal of the American Planning Association* (Winter): 77.

Fuerst, Franz. 2005. "Exogenous Shocks and Real Estate Rental Markets: An Event Study of the 9/11 Attacks and their Impact on the New York Office Market" (September 07). Russell Sage Foundation.

Fuglestvedt, Jan; Terje Berntsen; Gunnar Myhre; Kristin Rypdal; & Ragnhild Bieltvedt Skeie. 2008. "Climate Forcing from the Transport Sectors" (January 15). Center for International Climate and Environmental Research. <http://www.pnas.org/content/105/2/454.full.pdf>.

Fuller, R. 2011. "Impact of Past and Future Residential Housing Development Patterns on Energy Demand and Related Emissions." *Journal of Housing and the Built Environment*, 26 (2): 165–83.

Garten, Jeffrey E. 2008. "Stop the Bail Outs Now" (November 10). *Newsweek*: 19.

Gasser, Alexander. 2003. "World's Oldest Wheel Found in Slovenia" (March). Government Communication Office of the Republic of Slovenia. <http://www.ukom.gov.si/en/media_relations/background_information/culture/worlds_oldest_wheel_found_in_slovenia/>.

Gates, Anita. 2006. "Buildings Rise from Rubble while Health Crumbles" (September 11). *The New York Times*. <http://www.nytimes.com/2006/09/11/arts/television/11dust.html?_r=1&ref=nyregionspecial3>.

Gehl, J.; & L. Gemzoe. 1996. *Public Spaces and Public Life*. Copenhagen, Denmark: Danish Architectural Press.

Georgano, G. N. 1985. *Cars: Early and Vintage, 1886–1930*. London, England: Grange-Universal.

Gilbert, Alan. 1996. *The Mega-City in Latin America*. UN: United Nations University Press.

Gilliam, O. R.; C. M. Johnson; & W. Gordy. 1950. "Microwave Spectroscopy in the Region from Two to Three Millimeters." *Physical Review*, 78 (2): 140. <http://prola.aps.org/abstract/PR/v78/i2/p140_1>.

Goddard, Haynes. 1997. "Using Tradeable Permits to Achieve Sustainability in the World's Large Cities." *Environmental and Resource Economics* (Springer Netherlands), 10 (1): 63–99.

Goldstein, Allen H.; Charles D. Koven' Colette L. Heald; & Inez Y. Fung. 2009. "Biogenic Carbon and Anthropogenic Pollutants Combine to Form a Cooling Haze over the Southeastern United States" (May 05). *Proceedings of the National Academy of Sciences.*

Gott, J. Richard. 2002. *Time Travel in Einstein's Universe*. Boston : Houghton Mifflin.

Grady, Denise. 2010. "Lung Function of 9/11 Rescuers Fell, Study Finds" (April 07). *New York Times*. <http://www.nytimes.com/2010/04/08/nyregion/08lung.html>.

Grant, J. 2006. *Planning the Good Community: New Urbanism in Theory and Practice*. London: Routledge.

Grignaffini, S.; S. Cappellanti; & A. Cefalo. 2008. "Visualizing Sustainability in Urban Conditions." *WIT Transactions on Ecology and the Environment*, Vol. 1: 253-262. <http://md1.csa.com/partners/viewrecord.php?requester=gs&collection=ENV&recid=8642022&q=walkability+sustainability&uid=1015422&setcookie=yes>.

Guth, Alan. 1997. *The Inflationary Universe: The Quest for a New Theory Of Cosmic Origins*. New York: Helix Books.

Halsey, William D., ed. 1979. "Vehicle." *MacMillan Contemporary Dictionary*. London, UK: MacMillan Publishing.

Hanlon, Mike. 2005."BMW Unveils the Turbosteamer Concept" (December 14). <http://www.gizmag.com/go/4936/>.

Hanson, Phyllis. 2007. "FOD: A 3-Letter Acronym For Trouble" (November 14). <http://www.fodnews.com/article012908.html>.

Haslam, D. W.; W. P. James. 2005. "Obesity." *Lancet* 366 (9492): 1197–209. <http://www.sciencedirect.com/science/article/pii/S0140673605674831>.

Haynes, William M. 2010. *Handbook of Chemistry and Physics*. Boca Raton, Florida: CRC Press.

Heath, Thomas. 2011. "Bin Laden's War against the U.S. Economy" (May 03).

The Washington Post. <http://www.washingtonpost.com/blogs/ezra-klein/post/bin-ladens-war-against-the-us-economy/2011/04/27/AFDOPjfF_blog.html>.

Heilprin, John. 2003. "White House Edited EPA's 9/11 Reports" (June 13). *Seattle Post-Intelligencer*. <http://www.seattlepi.com/default/article/White-House-edited-EPA-s-9-11-reports-1122465.php?rand=26878.51>.

Henley, Jon. 2005. "Paris Drive to Cut Traffic in Centre by 75%" (March 17). *The Guardian.* <http://www.guardian.co.uk/world/2005/mar/15/france.jonhenley>.

Hensell, Lesley. 2001. "Tough Times Loom For Manhattan Commercial Market" (December 14). *Realty Times*. <http://realtytimes.com/rtpages/20011214_downtown.htm>.

Herlihy, David V. 2004. *Bicycle: The History*. CT: Yale University Press.

HowStuffWorks (HOW). 2011. "The Lifecycle of an Electric Car Battery" (July 23). <http://auto.howstuffworks.com/fuel-efficiency/vehicles/electric-car-battery4.htm>.

_____.2011a. "Advantages and Disadvantages of EVs" (July 23). <http://auto.howstuffworks.com/auto-parts/brakes/brake-types/regenerative-braking.htm>.

_____.2011b. "How Regenerative Braking Works" (July 23). <http://en.wikipedia.org/wiki/Vehicle#cite_note-regenerative-33>.

_____.2011c. "Can You Make a Rocket Engine using Hydrogen Peroxide and Silver?" (July 22). <http://www.howstuffworks.com/question159.htm>.

_____.2011d. "How Car Steering Works" (July 23). <http://www.howstuffworks.com/steering.htm>.

_____.2011e. "How Sailboats Move in the Water" (August 02). <http://adventure.howstuffworks.com/outdoor-activities/water-sports/sailboat3.htm>.

_____.2006. "How Do the Engines Breathe in Diesel Submarines?" (July 24). <http://science.howstuffworks.com/transport/engines-equipment/question286.htm.

Hylton, Stuart. 2007. *The Grand Experiment: The Birth of the Railway Age 1820-1845*. UK: Ian Allan Publishing.

Indianexpress.com (IND). 2011. "Post-9/11, US Policies Created Atmosphere of Fear for South Asians" (August 25). <http://www.indianexpress.com/news/post9-11-us-policies-created-atmosphere-of-fear-for-south-asians/836936/>.

Insight SRI Ltd (INS). 2012. "Runway Safety—FOD, Birds, and the Case for Automated Scanning" (March 13). <http://www.runway-safety.com/>.

_____. 2008. "The Economic Cost of FOD to Airlines" (March 08).

<http://insightsri.com/system/files/The+Ecomonic+Cost+of+FOD+-+Jul08.pdf>.

Jackson, Kenneth T. 1987. *Crabgrass Frontier: The Suburbanization of the United States.* Oxford, England: Oxford University Press.

International Size Acceptance Association (ISAA). 2009. "ISAA Mission Statement" (February 17). <http://www.size-acceptance.org/mission.html>.

Kaku, Michio. 1994. *Hyperspace: A Scientific Odyssey Through Parallel Universes, Time Warps, and The Tenth Dimension.* Illustrations by Robert O'Keefe. Oxford: Oxford University Press.

Kay, Jane Holtz. 1998. *Asphalt Nation: How the Automobile Took over America, and How We Can Take it Back.* CA: University of California Press.

Kenkifer.com (KEN). 1999. "How Much Do Bicycles Pollute? Looking at the Carbon Dioxide Produced by Bicycles." <http://www.kenkifer.com/bikepages/advocacy/bike_co2.htm>.

Kentucky Coal Education (KCE). 2011. "Coal and the Environment" (July 22). <http://www.coaleducation.org/lessons/twe/envi.pdf>.

Khimm, Suzy. 2011. "Osama bin Laden didn't Win, but He Was 'Enormously Successful'" (May 03). *The Washington Post.* <http://www.washingtonpost.com/business/economy/osama-bin-laden-didnt-win-but-he-was-enormously-successful/2011/05/02/AFexZjbF_story.html>.

Klein, Leighton W. 2012. "Fundamental Law of Road Congestion: Evidence from U.S. Cities" (February 17). <http://journalistsresource.org/studies/environment/transportation/fundamental-law-road-congestion-evidence-u-s-cities/>.

Knoflacher, Hermann. 2006. "A New Way to Organize Parking: The Key to a Successful Sustainable Transport System for the Future." *Environment and Urbanization* (International Institute for Environment and Development), 18 (2): 387–400.

KonSULT. 2008. "Regulatory Restrictions." Institute for Transport Studies, University of Leeds. <http://www.elseviersocialsciences.com/transport/konsult/private/level2/instruments/instrument009/l2_009a.htm>.

Lay, Maxwell G. 1992. *Ways of the World: A History of the World's Roads and of the Vehicles that Used Them.* NJ: Rutgers University Press.

Lefebre, Filip; Koen De Ridder; Stefan Adriaensen; Ute Arnold; Wolfgang Beckroege; Christine Bronner; Ole Damsgaard; Ivo Dostal; Jiri Dufek; Jacky Hirsch; Luc Int Panis; Zdenek Kotek; Thierry Ramadier; Annette Thierry; Stijn Vermoote; Annett Wania; & Christiane Weber. 2008. "Simulating the Impact of Urban Sprawl on Air Quality and Population Exposure in the German Ruhr Area. Part II: Development and Evaluation of an Urban Growth Scenario." *Atmospheric Environment*, 42 (30): 7070–7077.

Lightcraft Technologies International (LTI). 2011. "LTI-20 Flight Dynamics" (July 22). <http://www.lightcrafttechnologies.com/rpi_www/technical/flight_

dynamics.html>.

Littman, Todd. 2003. “Economic Value of Walkability.” *Transportation Research Board of the National Academies* (1828). <http://trb.metapress.com/content/m1573875u76t4223/>.

Lo, R. Hutabarat. 2009. “Walkability: What is It?” *Journal of Urbanism* (2) 2: 145-166. <http://www.tandfonline.com/doi/abs/10.1080/1754917090309286 7>.

Lopez, Russel P.; & H. Patricia Hynes. 2006. “Obesity, Physical Activity, and the Urban Environment: Public Health Research Needs.” *Environmental Health: A Global Access Science Source*. <http://www.ehjournal.net/content/5/1/25>.

Mahoney, Rebbecca. 2007. “Homeless Village or Leper Colony?” (January 20). *Orlando Sentinel*. <http://articles.orlandosentinel.com/2007-01-20/news/MHOMELESS20_1_volusia-county-homeless-problem-deland>.

Makinen, Gail. 2002. “The Economic Effects of 9/11: A Retrospective Assessment” (September 27). Congressional Research Service. <http://www.fas.org/irp/crs/RL31617.pdf>.

Mapawatt (MAPA). 2011. “Bicycle Power—How Many Watts Can you Produce?” (July 23).

Mattox, Brent S. 2006. “Investigative Report on Chemistry 301A Cylinder Explosion” (January 26). Texas A&M University. <http://ucih.ucdavis.edu/docs/chemistry_301a.pdf>.

McAleer, Neil. 1987. *The Mind-Boggling Universe*. New York: Doubleday & Co.

McArdle, P. 2004. “Substance Abuse by Children and Young People.” *Arch. Dis. Child.* 89: 701-704.

McCormick, Joseph; Susan Fisher-Hoch; & Leslie Alan Horvitz. 1997. *Virus Hunters of the CDC*. Nashville, TN: Turner Publishing.

McDougall, Walter A. 2010. “Shooting the Moon.” *American Heritage* (Winter).

McGoun, Skip. 2012. “Automobile Culture.” <http://www.pcaaca.org/areas/autoculture>.

McKinnon, Jim. 2001. “The Phone Line from Flight 93 was Still Open When a GTE Operator Heard Todd Beamer Say: 'Are You Guys Ready? Let's Roll'” (September 16). *Pittsburgh Post-Gazette*. <http://old.post-gazette.com/headlines/20010916phonecallnat3p3.asp>.

Meijaard, J. P.; Jim M. Papadopoulos; Andy Ruina; & A. Schwab. 2007. “Linearized Dynamics Equations for the Balance and Steer of a Bicycle: A Benchmark and Review.” *Proc. R. Soc. A*. 463 (2084): 1955–1982. <http://adsabs.harvard.edu/abs/2007RSPSA.463.1955M>.

Merriam-Webster's Collegiate Dictionary Online (MWD). 2012. “Network” (March 02). <http://www.m-w.com/dictionary/network>.

_____.2007. “Agency” (March 20). <http://www.m-w.com/dictionary/agency>.

Military Times (MT). 2011. “Week 04—Continuous Track” (July 23).

Miller, Bill. 2002. “Report Assesses Trade Center's Collapse” (May 01). *The Washington Post.* <http://www.washingtonpost.com/ac2/wp-dyn/A11614-2002Apr30?language=printer>.

Miller, Deborah. 2008. “When It Comes to FOD, 'Many Hands Make Light Work'” (September 18). <http://www.tinker.af.mil/news/story.asp?id=123115808>.

Monbiot, George. 2005. “They Call Themselves Libertarians; I Think They're Antisocial Bastards” (December 20). *The Guardian.* <http://www.guardian.co.uk/uk/2005/dec/20/politics.publicservices>.

Morlok, Edward K. 2005. “First Permanent Railroad in the U.S. and its Connection to the University of Pennsylvania” (May 11). <http://www.seas.upenn.edu /~morlok/morlokpage/transp_data.html>.

Munby, Julian. 2008. “From Carriage to Coach: What Happened?” *The Art, Science, and Technology of Medieval Travel*. Robert Bork and Andrea Kann, eds. UK: Ashgate.

NASA. 2011. “Historical Timeline” (July 22). <http://www.nasa.gov/centers/ kennedy/about/history/timeline/1950_prt.htm>.

_____.2011a. “Frequently Asked Questions about Ion Propulsion” (July 22). <http://nmp.nasa.gov/ds1/tech/ionpropfaq.html>.

_____.2011b. “Nozzles” (July 22). <http://www.grc.nasa.gov/WWW/K-12/airplane/nozzle.html>.

_____.2011c. “Three Forces on a Glider” (August 02). <http://www.grc.nasa.gov/WWW/K-12/airplane/glidfor.html>.

National Association to Advance Fat Acceptance (NAAFA). 2009. “What is NAAFA” (February 17). <http://govinfo.library.unt.edu/911/report/911Report _Ch7.htm>.

National Commission on Terrorist Attacks Upon the United States (NCTAUS). 2004. “The Attack Looms.” 9/11 Commission Report..

NHTSA.gov (NHTSA). 2012. “Appendix A: Standardized Field Sobriety Testing.” <http://www.nhtsa.dot.gov/People/injury/alcohol/SFST/appendix_a.htm>.

Nice, Karim. 2011. “How Car Steering Works” (July 23). *HowStuffWorks*. <http://www.howstuffworks.com/steering.htm>.

Norcliffe, Glen. 2001. *The Ride to Modernity: The Bicycle in Canada, 1869-1900*. Toronto, Canada: University of Toronto Press.

Nova Online (NO). 2000. “Time Can Vary.” <http://www.pbs.org/ wgbh/nova/time/thinktime.html>.

NYC. 2011. “New York City Commission on Human Rights.” <http://www.nyc.gov/html/cchr/html/report.html>.

OICA. 2011. “Production Statistics” (September 09). <http://oica.net/category/ production-statistics/>.

_____.2011a. “World Motor Vehicle Production by Manufacturer: World Ranking of Manufacturers 2010” (August). <http://oica.net/wp-content/uploads/ ranking-2010.pdf>.

Ogilvie, David; Matt Egan; Val Hamilton; & Mark Petticrew. 2004. "Promoting Walking and Cycling as an Alternative to Using Cars: Systematic Review" (September 22). *British Medical Journal* (BMJ Publishing Group), 329 (7469): 763. <http://www.ncbi.nlm.nih.gov/pmc/articles/PMC520994/?tool =pmcentrez>.

Omaye, S. T. 2002. "Metabolic Modulation of Carbon Monoxide Toxicity." *Toxicology*, 180 (2): 139–150. <http://www.sciencedirect.com/science/article/pii/S0300483X02003876>.

OSHA. 2009. "OSHA CO Guidelines" (May). <http://www.osha.gov/SLTC/healthguidelines/carbonmonoxide/recognition.html>.

Oxford English Dictionary (OED). 1982. "Bicycle." England: Oxford University Press.

Parrott, James. 2002. "The Employment Impact of the September 11 World Trade Center Attacks: Updated Estimates based on the Benchmarked Employment Data" (March 08). *The Fiscal Policy Institute*. <http://www.fiscalpolicy.org/Employment%20Impact%20of%20September%2011_Update.pdf>.

Patterson, L. Brooks. 2012. "Sprawl, Schmall...Give Me More Development" (April 05). <http://www.oakgov.com/exec/brooks/sprawl.html>.

Pennise, David; & Kirk Smith. 2012. "Biomass Pollution Basics" (March 15). WHO. <http://www.who.int/indoorair/interventions/antiguamod21.pdf>.

Piggott, Stuart. 1992. *Wagon, Chariot, and Carriage: Symbol and Status in the History of Transport*. London: Thames and Hudson.

_____.1983. *The Earliest Wheeled Transport*. Ithaca, NY: Cornell University Press.

Pfaff, William. 2003. "A Fiction Shattered by America's Aggression." *The International Herald Tribune* (Saturday, November 1).

Plunkett Research (PR). 2008. "Automobile Industry Introduction." <http://www.plunkettresearch.com/automobiles-trucks-market-research/industry-overview>.

PolicyLink (PL). 2008. "Equitable Development Toolkit: Transit Oriented Development." <http://www.dialogue4health.org/pdfs/wf1/transit-oriented-policylink.pdf>.

Popular Science Monthly (PSM). 1929. "U.S. Makes Ninety Percent of World's Automobiles" (November).

Prockop, L. D.; & R. I. Chichkova. 2007. "Carbon Monoxide Intoxication: An Updated Review." *J Neurol Sci*, 262 (1–2): 122–130. <http://www.sciencedirect.com/science/article/pii/S0022510X0700456X>.

Pulver, Adam. 2007. "An Imperfect Fit: Obesity, Public Health, and Disability Anti-Discrimination Law." Social Science Electronic Publishing. <http://papers.ssrn.com/sol3/papers.cfm?abstract_id=1316106>.

Quasiturbine (QUA). 2011. "Pneumatic Engine" (July 22). <http://sites.google.com/site/ quasiturbines/enginetypes/etypepneumatic>.

Raman, B. 2000. "Plane Hijacking: In Perspective." *South Asia Analysis Group.* <http://www.southasiaanalysis.org/%5Cpapers2%5Cpaper103.html>.

Raman, Shankar. 1997. Lectures on Literary Theory. Cambridge, MA: MIT (spring).

Ramirez, Laura, et al. 2006. "Indicators of Activity-Friendly Communities: An Evidence-Based Consensus Process" (December). *American Journal of Preventive Medicine* (December): 515–24. <http://www.ajpmonline.org/article/PIIS0749379706003059/fulltext>.

Reagan, Ronald. 1983. "Address to the Nation on the Soviet Attack on a Korean Civilian Airliner" (September 05). United States Government. <http://www.reagan.utexas.edu/archives/speeches/1983/90583a.htm>.

Reason Magazine (RM). 1998. "Plan Obsolescence" (June). <http://reason.com/archives/1998/06/01/plan-obsolescence>.

Rietveld, Piet; & Vanessa Daniel. 2004. "Determinants of Bicycle Use: Do Municipal Policies Matter?" *Transportation Research Part A: Policy and Practice* (Elsevier), 38 (7): 531–550.

Russell, James S. 2004. "Do Skyscrapers Still Make Sense?" (November 07). <http://archrecord.construction.com/innovation/2_Features/0411SkyscraperSense.asp>.

SAALT. 2003. "American Backlash: Terrorist Bring War Home in More Ways Than One." <http://www.saalt.org/attachments/1/American_Backlash_report.pdf>.

Salingaros, Nikos; & Federico Mena-Quintero. 2010. "A Brief History of Peer-to-Peer Urbanism" (October).

Sampson, Rod. 2008. "Brief History of Screw Development" (February 05).. <http://research.ncl.ac.uk/cavitation/archive/MAR2010%20-%20propeller%20history.pdf>.

Schmitt, Bertel. 2011. "Auto Industry Sets New World Record" (February 15). *The Truth About Cars*. <http://www.thetruthaboutcars.com/2011/02/auto-industry-sets-new-world-record-in-2010-will-do-it-again-in-2011/>.

ScienceDaily (SCI). 2009. "Mathematicians Take Aim At 'Phantom' Traffic Jams: New Model Could Help Design Better Roads} (June 08). <http://www.sciencedaily.com/releases/2009/06/090608151550.htm>.

Sears, Francis Weston; & Robert Brehme. 1968. *Introduction to the Theory of Relativity*. Boston, MA: Addison-Wesley.

Shen, Fern. 2010. "Highway to Nowhere Coming Down? Not Really" (September 24). *BaltimoreBrew*. <http://www.baltimorebrew.com/2010/09/24/highway-to-nowhere-coming-down-not-really/>.

Shlain, Leonard. 1991. *Art and Physics: Parallel Visions in Space,Time, and Light*. New York: William Morrow and Co., Inc.

Shukman, David. 2011. "Toxic Dust Legacy of 9/11 Plagues Thousands of People" (September 01). *BBC News*. <http://www.bbc.co.uk/news/world-us-canada-14738140>.

Siddiqi, Asif A..2003. *Sputnik and the Soviet Space Challenge*. Gainesville, Florida: The University of Florida Press.

Smith, C.; Allan Marks; & Michael Lieberman. 2005. *Basic Medical Biochemistry: A Clinical Approach*. Baltimore, MD: Lippincott Williams & Williams.

Smith, Robert. 1972. *A Social History of the Bicycle, its Early Life and Times in America*. NY: American Heritage Press.

Smith, Stephen. 2009. "9/11 'Wall Of Heroes.' To Include Sick Cops" (February 11). *CBS News*. <http://www.cbsnews.com/stories/2008/04/28/national/main4049362.shtml>.

Sputnik: A Digest of the Soviet Press (SPT). 1983. "The Truth and Lies about the South Korean Airliner" (December). Moscow, USSR: Novosti Printing House.

Stanford, Craig. 2003. *Upright: The Evolutionary Key to Becoming Human*. NY: Houghton-Mifflin.

Stopford, Martin. 1997. *Maritime Economics*. London, England: Routledge.

Strasser, Susan. 1999. *Waste and Want: A Social History of Trash*. New York: Metropolitan Books.

Swenson, L, Jr; J. M. Grimwood; & C. Alexander. 1966. *This New Ocean, A History of Project Mercury*, Washington D.C.. National Aeronautics and Space Adminstration.

Snyder, David. 2002. "Families Hear Flight 93's Final Moments" (April 19). *The Washington Post*. <http://www.washingtonpost.com/ac2/wp-dyn/A12262-2002Apr18>.

Tarr, Laszlo. 1969. *The History of the Carriage*. Elisabeth Hoch, tr. Budapest. Hungary: Corvina Press.

TDM Encyclopedia. (TDM). 2011. "Walkability Improvements: Strategies to Make Walking Convenient, Safe and Pleasant" (September 01). <http://www.vtpi.org/tdm/tdm92.htm>.

Thayil, Jeet. 2001. "645 Racial Incidents Reported in Week after September 11" (October 12). *India Abroad*. <http://www.highbeam.com/doc/1P1-79281024.html>.

Tikuisis, P; D. M. Kane; T. M. McLellan; F. Buick; & S. M. Fairburn. 1992. "Rate of Formation of Carboxyhemoglobin in Exercising Humans Exposed to Carbon Monoxide." *Journal of Applied Physiology*, 72 (4): 1311–9. <http://www.ncbi.nlm.nih.gov/pubmed/1592720>.

TIME. 1965. "Here Comes the Flying Stovepipe" (November 26). <http://www.time.com/time/magazine/article/0,9171,834721,00.html>.

Transportation Research Board (TRB). 2000. Highway Capacity Manual: HCM2000." Washington D.C.: National Research Council.

Tripp, H. A. 1942. *Town Planning and Road Traffic*. London, England: E. Arnold.

United Nations (UN). 2003. "Global Road Safety Crisis" (August 07). <http://www.searo.who.int/LinkFiles/whd04_Documents_un_secretary_general_report_on_orad_traffic_injuries.pdf>.

United States Bureau of Justice Statistics (USBJS). 1999. "DWI Offenders under Correctional Supervision" (June).

_____.1998. "Four in Ten Criminal Offenders Report Alcohol as a Factor in Violence: But Alcohol-Related Deaths and Consumption in Decline" (April 5).

Urrey, John. 2004. "The 'System' of Automobility." *Theory, Culture & Society*, 21: 4-5, 25-39. <http://tcs.sagepub.com/content/21/4-5/25.abstract>.

U.S. Centennial of Flight Commission (USCFC). 2011. "Early Helicopter Technology" (July 23). <http://www.centennialofflight.gov/essay/Rotary/early_helicopters/HE1.htm>.

van der Hoeven, Frank. 2012. "2 More Tunnels 2 Go" (March 11). <http://www.thinkdeep.nl/documents/Papers/Hoeven.pdf>.

Vandenbulcke, Grégory; Bas de Geus; Luc Int Panis; Isabelle Thomas; Bart Degraeuwe; Elke Cumps; Joris Aertsens; Rudi Torfs; & Romain Meeusen. 2011. "A Prospective Cohort Study on Minor Accidents Involving Commuter Cyclists in Belgium" (November 04). *Accident Analysis & Prevention*.

Walker, John. 2011. "Vacuum Propellers" (July 23). *Fourmilab Switzerland*. <http://www.fourmilab.ch/documents/vprop/>.

Walkonomics (WALK). 2011. "Rating Walkability by combining Open Data and Crowdsourcing." <http://walkonomics.com/blog/2011/06/rating-walkability-open-data-crowdsourcing/>.

Weber, Max. 1930. *The Protestant Ethic and the Spirit of Capitalism*. Talcott Parsons, tr. New York: Scribner.

Whitt, Frank R.; & David G. Wilson. 1982. *Bicycling Science*. Cambridge, MA: MIT Press.

WHO. 2011. "Indoor Air Pollution and Household Energy." <http://www.who.int/heli/risks/indoorair/indoorair/en/index.html>.

WHPSC. 2009. "Battle Mountain World Human Powered Speed Challenge" (September). <http://www.wisil.recumbents.com/wisil/whpsc2009/results.htm>.

Wikipedia (WK). 2012. "Effects of the Automobile on Societies" (March 02). <http://en.wikipedia.org/wiki/Effects_of_the_automobile_on_societies>.

_____.2012a. "Transport" (March 02). <http://en.wikipedia.org/wiki/Transport>.

_____.2012b. "Node" (March 02). <http://en.wikipedia.org/wiki/Node>.

______.2012c. “Intrastructure” (March 02). <http://en.wikipedia.org/wiki/Infrastructure>.

______.2012d. “Vehicle” (March 02). <http://en.wikipedia.org/wiki/Vehicles>.

______.2012e. “Driving under the Influence” (March 02). <http://en.wikipedia.org/wiki/Driving_under_the_influence>.

______.2012f. “Obesity” (March 03). <http://en.wikipedia.org/wiki/Obesity>.

______.2012g. “DUI” (March 03). <http://en.wikipedia.org/wiki/DUI>.

______.2012h. “Air Pollution” (March 03). <http://en.wikipedia.org/wiki/Air_pollution#Carbon_dioxide_emissions>.

______.2012i. “Future Car Technologies” (March 03). <http://en.wikipedia.org/wiki/Future_car_technologies>.

______.2012j. “Automobile Dependency” (March 03). <http://en.wikipedia.org/wiki/Automobile_dependency>.

______.2012k. “Air Safety” (March 03). <http://en.wikipedia.org/wiki/Air Safety>.

______.2012l. “Korean Air Lines Flight_007” (March 03). <http://en.wikipedia.org/wiki/Korean_Air_Lines_Flight_007>.

______.2012m. “United States Bill of Rights” (March 03). <http://en.wikipedia.org/wiki/United_States_Bill_of_Rights>.

______.2012n. “New Pedestrianism” (March 03). <http://en.wikipedia.org/wiki/New_pedestrianism>.

______.2012o. “Walkability” (March 05). <http://en.wikipedia.org/wiki/Walkability>.

______.2012p. “Bicycle” (March 06). <http://en.wikipedia.org/wiki/Bicycle>.

______.2012q. “Bicycle Safety” (March 06). <http://en.wikipedia.org/wiki/Bicycle_safety>.

______.2012r. “Kinetic Energy” (March 07). <http://en.wikipedia.org/wiki/Kinetic_energy>.

______.2012s. “Spacecraft” (March 08). <http://en.wikipedia.org/wiki/Spacecraft>.

______.2012t. “Outer Space” (March 08). <http://en.wikipedia.org/wiki/Outer_space>.

______.2012u. “Automobile Industry” (March 09). <http://en.wikipedia.org/wiki/Automobile_industry>.

______.2012v. “Traffic Collision” (March 09). <http://en.wikipedia.org/wiki/Traffic_collision>.

______.2012w. “Gasoline” (March 09). <http://en.wikipedia.org/wiki/Gasoline>.

______.2012x. “Platoon (Automobile)” (March 10). <http://en.wikipedia.org/wiki/Platoon_(automobile)>.

______.2012y. “Vehicle Infrastructure Integration” (March 10). <http://en.wikipedia.org/wiki/Vehicle_infrastructure_integration>.

_____.2012z. "Driverless Car" (March 10). <http://en.wikipedia.org/wiki/Driverless_car>.

_____.2012aa. "Liquid Nitrogen" (March 10). <http://en.wikipedia.org/wiki/Liquid_nitrogen>.

_____.2012bb. "Transit-Oriented Development" (March 11). <http://en.wikipedia.org/wiki/Transit_oriented_development>.

_____.2012cc. "Transit-Proximate Development" (March 11). <http://en.wikipedia.org/wiki/Transit_proximate_development>.

_____.2012dd. "Principles of Intelligent Urbanism" (March 11). <http://en.wikipedia.org/wiki/Principles_of_Intelligent_Urbanism>.

_____.2012ee. "New Urbanism" (March 11). <http://en.wikipedia.org/wiki/New_Urbanism>.

_____.2012ff. "Suburbanization" (March 11). <http://en.wikipedia.org/wiki/Suburbanization>.

_____.2012gg. "Foreign Object Damange" (March 13). <http://en.wikipedia.org/wiki/Foreign_object_damage>.

_____.2012hh. "Alcohol Intoxication" (March 14). <http://en.wikipedia.org/wiki/Alcohol_intoxication>.

_____.2012ii. "Drunk Driving Law by Country" (March 14). <http://en.wikipedia.org/wiki/Drunk_driving_law_by_country>.

_____.2012jj. "Short-Term Effects of Alcohol" (March 14). <http://en.wikipedia.org/wiki/Short-term_effects_of_alcohol>.

_____.2012kk. "Carbon Monoxide" (March 15). <http://en.wikipedia.org/wiki/Carbon_monoxide>.

_____.2012ll. "Industrial Revolution" (March 15). <http://en.wikipedia.org/wiki/Industrial_revolution>.

_____.2012mm. "Carriage" (March 17). <http://en.wikipedia.org/wiki/Carriage>.

_____.2012nn. "Horse Riding" (March 17). <http://en.wikipedia.org/wiki/Horse-riding#Criticism_of_horses_in_sport>.

_____.2012oo. "Aircraft Hijacking" (April 04). <http://en.wikipedia.org/wiki/Aircraft_hijacking>.

_____.2012pp. "September 11 Attacks" (April 04). <http://en.wikipedia.org/wiki/September_11_attacks>.

_____.2012qq. "Traffic Congestion" (April 05). <http://en.wikipedia.org/wiki/Traffic_congestion>.

_____.2012rr. "Urban Sprawl" (April 05). <http://en.wikipedia.org/wiki/Urban_sprawl>.

_____.2012ss. "Rail Transport" (April 06). <http://en.wikipedia.org/wiki/Rail_transport>.

_____.2012tt. “Rail Transport in Fiction” (April 06). <http://en.wikipedia.org/wiki/Rail_transport_in_fiction>.

_____.2012uu. “Ship Transport” (April 07). <http://en.wikipedia.org/wiki/Ship_transport>.

_____.2012vv. “Sailor” (April 07). <http://en.wikipedia.org/wiki/Sailor>.

_____.2012ww. “Seamanship” (April 07). <http://en.wikipedia.org/wiki/Seamanship>.

_____.2012xx. “RMS *Titanic*” (April 07). <http://en.wikipedia.org/wiki/Titanic>.

_____.2011nn. “Design Elements and Principles” (September 30). <http://en.wikipedia.org/wiki/Design_elements_and_principles>.

_____.2011oo. “Interpretation (Logic)” (April 13). <http://en.wikipedia.org/wiki/Interpretation_(Logic)>.

_____.2011pp. “Unsolved Problems in Linguistics” (February 20). <http://en.wikipedia.org/wiki/Unsolved_problems_in_linguistics>.

_____.2008. “Posthumanism” (October 20). <http://en.wikipedia.org/wiki/Posthumanism>.

_____.2008a. “Transhumanism” (October 20). <http://en.wikipedia.org/wiki/Transhumanism>.

_____.2008b. “Lowest Common Denominator” (March 26). <http://en.wikipedia.org/ wiki/Least_common_denominator>.

_____.2008c. “Infinity” (November 11). <http://en.wikipedia.org/wiki/Infinity>.

_____.2008d. “Transfinite Number” (November 10). <http://en.wikipedia.org/wiki/Transfinite_ number>.

_____.2008e. “Quantum Mechanics” (November 26). <http://en.wikipedia.org/wiki/Quantum_mechanics>.

_____.2008f. “Copenhagen Interpretation” (November 26). <http://en.wikipedia.org/wiki/Copenhagen_interpretation >.

_____.2008g. “Many Worlds Interpretation” (November 26). <http://en.wikipedia.org/wiki/Many_Worlds_Interpretation>.

_____.2008h. “Hyperspace (Science Fiction)” (November 23). <http://en.wikipedia.org/wiki/Hyperspace_(science_fiction)>.

_____.2008i. “Time Travel” (November 26). <http://en.wikipedia.org/wiki/Time_travel#Time_dilation>.

_____.2008j. “Wormhole” (November 25). <http://en.wikipedia.org/wiki/Wormhole>.

_____.2007. “Linguistics” (March 04). <http://en.wikipedia.org/wiki/Linguistics>.

Wikiversity (WKV). 2008. “Why 10 Dimensions” (November 23). <ttp://en.wikiversity.org/wiki/Why_10_dimensions>.

Wilgoren, Jodi; & Edward Wong. 2001. “On Doomed Flight, Passengers Vowed

To Perish Fighting" (September 13). *The New York Times*. <http://www.nytimes.com/2001/09/13/us/after-attacks-united-flight-93-doomed-flight-passengers-vowed-perish-fighting.html>.

Wilson, David Gordon; & Jim Papadopoulos. 2004. *Bicycling Science*. Cambridge, MA: The MIT Press.

Wilson, S. S.1973. "Bicycle Technology" (March). *Scientific American*.

Wittgenstein, Ludwig.1953. *Philosophical Investigations*. G. E. M. Anscombe and R. Rhees, eds. G.E.M. Anscombe, tr. Oxford: Blackwell.

World Health Organization (WHO). 2012. "Physical Inactivity: A Global Public Health Problem" (March 03). <http://www.who.int/dietphysicalactivity/factsheet_inactivity/en/index.html>.

_____.2000. "Technical Report Series 894: Obesity: Preventing and Managing the Global Epidemic." Geneva: World Health Organization. <http://whqlibdoc.who.int/trs/WHO_TRS_894_(part1).pdf>.

WorstPolluted.org (WORS). 2010. "Reports" (August 29). <http://www.worstpolluted.org/>.

Worldwatch Institute (WI). 2008. "Analysis: Nano Hypocrisy?" (January 16). <http://www.worldwatch.org/node/5579>.

INDEX

•A•

•B•

•C•

•D•

•E•

•H•

•I•

•M•

•N•

•O•

•P•

•Q•

•T•

•U•

•V•

•W•

•X•

•Y•